PERGAMON GENERAL PSYCHOLOGY SERIES

EDITORS

Arnold P. Goldstein, *Syracuse University*
Leonard Krasner, *Stanford University &*
SUNY at Stony Brook

HANDBOOK OF ALCOHOLISM
TREATMENT APPROACHES
(PGPS-157)

Pergamon Titles of Related Interest

Clarke ALCOHOLISM AND PROBLEM DRINKING: Treating Addictions
   or Modifying Bad Habits?

Ellis/McInerney/DiGiuseppe/Yeager RATIONAL-EMOTIVE THERAPY
   WITH ALCOHOLICS AND SUBSTANCE ABUSERS

Knott ALCOHOL PROBLEMS: Diagnosis and Treatment

Miller THE ADDICTIVE BEHAVIORS: Treatment of Alcoholism, Drug
   Abuse, Smoking and Obesity

Rhodes/Jason PREVENTING SUBSTANCE ABUSE AMONG CHILDREN
   AND ADOLESCENTS

Related Journals
(Free sample copies available upon request.)

ADDICTIVE BEHAVIORS
ALCOHOL
ALCOHOL AND ALCOHOLISM
CLINICAL PSYCHOLOGY REVIEW
JOURNAL OF SUBSTANCE ABUSE TREATMENT

HANDBOOK OF ALCOHOLISM TREATMENT APPROACHES

Effective Alternatives

Edited by

REID K. HESTER

Behavior Therapy Associates, Albuquerque,
New Mexico

WILLIAM R. MILLER

University of New Mexico, Albuquerque,
New Mexico

PERGAMON PRESS

New York • Oxford • Beijing • Frankfurt • São Paulo • Sydney • Tokyo • Toronto

Pergamon Press Offices:

U.S.A.　　　　　　　　Pergamon Press, Inc., Maxwell House, Fairview Park,
　　　　　　　　　　　　Elmsford, New York 10523, U.S.A.

U.K.　　　　　　　　　Pergamon Press plc, Headington Hill Hall,
　　　　　　　　　　　　Oxford OX3 0BW, England

PEOPLE'S REPUBLIC　　Pergamon Press, Qianmen Hotel, Beijing,
OF CHINA　　　　　　　People's Republic of China

FEDERAL REPUBLIC　　Pergamon Press GmbH, Hammerweg 6,
OF GERMANY　　　　　D-6242 Kronberg, Federal Republic of Germany

BRAZIL　　　　　　　Pergamon Editora Ltda, Rua Eça de Queiros, 346,
　　　　　　　　　　　　CEP 04011, São Paulo, Brazil

AUSTRALIA　　　　　Pergamon Press (Aust.) Pty., Ltd., P.O. Box 544,
　　　　　　　　　　　　Potts Point, NSW 2011, Australia

JAPAN　　　　　　　Pergamon Press, 8th Floor, Matsuoka Central Building,
　　　　　　　　　　　　1-7-1 Nishishinjuku, Shinjuku-ku, Tokyo 160, Japan

CANADA　　　　　　Pergamon Press Canada Ltd., Suite 271, 253 College Street,
　　　　　　　　　　　　Toronto, Ontario M5T 1R5, Canada

Library of Congress Cataloging in Publication Data

Handbook of alcoholism treatment approaches : effective alternatives /
　edited by Reid K. Hester, William R. Miller.
　　　p.　　cm.--(Pergamon general psychology series ; 157)
　　Includes bibliographies and indexes.
　　ISBN 0-08-036428-4 :
　　1. Alcoholism--Treatment. I. Hester, Reid K. II. Miller,
William R. III. Series
　　[DNLM: 1. Alcoholism--therapy.　　WM 274 H236]
　　RC565.H26　1989
　　616.86'1--dc19
　　DNLM/DLC　　　　　　　　　　　　　　　　　　　88-22391
　　for Library of Congress　　　　　　　　　　　　　　CIP

Printed in the United States of America

 The paper used in this publication meets the minumum requirements of
American National Standard for Information Sciences -- Permanence of
Paper for Printed Library Materials, ANSI Z39.48-1984

Dedication

To my parents, Larry and Eileen, who instilled in me a desire for knowledge,
To my mentors, Alan Marlatt, Warren Garlington, and Bill Miller, who challenged and encouraged me,
To my stepfather, Jim Steger, who has always been a great support to me in so many ways,
And to my wife, Shannon Donahue, light of my life

RKH

To E. Mansell Pattison, M.D.
Uncommon integrator
Undaunted innovator
Untimely silenced

WRM

Contents

Foreword

This handbook of treatment approaches for alcoholism hallmarks several conceptual and practical breakthroughs in alcoholism treatment.

First, it brings some measure of systematization, categorization, and conceptualization to various treatment regimens. Thomas Kuhn, a contemporary philosopher of science, has noted that science advances more by disproofs than by proofs. Only with a clear exposition of treatment procedures, as delineated in this volume, can the conduct of inquiry progress rather than regress. While fiscal concerns and the socio-emotional chauvinism of some treatment facilities has impeded progress, the contemporary treatment of the American alcoholic has been most impeded by a widespread conceptual oversimplification of the ailment we call alcoholism—in short, a conceptual myopia.

Second, this handbook signals that not all alcoholics are the same; that not all respond optimally, or at all, to a specific treatment; and that in fact, as Jacobson has noted elsewhere, we may do better to speak of the alcoholisms rather than alcoholism.

Third, at the core of this volume is the tenet that alcoholism is not a unidimensional ailment and hence that specific treatments should be matched to particular clients. The search for a single cause and/or cure is illusory and counterproductive, although appealing from administrative and cost-management perspectives. While the drug field quickly accepted this concept of multidimensional ailment, the alcoholism field has been slower to do so.

Fourth, this volume is of major importance on several practical counts. It admirably acquaints and instructs treatment personnel with a wide range of diverse treatment regimens. It alerts the attentive reader to the benefits of careful treatment–client matching. It can serve as both figure and ground for delineating the various types and dimensions of alcoholics and the alcoholisms. It clearly facilitates comparisons of treatment efficacy across diverse treatment regimens and clients. But perhaps the handbook's most significant and practical contribution will be to foster enhanced accountability of alcoholism treatment and, as a consequence, better serve the client.

Fifth, the handbook may foster productive debate. Implicit in many of the regimens presented is the notion that careful and particular training will be needed by treatment personnel. Alcoholism is a complex set of ailments, requiring diverse treatments rather than a generalized or generic approach. Thus, the watchword for the future of alcoholism treatment will be specialization—specialized not generalized approaches.

I want to thank Drs. Hester and Miller for the enormous effort in assembling this volume, and heeding my urgings and encouragements that such a volume was sorely needed. I am thankful that they took the challenge (and its attendant labors) and have succeeded so admirably.

Dan Lettieri, PhD
National Institute on Alcohol Abuse and Alcoholism

Preface

It was ten years ago, in the fall of 1978, that our paths first crossed in Albuquerque, New Mexico. In that year we began what has been a most enjoyable collaboration in reading, discussing, and reviewing the immense research literature available on how to treat people with alcohol problems.

When we set out to read everything that had been published in the way of alcoholism treatment outcome research, we had little appreciation for what lay in store for us. There had been a virtual explosion of studies in this area during the 1970s, and it took us six months just to read the 600 books and articles we found. It took another half year to write what became a 110-page review chapter summarizing the literature we found.

Several facts stood out for us as we completed this initial review in 1980. First, we were impressed with the sheer number of treatment methods that had been tried. This is a field with many alternative approaches. Second, we were nearly overwhelmed with the amount of information available, often with immediate practical implications. The intimidating size and scope of the literature suggested to us why so little of this knowledge has found its way into clinical practice. Third, we began to see the value of systematic, repeated, and programmatic research. For a number of tried treat-

ments, we saw a characteristic history: A few initial, uncontrolled studies yielded glowing reports of success, while later and more controlled studies found little or no specific benefit from the same technique. In other cases, a technique seemed to hold up well over a range of studies conducted by different teams in various locations. Improved methodology, in fact, seemed to show the treatment's power more clearly.

This led us, in 1983, to begin updating our original review. This time we decided to focus our attention only on studies with proper control or comparison groups. We excluded uncontrolled studies because the results of such research are confounded and often unreliable, making it difficult to draw firm inferences about the value of the treatment under study. Using this methodological filter, we were led to two surprising and seemingly unavoidable conclusions. First, we were pleased to see that a number of treatment methods had been rather consistently supported by the available controlled scientific research. On the other hand, we were dismayed to realize that virtually *none* of these treatment methods was in common use within U.S. alcoholism treatment programs.

Another conclusion of our review was there is no single superior treatment approach for alcohol problems. Rather, there are a number of very promising alternative approaches. This led us to a third collaboration to review the literature on matching clients to treatments. Here we found evidence that different people respond best to different approaches. This makes sense, of course. Why should any one approach be best for everybody? Yet in our observations, relatively few treatment programs were in reality putting this common-sense fact into practice. Instead, most programs offered a relatively consistent program to all comers. Worse, clients who failed to respond to the offered approach are often blamed for the failure because of "insufficient motivation." Would it not be more effective to offer a *range* of *alternative* approaches, from which each individual could be offered an optimal strategy for his or her particular personality and situation?

Our fourth review focused on the question of whether more "intensive" treatment programs would be superior in effectiveness to less intensive alternatives. Again we focused only on controlled studies using random assignment or matching designs. We found two dozen studies comparing longer with shorter treatment, residential with nonresidential programs, or more versus less intensive intervention. The results were startling. Without a single exception, the studies failed to show any advantage for the more intensive, longer, or residential approaches over less intensive and less expensive alternatives. It seems that the overall effectiveness of alcoholism treatment is not driven by where it is given or how long it takes. Rather, genuine differences seem to emerge from various alternative approaches, and from the matching of individuals to optimal treatment methods.

We then faced a vexing question: Why has all of this knowledge not been put into practice? Why are so many alcoholism treatment programs still offering very homogeneous programs which include neither scientifically validated options nor individualized treatment based on the available literature? One possibility is that the alternatives and the literature have not really been "available" to the average program or practitioner providing alcoholism treatment. Indeed, we have spent a decade unearthing this knowledge!

And so arose this, our fifth collaboration. We decided to assemble a handbook describing the variety of alternative treatment methods available for helping those with alcohol problems. We included every treatment approach for which we found promising scientific evidence. Our strategy was to identify some of the best clinical researchers in the world, asking each to write a practically focused chapter in the area of his or her central expertise. Our goal is to provide you, the practitioner, with enough working knowledge of each particular strategy to get you started.

Every clinical chapter includes several sections. It begins with an overview of the technique, to give you a general idea of how it works. Special clinical considerations are provided next, with particular focus on factors that may help you to match these treatment methods to the clients most likely to benefit from them. Cautions are also inserted regarding types of clients for whom the method may be inappropriate. The bulk of each chapter provides specific guidelines for the clinical application of the methods being described. A final section briefly outlines the scientific evidence currently available, to document the effectiveness of the methods discussed.

At the end of each chapter are two reference lists. The first offers clinical resources to which you can turn for further detail about how to administer each treatment approach. The second is a bibliography of research regarding the treatment strategy. These are meant to help you go beyond this handbook, to explore in greater depth the treatment alternatives that you find most helpful and feasible for your own clinical setting.

A book such as this is never finished. As we write this preface, dozens of new journal issues are in the mail, including important new research. The years ahead will doubtless reveal still more alcoholism treatment methods than we have included here, and further research will clarify the effectiveness of all these and other alternatives. We have done our utmost to give you state-of-the-art descriptions of what we believe are the best treatment alternatives available, each written by outstanding researchers with extensive firsthand experience in treating alcoholism. The ultimate value of this for you will be found in your own attempts to apply these methods in your day to day efforts with those who seek your help. We commend you for working in such a challenging area, and for the open-minded seeking that brought you to this book. May you find here some new alternatives to help you help others.

ACKNOWLEDGMENTS

Many have contributed to this volume. We are grateful first to all of the authors—highly competent and very busy professionals—who agreed to contribute their expertise to this project. We thank Nathan Azrin for his encouragement to us, which helped to get this volume started. Editor Jerome Frank worked closely with us as the book developed for Pergamon Press. During the editing process we appreciated the assistance of Janice Brown, who prepared a useful subject index to help you find material within the book. Our secretaries helped with the manuscript, and generally kept us on course: Vicki Roberts, Jo Ann Leitka and Heidi Hughes. Finally, we express our gratitude to Dan Lettieri, our longstanding colleague, who not only wrote the foreword but helped from the beginning to envision this volume and to find the right contributing authors.

R.K.H.
W.R.M.

PART I
Introduction

CHAPTER 1

Treating Alcohol Problems: Toward An Informed Eclecticism

William R. Miller
Reid K. Hester

THREE MYTHS ABOUT ALCOHOLISM TREATMENT

There was a time not long ago when therapists were trained in a "one true light" tradition. A would-be professional chose to be trained in one of several rival "schools" of treatment and was thoroughly indoctrinated into that perspective. The subtleties of practice in that mode were expounded, and an impelling rationale for the superiority of this approach was learned by heart along with the faults and failures of all other approaches to treatment. Each student of therapy was taught that his or hers was the one correct way toward the lasting alleviation of human suffering.

A more recent rival to this schoolish view is eclecticism, which acknowledges the potential value of a wide range of alternatives. Indeed, in some circles and professions "eclectic" has become the predominant orientation of helpers. On the surface this sounds enlightened, but an uncritical eclecticism easily gives way to aimless wandering or cynicism. The extremes are the naive position that all treatments have equal value and the embittered stance that none work at all. The undisciplined eclectic roams from one trend or fad to another, reaching into a bulging bag of tricks and drawing out whatever is in hand or intuitively meets the immediate moment. Trial-and-error reigns (Goldstein & Stein, 1976).

These perspectives reflect three different myths about alcoholism treatment:

1. Nothing works.
2. There is one particular approach which is superior to all others.
3. All treatment approaches work about equally well.

We have argued elsewhere (Miller & Hester, 1980, 1986a) that all of these assertions are mistaken. The large body of treatment research now available indicates that in fact there are several different approaches significantly better than no intervention or alternative treatments. No one approach stands out from all the rest, but neither are all treatments equally effective (or ineffective). The reason for hope and optimism in the alcoholism field is not the presence of a single outstandingly effective approach but rather an array of promising and effective alternatives, each of which may be most effective for different types of individuals. For most individuals, the chances are good for finding an acceptable and effective intervention among these choices.

CONCEPTUAL MODELS AND THEIR IMPLICATIONS FOR INTERVENTION

Unfortunately, the U.S. alcoholism treatment field remains largely mired in a competitive spirit, with each program or approach asserting its superiority. This may result in part from factors inherent in a for-profit health care economy; however, it also reflects disagreements and uncertainty regarding the nature and etiology of alcohol problems. Contemporary books confidently ascribe alcoholism to inherent biochemical abnormalities (Milam & Ketchum, 1981), social learning processes (Peele, 1985), family dynamics (Steiner, 1971), sociocultural influences (Cahalan, 1987) and personal choice (Fingarette, 1988). Given such disagreement about their essence and causes, it is little wonder that there has been such confusion about how alcohol problems should be treated.

As a context for the chapters that follow, we will describe briefly a developmental history of the ways in which people have thought about and addressed alcohol problems. This is directly relevant to the purpose of this volume because intervention efforts are necessarily informed and guided by how one thinks about the problem to be treated. As we describe eleven alternative models of alcohol problems and alcoholism, we invite you to consider which of these may best describe your own current thinking.

Moral Models

There haven't always been alcoholics. In fact there were no "alcoholics" prior to 1849, when the Swedish physician Magnus Huss intro-

duced the term to describe the adverse consequences of excessive drinking. Of course the dangers of alcohol abuse have been recognized from the beginning of recorded history, but until very recently these were understood as the natural consequences of unfortunate personal decisions to drink excessively. *Moral models emphasize personal choice as a cause of alcohol problems.*

Historically this view has taken various forms. Drunkenness has long been viewed by major religions as sinful behavior. A recent public policy statement of the Presbyterian Church in the United States (1986) has set forth a contemporary theological conception of alcohol abuse (but not use) as sin, by virtue of the harm caused to oneself or others. Some conceptions of alcoholism view it, at least in part, as a spiritual deficit (Alcoholics Anonymous, 1976). More rarely, alcohol problems have been understood as demonic possession. Overtones of such views persist in our language, describing alcoholic beverages as "spirits" or denouncing them as "demon rum."

Other moral conceptions of alcohol problems view them, either explicitly or implicitly, as willful violations of societal rules and norms. In modern society, drunk driving is clearly understood in this way, whether or not the driver is diagnosed as "alcoholic." Indeed, U.S. courts and juries have rarely excused criminal behavior because it was committed under the influence of alcohol or other drugs. This issue of personal responsibility for alcohol problems remains very much alive and unresolved (Fingarette, 1988). A 1988 Supreme Court case dealt with this question of whether alcoholism is a "disease" beyond the person's control and responsibility, or "willful misconduct" for which the individual is accountable. At various points in history, public intoxication has itself been a punishable crime. In some societies the mere possession or consumption of alcohol is a serious offense.

Whether understood as a spiritual or a criminal issue, these views agree in pointing to personal agency as a causal factor in problem drinking. The individual is seen as making choices and decisions to use alcohol in a problematic fashion, and as capable of making (and having made) other choices. When the emphasis is spiritual, the logical change agents would be the clergy or other representatives of the religious community. When seen as volitional violations of social codes, punishment becomes the appropriate intervention, with law enforcement personnel and systems being the agents of such intervention.

The Temperance Model

Often confused with moral models, the *temperance* model arises from a very different understanding of the causes of alcohol problems. In the United States, this view predominated from the late 19th century through the repeal of Prohibition in 1933. In its early years, the temperance movement emphasized just that: temperance, moderation, the temperate and cautious use of alcohol. The reason for exercising such caution was the hazardous nature of the drug itself. Alcohol was, quite correctly, seen as a drug with great potential for inflicting harm. Indeed, one must wonder if alcohol would ever be legalized if it were only now being introduced to society, and if we had access to current knowledge about its effects (e.g., over 100,000 alcohol-related deaths and $116 billion in social costs per year in the United States alone; National Institute on Alcohol Abuse and Alcoholism, 1987).

As the temperance movement gained political momentum, it became a prohibition movement. Alcohol came to be seen as an extraordinarily dangerous drug that no one could use safely or in moderation. Writings of the early 20th century asserted that it was impossible for anyone to be a moderate drinker: either one must return to the social norm of abstinence or progress on to alcoholism and death. A Prohibition Party emerged, and enormous political pressure was exerted upon the Congress to ban the manufacture, sale, transportation, and importation of alcoholic beverages. In 1919, the 18th Amendment to the U.S. Constitution, to make these criminal acts, was proposed, and in 1920 it was ratified into law. Alcohol use and related health problems dropped to the lowest levels in U.S. history, but the law proved very unpopular and difficult to enforce. In 1933, the 21st Amendment to the Constitution repealed the 18th Amendment, again legalizing alcohol.

The core assumption of the temperance model, whether or not directed toward prohibition, is that the cause of alcohol problems is *alcohol* itself. The drug is seen as so dangerous as to warrant great caution in use, if it is to be used at all. This is similar to the way in which drugs such as heroin and cocaine are currently viewed. The drug is understood to contain such addictive and destructive power that the emergence of problems can be explained simply by the pharmacologic properties of the drug itself. In first describing a syndrome of alcoholism, Magnus Huss construed it as the effects of excessive use of alcohol, a view akin to the temperance model.

How would one intervene to reduce and prevent alcohol problems from a temperance perspective? One approach is exhortation of others to practice temperance or abstinence. This would presumably be done by persons who are currently themselves temperate or abstinent. On a larger scale, social legislation can be enacted to control the cost, availability, and promotion of alcohol to the general public.

The American Disease Model

In 1933 the United States was in a conceptual quandary. The dominant view of alcohol problems had been that they were caused by the pernicious nature of alcohol itself. Yet the Congress had just voted to make alcohol freely available again, and a majority of states ratified it into law. A new model was needed.

It was just two years later that Alcoholics Anonymous came into being, and with it was born the *American disease* model of alcoholism. A central assertion of this model is that alcoholism is a unique and progressive condition that is qualitatively (not just quantitatively) different from normality. Alcoholics are regarded as substantially different from nonalcoholics, possessing a distinct condition that renders them incapable of drinking in moderation. The disease is sometimes likened to an allergy to alcohol, and is seen as arising from a combination of physical, psychological, and spiritual causes (Alcoholics Anonymous, 1976). The central symptom of alcoholism, in this view, is loss of control over alcohol, the inability to restrain oneself from further drinking once started ("One drink, one drunk"). The disease is understood as irreversible, incapable of being cured, but possible to arrest through total abstinence from alcohol. This view has achieved rather limited acceptance outside the United States (Miller, 1986).

The American disease model served as a useful transition from the period of prohibition. Moderate drinking was reconstrued as impossible not for *all* people, but only for certain people—namely, alcoholics. This model was beneficial to alcoholics, in that it absolved them of responsibility for their condition and justified humane treatment instead of punishment. It was likewise appealing to other drinkers, in its implication that only alcoholics are at risk and that nonalcoholics may drink with relative impunity. The medical profession ultimately embraced the idea of alcoholism as a disease requiring medical treatment. Lastly, the American disease model has often been promoted by the manufacturers of alcoholic beverages, in that it removes the blame from alcohol itself and shifts the emphasis to an abnormality within only certain individuals. It is sometimes said that "There are alcoholics in the world who have never had a drink, and so haven't discovered that they are alcoholic." The implication is that alcoholism is inherent in the physical or psychological makeup of the individual. In the context of the American disease model, it makes sense to assert that "Alcoholism is not caused by alcohol," a statement that seems absurd from other perspectives.

The intervention implications of this model are relatively straightforward. Persons with the disease of alcoholism must be identified, informed of their condition, brought to accept their diagnosis, and persuaded to abstain from alcohol for the remainder of their lives. Prevention efforts would focus on the early identification of persons with this unique condition, an endeavor now termed by one group "the quest for the test." Because of their personal experience with the condition, recovering alcoholics are seen as the optimal intervention agents to help others recognize, accept, and adjust to their disease. Peer support groups provide an ongoing resource for recovery.

Educational Models

Other approaches have relied upon education as a tool for prevention and treatment. U.S. alcoholism treatment often includes a series of lectures and films, as do programs dealing with drunk driving offenders. Efforts designed to prevent alcohol and drug abuse have long relied on educational approaches.

Implicit in such approaches is the assumption that alcohol problems evolve from a knowledge deficit, from a lack of accurate information. When armed with correct and up-to-date knowledge, individuals are presumed to be less likely to use alcohol (or other drugs) in a hazardous fashion and to suffer the consequences. Some educational approaches have included an "affective" component as well, seeking to instill motivation to change or avoid alcohol abuse. The appropriate intervention agents within this model would be educators.

Characterological Models

Characterological models emphasize the roots of alcoholism in abnormalities of personality. Psychoanalysts have proposed a variety of hypotheses regarding the causes of alcoholism. Some have asserted that it represents an early fixation of normal psychological development, involving severe unresolved conflicts regarding dependence. Arrested at the oral stage of development, the person acts out his or her dependence conflict by literally continuing to suck on a bottle. Other psychodynamic hypotheses have viewed alcoholism as arising from latent homosexuality, low self-esteem, sex-role conflicts, or a drive for power and control by persons who feel particularly impotent or powerless.

The central assumption here is that alcoholics are people with particular personality types, and that the resolution of alcoholism requires a restructuring of the personality. This has spawned the search for "the alcoholic personality" or "the addictive personality." A related assumption is that alcoholics display unusually high levels of certain character defense mechanisms, particularly the primitive defenses associated with disturbances early in development (e.g., denial). The logical intervention within characterological models is psychotherapy to resolve the basic underlying conflicts and bring the person to more mature levels of functioning. Preventive interventions would focus on fostering normal psychological development.

Conditioning Models

As basic principles of learning and conditioning were clarified during the first half of the 20th century, psychologists began to speculate that such processes may explain how alcohol problems develop. Proponents of classical or Pavlovian conditioning (S–R theory) emphasized the role of such learning in shaping drinking behavior and craving for alcohol. More recent research points to a significant role of classical conditioning in drug tolerance. Skinner's operant conditioning principles likewise showed a logical fit: if drinking alcohol leads to rewarding consequences, it is likely to continue or increase. A variety of potential incentives for drinking have been explored, including tension reduction, time out from social rules, and positive social reinforcement from companions. The contemporary concept of "enabling" suggests that those close to an alcoholic may inadvertently reinforce (or at least remove the negative consequences of) excessive drinking.

The premise of conditioning models is that excessive drinking is a learned habit, responding to ordinary principles of behavior. It follows that the same principles could be employed to help an individual relearn behavior patterns. A variety of treatment strategies rely upon classical (e.g., aversion therapies; see chapter 8) or operant learning principles (e.g., community reinforcement approach; see chapter 16). Prevention efforts from a learning perspective might focus on factors that create positive associations with alcohol (e.g., advertising) and contingencies that encourage heavy drinking.

Biological Models

Frequently confused with the American disease model, *biological* models emerged in the 1970's, placing strong emphasis on genetic and physiological processes as causes of alcoholism. Some have stressed the importance of hereditary risk factors, drawing on strong evidence that the offspring of alcoholics have a higher risk of alcohol problems themselves. Others have posited the existence of unique biological conditions (e.g., abnormal alcohol metabolism, unique brain sensitivity) which predispose some individuals to alcoholism—a version most similar to the American disease model. Still others have looked to the pharmacology of alcohol itself to explain how drinking can escalate into alcoholism. The popular "THIQ hypothesis" of the late 1970s and early 1980s was of this kind, describing a natural opiate-like chemical produced as a byproduct of alcohol metabolism. Pharmacologic addiction itself represents a biological model, when used to explain continued and escalating alcohol (or other drug) abuse.

The intervention implications of biological models vary. Where risk factors are emphasized, special caution in the use of alcohol may be advised for those at risk, and genetic counseling may be considered. Proponents of models which focus on the pharmacologic impact of alcohol on the body may counsel drinkers to avoid levels of consumption likely to cause bodily harm or activate the accelerating spiral of tolerance and dependence. If a unique susceptibility is posited, those found to be at risk might be counseled to abstain from alcohol altogether.

Social Learning Models

Principles of behavior have expanded beyond the basic conditioning processes, and with this maturing have come more complex learning models. Like the conditioning models, these focus on interactions between the individual and the environment in shaping patterns of alcohol use. The influence of peers and others has been examined more closely, emphasizing the importance of *modeling* of drinking behaviors and of peer pressure. Heavy-drinking companions have been shown to evoke increased consumption among those around them.

Social learning perspectives also emphasize the importance of *coping skills*. Alcohol can be used as a strategy for coping with problem situations or for altering one's psychological state. Reliance upon a drug for such a purpose defines the process of *psychological dependence*. In the absence of alternative and competing skills, the individual may continue to rely upon alcohol as a coping strategy.

Increased attention is also being devoted to *cognitive* processes, such as expectations about the effects of alcohol. Positive expectancies—beliefs that alcohol causes beneficial and desirable effects—may promote more frequent and heavy drinking (Brown, Goldman, & Christiansen, 1985). Recent models focusing on "relapse prevention" (see chapter 11) stress the importance of cognitive processes in evoking or averting relapse.

Interventions from a social learning perspective focus on altering the person's relationship to his or her environment. Changes may be made in the person's circle of friends, to avoid exposure to negative models and further reinforcement for problematic drinking. New skills may be taught so that the person need not rely upon a drug for coping purposes. Cognitive restructuring may be used in an attempt to alter positive expectancies. Preventive interventions within this model would be concerned with conditions of the social environment that foster positive expectations for alcohol use, provide heavy-drinking role models, or encourage the use of alcohol and other drugs to cope with problems.

General Systems Model

A *general systems* approach views individual behavior as an inherent part of a larger social system. Actions of the individual (such as problematic drinking) cannot be understood without considering their relationship to other members and levels of the systems to which the individual belongs. The person's actions are an inherent part of a bigger system, interlocking with this larger pattern of interactions. A general systems model maintains that a system (such as a family) tends to maintain an overall status quo, and will resist change. Working only with the individual, then, is a very limited endeavor because it overlooks the extent to which that person's behavior has functional importance within the system. What appears to be an individual's alcohol problem is, in fact, the malfunctioning or "dysfunction" of a larger system.

Most often the system considered is the family. A variety of theorists have argued that alcoholism is a family disorder, requiring that the whole family system be treated. Transactional analysts (Steiner, 1971), for example, have described alcoholism as the product of interactional "games" in which there are payoffs not only for the drinker but also for other family members. Family systems approaches argue similarly that the individual's alcoholism represents a coping strategy within the family structure. If the individual is treated alone, the family system may resist change, and if the individual does change, the family system may fall apart or another family member may become dysfunctional to compensate. From this perspective, only family therapy is likely to be effective in untangling the complex interactions that underlie alcoholism.

A more recent systems model asserts that the children of alcoholics (CoAs) manifest a unique kind of pathology as a result of the dysfunctional family atmosphere in which they were raised. Writers have hypothesized lists of "characteristics" of CoAs, or the various patho-

logical roles that they may adopt within the alcoholic family (Wegscheider, 1981). It is the dysfunctional family, this model asserts, which gives rise to the abnormal set of needs and traits in the CoA, in turn rendering him or her uniquely vulnerable to addictive behaviors or pathological relationships. Some have asserted that this pattern of personality pathology is passed even to the second generation, the grandchildren of alcoholics (Thanepohn, 1986). The usually recommended path to recovery is to recognize the CoA pattern, accept it as the cause of one's difficulties, and through therapy or peer support groups to work through one's dysfunctional history toward a more adaptive style.

Sociocultural Models

A still larger view points to the role of society and subculture in shaping the individual's drinking patterns and related problems. The level of per capita alcohol consumption in a society, for example, is powerfully influenced by the availability of alcoholic beverages: their cost, convenience of access, legal regulation and so forth. The more readily available, the more alcoholic beverages are consumed. A further key assumption is that the more alcohol a society consumes, the higher the level of alcohol problems it will experience. The social control of alcohol availability, then, becomes a key consideration. In the United States, this strategy has been dominant in addressing abuse of illicit drugs but relatively ignored in recent years with regard to alcohol.

The nature of drinking environments is also of interest within a sociocultural perspective. Certain characteristics of a drinking establishment favor heavier drinking. Recent legal trends have increased the liability of those who serve alcohol for any harm inflicted by the drinker who was served (e.g., in a vehicular crash). This development acknowledges the responsibility of the larger environment for the actions of the individual. Other cultural factors may also be important determinants of the level of alcoholism in a society. Among those often discussed are the level of societal stress or alienation, encouragement or punishment for drunkenness, attitudes about alcohol, and the symbolic or functional importance of alcohol within the society.

Interventions that follow from sociocultural

models are those which would impact all or a large part of the society. The availability of alcohol might be restricted by increasing taxation on (and thereby the price of) alcoholic beverages or tightly regulating the number, location, and hours of shops through which they are sold. Advertising which encourages unrealistic positive expectancies about alcohol may be prohibited. Establishments serving alcohol may be encouraged or required to follow "server intervention" guidelines to discourage intoxication and drunk driving. The means for enacting such social policy are often legislative, through the creation of appropriate laws or the actions of the courts.

Public Health Model

The history of alcoholism is largely a history of contention among the above-described models. Each has had its champions, who have defended it as the most (if not only) correct understanding of the nature of alcohol problems. Emotion-laden debates have often centered around a clash between two rival models of the nature of alcoholism.

Indeed, the practical implications of these models differ greatly (see Table 1.1). Consider, for example, the kinds of prevention measures that would be promoted by proponents of the American disease model and by those holding a sociocultural model. To the former, efforts to regulate the price and availability of alcohol appear futile, because the cause of alcoholism is seen as residing within the alcoholic and unrelated to alcohol. From a sociocultural perspective, on the other hand, the attempt to identify and intervene individually with a relatively small number of diagnosed alcoholics appears excessively narrow in focus.

It is far beyond the scope of this chapter to review the evidence regarding the validity of each of the ten models described above. Suffice it to say that evidence can be found in support of each of these models, and that each can likewise be shown to be limited in its ability to account for alcohol problems. No one of these models appears to be the whole truth, though each contains truth. No one of them is likely to be adequate in guiding efforts to intervene with and prevent alcohol problems.

A public health model, the last to be considered here, does offer some hope for integration. Public health professionals have espoused an approach that considers three types of causal factors in understanding and intervening with any disease. One important factor is the *agent*, often a germ but in this case ethyl alcohol. The agent itself contains a certain destructive potential. Some agents (e.g., the AIDS virus) take their toll on most or all individuals exposed to them. Others can be found in many or most human bodies, of whom only a few manifest the disease. This points to the importance of *host* factors as well, individual differences that influence susceptibility to the condition. These can be thought of as personal risk factors (e.g., family history) that increase or decrease one's susceptibility to the disease. A third important factor is the *environment*. With infectious diseases, attention might be directed to the water supply, insect populations, or other means by which the agent is spread to new hosts. In alcoholism, emphasis is on aspects of the environment which promote alcohol use and abuse. Within a public health perspective, then, the presence or absence of a disease or illness is a result of the interactions of the agent, host, and environment.

All of the above models can be understood as emphasizing one of these factors, usually to the exclusion of the other two. The temperance model points to the destructive power of the *agent* itself: alcohol. The moral, American disease, educational, characterological, and biomedical models all place strong emphasis on *host* factors. Emphasis on the *environment* can be found in the conditioning, social learning, general systems, and sociocultural perspectives.

A hallmark of the public health approach is its emphasis on the importance of considering and addressing all three components of the model. An approach which focuses on only one of the three components is likely to be very limited in its ability to eradicate the problem. A comprehensive effort acknowledges the importance of agent, host, *and* environment. Within the alcohol field, a public health approach acknowledges that alcohol is a hazardous drug, which places anyone at risk who consumes it unwisely or beyond moderation. It also recognizes that there are significant individual differences in susceptibility to alcohol problems, mediated by factors such as heredity, tolerance, brain sensitivity, and metabolic rates. Finally, it stresses the importance of environmental factors in determining rates of alcohol use and related problems, attending to influences such

Table 1.1. A Developmental History of Models of Addictive Behaviors
and Their Implications for Intervention

MODEL	EXAMPLES	EMPHASIZED CASUAL FACTORS	IMPLIED INTERVENTIONS	APPROPRIATE INTERVENTION AGENT
MORAL	Abuse as sin	Spirituality	Spiritual direction	Clergy
	Abuse as crime	Personal responsibility	Moral suasion Social sanctions	Law enforcement agents
TEMPERANCE	Prohibition WCTU	Alcohol	Exhortation Abstinence/ prohibition	Abstainers Legislators
AMERICAN DISEASE	A.A.	Irreversible constitutional	Identification/ confrontation	Recovering alcoholics
	N.A.	Abnormality of individual	Lifelong abstinence	Peer support
EDUCATIONAL	Lectures Affective educ.	Lack of knowledge Lack of motivation	Education	Educators
CHARACTERO-LOGICAL	Psychoanalysis	Personality Traits/dispositions Defense mechanisms	Psychotherapy Risk identification Self-image modification	Psychotherapists
CONDITIONING	Classical cond. Operant cond.	Conditioned response Reinforcement	Counterconditioning Altered contingencies Relearning "Disenabling"	Behavior therapists
BIOMEDICAL	Heredity Brain (THIQ)	Genetic Physiological	Risk identification Medical treatment	Diagnosticians Physicians
SOCIAL LEARNING	Cognitive therapy Relapse prevention	Modeling Expectancies Skill deficits	Appropriate models/goals Cognitive restructuring Skill training Self-control training	Cognitive-behavior therapists Appropriate models
GENERAL SYSTEMS	Transactional analysis "Adult children of alcoholics"	Family dysfunction	Family therapy Recognition, peer support	Family therapist Support groups
SOCIOCULTURAL	Control of consumption	Environmental Cultural norms	Supply-side intervention Social policy Server intervention	Lobbyists/legislators Social policy makers Retailers/servers
PUBLIC HEALTH	World Health Org. National Academy of Sciences	Interactions of host, agent, and environment	Comprehensive, multifaceted	Interdisciplinary

as the availability and promotion of alcohol products.

A public health model offers hope for integrating what have previously been rival and seemingly incompatible perspectives. It adopts from each perspective the factors that have been found to influence the occurrence of alcohol problems, integrating them into a complex and interactive model. The interventions that follow from a public health approach are necessarily diverse, addressing all three types of factors: agent, host, and environment. This perspective moves us away from the search for a single "correct" way to intervene, and toward a larger strategy which incorporates a variety of alternative strategies (Moore & Gerstein, 1981).

It is at this point that the relevance of these models to treatment becomes clear. Treatment approaches have often been guided by a single model, operating as if it were the only complete and accurate understanding of alcohol problems and their etiology. Yet alcohol problems and the individuals who manifest them are diverse, and effective treatment is likely to require not one but a range of effective alternatives. It is in this spirit that this book was prepared. Its chapters are meant to present you with alternatives, a variety of promising tools to use in working with different types of alcohol problems and individuals. No one chapter is "the answer." Each offers a piece of the larger solution.

AN INFORMED ECLECTICISM

We began this chapter by describing three myths of alcoholism treatment. One of these asserts that there is a single, outstandingly effective approach that is better than all others. The other two (nothing works, or everything works) reduce to the assertion that all approaches are equally valid. What lies beyond these too-simplistic orientations—one devoted to the exclusive truth of a single position, the others ascribing equal merit to all alternatives? At present, this is a frontier. Yet the guidelines for a more informed eclecticism are already beginning to emerge. Proposed systems have been variously described as prescriptive eclecticism (Dimond, Havens, & Jones, 1978), technical eclecticism (Lazarus, 1971), prescriptive psychotherapy (Goldstein & Stein, 1976), client–treatment matching (Miller & Hester, 1986b), and a cafeteria plan (Ewing, 1977). The central assumptions of an informed eclecticism, however, appear to be the following general assertions:

1. *There is no single superior approach to treatment for all individuals.* This is abundantly clear from the current alcoholism treatment outcome literature (Miller & Hester, 1980, 1986a). Instead we have an encouraging array of promising alternative interventions. There is no tried and true, "state-of-the-art" treatment of choice for alcoholism. Rather, the state of the art is an array of empirically-supported alcoholism treatment options.
2. *Different types of individuals respond best to different treatment approaches.* It is not the case that the same type of individual responds best to all forms of alcoholism treatment. Although a generic "good prognosis" profile could be described (e.g., socially stable, employed, married), there are also indications of differential response to alternative treatments (Miller & Hester, 1986b). For each treatment mode it is at least conceptually possible to describe the

profile of the optimal responder. A person who responds very well to treatment A might do poorly in treatment B, whereas for another person B may be a superior treatment to A. Even when treatments appear to be equivalent in their *overall* effects within a heterogeneous population, they may be very different in their appropriateness and effectiveness for a given subpopulation or individual. The appropriate question, then, is not "Which treatments are best?" but rather, "Which types of individuals are most appropriate for a given program?" or "For this individual, which approach is most likely to succeed?"

3. *It is possible to match individuals to optimal treatments, thereby increasing treatment effectiveness and efficiency.* From the first two assumptions, it follows that matching schemes could be developed to place individuals in different treatment approaches which are most likely to be effective for them. It is inappropriate to offer the same treatment for all individuals. Likewise, when empirical knowledge on matching is available, it is inappropriate to choose treatment arbitrarily or intuitively. Getting individuals into the right treatment the first time around can increase treatment efficacy, avoid unnecessary or ineffective treatment, and even improve staff morale.

Needless to say, this does not sound like something profoundly new. "Tailoring treatment to individual needs" has long been endorsed, and most professionals and programs give lip service to the value and importance of matching. Yet the fact is that very few programs even offer a range of alternative approaches, let alone match individuals to them. Though we recognize the value of matching, putting it into practice turns out to be much more difficult.

One obstacle is the unavailability of true alternatives. Professionals in remote or rural areas may be frustrated by the lack of treatment options. Even in a large metropolitan area, the alternatives are often sadly few. Our own community contains more than 50 different programs offering treatment for alcohol and drug abuse. Yet a close examination of these programs reveals that they are strikingly similar in content—virtually carbon copies of one another in most cases. A "standard formula" pervades what appear on the surface to be different programs. When there is only one treatment available, there is little opportunity for matching!

A second obstacle to the implementation of an informed eclecticism is the absence of criteria for matching individuals to treatments. Writers have variously proposed matching based on clients' preferences (Miller, 1987), personality patterns and the path of least client resistance (Dimond et al., 1978), empirical criteria (Goldstein & Stein, 1976; Miller & Hester, 1986b), or clinical judgment (Lazarus, 1971). The literature on matching clients to treatments is relatively young at this point. Though it does offer a few beginning guidelines for client–treatment matching (see chapter 17), much more knowledge is needed to provide criteria for triage.

A third substantial obstacle to effective matching persists even when treatment alternatives and plausible assignment criteria are available. This has to do with the health care economy. Factors of limited resources, economic competition, professional loyalties, third-party reimbursement, program linkages, and referral bias serve to constrain the range of options available or recommended to a given individual. Persons referred to program A for screening are likely to be judged as needing the services of program A (Hansen & Emrick, 1983). The pressure to fill beds or empty appointments may override attention to the individual's best interests. Health maintenance organizations (HMOs) and preferred provider organizations (PPOs) limit the range of professionals and programs from which a subscriber may seek treatment. Insurers reimburse treatment alternatives differentially. Finally, the counselor conducting screening may be strongly committed to a particular treatment program or approach, and uninformed about or even hostile toward alternatives.

Factors such as these have led some to propose that pretreatment assessment should be conducted by an independent evaluation agent with no affiliation or commitment to particular treatment programs, or approaches (Glaser et al., 1984). The evaluator, then, is free to assess each individual and make referrals within the full range of available options varying in content, setting, and intensity. Though relatively rare in past practice, such a scheme is becoming increasingly feasible. In employee assistance programs (EAPs) and some screening programs for drunk driving offenders, individuals are evaluated by a professional who typically will not be the treatment agent. Rather the evaluator's task is to assess the need for treatment and to recommend optimal intervention levels and options. Given adequate information, primary care physicians, clergy, or attorneys might serve a similar function.

One of the primary goals of this volume is to help the practicing clinician move toward a more informed eclecticism. The range of chapters is intended to help overcome the first obstacle by providing knowledge of treatment alternatives. Each chapter is a self-contained treatment manual which details the practicalities of one approach. The final chapter attempts a step toward overcoming the second obstacle by offering some tentative criteria for client–treatment matching. In passing, we would observe here that the staff member who sits "at the front door," the one who is responsible for steering individuals to treatments, ought to be the *most* knowledgable and highly trained professional in the system. Matching is one of the most challenging and important professional tasks. Inappropriate matching can result in wasted money, treatment and staff time, even lost families and lives. Appropriate matching, we believe, can substantially improve the effectiveness and efficiency of treatment within a system in general, as well as in the individual case. The more common practice, however, is to assign intakes to staff with relatively less training and experience.

The third obstacle may be the most formidable of all, but is not insurmountable. Even in a competitive health care market, matching is possible if alternatives and assignment criteria are available. Referral of appropriate clients to a competitor, for example, can go a long way toward establishing cooperative working relationships. To the extent that evaluation services can be disaffiliated from particular treatment providers, the opportunities for matching improve. Of course the "independent and objective" evaluator is corruptible too, if not accountable to peer or public review.

The most important reason to persist in pursuing true matching, however, is the welfare and interest of those who seek help. It is odd that consumer awareness has been so slow in coming to the field of mental health services in general and alcoholism treatment in particular. There is little doubt that inappropriately matched clients can be harmed, faring worse than if they had received no treatment at all. Individuals matched to the right treatment the first time can be spared years of needless suffering and impairment. A common concern for those who suffer from alcohol problems may, in the end, be the most persuasive ground for agreement and cooperation toward an informed eclecticism.

REFERENCES

Alcoholics Anonymous (1976). *Alcoholics Anonymous: The story of how many thousands of men and women have recovered from alcoholism* (3rd ed.). New York: Alcoholics Anonymous World Services.

Brown, S. A., Goldman, M. S., & Christiansen, B. A. (1985). Do alcohol expectancies mediate drinking patterns of adults? *Journal of Consulting and Clinical Psychology, 53*, 512–119.

Cahalan, D. (1987). *Understanding America's drinking problem.* San Francisco: Jossey-Bass.

Dimond, R. E., Havens, R. A., & Jones, A. C. (1978). A conceptual framework for the practice of prescriptive eclecticism in psychotherapy. *American Psychologist, 33*, 239–248.

Ewing, J. A. (1977). Matching therapy and patients: The cafeteria plan. *British Journal of Addiction, 72*, 13–18.

Fingarette, H. (1988). *Heavy drinking: The myth of alcoholism as a disease.* Berkeley: University of California Press.

Glaser, F. B., Annis, H. M., Skinner, H. A., Pearlman, S., Segal, R. L., Sisson, B., Ogborne, A. C., Bohnen, E., Gazda, P., & Zimmerman, T. (1984). *A system of health care delivery.* Toronto, Canada: Addiction Research Foundation.

Goldstein, A. P., & Stein, N. (1976). *Prescriptive psychotherapies.* New York: Pergamon.

Hansen, J., & Emrick, C. D. (1983). Whom are we calling "alcoholic"? *Bulletin of the Society of Psychologists in Addictive Behaviors, 2*, 164–178.

Lazarus, A. A. (1971). *Behavior therapy and beyond.* New York: McGraw-Hill.

Milman, J. R., & Ketchum, K. (1981). *Under the influence: A guide to the myths and realities of alcoholism.* Seattle, WA: Madrona Publications.

Miller, W. R. (1986). Haunted by the Zeitgeist: Reflections on contrasting treatment goals and conceptions of alcoholism in Europe and the United States. *Annalogs of the New York Academy of Sciences, 472*, 110–129.

Miller, W. R. (1987). Motivation and treatment goals. *Drugs & Society, 1*, 133–151.

Miller, W. R., & Hester, R. K. (1980). Treating the problem drinker: Modern approaches. In W. R. Miller (Ed.), *The addictive behaviors: Treatment of alcoholism, drug abuse, smoking, and obestiy* (pp. 11–141). Oxford: Pergamon.

Miller, W. R., & Hester, R. K. (1986a). The effectiveness of alcoholism research: What research reveals. In W. R. Miller & N. Heather (Eds.), *Treating addictive behaviors: Processes of change* (pp. 121–174). New York: Plenum.

Miller, W. R., & Hester, R. K. (1986b). Matching problem drinkers with optimal treatments. In W. R. Miller & N. Heather (Eds.), *Treating addictive behaviors: Processes of change* (pp. 175–204). New York: Plenum.

Moore, M. H., & Gerstein, D. R. (1981). *Alcohol and public policy: Beyond the shadow of prohibition.* Washington, DC: National Academy Press.

National Institute on Alcohol Abuse and Alcoholism (1987). *Alcohol and health: Sixth special report to Congress.* Rockville, MD: Author.

Peele, S. (1985). *The meaning of addiction.* Lexington, MA: Lexington Books.

Presbyterian Church U.S.A. (1986). *Alcohol use and abuse: The social and health effects.* New York: Program Agency, The Presbyterian Church (U.S.A.).

Steiner, C. (1971). *Games alcoholics play.* New York: Grove Press.

Thanepohn, S. G. (1986). Grandchildren of alcoholics at risk. *Changes, 5*, 6–7.

Wegscheider, S. (1981). *Another chance: Hope and health for the alcoholic family.* Palo Alto, CA: Science and Behavior Books.

PART II

Evaluation and Motivation

CHAPTER 2

A Comprehensive Approach to Pretreatment Evaluation: I. Detection, Assessment, and Diagnosis of Alcoholism

George R. Jacobson *

ACKNOWLEDGMENTS

The author is grateful to Ms. Pat Johnson for her assistance in preparing this chapter; and to Ms. Karen Roe for her assistance in providing research and reference materials.

The author is also grateful to all of the following individuals and organizations for their assistance and cooperation. Ms. Margaret Molinari and Ms. Carol Watson of National Computer Systems, Inc. were very helpful in providing information and materials pertaining to the revised Alcohol Use Inventory (AUI-R); Dr. John Horn graciously furnished a pre-publication draft of the new AUI user's *Manual*; Ms. Deborah Kay and Ms. Donna Hewin of the Addiction Research Foundation (Toronto, Ontario, Canada) were helpful in supplying copies of A Structured Addictions Assessment Interview for Selecting Treatment (ASIST); Dr. Norman G. Hoffman, Executive Director of the Chemical Abuse/Addiction Treatment Outcome Registry (CATOR) at St. Paul-Ramsey Hospital (St. Paul, Minnesota) furnished the Substance Use Disorder Diagnostic Schedule (SUDDS) and *Manual*; and Drs. Ken Winter and George Henly of the Chemical Dependency Adolescent Assessment Project (Northwest Area Foundation, St. Paul Foundation, and Amherst H. Wilder Foundation) generously forwarded the CDAAP materials.

*The opinions and conclusions expressed herein are solely those of the author and do not necessarily reflect the positions or policies of any institution with which he is affiliated.

CONCEPTUAL AND DEFINITIONAL ISSUES

In the 135 years since Magnus Huss (1852) enunciated his description of "chronic alcoholics" and coined the term "alcoholism," a gradual accumulation of clinical observations and research data has been slowly altering our views of this disorder. That alteration has not always been orderly or consistent, but has followed many different directions. When Jellinek (1960) summarized those views, he cited more than 200 definitions, conceptualizations, and theories of the etiology and treatment of alcoholism. These included, to name just a few, notions of sin and faulty religious training; nutritional deficiencies; allergies; abnormal biochemistry; brain pathology; neurosis; endocrinologic disorders; heredity and genetics; and social and cultural background.

Today, all of those views of alcoholism still claim a number of adherents and to one extent or another continue to influence our research studies and our approaches to treatment. By far the most widely accepted of these is the medical model, the conceptualization of alcoholism as a disease, which Jellinek (1952, 1960) himself advocated. He also noted, however, that there were several forms of alcoholism, only one of which clearly represented a disease in the classic sense of the term. (He also expressed his recognition that, in the end, a disease is anything that the medical profession chooses to identify as such.)

In much the same vein, I have emphasized the usefulness of the notion of *multiple alcoholisms* as a guide for our research, diagnosis, and treatment. I have documented the accumulating evidence pointing to several different alcoholisms, each with its own ultimately identifiable etiology, course and development, treatment, prognosis, and outcome (Jacobson, 1976, 1983b, 1987b). Similarly, Pattison (1979, 1980) has proposed a variety of *alcoholism syndromes* that may differ from one another in important dimensions. Of course, neither of us are without our critics (Rohan, 1978, 1982).

Be that as it may, there is indeed mounting evidence for the probable existence of several alcoholisms, which clinicians need to be aware of in order to provide accurate diagnosis and adequate and appropriate treatments. Epidemiologic studies of adopted-out children of alcoholic parents, raised in nonalcoholic foster families, have suggested the possible operation of hereditary mechanisms in an alcoholism referred to as *familial* (Bohman, 1978; Cadoret & Gath, 1978; Goodwin, 1982). Biochemical and behavioral research on nonalcoholic children of alcoholic parents reveal several possibilities for the development of new diagnostic approaches (Schuckit, 1979, 1985; Schuckit, Gold, & Risch, 1987). Other authors (e.g., Holden, 1987a, 1987b) have suggested that alcoholism may not be a disease in and of itself but rather a "final common pathway arrived at through a multitude of factors," or that one of the alcoholisms may be an expression of *depressive spectrum disease* (Lipton, 1979). Other research indicates that in some cases alcoholism is related to *attention deficit disorder* in childhood (Tarter, 1981).

Relatedly, Rudie and McGaughran (1961) have identified two alcoholisms, which they call *essential* and *reactive*. These bear certain similarities to expressions of alcoholism referred to as *primary* and *secondary* (Schuckit & Morrissey, 1979). Zucker (1987) has described the etiology of four alcoholisms, which he has named *antisocial* alcoholism, *developmentally cumulative* alcoholism, *developmentally limited* alcoholism, and *negative affect* alcoholism. Cooper (1987) has identified at least three (and possibly a fourth) types of alcoholics or other substance abusers; Cloninger (1987) has identified personality traits and behavioral, neurophysiological, and neuropharmacological characteristics which distinguish two types of alcoholisms.

Quite clearly, alcoholism is not the unitary clinical entity it was once believed to be. Nor does it appear to have a single specified etiology from physical causes that produce a consistent pattern of signs and symptoms for which there is a single best treatment. Neither can alcoholics any longer be considered a homogeneous clinical group who share a single common problem that can be best treated by a single common therapy. As Babor (1981) points out, "If at one time a major goal of the therapeutic process was to have the patient admit 'I am an alcoholic,' it may now be time to elaborate the confession to 'I am an alcoholic who is dependent on alcohol to a certain (slight, moderate, or severe) degree, who is disabled to a certain degree in certain areas of (physical, psychological, or social) functioning, and whose problem is primarily attributable to certain (physical, psychological, or environmentally induced) vulnerabilities.' . . . The problem, and the paradox, is that there seems not to be any one specific entity conforming to our current notions of alcoholism. Rather, there appears to be a whole group of related syndromes whose only common characteristics are drinking, dependence, and damage" (p. xiii).

If Babor's position is a valid one—and the weight of research data and clinical observation suggests that it is—then we must recognize the multivariate nature of alcoholism and the need to differentiate among alcoholisms—or alcoholism syndromes, or alcoholic subtypes—so that each may be treated by the method or methods most appropriate to each individual patient. The literature on diagnosis and assessment is filled with descriptive categories, classification schema, typological groupings, and so on: "There are gammas and deltas, primaries and secondaries, reactives and essentials, even 'precipitated' and 'screwed up' alcoholics" (Babor, 1981, p. xiii).

How are we to make sense of all these emerging ideas and apply them in a meaningful and systematic way that will allow us to achieve our common goals? Are we not just creating confusion and distracting ourselves from the process of providing the best diagnostic and treatment services for our patients? I think not; let me provide an analogy that may prove useful in guiding our diagnosis and treatment.

How we call a thing, the name we give it, influences our reactions to it, our perceptions of it, our feelings and attitudes toward it. Take, for example, that process we call *cancer*. Most people are likely to react with feelings of fear and dread, thoughts and images of wildly growing malignant cells invading the body, overcoming our natural defenses, and attitudes of hopelessness and helplessness, anticipation of disfiguring surgeries, or the certainty of a painful and lingering death.

At one time these reactions, perceptions, feelings, and attitudes may have been warranted. But medical and allied health scientists, researchers, and clinicians have made wonderful advances in understanding the etiology and development of cancer, as well as its diagnosis and treatment. Our current state of knowledge has led to an understanding that cancer is "a general term frequently used to indicate any of various types of malignant neoplasms, most of which invade surrounding tissues, may metastasize to several sites, and are likely to recur after attempted removal, and to cause death of the patient unless adequately treated" (Stedman's, 1982, p. 216).

We have learned, then, to think in terms of *cancers*, and we are aware of dozens of different carcinomas, leukemias, sarcomas, and other specific conditions which, although perhaps similar in a fundamental way, are also quite different in many important ways. Consequently, we have learned that cancers differ in etiology, course and development, patterns and outcome. Most importantly, through advances in diagnosis and treatment, we are learning which cancers respond best to which therapies. We know that some cancers may be more effectively treated by surgery, irradiation, one of several forms of chemotherapies, while others respond to combinations of such treatments. We have also learned that some treatments of cancer may in fact cause cancer or increase the likelihood of future malignancies.

We are also learning that an array of other variables must be taken into consideration for diagnosis and treatment. Has the patient been exposed to radiation? Does he smoke cigarettes? Does she drink alcohol? What stressors exist in his work environment? Is there a family history of malignancies? Did her mother ever use diethylstilbestrol? Does he have a supportive family willing to participate in his aftercare? Does she need to attend a support group for mastectomy patients?

This discussion of cancer and cancers serves as a useful metaphor for thinking about alcoholism and alcoholisms. While there is no single best or universally acceptable definition of alcoholism, Babor's idea of the elaborated therapeutic confession, and the cancer metaphor, suggest a definition that has been useful to me in my work: Alcoholism is a general term frequently used to indicate any of various types of alcohol use, misuse, abuse, or dependency problems, some of which may be progressive; may be of varying and multiple etiologies and may follow varying courses of development; may involve multiple organ systems to varying degrees; may pervade, to varying degrees, a variety of psychological, personal, interpersonal, occupational, spiritual, social, or other behavioral domains; may recur after attempted therapy; and may lead to decline or death of the patient unless adequately and properly treated.

This proposed working definition is intentionally broad and general, to accommodate the empirical phenomena associated with most conceptualizations of alcoholism. It allows for the construction of a variety of theoretic models and etiologic hypotheses, while serving as a guide for diagnosis and treatment. It permits, perhaps encourages, a multivariate, multidimensional mode of thinking about the varied nature of the problems we call alcoholism and the individual persons we call alcoholics. It facilitates a broader and more comprehensive vision than would a strictly interpreted medical model or disease concept, and encourages a multidisciplinary and interdisciplinary approach to diagnosis and treatment. It may even eliminate the parochial disputes so aptly described in the 19th-century poem by Saxbe:

> It was six men from Indostan,
> to learning much inclined,
> who went to see the elephant,
> though all of them were blind,
> that each by observation
> might satisfy his mind.

And we all know how that ended: The blind man who felt only the elephant's leg described a tree, the one who touched only the elephant's trunk insisted the animal was a snake, and so on. But none of them ever found out what an elephant really was.

Hence the need for, and value of, a multivariate approach to understanding the alcoholisms, a multidimensional approach to evaluating the alcoholic, and a multi- and interdisciplinary approach to treatment. We must recognize that it is no longer sufficient to merely feel the elephant's trunk or leg—to merely examine the alcoholic's drinking pattern or family constellation—to fully understand the complex nature of the organism we are dealing with. We must acknowledge that with alcoholism, as with cancer, we must know more than just whether or not the person has that generic health problem, so that we can provide more than a generic treatment. Our expanding knowledge, advancing technology, and increasing accountability permits—demands!—that we provide comprehensive diagnostic and evaluation procedures in which patients' needs, resources, characteristics, and problems are all fully considered. Only by so doing can we then plan and provide the most appropriate, constructive, cost-efficient, and effective treatments.

Our cancer metaphor instructs us to take a more ecological approach to evaluating our patients. Simply knowing about drunk driving arrests tells us nothing about cognitive deficits; knowing only about stressors in the workplace tells us nothing about antisocial personality traits. Many of these various aspects of the individual human being, his or her family, and the internal and external environment are independent of each other and all must be examined within the context of overall life circumstances and lifestyle before we can know how to act in the best interest of the patient. Our cancer metaphor further instructs us, then, that we can vastly improve treatment outcomes by prescribing for patients, with greater precision, those forms of therapy that will be most effective and efficient in arresting their disease; by increasing their motivation to change; or working through their pathological dependency; by modifying their drinking behavior; or doing whatever else our particular theories, models, and conceptualizations of alcoholism direct us to be doing.

The remainder of this chapter and all of the one which follows provide a pragmatic approach to comprehensive pretreatment evaluation. Experimental research data and empirical clinical observations, as well as my own experience, are all combined in varying proportions to suggest to clinicians ways in which a meaningful, comprehensive approach may be implemented.

DETECTION, ASSESSMENT, AND DIAGNOSIS OF ALCOHOL PROBLEMS

I have previously (Jacobson, 1976, 1983b) made a distinction among the procedures and purposes of the processes referred to as detection, assessment, and diagnosis, which can now be modified to reflect the role each may play in an overall comprehensive pretreatment evaluation.

Detection can be considered as functionally equivalent to *identification*, and as such it may serve a valuable first-level screening purpose. In terms of our cancer metaphor, detection procedures can tell us only about the presence or absence of the disease, and can suggest that the patient should be referred to a specialist in oncology for further examination.

Detection procedures are useful in settings where large numbers of people must be screened in short periods of time: overcrowded courtrooms filled with DWI offenders, general medical and mental health clinics, epidemiologic surveys, and the like. Of course, most detection procedures tend to be unidimensional, in that they usually focus primarily, if not solely, on the alcohol use and related problems, and they are therefore limited in that sense. Most such procedures are based on a medical model in which one must usually make a yes–no decision about the presence or absence of a particular disease. While a disease conceptualization may be appropriate for some alcoholism syndromes, that may not be the case for all alcoholisms (Holden, 1987a, 1987b). Nevertheless, detection procedures can be a useful first step in the continuum of pretreatment evaluation services. They should be viewed as performing a *triage* function—i.e., the screening and classification of sick, wounded, or injured persons for determining who will receive treatment.

Assessment procedures, by contrast, usually allow patients to be ranked along a particular continuum. Such continua also tend to be unidimensional, but may be used in combinations. If, following a medical model of alcoholism as a progressive disease, for example, the illness may be assessed as mild–moderate–severe in intensity or as early–middle–late in progression. Similarly, our metaphoric cancer may be assessed as Stage I, II, III, and so on. Alcoholism assessment procedures do permit some treatment-related decisions. For example, the Wisconsin State Medical Society (1981) has recommended assessment criteria for determining the need for detoxification procedures, inpatient rehabilitation services, or outpatient treatment. Similarly, a *Selective Severity Assessment* procedure has been developed for determining the need for medical intervention among patients experiencing alcohol withdrawal symptoms (Daley, 1987).

True *diagnosis* is defined by its quantitative and qualitative statements based on the correct application of appropriate scientific methods for establishing the cause and nature of the disorder, by evaluating its history, present signs and symptoms, laboratory data, and other special tests. Diagnosis, then, should lead to a clearer understanding of the etiology, development, expression, and purpose of the alcoholism; the formulation of adequate and appropriate treatment plans and programs; some notion of prognosis; and full appraisal of the efficacy and outcome of treatments (Jacobson, 1988). To fulfill these requirements, our metaphoric cancer patient would need the diagnostic services of an oncologist, who may consult with a radiologist, dietician, patholo-

gist, anesthesiologist, social worker, family members, and other persons who may play a role in the diagnosis and treatment of the patient. Our real-life alcoholic patient would, similarly, benefit from the attention of an analogously composed team of diagnostic and treatment personnel.

Babor and Kadden (1985) provide a valuable clarification, and an additional concept, that elaborates on the distinctions among detection, assessment, and diagnosis. They point out that *screening* is usually, but not necessarily, a medical procedure designed to identify a treatable disease, preferably in its early or presymptomatic stage. As such, it is usually initiated by the health care worker rather than by the patient. Screening involves the use of only a portion of the usual procedures required for formal diagnosis. Diagnosis "typically involves a broader evaluation of signs, symptoms, and laboratory data as these relate to the history of the patient's illness. Screening is designed primarily for initial identification, while the purpose of diagnosis is to provide a logical basis for establishing prognosis and planning treatment. In its ideal role, screening should lead to early diagnosis and thereby improved prognosis, but in many instances screening also serves to identify advanced cases that have not come to the attention of health care workers. When screening is applied selectively to patients seeking health care for disorders that may be unrelated to their chief complaint, we speak of *casefinding*" (p. 1).

Detection and Assessment

Because some instruments and techniques initially developed for detection purposes alone—i.e., for identifying a generic alcoholism—have assessment capabilities, we can consider both categories of functioning at once. Keep in mind, however, that the approaches considered in this section represent only a starting point in the continuum of comprehensive pretreatment evaluation procedures. They will answer only fundamental yes–no questions: Is this person an alcoholic? Is some form of treatment needed? In some cases they may also indicate a degree of severity or a patient's position on a progression continuum, but such information will generally not be suitable for prescribing optimally useful treatments, simply because these techniques do not generally elicit sufficient information for that purpose.

CAGE

One of the oldest and briefest of the direct identification techniques, the CAGE consists of only four questions, whose key words form the acronym (Ewing & Rouse, 1970). Only minutes are required to ask: (a) Have you ever felt you should *cut* down on your drinking? (b) Have people *annoyed* you by criticizing your drinking? (c) Have you ever felt *guilty* about your drinking? (d) Have you ever had a drink first thing in the morning (an *eye-opener*) to steady your nerves or get rid of a hangover? Of course, the very overt nature of the CAGE gives it high face validity, and therefore any person wishing to avoid being identified as an alcoholic can easily do so by giving false responses. It is very important, therefore, to seek corroborating information from other sources (e.g., spouse, family member, significant other).

Nevertheless, a year-long validation study (Mayfield, McLeod, & Hall, 1974) of 366 hospitalized psychiatric patients demonstrated that 90% of the 142 known alcoholics could be correctly identified by their CAGE responses. Although the validation study left many important questions unanswered (e.g., How were the initial alcoholism diagnoses made? How well would the CAGE work among persons who had reason to hide their drinking problem?), the authors found that scores of 2–3 provided the best result in terms of maximum number of true-positive (81%) and true-negative (89%) identifications. All things considered, that's a good rate of return on a five-minute investment.

While other clinical studies report similarly favorable results (e.g., Woodruff, Clayton, Cloninger, & Guze, 1976; Seixas, 1976), the CAGE appears to be less valid among DWI offenders (Mischke & Venneri, 1987). The high degree of face validity, as well as the social desirability response bias known to exist among DWI motorists, suggests that other approaches may be more suitable. A problem I have found with the CAGE stems from its lack of a temporal framework—i.e., the questions are not time-bound, and therefore one can not know if the client experienced drinking problems twenty years ago or twenty days ago. Therefore, it's wise to ask "When?" or "Tell me more about that" in response to any affirmative answer.

DIS

The Diagnostic Interview Schedule was developed under contract to the National Institute of Mental Health (NIMH) between 1979–1981. It contains relevant questions pertinent to a comprehensive psychiatric diagnostic interview, and is discussed in the following chapter in that context. For our purposes here, we need focus only on those 22 items pertaining to identifying persons said to be alcohol abusers or alcohol dependent.

Because I was a consultant to NIMH in the development of the alcohol and drug items in the current version of the Diagnostic Interview Schedule (DIS-III; Robins, Helzer, Croughan, Williams, & Spitzer, 1981; Robins, 1981), I have a biased view of it. It does cover most of the major problems and symptoms associated with a medical model of a generic alcoholism, and therefore has a good degree of content validity. Some reasonable time frames are specified where appropriate (e.g., "How long has it been since you drank seven or more drinks at least once a week, or do you still?"), and a suitable degree of quantification is possible for most items. Approximately 10–15 minutes should be sufficient for completion of the alcohol items, if one is a skilled, experienced interviewer.

There are several marked advantages to using the alcohol portion of the DIS-III as one's screening tool: (a) It is brief (but one must seek corroborating information); (b) It is exceptionally well standardized; (c) There is a great deal of data attesting to its favorable validity and reliability (Eaton & Kessler, 1985); (d) probably most important, the items are keyed to all of the major psychiatric diagnostic systems currently in use, including the *Diagnostic and Statistical Manual of Mental Disorders, 3rd. Ed.* (DSM-III; American Psychiatric Association, 1980) and its new revision (DSM-III-R; American Psychiatric Association, 1987), the Feighner criteria (Feighner et al., 1972), and the Research Diagnostic Criteria (RDC; Spitzer, Endicott, & Robins, 1978). A high degree of consistency in the outcome of screening can therefore be expected, if clients will respond candidly.

Neither the *DSM-III* nor the DIS is without its problems, however. Tarter and his colleagues (1987) found that the DIS items and the corresponding *DSM-III* criteria pertinent to identification of alcohol abuse are not highly related to self-reported pattern, severity, or consequences of alcohol use. They therefore question the validity and clinical utility of *DSM-III*'s alcohol abuse criteria, and suggest that persons so diagnosed would comprise a group so heterogeneous as to render the diagnosis virtually meaningless. Although this new finding should be kept in mind, the DIS still has an acceptable level of functional utility for screening purposes. When the DIS is used in conjunction with *DSM-III-R*, the screening function of DIS can be expanded to include assessment on a mild-moderate-severe continuum. Moreover, one can differentiate between alcohol *abuse* vs. *dependence* on the basis of quality, quantity, frequency, or duration of symptom(s) present.

MAST

The *Michigan Alcoholism Screening Test* (Selzer, 1971) is probably the most widely used direct detection approach available, and because it is so well known, comments here can be kept to a minimum (readers needing full information are referred to Jacobson, 1976, 1983b, 1988). The MAST is a 25-item list of common signs and symptoms of a generic alcoholism, which can be used as an interview structure or a self-administered questionnaire. A score of 5 or more represents the traditional cutoff point for positive identification. Self-administration requires only ten minutes or so, and interviews may take 15–20 minutes.

Many early clinical studies of the MAST (e.g., Moore, 1971, 1972) reported high levels of concurrent and discriminant validity ($r = .90$) and reliability ($\alpha = .95$). Others faulted the instrument for its susceptibility to "faking good" because of high face validity, its inherent biases, and an oversensitivity that led to false-positive rates of 33%–59% (Goldberg, 1974; Fisher, Mason, & Fisher, 1976; Selzer, Gomberg, & Nordhoff, 1979). Consequently, some changes in wording of items and scoring weights were introduced (Selzer *et al.*, 1979; Selzer, 1980) to correct those problems. Regardless of those alterations, however, our own studies (Jacobson, 1979; Jacobson & Lindsay, 1980; Jacobson, Moberg, & Lindsay, 1980; Jacobson, Niles, Moberg, Mandehr, & Dusso, 1979) of several hundred MAST-tested patients and clients show that using the traditional cutoff score of 5 results in unacceptably high false-positive rates (21%–34%) when checked against other criteria. Only by using a cutoff score of 12 did we achieve acceptably balanced rates of false positive (5%–8%) and false negatives (7%–12%). Among similar samples, Brown (1979) recommends that MAST scores of 4–10 be interpreted as suggestive of problem drinking but not alcoholism. Fleming and Barry (in press) used a cutoff score of 5 and found very high sensitivity (.96) but poor specificity

(.57). Cutoff scores of 10 reduced sensitivity somewhat (.92) but increased specificity dramatically (.90). Using our recommended cutoff of 12, sensitivity was .89 and specificity was .98.

As responsible clinicians, you will have to decide what is in the best interest of your patients or clients: high sensitivity (few false negatives), high specificity (few false positives), or a reasonable compromise. If the first is more suitable to your population, use 5 as a cutoff; if the second is more desirable, cut off at 12; if a compromise is acceptable, then 10 should be your cutting score. Alternatively, readers might apply a combination of determining the meaning of scores according to this scheme: 0–4 points = no problem, 5–9 = possible, 10–11 = probably, 12 = likely. Irrespective of which you select, do seek corroborating information in the manner suggested by others (Jacobson, 1976; McAuley, Longavaugh, & Gross, 1978), such as administering the MAST to spouse or family members using the third-person pronoun.

For settings in which time is at a premium, there is a 10-item brief MAST (BMAST; Pokorny, Miller, & Kaplan, 1972), a 13-item short MAST (SMAST; Selzer, Vinokur & Van Rooijan, 1975), and a totally self-administering MAST (SAAST; Morse & Hurt, 1979; Hurt, Morse, & Swenson, 1980). All of these modifications have reasonable validity and reliability indices, and have been widely implemented.

Several studies suggest that the MAST has actual and potential uses for assessment and for diagnostically differentiating several subtypes of alcoholics or a variety of alcoholism syndromes (Zung, 1978; Skinner, 1979; Snowden, Nelson, & Campbell, 1986). Because the test now appears to be capable of defining multidimensional severity continua and problem-drinking typologies, as well as fulfilling its initially intended screening function, it seems more versatile than originally assumed.

CRIT and MODCRIT

The Criteria Committee of the National Council on Alcoholism (NCA) developed its *criteria* (CRIT) *for the diagnosis of alcoholism* in response to three judicial opinions regarding the state of confusion and lack of consensus among health professionals as to what constitutes "alcoholism." NCA's Criteria Committee (1972) published and promoted a rather complex set of criteria that was intended to become the *sine qua non* in the field. The CRIT is essentially a checklist of 85 signs and symptoms ranked along two continua—severity and progression—and designated as either major or minor. The signs and symptoms are divided into two tracks—physiological–clinical and behavioral–psychological–attitudinal—and are identified as direct or indirect effects of alcohol ingestion, and are given differential weights indicating the degree of diagnostic certainty they provide. The presence of the diagnostic signs and symptoms can be determined by observation and interview, medical examination, laboratory tests, and other means. The CRIT possess the most favorable level of construct and content validity, provide both direct and indirect detection and assessment methods, and can be used by a wide range of health professionals.

The CRIT have been widely hailed and assailed (Jacobson, 1975, 1976, 1983a, 1983b; Pattison, 1979, 1980; Ringer, Küfner, Antons, & Feuerlein, 1977) and appear to have fallen into disuse. However, some components of the CRIT continue to be used in nearly all direct and indirect approaches to detection, assessment, and diagnosis. Its comprehensiveness and multivariate approaches (e.g., psychological–behavioral, medical, biochemical, social, and so forth) to identification of a generic alcoholism is both an advantage (parts of it can be applied in many varied situations) and a disadvantage (it appears to be a "laundry list" which many people have erroneously assumed must be used in its totality). However, if used according to NCA's original intent, some portions of the CRIT can be usefully applied as quick identification procedures in and of themselves, while other portions can serve as points of subjective and objective corroboration.

Attempted simplifications of the CRIT have resulted in a modified version (MODCRIT) that consists of 36 principal signs and symptoms elicited through observation and interview. When we tested it against other criteria among groups of patients, DWI offenders, and welfare recipients, we found acceptable levels of validity and reliability (Jacobson et al., 1979; Jacobson & Lindsay, 1980; Jacobson et al., 1979; Herrington et al., 1981). The 30–40 minute MODCRIT interview seems to have acceptable sensitivity (6.5% false negatives) and specificity (7.5% false positives). Users are advised to use a scoring system that gives a 5-point weighting to each Diagnostic Level 1 (DL1) item and 1 point to each DL 2 item. The few DL 3 items included are not currently weighted, but serve to arouse suspicion and focus attention on possible symptomatic behaviors that need to be investigated further in your interview or in subsequent evaluation. Scores of 6 or higher will identify 90% of alcoholics, and correspond well to a MAST criterion score of 12. For maximum effectiveness, use the entire MODCRIT rather than stopping when the 6-point criterion has been met. Appendix 2.1 (at the end of this chapter) shows the MODCRIT items and their DLs as well as corresponding items from the *DSM*, DIS, and MAST.

As with other direct screening approaches, the face validity of the MODCRIT renders it vulnerable to intentional falsification. Therefore, it is advisable to seek corroborating information from a spouse, family member, or other knowledgeable informant.

MAC

The *MacAndrew Scale* is one of the most widely used *indirect* techniques for use with actual and potential alcoholic individuals, who should subsequently be referred for comprehensive evaluation. It is indirect in the sense that it has no face validity—i.e., the item content of the MAC is devoid of references to alcohol and alcohol-related problems (and therefore is not generally susceptible to distortion or "faking" and does not arouse suspicion or provoke defensiveness on the part of the client). It does not detect alcoholics or alcoholism *per se* but is sensitive to a pattern of responding which MacAndrew (1965) and others (see Jacobson, 1976, 1983b, 1988 for reviews) have demonstrated to be typical both of known alcoholics and potential future alcoholics.

Unfortunately, the MAC also has no construct validity in the customary sense of that term; simply put, we don't know what it really measures. Some sort of common underlying general addictive propensity has been suggested by the research literature, but this idea remains questionable (Lachar, Berman, & Grisell, 1976; Burke, 1983). Nevertheless, the MAC scale has a generally favorable level of sensitivity (i.e., few false-negative identifications) but a questionable degree of specificity (false-positive identifications may be unacceptably high), because it also is sensitive to nonalcoholic drug users, delinquency or criminality, heavy cigarette smoking, and coffee use. Be aware also that black psychiatric patients who are not substance abusers are frequently among the false positives (Graham, 1987). Therefore the MAC should not be used in isolation, and a positive score requires further evaluation.

Other studies summarized by MacAndrew (1983) now lead us to believe that his scale may have value for diagnostic and treatment-prescription purposes as well. Statistical studies show that the MAC can identify many different factors descriptive of putative traits of alcoholics, such as "boredom with or lack of concern about the proprieties of daily living." MacAndrew reports the identification of two subtypes of alcoholics on his scale: *primaries*, who are reward-seekers and who drink impulsively; and *secondaries*, who are punishment avoiders, drink to cope with negative feelings, are fearful, reticent, and have constricted interests. The two types are reported to occur in a ratio of .85:.15 in samples of known alcoholics.

Those are basically the pros and cons of using the MAC scale. In appearance, the scale is a 49-item, forced-choice, true–false questionnaire that is totally self-administering. It is suitable for individual or group administration, requires only 15–20 minutes for completion, can be scored in a minute or two, and requires no special training for use. Because it is derived from the Minnesota Multiphasic Personality Inventory (MMPI) it can be scored as part of that test if used in its entirety (see chapter 3). However, for quick screening it can be used off-scale (i.e., administered independently of the full MMPI) with only about a 2% loss of classificatory accuracy (Burg, 1973; MacAndrew, 1979). If used off-scale, then the 15 items of the MMPI's L scale should be added. We (Jacobson, Hedlund, Lyttle, & MacLaughlin, 1986) insert an L-scale item after every three MAC items; if the L score is 9 or higher, we consider the MAC to be invalid (usually because of a reading problem, failure to understand instructions, or some intentional response bias).

The issue of cutoff scores has not been satisfactorily resolved yet (see Graham, 1987 for a review of this controversy), and each reader will have to decide whether to opt for maximum sensitivity (cut off at MAC = 24) or maximum specificity (cut off at MAC = 27). For the best compromise, try this scheme: MAC score of ≤23 = negative; MAC score of 24–27 = possible; MAC score of ≥28 = positive.

For those needing greater brevity, a 20-item MAC scale is now available (Rathus, Fox, & Ortins, 1980). It seems to be particularly useful with adolescent clients, but the problem of over-sensitivity of the scale has not yet been resolved.

Others

It is impossible in a chapter of this length to do justice to the variety of other direct and indirect detection and assessment approaches available for screening purposes. There are pencil-and-paper questionnaires, symptom checklists, quantity–frequency scales of actual ethanol ingestion, medical examination formats, biochemical lab tests, self-reports, interview formats, and others. Some purport to identify that elusive and chimeric "alcoholic personality"; others mechanically analyze blood samples to determine alcohol-induced changes in liver enzymes or blood alcohol concentration in the absence of behavioral signs of intoxication.

Some interesting examples, however, should give readers an idea of the variety of other methods available to them. A simple "trauma scale" described by Skinner and his co-workers (1985) was successful in detecting 70% of "excessive drinkers" in their clinical sample. By asking five direct questions—(a) Have you had any fractures or dislocations of your bones or joints? (b) Have you been injured in a road traffic accident? (c) Have you injured your head? (d) Have you been injured in an assault or fight (exclude sports injuries)? and (e) Have you been injured after drinking?—they achieved a greater degree of sensitivity and only slightly less specificity than sophisticated biochemical tests. Skinner et al. recommend the use of the trauma scale in addition to laboratory tests, and indicate that thereby one can reasonably expect to identify 80% of excessive drinkers. These indirect methods, of course, prevent patients from becoming resistant or defensive. Sanchez-Craig and Annis (1981) have reported decreased levels of high density lipoprotein cholesterol (HDLC) in alcoholics who are drinking heavily and/or have liver disease and have recommended that as a possible marker. Several sources provide reviews of the multiplicity of techniques and approaches one may want to consider—e.g., Jacobson (1975, 1976, 1983b, 1988); Herrington, Jacobson, & Benzer (1987); Lettieri, Nelson, Sayers (1985); Miller (1976); and Chang & Chao (1985).

Diagnosis

Once the screening procedure indicates the possible or probable presence of a drinking or drinking-related problem, one may then refer the client or patient for a more thorough and comprehensive evaluation. Alternatively, depending on circumstances, one may begin the pretreatment evaluation with a diagnostic approach that will closely fulfill the criteria of true diagnosis discussed earlier. The measures included below are those which research and clinical experience have shown to be of value in understanding etiology, planning and implementing individualized treatment programs, and assessing treatment outcome.

Principles of validity—particularly construct validity—and reliability, as well as other psychometric properties, were taken into consideration in making this selection of recommended diagnostic procedures. Practical matters were also considered, such as time and expense of administration and scoring, accessibility of source materials, applicability of results, and related concerns. Theoretic rationale of instrument development was also considered, because of the relationships among how one conceptualizes alcoholic disorders, how one understands the various multifactorial etiologies, and how one assigns particular patients to specific treatments. The body of research data underlying and supporting the diagnostic and therapeutic implications of the measures have also been weighed in the balance. Where instrument development has proceeded empirically, without major obstacles in obtaining sound diagnostic results, such instruments are also included here.

Please keep in mind that none of the recommended diagnostic procedures will be totally acceptable to all clinicians in all settings. Some problems in validity and reliability are unavoidable, some tests may be too time-consuming, and so forth. Nevertheless, all of the materials discussed here hold the promise of expanding our knowledge, increasing our understanding, and improving our capacity for delivering appropriate and beneficial clinical services.

ERA

The *Essential–Reactive Alcoholism* interview has been described, reviewed, and evaluated elsewhere (Jacobson, 1976, 1983b). Suffice it to say here that it is a structured interview format comprised of 55 scorable items and 14 "fillers," which can be administered and scored in approximately 30 minutes. Experience in interviewing is useful, but beginners should not have much problem in following the author's instructions. Some degree of subjective judg-

ment will be needed in scoring or interpreting patients' responses that deviate substantially from the examples provided. The principal source document (Rudie, 1959) is readily accessible, as are several related publications describing its applications (Rudie & McGaughran, 1961; Treffert, Ansfield, & Hughes, 1974; Sugerman, Reilly, & Albahary, 1965; Levine & Zigler, 1973; Zigler & Phillips, 1962; Templer, Ruff, & Ayers, 1974).

The hypothetical constructs underlying the ERA are based on psychoanalytic theory, for which there has been insufficient validation. For practical purposes, however, acceptance of the theory is of little importance in successfully using the diagnostic and treatment-matching indications the ERA provides. Because the theory is an old one and the hypothetical constructs were developed in the context of the belief that most alcoholics were males, ERA-users may want to update the language of some of the interview items.

The interview purports to assess eight dimensions of patient characteristics relevant to diagnosis and treatment: economic dependence, emotional dependence, persistent application to reality tasks, age at onset of abusive drinking and precipitating circumstances, relationships with friends, character traits, gastrointestinal symptoms and need for oral gratification, and use of nonbeverage alcohol ("products"). Higher scores are indicative of essential alcoholism, and lower scores suggest reactive alcoholism. Because the essential–reactive dimension may be a continuum rather than a dichotomy, there are no inviolable rules about diagnostic cutoff scores. Fairly consistently, however, scores of 16–18 seem satisfactory for making diagnostic and treatment-matching decisions (Rudie, 1959; Rudie & McGaughran, 1961; Treffert, Ansfield, & Hughes, 1974; Templer, Ruff, & Ayers, 1974), and our own research supports a cutoff of 16 for men and women (Jacobson, Riedel, & Ryba, in preparation; Jacobson, Sternbach, Wallace, Brethauer, & Clark, in preparation).

Practical implications of the ERA for understanding etiology, as well as for diagnosis and treatment-matching, lie in the observations that essential alcoholics (a) are likely to have a longer history of abusive drinking; (b) generally can not identify any significant precipitating circumstances; (c) have difficulty in establishing or maintaining long-term or intimate interpersonal relationships; (d) do not establish or consistently maintain long-term goals; (e) have difficulty in assuming personal responsibilities; and (f) are unlikely to experience the behavior-controlling effects of anxiety or guilt (Rudie & McGaughran, 1961). By contrast, reactive alcoholics tend to fall at the other end of the spectrum on all of these factors, frequently have achieved a more satisfactory level of premorbid adjustment, and often have a more favorable prognosis.

Our studies (Jacobson et al., in preparation) of the ERA's treatment-related implications revealed that high scores on subscale 3 (Persistent application to reality tasks) were positively correlated with multiple readmissions for detoxification, and that higher overall scores were associated with a greater likelihood of cognitive deficits or dysfunctions. Tarter (1981) reported that essential alcoholics had more of the cognitive and behavioral traits associated with hyperactivity or minimal brain dysfunction, which certainly has important implications for treatment. He saw a similarity between the essential–reactive dimension and the primary–secondary distinction mentioned eaerlier, and Templer et al. (1974) suggested that essential alcoholism may be familial. Male alcoholics with one or more alcoholic parents or grandparents had significantly higher ERA scores, and the number of alcoholics in a patient's family was positively correlated with ERA scores.

Treffert and his colleagues (1974) studied 311 hospital-treated male alcoholics, during their inpatient stay and for a year after discharge, to test the diagnostic and treatment-matching value of the ERA, and reported favorable results. Essential alcoholics (E/; ERA scores = 1–15) and reactives (R/; ERA scores = 16–30) were randomly assigned to essential (/E), reactive (/R), or control (/C) treatments during their inpatient stay. Treatment /R, conducted by non-AA-oriented staff, included (a) psychotherapy focused on psychological problems assumed to be independent of, or underlying, the alcoholism; (b) little or no focus on the alcoholism per se; (c) didactic lectures on alcoholism; (d) pharmacotherapy with tranquilizers, antidepressants, or other appropriate medications; (e) no use of Antabuse or other aversive medications. Available aftercare focused on maximizing insight and self-understanding. Treatment /E was a generally traditional one, emphasizing abstinence and based on AA concepts. Mandatory aftercare involved strong social controls. Treatment /C was a mixture of both approaches.

Independent followup interviews and ratings at 2-, 6-, and 12-month post-discharge intervals showed that properly matched patients (R/R, E/E) generally had better outcomes than mismatched groups (R/E, R/C, E/R, E/C) on all variables: drinking or abstinence, employment, arrests, social and family relations, health, and overall improvement. The R/R group had a generally more favorable outcome than E/E patients.

Clinical personnel interested in using the ERA may want to consider the following suggestions. Because of the uncertainty over the dichotomous versus continuous nature of the essential–reactive dimension, use the full range of ERA scores for treatment-matching. Patients in the lowest-scoring quartile may be suitable for R/R groups; the highest quartile may be good E/E candidates; and the middle two quartiles may be C/C patients.

AUI, AUI-R, ADS

The *Alcohol Use Inventory* and precursive *Alcohol Use Questionnaire (AUQ)* have been extensively and favorably reviewed in the past (Jacobson, 1974, 1976, 1983b) as being excellent examples of the multivariate approach to assessment and the multifactorial approach to determining diagnosis, understanding etiologies, and making rational assignment of individuals to appropriate differential treatments. The authors' continuing interests in clinical and experimental research have recently led to some significant revisions and modifications, and a new and expanded version (the *AUI-R*, to distinguish it from the original AUI) is now available. Interested readers will find it useful to refer to the source documents for both the AUI-R (Horn, Wanberg, & Foster, 1987) and the original AUI (Wanberg, Horn, & Foster, 1977).

Fifteen years ago Wanberg, Horn, and Foster (1973) advanced the ideas of multifactorial etiololgy and a number of alcoholism syndromes. In these syndromes, alcohol was seen to provide a variety of different effects, drinking was shown to have occurred in a multitude of different patterns, and the misuse and abuse of alcohol had created a diversity of different problems. The three respective domains were referred to as *benefits, styles, and consequences*, all of which interacted to produce many constellations of causes, symptoms, and characteristics; in turn, such characteristics were representative of different predisposing, precipitating, and perpetuating factors, requiring (and making possible) different treatment approaches.

The AUQ, AUI, and AUI-R have all quite logically followed from their hypothetic (and empirically supported) position, and each generation of diagnostic materials represents an improvement over its predecessor. In its current incarnation, the AUI-R is a 228-item, forced-choice, self-report questionnaire suitable for individual or group administration with persons age sixteen or older. The last twenty items need not be answered by unmarried individuals, so administration time will vary between 40–60 minutes. It is written at a sixth-grade reading level, so few individuals should have difficulty with the language. Hand-scoring is primarily a clerical function, requiring ten minutes or so. Interpretation of profiles requires a good deal of knowledge and experience, as well as a firm grasp of the theory and purpose of the test. However, computer-based scoring and interpretation of the AUI-R is available, as are different test formats and other services. Validity and reliability studies have had consistently favorable outcomes, and psychometrically the AUI-R is a virtual paragon. It is not infallible, of course, and a sophisticated patient could distort the results in a favorable or unfavorable direction. As with all diagnostic procedures, therefore, collection of corroborating information is useful.

The AUI-R differs from the AUI in a number of ways which are worthy of some elaboration here. There are now seventeen primary scales (principal factors) rather than the sixteen found in the AUI; six second-order scales (rather than the AUI's five); and a third-order "general alcoholism" scale. The primary scales have also been reorganized and are now grouped into four domains: *benefits* (i.e., reasons for drinking, such as to improve sociability, decrease feelings of inferiority); *styles* (i.e., patterns of drinking, such as gregariously, compulsively); *consequences* (i.e., negative effects, such as becoming belligerent, harming oneself or others); and (the new domain) *concerns and acknowledgments*, which encompasses two new and potentially valuable treatment indicators, assessing readiness to accept help and awareness of drinking problems. The new second-level scale was apparently developed to accommodate current information pertaining to acknowledgement of problems and acceptance of treatment.

The very broad third-level factor appears to be relatively unchanged, at least in concept.

An interesting derivative of the AUI-R, warranting brief mention here, is the *Alcohol Dependency Scale* (ADS, Skinner & Horn, 1984), which identifies and assesses an alcohol dependence syndrome that is consonant with several widely accepted definitions of alcoholism (Criteria Committee, National Council on Alcoholism, 1972; World Health Organization, 1952; American Psychiatric Association, 1980, 1987). It includes twenty-five AUI items pertaining to the compulsion to drink excessively, repetitive experiences of withdrawal symptoms, and loss of control over one's behavior while drinking. Information is available on the relation between the ADS and physical symptoms, psychosocial problems, participation in treatment, and other treatment-related variables (Skinner & Allen, 1982). For example, high scorers are less likely to keep their appointments for treatment sessions; higher scores are associated with greater ingestion of alcohol and more psychosocial problems and physical symptoms; and increased probability of liver disease is associated with higher scores. Patients with lower scores felt that they could control their drinking, while those with higher scores believed that abstinence was necessary for their improvement (Lettieri, Nelson, & Sayers, 1985).

Both the AUI-R and the ADS have been favorably received (Nathan & Skinstad, 1987) as valuable alternatives to traditional "diagnostic" (i.e., dichotomous decisionmaking) procedures, and readers are encouraged to consult the literature to determine how these approaches can be applied to their own clinical settings and clientele (Horn, Wanberg, & Adams, 1982; Wanberg & Horn, 1983, 1987).

The AUI-R has the potential for accelerating the evolution of diagnostic and treatment-assignment procedures and placing them on a sound and rational footing. Skinner and Allen (1983) certainly agree: "To date, the AUI has been one of the most comprehensive assessment instruments available to researchers and clinicians in the alcoholism field" (p. 852). They reported favorable findings regarding the scale's reliability, robustness, concurrent validity, and construct validity when they administered the AUI to 274 patients at the Addiction Research Foundation (ARF) in Toronto.

In our own studies (Jacobson, Hedlund, Lyttle, & MacLaughlin, 1986), using the AUI in a mixed population of adult substance abuse inpatients, we found that the 99 alcoholics scored significantly higher than the 76 drug abusers on ten of the AUI's subscales but significantly lower on subscale 3 (i.e., the alcoholics were more likely to drink alone; the drug abusers used alcohol gregariously) and 13 (nonalcoholic drug usage), providing evidence of concurrent validity. When we compared alcoholics with and without history of conviction for driving while intoxicated (DWI), the drunk drivers showed significantly greater social role maladaptation and alcohol-related deterioration, as expected. With another group of 89 adult alcoholics we (Jacobson & Rubin, 1981) predicted that individuals with a prominent spike on subscale 4 (obsessive-compulsive drinking style) of their AUI profile would be better risks for outpatient treatment. We found that the subscale-4 spike successfully discriminated between treatment remainers and treatment dropouts, while number of outpatient sessions attended was significantly correlated with subscale-4 scores for treatment remainers. And while obsessive-compulsive drinking style correlated significantly with MMPI-measured obsessive-compulsive personality traits, the latter was not at all predictive of dropping out of treatment.

When comparing AUI profiles of alcoholic adolescents with those of alcoholic adult females, the teenagers used alcohol to fulfill their needs for socializing with peers (subscale 3) while the women were more likely to be solitary drinkers (Jacobson, 1983a). Short-term follow-up (3 and 6 months post-discharge) indicated that adolescents whose subscale-3 scores decreased were more likely to have remained abstinent.

Interestingly, other AUI studies (Skinner & Allen, 1983) suggest that denial, as a symptom of alcoholism, may indeed be far less common than once believed. The social undesirability of many alcohol-related behaviors and symptoms notwithstanding, defensiveness, denial, and minimization seem to be of little impact in AUI self-reports.

Clinicians needing a means of evaluating and intervening with nonalcoholic heavy social drinkers may also find the AUI (and AUI-R) suitable for their purposes, as demonstrated by Rohsenow (1982). For example, "if one wanted to use a scale to target a group of heavy college drinking men who were potentially at highest

risk for developing serious drinking problems, it would appear that the Sustained Drinking scale of the AUI is a good candidate" (p. 394). And regarding the nature of the intervention, she recommends that "This group may be best able to benefit from a *prevention program* designed toward teaching skills for coping with situations that commonly lead to depression and anger . . . Young men scoring highly on Self-Benefit Drinking may not particularly be at risk for alcohol problems, but would probably benefit from treatment for their chronic dysphoric affect" (p. 395).

A huge array of clinical improvements and research opportunities await treatment personnel who recognize the prescriptive value of the AUI-R, and the test's authors have provided guidelines for doing so (Horn et al., 1987; Wanberg et al., 1977; Skinner & Allen, 1983). These authors have elaborately described the meanings and clinical implications of the individual scales. For example, high scorers on the SOCIALIM subscale may benefit from social skills training, or may need therapy to help gain confidence in their existing social skills and to overcome shyness; group therapy may be useful for these purposes. Elevations on the MANGMOOD subscale suggest the need for treatment aimed at helping patients deal with negative affect, particularly anxiety, depression, or both; particular forms of psychotherapy or pharmacotherapy may be appropriate in such cases.

The authors (Horn, et al., 1987; Wanberg & Horn, 1987) recommend a "BSCC approach" to interpreting etiologic and therapeutic implications of the AUI-R, rather than looking at just the isolated subscales. That is, one must consider all four domains assessed by the questionnaire: *Benefits, Styles, Consequences,* and *Concerns*. By so doing, the authors have begun developing typologies (alcoholism syndromes or alcoholisms) which they feel may serve as suggested guidelines for understanding one's patients and individualizing treatment. Again, examples may provide clarification: The *Committed Type*, — likely to be male, drinking is used in his work, abstinence is not likely to be acceptable to him, regulating his drinking may be a reasonable goal, and he is unlikely to comply with a program that demands permanent abstinence; or the *Rebellion Type*, — likely to be a young male, possibly a member of an ethnic minority, with a history of antisocial activities, distrustful of and resentful toward authority, may use drinking as a way of striking back.

As part of a comprehensive pretreatment evaluation procedure, the AUI-R has demonstrated its value, and its applications in assessing treatment outcome, also should not be overlooked. As Nathan and Skinstad (1987) have pointed out, "the scales [of the AUI-R] provide a picture of patients entering or emerging from treatment that is more comprehensive than that provided by assessment instruments that tap only a portion of this information" (p. 334).

ASI

McLellan and his colleagues (1980) have responded to the perceived need for a multifactorial diagnostic procedure by developing the *Addiction Severity Index* (ASI; Cacciola, Griffith, & McLellan, 1987), which can also be used for treatment-matching and outcome assessment, for alcoholics and other substance abuse patients. The ASI is a highly structured individual interview procedure requiring approximately 30–40 minutes, to be completed jointly by the patient and a properly trained technician (the authors provide training materials and instructional sessions at very reasonable costs) or a mental health professional skilled in interviewing. Approximately 180 items provide pertinent information in six diagnostic and treatment-related domains: medical, employment/support, drug/alcohol use, legal status, family/social relations, and psychological/psychiatric status. The initial section of the interview protocol provides for the collection of standard sociodemographic information. Key features of the ASI include (a) a five-point rating scale which requires the patient to numerically assess the perceived severity of his or her own problems in each domain; (b) a ten-point rating scale, to be used by the interviewer; (c) interviewer confidence–rating scales, pertaining to patients' ability to understand the questions and the likelihood of intentional misrepresentation; and (d) the generation of a multidimensional severity profile. Of special importance to users of the ASI is the authors' conceptualization of *severity*, which is operationally defined as the *need for additional treatment*, regardless of the availability of any particular therapeutic modality and irrespective of the assumed capacity of the patient to benefit from a particular treatment.

Several large-scale studies and years of actual use of the instrument, involving more than 4,000 substance abuse patients at several different treatment facilities, provide generally favorable evidence for the clinical and experimental utility of the ASI (for details and further references, see McLellan et al., 1985a; McLellan, Luborsky, O'Brien, Barr, & Evans, 1985b). Data on inter-rater reliability, test–retest reliability, independence of subscales, concurrent validity, and discriminant validity all show consistently positive results. Both retrospective and prospective (predictive) studies using the ASI are reasonably convincing of the instrument's value in making diagnostic and prognostic statements, assigning patients to specific treatment programs, and assessing treatment outcomes. Moreover, the authors (McLellan, et al., 1985a) report that the Joint Commission on Accreditation of Hospitals (JCAH) has named the ASI as "a model instrument for satisfying its requirements for a comprehensive patient admission assessment leading to an individualized treatment plan" (p. 422).

In prospective studies of the validity and utility of the ASI, McLellan et al. (1983a) used six different treatment programs (alcohol therapeutic community, fixed-interval drinking decisions, combined treatment, drug abuse therapeutic community, alcohol outpatient, and methadone maintenance) and a three-level decision hierarchy (alcohol and/or drug dependence, ASI-assessed severity of psychiatric problems, and ASI-assessed severity of other problems) to develop specific treatment-matching protocols and decision rules. Treatment-process and six-month post-admission followup data, collected on a double-blind basis for matched and mismatched patients (47% of patients could not be matched to most-appropriate treatments because of lack of beds or treatment slots, patient noncompliance, errors, and clinical overriding of the decision strategy), indicated significantly less resistance to treatment, more favorable motivation for treatment, greater length of treatment, and a higher proportion of favorable discharges, among the matched patients. Seventeen of the nineteen post-treatment outcome criteria were generally more favorable for the matched patients, and eight of the comparisons attained statistical significance.

It is important to note the reported significance of the psychiatric severity subscale. It has been repeatedly demonstrated that this particular portion of the ASI may be the best pre-dictor of treatment outcome (McLellan, et al., 1983a, 1983b, 1984, 1985a). In fact, substance abuse patients "with low psychiatric severity improved in every treatment program. Patients with high psychiatric severity showed virtually no improvement in any treatment. Patients with midrange psychiatric severity . . . showed outcome differences from different treatments and especially from specific patient–program matches" (McLellan, et al., 1983a, p. 620). It is not sufficient, however, to rely solely on ASI subscale scores, which indicate the nature and severity of psychiatric or psychological prob-lems but do not permit a specific psychiatric diagnosis. A separate psychiatric evaluation is necessary to develop a diagnosis and provide an appropriate patient–treatment match. McLellan's data support our own observations (Jacobson, 1987a; Herrington, Benzer, Jacob-son, & Hawkins, 1982; Bedi, 1987) of a 20%–66% frequency of concomitant psychiatric problems in substance abuse populations, and underscore the importance of *comprehensive* pretreatment evaluation (as further discussed in chapter 3).

Although nearly all of the clinical studies in the literature have been reported by the ASI's authors themselves, Emrick and Hansen (1983) consider the instrument quite useful, and other professionals (Gottheil, McLellan, & Druly, 1981; Pattison, 1982) have recommended it. To their credit, McLellan and his colleagues have recognized and discussed the limitations of the ASI (e.g., some of the assumptions underlying the family/social severity items may not be valid for some patients, and the authors en-courage others in the field to approach this difficult and important problem area by col-lecting additional information). They have also identified three subgroups of substance abuse patients for whom the ASI may not be appro-priate: older alcoholics with overt cognitive impairments, younger drug abuse patients with histories of criminal activity, and adoles-cents younger than sixteen who are still sup-ported by their parents. Moreover, there ap-pear to be no followup studies of more than six month's duration, and hence little is known about longer-term treatment effects predicated on ASI scores and profiles. Also, there are few data dealing specifically with female patients, whose severity scores and concerns may differ from men's.

Even with these observations and caveats in mind, the clinical and experimental evidence favoring the ASI as part of a comprehensive pretreatment evaluation procedure remains solid. McLellan and his co-workers (1983b) have demonstrated that treatment can not only be efficacious but cost-efficient and cost-effective. One must first, however, master the skills of proper diagnosis and differentiation of substance abuse patients.

CDP

The *Comprehensive Drinker Profile* (CDP; Miller & Marlatt, 1984) is a highly structured individual interview requiring 1–2 hours for completion by patient and clinician jointly. Training, practice, and experience on the part of the interviewer—as well as an empathic, nonjudgmental, nonconfrontive attitude—are recommended for successful use of the CDP. A marked advantage of the CDP is the extent to which the authors intended the patient to be perceived and treated as a unique individual. This intention is reflected in the way in which the CDP invites the patient to participate and cooperate in his or her diagnosis, self-understanding, and treatment-selection. The several card-sorting tasks, given the patient to complete in the course of the process, provide a unique and captivating manner of involving the patient.

The interview—88 items, some with several subcomponents—is organized to systematically collect objective and subjective information classified as *demographic* (e.g., residential ar-rangements, occupational and educational his-tories), *drinking* (e.g., consumption levels and patterns, alcohol-related life problems, drinking settings, associated behaviors), and *motivational* (e.g., reasons for drinking, effects of drinking, associated life problems). This last section invites the patient to set his or her own treatment goals, assess the likelihood of achieving those goals, and describe how failure might affect him or her. The content of the interview is a balanced combination of straight-forward self-reporting (e.g., date of birth, names of medications used) and open-ended questions requiring some thought and elabora-tion (e.g., "What do you see as the most ideal outcome of treatment for you here? What would you like to happen?"). Rules for ana-lyzing and interpreting clients' open-ended re-sponses, along with instructions for scoring other items, a model data-entry form for computer encoding, and statistical data from the authors' own patient samples, are all included in the *Manual* (Miller & Marlatt, 1984).

Users of the CDP will find particularly helpful the many treatment-matching suggestions liberally but inconspicuously included in the *Manual*. Many of the recommendations are data-based (and consequently readers are encouraged to make use of the clinical references listed by the authors), while others seem more speculative. Some illustrative examples may be useful. Regarding the CDP-derived demographic domain, married patients may be more successful in maintaining long-term abstinence, while those who are single may more successfully maintain moderated non-problem drinking, particularly if they are young (under 40) and male. Regarding the drinking domain, clients offered a choice of treatment options are generally more successful than those assigned to a single treatment, with lower dropout rates, less resistance to treatment, and better compliance. Patients with lower levels of alcohol dependence are more likely to relapse from abstinence than from moderation; past drinking patterns may be predictive of success in aversive conditioning (e.g., covert sensitization) programs. Regarding the motivational domain, response patterns are differentially indicative of a client's need to acquire nonchemical means of achieving positive affective states versus nonchemical ways of coping with negative emotions (similar to the *primaries* and *secondaries* described by MacAndrew [1983] in the earlier discussion of the MAC). Other responses enable the clinician to avoid recommending treatments that have been unsuccessful in the past and about which the patient may be quite pessimistic; finding out that a patient often feels bored, depressed, fatigued, and unassertive can help the clinician–client team to establish appropriate cognitive–behavioral interventions.

A shorter form of the CDP (BDP, *Brief Drinker Profile*), a companion form for assessing treatment outcome (FDP, *Followup Drinker Profile*), and an interview technique for collecting information from patients' significant others (CIF, *Collateral Interview Form*) are all available from the same source (see Miller & Marlatt, 1984). The BDP and FDP each require less than one hour for administration. The CIF has the value of providing corroborating information regarding the validity of patients' self-reports, and also involves the patient's significant other in the therapy process.

ASIST

A Structured Addictions Assessment Interview for Selecting Treatment (Addiction Research Foundation, 1985) is another very comprehensive and thorough structured interview technique for individual use with alcoholic persons and other drug abusers. Up to two hours may be required for completion; this procedure is viewed as a wise investment of time, since Edwards and his co-workers (1977) observed that their patients generally agreed that their lengthy pretreatment evaluation interview had been the most therapeutic aspect of treatment. Cooper and Zarebski (1985) concur regarding that particular value of comprehensive evaluation, and make specific reference to the ASIST in the context of discussing pretreatment "screening and referral" as the key to successful patient–treatment matching. Although American readers may find that some aspects of the ASIST questionnaire and *Manual* may not be fully relevant in the United States, that should not significantly reduce its value.

In content and format, ASIST has much in common with the ASI and CDP, but is somewhat more complex than either. Obviously written with computer encoding in mind, the interview schedule is organized into eleven distinct areas: identifying information; basic information; living arrangements and marital and family relationships; other social relationships; education and employment; finances; leisure; legal problems; alcohol use; other drug use; and physical and emotional health. Space and formats are provided for interviewer's notes and observations, summary scores, recommended treatment plans or options, and other pertinent data.

Useful and novel features include the prospective patient's numerical ratings of the negative and positive effects of alcohol (and other drugs) in each of the life areas surveyed, the extent of his or her concern about problems in those life areas, and his or her perception of the urgency of those problems. Relatedly, the interviewer provides a numerical indication of his or her estimate of problem severity (1 = client strength/support system, 6 = extreme problem, assistance essential). Then the prospective patient's problem-urgency ratings are ranked, the interviewer follows suit, and the two individuals then work together to arrive at a negotiated ranking of the problems. Thus, "a priority ranking was undertaken to ascertain which areas required immediate attention. The recommended treatment plan addressed the most urgent problems initially, secondary problems next, and so forth" (Cooper & Zarebski, 1985, p. 5). These rating and ranking procedures, and the mutuality of the process, may well fulfill Baekeland and Lundwall's (1977) recommendations to provide what the patient perceives as essential to meeting his or her needs, rather than just providing what is easiest or what is available.

Proper and full use of ASIST requires knowledge of the Alcohol Dependency Scale (ADS, Skinner & Horn, 1984), the Drug Abuse Screening Test (DAST, Skinner, 1982), and the General Health Questionnaire (GHQ), all of which are available from the Addiction Research Foundation in Toronto.

SUDDS

Although not as wide-ranging a diagnostic and treatment-matching instrument as the AUI, the *Substance Use Disorder Diagnostic Schedule* (Harrison & Hoffman, 1985) is useful for its very specific application to establishing and clarifying a *DSM-III* or *DSM-III-R*-based identification of substance use disorders. It goes beyond that function, however, in examining alcohol- and other drug-related behaviors which the authors feel are relevant to fulfilling the demands of third-party payers, need for admission and continued-stay documentation, the needs of EAP and court personnel, collection of corroborating information from collateral sources, and other purposes. Moreover, the SUDDS can be used to collect baseline (treatment–admission) data against which one can assess treatment-outcome results at follow up. The SUDDS is tied into the highly regarded, nationwide, computerized treatment-outcome system called CATOR (Chemical Abuse/Addiction Treatment Outcome Registry).

The principal purpose of the SUDDS, however, is to provide a systematic and uniform, valid, reliable, and replicable method of collecting clinically relevant information for identification of a variety of substance use disorders, and it does so admirably. The interview requires approximately 20–35 minutes, and contains 94 items (some having several subparts) dealing with a vast array of alcohol and other drug use behaviors, environmental stressors, symptoms of depression, health problems, legal problems, social and occupational dysfunctions, and related matters.

Regarding its utility for treatment-matching,

in addition to its own merits the SUDDS is a useful adjunct to the ERA interview. For example, one SUDDS item identifies twenty-two specific environmental stressors which may serve to establish the occurrence of precipitating events in the life of the reactive alcoholic. Additionally, the SUDDS identifies nine major symptoms of depression, and therefore may suggest a treatment-matching strategy for an affective or mood disorder, involving psychotherapy, pharmacotherapy, or both. Its capacity for identifying polydrug abuse, which is becoming more commonly observed among alcoholics, enhances its treatment-assignment potential in much the same manner as the ASI.

CDAAP Scales

Inclusion of the *Chemical Dependency Adolescent Assessment Project* scales (Winters & Henly, 1987), which are just now becoming commercially available at the time of this writing, may seem premature. However, the value of the materials warrants alerting readers to their imminent public distribution. The CDAAP represents the best attempt to date at addressing the special diagnostic and treatment needs of children and adolescents, a growing proportion of whom are presenting themselves for professional attention. The *Adolescent Alcohol Involvement Scale* (AAIS; Mayer & Filstead, 1979) is the only other serious attempt to deal with the problems of this special population, but the CDAAP is far more comprehensive and utilitarian for this purpose.

Under development since 1982, the CDAAP is directed toward identification and assessment of predisposing, precipitating, and perpetuating factors underlying the etiology and development of alcoholism and other drug problems, with the goal of providing diagnostically useful information that can be applied to determining the most appropriate levels and styles of treatment for each youngster. As such, it draws heavily on theoretical and applied sources pertaining to developmental psychology, personality theory, social psychology, and related areas. It incorporates current knowledge of emotion, motivation, cognition, family and peer relations, and other psychosocial variables as they relate to normal and deviant child and adolescent behaviors.

Two related self-administering questionnaires, each requiring 30–45 minutes for completion, are designed to be used in conjunction with a *DSM-III-R*-based clinical interview. The first of these, the *Personal Experience with Chemicals Scales* (PECS), assess the types of chemicals used, pattern and severity of use, and purposes and effects of use (e.g., social consequences, physiological consequences, social–gregarious use), through the inclusion of 125 items. The second, the *Personal Experience with Living Scales* (PELS) uses 205 items to identify predisposing and perpetuating factors such as general maladjustment, social skills deficits, self-control deficits, rebelliousness, family support for use of chemicals, and several others. In addition, validity scales are embedded in the questionnaire.

Patterns of responding to the PELS (a 22-scale profile graphically displays all results of testing) are particularly useful for developing differential treatment-matching recommendations. The need for psychiatric care, social skills training, impulse-control measures, family counseling, removal from the home environment, and other specific treatment concerns can be inferred from the PELS, while the PECS allows inferences specific to the substance use disorders per se.

The psychometric properties of reliability and validity (specifically, content, construct, convergent, and discriminant) have all been adequately addressed, as have the standardization and normative procedures, through extensive sampling with a variety of clinical and nonclinical populations. The materials have all gone through several revisions, and language, reading level, and format are suitable for a wide range of children and adolescents. The developmental, validation, and standardization procedures have recently been described by Winters and Henly (1987), and readers are encouraged to review that information.

Diagnosis: Other Suggested Resources

For more than ten years Gibbs and Flanagan (1977) and Gibbs alone (1980, 1981) have systematically worked toward identifying predictors of treatment outcome, specifying the relationships between treatment-outcome predictors and specific treatment-assignment criteria, and developing a design for evaluating the efficacy of type-specific treatments based on alcoholic-type/treatment-characteristic interactions. After identifying fifty putative treatment-outcome predictors and applying rigorous statistical methods, two principal clusters were identified and confirmed—social stability and intellectual/cognitive functioning—and a third ("general severity" of alcohol problem) also emerged and was incorporated with the other two.

A 2 × 2 matrix of social stability and intellectual/cognitive functioning allowed Gibbs and Flanagan (1977) to identify four types of alcoholics and their respectively recommended treatment programs. Type I (high social stability, low intellectual functioning) should be selected for outpatient treatment, use of Antabuse, antianxiety or antidepressant medications, and frequent monitoring by a physician. Type II patients (high social stability, high intellectual functioning) are recommended for outpatient treatment with group or individual insight-oriented therapies. Type III individuals (low social stability, low intellectual functioning) are best suited to highly structured residential programs, supervised work arrangements, and vocational counseling and training. Type IV alcoholics (low social stability, high intellectual functioning) would probably be most suitable for inpatient treatment, individual or group insight-oriented therapies, structured work-release arrangements, and continued outpatient therapy after discharge from inpatient programs.

Gibbs' classification and treatment schemata contain important elements seen in the related work of cognitive theorists (Harvey, Hunt, & Schroder, 1961) and personality and social psychologists (Rudie, 1959; Rudie & McGaughran, 1961; Sugerman, Reilly, & Albahary, 1965; Levine & Zigler, 1973; Zigler & Phillips, 1962) whose work is discussed in other contexts in this chapter.

Although not formalized or standardized to the extent of those diagnostic procedures discussed earlier in this chapter, Gibbs (1980) does refer to a questionnaire he has developed for use in testing his hypotheses. Because of the potential seen in Gibb's work and the implications for continued development, readers are encouraged to try his system in their own clinical settings.

Several other matters relevant to present and future concerns about comprehensive pretreatment evaluation are worthy of brief recognition here. Dean (1985) makes a convincing case for multivariate assessment and treatment techniques, and he recommends a combination of detection and identification instruments that may at least partially fulfill those purposes. O'Leary and his colleagues (1979) identify and clarify some of the implicit biases by means of which many generic alcoholism treatment programs admit and exclude prospective patients, and clinicians responsible for selection procedures are well advised to be aware of those biases. Wallace (1986) will certainly enhance one's awareness of the heterogeneity of alcoholics and the need for recognizing various conceptualizations of alcoholism, their diagnoses, and their treatments. Watson and his group (1986) provide outstandingly detailed advice regarding identification of medical and biological signs of alcoholism and relevant laboratory tests for inclusion among one's comprehensive evaluation procedures. Giuliani and Schnoll (1985) provide a model for treatment-program selection which goes beyond the traditional concerns, and they identify specific criteria for assigning patients to four types of programs/levels of care. Cohen and Harrison (1986) review our "urge to classify" substance abusers and recommend "psychosocial classifications" as being most meaningful for understanding etiology and prescribing relevant and appropriate treatments.

Finally—and I considered this must reading—Einstein (1986) coherently and exhaustively examines seventeen selected types of therapies for substance abusers (e.g., verbal, behavioral, chemotherapeutic). He identifies thirteen selected change and treatment factors (e.g., compliance potential, beliefs and attitudes of therapists, temporal demands of treatment), which he casts into a giant matrix to demonstrate the variety and complexity of factors that should be taken into consideration as part of the patient-treatment matching process.

Detection, Assessment, and Diagnosis: The Need for Corroboration

The literature is replete with references to *denial* as a defense mechanism believed to be typical of alcoholics (e.g., Jacobson, 1988; Herrington, Jacobson, & Benzer, 1987). For whatever reason—fear of retribution, protection of self-esteem, potential loss of job or family—many alcoholics are unwilling and/or unable to veridically perceive, report, and accept their own drinking as a problem or as a cause of problems. They may deny, minimize, project, rationalize, and in other ways distort or misrepresent the extent to which they use alcohol and the degree to which it has negatively affected their lives. Although some alcoholics do provide valid self-reports (Sobell & Sobell, 1975), this is not to be expected under all circumstances. While it has been suggested that denial or other unconscious or conscious defensive behaviors are often misunderstood by health care workers (Jacobson, 1988), their utilization by alcoholics must be taken into consideration. Pattison (1985) has written some excellent guidelines for establishing attitudes of trust and confidentiality between patient and health care worker which can be very useful in assuring an increased degree of candid self-disclosure and honest self-reports.

Nevertheless, clinicians must be prepared to seek corroborating information from patients' spouse, family members, employers, and other collateral sources. Miller, Crawford, and Taylor (1979) have recommended interviewing patients' significant others as a source of validating information. Jacobson (1976) has suggested administering the MAST to the patient's spouse or significant other by simply changing the wording of appropriate items to use the third-person singular pronoun (e.g., Has he ever gotten into fights while drinking? Has she ever neglected her obligations, family, or work for two or more days because she was drinking?). Mortimer and his colleagues (1973) routinely seek corroborating information from arrest records and police reports, Department of Motor Vehicles files, records of blood alcohol concentration (BAC) at time of arrest for driving while intoxicated (DWI), school records, employment histories, and other sources. Miller and Marlatt's (1984) CIF was developed specifically for the purpose of gathering confirming data from significant others in the patient's life.

Other direct and indirect techniques of substantiating the presence of drinking and drinking-related problems are available. Biochemical tests and laboratory analyses are valued for their objectivity, tend not to arouse suspiciousness or evasiveness on the part of the client, and can be part of an overall pretreatment health examination. Tests for decreased high density lipoprotein cholesterol (Sanchez-Craig & Annis, 1981), BAC levels (Lipo, 1987), abnormal liver enzymes (Shaw, Lee, Fuller, & Lieber, 1985), and other laboratory procedures can all be useful (see Chang & Chao, 1985, for a comprehensive review). Benzer (1987) has detailed disorders of gastrointestinal, cardiovascular, neurologic, and other physical systems which often reflect signs of abusive drinking, and which can be incorporated into a pretreatment examination process.

For corroboration of alcohol or other drug problems among DWI offenders, we (Jacobson et al., 1986) have been using an indirect, inferential battery of self-administering pencil-and-paper measures which include the MAC and scales of impulsiveness, dependency and repression/denial of dependency from the Minnesota Multiphasic Personality Inventory (MMPI), portions of the Tennessee Self Concept Scale (TSCS), several subscales of the Sixteen Personality Factors questionnaire (16–PF), and other measures (see chapter 3 for all of the above). Requiring approximately one hour for completion and used in conjunction with the direct techniques of the MAST and MODCRIT, the battery discriminates well among alcoholics, other drug abusers, DWI offenders, risky drivers, and normals.

For a comprehensive survey of potential corroborating methods, see Miller (1976). Although his review is directed principally toward techniques of detection, assessment, and diagnosis, some of the methods and tools he discusses are applicable for validating and authenticating the direct self-reports of alcoholics.

CONCLUSION

This chapter does not exhaust the possibilities for detection, assessment, and diagnosis. There is a large number of potentially useful methods, techniques, and approaches available, which are beyond the scope of a single chapter. Interested readers should consult the inclusive volume by Lettieri et al. (1985), which briefly describes and reviews approximately forty-five instruments that are of varying degrees of utility for detection, assessment, diagnosis, treatment planning, determination of treatment outcome, or all of the above. Relatedly, Chang and Chao (1985) provide an excellent, detailed presentation of a variety of approaches that may be useful in many different clinical and research applications. Most of the methods they present are medical and biochemical in nature, and can be welcome additions to the clinical armamentarium.

Recent advances in our knowledge of alcoholism and the many guises and appearances it can assume places new demands on clinicians. One such demand is a continuing awareness of, and ongoing education in, the development of methods of detection, assessment, and diagnosis. Another of those demands requires a high degree of intellectual flexibility—the ability to change our attitudes toward, and our approaches to, understanding and dealing with a variety of alcoholisms and a vastly heterogeneous population of alcoholics. As our cancer metaphor has amply illustrated, technical achievements that were valid yesterday may not be so by tomorrow. Additional demands are placed on us for increasing accountability. Legislatures, managed health-care systems, professional accreditation groups, decreasing health-care dollars, and knowledgeable and sophisticated health-care consumers are all requiring (and rightly so in most cases) that we be held accountable to justify our procedures and practices.

These are only a few of the scientific, social, political, and economic forces acting on us. We must not only be appropriately reactive but proactive as well. We must take every opportunity to advance our knowledge, enrich our skills, improve our services, and enhance the quality of care we bring to our patients or clients. It is hoped that this chapter may, in part, respond to those forces and serve those purposes.

REFERENCES

Clinical Guidelines: Detection and Assessment

CAGE

Mayfield, D., McLeod, G., & Hall, P. (1974). The CAGE questionnaire: validation of a new alcoholism screening instrument. *American Journal of Psychiatry, 131,* 1121–1123. Contains information on the content and administration of the four-item CAGE and the results of a one-year validation sample, and is more readily accessible to readers than the original CAGE presentation (Ewing & Rouse, 1970).

DIS

Robins, L. N., Helzer, J. E., Croghan, J., Williams, J. B. W., & Spitzer, R. L. (1981). *NIMH Diagnostic Interview Schedule: Version III.* Rockville, MD: National Institute of Mental Health.

Robins, L. N. (1981). *NIMH Diagnostic Interview Schedule: Version III. Instructions for Use.* Rockville, MD: National Institute of Mental Health.

The first of these two publications contains the complete content of the 263-item DIS: the questions to be asked, a computer-encoding format, and a few ancillary materials. The second publication contains complete instructions for conducting the interview, scoring, and related matters. All materials are in the public domain and are available at no charge from NIMH.

MAST

Selzer, M. L. (1971). The Michigan Alcoholism Screening Test: the quest for a new diagnostic instrument. *American Journal of Psychiatry, 127,* 89–94. Describes the development, content, administration, and scoring of the MAST. For similar information on two brief forms of the MAST see Pokorny, Miller, and Kaplan (1972) and Selzer, Vinokur, and Van Rooijan (1975).

CRIT, MODCRIT

Criteria Committee, National Council on Alcoholism. (1972). Criteria for the diagnosis of alcoholism. *American Journal of Psychiatry, 129,* 127–135. Describes the rationale, purpose, content, and use of the entire CRIT system. Provides information on the presumed course of alcoholism, at-risk characteristics, and related materials. For information on the development, content, and use of the MODCRIT, see Jacobson, Niles, Moberg, Mandehr, and Dusso (1979); Jacobson and Lindsay (1980); and Jacobson, Moberg, and Lindsay (1980). A format for administering and scoring the MODCRIT as an interview is available from the Ralph G. Connor Alcohol Research Reference File, Center of Alcohol Studies, Rutgers University, New Brunswick, New Jersey, 08903.

MAC

MacAndrew, C. (1965). The differentiation of male alcoholic outpatients from nonalcoholic psychiatric outpatients by means of the MMPI. *Quarterly Journal of Studies on Alcohol,* 1965, *26,* 238–246. Reports on content, administration,

and scoring of the MAC, statistical data on discriminant validity of scale items, and related information.

Clinical Guidelines: Diagnosis

ERA

Rudie, R. R. (1959). Developmental and behavioral differences between essential and reactive alcoholics. Doctoral dissertation, University of Houston. Contains complete details on theory, construction, content, administration, and scoring of the ERA interview schedule and related information. Copies are available through University Microfilms, Ann Arbor, Michigan.

AUI, AUI-R

Horn, J. L., Wanberg, K. W., & Foster, F. M. (1987). *Guide to the Alcohol Use Inventory.* Minneapolis, MN: National Computer Systems.

Wanberg, K. W., Horn, J. L., & Foster, M. F. (1977). A differential assessment model for alcoholism: the scales of the Alcohol Use Inventory. *Journal of Studies on Alcohol, 38,* 512–543.

The first of these two source documents is an outstanding example of how a user's guide should be written. In a clear and concise fashion the authors provide useful and interesting information about background and theoretic rationale, test development, content and meaning of the instrument and all of its subscales; data on validity and reliability; instructions for administration and scoring; clinical applications of the diagnostic instrument; interpretation of scores and profiles; indications for treatment; and other information that clinicians and researchers will find valuable. The manual pertains to the revised AUI, which has been available for approximately two years. Test booklets, answer sheets and profile forms, scoring templates, and other materials and services must be purchased from the publisher. The second source document is actually the manual for the original AUI, which has been in reasonably wide use for nearly fifteen years. It provides a more detailed description of the history and development of the AUI, as well as clinically and experimentally useful interpretations of the instrument and its implications for treatment-planning and individualized treatment assignment.

ADS

Skinner, H. A., & Horn, J. L. (1984). *Alcohol Dependence Scale (ADS) Users Guide.* Toronto, Ontario: Addiction Research Foundation. This source document provides, in a concise and definitive manner, the background and development of the ADS, information on its psychometric properties, and instructions for administration, scoring, and interpretation. Test booklets are available for purchase from the publisher.

ASI

Cacciola, J., Griffith, J., & McLellan, A. T. (Eds.) (1987). *Addiction Severity Index Instruction Manual (4th ed.)* (Mimeo). Philadelphia, PA: University of Pennsylvania, School of Medicine, Department of Psychiatry/Veterans Administration Medical Center. This informal, mimeographed 33-page manual provides exceptionally detailed step-by-step instructions on the administration, scoring, and interpretation of the ASI interview schedule. Highly specific suggestions are provided regarding how to phrase questions, develop rapport with patients, clarify the meaning of patients' responses, and so on. The ASI, Manual and related documents, and training materials and services can be obtained directly through the authors. (Contact Dr. A. T. McLellan, VA Medical Center [116], University Avenue, Philadelphia, PA, 19104).

CDP,BDP, CIF, FDP

Miller, W. R., & Marlatt, G. A. (1984). *Manual for the Comprehensive Drinker Profile.* Odessa, FL: Psychological Assessment Resources, Inc. A well-written, detailed manual providing a bit of background information on development and purpose of the CDP, an extremely thorough and precise explanation of how to administer the interview, complete instructions for scoring, and very useful guidelines for interpretation of results, with some useful suggestions for treatment assignment. Interview booklets, card-sort materials, and additional information are available from the publisher. The Brief Drinker Profile (BDP), an abbreviated version of the CDP, is also available. A Followup Drinker Profile (FDP) and a Collateral Interview Form (CIF) are also available from the same source.

ASIST

Addiction Research Foundation (1985) *A Structured Addictions Assessment Interview for Selecting Treatment (ASIST).* Toronto, Ontario, Canada: Author. Contains explicit instructions for administering, scoring, and interpreting the questionnaire. All necessary materials are available from the publisher. Some aspects of ASIST may be inappropriate or irrelevant to U.S users.

SUDDS

Harrison, P. A., & Hoffmann, N. G. (1985). *Substance Use Disorder Diagnostic Schedule (SUDDS) Manual.* St. Paul, MN: Medical Education and Research Foundation, St. Paul-Ramsey Medical Center. A well-developed and thoughtful *Manual* that focuses on leading the interviewer through the step-by-step, question-to-question process of administering the SUDDS, querying the patient, clarifying responses, recording the data, and making decisions about classifying and quantifying the patient's problems. All necessary materials and ancillary services are available from the publisher.

CDAAP

Winters, K. C., & Henly, G. A. (1987, March). Scales of the Chemical Dependency Adolescent Assessment Project. Paper presented at the Fifth Annual Conference of the State of Wisconsin Alcohol and Drug Abuse Research Advisory Committee, Milwaukee, Wisconsin. Provides information on theory, history, and development of CDAAP materials; content and structure of questionnaires; psychometric properties of the instruments; and outcome of use with several clinical and comparative populations. Copies of the questionnaire, instructions for administration and scoring, interpretation, clinical applications, and other information are available from the authors (CDAAP, 1295 Bandana Blvd., N., Suite 210, St. Paul, MN 55108).

RESEARCH

American Psychiatric Association (1980). *Diagnostic and statistical manual of mental disorders (3rd. ed.).* Washington, D.C.: Author.

American Psychiatric Association (1987). *Diagnostic and statistical manual of mental disorders (3rd. ed., rev.) DSM-III-R*. Washington, D.C.: Author.

Babor, T. F. (1981). Evaluating the evaluation process. In R. E. Meyer, B. C. Glueck, J. E. O'Brien, T. F. Babor, J. Jaffe, & J. R. Stabenau (Eds.), *Research monograph No. 5. Evaluation of the alcoholic: Implications for research, theory, and treatment* (pp. x–xvi). Rockville, MD: National Institute on Alcohol Abuse and Alcoholism.

Baekeland, F., & Lundwall, L. K. (1977). Engaging the alcoholic in treatment and keeping him there. In B. Kissin, & H. Begleiter (Eds.), *The biology of alcoholism—Vol. 5, Treatment and rehabilitation of the chronic alcoholic* (pp. 161–195). New York: Plenum.

Bedi, A. (1987). Alcoholism, drug abuse, and other psychiatric disorders. In R. E. Herrington, G. R. Jacobson, & D. G. Benzer (Eds.), *Alcohol and drug abuse handbook* (pp. 346–384). St. Louis, MO: Warren H. Green, Inc.

Benzer, D. G. (1987). Medical complications of alcoholism. In R. E. Herrington, G. R. Jacobson, & D. G. Benzer (Eds.), *Alcohol and drug abuse handbook* (pp. 219–253). St. Louis, MO: Warren H. Green, Inc.

Bohman, M. (1978). Some genetic aspects of alcoholism and criminality; a population of adoptees. *Archives of General Psychiatry, 35*, 269–276.

Brown, R. A. (1979). Use of the Michigan Alcoholism Screening Test with hospitalized alcoholics, psychiatric patients, drinking drivers, and social drinkers in New Zealand. *American Journal of Drug and Alcohol Abuse, 6*, 375–381.

Burg, E. (1973). The reliability of the MacAndrew alcoholism scale, administered separately and as part of the Minnesota Multiphasic Personality Inventory. Master's thesis, University of Wisconsin—Oshkosh.

Burke, H. R. (1983). "Markers" for the MacAndrew and the Cavior Heroin Addiction MMPI scales. *Journal of Studies on Alcohol, 44*, 558–563.

Cadoret, R. J., & Gath, A. (1978). Inheritance of alcoholism in adoptees. *British Journal of Psychiatry, 132*, 252–258.

Chang, N. C., & Chao, H. M. (Eds.). *Early identification of alcohol abuse: Proceedings of a workshop, October 32–November 1, 1983* (Research Monograph No. 17, DHSS Pub. No. [ADM]85–1258). Rockville, MD: National Institute on Alcohol Abuse and Alcoholism.

Cloninger, C. R. (1987). Neurogenetic adaptive mechanisms in alcoholism. *Science, 236*, 410–416.

Cohen, A., & Harrison, M. D. (1986). The "urge to classify" the drug user: a review of classification by patterns of abuse. *International Journal of the Addictions, 21*, 1249–1260.

Cooper, D. E. (1987). The role of group psychotherapy in the treatment of substance abusers. *American Journal of Psychotherapy, 41*, 55–67.

Cooper, H., & Zarebski, J. (1985, August). A promising technique for successful patient–treatment matching: the addiction assessment process. Paper presented at the 34th International Congress on Alcoholism and Drug Dependence, Calgary, Alberta, Canada.

Criteria Committee, National Council on Alcoholism (1972). Criteria for the diagnosis of alcoholism.

American Journal of Psychiatry, 129, 127–135.

Daley, M. (1987). The role of nursing in the treatment of substance use disorders. In R. E. Herrington, G. R. Jacobson, & D. Benzer (Eds.), *Alcohol and drug abuse handbook* (pp. 269–292). St. Louis, MO: Warren H. Green, Inc.

Dean, J. (1985). A multivariant assessment and treatment technique for alcohol problems. *International Journal of the Addictions, 20*, 1281–1290.

Eaton, W. W., & Kessler, L. G. (Eds.). (1985). *Epidemiologic field methods in psychiatry: The NIMH epidemiologic catchment area program*. Orlando, FL: Academic Press.

Edwards, G., Orford, J., Egert, S., Guthrie, S., Hawker, A., Heneman, C., Mitcheson, M., Oppenheimer, E., and Taylor, C. (1977). Alcoholism: a controlled trial of "treatment" and "advice." *Journal of Studies on Alcohol, 38*, 1004–1031.

Einstein, S. (1986). Treatment of the drug user: considering the "demands" of therapeutic technologies and their implications for treatment planning, implementation, and outcome. *International Journal of the Addiction, 21*, 1339–1358.

Emrick, C. D. (1975). A review of psychologically oriented treatment of alcoholism. II. The relative effectiveness of different treatment approaches and the effectiveness of treatment versus no treatment. *Journal of Studies on Alcohol, 36*, 88–108.

Emrick, C. G., & Hansen, J. (1983). Assertions regarding effectiveness of treatment for alcoholism: fact or fantasy? *American Psychologist, 38*, 1078–1088.

Ewing, J. A., & Rouse, B. A. (1970, February). Identifying the hidden alcoholic. Paper presented at the 29th International Congress on Alcoholism and Drug Dependence, Sydney Australia.

Favazza, A. R., & Pires, J. (1974). The Michigan Alcoholism Screening Test: application in a general military hospital. *Quarterly Journal of Studies on Alcohol, 35*, 925–929.

Feighner, J. P., Robins, E., Guze, S. B., Woodruff, R. A., Winokur, G., & Munoz, R. (1972). Diagnostic criteria for use in psychiatric research. *Archives of General Psychiatry, 26*, 57–63.

Fleming, M. F., & Barry, K. L. (in press). A study examining the psychometric properties of an abbreviated form of the Michigan Alcoholism Screening Test. *Journal of Family Practice.*

Gibbs, L. E. (1980). A classification of alcoholics relevant to type-specific treatment. *International Journal of the Addictions, 15*, 461–488.

Gibbs, L. E. (1981). The need for a new design for evaluating alcoholism treatment programs. *Drug and Alcohol Dependence, 8*, 287–299.

Gibbs, L., & Flanagan, J. (1977). Prognostic indicators of alcoholism treatment outcome. *International Journal of the Addictions, 12*, 1097–1141.

Giuliani, D., & Schnoll, S. H. (1985). Clinical decision making in chemical dependence treatment: a programmatic model. *Journal of Substance Abuse Treatment, 2*, 203–208.

Goodwin, D. W. (1982). Alcoholism and heredity: update on the implacable fate. In E. L. Gomberg, H. R. White, & J. A. Carpenter (Eds.), *Alcohol, science, and society revisited* (pp. 162–170). Ann Arbor, MI: University of Michigan Press.

Gottheil, E., McLellan, A. T., & Druly, K. A. (Eds.).

(1981). *Matching patient needs and treatment methods in alcoholism and drug abuse.* Springfield, IL: Charles C. Thomas.

Graham, J. R. (1987). *The MMPI: A practical guide (2nd ed).* New York: Oxford University Press.

Harvey, O. J., Hunt, D. E., & Schroder, M. H. (1961). *Conceptual systems and personality organization.* New York: J. Wiley.

Herrington, R. E., Benzer, D. G., Jacobson, G. R., & Hawkins, M. K. (1982). Treating substance use disorders among physicians. *Journal of the American Medical Association, 247,* 2253–2257.

Herrington, R. E., Jacobson, G. R., & Benzer, D. (Eds.). (1987). *Alcohol and drug abuse handbook.* St. Louis, MO: Warren H. Green, Inc.

Herrington, R. E., Jacobson, G. R., Daley, M. E., Lipo, R., Biller, H., & Weissgerber, K. (1981). Use of the plasma alpha-amino-n-butyric acid to leucine ratio in identifying alcoholics: an unsuccessful test. *Journal of Studies on Alcohol, 42,* 492–499.

Holden, C. (1987a). Alcoholism and the medical cost crunch. *Science, 235,* 1132–1133.

Holden, C. (1987b). Is alcoholism treatment effective? *Science, 236,* 20–22.

Horn, J. L., Wanberg, K. W., & Adams, G. (1982). Diagnosis of alcoholism: factors of drinking, background and current conditions in alcoholics. In E. M. Pattison (Ed.), *Selection of treatment for alcoholics* (pp. 53–78). New Brunswick, NJ: Rutgers Center of Alcohol Studies.

Hurt, R. D., Morse, R. M., & Swenson, W. M. (1980). Diagnosis of alcoholism with a self-administered alcoholism screening test: results with 1,002 consecutive patients receiving general examinations. *Mayo Clinic Proceedings, 55,* 365–370.

Huss, M. (1852). *Chronische Alkoholskrankheit, oder Alcoholismus chronicus. Ein Beitrag zur Kenntris der Vergiftungs-Krankheiten nach eigener und anderer Erfahrung.* Stockholm, Sweden and Leipzing, Germany: C. E. Fritze.

Jacobson, G. R. (1975). *Diagnosis and assessment of alcohol abuse and alcoholism* (DHEW Pub. No. [ADM] 80–228). Rockville, MD: National Institute on Alcohol Abuse and Alcoholism.

Jacobson, G. R. (1976). *The Alcoholisms: Detection, Assessment, and Diagnosis.* New York: Human Sciences Press.

Jacobson, G. R. (1979). Identification and assessment of problem drinkers. In *Proceedings of the 2nd National DWI Conference,* (pp. 35–43). Falls Church, VA: AAA Foundation for Traffic Safety.

Jacobson, G. R. (1983a, October). Evaluation and assessment of the individual alcoholic. Paper presented at the Fourth Annual University of New Mexico Department of Psychiatry/National Council on Alcoholism Institute on Alcoholism, Albuquerque, NM.

Jacobson, G. R. (1983b). Detection, assessment, and diagnosis of alcoholism: current techniques. In M. Galanter (Ed.), *Recent developments in alcoholism, vol. I* (pp. 377–413). New York: Plenum.

Jacobson, G. R. (1987a). Alcohol and drug dependency problems in special populations: children and adolescents. In R. E. Herrington, G. R. Jacobson, & D. G. Benzer (Eds.), *Alcohol and drug abuse handbook* (pp. 405–432). St. Louis, MO: Warren H. Green, Inc.

Jacobson, G. R. (1987b, June). Alcoholism or alcoholisms? Treatment or treatments? Paper presented at A Symposium on Alcohol Treatment: Examining the Alternatives. Milwaukee, WI: University of Wisconsin-Milwaukee.

Jacobson, G. R. (1988). Identification of problem drinkers and alcoholics. In R. R. Watson (Ed.), *Diagnosis of alcohol abuse.* Boca Raton, FL: CRC Press, Inc.

Jacobson, G. R., Hedlund, R. D., Lyttle, M., & MacLaughlin, S. (1986). Development of Wisconsin's Drug Abuse Screening Inventory (Highway Safety Project No. 00-84-00-02-037-130.). Final Report to Wisconsin Department of Transportation. Madison, WI: DOT Office of Highway Safety.

Jacobson, G. R., & Lindsay, D. (1980). Screening for alcohol problems among the unemployed. In M. Galanter (Ed.), *Currents in alcoholism, vol. VII: Recent advances in research and treatment* (pp. 357–371). New York: Grune & Stratton.

Jacobson, G. R., Moberg, D. P., & Lindsay, D. (1980). Screening for alcohol problems among the unemployed: II. Further developments of rapid identification procedures, referral for treatment, and outcome of treatment. Final Report to the Governor's Employment and Training Office.

Jacobson, G. R., Niles, D. H., Moberg, D. P., Mandehr, E., & Dusso, L. (1979). Identifying alcoholic problem-drinking drivers: Wisconsin's field test of a modified NCA Criteria for the diagnosis of alcoholism. In M. Galanter (Ed.), *Currents in alcoholism, vol. VI: Treatment, rehabilitation, and epidemiology* (pp. 273–293). New York: Grune & Stratton.

Jacobson, G. R., Riedel, J., & Ryba, S. (in preparation). The essential–reactive alcoholism distinction among female inpatients.

Jacobson, G. R., & Rubin, E. M. (1981). Premature termination of treatment among alcoholics: predicting outpatient clinic dropouts. In M. Galanter (Ed.), *Currents in alcoholism, vol. VIII: Recent advances in research and treatment* (pp. 162–174). New York: Grune & Stratton.

Jacobson, G. R., Sternbach, T. G., Wallace, A., Brethauer, R., & Clark, B. (in preparation). Characteristics of male and female alcoholics prematurely terminating inpatient treatment.

Jellinek, E. M. (1952). Phases of alcohol addiction. *Quarterly Journal of Studies on Alcohol, 13,* 673–684.

Jellinek, E. M. (1960). *The disease concept of alcoholism.* New Haven, CT: College and University press.

Lachar, D., Berman, W., & Grisell, J. L. (1976). The MacAndrew Alcoholism Scale as a general measure of substance misuse. *Journal of Studies on Alcohol, 37,* 1609–1615.

Lettieri, D. J., Nelson, J. E., & Sayers, M. A. (Eds.). (1985). *Treatment Handbook Series: 2. Alcoholism Treatment Assessment Research Instruments* (DHHS Pub. No. [ADM 85 1380]). Rockville, MD: National Institute on Alcohol Abuse and Alcoholism.

Levine, J. And Zigler, E. (1973). The essential–reactive distinction in alcoholism: a developmental approach. *Journal of Abnormal Psychology, 81,* 242–249

Lipo, R. F. (1987). Drug screening for presence of substance of abuse. In R. E. Herrington, G. R. Jacobson, & D. Benzer (Eds.), *Alcohol and drug abuse handbook* (pp. 134–149). St. Louis, MO: Warren H. Green, Inc.

Lipton, M. A. (1979). Diverse research strategies for depression and alcoholism. *American Journal of Psychiatry, 136,* 497–501.

MacAndrew, C. (1983). Alcoholic personality or personalities: scale and profile data from the MMPI. In W. M. Cox (Ed.), *Identifying and measuring alcoholic personality characteristics* (pp. 73–85). San Francisco, CA: Jossey-Bass.

Mayer, J. E., & Filstead, W. J. (1979). The Adolescent Alcohol Involvement Scale: an instrument for measuring adolescent use and misues of alcohol. *Journal of Studies of Alcohol, 40,* 291–300.

McAuley, R., Longavaugh, R., & Gross, H. (1978). Comparative effectiveness of self and family forms of the Michigan Alcoholism Screening Test. *Journal of Studies on Alcohol, 39,* 1622–1627.

McLellan, A. T., Childress, A. R., Griffith, J., & Woody, G. E. (1984). The psychiatrically severe drug abuse patient: methadone maintenance or therapeutic community? *American Journal of Drug and Alcohol Abuse, 10,* 77–95.

McLellan, A. T., Luborsky, L., Cacciola, J., Griffith, J., Evans, F., Barr, H. L., & O'Brien, C. P. (1985a). New data from the Addiction Severity Index: reliability and validity in three centers. *Journal of Nervous and Mental Disease, 173,* 412–423.

McLellan, A. T., Luborsky, L., O'Brien, C. P., Barr, H. L., & Evans, F. (1985b). The Addiction Severity Index in three different populations. In Committee on Problems of Drug Dependence, Inc. (Research Monograph Series, No. 55 DHHS Pub. No. [ADM] 85-1393.). *Problems in Drug Dependence, 1984: Proceedings of the 46th Annual Scientific Meeting.* Rockville, MD: National Institute on Drug Abuse.

McLellan, A. T., Luborsky, L., Woody, G. E., & O'Brien, C. P. (1980). An improved diagnostic evaluation instrument for substance abuse patients: the Addiction Severity Index. *Journal of Nervous and Mental Disease, 168,* 26–33.

McLellan, A. T., Luborsky, L., Woody, G. E., O'Brien, C. P., & Druly, K. A. (1983a). Predicting response to alcohol and drug abuse treatments: role of psychiatric severity. *Archives of General Psychiatry, 40,* 620–625.

McLellan, A. T., Woody, G. E., Luborsky, L., O'Brien, C. P., & Druly, K. A. (1983b). Increased effectiveness of substance abuse treatment: a prospective study of patient–treatment "matching." *Journal of Nervous and Mental Disease, 171,* 597–605.

Miller, W. R. (1976). Alcoholism scales and objective assessment methods: a review. *Psychological Bulletin, 83,* 649–674.

Miller, W. R., Crawford, V. L., & Taylor, C. A. (1979). Significant others as corroborative sources for problem drinkers. *Addictive Behaviors, 4,* 67–70.

Miller, W. R., & Hester, R. K. (1986). Inpatient alcoholism treatment: who benefits? *American Psychologist, 41,* 794–805.

Mischke, H. D., & Venneri, R. L. (1987). Reliability and validity of the MAST, Mortimer-Filkins questionnaire, and CAGE in DWI assessment. *Journal of Studies on Alcohol, 48,* 492–501.

Morse, R. M., & Hurt, R. D. (1979). Screening for alcoholism. *Journal of the American Medical Association, 242,* 2688–2690.

Mortimer, R. G., Filkins, L. D., Kerlan, M. W., & Lower, J. S. (1973). Psychometric identification of problem drinkers. *Quarterly Journal of Studies on Alcohol, 34,* 1322–1335.

Nathan, P. E., & Skinstad, A-H. (1987). Outcomes of treatment for alcohol problems: current methods, problems, and results. *Journal of Consulting and Clinical Psychology, 55,* 332–340.

O'Leary, M. R., Speltz, M. L., Donovan, D. M., & Walker, R. D. (1979). Implicit preadmission screening criteria in an alcoholism treatment program. *American Journal of Psychiatry, 136,* 1190–1193.

Pattison, E. M. (1979, October). The NCA Criteria after nearly ten years. Paper presented at the conference on Evaluation of the Alcoholic: Implications for Research, Theory, and Treatment. Hartford, CT: University of Connecticut Health Center and Alcohol Research Center.

Pattison, E. M. (1980). The NCA diagnostic criteria: critique, assessment, alternatives. *Journal of Studies on Alcohol, 41,* 965–981.

Pattison, E. M. (Ed.). (1982). *Selection of Treatment for Alcoholics.* New Brunswick, NJ: Rutgers Center of Alcohol Studies.

Pattison, E. M. (1985). The selection of treatment modalities for the alcoholic patient. In J. H. Mendelson & N. K. Mello (Eds.), *The diagnosis and treatment of alcoholism* (2nd ed.) (pp. 189–294). New York: McGraw-Hill.

Pokorny, A. D., Miller, B. A., & Kaplan, H. B. (1972). The brief MAST: a shortened version of the Michigan Alcoholism Screening Test. *American Journal of Psychiatry, 129,* 342–345.

Rathus, S. A., Fox, J. A., & Ortins, J. B. (1980). The MacAndrew Scale as a measure of substance abuse and delinquency among adolescents. *Journal of Clinical Psychology, 36,* 579–583.

Ringer, C., Küfner, H., Antons, K., & Feuerlein, W. (1977). The NCA Criteria for diagnosis of alcoholism: an empirical evaluation study. *Journal of Studies on Alcohol, 38,* 1259–1273.

Rohan, W. P. (1978). Comments on "The NCA criteria for the diagnosis of alcoholism: an empirical evaluation study." *Journal of Studies on Alcohol, 39,* 211–218.

Rohan, W. P. (1982). The concept of alcoholism: assumptions and issues. In E. M. Pattison & E. Kaufman (Eds.), *Encyclopedic handbook of alcoholism* (pp. 31–39). New York: Gardner Press.

Rohsenow, D. J. (1982). The Alcohol Use Inventory as predictor of drinking by male heavy social drinkers. *Addictive Behaviors, 1,* 387–395.

Rudie, R. R., & McGaughran, L. S. (1961). Differences in developmental experience, defensiveness, and personality organization between two classes of problem drinkers. *Journal of Abnormal and Social Psychology, 62,* 659–665.

Sanchez–Craig, M., Annis, H. (1981). Gamma–Glutamyltranspeptidase and high–density lipoproteins cholesterol in male problem drinkers: Advantages of a composite index for predicting alcohol consumption. *Alcoholism: Clinical and Experimental Research, 5,* 540–544.

Schuckit, M. A. (1979). *Drug and alcohol abuse: A clinical guide to diagnosis and treatment.* New York: Plenum.

Schuckit, M. A. (1985). Genetics and the risk for alcoholism. *Journal of the American Medical Association, 254,* 2614–2617.

Schuckit, M. A., Gold, E., & Risch, C. (1987). Serum prolactin levels in sons of alcoholics and control subjects. *American Journal of Psychiatry, 144,* 854–859.

Schuckit, M. A., & Morrissey, E. R. (1979). Psychiatric problems in women admitted to an alcoholic detoxification center. *American Journal of Psychiatry, 136,* 611–617.

Seixas, F. (1976). Afterword. In G. R. Jacobson, *The alcoholisms: Detection, assessment, and diagnosis* (pp. 407–414). New York: Human Sciences Press.

Selzer, M. L., Vinokur, A., & Van Rooijan, L. (1975). A self-administered short Michigan Alcoholism Screening Test (SMAST). *Quarterly Journal of Studies on Alcohol, 36,* 117–126.

Shaw, S., Lee, K., Fuller, R. K., & Lieber, C. S. (1985). Sequential measurement of plasma alpha amino-n-butyric acid and gamma glutamyl transpeptidase for the diagnosis of relapse following treatment for alcoholism (Research Monograph No. 17, DHSS Pub. No. [ADM] 85-1258). In N. C. Chang & H. H. Chao (Eds.), *Early identification of alcohol abuse; Proceedings of a workshop, October 31–November 1, 1983* (pp. 100–107). Rockville, MD: National Institute on Alcohol Abuse and Alcoholism.

Skinner, H. (1979). A multivariate evaluation of the Michigan Alcoholism Screening Test. *Journal of Studies on Alcohol, 40,* 831–844.

Skinner, H. A. (1982). The Drug Abuse Screening Test. *Addictive Behaviors, 7,* 363–371.

Skinner, H. A., & Allen, B. A. (1982). Alcohol dependence syndrome: measurement and validation. *Journal of Abnormal Psychology, 91,* 199–209.

Skinner, H. A., & Allen, B. A. (1983). Differential assessment of alcoholism: evaluation of the Alcohol Use Inventory. *Journal of Studies on Alcohol, 44,* 852–862.

Skinner, H. A., Holt, S., Schuller, R. Roy, J., & Israel, Y. (1985). Identification of alcohol abuse: trauma and laboratory indicators. In N. C. Chang & H. M. Chao (Eds.), *Early identification of alcohol abuse; Proceedings of a workshop, October 31–November 1, 1983* (pp. 285–301). (Research Monograph No. 17, DHSS Pub. No. [ADM] 85-1258). Rockville, MD: National Institute of Alcohol Abuse and Alcoholism.

Snowden, L. R., Nelson, L. S., & Campbell, D. (1986). An empirical typology of problem drinkers from the Michigan Alcoholism Screening Test. *Addictive Behaviors, 11,* 37–48.

Sobell, L. C., & Sobell, M. B. (1975). Outpatient alcoholics give valid self-reports. *Journal of Nervous and Mental Disease, 161,* 32–42.

Spitzer, R. L., Endicott, J., & Robins, E. (1978). Research diagnostic criteria: rationale and reliability. *Archives of General Psychiatry, 35,* 733–783.

Stedman's Medical Dictionary, 24th Edition (p. 216).

(1982). Baltimore, MD: Williams & Wilkins.

Sugarman, A. A., Reilly, D., & Albahary, F. S. (1965). Social competence and the essential–reactive distinction in alcoholism. *Archives of General Psychiatry, 12,* 552–556.

Tarter, R. E. (1981). Minimal brain dysfunction as an etiological predisposition to alcoholism. In R. E. Meyer, B.C. Glueck, J. E. O'Brien, T. F. Babor, J. Jaffe, & J. R. Stabenau (Eds.), *Research Monograph No. 5 Evaluation of the Alcoholic: Implications for Research, Theory, and Treatment* (pp. 167–191). Rockville, MD: National Institute on Alcohol Abuse and Alcoholism.

Tarter, R. E., Arria, A. M., Moss, H., Edwards, N. J., & Van Thiel, D. H. (1987). DSM-III criteria for alcohol abuse: associations with alcohol consumption behavior. *Alcoholism: Clinical and Experimental Research, 11,* 541–543.

Templer, D. I., Ruff, C. F., & Ayers, J. (1974). Essential alcoholism and family history of alcoholism. *Quarterly Journal of Studies on Alcohol, 35,* 655–657.

Treffert, D. A., Ansfield, P. J., & Hughes, G. B. (1974). Different strokes for different folks: an analysis of specific treatment in two subgroups of alcoholics (Research Grant No. MH 18441-02). Final Report to National Institute of Mental Health.

Wallace, J. (1986). The other problems of alcoholics. *Journal of Substance Abuse Treatment, 3,* 163–171.

Wanberg, K. W., & Horn, J. L. (1983). Assessment of alcohol use with multidimensional concepts and measures. *American Psychologist, 38,* 1055–1069.

Wanberg, K., & Horn, J. L. (1987). The assessment of multiple conditions in persons with alcohol problems. In W. M. Cox (Ed.), *Treatment and prevention of alcohol problems: A resource manual* (pp. 27–55). Orlando, FL: Academic Press.

Wanberg, K. W., Horn, J. L., & Foster, F. M. (1973, September). A differential model for the diagnosis of alcoholism: scales of the Alcohol Use Questionnaire. *Selected papers: Twenty-Fourth annual meeting of the Alcohol and Drug Problems Association of North America.* Washington, D.C.: ADPANA.

Watson, R. R., Mohs, M. E., Eskelson, C., Sampliner, R. E., & Hartmann, B. (1986). Identification of alcohol abuse and alcoholism with biological parameters. *Alcoholism: Clinical and Experimental Research, 10,* 364–385.

Winters, K. C., & Henley, G. A. (1987). Advances in the assessment of adolescent chemical dependency: development of a chemical use problem severity scale. *Psychology of Addictive Behaviors, 1,* 146–153.

Wisconsin State Medical Society, Committee on Alcohol and Other Drug Abuse (1981). Guideline admission criteria for chemical dependency treatment services. *Wisconsin Medical Journal, 80,* 5–7.

Woodruff, R. A., Clayton, P. J., Cloninger, C. R., & Guze, S. B. (1976). A brief method of screening for alcoholism. *Diseases of the Nervous System, 37,* 434–435.

World Health Organization (1952). *Expert Committee Report, No. 48.* Geneva, Switzerland: Author.

Zigler, E., & Phillips, L. (1962). Social competence and the process–reactive distinction in psychotherapy. *Journal of Abnormal Psychology, 65,* 215–222.

Zucker, R. A. (1987). The four alcoholisms: a developmental account of the etiologic process. In P. C. Rivers (Ed.), *Alcohol & addictive behavior, Nebraska Symposium on Motivation, 1986* (pp. 27–83). Lincoln, NE: University of Nebraska Press.

Zung, B. J. (1978). Factor structure of the Michigan Alcoholism Screening Test. *Journal of Studies on Alcohol, 39,* 56–57.

Appendix. Comparison of Major Screening Instruments.

MODCRIT Items	Corresponding MAST Items	Corresponding DSM-III-R Criterion	Corresponding DIS Items
A. Psychological and Attitudinal Indicators (Track II) Minor Criteria			
1. Client admits a drinking problem, wonders about or questions the normalcy of his or her drinking, or in other ways implies a concern about his/her drinking in terms of quantity, frequency, or duration of drinking episodes, inability to regulate drinking, inability to abstain from drinking, etc. (DL 2)	Do you feel you are a normal drinker? (2) Can you stop drinking without a struggle after one or two drinks? (2) Are you always able to stop drinking when you want to? (2)	Substance often taken in larger amounts or over a longer period than the person intended. Persistent desire or one or more unsuccessful efforts to cut down or control substance use.	Did you ever think that you were an excessive drinker? Have you ever wanted to stop drinking but couldn't? Some people promise themselves not to drink before 5 o'clock or never to drink alone, in order to control their drinking. Have you ever done anything like that? Have you ever gone on binges or benders, where you kept drinking for a couple of days or more without sobering up?
2. When talking freely during assessment, makes frequent reference to drinking, people (including self) being "bombed," "stoned," etc., or admits to drinking more than peers. (DL 2)			
3. Drinking to relieve anger, insomnia, fatigue, depression, social discomfort, etc. (DL 2)			
4. Psychological symptoms consistent with organic brain impairment, reported by client, significant other(s), and/or as observed in assessment (e.g., impairment in memory, attention, concentration, reasoning, judgment). (DL 2)	Have you ever been seen at a psychiatric or mental health clinic, or gone to any doctor, social worker, or clergyman for help with an emotional problem related to drinking? (2)	Continued substance use despite knowledge of having a persistent or recurrent . . . psychological . . . problem that is caused or exacerbated by the use of the substance.	There are several health problems that can result from long stretches of pretty heavy drinking. Did drinking ever cause you to have . . . memory trouble when you haven't been drinking (not blackouts)?

44

5. Unexplained changes in family, social, school, business, and/or other relationships and activities, reported by client and/or significant other(s). (DL 3)		
6. Complaints about family members and/or significant others, job, school, friends. (DL 2)		
7. Spouse, significant other, and/or family member(s) complain about client's drinking, as reported by client, spouse, significant other(s), and/or family member(s). (DL 2)	Does your wife (husband), girlfriend (boyfriend), and/or parents ever worry or complain about your drinking? (1) Do friends and relatives think you are a normal drinker? (2) Has your wife (husband), girlfriend (boyfriend), or other family member ever gone to anyone for help about your drinking? (2)	Continued substance use despite knowledge of having a persistent or recurrent social . . . problem that is caused or exacerbated by the use of the substance . . . Has your family objected because you were drinking too much?
8. Major family disruptions, (e.g., separation or threat of separation, divorce or threat of divorce), not specifically related to drinking. (DL 3)		
8.1. Major family disruptions, (e.g., separation or threat of separation, divorce), specifically related to drinking. (DL 2)	Does your wife (husband) or girlfriend (boyfriend) ever worry or complain about your drinking? (1) Has your drinking ever created problems with you and your wife (husband) or girlfriend (boyfriend)? (2)	Continued substance use despite knowledge of having a persistent or recurrent social . . . problem that is caused or exacerbated by the use of the substance . . . Has your family ever objected because you were drinking too much?

Continued

45

Appendix. Comparison of Major Screening Instruments (*Continued*)

MODCRIT Items	Corresponding MAST Items	Corresponding DSM-III-R Criterion	Corresponding DIS Items
A. Psychological and Attitudinal Indicators (Track II) Minor Criteria (cont'd)			
9. Job loss (due to increasing interpersonal difficulties), frequent job changes, financial difficulties, failure to meet social, personal, and/or family obligations, for reasons unexplained or unrelated to drinking. (DL 3)			
9.1. Job loss (due to increasing interpersonal difficulties), frequent job changes, financial difficulties, failure to meet social, personal, and/or family obligations for reasons related to drinking. (DL 2)	Have you ever neglected your obligations, your family, or your work for two or more days because you were drinking? (2)	Frequent intoxication or withdrawal symptoms when expected to fulfill major role obligations at work, school, or home . . . A great deal of time spent in activities necessary to get the substance, and/or recovering from its effects.	Have you ever had job (or school) troubles because of drinking—like missing too much work or drinking on the job (or at school)? Did you ever lose a job (or get kicked out of school) on account of drinking? Have you ever gone on binges or benders, where you kept drinking for a couple of days or more without sobering up?
10. Open expression of regressive defensive mechanisms, (e.g., denial, projection), in attempt to explain problems. (DL 3)			
11. Open expression of feelings of resentment, jealousy, paranoid (suspicious, blaming) attitudes or ideas. (DL 3)			

12. Expressions of feelings of isolation, sadness, guilt, self-blame; suicidal thoughts or ideas. (DL 3)			
12.1. Expression of feeling isolation, sadness, guilt, self-blame, related to drinking; suicidal thoughts or ideas related to drinking. (DL 2)	Continued substance use despite knowledge of having a persistent or recurrent . . . psychological problem that is caused or exacerbated by the substance. . .	Do you ever feel guilty about your drinking? (1)	
13. Feelings of "losing one's mind" or losing control over one's feelings. (DL 2)	Continued substance use despite knowledge of having a persistent or recurrent . . . psychological problem that is caused or exacerbated by the substance. . .		
B. Behavioral Indicators (Track II) Minor Criteria			
14. Gulping drinks. (DL 3)		Do you ever drink in the morning? (1)	
15. Surreptitious (secret or hidden) drinking. (DL 2)			
16. Morning drinking (assess nature of peer group, work shift, and other circumstances, recreations, etc.). (DL 2)	Substance often taken to relieve or avoid withdrawal symptoms		Did you ever need a drink just after you had gotten up (i.e., before breakfast)?
17. Repeated conscious attempts at *abstinence* (as distinguished from Criterion A.1.). (DL2)	Persistent desire or one or more unsuccessful attempts to eliminate (rather than merely cut down or control) substance use.	Are you always able to stop drinking when you want to? (2)	Have you ever wanted to stop drinking but couldn't?
18. Blatant or conspicuous and inappropriate use of alcohol as explained by client or significant other, or by observation during assessment (e.g., intoxication, odor of alcohol, possession of alcohol). (DL 1)	Recurrent use in situations in which use is physically hazardous.	Have you ever neglected your obligations, your family, or your work for two or more days because you were drinking? (2) Have you ever been arrested, even for a few hours, because of drunk behavior? (2)	Have you ever gotten into trouble because of drinking—like having an accident or being arrested for drunk driving?

Continued

Appendix. Comparison of Major Screening Instruments (*Continued*)

MODCRIT Items	Corresponding MAST Items	Corresponding DSM-III-R Criterion	Corresponding DIS Items
B. Behavioral Indicators (Track II) Minor Criteria (cont'd)			
19. Skid Row or equivalent socio-economic level, attributable to drinking. (DL 1)		Important social, occupational, or recreational activities given up or reduced because of substance use.	
20. Frequent and various medical excuses from work. (DL 2)			
21. Shifting from one alcoholic beverage to another, unexplained. (DL 2)			
22. Preference for drinking companions, bars, taverns, etc. (DL 2)	Have you ever lost friends because of your drinking? (2)	Important social, occupational, and/or recreational activities given up or reduced because of substance use.	
23. Loss of interest in activities unassociated with drinking. (DL 2)	Have you ever gotten into trouble at work because of drinking? (2)		
24. Choice of employment that facilitates drinking as part of the job, or allows wider latitude for surreptitious drinking. (DL 3)	Have you ever lost a job because of drinking? (2) Have you ever neglected your obligations, your family, or your work for two or more days because you were drinking? (2)		
25. Frequent automobile accidents and/or other traffic violations not known to involve alcohol. (DL 3)			
26. Legal problems (civil or criminal) attributable to drinking, such as non-payment of bills, default in child support, arrests for drunk and disorderly behavior, assault/battery, etc. (DL 2)	Have you ever been arrested, even for a few hours, because of drunk behavior? (2) Have you gotten into fights when drinking? (1)	Continued substance use despite knowledge of having a persistent or recurrent social . . . problem that is caused or exacerbated by the use of the substance.	Have you ever gotten into trouble driving because of drinking—like having an accident or being arrested for drunk driving?

		Have you ever been arrested or held at the police station because of drinking or disturbing the peace while drinking? Have you ever gotten into physical fights while drinking?
27. History of family members undergoing psychiatric treatment; school and/or behavioral problems in children. (DL 3)		
27.1. History of family members undergoing treament for alcoholism; alcohol-related school and/or behavioral problems in children. (DL 2)		
28. Frequent change in residence for poorly defined reasons ("geographic escape"). (DL 3)		
29. Anxiety-relieving mechanisms, such as telephone calls that are inappropriate in time, distance, person, or motive ("telephonitis"). (DL2)		
30. Outbursts or rage, suicidal gestures, and/or other inappropriate or uncontrolled expressions of emotion, reported by the client and/or significant other, and related to drinking. (DL 2)	Has your drinking ever created problems with you and your wife (husband), or girlfriend (boyfriend)? (2) Have you gotten into fights when drinking? (1)	Continued substance use despite knowledge of having a persistent or recurrent . . . psychological problem that is caused or exacerbated by the use of the substance. . .	Have you ever been arrested or held at the police station because of drinking or disturbing the peace while drinking? Have you ever gotten into physical fights while drinking?

Continued

Appendix. Comparison of Major Screening Instruments (*Continued*)

MODCRIT Items	Corresponding MAST Items	Corresponding DSM-III-R Criterion	Corresponding DIS Items
C. Behavioral, Psychological, and Attitudinal Indicators (Track II) Major Criteria			
31. History of previous treatment(s) for substance use disorder, reported by client and/or significant other. (DL 1)	Have you ever attended a meeting of Alcoholics Anonymous because of your own drinking? (5)	Continued substance use despite knowledge of having a persistent or recurrent social, psychological, or physical problem that is caused or exacerbated by use of the substance.	Have you ever told a doctor about a problem you had with drinking?
	Have you ever gone to anyone for help about your drinking? (5)		Have friends, your doctor, your clergyman, or any other professional ever said you were drinking too much for your own good?
	Have you ever been in a hospital because of drinking? (5)		
	Have you ever been seen at a psychiatric or mental health clinic, or gone to any doctor, social worker, or clergyman for help with an emotional problems related to drinking? (2)		
32. Drinking despite strong medical contraindications known to the client. (DL 1)	Have you ever been told you have liver trouble? Cirrhosis? (2)	Continued substance use despite knowledge of having a persistent or recurrent . . . physical problem that is caused or exacerbated by use of the substance.	Have you ever continued to drink when you knew you had a serious physical illness that might be made worse by drinking?
	Have you ever gone to anyone for help about your drinking? (5)		Have friends, your doctor, your clergyman, or any other professional ever said you were drinking too much for your own good?

Criterion	Questions	Questions
33. Drinking despite strong, identified social contraindications (family, legal, and occupational problems directly attributable to alcohol; all three types of problems must be present; related DL 2 and DL 3 symptoms must have been endorsed). (DL 1)	Have you ever lost friends because of your drinking? (2) Have you ever gotten into trouble at work because of your drinking? (2) Have you ever lost a job because of drinking? (2) Have you ever been arrested for drunk driving? (2) Have you ever been arrested . . . because of drunk behavior? (2)	There are several health problems that can result from long stretches of pretty heavy drinking. Did drinking ever cause you to have: a. liver disease or yellow jaundice, b. vomiting blood or other stomach troubles, c. trouble with tingling or numbness in your feet, d. memory trouble when you haven't been drinking (not blackouts), e. inflammation of your pancreas or pancreatitis?
	Continued substance use despite knowledge of having a persistent or recurrent social (or) psychological . . . problem that is caused or exacerbated by use of the substance.	Have you ever had job (or school) troubles because of drinking—like missing too much work or drinking on the job (or at school)? Did you ever lose a job (or get kicked out of school) on account of drinking? Have you ever gotten into trouble driving because of drinking—like have an accident or being arrested for drunk driving? Have you ever been arrested or held at the police station because of drinking or disturbing the peace while drinking? Have you ever gotten into physical fights while drinking?

Continued

51

Appendix. Comparison of Major Screening Instruments (*Continued*)

MODCRIT Items	Corresponding MAST Items	Corresponding DSM-III-R Criterion	Corresponding DIS Items
D. Physiological and Clinical (Track I) Major Criteria			
34. Alcoholic "blackout" periods (differentiated from psychological fugue states, psychomotor seizures) as described by client and/or significant other. (DL 2)	Have you ever awakened the morning after some drinking . . . and found that you could not remember a part of the evening before? (2)	Continued substance use despite knowledge of having a persistent or recurrent . . . psychological or physical problem that is caused or exacerbated by use of the substance.	Have you ever had blackouts while drinking, (i.e., where you drank enough) so that you couldn't remember the next day what you had said or done? Have you ever continued to drink when you knew you had a serious physical illness that might be made worse by drinking?
35. Client and/or significant other reports withdrawal syndrome (when alcohol intake is abruptly discontinued or significantly reduced without substitution of other drugs or medications), including:	Have you ever had delirium tremens (DTs), severe shaking, heard voices, or seen things after heavy drinking? (2)	Characteristic withdrawal symptoms, including coarse tremor of hands, tongue, or eyelids; nausea or vomiting; malaise or weakness; autonomic hyperactivity (increased blood pressure, rapid heart rate, sweating); anxiety; depressed mood or irritability; transient hallucinations or illusions; headache; insomnia.	Have you ever had "the shakes" after stopping or cutting down on drinking (e.g., your hands shake so that your coffee cup rattles in the saucer or you have trouble lighting a cigarette)?
35.1. Gross tremor (differentiated from other causes of tremor). (DL 1)			Have you ever had fits or seizures after stopping or cutting down on drinking?

35.2. Hallucinosis (differentiated from schizophrenic hallucinations, other psychoses, and other substance-induced hallucinations). (DL 1)

Have you ever seen or heard things that weren't really there after cutting down on drinking?

35.3. Withdrawal seizures (differentiated from epilepsy, other seizure disorders, and other substance-induced seizures). (DL 1)

35.4. Delirum tremens (DTs) usually beginning 1-3 days after cessation of drinking and including tremors, disorientation, and hallucinations. (DL 1)

Have you ever had DTs (hallucinations and fever) when you quit drinking?

36. Client and/or significant other reports marked increases in tolerance (although there may be a decreased tolerance later, in the presence of liver disorders). (DL 2)

Marked tolerance; need for markedly increased amounts of the substance (e.g., at least a 50% increase) in order to achieve intoxication or desired effect, or markedly diminished effect with continued use of the same amount.

Notes

Numbers in parentheses indicate diagnostic significance (weighting) of the item. Use recommended cutoff scores of ≤ 4 = no problem, 5-9 = possible, 10-11 = probable, ≥ 12 = likely.

Some symptoms of the disturbance must have persisted for at least one month, or must have occurred repeatedly over a longer period of time.

DL numbers in parentheses refer to NCA's diagnostic levels. (DL 1 = classical, definite, obligatory) (clearly associated with alcoholism) (DL = 2 probable, frequent, indicative, lends strong suspicion, seek corroborative information) (DL = 3 potential, possible, incidental, should arouse suspicion). Use recommended cutoff score of ≥ 6 when DL 1=5, DL 2=1, DL 3=0.

CHAPTER 3

A Comprehensive Approach to Pretreatment Evaluation: II. Other Clinical Considerations

George R. Jacobson [*]

ACKNOWLEDGMENTS

The author is grateful to Ms. Patricia Johnson for her assistance in preparing this chapter, and to Ms. Karen Roe for her assistance in providing research and reference materials.

CONCEPTUAL ISSUES IN COMPREHENSIVE EVALUATION

Just as the preceding chapter detailed a variety of approaches to detection, assessment, and diagnosis of alcoholism and alcohol-related problems, this chapter highlights and summa-

[*]The opinions and conclusions expressed herein are solely those of the author and do not necessarily reflect the positions or policies of any institution with which he is affiliated.

rizes clinically useful methods of assessment and diagnosis of related and relevant aspects of human functioning. In selecting materials for inclusion herein, the same considerations of validity, reliability, availability of materials, time and expense, ease of administration and scoring, and related matters were equivalently emphasized. Instruments and techniques with substantial underlying data bases and of demonstrated clinical value were given preference.

Ultimate selection of the components of a comprehensive clinical evaluation battery must, however, remain the responsibility of individual practitioners. That selection will be guided by how one conceptualizes alcoholism, and one's awareness of the overall context of human functioning within which the alcohol-related problems are embedded. That is, it is no longer a tenable stance to look at just the alcoholism, as though it had an autonomous existence of its own, apart from the biopsychosocial environment in which it occurs. Concomitant psychopathology, personality, perception, self-concept, cognitive style, intellectual performance, physical health status, and other domains of human functioning must all be part of the descriptive, diagnostic, prognostic, and prescriptive processes by means of which the individual patient is assigned to the most effective treatment(s).

How one conceptualizes alcoholism is no less important in the context of this chapter than it was in the preceding chapter. If, for example, one conceptualizes it as a disease, in terms of a strictly constructed medical model, then physical examination and laboratory procedures would take precedence. But if alcoholism is understood as being symptomatic of some underlying or concomitant psychopathology, then the psychiatric evaluation and psychological assessment methods will be of higher priority. For clinicians who think of alcoholism primarily in terms of perceptual and cognitive deficits or dysfunctions, then other, more relevant objects of evaluation would be targeted.

The thrust of this chapter, however, is that to be most effective and useful, pretreatment evaluation must in fact be truly comprehensive, and therefore it must be multidisciplinary and interdisciplinary. The cancer metaphor woven through the preceding chapter remains operative here as well. Alcoholism is truly a *biopsychosocial* phenomenon, and optimum treatments depend on an overall ecological approach to assessment of all relevant aspects of the organism and his or her environment.

There are data, cited below and in the preceding chapter, indicating that genetic, biochemical, and neuroendocrinologic variables may play some causal role in the etiology of one or more forms of *familial* alcoholism. And it is certainly known that alcohol abuse causes disease. Hence the need for a medical component in a comprehensive pretreatment evaluation, and in treatment *per se*. There is an equivalent body of data suggesting that *essential* alcoholism may be a *primary* psychiatric disorder, while *reactive* alcoholism may be a *secondary* one. There are frequent associations between alcoholism and personality disorders or mood disorders in adults and attention deficit disorders or conduct disorders in children and adolescents. Nationwide epidemiologic studies (Eaton & Kessler, 1985) show that individual psychiatric disorders tend to occur in patterns; hence the need for a psychiatric evaluation

component. Other studies point to the possibility that another form of alcoholism may be related to particular styles of perception and levels of cognitive function. Meldman's (1970) studies suggest that alcoholism may be attributable to "diseases of attention and perception," and my own clinical and experimental observations point in a similar direction. Thus, evaluation of perceptual and cognitive variables is recommended, particularly since learning, memory, attention, and concentration are involved in virtually all successful forms of "talk treatment." Other clinicians operate on the assumption that low self-esteem is both a cause and an effect of alcohol abuse and must therefore be a focus of evaluation and treatment.

It should be clear, then, that multiple conceptualizations of alcoholism exist, and guide our understanding of, thinking about, and treatment for our patients. However, none of these conceptualizations are totally valid for all alcoholics or for all expressions of the alcoholisms. Nor have any of them been conclusively demonstrated to be irrelevant or unsupportable. We are well advised to conscientiously consider all of them.

The remainder of this chapter focuses on how (and, to some extent, why) an appropriate comprehensive pretreatment evaluation may be conducted. Implications for treatment-matching are also suggested, as are criteria for treatment-outcome determination.

MEDICAL AND LABORATORY PROCEDURES

Good clinical practice demands a thorough and comprehensive medical examination, laboratory studies, and related procedures. A variety of medical complications, affecting virtually all systems of the body, can sometimes result from long-term abusive drinking, dietary and nutritional neglect, and related factors. Guidelines for medical, laboratory, and other diagnostic and treatment-planning procedures are available elsewhere (Criteria Committee, National Council on Alcoholism, 1972; Herrington, Jacobson, & Benzer, 1987; Kissin, 1977; Kissin & Begleiter, 1971, 1972, 1974; Pattison & Kaufman, 1982; Chang & Chao, 1985; Watson, Mohs, Eskelson, Sampliner, & Hartmann, 1986). The outcomes of the medical diagnostic studies will, of course, suggest prognoses, and the patient's response to treatment is a vital index of his or her progress in recovery.

PSYCHIATRIC EVALUATION

Most personnel at treatment agencies and institutions are aware of the importance of a complete psychiatric examination as part of a comprehensive pretreatment evaluation for patients. Relatively high proportions of alcoholic patients have shown other, concomitant psychopathologies requiring additional treatment arrangements (Jacobson, 1987a; Herrington, Benzer, Jacobson, & Hawkins, 1982; Bedi, 1987). Between 20%–67% of patients were found to be in need of psychiatric care beyond that usually provided for alcoholic patients. Antisocial personality disorders and affective or mood disorders appeared to be most common. Since it is known that treatment for alcoholism is less likely to be fully effective if concomitant disorders go undiagnosed and untreated, readers are strongly urged to consider psychiatric diagnosis as a routine component of pretreatment evaluation, if possible. In fact, Donovan (1986) has gone so far as to state that a personality disorder diagnosis should be a mandatory consideration in every psychiatric diagnosis of alcoholism, because traditional approaches to diagnosis may not be adequate. Moreover, Donovan recommends looking at the etiologies and diagnoses of "the alcoholisms," and has constructed a tentative, tripartite, multifactorial model for doing so. Many of his diagnostic and etiologic observations have direct implications for treatment, particularly those regarding a *familial* alcoholism, which he discusses briefly. Relatedly, it has been shown that persons having one psychiatric diagnosis (e.g., alcohol abuse or dependence) are more likely to be found with two or more concomitantly (Eaton & Kessler, 1985).

Therefore, a full-spectrum, systematic psychiatric examination for every patient can be useful. The previously mentioned diagnostic criteria established by the American Psychiatric Association (1980, 1987) are the most widely used for this purpose. The *DSM-III* or *DSM-III-R* criteria can be used in conjunction with the Diagnostic Interview Schedule (DIS; Robins, 1981; Robins, Helzer, Croghan, Williams, & Spitzer, 1981). In its entirety, the DIS-III has 263 very specific and well-structured questions covering the gamut of psychiatric symptoms. Experience in interviewing is mandatory, and 1.5–2 hours should be allowed for completion of the procedure. We (Jacobson, Hedlund, Lyttle, & MacLaughlin, 1986) have found that students with some background in interviewing can be trained to use the DIS-III after 3–6 hours of supervised patient interaction. Complete instructions (Robins, 1981) for use of the DIS-III are available on request, at no cost. The advantages and disadvantages of using the DIS and DSM-III or DSM-III-R are discussed in the preceding chapter. Acceptable alternative procedures include the Feighner criteria (Feighner, Robins, Guze, Woodruff, Winokur, & Munoz, 1972) and the Research Diagnostic Criteria (RDC; Spitzer, Endicott, & Robins, 1978).

PSYCHOLOGICAL AND NEUROPSYCHOLOGICAL PROCEDURES

So much has been written about psychological and neuropsychological characteristics of alcohol abusers that it is difficult to simply summarize those data and make specific recommendations for useful procedures. The decision as to what information may be most useful must be guided, in part, by the treatment resources available to the clinician in his or her particular treatment setting. However, many alcoholics show a variety of cognitive and neuropsychological deficits and dysfunctions (Parsons, Butters, & Nathan, 1987). Many of those problems can interfere with treatment; however, they are also more treatable than once thought (e.g., Løberg, 1980; Hansen, 1980). Therefore, sound psychological and neuropsychological data are essential to comprehensive pretreatment evaluation. Brief descriptions of widely used testing procedures follow.

The *Shipley Institute of Living Scale* (SILS; Shipley, 1940; Zachary, 1987) is a brief (maximum timed administration is twenty minutes, scoring requires only a minute or two), self-administering, inexpensive (less than $1.00 per patient), well-researched, reasonably valid, and reliable test that provides quantitative measures of verbal skills and abstract thinking. The combined scores provide an inferred or estimated overall IQ (Paulson & Lin, 1970), while the difference between the two scores provides a conceptual quotient (CQ). The CQ is an index of cognitive development or cognitive dysfunction, theoretically relevant to the etiology of alcohol abuse (Harvey, Hunt, & Schroder, 1961), attributable to the effects of alcohol abuse, and directly applicable to developing a patient's treatment program.

The *Bender Visual Motor Gestalt test* (BG; Bender, 1938) is another brief assessment tool. It takes approximately ten minutes for individual administration of visual stimuli and an additional ten minutes or so for scoring (Pascal & Suttel, 1951). Although widely used, it is only a gross measure of brain dysfunction and not specific at all to alcohol-related impairment. Nevertheless, in using this test in our own studies of 500 consecutively admitted inpatients, we found that more impaired individuals (higher BG scores) were significantly more likely to drop out of hospital treatment (Jacobson, Sternbach, Wallace, Brethauer, & Clark, in preparation). Some degree of organic dysfunction may be transient, signifying residual toxicity and suggesting that involvement in cognitive–intellectual aspects of treatment should be postponed by 1–4 weeks after cessation of drinking (Tarter & Sugerman, 1976). More enduring residual dysfunction may be an indicator for routing a patient into a treatment track that is more explicit, concrete, or directive.

Valuable clinical information is also derived from routine use of the *Memory for Designs Test* (MFD; Graham & Kendall, 1960). and the Digit Span subtest of the *Wechsler Adult Intelligence Scale* (WAIS; Wechsler, 1955). The former requires approximately fifteen minutes for individual presentation and reproduction of visual stimuli and perhaps ten minutes for scoring, and yields useful information regarding dysfunctions of attention, concentration, and short-term retention and recall. The latter provides similar information using auditory stimuli and requires only ten minutes or less for individual oral presentation and repetition of increasingly longer series of numbers (administration and scoring are simultaneous). Bergman (1987) reports favorable use of the MFD, and Wilson (1987) describes the value of the WAIS's Digit Span subtest, in their respective clinical settings.

A number of other practical alternatives for testing attention, concentration, learning, retention and memory, and related abilities are described by Small (1973). A wide-ranging review by Miller and Saucedo (1985) summarizes the clinical value of a battery comprised of the *Digit Symbol* and *Block Design* subtest of the original WAIS or its current revision (WAIS-R) (Wechsler, 1955, 1981), and the *Category, Tactual Performance,* and *Trail Making* components of the Halstead–Reitan Neuropsychological Test Battery (Halstead, 1947; Reitan & Davison,

1974). Administration and scoring of the Digit Symbol test requires five minutes or so, as the patient learns to substitute geometric figures in place of numbers. The Block Design subtest requires the patient to duplicate a series of increasingly difficult geometric patterns using red and white cubes while he or she looks at a two-dimensional picture of the finished product. Time limits are specified for each of the designs to be reproduced. In the Category Test, the patient is given seven series of visual stimuli which must be sorted into four classes (categories), based on principles that he or she must discover as the test-administrator provides verbal feedback on the correctness and incorrectness of the patient's sortings. The Tactual Performance Test is administered while the patient is blindfolded. The patient handles a wooden three-dimensional geometric object (e.g., star, square) and then must place it in its corresponding recess on a form-board, first using the dominant, then the non-dominant, then both hands. Subsequently the patient's blindfold is removed, and he or she is asked to draw the shapes he or she has been handling and their respective locations on the form-board. In the Trail Making Test, the patient first performs a timed connect-the-dots type of task, thereby making a trail of circled numbers. The second part of the test requires the patient to make a similar trail by alternately connecting numbers and letters. The diagnostic and treatment-related applications of this five-part battery have been substantiated by other clinicians and researchers (see Parsons, et al., 1987).

When more comprehensive and sophisticated neuropsychological diagnostic measures are warranted, the Luria (Christensen, 1975) or complete Halstead–Reitan batteries are often recommended for evaluation of cognitive-intellectual functioning. The data derived from these measures do provide information relevant to treatment-assignment, and have been related to recovery of function in a variety of alcoholic populations (Parsons et al., 1987).

PERSONALITY, PERCEPTION, AND SELF-CONCEPT

Meaningful and comprehensive pretreatment evaluation should include valid, reliable, and clinically relevant measures of personality, perception, self-concept, and related variables.

Clinically relevant data, directly applicable to

understanding the possible etiologies of the patient's alcohol abuse and planning an appropriate treatment program, can be derived from the *Sixteen Personality Factors Questionnaire* (16-PF; Cattell, Eber, & Tatsouka, 1970). A self-administering, forced-choice, 187-item questionnaire, suitable for individual or group use, the 16-PF can be completed in approximately 45–60 minutes. Scoring and profiling requires 10–15 minutes, but machine scoring and computerized profiling and interpretive reporting services are commercially available at reasonable costs. Several different forms are available, depending on education and reading level, thus facilitating pre- and post-treatment evaluations.

Sixteen pairs of bipolar first-order personality traits, four second-order clusters, and other ancillary data emerge from this factor analytically constructed test, which has been well researched since its appearance in 1949 (see Meyer, 1983, for a review). The test provides descriptive, predictive, and prescriptive information in the hands of a skilled and experienced user. One approach to the utilization of this information is the actuarial overall profile analysis (Krug, 1981), while another emphasizes individual subscales (Karsen and O'Dell, 1976). There is much to recommend both processes, but the latter may be better suited to the purposes of this chapter. For example, scores on Factor H (colloquially called *boldness*; technically referred to as *threctia* at one pole and *parmia* at the other) suggest that at one extreme the individual is "shy, timid, restrained, threat-sensitive" and at the other extreme "adventurous, thick-skinned, socially bold." Cattell et al. (1970) suggest that *threctia* (high susceptibility to threat) may be an inherited trait, having its biogenesis in an over-responsive or sensitive sympathetic nervous system. Alcoholic individuals with low Factor H scores are often very shy, experience strong feelings of inferiority, have difficulty in expressing themselves, are uncomfortable and distressed in group settings, and may feel threatened by what they perceive as a frightening treatment environment.

Costello (1978) used the 16-PF to identify two types of alcoholics, one being anxious, introverted, and dependent and the other being more aggressive and socialized and less anxious. Zivich (1981) identified at least five, and perhaps as many as eight, subtypes of alcohol-

ics, and then was partially successful in relating the typology to treatment outcome.

In our own clinical research (Jacobson, 1985; Jacobson, Halikas, Morse, & Lyttle, 1984; Halikas, Jacobson, Morse, & Lyttle, 1984) with juvenile substance abusers (82% had a *DSM-III*-defined psychiatric diagnosis of alcohol abuse or dependence) we found several 16-PF patterns relevant to differential treatment assignment. Teenagers who were more emotionally unstable, less conscientious, more conservative, less controlled, and more tense were more likely to have a diagnosable attention deficit disorder (ADD) that could interfere with their ability to benefit from conventional alcoholism treatment approaches. Adolescents (especially girls) who were more emotionally unstable and less extroverted or more socially withdrawn on the 16-PF were more likely to be in need of medical and psychiatric treatment for an affective disorder (depression) in addition to their substance use disorder.

The 16-PF also offers the advantage of providing information about "normal" personality traits, thereby giving clinicians valuable data about positive aspects of the patient, his or her strengths and resources, which can be harnessed to the tasks and goals of treatment. Of course, a variety of other personality tests are capable of providing similar information, and many of them have also been used with alcoholics for diagnostic and treatment-planning purposes. Cox (1983, 1985, 1987) has reviewed a number of studies involving the *Thematic Apperception Test* (TAT), *Eysenck Personality Inventory* (EPI), *Personality Research Form* (PRF), *California Psychological Inventory* (CPI), *Differential Personality Inventory* (DPI), and others. Overall, however, his extensive surveys suggest that the 16-PF, PRF, and DPI currently have the greatests clinical applicability.

Only the *Minnesota Multiphasic Personality Inventory* (MMPI) has been so extensively researched and so widely applied in a variety of clinical settings as to warrant what appears to be Cox's endorsement. Literally thousands of studies on MMPI patterns and profiles of alcoholic patients have been generated since the test appeared in 1948. Many useful alcoholic typologies relevant to diagnosis and treatment have emerged. Goldstein and Linden (1969) studied 513 alcoholics and identified four consistent clinical profiles relevant to diagnosis and treatment; Goss and Morosko (1969) used the MMPI to identify alcoholics who might benefit from pharmacotherapy versus those more appropriate to alteration of drinking behavior by alternative techniques (e.g., aversive conditioning). Many other clinical and experimental studies have suggested further relationships between MMPI profiles and treatment-assignment and outcome, and possible etiologies (see Cox, 1983, 1985, 1987 for reviews). The MMPI has an added advantage in the availability of more than 400 experimental subscales, some of which (e.g., Dependency, Denial of Dependency, Impulsivity) may be of value in determining treatment assignments and assessing treatment outcomes for alcoholic patients.

Three principal source books (Dahlstrom & Welsh, 1960; Dahlstrom, Welsh, & Dahlstrom, 1972, 1975) are available to interested readers. The test itself is a 566-item forced-choice questionnaire, requiring up to three hours for administration and yielding a profile comprising four validity scales and ten principal clinical scales. English and foreign-language versions of the test are available in a variety of formats (e.g., booklet, tape recording), computer software is available for administration and scoring, and many commercial services provide automated scoring, profiling, and clinical interpretation. An excellent source of basic information on understanding and interpreting MMPI profiles is also available (Graham, 1987).

A measure of self-concept is a very important part of a comprehensive pretreatment evaluation battery, as indicated in Cox's (1985) review of numerous studies relating self-concept and self-esteem to treatment-related characteristics of alcoholics. Cox's review indicates the *Tennessee Self Concept Scale* (TSCS; Fitts, 1965) as the preferred instrument. The reusable test booklet provides 100 self-descriptive statements, to which the patient responds on a five-point Likert scale, using a disposable three-page combination answer sheet, scoring form, and profile form (with a self-contained carbon paper insert). Self-administration requires 45–60 minutes; scoring and profiling may take 15–20 minutes. Both a *Counseling* and a *Research* form is available, and the latter is preferred for the added information it yields. By providing an overall or "total self concept score," three dimensions of self-evaluation and self-acceptance, a measure of self-criticism, five

component subscales of self-concept, and a number of other ancillary measures, the TSCS enables the clinician to more precisely recommend specific treatment approaches. Be warned, however, that the design of the test booklet and answer sheet almost guarantees a bit of confusion on the part of most patients, and many tedious mathematical operations are required for scoring and profiling the completed test.

In several of our studies (Jacobson, 1985; Jacobson, Halikas, Morse, & Lyttle, 1984; Jacobson, Hedlund, Lyttle, & McLaughlin, 1986; Halikas, Jacobson, Morse, & Lyttle, 1984) we have identified subgroups of alcoholics who differ significantly in defensiveness, sense of personal identity, family-self, moral/ethical-self, and other TSCS-identified variables. One subgroup of adolescents showed a very poor or undeveloped sense of personal identity, leading us to conclude that their alcohol (and other drug) use may have been motivated by a heightened need to establish their identity through affiliation with a substance-abusing subculture. Another of our alcoholic subgroups was found to be significantly lacking in TSCS-identified "positive defensiveness;" this certainly could provide a basis for differential treatment.

Locus of Control (LOC), as defined in terms of social learning theory by Rotter (1966) in his original monograph, is another clinical concept relevant to assigning alcoholic individuals to appropriate treatment. The LOC test is a 29-item forced-choice questionnaire requiring only 10–15 minutes for self-administration and subsequent scoring. The two extremes of the scoring distribution define rather consistent personality–perceptual–behavioral styles that are referred to as *internal* (*I*) or *external* (*E*), pertaining to the manner in which the individual perceives the value of his or her own efforts in having some impact on the environment. Low scorers (*I*) believe that their own skills and efforts are influential in achieving their goals, creating success, and having impact on the environment; they feel that they are able to exercise control over their own lives, and acknowledge a sense of responsibility for themselves. High scorers (*E*) are more likely to believe in fate or luck, that "things just happen" to them, that their efforts are unlikely to be rewarded, and that they are victims of circumstances and not responsible for themselves.

They appear to be unmotivated by a need for achievement and seem to have difficulty in learning from experience, often failing to see a causal link between their own behavior and environmental consequences.

E-oriented alcoholics have been shown to experience greater psychological distress and psychopathology, including feelings of helplessness, depression, and isolation, for which special treatment attention may be needed (Rohsenow & O'Leary, 1978). In our own studies (Jacobson, 1985) of substance-using adolescents we found an overall tendency toward an E-orientation, which was significantly more marked for teenagers also diagnosed with an ADD. Relatedly, I-oriented alcoholics are often disliked by treatment personnel in traditional programs, and may be inappropriate candidates for activities that require a belief in personal powerlessness and inability to manage one's life. Intermediate and E-oriented patients tend to have a higher rate of abstinence one year after conventional inpatient treatment (Rohsenow, 1983; Abbott, 1984). Other research suggests that a specific drinking-related LOC may be more appropriate as a partial basis for treatment assignment (Donovan & O'Leary, 1978). Cox (1985) summarizes other useful studies regarding the LOC and alcoholism.

Two additional patient variables that have shown promise as potentially valuable indicators for differential treatment-track assignment and treatment outcome are *sensation seeking* and *field dependence*. Zuckerman (1979, 1983) has collected clinical and experimental data regarding sensation-seeking motivation and behavior and its biochemical and neurophysiologic substrates, some of which are applicable to understanding and differentially treating alcohol-abusing patients. The current version (Form V) of the *Sensation Seeking Scale* (SSS; Zuckerman, 1979) is a rapidly (15–20 minutes) self-administering, 40-item, forced-choice questionnaire describing a variety of exciting, interesting, stimulating, risk-taking activities. Scoring (less than 10 minutes) provides an overall index of the strength of the sensation-seeking motive, and its constituent subparts: thrill and adventure seeking (TAS), experience seeking (ES), disinhibition (DIS), and boredom susceptibility (BS). Rich in etiologic and therapeutic implications for a variety of substance use disorders, several implications for alcohol abuse patients can be derived from existing data.

Hospitalized problem drinkers are significantly lower on all aspects of sensation seeking, except boredom susceptibility, when compared to drug users, but significantly higher than nonusers (Zuckerman, 1979). Other studies tend to confirm the observation that alcoholics in general are not high sensation seekers (Kish, 1970) and that older alcoholics are even less so (Schwarz, Burkhart, & Green, 1978). But the experience-seeking component tends to increase with age, and is positively correlated with length of stay in traditional treatment (Rubin, 1987).

Among adolescent alcohol abusers (Jacobson, 1985), disinhibition subscale scores were found to be elevated; even more so, adolescent alcoholics with ADD showed significant elevations on disinhibition, boredom susceptibility, and overall sensation seeking. Clinically depressed adolescent alcohol abusers were significantly higher on experience seeking. High sensation-seeking adolescents also performed better on the SILS and on the intelligence-related subscale of the 16-PF, were more liberal and free-thinking, were more tense and driven, and had lower positive-defensiveness scores on the TSCS. Because of the many differences between high and low sensation-seeking adolescents, Jacobson (1987a, b) has suggested separate treatment tracks. For example, high sensation seekers may benefit from activity therapies which provide excitement and physical challenge (e.g., Outward Bound programs). Dance and movement therapies also may be beneficial. Art and music therapies and psychodrama may be appropriate for experience-seekers.

The final patient variable to be considered in the comprehensive pretreatment evaluation is referred to as *field dependence–independence* (FD–FI), the two extremes of a continuum of perceptual style that represents one particular aspect of the more comprehensive construct of psychological differentiation (Witkin, Dyk, Faterson, Goodenough, & Karp, 1962). A number of studies have consistently demonstrated that alcoholics in general are quite field dependent in their perceptual style (Bailey, Hustmyer, & Kristofferson, 1961; Goldstein & Chotlos, 1965; Karp, Witkin, & Goodenough, 1965), and norms have been developed for alcoholics' performance on one particular measure of FD–FI (Jacobson, 1974; Jacobson, Van Dyke, Sternbach, & Brethauer, 1976). Several others have all independently implicated field dependence as a possible etiologic factor in the biopsychogenesis of alcohol abuse (Pisani, Jacobson, & Berenbaum, 1973; Bergman, Holm, & Agran, 1981; Goldstein, 1987). Field dependence is associated with more primitive defenses (e.g., repression and denial); a less analytic problem-solving style; a less differentiated self-concept and body image; a greater dependence on external environmental cues for spatial orientation; lack of foresight, inability to anticipate the consequences of one's own behavior, and other variables relevant to treatment assignment and outcome (Karp, Kissin, & Hustmyer, 1970; Witkin, 1965; Witkin & Goodenough, 1981; Bertini, Pizzamiglio, & Wapner, 1986).

Jacobson (1981) has suggested the special therapeutic roles of restricted environmental stimulation treatment (REST, also referred to as sensory deprivation), clinical biofeedback, meditation, and hypnosis in increasing body- and self-awareness for selected field-dependent alcoholics. Fisk (1970) found that more field-dependent alcoholics were more psychologically dependent in general, and that FD–FI is related to the ability of male alcoholics to establish and maintain treatment relationships. Abbott (1984) reported interactions between LOC and FD–FI to be predictive of recidivism among alcoholics treated in conventional (group therapy and Alcoholics Anonymous) abstinence-oriented programs. In general, alcoholics who are relatively more field-independent can be expected to benefit more from insight–oriented and cognitive therapies, while relatively more field-dependent alcoholics may benefit from treatments that are directive, concrete, and oriented toward short-term goals. Cox (1985) summarizes other treatment-related research involving the field dependence–independence continuum.

FD–FI is traditionally assessed by several pencil-and-paper tests referred to as the *Hidden* or *Embedded Figures Test* (EFT; French, Ekstrom, & Price, 1963), and many varieties are available (children's and adults' forms, individual and group forms, color forms, and so on). Basically, all require the individual to locate and identify a series of geometric shapes or other forms that are hidden or embedded in a complex or distracting background context. Performance is scored as time to completion, or number of errors, or correct solutions per unit time. Better performance defines the FI end of the continuum. Although there is some controversy over the validity and purity of the EFTs (Witkin &

Goodenough, 1981), they remain very widely used because they are relatively quick and inexpensive. Of greater validity and purity of measurement are the various forms of the *Rod and Frame* tests (RFTs), which involve a square frame or box that can be rotated in the fronto-parallel plane, within which there is an independently rotatable rod or pointer. Patients are asked to align the rod to the vertical, regardless of the false and misleading cues presented by the visual surround of the tilted frame. Patients may be tilted, standing, or seated, and veridical performance defines the FI end of the scoring distribution. Commercially produced RFTs are available; procedures require individual administration, usually taking not more than ten minutes.

One final note in closing this section of the chapter. While clinicians are encouraged to apply the above-described battery for the purpose of determining how their patients may be best served through assignment to appropriate and relevant treatments, many components of the evaluation procedures may also be used for appropriate assignment of clinicians to patients. McLachlan (1972, 1974) and Skinner (1981) argue convincingly for the importance of matching patients and therapists on several dimensions, especially cognitive level (as defined by Harvey, Hunt, & Schroder, 1961). When treated alcoholic patients were followed up for 12–16 months, those who had been matched to their primary therapists and aftercare counselors by cognitive levels showed the most favorable recovery rates. Of the variables recommended in the earlier-described battery, SILS abstraction performance, LOC, and FD–FI may be the most relevant as a basis for patient-therapist match. Conceptual levels of treatment and recovery milieu are also of importance, but are beyond the scope of this chapter.

CONCLUSION

The various components of the recommended comprehensive pretreatment evaluation procedures are, quite clearly, beyond the scope of any single individual. A multidisciplinary team, working in collegial and interdisciplinary cooperation, is required. Perhaps such a requirement is an inevitable development, given the expansion of current knowledge about alcoholisms and their possible etiologies and treatments. Again, the cancer metaphor carried forward from the preceding chapter is an appropriate one. The many and varied forms of the disease(s) subsumed under that singular noun, and what we know about their causes, treatments, and outcomes, demands the attention of an array of professionals.

The cancer patient's wife may be first to detect a lump in her husband's neck (the alcoholic's husband may first to detect a change in his wife's drinking pattern), and the family physician may confirm her suspicions. But a surgeon may do the biopsy, and a pathologist may make the actual diagnosis. An oncologist will be consulted, and if surgery is the recommended treatment an anesthesiologist will participate in the procedures. A psychiatrist or psychologist may assess the patient's state of mind, a social worker may discuss with the family their role in the patient's recovery, and so on. It should be no surprise, then, that a multidimensional biopsychosocial disorder of the complexity of alcoholism should be approached in a similar manner.

A single chapter or two cannot be expected to exhaustively elaborate all components of a comprehensive evaluation process. Other valuable resources are recommended in the Clinical Guidelines that follow, and attention to the References will suggest further readings to guide your efforts.

REFERENCES

Clinical Guidelines: Medical and Laboratory Procedures

Herrington, R. E., Jacobson, G. R., & Benzer, D. (Eds.) (1987). *Alcohol and drug abuse handbook.* St. Louis, MO: Warren H. Green, Inc.

Kissin, B. (1977). Medical management of the alcoholic patient. In B. Kissin & H. Beglieter (Eds.), *The biology of alcoholism, vol. 5: Treatment and rehabilitation of the chronic alcoholic* (pp. 53–100). New York: Plenum.

Kissin, B., & Begleiter, H. (Eds.) (1971). *The biology of alcoholism, vol. 1: Biochemistry.* New York: Plenum.

Kissin, B., & Begleiter, H. (Eds.) (1972). *The biology of alcoholism, vol. 2: Physiology and behavior.* New York: Plenum.

Kissin, B., & Begleiter, H. (Eds.) (1974). *The biology of alcoholism, vol. 3: Clinical pathology.* New York: Plenum.

Pattison, E. M., & Kaufman, E. (Eds.) (1982). *Encyclopedic handbook of alcoholism.* New York: Gardner Press.

These six references contain specific information (and in some cases, step-by-step instructions) regarding diagnosis, treatment, and clinical implications of virtually all known medical consequences of acute and chronic alcohol abuse, including neurologic impairments, liver and pancreatic disorders, endocrine disturbances, sleep problems, hematopoietic disorders, and infectious diseases.

Clinical Guidelines: Psychiatric Evaluation

DSM

American Psychiatric Association (1980). *Diagnostic and Statistical Manual of Mental Disorders* (3rd ed.) Washington, D.C.: Author.

American Psychiatric Association. (1987). *Diagnostic and Statistical Manual of Mental Disorders* (3rd ed., rev.) DSM-III-R. Washington, D.C.: Author.

The source books for psychiatric diagnosis in the United States. Contains descriptive criteria for all known (and some hypothesized) psychiatric disorders, including alcohol abuse or dependence and other "Psychoactive Substance Use Disorders," instructions for use of the multi-axial diagnostic system, processes for conducting differential diagnoses, and a wealth of related clinical information.

DIS

Robins, L. N., Helzer, J. E., Croghan, J., Williams, J. B. W., & Spitzer, R. L. (1981). *NIMH Diagnostic Interview Schedule: Version III.* Rockville, MD: National Institute of Mental Health.

Robins, L. N. (1981). *NIMH Diagnostic Interview Schedule: Version III. Instructions for use.* Rockville, MD: National Institute of Mental Health.

The first of these two publications contains the complete content of the 263-item DIS, the questions to be asked, a computer-encoding format, and a few ancillary materials. The second publication contains complete instructions for conducting the interview, scoring, and related matters. All materials are in the public domain and are available at no charge from NIMH.

Clinical Guidelines: Psychological and Neuropsychological Procedures

SILS

Zachary, R. A. (1987). *Revised Manual for the Shipley Institute of Living Scale.* Los Angeles, CA: Western Psychological Services. Complete instructions for the administration, scoring, and interpretation of the SILS. All materials can be ordered from the publisher (Western Psychological Services, 12031 Wilshire Boulevard, Los Angeles, California 90025)

Paulson, M. G., & Lin, L-L. (1970). Predicting WAIS IQ from Shipley-Hartford scores. *Journal of Clinical Psychology, 26,* 453–461. Provides information on rationale and research, formulas, statistical operations, and complete age-related tables for transforming SILS total raw scores to estimated WAIS full-scale IQ scores.

BG

Bender, L. (1938). *A Visual motor Gestalt test and its clinical use.* New York: American Orthopsychiatric Association. Provides complete information on development, standardization, administration, interpretation, and clinical applications of the test.

Pascal, G. R., & Suttell, B. J. (1951). *The Bender-Gestalt test: Quantification and validity for adults.* New York: Grune & Stratton. A fully illustrated and comprehensively detailed manual for scoring the test. Includes norms for adults, conversion of raw scores to standard scores, examples of all possible scoreable deviations, and sample scoring sheets. Several complete test protocols are included in which readers may compare their own scoring with that of the authors, allowing for practice and a determination of interrater reliability.

MFD

Graham, F. K., & Kendall, B. S. (1960). Memory for Designs Test (Revised). *Perceptual and Motor Skills,* Monograph Supplement 11. Contains the rationale, description, and admin-

istration and scoring of the test, and clinical implications of test performance. Test materials must be purchased separately.

WAIS subtests

Wechsler, D. (1955). *Manual for the Wechsler Adult Intelligence Scale.* New York: The Psychological Corporation. Provides the rationale, description, norms, instructions for administration and scoring of the entire WAIS. No materials are needed for the Digit Span subtest. Although the WAIS has been recently revised (WAIS-R), this particular subtest remains essentially unchanged. The revised *Manual* (Wechsler, 1981) is available from the same source.

Others

Small, L. (1973). *Neuropsychodiagnosis in psychotherapy.* New York: Brunner/Mazel. Describes a wide range of neurological and neuropsychological deficits, their diagnostic signs and symptoms, the significance of diagnosis for treatment, and recommendations for a variety of appropriate diagnostic approaches. The Bibliography and Appendix (Some Additional Tests for Evaluating Brain–Behavior Relationships) are particularly useful.

Halstead, W. C. (1947). *Brain and intelligence.* Chicago, IL: University of Chicago Press.

Reitan, R. M., & Davison, L. A. (Eds.) (1974). *Clinical neuropsychology: Current status and applications.* Washington, DC: Winston. Description of the theory, principles, and procedures of neuropsychological assessment of organic brain damage and dysfunction. Test materials must be purchased separately. A high level of training and skill is required of the administrator.

Christensen, A.L. (1975). *Luria's Neuropsychological Investigation. Text and manual.* New York: Spectrum Publications. Comprehensive and definitive information regarding theory and practice, administration, and interpretation. Actual test materials must be purchased separately, and a high level of training and skill is demanded of the administrator.

16-PF

Cattell, R. B., Eber, H. W., & Tatsuoka, M. M. (1970). *Handbook for the Sixteen Personality Factor Questionnaire (16-PF).* Champaign, IL:

Institute for Personality and Ability Testing. Comprehensive and definitive information on design, construction, standardization, and psychometric properties of the test; purposes and applications of the test; meanings and interpretations of the component scales; data on clinical prediction, and so on. Test booklets, answer sheets, scoring templates, norms for converting raw scores to profile scores, and other materials must be purchased separately. Six forms of the 16-PF are available, as are tape-recorded versions, and computerized scoring, profiling, and interpretive services.

MMPI

Dahlstrom, W. G., & Welsh, G. S. (1960). *An MMPI handbook: A guide to use in clinical practice and research*. Minneapolis, MN: University of Minnesota Press.

Dahlstrom, W. G., Welsh, G. S., & Dahlstrom, L. E. (1972). *An MMPI handbook: Vol. I, clinical interpretations*. Minneapolis, MN: University of Minnesota Press.

Dahlstrom, W. G., Welsh, G. S., & Dahlstrom, L. E. (1975). *An MMPI handbook: Vol. II, research applications*. Minneapolis, MN: University of Minnesota Press. These three volumes provide comprehensive information and documentation regarding test development and standardization, validity and reliability, administration and scoring, meaning of individual scales, interpretation of profiles, and so forth. Test materials must be purchased separately. A revised MMPI, the first since 1948, is expected soon, but the current versions will probably remain an "industry standard" through the 1980s.

TSCS

Fitts, W. H. (1965). *Manual for the Tennessee Self Concept Scale*. Nashville, TN: Counselor Recordings and Test. Provides information on theory, test construction, standardization, norms, administration, scoring, and interpretation. Test materials must be purchased separately. The original copyright was recently purchased by Western Psychological Services (Los Angeles, California), and some improvements have already been made in the scoring procedures. A comprehensive computerized scoring and interpretation service is now offered, and one looks forward to other anticipated improvements.

LOC

Rotter, J. B. (1966). Generalized expectancies for internal versus external control of reinforcement. *Psychological Monographs, 80*, whole No. 609. Provides theory and rationale, information on test development and standardization, test items and scoring norms, and the relationship of LOC scores to other psychological characteristics and behaviors. No special materials are needed.

SSS

Zuckerman, M. (1979). *Sensation seeking: Beyond the optimal level of arousal*. Hillsdale, NJ: Lawrence Erlbaum Associates. Contains a complete description of theory and rationale, test construction and standardization, experimental and clinical correlates and meanings of sensation seeking, and related information. Copies of the Sensation Seeking Scale, instructions for administration, scoring, norms, and other related materials are contained in Appendices. No other materials are needed.

RFT, EFT

Witkin, H. A., Dyk, R. B., Faterson, H. F., Goodenough, D. R., & Karp, S. A. (1962). *Psychological Differentiation: Studies of Development*. New York: Wiley. Primary a research-oriented volume describing the experimental bases, theoretic rationale, derivation, and development of the field dependence–independence construct. Much clinically useful information is also available. Descriptions of the principal tests of FD–FI (rod and frame test, RFT; embedded figures test, EFT) are also included, along with material pertaining to administration and scoring, performance, meaning and interpretation of scores, clinical applications and implications, and so forth. Test materials must be purchased separately: Several standardized forms of the EFT are commercially available, and some equipment manufacturers are still producing the RFT apparatus.

French, J. W., Ekstrom, R. B., & Price, L. A. (Eds.) (1963). *Kit of reference tests for cognitive factors (rev. ed.)*. Princeton, NJ: Educational Testing Service. Provides samples of tests, manual of instructions for administration and scoring, meaning and interpretation of the test materials, and related information. Several forms of Hidden and Embedded Figures Tests

(EFTs) are included, as are tests of cognitive flexibility, speed of closure, and kindred cognitive performance measures.

RESEARCH

Abbott, M. W. (1984). Locus of control and treatment outcome in alcoholics. *Journal of Studies on Alcohol, 45*, 46–52.

Bailey, W., Hustmyer, F., & Kristofferson, A. (1961). Alcoholism, brain damage, and perceptual dependence. *Quarterly Journal of Studies on Alcohol, 22*, 387–393.

Bedi, A. (1987). Alcoholism, drug abuse, and other psychiatric disorders. In R. E. Herrington, G. R. Jacobson, & D. G. Benzer (Eds.), *Alcohol and drug abuse handbook* (pp. 346–384). St. Louis, MO: Warren H. Green, Inc.

Bergman, H. (1987). Brain dysfunction related to alcoholism: some results from the KARTAD Project. In O. A Parsons, N. Butters, & P. E. Nathan (Eds.), *Neuropsychology of alcoholism: Implications for diagnosis and treatment* (pp. 21–44). New York: Guilford Press.

Bergman, H., Holm, L., & Agran, G. (1981). Neuropsychological impairment and a test and the predisposition hypothesis with regard to field dependence in alcoholics. *Journal of Studies on Alcohol, 42*, 15–23.

Bertini, M., Pizzamiglioi, L., & Wapner, S. (Eds.) (1986). *Field dependence in psychological theory, research, and application: Two symposia in memory of Herman A. Witkin*. Hillsdale, NJ: Lawrence Erlbaum Associates.

Chang, N. C., & Chao, H. M. (Eds.) (1985). *Early identification of alcohol abuse: Proceedings of a workshop, October 31–November 1, 1983* (Research Monograph No. 17, DHSS Pub. No. [ADM] 85-1258). Rockville, MD: National Institute on Alcohol Abuse and Alcoholism.

Costello, R. (1978). Empirical derivation of a partial personality typology of alcoholics. *Journal of Studies on Alcohol, 39*, 1258–1266.

Cox, W. M. (1983). *Identifying and measuring alcoholic personality characteristics*. San Francisco, CA: Jossey-Bass.

Cox, W. M. (1985). Personality correlates of substance abuse. In M. Galizo & S. A. Maisto (Eds.), *Determinants of substance abuse: Biological, psychological and environmental factors* (pp. 209–246). New York: Plenum.

Cox, W. M. (1987). Personality theory and research. In H. T. Blane & K. E. Leonard (Eds.), *Psychological theories of drinking and alcoholism* (pp. 55–89). New York: Guilford Press.

Criteria Committee, National Council on Alcoholism (1972). Criteria for the diagnosis of alcoholism. *American Journal of Psychiatry, 129*, 127–135.

Donovan, J. M. (1986). An etiologic model of alcoholism. *American Journal of Psychiatry, 143*, 1–11.

Donovan, D. M., & O'Leary, M. R. (1978). The drinking-related locus of control scale: reliability, factor structure, and validity. *Journal of Studies on Alcohol, 39*, 759–784.

Eaton, W. W., & Kessler, L. G. (Eds.) (1985). *Epidemiologic field methods in psychiatry: The NIMH Epidemiologic Catchment Area Program*. Orlando, FL: Academic Press.

Feighner, J. P., Robins, E., Guze, S. B., Woodruff, R. A., Winokur, G., & Munoz, R. (1972). Diagnostic criteria for use in psychiatric research. *Archives of General Psychiatry, 26*, 57–63.

Fisk, C. B. (1970). Psychological dependence, perceptual dependence, and the establishment of a treatment relationship among male alcoholics. Unpublished PhD dissertation, Boston University.

Goldstein, G. (1987). Etiological considerations regarding the neuropsychological consequences of alcoholism. In O. A. Parsons, N. Butters, & P. E. Nathan (Eds.), *Neuropsychology of alcoholism: Implications for diagnosis and treatment* (pp. 227–246). New York: Guilford Press.

Goldstein, G., & Chotlos, J. W. (1965). Dependency and brain damage in alcoholics. *Perceptual and Motor Skills, 21*, 135–150.

Goldstein, S. G., & Linden, J. D. (1969). Multivariate classification of alcoholics by means of the MMPI. *Journal of Abnormal Psychology, 74*, 661–669.

Goss, A., & Morosko, T. E. (1969). Alcoholism and clinical symptoms. *Journal of Abnormal Psychology, 74*, 682–684.

Graham, J. R. (1987). *The MMPI: A practical guide (2nd ed)*. New York: Oxford University Press.

Halikas, J. A., Jacobson, G. R., Morse, C., & Lyttle, M. (1984, June). Substance use disorders and concomitant psychiatric diagnoses among juvenile offenders. Paper presented at the Second Congress of the International Society for Biomedical Research on Alcoholism, Sante Fe, New Mexico.

Hansen, L. (1980). Treatment of reduced intellectual functioning in alcoholics. *Journal of Studies on Alcohol, 41*, 156–158.

Harvey, O. J., Hunt, D. E., & Schroder, H. M. (1961). *Conceptual Systems and Personality Organization*. New York: Wiley.

Herrington, R. E., Benzer, D. G., Jacobson, G. R., & Hawkins, M. K. (1982). Treating substance use disorders among physicians. *Journal of the American Medical Association, 247*, 2253–2257.

Jacobson, G. R. (1974). Field dependence among male alcoholics: establishing norms for the Rod and Frame Test. *Perceptual and Motor Skills, 39*, 1015–1018.

Jacobson, G. R. (1981, March). Alternative states of awareness: new possibilities in the treatment of alcoholics. Paper presented at Second Annual Symposium on Advances in Alcoholism, Newport Beach, California.

Jacobson, G. R. (1985, March). Characteristics of personality, self-perception, and psychiatric diagnoses among court-referred juveniles with substance use disorders. Paper presented at the Ninth International Conference on Personality Assessment, Honolulu, Hawaii.

Jacobson, G. R. (1987a). Alcohol and drug dependency problems in special populations: children and adolescents. In R. E. Herrington, G. R. Jacobson, & D. G. Benzer (Eds.), *Alcohol and drug abuse handbook* (pp. 405–432). St. Louis, MO: Warren H. Green, Inc.

Jacobson, G. R. (1987b, June). Alcoholism or alcoholisms? Treatment or treatments? Paper presented at A Symposium on Alcohol Treatment: Examining the Alternatives. Milwaukee, WI: University of Wisconsin–Milwaukee.

Jacobson, G. R., Halikas, J. A., Morse, C., & Lyttle, M. (1984, May). Psychological characteristics and psychiatric diagnoses among juvenile offenders with substance use disorders. Paper presented at the 30th International Institute on the Prevention and Treatment of Alcoholism, Athens, Greece.

Jacobson, G. R., Hedlund, R. D., Lyttle, M., & MacLaughlin, S. (1986). Development of Wisconsin's Drug Abuse Screening Inventory (Highway Safety Project No. 00-84-00-02-037-130.). Final report to Wisconsin Department of Transportation. Madison, WI: DOT Office of Highway Safety.

Jacobson, G. R., Van Dyke, A., Sternbach, T. G., & Brethauer, R. (1976). Field dependence among male and female alcoholics: II. Norms for the Rod-and-Frame Test. *Perceptual and Motor Skills, 43*, 399–402.

Jacobson, G. R., Sternbach, T. G., Wallace, A., Brethauer, R., & Clark, B. (in preparation). Characteristics of male and female alcoholics prematurely terminating inpatient treatment.

Karp, S. A., Kissin, B., & Hustmyer, F. E. (1970). Field dependence as a predictor of alcoholic therapy dropouts. *Journal of Nervous and Mental Disease, 150*, 77–83.

Karp, S. A., Witkin, H., & Goodenough, D. (1965). Alcoholism and psychological differentiation: effect of achievement of sobriety on field dependence. *Quarterly Journal of Studies on Alcohol, 26*, 580–585.

Karsen, S., & O'Dell, J. W. (1976). *A guide to the clinical use of the 16-PF*. Champaign, IL: Institute for Personality and Ability Testing.

Kish, G. B. (1970). Correlates of active–passive food preferences: failure to confirm a relationship with alcoholism. *Perceptual and Motor Skills, 31*, 839–847.

Krug, S. E. (1981). *Interpreting 16 PF profile patterns*. Champaign, IL: Institute for Personality and Ability Testing.

Lóberg, T. (1980). Alcohol misuse and neuropsychological deficits in men. *Journal of Studies on Alcohol, 41*, 119–128.

McLachlan, J. F. (1972). Benefit from group therapy as a function of patient–therapist match on conceptual level. *Psychotherapy Theory, Research, and Practice, 9*, 317–323.

McLachlan, J. F. (1974). Therapy strategies, personality orientation, and recovery from alcoholism. *Canadian Psychiatric Association Journal, 19*, 25–30.

Meldman, M. J. (1970). *Diseases of attention and perception*. New York: Pergamon Press.

Meyer, R. G. (1983). *The clinician's handbook: The psychopathology of adulthood and late adolescence*. Boston: Allyn & Bacon.

Miller, W. R., & Saucedo, C. F. (1985). Assessment of neuropsychological impairment and brain damage in problem drinkers. In W. R. Miller (Ed.), *Alcoholism: Theory, research, and treatment* (pp. 141–195). Lexington, MA: Ginn Press.

Parsons, O. A. Butters, N., & Nathan, P. E. (Eds.) (1987). *Neuropsychology of alcoholism: Implications for diagnosis and treatment*. New York: Guilford Press.

Pisani, V. D., Jacobson, G. R., & Berenbaum, H. L. (1973). Field dependence and organic brain deficit in chronic alcoholics. *International Journal of the Addictions, 8*, 559–564.

Rohsenow, D. J. (1983). Alcoholics' perceptions of control. In W. M. Cox (Ed.), *Identifying and measuring alcoholic personality characteristics* (pp. 37–51). San Francisco: Jossey-Bass.

Rohsenow, D. J., & O'Leary, M. R. (1978). Locus of control research on alcoholic populations: a review, II. Relationship to other measures. *International Journal of the Addictions, 13*, 213–226.

Rubin, E. (1987). Personality correlates and drug of choice. Unpublished doctoral dissertation, Wisconsin School of Professional Psychology, Milwaukee, Wisconsin.

Schwarz, R. M., Burkhart, B. R., & Green, B. (1978). Turning on or turning off: sensation seeking or tension reduction as motivational determinants of alcohol use. *Journal of Consulting and Clinical Psychology, 46*, 1144–1145.

Shipley, W. C. (1940). A self-administering scale for measuring intellectual impairment and deterioration. *Journal of Psychology, 9*, 371–377.

Skinner, H. A. (1981). Different strokes for different folks: differential treatment for alcohol abuse (U.S. DHHS Pub. No. [ADM] 81-1033). In *Research monograph No. 5. Evaluation of the alcoholic: Implications for research, theory, and treatment* (pp. 349–367). Rockville, MD: National Institute on Alcohol Abuse and Alcoholism.

Spitzer, R. L., Endicott, J., & Robins, E. (1978). Research diagnostic criteria: rationale and reliability. *Archives of General Psychiatry, 35*, 773–783.

Tarter, R. E., & Sugerman, A. A. (1976). *Alcoholism: Interdisciplinary approaches to an enduring problem*. Reading, MA: Addison-Wesley.

Watson, R. R., Mohs, M. E., Eskelson, C., Sampliner, R. E., & Hartmann, B. (1986). Identification of alcohol abuse and alcoholism with biological parameters. *Alcoholism: Clinical and Experimental Research, 10*, 364–385.

Wilson, B. (1987). Identification and remediation of everyday problems in memory-impaired patients. In O. A. Parsons, N. Butters, & P. E. Nathan (Eds.), *Neuropsychology of alcoholism: Implications for diagnosis and treatment* (pp. 322–338). New York: Guilford Press.

Witkin, H. A. (1965). Psychological differentiation and forms of pathology. *Journal of Abnormal Psychology, 70*, 317–336.

Witkin, H. A., & Goodenough, D. R. (1981). *Cognitive styles: Essence and origins. Field dependence and field independence*. New York: International Universities Press.

Zivich, J. M. (1981). Alcoholic subtypes and treatment effectiveness. *Journal of Consulting and Clinical Psychology, 49*, 72–80.

Zuckerman, M. (1983). *Biological bases of sensation seeking, impulsivity, and anxiety*. Hillsdale, NJ: Lawrence Erlbaum Associates.

CHAPTER 4

Increasing Motivation for Change

William R. Miller

WHAT IS MOTIVATION?

The treatment of alcoholism now involves a wide range of professionals: psychologists and physicians, nurses and social workers, clergy and certified alcoholism counselors. Between and within these professional groups there are wide differences in how alcohol problems are viewed, and in approaches to treatment and rehabilitation. If there is one point on which all seem to agree, however, it is that client *motivation* is a key issue in recovery.

Perhaps the most common conception of motivation within the alcoholism field is that it is a characteristic of the client, a personal trait or state. He or she comes to treatment with a certain level of motivation. Those who refuse, do not comply with, or fail in treatment are often said not to have been "motivated enough." The notion of "hitting bottom" refers to reaching a point where the person is sufficiently motivated to admit having a problem and to accept help.

Lack of motivation has most often been explained as the result of strong defense mechanisms inherent in the alcoholic, which are themselves part of the disease. Most familiar of these is *denial*, refusing to accept reality that is plain to others. Alcoholics have also been described as overusing the defense mechanisms of projection, rationalization, and regression (Fox, 1967). These defense mechanisms have been seen as inherent in the character structure of the alcoholic, and as posing a substantial obstacle to recovery (Clancy, 1961; Moore & Murphy, 1961).

A Shift in Thinking

Over the past twenty years, however, there has been a gradual shift in thinking about motivation. The reasons for this shift are several.

High bottoms

One early recognition was that many alcoholics do not have to deteriorate all the way to a disastrous "bottoming out;" rather, they turn their lives around earlier. Such individuals came to be called "high bottom" alcoholics. At first, there was interest in what natural life circumstances led to high-bottom turnarounds. Life crises were recognized as often corresponding to such changes. Then professionals

67

began to ask whether it would be possible to intervene in a way to "raise the bottom," to help a person before he or she reached a disastrous low bottom.

Enabling and Co-Dependence

Gradually it was recognized that factors external to the alcoholic contributed to his or her motivation for change. The concept of "enabling" emerged to describe the behaviors of those close to an alcoholic which reinforce the continuation of his or her alcohol abuse. Interlocking behavior patterns of alcoholics and "codependents" were described as a source of continued denial and low motivation for change. Alcoholism came to be seen not just as the pathology of one individual but as a complex pattern involving interactions between the individual and those around him or her.

Interventions

This led naturally to the exploration of a variety of strategies for precipitating the kind of life crises that could lead an alcoholic to seek and accept help. If external factors can prolong alcoholism, increase denial, and diminish motivation for change, then surely the opposite can be true as well. Employee assistance programs appeared in industry, making use of contingent pressure from employers to increase motivation for change in problem drinking employees. Alcoholism information and treatment centers began dispensing advice to family members on how to increase an alcoholic's motivation to seek help. A method which has come to be known, in the United States, as "the intervention" evolved as a specific approach to precipitating a motivating life crisis (Johnson, 1980). By the 1980s, it was clearly recognized that external factors have a great deal to do with an alcoholic's motivation for change.

Research on the "Alcoholic Personality"

Another factor which contributed to the shift away from a character-trait view of motivation was the consistent finding that alcoholics do not manifest a characteristic type of personality. Forty years of both psychological (Miller, 1976) and longitudinal studies (Jones, 1968; Vaillant, 1983) have failed to reveal a consistent "alcoholic personality." Attempts to derive a set of alcoholic personality subtypes have yielded profiles very similar to those found when subtyping a general population (Løberg & Miller, 1986). That is, alcoholics appear to be as variable in personality as are nonalcoholics. Psychometric studies of character defense mechanisms among alcoholics have yielded a similar picture. Denial and other defense mechanisms have been found to be no more or less frequent among alcoholics than among people in general (Chess, Neuringer, & Goldstein, 1971; Donovan, Rohsenow, Schau, & O'Leary, 1977; Skinner & Allen, 1983).

Research on Therapist Effects

Yet another bit of evidence questioning a client-trait view of motivation emerged from studies of the effects of therapist characteristics in alcoholism treatment. An early observation was that the "motivation" of alcoholics for treatment varied widely among the caseloads of therapists. One common index of motivation, for example, is dropout from treatment. Early studies recognized that treatment staff differed greatly in the number of their patients who dropped out. Some lost very few patients, while for others nearly half of their patients failed to return. Within a given treatment center, a majority of dropouts were accounted for in the caseloads of a relatively small number of staff (Greenwald & Bartmeier, 1963; Raynes & Patch, 1971; Rosenberg, Gerrein, Manohar, & Liftik, 1976; Rosenberg & Raynes, 1973). As will be discussed later in this chapter, staff with more "motivated" patients have predictable characteristics and styles themselves.

All of these factors have led to a shift in thinking about client motivation. No longer do therapists need to feel helpless if a client is "not motivated." No longer is it appropriate to blame clients for having insufficient motivation, or for failing to respond to treatment because of character defense mechanisms. No longer is it necessary to wait for alcoholics to hit bottom. Motivation is recognized as the result of an interaction between the alcoholic and those around him or her. This means that there are things a therapist can do to increase motivation for change.

Before turning to a description of effective methods for increasing client motivation, however, it is appropriate to clarify what is meant by "motivation." If, as is increasingly recognized, motivation is *not* a client trait, a personality characteristic, a set of overused defense mechanisms, then what *is* it?

For clues, we can look to the experience of

alcoholism treatment professionals, who express common frustrations related to motivation. In listening to these frustrations and complaints, I find that therapists are not describing generalized defense mechanisms in the sense that I would understand them as a psychologist. Rather they are describing particular practical problems. "How can I get a client to recognize the seriousness of her problem?" "Why does this client continue to insist that he is not an alcoholic, and that he can drink without losing control?" "How can I help this client to do what he needs to do to recover, and to stop procrastinating?"

The problems of client motivation are problems of compliance. They are not absolutely unique to alcoholism. Physicians express the same frustrations in trying to get overweight patients to lose weight, heart patients to quit smoking, hypertensives and diabetics to take their medications and maintain a proper diet. Dentists and dental assistants complain that their patients won't floss and brush properly. World religions have long recognized the difficulty of faithfully following a set of precepts and teachings, and the human tendency to ignore rather than see and confess one's shortcomings.

In this broader view, motivation can be understood not as something one *has* but rather as something one *does*. It involves recognizing a problem, searching for a way to change, and then beginning, continuing, and complying with that change strategy.

Stages of Change

A very helpful model of change has been described by Prochaska and DiClemente (1982, 1986). They developed their model by studying how change occurs naturally, outside of treatment. They studied people who were self-changers, who accomplished significant change (e.g., stopping smoking) on their own, without formal outside help. When comparing self-change to what occurs in therapy, they found many similarities. This led them to describe change as occurring in *stages* or steps. Change is rarely a sudden event, occurring in a moment of transformation like that of Ebenezer Scrooge in the familiar Dickens tale, *A Christmas Carol*. Instead, it happens in stages or cycles.

Figure 4.1 shows a wheel of change reflecting the stages described by Prochaska and DiClemente. In *Precontemplation* the person is not

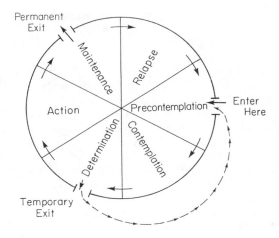

Figure 4.1. A stage model of the process of change. Adapted from James O. Prochaska and Carlo C. DiClemente (1982), "Transtheoretical therapy: Toward a more integrative model of change." *Psychotherapy: Theory, Research, and Practice, 19;* 276–288. Reprinted with permission from W. R. Miller & K. A. Jackson (1985), *Practical Psychology for Pastors.* Englewood Cliffs, NJ: Prentice-Hall, page 130.

even considering change. Told that he or she has a problem, the precontemplator may be more surprised than defensive. The person is just not considering (contemplating) that there might be a problem, or that change is possible. To hear that there is a problem or a way to change is news. To call the person a precontemplator, by the way, implies that there really *is* a problem, and that someone else perceives it while the person does not. Precontemplators would not ordinarily be seen in treatment, because they do not perceive that they have a problem or need help.

Contemplation, by contrast, describes a stage in which the person is at least somewhat ambivalent. Allowed to talk and explore freely, a contemplator might say something like this:

> Sometimes I wonder if I drink too much, though I don't really drink more than most of my friends. It's just that when I wake up with a hangover, I feel like maybe I'm doing myself some serious damage. I don't think I'm an alcoholic, because I can stop drinking when I want to. But it worries me that sometimes I can't remember what happened the night before, and that's not normal. I like drinking, though, and I'd hate to give it up.

The characteristic style of the contemplator is "yes, but." It reflects that fact that part of the person wants to change, and part does not. It's as if there were an internal balance or seesaw which rocks back and forth between motivations to change on one side and to stay the same on the other.

Determination is a hypothetical point where the seesaw or balance tips in favor of change. Enough weights are placed on the "change" side—or taken off the status quo side—that there is an imbalance in favor of change. Sometimes this occurs suddenly, as when one's partner jumps off the other end of a seesaw. Sometimes it is a gradual process of slowly tipping further and further in the direction or change. At some point, a decision or determination is reached that it is time to change. Unlike contemplators, those in determination say things like, "Something's got to change! I can't go on like this! What can I do?" My experience is that this stage is like a window or a door that opens up for a period of time. If the person gets through to the next stage, the process of change continues. If not, the door closes and he or she is back to contemplation or (if completely discouraged that change is impossible) to precontemplation.

Action is the process of doing something. The person chooses a strategy for change and pursues it. What we ordinarily call treatment would come at this point.

Maintenance is the real challenge in all of the addictive behaviors (Marlatt & Gordon, 1985). It is not difficult to stop drinking; it's hard to *stay* sober. It is not hard to quit smoking or using drugs, but it is challenging to stay away. It is easy to go on a diet and lose weight, but harder to keep it off. During the maintenance stage, the person's challenge is to maintain the gains that he or she has made, to keep from relapsing.

Relapse, as every alcoholism professional knows, is a very common phenomenon in addictive behaviors. Long-term followup data suggest that more than 90% of those who leave alcoholism treatment will drink again at some time in the future (Helzer et al., 1985; Polich, Armor, & Braiker, 1981). A slip, however, need not turn into a disastrous relapse (see chapter 11). The challenge in this stage is to recover from the slip or relapse as quickly as possible and to resume the change process. In this sense, relapse is just another step in the process of change that leads to stable recovery. It is typical for alcoholics (as well as smokers, dieters, drug abusers, and so forth) to go around the wheel several times before finally escaping through the permanent exit of maintenance.

The important point for a therapist to recognize is that clients need different kinds of help, depending upon where they are in this cycle. The precontemplator needs to have his or her awareness raised, starting the change balance moving. In the contemplation stage, the client needs to have weights placed on the change side of the balance and taken off the side of the balance favoring status quo. At the point of determination, however, the key help needed is in sorting out the alternative change strategies that are available and choosing the one most likely to be effective for this individual (Miller & Hester, 1986b). In action, the client may need help in carrying out and complying with strategies for change. In maintenance, the client may need to develop new skills to maintain a sober lifestyle. If relapse occurs, the therapist's job is to help the person recover from it as quickly as possible rather than prolonging it, and to resume the journey around the wheel of change again.

The chapters of Parts III and IV of this book provide a wide array of strategies appropriate to use with clients in the action, maintenance, and relapse stages. This chapter is devoted to strategies to increase motivation, helping clients to move from the point of precontemplation or contemplation into determination and action. The effectiveness of a motivation strategy is judged by whether the client begins, continues, and complies with a change strategy. The client's ultimate outcome with regard to recovery will be determined by the effectiveness of the change strategy itself. Helping clients to comply with an ineffective change strategy is, of course, of little use. The central concern in this chapter, however, will be with how therapists can help to increase client motivation.

It is important to note here that no *one* of these motivational strategies may be sufficient in itself. Although advice, for example, may be enough for some, an effective motivational package is more likely to consist of a combination of the elements discussed below.

INCREASING CLIENT MOTIVATION: AN INTERVENTION TOOLBOX

Several years ago I set out to review the available research on how to motivate alcoholics for change. To my amazement, I found hundreds of articles and a very encouraging amount of data on what works (Miller, 1985). There are a number of different tools or approaches that a therapist can use in seeking to instill motivation for change. I will describe these tools under eight headings, which are arranged in alphabetical order.

Advice

A relatively simple strategy to increase motivation for change is to give the client clear and direct advice as to the need for change and how it might be accomplished. Smokers, for example, are significantly more likely to quit if a physician clearly advises them to do so for health reasons, and provides sound recommendations for how to do so (e.g., Russell, Wilson, Taylor, & Baker, 1979). One surprising finding is that a relatively minimal advice intervention is sometimes sufficient to motivate change in problem drinkers, and may be as effective as more extensive interventions (Edwards et al., 1977; Heather, 1986; Miller, Gribskov, & Mortell, 1981; Miller & Taylor, 1980; Miller, Taylor, & West, 1980; Ritson, 1986).

Barriers

A practical consideration in assessing client motivation is the removal of significant barriers to change. The need for child care may prevent a parent from seeking treatment. Attendance at aftercare meetings has been found to be most strongly predictable not from client characteristics but rather from the distance a client has to travel to reach the meeting (Prue, Keane, Cornell, & Foy, 1979). The cost of treatment is an obvious obstacle for many. Accessibility to handicapped persons, women, minorities, and economically disadvantaged populations is an important consideration for a treatment center. The more practical obstacles one can remove, the more likely it is that a client will participate.

Choice

A strong and consistent finding in research on motivation is that people are most likely to persist in an action when they perceive that they have personally chosen to do so. In order to perceive that one has a choice, there must first be *alternatives* from among which one can choose. Research suggests that a particular alcoholism treatment approach is more effective when a client chooses it from among alterna-

tives than when it is assigned to the client as his or her only option (Kissin, Platz, & Su, 1971). Perceived freedom of choice also appears to reduce client resistance and dropout (Costello, 1975; Parker, Winstead, & Willi, 1979). In practice, this amounts to presenting clients with options and negotiating with them as to which approach(es) are most acceptable and promising.

Decreasing Attractiveness

One way to tip the contemplation balance in favor of change is to decrease the attractiveness of drinking. Helping clients to be vividly aware of the negative consequences and risks associated with excessive drinking is thus a sound motivational strategy. Methods which invoke vivid negative images of alcohol have been found to be helpful (see chapter 8). The practical procedure here is to raise the client's awareness of the *costs* of drinking, particularly those which are most relevant and worrisome to the individual client. One of the few preventive interventions shown to be effective in combatting alcohol and drug abuse included a component in which children were taught to detect and debunk the pro-drug messages in alcohol and tobacco advertising (Botvin, Baker, Renick, Filazzola, & Botvin, 1984).

External Contingencies

This is, in a way, the opposite side of the coin from choice. External contingencies rely on pressure from the outside to persuade or coerce a client to seek help. Such contingencies can and do work. Faced with the options of seeking treatment versus losing one's job or going to jail, most people will choose the former. Spouses of alcoholics are sometimes counselled to pose an alcoholic with the ultimatum of staying sober or losing the marriage. Abstinence or taking disulfiram may be assigned by judges during sentencing as a condition of probation. Participation in treatment may be placed as a condition for restoration of a driver's license.

There is evidence that problem drinkers brought into treatment by such external contingencies respond with about the same rate of success as those who are self-referred. A caution here, however, is that if an external contingency is to be used, one should ensure that it will be enforced, or at least that the client believes it will be. Further, brief contingencies are likely to yield a rebound effect. It is a common phenomenon, for example, that a 90-day mandate to monitored disulfiram will be followed by a discontinuation of medication on day 91. When external contingencies are used rather than personal choice, the contingency should be a firm and long-lasting one.

External contingencies and personal choice are not necessarily mutually exclusive. Even within a population required to seek treatment (e.g., drunk driving offenders), it is feasible to offer a choice among a variety of alternative treatments and to foster the perception of personal control over the change process.

Feedback

Another general finding in the motivation literature is the persuasiveness of personal, individual feedback. Lectures about the detrimental effects of alcohol on people *in general* seem to have little or no impact on drinking behavior, either in treatment or in prevention settings. *Personal* feedback of ways in which alcohol is harming the individual, however, has been found in a number of studies to have a strong motivational effect. Kristenson (1983), for example, identified from a health screening those individuals who had an elevated liver enzyme (GGTP) indicative of excessive and health-damaging drinking. He briefly intervened with half of these individuals by giving them personal feedback of this finding and advising them to change their drinking. Five years later, those receiving this intervention (as compared to the other half of the group not given brief intervention) showed lower rates of disease, death, hospitalization, sick days and work absence. Personal feedback or impairment has been an element in other effective minimal interventions (e.g., Edwards et al., 1977).

A very feasible way to implement this in practice is to do a structured and objective intake evaluation with every client, and then to provide individual feedback of results (Miller, Sovereign, & Krege, 1988). The client's individual scores can be compared with normative data from a general population or from groups of clients already in treatment. Measures of alcohol consumption, dependence, family history, and problem severity are useful in this regard. We have also used serum chemistry profiles and neuropsychological testing to examine for the physical effects of excessive drinking. When follow-up evaluations are completed, clients can be given feedback of their improvement as a reinforcement of their progress.

Goal Setting

A seventh tool involves helping the client to set a clear goal for change. Research on motivation clearly points to the strong effect of goal setting on change. Feedback of present personal state, for example, will have little impact if the client does not recognize it as being discrepant from where he or she would *like* to be. It is a perceived discrepancy between one's goal and one's present state that strongly motivates change.

Consideration of personal choice, described earlier, is relevant in the setting of goals. Clients come to treatment with a wide variety of personal goals. Some choose to pursue total abstinence. Some want to try cutting down on their drinking before or instead of committing to lifelong absintnence. Some are aware of their excessive drinking, but are more concerned with other life problems they are having. It is more likely to be effective, from a motivational perspective, to acknowledge the client's own goals and negotiate treatment objectives than to insist *a priori* that the client accept a particular goal (Miller, 1987). If therapist's goal for a client is total abstinence, the question still remains as to what may be the most effective means for helping the *client*. Direct persuasion is not necessarily the most effective strategy for motivation. Neither the therapist's nor the client's initial goal appears to be a strong determinant of outcome.

For motivational purposes, the strategy is to help the client clarify his or her goals and to compare these with the present state of affairs. The goal of treatment, like the method to be used to pursue that goal, is better negotiated than prescribed.

Helping Attitude

The final tool for motivating clients might be called a "helping attitude." This is meant to summarize a number of findings regarding therapist characteristics which increase client motivation.

One of the strongest predictors of therapist

success in motivating and treating alcoholic clients is *empathy*, as defined by Carl Rogers and his students (Truax and Carkhuff, 1967). An empathic therapist, in this definition, is one who maintains a more client-centered approach, listening to and reflecting the client's statements and feelings. Empathic counselors in this sense are characterized as warm, supportive, sympathetic, and attentive. The opposite of this type of empathy is a highly confrontational, aggressive, suspicious style of dealing with clients. "Empathy" should not be confused with the tendency to *identify* with one's clients, or whether one has been through similar experiences. The effectiveness of counselors has been found to be unaffected by whether or not they are themselves alcoholics. Being in early stages of one's own recovery may, in fact, be associated with lower levels of therapeutic empathy as a counselor (Manohar, 1973).

An empathic approach is one common element in a variety of interventions that have been shown to yield favorable long-term outcomes with problem drinkers (Chafetz, 1961; Edwards et al., 1977; Kristenson, 1983). A comparison of alternative styles of group therapy favored a client-centered approach over three others (Ends & Page, 1957). Two research teams have found a positive relationship between therapist empathy and favorable long-range client outcomes (Miller & Baca, 1983; Miller et al., 1980; Valle, 1981). A hostile-confrontational style of counseling, by contrast, has been found in general to be associated with poor long-term results (Lieberman, Yalom, & Miles, 1973). One study identified hostility of the therapist's vocal *tone* as a predictor of dropout among alcoholics (Milmoe, Rosenthal, Blane, Chafetz, & Wolf, 1967).

A therapist's *optimism* may also powerfully influence client motivation and outcome. Clients in general who perceive their therapist as wanting to help are more likely to stay in treatment and be receptive to change (Thomas, Polansky, & Kounin, 1955). Leake and King (1977) demonstrated experimentally that therapist expectations of good prognosis are predictive of favorable outcomes among alcoholic clients.

Beyond these characteristics of therapist style, there are also specific therapist behaviors that can powerfully influence a client's persistence and compliance. Consider the following situation. An alcoholism clinic decides to experiment with a simple procedure. Following a first visit for evaluation, clients are (without their knowledge) assigned at random to one of two conditions. Those in one group are sent a handwritten letter the next day, in which the intake staff member says, in essence, "I'm glad you came in. I think you do have a problem to work on, and I am concerned about you. I hope you will come back, and we'll be glad to work with you if you do." Those in the other group are sent no letter. This was actually done, with the finding that 50% of those receiving the single letter returned, as compared with 31% of those getting no letter (Koumans & Muller, 1965). A similar letter, sent when a client missed an appointment, decreased dropout from 51% to 28% (Panepinto & Higgins, 1969). Similarly, a group receiving a single personal telephone call during the week after initial consultation returned for treatment 44% of the time, as compared with 8% of those receiving no call (Koumans, Muller, & Miller, 1967). Personal calls have also been shown to increase aftercare attendance (Intagliata, 1976). These very small investments of time may yield a substantial increase in outpatient treatment retention.

Consider another issue relevant to the therapist's helping attitude. An alcoholic has been evaluated, and it is recommended that the person go for treatment. Is it better to place a referral call and make an appointment *for* the person, or to give him or her the number of the treatment program and the responsibility for placing the call? Some believe that personal responsibility is so vital that the latter procedure should be used. An experimental comparison of these two referral procedures yielded an enormous difference: the referral was completed in 82% of cases where the counselor made the call, as compared with 37% of cases where the client was told to call (Kogan, 1957).

To summarize, client motivation and compliance appear to be substantially increased by contact with a therapist who is empathic, optimistic, and who takes an *active* interest in the alcoholic's welfare.

MOTIVATIONAL INTERVIEWING

Rationale

In an initial attempt to devise a practical therapeutic approach combining these elements, I derived a system called "motivational interviewing" (Miller, 1983). Its purpose is to increase client motivation for change; that is, to increase the likelihood that the client will enter into, continue, and comply with actions needed for recovery. Its primary usefulness would be during initial sessions, although it is a style that can be used throughout a therapeutic intervention process.

Motivational interviewing *is* a confrontational process, but not in the usual sense. It is intended to bring a client to greater awareness of and personal responsibility for his or her problem with alcohol, and to instill a commitment to change. In the language of Prochaska and DiClemente's model, it is intended to move the individual from precontemplation or contemplation to determination and action. The underlying strategy for doing so is to create a dissonance or discrepancy between the person's current behavior and important personal goals (e.g., self-esteem, self-protection, health).

What are the optimal methods for accomplishing this? Although direct and forceful persuasion is effective with some, motivational interviewing relies upon a somewhat different strategy. A goal is to have the client express verbally his or her own concerns about drinking and its effects, to state perceptions that drinking is a problem, and to express a need for willingness to change. The therapist specifically avoids taking responsibility for these statements, for persuading the client that he or she has a serious problem and needs to change. Instead the therapist seeks to evoke these perceptions from the client.

There are several reasons for considering this approach. One is the fact that clients tend to be more committed to a plan that they perceive as their own, addressing personal concerns. A social psychological principle is that "As I hear myself talk, I learn what I believe." It is in the client's interest, then, to have the *client* rather than the therapist express perceptions of the problems and the need for change. A second is the paradoxical effect of therapist assertions. A therapist statement that "You have a serious problem and you need treatment" is likely to evoke from the client the opposite, countering argument: "No, I don't." These are exactly the *wrong* words to evoke from the client. Although client statements of this kind are often understood as the product of alcoholic systems of denial, there is persuasive evidence that they are powerfully evoked by the way in which the therapist approaches the client (Patterson &

Forgatch, 1984; Sovereign & Miller, 1987). Remember, also, that current research points to no particular personality or defensive character structure unique to alcoholics. The resistant behavior that is labeled "denial" is strongly influenced by the way in which the therapist approaches the alcoholic.

As an example, consider the issue of the client "admitting" the problem. Many counselors place great importance on the client admitting and accepting the label "alcoholic." Power struggles emerge in which the client and therapist clash on whether the label is appropriate. Unfortunately, research suggests no strong relationship between self-labeling and outcome. Many treatment failures are quite willing to accept the label "alcoholic," and many people respond favorably to treatment without ever calling themselves alcoholic (e.g., Miller & Joyce, 1979; Polich et al., 1981). In our clinic, where we have de-emphasized labeling, we have experienced very little of this kind of client resistance. It is common for our clients to say, "I don't think I'm alcoholic, but . . ." The recognition of a serious problem in need of change does not require the acceptance of a particular diagnostic label. To struggle against a client's reluctance to accept a label is one way to evoke unnecessary resistance.

Motivational interviewing is intended to minimize such client resistance. Table 4.1 contrasts this approach with a more familiar strategy of "confronting denial." The two approaches are intentionally stated in opposite terms, but realize that *both* are confrontational methods, differing only in strategy for accomplishing the confrontation. Likewise it should be recognized that both are valid approaches, each likely to work with some but not all individuals. My intention is to present motivational interviewing as an alternative to but not a replacement for "head-on" tactics.

Contemplation Strategies

One primary goal of motivational interviewing is to increase the individual's personal, salient awareness of his or her problems and risk. One way of eliciting such statements from clients is to *ask* for them: "Tell me what things you have noticed about your drinking that concern you, or that you think might become problems." Similarly, with regard to the need for change, a therapist can ask, "What makes you think that maybe you should do something about your

Table 4.1. Contrasting Approaches to Motivation

CONFRONTATION-OF-DENIAL	MOTIVATIONAL INTERVIEWING APPROACH
Heavy emphasis on acceptance of self as "alcoholic"; acceptance of diagnosis seen as essential for change	Deemphasis on labels; acceptance of "alcoholism" label seen as unnecessary for change to occur
Emphasis on disease of alcoholism which reduces personal choice and control	Emphasis on personal choice regarding future use of alcohol and other drugs
Therapist presents perceived evidence of alcoholism in an attempt to convince the client of the diagnosis	Therapist conducts objective evaluation, but focuses on eliciting the client's own concerns
Objective assessment data are used in a confrontive fashion, as proof of a progressive disease and the necessity of abstinence	Objective assessment data are presented in a clear but low-key fashion, not imposing conclusions on the client
Resistance seen as "denial," a trait characteristic of alcoholics, requiring confrontation	Resistance seen as an interpersonal behavior pattern influenced by the therapist's behavior
Resistance is met with argumentation and correction	Resistance is met with reflection
Goal of treatment is always total and lifelong abstinence; client seen as in denial and incapable of making sound decisions	Treatment goals are negotiated between client and therapist based on data and acceptability; client seen involvement in and acceptance of goals seen as vital

drinking?" Though some clients stonewall in response to such questions, many will volunteer at least a few tentative concerns, often qualifying them with "buts," representing the other side of their ambivalence (typical of contemplators).

How the therapist responds to these initial offerings will determine whether the client risks exploring and exposing further concerns. If the initial revelations are immediately seized upon as evidence of alcoholism and thrown back to the client as such, additional disclosures may not be forthcoming. If, on the other hand, the client's concern statements are met with empathic reflection (Truax & Carkhuff, 1967), the client may be more likely to continue exploring these and other concerns. The skillful therapist will reflect *both* sides of the client's ambivalence, but place greater stress on the perceived problems. ("So on the one hand you don't think of yourself as an alcoholic, but on the other you can see that your drinking is having some scary effects on you, and you worry that you may be doing serious damage to yourself.") A simple "What else?" can also help the client to continue expressing worrisome aspects of his or her drinking.

With some clients, I find it useful to employ a mildly paradoxical strategy by taking a devil's advocate role and asking the client to persuade me that there really is a problem here in need of attention. I may say, "Surely there must be more than this for you to be concerned enough to come here." In screening a client for treatment, I may also pose a paradoxical challenge: "This program requires a great deal of motivation, and the person must really want to change. Frankly, I wonder whether you are clear enough about your problem, and whether you're motivated enough to stick with a program like this." Such paradoxical statements must be handled carefully, but often they have an effect of eliciting additional client statements of concern and commitment.

The therapist skill of empathic reflection is a key element in this approach. The therapist repeats and rephrases the client's concerns, reinforcing them and letting the client hear them twice—once from his or her own mouth, and once from the therapist's as a reflection. Periodically, in an initial interview, the therapist summarizes the client's stated concerns and reservations.

Feedback of objective assessment findings can be integrated nicely into a motivational interviewing approach. When doing so, the therapist presents the findings to the client in a low-key, objective fashion. Instead of employing the findings as proof and attempting to persuade the client (a strategy likely to evoke resistance), the therapist presents the data and asks the client what he or she makes of them. Again, client statements of concern are likely to be evoked, and can be reflected empathically.

Determination Strategies

If the process goes well, a critical mass of motivational discrepancy accumulates, and the client begins to consider what alternatives may be available. The transition in client speech is from "Is there a problem?" to "What can I do?" The work of Prochaska and DiClemente (1986) suggests that these two questions (and indeed the contemplation and action stages) overlap considerably. In fact, the client's willingness to admit that there is a problem may, in part, be determined by the perceived availability of acceptable alternatives for resolving it. Why go through the pain of admitting that there is a serious problem if there is nothing to be done about it, or if the change strategies are unacceptable?

This raises another important point from motivational research. Once a perceived discrepancy has been created, once the person perceives a risk, several things happen. One of them is emotional. Seeing personal risk and problems is upsetting. The client may become more anxious, depressed, agitated, sad, or angry. This is an *uncomfortable* state, which is one reason why it is motivating. From here, the process can go one of two ways. The client may resolve the discrepancy either by *risk-reduction* or by *fear-reduction*. The risk-reduction route involves changing behavior, doing something to reduce the risk (e.g., stopping drinking). That is, the person moves on to the action stage of change. The fear-reduction route, by contrast, involves *cognitive* changes to decrease the perceived discrepancy: denial, rationalization, projection, and other defensive strategies. That is, the person copes by reducing the perceived problem, thus returning to a contemplation stage of change. Because the perceived discrepancy (determination) state is fear-evoking, the person will use one or the other route to escape from it. The therapist, obviously, is interested in promoting risk reduction rather than fear reduction.

What makes the difference in which approach a client will choose? The work of Rogers suggests that self-efficacy is a key (Rogers, Deckner, & Mewborn, 1978; Rogers & Mewborn, 1976). Self-efficacy refers to the client's perception that there is an effective and realistic change strategy available, and that he or she is capable of carrying it out. If the client perceives that such a change method is available, he or she is likely to pursue it as a risk reduction

strategy. If not, then the client is likely to use defense mechanisms to reduce the discomfort of perceiving the discrepancy.

The key, then, is to encourage self-efficacy in the client, to assure him or her that there are available, effective, acceptable, and realistic avenues for change. A good strategy for doing this is to provide the client with a set of *alternatives*. Current research on treatment outcome clearly indicates that there is no single, outstandingly effective approach for overcoming alcoholism (Miller & Hester, 1986a). Rather there are a variety of promising strategies for change, each of which is effective for some individuals. The chapters of Parts III and IV of this book present a menu of such strategies. It is possible, then, to describe to a client the range of options available, and together to discuss which of these alternatives might be the best place to start.

This approach has a number of advantages. First, the therapist is not in the position of "selling" a single particular approach, thus running the risk of evoking client resistance. Any one approach may be unacceptable to a client for various reasons. The menu approach defuses the resistance related to accepting versus refusing a particular treatment. Secondly, research indicates that treatments chosen by a client from among alternatives are more likely to be effective. The choice process increases the client's perception of personal control, and enhances motivation for compliance. Thirdly, research on matching of clients to treatments similarly suggests that individualized strategies lead to increased positive outcomes (Miller & Hester, 1986b). Finally, clients can be valuable resources in choosing optimal change strategies, in that they have direct knowledge of the acceptability of different approaches. Although the client's preferences are not the only consideration in choosing a change strategy, to ignore or violate these preferences is to sacrifice motivational potential and to increase the likelihood of resistance.

Moderation as an Option

In considering alternatives, it is worthwhile here to discuss briefly the issue of treatment goal. Clients often present with the desire to reduce their alcohol consumption to a safe level, rather than abstaining totally. Such outcomes unquestionably do occur following alcoholism treatment, although their frequency is a matter of heated debate (Heather & Robertson, 1983; Helzer et al., 1985; Polich et al., 1981). The practical consideration for the clinician is whether to oppose adamantly even a consideration of this goal, thereby increasing the likelihood of evoking client resistance and dropout, or to discuss this as one option among many.

From my perspective, the goal of client and therapist in this situation is, in fact, the same: to eliminate the problems and risks associated with the client's current drinking. They may disagree, however, as to how best to pursue this common objective. My own perspective is that there is little sense in losing a client by a standoff on this issue. There appears to be no strong relationship between a client's prognosis and his or her beliefs about the necessity of abstinence (Watson, Jacobs, Pucel, Tilleskjor, & Hoodecheck-Schow, 1984). Effective strategies for teaching moderation are available (see chapter 8), at least for a subset of problem drinkers. It has been my clinical experience that an unsuccessful trial at "controlled drinking" may be a more persuasive confrontation of the need for abstinence than any amount of direct argumentation between therapist and client. Our long-term follow-up research with clients treated with a moderation goal found that more wound up abstaining than moderating their drinking without problems (Miller, Leckman, & Tinkcom, 1988). A more thorough discussion of this treatment strategy can be found in chapter 8. The point here is that within a motivational interviewing approach, the option of seeking a moderation outcome is a proper subject for consideration, and head-to-head opposition of a client's goals in this regard may be detrimental (Sanchez-Craig & Lei, 1986).

THE DRINKER'S CHECK-UP

From our initial work with motivational interviewing, we evolved an early intervention approach that we have called the Drinker's Check-up (DCU; Miller, Sovereign, & Krege, 1988). This is a two-session intervention appropriate as a motivational prelude to treatment. It also has potential uses as a minimal intervention itself, applicable to settings where one has only relatively brief contact with problem drinkers (e.g., family practice, employee assistance programs, screening programs, health maintenance systems).

As we have offered it, the DCU consists of a two-hour evaluation that yields several dozen objective indicators of alcohol-related problems. We have combined the Brief Drinker Profile (Miller & Marlatt, 1987), the Alcohol Use Inventory (Horn, Wanberg, & Foster, 1987), a serum chemistry panel of tests sensitive to alcohol's impact on physical systems, and a neuropsychological evaluation comprised of measures sensitive to alcohol's chronic effects on the brain (Miller & Saucedo, 1983). The evaluation is done in a single session, and the client returns one week later for a feedback visit.

We have advertised this check-up through local news media, describing it in a fashion we believed likely to evoke minimal resistance and threat. The DCU is described as being for drinkers (not for alcoholics) who would like to find out whether alcohol is harming them in any way. The check-up is free, confidential, and not part of any treatment program. Objective results are given, and it is up to the drinker to decide what, if anything, to do with the findings.

Our recruitment strategy worked, in that we received a substantial number of calls. Those who referred themselves for the DCU proved to be alcohol-impaired in almost every case, yet few had ever consulted anyone to seek help. Most said they had never been treated for alcohol problems, and were not eager to enter treatment. Less than one third considered themselves even to be problem drinkers.

Following treatment, at follow-ups of 3 and 18 months, we found that participants in the check-up perceived their problems to be more serious than they thought prior to the DCU and showed a significant reduction in their alcohol consumption. If such a check-up were offered not as a self-contained intervention but as the first phase of treatment, it could provide a motivational head start.

In a second controlled evaluation, we compared two different styles of providing feedback of findings from the DCU. One group received feedback in the motivational interviewing style described above. The other received a confrontation-of-denial approach, as outlined in Table 4.1. The same therapists administered both styles. Examining long-term impact on drinking behavior, we found that clients whose therapists employed the confrontation-of-denial approach showed less change than those employing the more empathic strategy of feedback. Overall, participants in the DCU again showed a significant decrease in their use of alcohol (Sovereign & Miller, 1987).

MORE DIRECTIVE APPROACHES

Motivational strategies with a more directive flavor have enjoyed greater popularity in the alcoholism field to date. As discussed earlier, firm contingencies from the employer, family, or legal authorities are often successful in persuading an individual to accept treatment against his or her initial wishes. The impact of such treatment will depend upon the appropriateness of the client–treatment match, but overall outcomes appear to be roughly comparable to outcomes for voluntary clients in similar programs.

One particularly coercive motivational approach, associated with the Johnson Institute and its training efforts, emphasizes a dramatic intervention in which multiple members of the alcoholic's family and community simultaneously confront the person with his or her problems. Greenberger (1983), in a front-page story for the *Wall Street Journal*, offered the following description of such an intervention arranged through an employee assistance program:

> They called a surprise meeting, surrounded him with colleagues critical of his work and threatened to fire him if he didn't seek help quickly. When the executive tried to deny that he had a drinking problem, the medical director . . . came down hard. "Shut up and listen," he said. "Alcoholics are liars, so we don't want to hear what you have to say." (p. 1).

Many interventions of this kind would have less of a hostile tone, and would place greater emphasis on compassionate concern. Indeed, there seems to be a trend away from highly confrontational approaches, even within the "Minnesota model" programs with which they are often associated (Hazelden, 1985). The core of this intervention seems to be the arranging of a surprise meeting which the alcoholic is not allowed to leave, and in which a number of significant others express directly their observations and concerns. In the absence of outcome data (I am aware of no outcome studies)

the ultimate impact of such interventions on the alcoholic and on the family remains unknown. The widespread popularity of this intervention method, particularly in residential treatment centers, suggests that it is at least effective in transporting the alcoholic into treatment.

Perhaps at this point the most appropriate view of motivational approaches is the same view as seems warranted with regard to treatment. There are a number of promising alternative methods available. We have at our disposal a large literature on the psychology of motivation, and an encouraging number of studies on the effectiveness of particular strategies with alcoholics. It seems sensible to begin with less intrusive strategies for motivating change, and then move to the use of more dramatic interventions and external contingencies if these fail. Informed judgment about which strategies are optimal for which types of problem drinkers must await the emergence of new research.

REFERENCES

Clinical Guidelines

Jacobs, M. R. (1981). *Problems presented by alcoholic clients: A handbook of counseling strategies.* Toronto, Canada: Addiction Research Foundation.

Miller, W. R. (1983). Motivational interviewing with problem drinkers. *Behavioral Psychotherapy, 11,* 147–172.

Miller, W. R. (1987). Motivation and treatment goals. *Drugs and Society, 1,* 133–151.

Miller, W. R., Sovereign, R. G., & Krege, B. (1988). Motivational interviewing with problem drinkers: II. The Drinker's Check-up as a preventive intervention.*Behavioral Psychotherapy.*

Reviews

Appel, C-P. (1986). From contemplation to determination: Contributions for cognitive psychology. In W. R. Miller & N. Heather (Eds.), *Treating addictive behaviors: Processes of change* (pp. 59–89). New York: Plenum.

Miller, W. R. (1985). Motivation for treatment: A review with special emphasis on alcoholism. *Psychological Bulletin, 98,* 84–107.

Parker, M. W., Winstead, D. K., & Willi, F. J. P. (1979). Patient autonomy in alcohol rehabilitation: I. Literature review. *International Journal of the Addictions, 14,* 1015–1022.

RESEARCH

Botvin, G. J., Baker, E., Renick, N. L., Fillazola, A. D., & Botvin, E. M. (1984). A cognitive–behavioral approach to substance abuse prevention. *Addictive Behaviors, 9,* 137–147.

Chafetz, M. E. (1961). A procedure for establishing therapeutic contact with the alcoholic. *Quarterly Journal of Studies on Alcohol, 22,* 325–328.

Chess, S. B, Neuringer, C., & Goldstein, G. (1971). Arousal and field dependence in alcoholics. *Journal of General Psychology, 85,* 93–102.

Clancy, J. (1961). Procastination: A defense against sobriety. *Quarterly Journal of Studies on Alcohol, 22,* 269–276.

Costello, R. M. (1975). Alcoholism treatment and evaluation: In search of methods. *International Journal of the Addictions, 10,* 251–275.

Donovan, D. M., Rohsenow, D. J., Schau, E. J., & O'Leary, M. R. (1977). Defensive style in alcoholics and nonalcoholics. *Journal of Studies on Alcohol, 38,* 465–470.

Edwards, G., Orford, J., Egert, S., Guthrie, S., Hawker, A., Hensman, C., Mitcheson, M., Oppenheimer, E., & Taylor, C. (1977). Alcoholism: A controlled trial of "treatment" and "advice." *Journal of Studies on Alcohol, 38,* 1004–1031.

Ends, E. J., & Page, C. W. (1957). A study of three types of group psychotherapy with hospitalized male inebriates. *Quarterly Journal of Studies on Alcohol, 18,* 263–177.

Fox, R. (1967). A multidisciplinary approach to the treatment of alcoholism. *American Journal of Psychotherapy, 123,* 769–778.

Greenberger, R. S. (1983). Sobering method: Firms are confronting alcoholic executives with threat of firing. *The Wall Street Journal, 201,*(9), 1, 26.

Greenwald, A. F., & Bartmeier, L. H. (1963). Psychiatric discharges against medical advice. *Archives of General Psychiatry, 8,* 117–119.

Hazelden Foundation (1985). You don't have to tear 'em down to build 'em up. *Hazelden Professional Update, 4*(2), 2.

Heather, N. (1986). Change without therapists: the use of self-help manuals by problem drinkers. In W. R. Miller & N. Heather (Eds.), *Treating addictive behaviors: Processes of change* (pp. 331–359). New York: Plenum Press.

Heather, N., & Robertson, I. (1983). *Controlled drinking* (rev. ed.). London: Methuen.

Helzer, J. E., Robins, L. N., Taylor, J. R., Carey, K., Miller, R. H., Combs-Orme, T., & Farmer, A. (1985). The extent of long-term moderate drinking among alcoholics discharged from medical and psychiatric treatment facilities. *New England Journal of Medicine, 312,* 1678–1682.

Horn, J. L., Wanberg, K. W., & Foster, F. M. (1987). *Guide to the Alcohol Use Inventory.* Minneapolis, MN: National Computer Systems.

Intagliata, J. (1976). A telephone follow-up procedure for increasing the effectiveness of a treatment program for alcoholics. *Journal of Studies on Alcohol, 37,* 1330–1335.

Johnson, V. (1980). *I'll quit tomorrow.* (Rev. ed.) New York: Harper & Row.

Jones, M. C. (1968). Personality correlates and antecedents of drinking patterns in adult males. *Journal of Consulting and Clinical Psychology, 32,* 2–12.

Kissin, B., Platz, A., & Su, W. H. (1971). Selective factors in treatment choice and outcome in alcoholics. In N. K. Mello & J. H. Mendelson (Eds.), *Recent advances in studies of alcoholism* (pp. 781–802). Washington, DC: U. S. Government Printing Office.

Kogan, L. S (1957). The short-term case in a family agency: Part II. Results of study. *Social Casework, 38,* 296–302.

Koumans, A. J. R., & Muller, J. J. (1965). Use of letters to increase motivation in alcoholics. *Psychological Reports, 16,* 1152.

Koumans, A. J. R., Muller, J. J., & Miller, C. F. (1967). Use of telephone calls to increase motivation for treatment in alcoholics. *Psychological Reports, 21,* 327–328.

Kristenson, H. (1983). *Studies on alcohol related disabilities in a medical intervention* (2nd ed.). Malmö, Sweden: University of Lund.

Leake, G. J., & King, A. S. (1977). Effect of counselor expectations on alcoholic recovery. *Alcohol Health and Research World, 1*(3), 16–22.

Lieberman, M. A., Yalom, I. D., & Miles, M. B. (1973). *Encounter groups: First facts.* New York: Basic Books.

Løberg, T., & Miller, W. R. (1986). Personality, cognitive and neuropsychological dimensions of harmful alcohol consumption: A cross-national comparison of clinical samples. *Annals of the New York Academy of Sciences, 472,* 75–97.

Manohar, V. (1973). Training volunteers as alcoholism treatment counselors. *Quarterly Journal of Studies on Alcohol, 34,* 869–877.

Marlatt, G. A., & Gordon, J. R. (1985). *Relapse prevention: Maintenance strategies in the treatment of addictive behaviors.* New York: Guilford Press.

Miller, W. R. (1976). Alcoholism scales and objective assessment methods: A review. *Psychological Bulletin, 83,* 649–674.

Miller, W. R. (1983). Motivational interviewing with problem drinkers. *Behavioral Psychotherapy, 11,* 147–172.

Miller, W. R. (1985). Motivation for treatment: A review with special emphasis on alcoholism. *Psychological Bulletin, 98,* 84–107.

Miller, W. R. (1987). Motivation and treatment goals. *Drugs and Society, 1,* 133–151.

Miller, W. R., & Baca, L. M. (1983). Two-year follow-up of bibliotherapy and therapist-directed controlled drinking training for problem drinkers. *Behavior Therapy, 14,* 441–448.

Miller, W. R., Gribskov, C. J., & Mortell, R. L. (1981). Effectiveness of a self-control manual for problem drinkers with and without therapist contact. *International Journal of the Addictions, 16,* 1247–1254.

Miller, W. R., & Hester, R. K. (1986a). The effectiveness of alcoholism treatment: What research reveals. In W. R. Miller & N. Heather (Eds.), *Treating addictive behaviors: Processes of change* (pp. 121–174). New York: Plenum.

Miller, W. R., & Hester, R. K. (1986b). Matching problem drinkers with optimal treatment methods. In W. R. Miller & N. Heather (Eds.), *Treating*

addictive   behaviors: Processes   of   change
(pp. 175–204). New York: Plenum.

Miller, W. R., & Joyce, M. A. (1979). Prediction of
abstinence, controlled drinking, and heavy
drinking outcomes following behavioral self-
control training. *Journal of Consulting and Clinical
Psychology, 47*, 773–775.

Miller, W. R., Leckman, A. L., & Tinkcom, M. (1988).
Long-term follow-up of controlled drinking therapies. Manuscript submitted for publication.

Miller, W. R., & Marlatt, G. A. (1984). *Manual for the
Comprehensive Drinker Profile.* Odessa, FL: Psychological Assessment Resources.

Miller, W. R., & Marlatt, G. A. (1987). *Manual supple-
ment for the Brief Drinker Profile, Follow-up Drinker
Profile,* and *Collateral Interview Form.* Odessa, FL:
Psychological Assessment Resources.

Miller, W. R., & Muñoz, R. F. (1982). *How to control
your drinking.* (Rev. ed.) Albuquerque, NM: University of New Mexico Press.

Miller, W. R., & Saucedo, C. F. (1983). Assessment of
neuropsychological   impairment   and   brain
damage in problem drinkers. In C. J. Golden, J. A.
Moses, Jr., J. A. Coffman, W. R. Miller, & F. D.
Strider (Eds.), *Clincal neuropsychology: Interface
with   neurologic   and   psychiatric   disorders,*
(pp. 141–195). New York: Grune & Stratton.

Miller, W. R., Sovereign, R. G., & Krege, B. (1988).
Motivational interviewing with problem drinkers:
II. The Drinker's Check-up as a preventive inter-
vention. *Behavioral Psychotherapy 16*, 251–268.

Miller, W. R., & Taylor, C. A. (1980). Relative effectiveness of bibliotherapy, individual and group
self-control training in the treatment of problem
drinkers. *Addictive Behaviors, 15*, 13–24.

Miller, W. R., Taylor, C. A., & West, J. C. (1980).
Focused versus broad-spectrum behavior therapy
for problem drinkers. *Journal of Consulting and
Clinical Psychology, 48*, 590–601.

Milmoe, S., Rosenthal, R., Blane, H. T., Chafetz, M.
E., & Wolf, I. (1967). The doctor's voice: Postdictor
of successful referral of alcoholic patients. *Journal
of Abnormal Psychology, 72*, 78–84.

Moore, R. C., & Murphy, T. C. (1961). Denial of
alcoholism as an obstacle to recovery. *Quarterly
Journal of Studies on Alcohol, 22*, 597–609.

Panepinto, W. C., & Higgins, M. J. (1969). Keeping
alcoholics in treatment: Effective follow-through
procedures. Quarterly Journal of Studies on Alcohol, 30, 414–419.

Parker, M. W., Winstead, D. K., Willi, F. J. P. (1979).
Patient autonomy in alcohol rehabilitation: I. Literature review. *International Journal of the Addictions, 14*, 1015–1022.

Patterson, G. A., & Forgatch, M. S. (1984). Therapist
behavior as a determinant for client noncompliance: A paradox for the behavior modifier. *Journal
of Consulting and Clinical Psychology, 53*, 846–851.

Polich, J. M., Armor, D., & Braiker, H. B. (1981). *The
course of alcoholism: Four years after treatment.* New
York: Wiley.

Prochaska, J. O., & DiClemente, C. C. (1982). Transtheoretical therapy: Toward a more integrative
model of change. *Psychotherapy: Theory, Research,
and Practice, 19*, 276–288.

Prochaska, J. O., & DiClemente, C. C. (1986). Toward
a comprehensive model of change. In W. R. Miller
& N. Heather (Eds.), *Treating addictive behaviors:
Processes of change* (pp. 3–27). New York: Plenum.

Prue, D. M., Keane, T. M., Cornell, J. E., & Foy, D.
W. (1979). An analysis of distance variables that
affect aftercare attendance. *Community Mental
Health Journal, 15*, 149–154.

Raynes, A. E., & Patch, V. D. (1971). Distinguishing
features of patients who discharge themselves
from psychiatric ward. *Comprehensive Psychiatry,
12*, 473–479.

Ritson, B. (1986). The merits of simple intervention.
In W. R. Miller & N. Heather (Eds.), *Treating
addictive   behaviors: Processes   of   change*
(pp. 375–387). New York: Plenum.

Rogers, R. W., Deckner, C. W., & Mewborn, C. R.
(1978). An expectancy-valve theory approach to
the long-term modification of smoking behavior.
Journal of Clinical Psychology, 34, 562–566.

Rogers, R. W., & Mewborn, C. R. (1976). Fear ap-
peals and attitude change: Effects of a threat's
noxiousness, probability of occurrence, and the
efficacy of coping responses. *Journal of Personality
and Social Psychology, 34*, 54–61.

Rosenberg, C. M., Gerrein, J. R., Manohar, V., &
Liftik, J. (1976). Evaluation of training of alcoholism counselors. *Journal of Studies on Alcohol, 37*,
1236–1246.

Rosenberg, C. M., & Raynes, A. W. (1973). Dropouts
from treatment. *Canadian Psychiatric Association
Journal, 18*, 229–233.

Russell, M. A. H., Wilson, C., Taylor, C., & Baker, C.
D. (1979). Effects of general practitioners' advice
against smoking. *British Medical Journal, 2*,
231–235.

Sanchez-Craig, M., & Lei, H. (1986). Disadvantages
to imposing the goal of abstinence on problem
drinkers: An empirical study. *British Journal of
Addiction, 81*, 505–512.

Skinner, H. A., & Allen, B. A. (1983). Differential
assessment of alcoholism. *Journal of Studies on
Alcohol, 44*, 852–862.

Sovereign, R. G., & Miller, W. R. (1987). Effects of
therapist style on resistance and outcome among
problem drinkers. Paper presented at the Fourth
International Conference on Treatment of Addictive Behaviors, Os/Bergen, Norway.

Thomas, E., Polansky, N., & Kounin, J. (1955). The
expected behavior of a potentially helpful person.
Human Relations, 8, 165–174.

Truax, C. B., & Carkhuff, R. R. (1967). *Toward effective
counseling and psychotherapy.* Chicago: Aldine.

Vaillant, G. M. (1983). *The natural history of alcoholism:
Causes, patterns, and paths to recovery.* Cambridge,
MA: Harvard University Press.

Valle, S. K. (1981). Interpersonal functioning of alcoholism counselors and treatment outcome. *Journal
of Studies on Alcohol, 42*, 783–790.

Watson, C. G., Jacobs, L., Pucel, J., Tilleskjor, C., &
Hoodecheck-Schow, E. A. (1984). The relationship of beliefs about controlled drinking to recidivism in alcoholic men. *Journal of Studies on Alcohol, 45*, 172–175.

CHAPTER 5

Follow-up Assessment

William R. Miller

The term "follow-up" has had many meanings. For some treatment programs it refers to the availability of additional treatment or "booster" sessions for clients who desire them. Other programs think of follow-up as ongoing after-care groups which former patients are invited to attend. Still others follow up by mailing their clients newsletters or satisfaction question-naires.

What I mean by follow-up, however, is a *systematic, structured, individual contact at one or more designated intervals following treatment.* There are, I will argue, substantial benefits that can be uniquely derived from this kind of follow-up, benefits both for patients and for those who treat them. An organized system of follow-up provides gains that are difficult to achieve in any other way.

I also hope to persuade you that the gains to be derived from systematic follow-up by far outweigh the costs involved. Follow-up need not be expensive, and considering the time and effort spent in treatment itself it can be a very cost-effective investment. This chapter will dis-cuss some of the major theoretical and practical issues encountered in implementing systematic follow-up.

REASONS FOR SYSTEMATIC FOLLOW-UP

The staff of alcoholism treatment programs often recognize that it would be beneficial to do systematic follow-up, but maintain that they just don't have the time. "Our first priority is to treatment, and if we had more time or staff then maybe we could do follow-up."

Yet one of the primary reasons for con-ducting systematic follow-up is a *commitment to treatment.* Follow-up is an essential link to treat-ment effectiveness. Without the crucial infor-mation that follow-up can provide, treatment personnel are working in a vacuum. They have no reliable feedback to help them discover and evaluate new approaches, to assess the effec-tiveness of what they are doing, to learn how to match new clients with optimal approaches. Treatment without feedback has been likened to practicing golf in the fog (Ziskin, 1970). One may stand at the tee and drive dozens of golf balls off into the mist. One may imagine where each ball went, fantasize what a good drive it was, and congratulate oneself on being a good golfer. Yet without being able to see where the drives land, the golfer will improve very little, if at all. In order to learn, people need feedback. Without such feedback it is difficult or impossible to know who is helped, who is harmed, and who is unchanged by treatment. A first important reason for making a commitment to systematic follow-up, then, is to provide this kind of feedback, which helps treatment staff improve their skills and ultimately to be more effective in treating alcoholism.

A second, equally important benefit of systematic follow-up is its direct impact on the clients themselves. Clients often appreciate follow-up visits, perceiving them as continued concern and care from the treatment center. Planned follow-up interviews, particularly at peak risk intervals following treatment, may also serve as booster sessions, reinforcing the treatment process. An impending relapse may be detected, allowing the client and therapist to renew efforts to prevent it. Clients who have slipped can be redirected toward recovery. New issues may be revealed, suggesting additional steps that the client needs to take to maintain sobriety. In a real sense, *systematic follow-up is aftercare.*

A third important benefit is to be found in *documentation* of outcome. Without systematic follow-up, treatment programs must rely upon anecdotal reports, questionnaires, and staff impressions to document their effectiveness. Such forms of evidence, while useful, are increasingly regarded as inadequate by those responsible for decisions about funding of treatment. In an era of great concern about health care cost containment, accountability is a growing issue. The Joint Commission on Accreditation of Hospitals (JCAH) is moving toward requiring outcome evaluation for accreditation. A systematic follow-up process can provide clear documentation of benefits deriving from a program.

Finally, structured follow-up permits programs to *share new knowledge* with each other. When information is collected in a systematic way following treatment, it is possible to provide summaries of this information in a way that they can be helpful to other programs in designing future treatment approaches. What are the results of a particular approach to treatment? Are certain types of individuals most likely to respond, and others to relapse? Do different types of treatment work better with one kind of person than with another? How effective is a brief, well-planned intervention in comparison with a more intensive (and expen-

sive) approach? Answers to such important clinical questions can be derived from systematic follow-up.

In short, follow-up offers a variety of important benefits. It can help staff to discover the aspects of their treatment that are particularly effective, providing the feedback needed to become better therapists. It can help patients to maintain a relationship with the treatment program and to avoid relapse. It can help administrators to document the benefits which derive from a program's services and to shape the program toward more effective and efficient treatment. Finally, it can provide new knowledge which ultimately benefits those who seek treatment in the future.

PRACTICAL ISSUES

There are a number of practical details to be decided in implementing a system of patient follow-up. One is the *format* of the follow-up contact. Questionnaires are used by some programs, and do provide a certain amount of information. Mailed questionnaires have several important disadvantages, however. First they lack the face-to-face contact that can offer clinical benefits for clients. There is no one to ask the additional questions, to pursue a concern that emerges, to suggest new strategies or renewed treatment. The return rate may be low, and there is little verification of the accuracy of information provided. There is no process for explaining questions that are unclear to the client or for probing further for clarification. An in-person interview, by contrast, permits individualized inquiry and intervention. A telephone interview offers an intermediate option, particularly for those unable or unwilling to return for an interview.

A second issue is the *timing* of follow-up interviews. The majority of relapses following alcoholism treatment occur within the first 6–12 months. The percentage of "successful" outcomes, then, will be strongly influenced by the point at which follow-up is conducted. Interviews conducted shortly after treatment discharge or termination will invariably yield much higher success rates than those completed one year later (Costello, Biever, & Baillargeon, 1977). From the viewpoint of relapse prevention, it is desirable to have regular follow-ups during the period of peak risk; for example, at 3, 6, and 12 months after treatment. To provide treatment staff with feedback of the ultimate impact of their interventions, a follow-up of at least 12 months is required. Shorter-term follow-ups will produce misleadingly high rates of success, and will not differentiate well between those for whom treatment effects hold and those who relapse. If only one follow-up point can be managed, the one-year anniversary of treatment might be a good choice.

A third issue regards *who* should conduct the follow-up. There are advantages and disadvantages to having the interview conducted by a staff member who was involved in the person's treatment. Familiarity, rapport, and the therapist's knowledge of the case argue in favor of this approach. A personal interview may also provide the therapist with more salient and direct feedback about what works and with whom it works. On the other hand, clients may be more likely to be candid with an independent interviewer, who has less personal investment in hearing a positive report. Therapists may similarly have difficulty in conducting objective follow-up evaluations of their own work.

A fourth practical detail is integration of follow-up into the regular treatment program plan. It is wise to have clients expect from the very beginning of treatment that they will be having follow-up visits, and to present these as a routine part of treatment. One practical aid useful in locating clients for follow-up is to obtain, at intake, the names, addresses, and telephone numbers of at least two people who do not live with the client, who are likely to remain at the same address, and who would always know how to get in touch with the client. There are substantial advantages in having parallel measures administered at intake and at follow-up, allowing direct comparisons of pretreatment and post-treatment functioning. Staff and patients should come to view follow-up as a vital and integral part of treatment.

OUTCOME MEASURES

Another complicated issue is *what to measure* at follow-up. The most simplistic question is whether or not the client is drinking. The all-or-none simplicity of this question is appealing, but it falls far short of reflecting the client's overall situation. In fact, a comprehensive evaluation of a person's current status involves assessing several different dimensions (see chapters 2 and 3).

There is no single measure which adequately captures the complexity of treatment outcome. It is tempting to think of alcoholism as a single, unitary phenomenon which could be measured with a single yardstick. The truth appears to be more complicated. The abuse of alcohol inflicts a variety of kinds of damage to a person's life and health. Having a good measure of one type of impairment, unfortunately, tells one relatively little about the individual's wellness on other dimensions (Horn, 1978; Skinner, 1981). For this reason, I will discuss a number of different dimensions that are important to assess in evaluating the outcome of alcoholism treatment. For each dimension I will describe, briefly, some state-of-the-art measures. Recognize, however, that the particular measures described here are only some of the possible approaches to assessment. Larger catalogs of alcoholism assessment methods have been published elsewhere (Jacobson, 1976; Lettieri, Nelson, & Sayers, 1985; Miller, 1976).

Alcohol Consumption

Although total abstinence from alcohol remains the most emphasized goal of alcoholism treatment, it is now recognized that at least some problem drinkers manage to moderate their use of alcohol and to sustain problem-free drinking over long spans of time (Heather & Robertson, 1983; Miller, Leckman, & Tinkcom, 1988). As treatment systems reach out to a broader range of problem drinkers, encompassing the realm of secondary prevention, moderate and problem-free drinking is an outcome that will be increasingly observed. Even within traditional treatment settings, sustained total abstinence is achieved by a minority of alcoholics (Helzer et al., 1985; Polich, Armor, & Braiker, 1981), and "improved" states falling short of complete abstinence have accounted for about half of the favorable outcomes reported in many treatment studies (Emrick, 1974).

For these reasons, it is increasingly recognized that the quantification of alcohol consumption represents an important dimension for assessment at intake and follow-up. Simply asking, "How much do you drink?" is unlikely to yield reliable information. A widely used approach is a structured interview procedure which reconstructs a specified time period. The "time-line follow-back" method uses a monthly calendar and memory anchor points to reconstruct daily consumption (Sobell et al., 1980). Miller and Marlatt (1984, 1987) have developed a procedure to characterize consumption during a specified interval by quantifying typical weekly drinking and additional episodic drinking. A questionnaire approach described by Cahalan, Cisin, and Crossley (1969) reconstructs alcohol use by specifying the frequency of drinking episodes and the quantity consumed on each occasion, using the cross-product of these to reflect total consumption.

Quantity of alcohol consumption can be monitored on an ongoing basis through the use of daily record cards (Miller & Muñoz, 1982) on which the time, type, and amount of each drink is recorded at the time of consumption. From such records it is possible, by computer or hand calculation, to project the client's probable blood alcohol concentration resulting from consumption (Matthews & Miller, 1979; Rutgers Center of Alcohol Studies, 1983). In this way, degree of intoxication can be assessed, providing a more sensitive measure than the number of drinks consumed. A consumption level of seven drinks per week, for example, is less worrisome if it reflects one drink per day (resulting in a blood alcohol peak of less than 10 mg%) than when it involves a single weekly episode of seven drinks (resulting in a peak of 150 mg%).

Because the truthfulness of alcoholics' self-reports about drinking is often questioned, it is useful to obtain some independent verification of self-reported consumption. One relatively simple method for doing this is to interview significant others (spouse, family, friends) with the client's permission. Through a structured telephone or in-person interview, it is possible to construct a quantitative picture of alcohol consumption which can be compared with the client's own reports on the same measures (Miller, Crawford, & Taylor, 1979; Miller & Marlatt, 1987). The use of routine breath tests prior to each follow-up interview likewise serves as a verification of self-report, and ensures that one is interviewing a sober subject. Others have advocated the use of additional biomedical verification procedures such as blood or urine tests (O'Farrell & Maisto, 1987; Reyes & Miller, 1980).

Urges to Drink

Independently of actual consumption, it can be instructive to inquire about a client's experienced *urges* to drink. These can be assessed by interview, asking about the frequency of urges and the situations in which they occur, or by daily monitoring on a record card. The pattern of continued urges to drink may provide clues as to the probability of relapse, and the likely steps needed to prevent relapse. In residential treatment programs, it is common for patients to experience no urges while in the hospital but to be plagued by them upon discharge. Urges to drink may persist through months or even years of continuous abstinence.

Symptoms and Consequences

The measurement of alcohol consumption alone does not yield a complete picture of a client's drinking at intake or follow-up. Drinking which may, by quantity, appear to be "moderate" or "controlled" may nevertheless still be resulting in life problems or worrisome pathological symptoms such as blackouts (Miller et al., 1988; Polich et al., 1981).

Many "alcoholism scales" consist of a checklist of possible symptoms and consequences of pathological drinking. Most familiar of these is Selzer's (1971) Michigan Alcoholism Screening Test (MAST), which assigns various numbers of points based on the presence of specific symptoms or problems. Because these "laundry list" scales often ask whether the symptoms have *ever* occurred, however, they are not appropriate for readministration at follow-up, since the cumulative score would not be expected to decrease. Other instruments are available which can be used to assess alcohol-related symptoms and consequences before and after treatment (Cahalan, 1970; Horn, Wanberg, & Foster, 1987; Miller & Marlatt, 1984, 1987; Polich et al., 1981). Like the MAST and the familiar "Johns Hopkins 20 Questions," these are checklists of specific symptoms and consequences. The presence or absence of each item can be established for a specific follow-up interval. Significant others can be interviewed for collateral verification.

Dependence Syndrome

The DSM-III-R (American Psychiatric Association, 1987) places heavy emphasis on the concept of alcohol dependence, specifying a list of symptoms of the dependence syndrome. The items of this list overlap somewhat with items of "laundry lists" of symptoms and consequences. Researchers sometimes distinguish between symptoms of pathological drinking (e.g., memory blackouts, nausea and vomiting), adverse life consequences (e.g., job loss, family problems, legal difficulties), and alcohol dependence syndrome (e.g., tolerance, withdrawal, subjective compulsion). Severity of dependence appears to be an important predictor of treatment outcome (e.g., Miller et al., 1988), and deserves separate assessment.

Several scales are now available for evaluating alcohol dependence. The Alcohol Dependence Scale (Skinner & Horn, 1984) has achieved wide usage as a relatively brief but reliable and valid measure of dependence. A British dependence scale focuses more narrowly on the symptoms of severe withdrawal syndrome (Stockwell, Hodgson, Edwards, Taylor & Rankin, 1979). Subscales of more comprehensive assessment instruments also measure dependence syndrome (Horn, Wanberg, & Foster, 1987; Miller & Marlatt, 1984, 1987).

Neuropsychological Status

There is a relatively clear pattern of brain damage and neuropsychological impairment associated with alcoholism (Miller & Saucedo, 1983). Statistical relationships between neuropsychological functioning and other outcome dimensions are present but modest. That is, the only reliable way to assess the extent of a client's neuropsychological status is to measure it directly. It cannot, for example, be reliably inferred from measures of consumption or dependence. Neuropsychological assessment may be particularly important because it appears to be one of the earliest and most sensitive indicators of alcohol-related impairment.

On the Revised Wechsler Adult Intelligence Scale (WAIS-R), alcoholics show relatively normal performance on subscales of verbal intelligence. Impaired scores are commonly observed in alcoholics, however, on performance measures such as Block Design, Digit Symbol, Picture Arrangement, and Object Assembly, often resulting in a lower Performance IQ relative to Verbal IQ.

Subscales of the Halstead–Reitan Neuropsychological Test Battery for Adults are also highly sensitive to alcohol-related brain impairment. Among the most frequently impaired measures are the Categories Test, total time and location scores on the Tactual Performance Test, versions A and B of the Trail-Making Test, and the Finger Oscillation (Tapping) Test.

Other measures of visuospatial performance and information processing likewise commonly reflect alcohol-related impairment. The Wisconsin Card Sorting Test, the Benton Visual Retention Test, and Raven's Progressive Matrices appear to detect deficits in alcoholics. Measures of field dependence such as the Embedded Figures Test are also sensitive to alcohol's effects.

An advantage of neuropsychological assessment is that brain impairment may be detected well before alcohol's chronic effects become obvious on other dimensions. Neuropsychological deficits appear to emerge in a gradual fashion over the drinking career, with major syndromes (e.g., Wernicke-Korsakoff) representing only the endpoint of a continuous process of impairment.

Health Status

Chronic alcohol abuse also takes its toll on the body's other organ systems. A comprehensive intake and follow-up evaluation includes assessment of the patient's physical health. It is quite possible for a person to be drinking in a manner that damages the body without showing major life problems or dependence symptoms. Jellinek (1960), in fact, proposed the specific subtype of "beta" alcoholism to describe such persons. A full medical examination may be desirable as part of follow-up with certain populations. A serum chemistry panel can be obtained from a small blood sample, and may reflect alcohol-related abnormalities. Liver enzymes such as glutamic oxalcetic transaminase (SGOT) and gamma glutamyl transpeptidase (GGTP) should be included. Other serum measures which may reflect alcohol-related effects are high density lipoprotein cholesterol (HDL), mean corpuscular volume (MCV), bilirubin, uric acid, and alkaline phosphatase.

Other Problems

Individuals with diagnosable alcohol abuse or dependence frequently show concomitant problems as well. Anxiety and affective disorders, marital and sexual dysfunction, family problems, financial difficulties, and sleep disorders are all common within alcoholic populations. Remission from alcoholism, even by total abstinence, does not guarantee improvement in these other problem areas. Indeed, undetected and untreated concomitant problems may contribute significantly to relapse. The phenomenon of psychological dependence (Miller & Pechacek, 1987) implies a reliance on alcohol for coping purposes and a need for the development of alternative coping strategies.

The time and cost involved in administering separate assessment instruments to evaluate all major potential concomitant problems would be prohibitive. An alternative approach is the use of Kiresuk's method of "goal attainment scaling," which provides individualized change measures. At intake, additional life problems are identified and a baseline status is established. Relative to this baseline, three degrees of potential improvement (+1, +2, +3) and deterioration (−1, −2, −3) are specified in quantitative terms. At follow-up, then, the interviewer simply establishes the range into which the client's status currently falls on each of these problem dimensions. This approach has proved useful in following up problem drinkers after treatment (Miller, Hedrick, & Taylor, 1983). Where particular problems (e.g., depression) are of major concern, an appropriate specific instrument (e.g., Beck Depression Inventory) could be employed for evaluation purposes.

It is also useful to query all clients with regard to the occurrence of specific problems. Commonly included in this category are employment status and problems, legal difficulties, marital status, and family problems. The Addiction Severity Index (McLellan, Luborsky, Woody & O'Brien, 1980) yields scores in seven areas of adaptive functioning.

Finally, other addictive behaviors should be explored. These include the client's current use of tobacco, caffeine, and other prescription and nonprescription drugs and his or her eating and nutritional patterns. A concern here is the substitution of one form of substance abuse for another.

Comprehensive Assessment Systems

Because it is often not practical to administer a large number of different measures at follow-up, comprehensive systems for intake and follow-up assessment have been developed. These incorporate several of the above dimensions into a single interview or questionnaire format, providing parallel pretreatment and follow-up measures.

The most time-efficient of these is the Alcohol Use Inventory, recently reissued in revised form (Horn, Wanberg, & Foster, 1987). This instrument has undergone extensive psychometric development over a span of 20 years. As a paper and pencil questionnaire, it can be administered at very little cost to clients who have adequate reading ability. Both hand-scoring and computer-scoring systems are available. It yields a range of clinically relevant scale scores, based on a factor analysis of a large sample of individuals in treatment for alcohol problems. Parallel intake and follow-up forms are available.

The Addiction Severity Index (McLellan et al., 1980) is a structured interview yielding ratings on seven dimensions including medical, employment, legal, family, and psychological status, alcohol use, and drug use. Outcome can be judged by comparing subscale scores at intake with those at follow-up.

The Comprehensive Drinker Profile (Miller & Marlatt, 1984) is a two-hour structured intake interview that yields both qualitative and quantitative indices of alcohol and drug use, symptoms and consequences, dependence, other life problems, medical and family history, and motivation. The Brief Drinker Profile (Miller & Marlatt, 1987) is a one-hour version of the same interview, retaining most of the quantitative measures. Parallel measures are provided by the Follow-up Drinker Profile and the Collateral Interview Form (Miller & Marlatt, 1987).

Another comprehensive evaluation approach is the Structured Addictions Assessment Interview for Selecting Treatment, developed by the Addiction Research Foundation (1984). It consists of an integrated series of questions designed to assist in client–treatment matching.

The National Alcohol Program Information System (NAPIS; National Institute on Alcohol Abuse and Alocholism, 1979) is a briefer, 34-item multiple choice intake interview with a parallel follow-up assessment interview. This instrument was developed for use by federally funded alcoholism treatment programs, and a data base for over 100,000 clients exists for this instrument.

CLINICAL INTERVIEWING GUIDELINES

The style of follow-up interviewing may influence the amount and accuracy of information obtained. It is useful to interview clients in a non-judgmental manner, responding in a reflective and empathic manner to whatever information is divulged. Criticism, disapproval, advice, warnings, shock, and dismay should be avoided in the process of completing the follow-up interview. Once information has been obtained, it may then be appropriate to discuss the client's status and what steps, if any, need to be taken. A structured interview format provides a standard set of questions to be asked of all clients, and helps keep the interview on track.

Any penalties for divulging information will, of course, also bias clients' reports. If the client believes that reporting alcohol or drug use is likely to result in legal penalties (e.g., revoked probation, continued suspension of driver's license), honesty is jeopardized. Some treatment programs offer free aftercare or booster sessions to clients as long as they have remained totally abstinent. Relapse, in this case, results in the loss of free treatment services. Again, candid reports of drinking are less likely under these circumstances. To increase the likelihood of obtaining accurate follow-up data, it is wise to assure the client (assuming it is true) that the information provided will have no adverse effects upon him or her, and will not prejudice future treatment.

WHAT IS "SUCCESS"?

The criteria for treatment success are variable. A client's goals may focus on mere relief from discomfort, compliance with legal requirements, regaining of a jeopardized marriage or job, alleviation of depression, or enhanced personal functioning. A therapist's goals may center on abstinence from alcohol and other drugs, enhanced self-esteem, improved working skills, or overall life satisfaction. The agenda of courts, schools, or employers making referrals are likely to revolve around the absence of future violations of rules and standards. Program administrators may be concerned with the promotion of a favorable image of the treatment program to enhance future marketing, referrals, and funding, and the avoidance of adverse sensational publicity or lawsuits. Law enforcement officials and the larger community may have, as primary goals for treatment systems, the reduction of drunk driving and the removal of inebriates from public streets. These goals may converge or conflict, depending upon individuals and circumstances.

How, then, is one to judge when treatment has been successful? There is no gold standard. When entire programs are being assessed, outcomes are evaluated relative to the hopes or expectations for the program. A drunk driver screening and treatment program, for example, may be judged by its impact on alcohol-related traffic fatalities in the community at large. Cost-effectiveness considerations enter into the evaluation of programs: How much impact is occurring relative to the cost of services?

At an individual level, however, outcome becomes a bit easier to evaluate. For the alcohol-impaired person, a *sine qua non* of successful outcome is a change in drinking behavior such that it no longer causes adverse consequences or places the person or others at significant risk of harm. The easiest outcome to understand in this regard is total abstinence. The person who never drinks again will never encounter risk or problems as a result of future drinking. For some, abstinence is the only way to ensure freedom from alcohol dependence and problems. Others succeed in reducing their alcohol use to a low level, avoiding the risks and problems associated with their formerly excessive drinking. In both cases, the individual is no longer troubled by the health and social problems previously suffered in relation to drinking.

In most outcome studies, however, the larger category consists of people with less straightforward outcomes. They are not consistently abstinent; they may be drinking much less or less often, but they continue to experience alcohol-related symptoms and problems, albeit at a lesser level. On some classification systems they may be called "improved." By other standards, these are treatment failures. What of individuals who successfully sustain total abstinence but experience continued or exacerbated depression and social maladjustment? What of the person who goes from years of unemployment and daily intoxication to a pattern of stable employment with four weekend binges a year during vacation and holidays?

It becomes difficult to apply a black-and-white, all-or-none test of success. Like alcohol problems themselves, outcomes come in a range of shades and degrees. Systematic follow-up reveals this rich array of outcomes. It is perhaps, less important to lay on an all-or-none template of success versus failure than to learn from follow-up what components of treatment seem to help what kinds of people.

A FINAL PLEA

Follow-up takes time, and involves some complex problems and issues. Nevertheless it is, I believe, one of the very best investments on staff time. It is good for one's clients, who experience continuing concern and contact, and may be helped to anticipate or avert an impending relapse. It can provide useful information with which to respond to demands for program accountability.

From the therapist's perspective the most persuasive value of follow-up is the learning that it permits. Imagine a school in which students never received feedback on their work, in which tests were given regularly but never returned. Imagine being a radio talk-show host who never received any calls. Consider what the state of medicine would be if diseases such as cancer were treated but no one bothered to follow up to see which treatments worked.

Without knowledge of results, we stop learning and growing. Without regular feedback we are left to our personal fears and fantasies about our own effectiveness. Without follow-up we can speculate and quarrel for years on end about which treatment method is "best" or "most effective." Without new knowledge from follow-up we go on year after year practicing the same approaches and teaching them to the next generation of helpers. We stay largely the same, blending brilliance and blunders, with no reliable way to know the difference.

Can't afford to do follow-up? The truth is that we can't afford *not* to include follow-up in our regular practice. The cost—to our clients and to our own learning—of working without reliable feedback is just too high

REFERENCES

Addiction Research Foundation. (1984). *A structured addictions assessment interview for selecting treatment.* Toronto, Canada: Author.

American Psychiatric Association. (1987). *Diagnostic and statistical manual of mental disorders.* (3rd ed., revised). Washington, DC: Author.

Cahalan, D., Cisin, I. H., & Crossley, H. M. (1969). *American drinking practices: A national study of drinking behavior and attitudes.* New Brunswick, NJ: Rutgers Center of Alcohol Studies.

Cahalan, D. (1970). *Problem drinkers.* San Francisco, CA: Jossey-Bass.

Costello, R. M., Biever, P., & Baillargeon, J. G. (1977). Alcoholism treatment and programming: Historical trends and modern approaches. *Alcoholism: Clinical and Experimental Research, 1,* 311–318.

Emrick, C. D. (1974). A review of psychologically oriented treatment of alcoholism: I. The use and interrelationships of outcome criteria and drinking behavior following treatment. *Quarterly Journal of Studies on Alcohol, 35,* 523–549.

Heather, N., & Robertson, I. (1983). *Controlled drinking.* (Rev. ed.) New York: Methuen.

Helzer, J. E., Robins, L. N., Taylor, J. R., Carey, K., Miller, R. H., Combs-Orme, T., & Farmer, A. (1985). The extent of long-term moderate drinking among alcoholics discharged from medical and psychiatric treatment facilities. *New England Journal of Medicine, 312,* 1678–1682.

Horn, J. L. (1978). Comments on the many faces of alcoholism. In P. E. Nathan, G. A. Marlatt, & T. Loberg (Eds.), *Alcoholism: New directions in research and treatment* (pp. 1–40). New York: Plenum.

Horn, J. L., Wanberg, K. W., & Foster, F. M. (1987). *Guide to the Alcohol Use Inventory.* (Rev. ed.) Minneapolis: National Computer Systems.

Jacobson, G. R. (1976). *The alcoholisms: Detection, diagnosis, and assessment.* New York: Human Sciences Press.

Jellinek, E. M. (1960). *The disease concept of alcoholism.* New Haven, CT: Hillhouse Press.

Lettieri, D. J., Nelson, J. E., & Sayers, M. A. (Eds.) (1985). *Alcoholism treatment assessment research instruments.* NIAAA Treatment Handbook Series, No. 2. Rockville, MD: National Institute on Alcohol Abuse and Alcoholism.

Matthews, D. B., & Miller, W. R. (1979). Estimating blood alcohol concentration: Two computer programs and their applications in therapy and research. *Addictive Behaviors, 4,* 55–60.

McLellan, A. T., Luborsky, L., Woody, G. E., & O'Brien, C. P. (1980). An improved diagnostic instrument for substance abuse patients: The Addiction Severity Index. *Journal of Nervous and Mental Disorders, 168,* 26–33.

Miller, W. R. (1976). Alcoholism scales and objective assessment methods: A review. *Psychological Bulletin, 83,* 649–70.

Miller, W. R., Hedrick, K. E., & Taylor, C. A. (1983). Addictive behaviors and life problems before and after behavioral treatment of problem drinkers. *Addictive Behaviors, 8,* 403–412.

Miller, W. R., Leckman, A. L., & Tinkcom, M. (1988). Long-term follow-up of controlled drinking therapies. Manuscript submitted for publication.

Miller, W. R., & Marlatt, G. A. (1984). *Manual for the Comprehensive Drinker Profile.* Odessa, FL: Psychological Assessment Resources.

Miller, W. R., & Marlatt, G. A. (1987). *Comprehensive Drinker Profile manual supplement.* Odessa, FL: Psychological Assessment Resources.

Miller, W. R., & Muñoz, R. F. (1982). *How to control your drinking*. (Rev. ed.) Albuquerque, NM: University of New Mexico Press.

Miller, W. R., & Pechacek, T. F. (1987). New roads: Assessing and treating psychological dependence. *Journal of Substance Abuse Treatment, 4*, 73–77.

Miller, W. R., & Saucedo, C. F. (1983). Assessment of neuropsychological impairment and brain damage in problem drinkers. In C. J. Golden, J. A. Moses, Jr., J. A. Coffman, W. R. Miller, & F. D. Strider (Eds.), *Clinical neuropsychology: Interface with neurologic and psychiatric disorders* (pp. 141–195). New York: Grune & Stratton.

National Institute on Alcohol Abuse and Alcoholism, Office of Program Development and Analysis (1979). *National Alcoholism Program Information System (NAPIS)*. Washington, DC: U.S. Government Printing Office.

O'Farrell, T. J., & Maisto, S. A. (1987). The utility of self-report and biological measures of alcohol consumption in alcoholism treatment outcome studies. *Advances in Behavior Research and Therapy, 9*, 91–125.

Polich, J. M., Armor, D. J., & Braiker, H. B. (1981). *The course of alcoholism: Four years after treatment*. New York: Wiley.

Reyes, E., & Miller, W. R. (1980). Serum gamma-glutamyl transpeptidase as a diagnostic aid in problem drinkers. *Addictive Behaviors, 5*, 59–65.

Rutgers Central of Alcohol Studies (1983). *Alcocalculator: An educational instrument* (Rev. ed.). New Brunswick, NJ: Author.

Selzer, M. L. (1971). The Michigan Alcoholism Screening Test: The quest for a new diagnostic instrument. *American Journal of Psychiatry, 127*, 1653–1658.

Skinner, H. A. (1981). Primary syndromes of alcohol abuse: Their measurement and correlates. *British Journal of Addiction, 76*, 63–76.

Skinner, H. A., & Horn, J. W. (1984). *Alcohol Dependence Scale: a user's guide*. Toronto, Canada: Addiction Research Foundation.

Sobell, M. B., Maisto, S. A., Sobell, L. C., Cooper, A. M., Cooper, T. C., & Sanders, B. (1980). Developing a prototype for evaluating alcohol treatment effectiveness. In L. C. Sobell, M. B. Sobell, & E. Ward (Eds.), *Evaluating alcohol and drug abuse treatment effectiveness: Recent advances* (pp. 129–150). Elmsford, NY: Pergamon Press.

Stockwell, T., Hodgson, R., Edwards, G., Taylor, C., & Rankin, H. (1979). The development of a questionnaire to measure severity of alcohol dependence. *British Journal of Addiction, 74*, 79–87.

Ziskin, J. (1970). *Coping with psychiatric and psychological testimony*. Beverly Hills, CA: Law and Psychology Press.

PART III

Primary Treatment Approaches

The following four chapters focus directly on the suppression of drinking behaviors. Once a client is motivated for treatment and a goal has been negotiated, the first interventions should be aimed at the cessation of abusive drinking. These chapters provide you with concrete strategies to achieve that goal.

CHAPTER 6

Brief Intervention Strategies

Nick Heather

INTRODUCTION

Unlike other contributions to this book, the present chapter is not concerned with a specific treatment method but with a range of intervention strategies that have come to be called "brief" or "minimal" interventions. It is therefore impossible to provide a hard and fast definition or concise description of this approach. For example, to ask how short an intervention must be before it can reasonably be called brief is rather like asking how long is a piece of string!

The main reason brief interventions are important, however, is that they offer the promise of making our attempts to alter drinking behavior much more cost-effective. The evidence strongly suggests that many of our clients simply do not need a protracted and expensive course of individual or group treatment in order to benefit. By identifying these clients and offering them a brief intervention appropriate to their requirements, more time and energy can be devoted to those with more severe problems who do need a more intensive approach. Thus valuable treatment resources can be more efficiently used. At the same time, brief interventions provide the opportunity to help clients early in the course of their drinking

problem, before alcohol dependence has developed to a level that makes conventional treatment difficult and before excessive drinking has produced permanent damage. Generally speaking, brief interventions are not intended for people whose problems are sufficiently serious to deserve the label of "alcoholism" but for those with earlier or less serious problems. Such clients are typically unwilling to attend regular treatment programs; indeed, the evidence shows that it is often unnecessary for them to do so.

Although a concise definition is not possible, brief interventions do have certain general characteristics which give them some conceptual coherence (see Heather, 1986). If delivered by personnel with expertise in the alcohol problems area, they involve less specialist time than would normally be devoted to intensive treatment—say, one or two sessions of assessment and advice at the most. On the other hand, brief interventions are often developed by alcohol problems specialists for delivery by other professional groups, such as general medical practitioners, hospital physicians, ward and community nurses, health visitors, social workers, probation officers, employee counselors, and so on, who deploy them along with the many other duties for which they are responsible. Paraprofessional workers, voluntary counselors and clients' relatives and friends are also important elements in these strategies. One of the main modes of brief intervention is by self-help manuals and other forms of "bibliotherapy." Even where some personal contact with clients is involved, this is often supported by written materials for home study. Although there are exceptions, brief interventions thus far have most often been aimed at a goal of moderate drinking rather than total abstinence. The corollary of this is, of course, that they are normally directed at problem drinkers with only low or moderate levels of alcohol dependence or alcohol-related problems.

The recent boom in interest in brief interventions is a result of several influences. First, there is evidence, to be described later in the chapter, that they are often no less effective in modifying drinking behavior than more traditional forms of therapy. Second, there has recently been a growing recognition that the damage caused by excessive drinking—for example, problems due to acute intoxication or adverse physical health consequences—often do not entail a high degree of alcohol dependence, and also that the lives of large numbers of people in society are impaired by excessive consumption, quite apart from those who would traditionally be termed "alcoholics." This has led to a shift away from an exclusive preoccupation with problems involving high alcohol dependence and to a tendency to move interventions out into community settings and away from the specialized alcohol problems clinic (Department of Health and Social Security, 1978). Finally, in view of the ever-increasing costs of specialist treatment and the shrinking health expenditure budgets of many countries, there has been a need to develop less expensive and labor-intensive modes of intervention, provided these can be justified by evaluative research. These influences have conspired to focus attention on the use of brief, low-cost interventions as alternatives to intensive, individual or group treatment of problem drinkers.

In the area of brief interventions, the conventional distinction between treatment and education for problem drinkers breaks down. Indeed, many brief interventions, particularly those delivered in community-based settings or not involving personal contact with helpers, are best described to the public as "education" rather than "treatment." Of course, in this context, education is much more than merely providing information; it includes methods of behavioral change drawn from the same set of social learning principles that form many of the intensive treatment methods described in this volume. However, by emphasizing the educational aspect of brief interventions, much can be done to avoid the labeling process involved in the diagnosis of problem drinking, thereby reducing the stigma attached to the admission of an alcohol problem that often deters potential clients from tackling their problems. The most promising mode of delivery for many brief interventions is as part of health education and general health promotion initiatives.

SPECIAL CONSIDERATIONS

Because brief interventions are usually directed at a reduced drinking goal and also because there is often a limited degree of control over progress, the most suitable clients for the majority of brief interventions are those with low levels of alcohol dependence. (This will be operationally defined in the next section.) Those with moderate levels of dependence may also be suitable for relatively brief interventions, but usually there will be somewhat more direct involvement of specialized personnel. At the present state of knowledge, clients in contact with agencies who show a high level of dependence and/or a high degree of alcohol-related harm should normally be excluded from brief interventions and referred for intensive treatment. Strictly speaking, degree of alcohol dependence is a more important criterion than the extent of alcohol-related problems, because it is more relevant to the possibility of change and how much effort needs to be expended to bring this change about.

Another important target for brief interventions is the large group of people who are drinking above guidelines for safe drinking recommended by medical authorities but who do not yet show overt signs of alcohol-related problems. These are the "hazardous" drinkers described in recent World Health Organization (WHO) reports (Edwards, Arif, & Hodgson, 1982).

In addition to those with lower levels of alcohol dependence and less severe or no alcohol-related problems, clients with more serious problems may make use of brief interventions when access to intensive treatment is limited or where there are psychological barriers to the seeking of help from specialist services. It is likely that only a minority of people with alcohol problems ever come into contact with specialist services (see, e.g., Hingson, Scotch, Day, & Culbert, 1980). There are probably many reasons for this, including feelings of shame and guilt at the admission of a problem, a difficulty in conceding that drinking behavior is out of control and outside help is needed, and a fear of hospitals and treatment, especially if associated with psychiatric diagnosis (Thom, 1986; see also Miller, Sovereign, & Krege, 1987). The geographical inaccessibility of treatment centers simply may be a barrier in some cases. The effects of all these factors can be mitigated by the use of non-specialist, brief interventions. Since it can be reasonably assumed that many clients would otherwise receive no help at all, this use of brief interventions can be ethically justified. Moreover, most contain advice on the conditions where more intensive help should be sought and procedures for channelling more serious problem drinkers into specialist services if necessary.

To summarize, there are three target groups for brief interventions: (a) hazardous drinkers; (b) low- or moderate-dependence problem drinkers; and (c) high-dependence problem drinkers who are not reached by conventional treatment services.

DESCRIPTION

In providing a description of the main types of brief intervention strategies and recommendations for their application, two important caveats must be stated at the outset. First, many of the interventions to be described here are based on British experience and therefore reflect British conditions. Particular conditions in other countries (for example, the circumstances under which primary health care is delivered) may be different and adjustments should be made for this. Second, although there is evidence for the effectiveness of brief interventions in general, research on optimal practical applications has only just begun. Thus, we have little firm evidence regarding just how brief interventions may become while remaining effective. We cannot yet determine from research what levels of severity of dependence and problems should result in clients being excluded from brief interventions in favor

of more intensive treatments. Therefore, many of the recommendations in this section are based on informed guesses as to the best chances for success. However, many of these procedures await firm evidence of their effectiveness, and in other instances, they may have to be revised in the light of research findings. In this situation, it is advisable to err, if anything, on the side of caution.

Three main categories of brief intervention will be described here: agency-based interventions; community-based interventions; and self-help manuals. Each will be discussed in terms of issues relating to recruitment and screening of clients, exclusion criteria, and optimal methods of implementation, as well as specific contents.

AGENCY-BASED INTERVENTIONS

This section will deal with brief interventions given by specialist alcohol problems agencies—either hospital-based clinics or voluntary counseling services. Compared with other types of brief intervention that do not involve direct therapist contact, there is an opportunity here for more personal involvement by staff in brief interventions, more accurate assessment, and more control over the effects of the intervention. Particularly important, as we shall see, is an assessment of the level of alcohol dependence shown by the client.

A Basic Treatment Scheme

Orford and Edwards (1977) provide an outline for a "basic treatment scheme," consisting of assessment and one session of counseling. The scheme has the following elements:

Comprehensive assessment

The continued necessity for this is justified by three needs: (a) to establish a sufficient basis of information to help clients and their families formulate a plan of action; (b) for the client (and spouse) to engage in a broad review of the situation, which may in itself have some therapeutic value; and (c) for the advisory team to establish their credibility and hence their persuasiveness. One critical aspect of the assessment process is the measurement of level of alcohol dependence, which will be dealt with below. (See chapter 2 for specific assessment tools.)

A single, detailed counseling session for the client and, when the client is married, the spouse.

This is the basic treatment, replacing more intensive forms of care. However, it "in no way contradicts the notion that each person requires an individually formulated approach, and there will be circumstances in which clinical judgment leads to the conclusion that more (or very much more) than the basic intervention is needed" (Orford & Edwards, 1977, p. 110). The counseling session itself involves a discussion between counselor, client, and spouse to define a set of goals. These goals should be seen by those being counseled as logically related to their perception of their problems as derived from assessment and discussion, and should cover drinking, marital cohesiveness, and other goals for work, leisure, finances, and housing. Counseling should also strongly emphasize both the self-responsibility of the client and the shared engagement of the spouse, but these should be discussed and explained rather than merely stated. An open and definite commitment towards the agreed goals should be aimed for.

Some follow-up system to check on progress.

Apart from any extra therapeutic value such regular contact might have, it also serves as a "safety net" for clients who may develop more serious or life-threatening problems. Whatever type of follow-up method is used, however, it should fall well short of the traditional system of active community care.

Common reasons for going beyond the basic approach.

The decision to increase the intensity of care for an individual client who has been given basic treatment must obviously be a matter of clinical judgment. However, a few common circumstances are: (a) brief admission for detoxification where, for example, there is evidence of reinstatement of severe dependence, concomitant sedative misuse, or poor social sup-

port; (b) underlying or concomitant psychological illness or distress, such as depressive illness or phobic disorder; (c) physical illness requiring referral or admission; (d) life-threatening situations or acute dangers to family requiring immediate admission; (e) homelessness, which may require extensive social services and/or halfway house placement.

This basic treatment is proposed by Orford and Edwards as being suitable for the broad range of clients who attend specialized alcohol clinics, bearing in mind the exceptions and qualifications given above. However, there is some evidence that clients with high levels of dependence are more likely to benefit from a more intensive approach, and this will be discussed in more detail below. Moreover, the basic treatment scheme is based on experience with married, male clients of relatively high social stability. Thus a conservative choice of client group for this basic treatment would be men with intact marriages, secure employment, and low or moderate levels of alcohol dependence. Counseling and advice would normally involve the spouse.

It is important to establish here that, especially if associated with conservative criteria for client-selection, there is nothing unethical or uncaring in offering the type of basic treatment described above. This is sometimes difficult for treatment providers to accept, since they are often deeply committed to the style of treatment they practice and are convinced that the more treatment their clients receive the greater will be their chances of recovery. However, this understandable commitment to intensive treatment for all clients is simply contradicted by the evidence. Provided that safeguards for checking on progress and for offering more intensive treatment when necessary are incorporated in the treatment plan, the attempt to give intensive treatment to all who attend is a waste of precious resources, which could more profitably be directed at providing a greater number of clients with less intensive treatment and in ensuring that those who do need more therapeutic attention are adequately provided for. Moreover, involving as it does three or four hours of detailed assessment and advice, the kind of basic approach described by Orford and Edwards can hardly be called "minimal." Indeed, it probably represents more sustained and devoted attention to their problems than most clients have received in their lifetimes (Ritson, 1986).

Assessment of Level of Dependence

So far in this chapter, levels of alcohol dependence have been spoken of generally, without any attempt to specify these levels in operational terms. There now exist many instruments for measuring dependence, including the following:

Severity of Alcohol Dependence Questionnaire. (SADQ) (Stockwell, Hodgson, Edwards, Taylor, & Rankin, 1979).

A 20-item self-administered scale referring to the last month of heavy drinking. The main advantages of the SADQ are that it is easy to administer and score and is in wide use. Disadvantages include a relative insensitivity to lower degrees of dependence and the fact that—given the focus on a recent heavy drinking month—the duration of dependent drinking is not taken into account.

Alcohol Dependence Scale (ADS) (Skinner and Allen, 1982).

A 34-item scale which can be either self- or therapist-administered, the ADS is somewhat more complex to administer and score than the SADQ; however, this is compensated for by more attention to psychological, as well as physical, aspects of dependence.

Short-form Alcohol Dependence Data Questionnaire (SADD) (Raistrick, Dunbar, & Davidson, 1983).

A 15-item self-administered scale, the SADD is the quickest and most convenient of the scales listed here and was especially constructed to be sensitive to early signs of dependence. Its main disadvantage is that it is less frequently used than other scales, and comparative data are therefore less available.

Ph Score from the Comprehensive Drinker Profile (CDP) (Miller and Marlatt, 1984).

An 11-point scale included in a section on Alcohol-Related Life Problems of the CDP. The main point in using the Ph score is that it can be measured at the same time as alcohol-related problems in general and, if the full CDP is used, as part of a thorough assessment of

alcohol-related problems. However, its major limitation is that it is confined to physical aspects of dependence.

Edinburgh Alcohol Dependence Scale (EADS) (Chick, 1980).

A 34-item interviewer-administered scale for use in circumstances where self-administration is not desired. Its main advantage is that it makes use of clinical skills and sensitivity in the measurement of dependence. The EADS also comes in a brief 7-item form, allowing a dichotomous classification into "early" and "late" dependence.

The choice of measuring instrument will depend on local factors. If time and convenience are pressing considerations, one of the shorter scales (SADQ, SADD) may be preferred. On the other hand, if there are trained staff available to administer it, the EADS offers a more accurate and refined assessment. It may be desired to place the measurement of dependence within the context of a self-contained, thorough assessment of the client's problem, in which case the Ph Score should be used. If the majority of clients coming for help can be assumed to show only low to moderate levels of dependence, the ADS, SADD, or EADS are the best instruments. There is no reason, of course, why any of the scales (except the EADS) could not be adapted to automated testing.

Treatment Goals and Levels

The measurement of dependence can be used to assess clients with respect to two major and linked treatment decisions—the goal and the intensity of treatment. Table 6.1 gives the range of scores on four of the instruments listed above which correspond to three categories of the treatment goal–treatment intensity interaction. These recommendations are not based on empirical data but on the comments of the authors of the scales (in their manuals or publications) and on some practical experience with using them. Moreover, there is no evidence that the corresponding ranges on the various scales shown in Table 6.1 are empirically equivalent; their correspondence is simply as rules of thumb with a similar purpose in each case.

It cannot be emphasized too strongly that allocation to moderate drinking or abstinence goals and to brief or intensive interactions are

Table 6.1. Suggested Ranges of Scores on Four Measures of Alcohol Dependence for Determining Goal and Intensity of Intervention

INSTRUMENT	LOW DEPENDENCE/BRIEF, MODERATE DRINKING INTERVENTION	MODERATE DEPENDENCE/BRIEF OR INTENSIVE INTERVENTION; MODERATE DRINKING OR ABSTINENCE	HIGH DEPENDENCE/INTENSIVE, ABSTINENCE INTERVENTION
SADQ	0–20	21–40	41–60
ADS	0–13	14–30	31–51
SADD	0–9	10–19	20–45
Ph. Score	0–4	5–14	15–20

essentially clinical decisions, depending critically on the unique circumstances and characteristics of the individual client. Nevertheless, Table 6.1 gives broad guidelines for making these decisions with respect to level of dependence. If measured dependence is below a certain level, a brief intervention with a goal of moderation would normally be the treatment of choice. The major exceptions to this would be the presence of organic illness which precluded further drinking, or perhaps the strenuous objections of spouse or relatives to any drinking whatsoever, which may make abstinence more advisable. There may also be certain occupations which make abstinence a preferred option. Above all, if the client expresses a preference for abstinence, this should be accepted irrespective of level of dependence or any other factor.

For those above a defined level of measured dependence, intensive treatment aimed at abstinence is normally the rule. Again, however, there may be a few exceptions. If the client insists on continuing to drink despite strong advice to the contrary, then obviously every effort should be made to assist him or her to drink at safer levels. If there have been many failed attempts at abstinence-oriented treatment in the past, a moderation training program may be well worth trying, provided there are no contraindications such as alcohol-related organic damage. If a goal of moderation for a high-dependence client is decided on, for whatever reason, it should be accompanied by intensive treatment, assuming the client is agreeable to this.

In the middle range of dependence, the two key treatment decisions are more difficult to make. This is not the place to discuss the many issues bearing on the choice between the goals of abstinence versus moderation (see Heather & Robertson, 1983). Suffice it to say that as the

dependence score increases within the moderate range, abstinence should become more favored. Offering clients a role in negotiating the goal with the therapist is more likely to enlist their cooperation in treatment. Where the client has no definite preference, the choice of goal should also reflect the predelictions of the therapist or counselor; there is no point in treatment with a goal of moderation being carried out by someone who has no confidence in the viability of this goal for problem drinkers.

Self-help Manuals in Agency Settings

The use of self-help manuals in general will be described later in the chapter. Here we will consider the possible use of manuals from the base of a specialist agency. Self-help manuals may be especially appropriate when there is no spouse or partner to assist the change process; there is also a suggestion that the self-help approach is particularly suited to female clients. The use of manuals in agency settings therefore represents one alternative to the basic treatment program described above. There are several ways in which they can be used, involving different levels of counselor contact. Here is a suggested scheme for the relationship between the use of self-help manuals and degree of counselor contact:

A. Manual instead of counselor contact when there are no signs of alcohol dependence;

B. Manual in addition to minimal counselor contact when there are signs of low alcohol dependence;

C. Manual in addition to intensive counselor contact when there is moderate alcohol dependence.

The first use of manuals, (A) involves a very brief assessment, from which it can be established that alcohol dependence is either not present or is at a negligible level, and that there are no alcohol-related problems of any consequence (i.e., "hazardous" drinking). In these circumstances, it is justifiable to simply hand out a self-help manual without any counselor contact, provided the manual contains advice and encouragement about seeking further help if necessary. It may be unlikely that many clients fitting this description will be found at an alcohol problems clinic, but this is the kind of self-referral that could be encouraged by the agency through media advertisements and specially arranged events, displays, and so on. A full and detailed self-help manual may be too long for this purpose and a shorter booklet, concentrating on self-monitoring and drinking guidelines (e.g., as in the Scottish Health Education Council leaflet "That's the Limit") is preferable.

The second use, B, is aimed at individuals with low alcohol dependence and entails minimal counselor contact—e.g., the provision of one session of detailed assessment and concrete advice. The client's attention is then drawn to the parts of the self-help manual especially relevant to his or her case and invited to take it home for further work. Again, provided a good follow-up system is in operation, this very limited intervention is perfectly justifiable.

The third and last use of manuals, C, refers to individuals who have somewhat higher levels of dependence but are still suitable for a goal of moderate drinking. Here manuals may be used as workbooks for homework assignments as an aid to counseling. In between counseling sessions, clients are asked to read certain sections or to carry out exercises described in the manual, and results are discussed at the next meeting. Many counselors, especially those who are relatively inexperienced, find the structure and guidance provided by manuals to be useful for counseling. The manual may also be given to the client to take home after counseling has terminated, as an aid to maintenance.

Other Relevant Variables

In deciding between brief and intensive interventions, the following variables are relevant in addition to level of dependence:

Client choice.

As with treatment goal, clients should have an important say in deciding the intensity of treatment. There may be several reasons (e.g.,

a marked sensitivity to the stigma of acknowledging an alcohol problem) which make some clients prefer only minimal contact with the agency. Although in many cases an attempt should be made to persuade the client of the advisability of more frequent contact, in the last resort treatment is only likely to be successful if it fits with the client's wishes and expectations. Again, an efficient follow-up system will always be an advantage in ensuring that clients have received a sufficient level of help for their needs.

Client personality.

Clients with a higher internal locus of control (i.e., who see themselves as being more in control of their lives, rather than at the mercy of external events or "fate") are likely to do better with treatment requiring self-management skills. Other personality variables may also be relevant (Dow, 1982).

Client social stability.

As implied above, when there is a high level of social stability, in terms of secure employment, stable living arrangements, and a cohesive marriage or partnership, the prospects for the success of a brief intervention are greatly increased.

Client cognitive functioning.

When there is any suggestion of irreversible neuropsychological impairment, an intensive intervention should be preferred. This is because it will be difficult for cognitively impaired clients to implement self-management procedures. Alcohol-related cognitive impairment may be assessed by a range of tests which are especially sensitive to alcohol's effects on the brain (see Miller & Saucedo, 1983).

Client reading skills and habits.

Where the brief intervention contains an important element of bibliotherapy, it is obvious but important that the client's reading skills and habits must be up to a required level.

Personality of spouse or partner and relationship variables.

Since the spouse or partner of the client may be involved in the change process, these variables may well affect the likelihood of success of a brief intervention. If the partner acts in such a way as to reinforce only behavioral changes and does not inadvertently reinforce excessive drinking, intensive counselor involvement may be unnecessary.

Stage of change.

The stage in the change process the prospective client is deemed to have reached(Prochaska & DiClemente, 1986) is a most important criterion for deciding on the intensity of intervention. If he or she has reached the Action stage and is determined to try to solve the alcohol problem, a brief intervention with practical guidance and advice may be all that is necessary. On the other hand, if it is suspected that the client still has some doubts about the need for cutting down or stopping drinking—if, in other words, he or she is still in the Contemplation stage—then more protracted contact may be necessary to help the client come to a firm decision (see Miller, 1983).

Counselor or therapist skills.

There is evidence to suggest that when counseling is carried out by personnel with high levels of empathy, it is on the whole more successful than bibliotherapy alone, whereas the reverse is the case with counselors low on empathy (Miller et al., 1981). This should therefore be taken into account in decisions as to whether to use self-help manuals rather than intensive counseling.

Complicating factors.

There may be a number of unique client factors—for example, aspects of the employment situation, highly abnormal attitudes to the use of alcohol, or the presence of associated life problems—which may make a more intensive approach advisable.

COMMUNITY-BASED INTERVENTIONS

Included in this category are some of the most innovative and potentially important types of brief intervention. However, there arises a special problem in intervening in community settings which does not normally occur in specialist agencies. This stems from the fact that

the intervention will be "opportunistic"—i.e., that it attempts to modify drinking behavior in contexts where clients have attended for reasons unconnected with problem drinking. Thus, many potential clients will not be seeking help for an alcohol problem and may not recognize the existence of such a problem. Indeed, they may resent the suggestion and underestimate drinking quantities or deny the existence of any problems that may exist.

Identification

Since most of the work to date has concentrated on the potential of brief interventions in medical settings, the major part of this discussion will focus on screening procedures for use in such settings before briefly describing screening in other contexts. It should be noted that screening is not intended to be definitive of alcohol problems but is merely a first stage in the identification process, to be followed by more intensive assessment. There are several sources of data which may be utilized in screening, as follows:

Questionnaires.

Unfortunately, most questionnaires available at present were developed for the purpose of identifying "alcoholics." For example, the most widely used instrument, the Michigan Alcoholism Screening Test (MAST), of which several versions now exist, was standardized on diagnosed alcoholics and contains questions unsuitable for those with less severe problems (e.g., experience of delirium tremens, attendance at AA meetings). Its usefulness as a detection instrument in community settings is therefore limited, although it can still form a relevant part of a lengthier assessment procedure. Another widely used instrument, the CAGE (Ewing, 1984) is more applicable to brief interventions. CAGE is an acronym for four questions: have you ever felt you ought to Cut down on your drinking?; have people Annoyed you by criticizing your drinking?; have you ever felt bad or Guilty about your drinking?; have you ever had a drink first thing in the morning to steady your nerves, or get rid of a hangover (Eye-opener)? Two or more positive responses is taken to suggest a drinking problem. To take account of the changeability of drinking problems, however, these questions should be preceded by "in the last year" or a shorter period where appropriate.

Laboratory tests.

An obvious problem with the use of questionnaires in this area is that they ask straightforwardly about drinking and alcohol problems and are therefore easy to fake by someone who wishes to do so. Although, if obtained in the right manner, self-reports of drinking are more valid and reliable than is often supposed, there may be particular circumstances where it is suspected that potential clients will be less than frank. Hence the great amount of attention paid in recent years to developing more objective measures for use in screening. The most popular laboratory test is a measure of the liver enzyme gamma-glutamyl transferase (GGT). This is known to reflect alcohol consumption without, up to a certain level, indicating liver damage. The main problem with its use in detection is that GGT returns to normal after a relatively short period of abstinence and for this reason the haematological marker mean cellular volume (MCV) may be preferred, since it reflects longer-term changes in drinking levels. However, although the sensitivities (i.e., the ability to detect positive cases) of both measures vary widely according to the setting in which they are employed, GGT is generally speaking more sensitive to the presence of excessive drinking than MCV. (For a review, see Holt, Skinner, & Israel, 1981.) Combinations of MCV and GGT or combinations involving several other laboratory tests appear to provide better detection than single tests (Bernadt, Mumford, Taylor, Smith, & Murray, 1982; Ryback, Eckhardt, & Paulter, 1980).

Medical history.

Physical complaints, such as nausea, retching, dyspepsia, and diarrhea are common among heavy drinkers and may be used in detection (see Skinner, Holt, Sheu, & Israel, 1986). One recent approach concentrates on the fractures and other injuries which are also common among excessive drinkers and is known as the "trauma scale" (Skinner, Holt, Schuller, Roy, & Israel, 1984). This refers to experience of fractures or dislocations, injuries in road traffic accidents, head injuries, assaults

or fights, and injuries after drinking, with two or more positive items suggesting a drinking problem.

Clinical examination.

Probably even more effective in detection are physical signs recorded from clinical examination (see Skinner et al., 1986). The French physician Le Gô has developed a systematic procedure to guide this examination and calculate a score that may indicate heavy alcohol consumption (Le Gô, 1976).

Composite instruments.

There has recently been a recognition that a composite of the above types of data is likely to improve the effectiveness of screening. For example, the Alcohol Clinical Index (Skinner et al., 1986) combines clinical signs from examination by a physician with medical history from a self-completed questionnaire or interview. Laboratory investigations and alcohol questionnaires are employed as corroborating data. The most recent composite instrument is one developed in a WHO Collaborative Project on the identification and treatment of harmful alcohol consumption (Saunders & Aasland, 1987). This provides a ten-item core screening instrument, consisting of three items on frequency and amount of drinking, three on early alcohol dependence, and four on alcohol-related problems. All questions refer directly to alcohol consumption, but also provided is a more disguised screening procedure, using two items from trauma history, five from clinical examination, and a blood test for the measurement of GGT. Although this latter procedure is less sensitive and specific to drinking problems than the core instrument, it may be used in situations where the validity of the latter is in doubt. The chief virtues of the WHO approach are that it was developed and standardized with the specific purpose of detecting harmful and hazardous drinkers rather than alcoholism as such, and that it is intended to be easily translatable across different cultures. Moreover, the core screening instrument may be used in combination with other lifestyle assessment procedures inquiring about health issues such as cigarette smoking, dieting, and exercise. Apart from providing useful information about other health risks, placing screening in this wider health context makes it more likely that potential clients will cooperate with it.

The type of screening device used in conjunction with a brief intervention will obviously depend on very practical matters. These include the time which may be allocated; the availability of qualified personnel to conduct clinical examinations or take medical histories; and access to laboratory facilities. The setting in which the screening takes place and the type of client contacted there will influence the acceptability of the screening procedure to its potential targets.

In nonmedical situations, screening may be adjusted in an *ad hoc* fashion to particular requirements. For example, Robertson and Heather (1982), in recruiting candidates for an "alcohol education course" for young offenders, asked court personnel to identify young men who either (a) agreed they had a drinking problem; (b) said they were worried about their drinking; (c) thought they would get into less trouble if they did not drink so much; or (d) had committed more than half of their previous offenses under the influence of alcohol. Referrals were then given a more thorough assessment. In similar fashion, screening in an industrial context could take into account a decline in work performance, number of days of sick absenteeism, or failure to show up for work on Monday mornings. These are all indicators of a possible alcohol problem. Some potential clients for brief intervention will obviously self-select, such as persons arrested for drunk-driving offenses. When other methods are not feasible, the CAGE questionnaire can form a quick, rough-and-ready first step in the identification process.

Interventions at Primary Care Level

Babor, Ritson, and Hodgson (1986) have summarized the advantages of locating early intervention strategies at the primary care level: excessive drinkers make more than average use of health facilities; primary health care workers are usually accessible to the community and have an established credibility within it; problems of stigma and labeling are largely avoided; and there is often an opportunity for the family contact which is an important element in the change process.

One example of a brief intervention at this level is the Scottish Health Education Group's DRAMS Scheme (see Heather, 1987). DRAMS stands for *Drinking Reasonably And Moderately with Self-control*. It makes available to the general practitioner (GP) or family practitioner a simple, interactive method that provides a clear structure for intervening with problem drinkers. The DRAMS Kit consists of: (a) a four-page introductory leaflet for the physician; (b) a Medical Record Card with spaces for the doctor to enter patient details, results of blood tests, a record of weekly self-monitored consumption, and a 10-item Medical Questionnaire (MQ) comprising adverse medical and social consequence of heavy drinking; (c) a two-week Drinking Diary Card for use by the patient; and (d) a 59-page booklet which is an abbreviated version of Robertson and Heather's (1985, 1986) self-help manual. It is suggested that if the doctor suspects the presence of a drinking problem he or she should check the 10 items of the MQ. In the event of any positive response, the possibility of a problem is raised with the patient. If the patient agrees, a blood sample is taken for the measurement of GGT, MCV, and blood alcohol concentration, and the patient is handed the Drinking Diary Card and asked to fill it in as honestly as possible. A follow-up consultation in two weeks time is arranged, at which the results of the Drinking Diary Card and the blood test are reviewed. If the existence of a problem is confirmed, the doctor advises the patient of the need to reduce drinking. He or she then introduces the self-help booklet and encourages the patient to work out a realistic plan of action based on guidelines given in the booklet and using further self-monitoring diary sheets. Appointments for further consultations are made at which the patient's medical condition and progress at cutting down are reviewed. The results of further blood tests and, in particular, feedback of GGT levels are used to reinforce progress.

In pilot work with DRAMS, many general practitioners found it useful and were glad to have an alternative to total abstinence to offer appropriate patients. However, one problem which soon became apparent was that a high proportion of patients given DRAMS did not return for the two-week consultation. In retrospect, it is obvious that this was due to the fact that DRAMS did not take account of the motivational level of the patient. As a result, a revised DRAMS is now being developed which takes account of the patient's stage of change according to Prochaska and DiClemente's model and a flow diagram describing this revised scheme is shown in Figure 6.1. This is intended merely as a guide to thinking about some of the issues arising from the application of brief interventions in a primary care setting.

From Figure 6.1 it will be seen that screening for alcohol-related problems or excessive consumption is followed by further assessment designed to exclude those not suitable for the DRAMS Scheme. The doctor then raises the issue of the harm, actual or potential, which is being caused in the patient's life by alcohol. Eventually the patient is asked whether, with the doctor's help, he or she wishes to try to cut down drinking. The next stage in the procedure depends upon the answer to this question. If this can be classified under the heading of "Definitely no," the patient is regarded as being in the Precontemplation stage; short reading material on the risks of excessive drinking is provided but is left to the patient to make a further appointment. If, on the other hand, the answer to the key question is classified as "definitely yes," the Action stage is immediately entered. This involves a method similar to the original DRAMS, with the addition of an explicit procedure for involving the patient's partner, including a short leaflet written for the partner and containing instructions for "contractual" exercises. After the doctor has started off the Action procedure, regular visits are scheduled with the practice nurse, who gives feedback and reinforcement for changes in self-reported consumption and GGT levels. Eventually, after a general review of progress by the doctor, the Action phase is terminated and the Maintenance phase entered. This consists of self-help literature covering the identification of high-risk relapse situations, some instruction in coping skills, and an attempt at cognitive restructuring of unhelpful beliefs and expectations (see Marlatt & Gordon, 1985). The patient is encouraged to make other appointments if and when necessary.

The area of chief difficulty concerns patients whose reply to the question—of whether they wish to cut down drinking—falls into neither of the above categories but can only be classified as "Maybe". In this case the patient is regarded as being in the Contemplation stage. The procedure here includes self-help material with a "balance sheet" exercise on the advantages and disadvantages of cutting down versus continuing to drink heavily. It also depends crucially on the skill of the doctor in the interview situation. Here the principles of motivational interviewing, as described by Miller (1983), are used to gently sway the patient towards increased motivation and a readiness to enter the Action stage. The results of self-monitored consumption and of blood tests may be used by the doctor as allies in this process. Figure 6.1 shows that the patient may move from the Contemplation stage in either direction when a decision as to the attempt to cut down has eventually been made. The revised DRAMS Scheme has the advantage of greater flexibility in meeting the particular needs of individual patients, and also makes more use of the skills of medical and nursing staff in the change process.

The DRAMS Scheme is, of course, only one example among a wide range of intervention strategies which may be used at the primary care level. As well as variations in the type of worker who delivers the intervention and in the balance between self-help and personal contact, methods of recruiting excessive drinkers may also vary. For instance, as well as the opportunistic kind of approach used in DRAMS, potential clients may be identified by means of a screening instrument mailed to all patients on a general practitioner's list, or at least those in high risk categories. Those who reply could be invited to a preliminary meeting before more extended involvement takes place. The many issues involved in early intervention in the primary care setting have been discussed by the Royal College of General Practitioners (1986), and specific intervention strategies have been described by Skinner and Holt (1983) and Anderson (1987).

Interventions in General Hospital Wards

Hospital wards are a potentially very fertile source of candidates for brief interventions, since research suggests that between 10% and 30% of general inpatients are excessive drinkers (Jarman & Kellett, 1979; Quinn & Johnston, 1976). In the past, the majority of such cases have tended to be missed by medical staff, but there is now growing concern about the identification of problem drinkers in hospitals, as witnessed in a recent report by the Royal College of Physicians (1987). Barrison, et al. (1982) reported satisfactory identification by

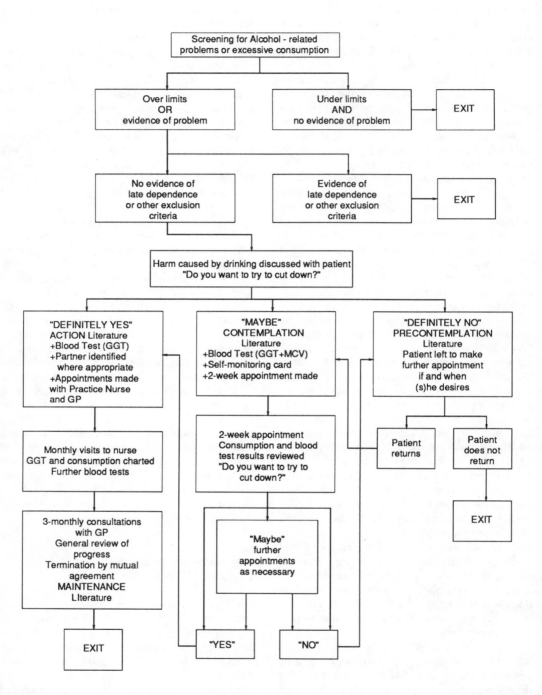

FIGURE 6.1. Flow diagram for revised DRAMS scheme based on Prochaska and DiClemente's model of change.

using a combination of simple questions about quantity and frequency of drinking and the CAGE questionnaire. Chick, Lloyd, & Crombie (1985) identified problem drinkers by a weighted combination of questions relating to consumption, alcohol-related problems, and dependence symptoms.

With regard to intervention, Chick et al. (1985) have demonstrated the effectiveness of a single session of counseling given by an experienced nurse and lasting up to 60 minutes. During this session, the nurse gives the patient a specially prepared booklet and engages him or her in a discussion about lifestyle and health, which helps the patient to weigh up the drawbacks of the current pattern of drinking and come to a decision about future consumption. The objective is problem-free drinking, although abstinence may be agreed in some cases. The best target for this type of intervention is male patients with good social support, since it is this group on which the effectiveness of the method was established, but other patients may be included provided there is a means of checking on progress after discharge. The relative contributions to beneficial change of counseling on the ward and self-help materials to take home are unknown, as are the possible additions to effectiveness of home visits following discharge to reinforce progress and regular feedback of GGT results, but these variations are worth trying if there are suitable staff members available. The roles played by medical staff, ward nurses, community nurses, and health visitors will depend on the type of approach being used.

Community Health Programs

Two recent approaches to early intervention for alcohol problems, in different parts of Europe, are of great potential importance. The first is the general health screening project in Malmö, Sweden (Kristenson, Trell, & Hood, 1982; Kristenson, Ohlin, Hulten-Nosslin, Trell, & Hood, 1983) in which problem drinkers were identified by a raised GGT on two occasions three weeks apart. The intervention consisted of a detailed physical examination and-interview regarding drinking history, alcohol-related problems, and symptoms of dependence. Subjects were offered appointments with the same physician every three months and monthly visits to a nurse who gave feed-

back of GGT results. Once drinking had reached moderate levels, frequency of clinical contacts was reduced.

The other important European innovation followed the establishment by the French government in 1970 of three experimental clinics known as *Centres D'Hygiene Alimentaire* (CHAs). These clinics received referrals from the courts, social service agencies, physicians, hospitals, and various other sources. Their remit was to stress to patients the importance of diseases related to nutrition, to offer help to chronic excessive drinkers without serious psychological or social problems, and also to help those alcoholics who rejected psychiatric treatment. Clinic staff furnished drinkers with proof of alcohol abuse, gained their confidence in order to reach an acknowledgment of a problem, persuaded them to make a radical change in drinking, and demonstrated that a reduction in drinking, when it does occur, leads to improvements in health. Although the CHAs have not yet been subjected to controlled evaluation, two reviews (Babor et al., 1983; Chick, 1984) have concluded that this method of intervention is very promising in view of its cheapness, accessibility, and widespread contact with problem drinkers. Similar programs deserve exploration, with suitable adjustments to local conditions, in other countries.

The Drinker's Check-Up

Following Miller's (1983) description of the "motivational interviewing" approach to problem drinking, Miller et al. (1987) have recently described a procedure known as The Drinker's Check-up (DCU), which is offered to drinkers as a means of discovering what adverse effects alcohol may be causing to their lives. It provides objective feedback from a battery of measures, with the intention of increasing the client's awareness of risk.

The DCU is promoted in the local news media through advertisements which stress that it (a) is free and confidential; (b) is not part of a treatment program; (c) is intended for drinkers in general, not alcoholics; (d) does not involve a label or diagnosis; and (e) gives clear and objective feedback which drinkers may use as they please. The complete DCU requires two visits: the two-hour check-up itself and a return visit a week later when clients receive information and motivational feedback, presented in an objective and empathic manner. The battery of tests used include: (a) the Brief Drinker Profile (Miller & Marlatt, 1987); (b) a blood test for the measurement of indicators of alcohol-related physical impairment; (c) eight neuropsychological tests of particular sensitivity to the effects of alcohol on the brain (Miller & Saucedo, 1983); (d) interviews with up to three collateral sources to confirm the client's self-report; and (e) the Alcohol Use Inventory (Horn, Wanberg, & Foster, 1987). The authors emphasize that this list of tests and procedures is not definitive for the DCU, and that other types of measure are potentially useful.

Miller et al. (1987) suggest that the DCU has several possible applications. It could be used as part of routine health screening procedures in medical settings as an aid to early intervention and secondary prevention. It could also be employed in specialist agencies to assist treatment matching, especially with regard to the appropriate level of intervention. The most original use, however, is as a non-threatening means of self-assessment which is made available to the general public and may be effective in starting a motivational process leading to eventual change in drinking habits. In appropriate cases, a range of alternative methods of behavior change can be discussed with the client at the end of the feedback session, and a counseling relationship or some other form of intervention set up. The Drinker's Check-up is an exciting and potentially valuable addition to the range of brief intervention strategies.

Interventions in Nonmedical Settings

A model of an "alcohol education course" for young offenders with alcohol-related problems referred from the courts was described by Robertson and Heather (1982). In this context, of course, "education" means much more than merely providing information and includes many of the procedures listed in the typical contents of self-help manuals (see Robertson and Heather, 1985). However, the group setting allows useful discussion of various aspects of the change process and the opportunity for mutual feedback on progress among group members. The optimum number in a group is probably between six and eight. In a recent survey, Baldwin and Heather (1987) reported

the existence of at least 20 alcohol education courses in the United Kingdom using a variety of methods, although none has been properly evaluated.

Another obvious source of clients for this type of alcohol education course is drunk driving offenders. The use of education as an alternative to legal sanctions in this area has become increasingly popular, particularly in the United States, but the education offered is typically of a didactic kind and ignores performance based procedures. The systematic application of brief, behaviorally based training programs in this area is urgently needed. In addition to behavioral programs in group settings, home study programs could be used (see Swenson & Clay, 1980).

Apart from court referrals, the other major nonmedical source of candidates for brief interventions is the industrial setting. Again, there has been a rapid increase in the number of Employee Assistance Programmes in the United States aimed at problem drinkers identified in the workplace. Unfortunately, however, the great majority of these programs are based on the disease view of alcoholism and are aimed at total abstinence. Rather than being conducive to early intervention, as is usually the claim, such a background might be seen as a discouragement to early identification and behavior change. As in the case of drunk driver programs, what is needed is the systematic application of moderate drinking training courses and other types of brief intervention aimed at reduced drinking, for employees with lower levels of dependence and less severe problems (see Walker & Shain, 1983).

Drinkwatchers

A self-help organization called "Drink-Watchers" was founded in the United States by Winters (1978) during the 1970s. However, the development and rationale of a completely independent, non-profit organization with the same name in Britain has recently been described by Ruzek (in press). This Drink-Watchers service is based on the same behavioral principles, aimed at a goal of moderate drinking described in this chapter, with the added ingredient of group meetings as the principal mode of delivery. The essence of the service is a single individual screening session followed by group participation. Clients whose drinking problems are sufficiently severe to require abstinence-oriented treatment are referred elsewhere, as are those clients with a goal of moderation who request or require additional counseling. For the majority, however, progress in cutting down is encouraged by attendance at open groups, meeting on average one evening a week for about two and one-half hours. Self-monitoring and goal setting are aided by mutual feedback among group members. A group leader is used to focus discussion along appropriate channels and to set group exercises involving identification of high-risk situations and practice in coping skills (see Ruzek, in press).

Implicit in the Drinkwatchers program is the dissemination of autonomous groups throughout the country. To date, there are 14 branches in 11 cities in Britain, with four more branches in the planning stage. Provided they are supplied with adequate medical and other professional advice, these local branches, mirroring and complementing in many respects the activities of Alcoholics Anonymous with a different range of problem drinkers, represent a very exciting development in early intervention strategies. The Drinkwatchers concept deserves attention in other countries.

Involvement of Professional Groups

One advantage of the Drinkwatchers strategy and of self-help manuals sent through the mail is that no cooperation is needed from any group of professionals in order to implement the intervention. Unfortunately, however, these strategies can never substitute completely for interventions in community settings where the involvement of medical, nursing, social work, and other personnel is essential. It may be an exaggeration to say that difficulties relating to the involvement of these professional groups represent a greater obstacle to progress than those inherent in changing the behavior of problem drinkers themselves, but there is no doubt that a lack of willingness to become involved in brief intervention work is a serious problem.

As a consequence, there has been a great deal of attention paid in recent years to analyzing these difficulties and suggesting solutions (e.g., Shaw, Cartwright, Spratley, & Harwin, 1978). General practitioners have been the most inten-

sively studied group in Britain. It has been concluded that, in dealing with problem drinkers, GPs may lack "role adequacy," "role legitimacy," and "role support"; in plainer language, they do not know how to respond, are unsure whether to respond or not, and feel unsupported when they do respond (Clement, 1986). The same considerations apply to other professional groups. In addition, there may be moral or ideological objections to working with problem drinkers; for example, some physicians feel that their job is to provide a technical, medical intervention and that changes in behavior are a matter entirely for the patient and outside their own professional responsibility.

The only remedy for these difficulties is, of course, a patient and concerted program of education aimed at enabling professional workers to realize the importance of changing the behavior of excessive drinkers and of the vital role they can play in such a process. The evidence shows that those helpers who have had successful experiences in the past are more likely to wish to be involved than those with less experience (Shaw et al., 1978). It is essential also to convey changes in thinking about alcohol problems, since the views of many professionals reflect outmoded concepts. For example, as members of the general public, many non-specialist workers share the dichotomous view of alcohol problems as involving only "alcoholics" and "normal drinkers." One of the first tasks for an educational program is, therefore, to break down this oversimplified model and introduce the concept of the early or low-dependence problem drinker and the possibility of moderate drinking as a goal. If methods are available for intervening with such a population, such as the DRAMS Scheme for general practitioners, this will create a "virtuous circle," in which the more often the interventions are applied the more frequently will opportunities for their use arise and be recognized as such. In more general terms, so great are the potential benefits from the active involvement of the major professional groups in brief interventions for problem drinking that a considerable expenditure of resources is justified in the attempt to realize this potential.

SELF-HELP MANUALS

Apart from making self-help manuals commercially available in the local bookstore, the most direct form of brief intervention is simply to advertise help and advice for excessive drinking in the press, television, or other media and send a self-help manual aimed at reduced consumption to those replying. An example of such an advertisement, from a self-help project in Dundee, Scotland is given in Figure 6.2.

With this type of intervention, there are obvious restrictions on the ability to screen suitable clients and exclude those who are not suited to a brief intervention or a goal of moderate drinking. However, it will be noted that the advertisement shown in Figure 6.2 stresses that the advice offered "is not for alcoholics." A more refined explanation of what is meant by alcoholism in this context (i.e., the presence of marked withdrawal symptoms and relief drinking) may be made in the opening pages of the self-help manual itself. Needless to say, all self-help manuals should contain an appendix giving addresses of specialist agencies to which clients may turn if there is no improvement.

The distribution of self-help manuals can be supported by various degrees of contact with helping agencies. For example, clients could be asked to mail the results of each week's self-monitored alcohol consumption to the agency, using sheets specially prepared for this purpose (see Miller, 1978). Alternatively, clients might be asked to telephone at set times to record this information and discuss difficulties which may have arisen, either to a telephone answering service or in a personal interview. The added costs of such contact must be weighed against any additional gain which might be expected.

Self-help manuals need not be aimed at a controlled goal of moderate drinking but can be directed at total abstinence, either permanent or temporary. Such a manual has been developed by Murray, McGarva, and Heather (1986) for use with problem drinkers identified on general hospital wards whose abstinence is advisable on grounds of organic illness rather than a high level of alcohol dependence. It is also important to point out that self-help methods need not be limited to the written word. Especially if clients have poor reading skills or habits, audiotapes are an interesting alternative, (while in view of the recent increase in home video equipment) videotapes may have an even more exciting potential. The use of interactive computer programs for use in the home should also be explored.

DRINKING TOO MUCH?

If you have the feeling that you are drinking more alcohol than you should, you can get free help and advice through the post now.

This is not for alcoholics, but for people who genuinely feel they should cut down their drinking and are having some difficulty doing so.

The advice which will be sent to you is absolutely free. This is not a trick to try to sell you something. It's an official health education project to help people reduce their drinking.

If you think you would benefit from drinking less, just write your name and address in the space provided below, cut it out and send it to **SELF-HELP PROJECT, FREEPOST, NINEWELLS MEDICAL SCHOOL, DUNDEE, DD1 9XT.** No postage is required if the word FREEPOST is clearly written on the envelope.

Please note that your name and address will be kept STRICTLY PRIVATE AND CONFIDENTIAL. No unauthorised person will ever know that you have responded to this advertisement.

If you are on the telephone, please enter your number below so that we can contact you, again on a STRICTLY CONFIDENTIAL basis.

I would like advice on how to cut down my drinking. **SEND TO: SELF-HELP PROJECT, FREEPOST, NINEWELLS MEDICAL SCHOOL, DUNDEE, DD1 9XT. (Block letters, please.)**

NAME (Mr/Mrs/Miss) ____________________

AGE ____________________

ADDRESS ____________________

____

TELEPHONE NUMBER: ____________________

FIGURE 6.2. Advertisement for self-help manual.

EFFECTIVENESS

Evidence suggesting that brief interventions may be as effective as more intensive treatments first came to prominence as a result of Emrick's (1975) review of alcoholism treatment outcome studies. From an inspection of studies comparing treatment with no treatment, or at least only minimal treatment contact, Emrick concluded that there was no evidence that treatment improved abstinence rates. However, he also noted that more treated than untreated clients showed some improvement in their drinking problems, suggesting that formal treatment does at least increase the probability of some amelioration in the adverse consequences of drinking. Unfortunately, even this inference is made suspect by the possible existence of selective client characteristics which may have biased the comparison between formally and minimally treated groups.

The second influential piece of work to raise the status of brief intervention was Orford and Edwards' (1977) controlled comparison of treatment and advice among 100 married, male alcoholics seen at the Maudsley Hospital, London. Following a comprehensive three-hour assessment, clients were randomly assigned either to a group which received a single counseling session together with their wives and were then told, "in constructive and sympathetic terms," that the responsibility for solving their problem lay in their own hands or to a group which received a mixture of outpatient and inpatient, psychiatric, and social work care representing the standard package of help available at any well-supported treatment center. At follow-up 12 months after initial assessment, there was no evidence of any significant differences between these groups in drinking behavior, alcohol-related problems, social adjustment, or any other outcome measure. A long-term follow-up (Taylor, et al., 1985) continued to show no difference between groups after ten years. As in the case of Emrick's (1975) review, however, a closer inspection of the data revealed some grounds for more confidence in the effects of conventional treatment. Thus, a two-year follow-up of the same cohort suggested that those with more severe levels of alcohol dependence were more likely to attain the stated goal of abstinence if they had received treatment than if they had received advice (Orford, Oppenheimer, & Edwards, 1976). Moreover, it is often pointed out that the married and socially stable alcoholics without psychiatric disturbance studied by Orford and Edwards had a generally good prognosis and may therefore have been more likely to benefit from the brief intervention than the unmarried or less socially stable individuals frequently seen in treatment (e.g., Kissin, 1977).

A recently completed study by Chick et al. (1988) was based on Orford and Edwards' design but with a few important modifications. Following a comprehensive client and informant assessment, 152 of those attending an alcohol problems clinic were randomly assigned to receive either extended inpatient or outpatient treatment, typical of that offered in British treatment centers, or, alternatively, one session of advice. The advice group was itself divided into subgroups, receiving either very brief, standardized advice lasting about five minutes or a more comprehensive advice session lasting an hour. Unlike Orford and Edwards' sample, this included women and unmarried clients. The results showed that, at one-year follow-up, there was no difference between extended treatment and advice groups in abstinence rates or in terms of employment and marital status. However, the extended group showed evidence of less alcohol-related damage in the year since intake. This study therefore supported, in a controlled trial, Emrick's suggestion that, compared with brief intervention, extended treatment does not affect the likelihood of successful abstinence but may reduce the amount of harm caused by drinking. Chick et al. also found no differences in outcome between the very brief and comprehensive advice groups, but this finding is difficult to interpret because both groups received numerous research visits in the follow-up period from social work personnel and this may have obscured any potential difference between the two groups in question.

Interventions With a Goal of Moderation

Although the earlier work on brief interventions was concerned with the abstinence treatment goal, it is in conjunction with the goal of moderate, nonproblematic drinking and low-dependence problem drinkers that research interest has subsequently focused. Research by Sanchez-Craig and her colleagues in Toronto demonstrated that, among early or low-dependence problem drinkers, moderate drinking is preferable to abstinence as a treatment goal. Sanchez-Craig (1980) randomly assigned problem drinkers to two similar behavioral conditions which differed mainly in terms of treatment goal, abstinence or moderate drinking. All clients were asked to abstain during the period of treatment itself, which consisted of six individual 90-minute sessions. At the end of the treatment period, it was found that the moderate drinking goal clients had drunk only one-third the amount of alcohol that the abstinence group had consumed and also had drunk on significantly fewer days and less often to excess. Although at two year follow-up there were no significant differences between groups, moderate drinking was considered to be the more appropriate goal since it was more acceptable to the majority of clients, and most of those assigned to abstinence had developed moderate drinking patterns on their own (Sanchez-Craig, Annis, Bornet, & McDonald, 1984). On the basis of further analyses, Sanchez-Craig and Lei (1986) concluded that among the heavier drinkers taking part in the study, imposition of the goal of abstinence was ineffective in promoting abstinence and counterproductive in encouraging moderate drinking.

Apart from the research of Miller and his colleagues using self-help manuals, which will be described below, at least two well-designed studies have compared brief with more intensive interventions with a goal of moderation. Vogler, Weissbach, Compton, and Martin (1977) studied 80 problem drinkers, most of whom had been referred from the courts after drunk-driving convictions. There was clear evidence of alcohol-related problems in all cases, but mean pretreatment consumption was relatively low, at about 7 units per day. Clients were randomly assigned to one of four groups receiving the following: (a) videotape feedback of drunken behavior, BAC discrimination training, aversive conditioning, assertiveness training, problem solving skills training, counseling in non-vocational interests, and alcohol education; (b) as above but without videotape feedback and aversive conditioning; (c) as for b but without BAC discrimination training; (d) alcohol education only. At one year follow-up, all groups showed a significant improvement, but there were no significant differences between groups.

More recently, a similar finding was obtained by Skutle and Berg (1987) from Bergen, Nor-

way. These authors randomly assigned 48- "earlystage" problem drinkers recruited through newspaper advertisements to one of four groups, as follows: (a) therapist-directed "behavioral self-control training" (BSCT; see Miller, 1978 and Chapter 9); (b) training in coping skills; (c) a combination of BSCT and coping skills training; (d) bibliotherapy based on BSCT. At follow-up 3, 6, and 12 months following the end of treatment, although all groups showed significant reductions in consumption, there were again no significant-differences between groups. Lack of blind follow-up was the only major fault in the design of this study.

In another study randomly assigning problem drinkers to intensive and brief moderate drinking goal interventions, evidence was found for the superior effectiveness of the former. Robertson, Heather, Dzialdowski, Crawford, and Winton (1986) compared 16 clients given individually tailored behavior psychotherapy, aimed at moderate drinking and lasting an average of 9 sessions, with 21 clients given 3 or 4 sessions of assessment and advice. At follow-up a mean of 15.5 months after termination of treatment, the intensive group was found to show a significantly greater reduction in consumption and in the number of days of abstinence in the month before assessment. The discrepancy between this finding and those cited above may be due to several factors, including different sample characteristics in terms of level of dependence, pretreatment consumption, and problems. Another possibility is suggested by the finding of Miller et al. (1980) that clients given a self-help manual fared worse than those who received individual attention from counselors high on empathy but better than those whose counselors were low on empathy. It could be that the therapists used in the Robertson et al. study possessed above-average therapeutic skills. It should also be noted that it took Robertson et al. over four years to achieve a figure of 37 treated clients, and that others have commented on the difficulties in attracting referrals of low-dependence problem drinkers for moderate drinking treatment in hospital settings (e.g., Vogler, Compton, & Weisbach, 1976).

Self-help Manuals

Research on the use of self-help manuals in the alcohol problems field was pioneered by William Miller and his colleagues. The original intention of the study by Miller (1978) was to compare the effectiveness of three behavioral treatment modalities. However, as an afterthought, the self-help manual written by Miller and Muñoz (1982) was randomly distributed to half the clients at the end of treatment, with the other half receiving it three months later. The result was that the manual group continued to show therapeutic gains during the follow-up period, in contrast to the non-manual group who remained at the level reached at termination of treatment and were significantly more improved at three months follow-up. This "serendipitous" finding thus showed that a self-help manual was an effective supplement to treatment. The question posed by Miller, Gribskov, and Mortell (1981) was how effective could a manual be when used on its own, without therapist involvement? Thirty-one clients were randomly assigned either to be interviewed and then given a manual plus self-monitoring cards to mail in to the clinic or to enter a group receiving ten individual treatment sessions using the same BSCT method covered by the manual. There were no significant differences in outcome between these two groups at three months follow-up; indeed, such differences as there were tended to be in favour of the manual only group.

In another study, Miller and Taylor (1980) compared a manual only (bibliotherapy) group with three types of behavioral treatment. At one year follow-up, all four groups showed significant reductions in consumption but, once more, there were no significant differences between groups on any type of outcome measure. In a similar study, Miller et al. (1980) randomly allocated 56 problem drinkers to: (a) bibliotherapy; (b) six weekly sessions of BSCT; (c) BSCT plus 12 sessions of relaxation, communication, and assertiveness training; (d) BSCT plus 12 weeks of individually tailored broad-spectrum treatment modules focusing on anxiety, depression, insomnia, and so forth. At one year follow-up, while all groups showed a significant reduction in consumption, there were no significant differences between groups except that the bibliotherapy group reported more hours per week with a BAC exceeding 80 mg/100 ml. However, the higher mean consumption of the bibliotherapy group at intake must be borne in mind here. Success rates for the four groups above were: (a) 60%, (b) 70%, (c) 89%, (d) 89%. Thus there is an association here between outcome and increasing amount of therapist contact, with the more costly and intensive treatments producing the best results. However, the success rate for bibliotherapy alone is high and the use of bibliotherapy could be justified from this study on the basis of cost-effectiveness.

In a two-year follow-up of the accumulated cohort from the Miller and Taylor (1980) and Miller et al. (1980) studies (Miller & Baca, 1982), improvement rates for bibliotherapy clients were equivalent or better than for those in the various treatment conditions, except for those given BSCT in groups. Generally speaking, stability of outcome among these clients was found to be good, with more than 80% showing equal or greater improvement at two years compared with earlier follow-up points. There was no greater risk of relapse from a moderate drinking outcome than from abstinence.

Buck and Miller (1981) moved on to the next stage in their research program by hypothesizing the superiority of a self-help manual to two control conditions. These authors compared a manual group to one involving only the self-monitoring of alcohol consumption and a further group of no-treatment, waiting-list controls. Follow-up was restricted to the end of the ten-week treatment phase because of the ethical requirement of offering the control clients some form of treatment, in this case therapist-administered treatment in a group format. It was found that the bibliotherapy group was superior to the other two on measures of consumption at the 10-week follow-up point but that this superiority disappeared after controls had received treatment. It must be pointed out that there are well-known problems with the use of waiting-list controls, who may simply defer a decision to cut down drinking to the time when they know they will begin receiving treatment. Nevertheless, this study shows that self-monitoring alone is insufficient to explain the beneficial effects of bibliotherapy aimed at controlled drinking.

Although the work of the Miller group has clearly demonstrated the viability of a self-help approach for low-dependence problem drinkers, it does have certain limitations, related mainly to the fact that self-help materials were evaluated within the context of a conventional service delivery system. Most clients in bibliotherapy groups were self-referrals to an-outpatient clinic and were presumably highly motivated to change. They were all seen at least once by a therapist for assessment interviewing and were given self-monitoring cards to be filled in and mailed to the clinic each week.

Thus, minimal therapist contact was present rather than the manual being entirely self-administered (see Glasgow & Rosen, 1978).

This was the main rationale for a study by Heather, Whitlon, and Robertson (1986). A total of 785 individuals responded to advertisements in the Scottish national press offering free help to cut down drinking and were sent alternatively either a self-help manual based on behavioral principles (Robertson & Heather, 1985) or a general advice and information booklet that included addresses of helping agencies. A subsample of respondents was interviewed by telephone, but the only contact with the main sample was through the mail. At six months follow-up, it was found that the manual group showed a significantly greater reduction in mean alcohol consumption than the controls and also greater improvement on variables measuring physical health and the extent of alcohol-related problems. Within the limits of the consumption and dependence levels shown in the sample, there was no evidence that improvement was confined to only those showing relatively lower consumption or early as opposed to late dependence. At a one year follow-up of the same cohort (Heather et al., 1987), the gains observed at the earlier follow-up had been maintained and there was further evidence of the superiority of manual over control groups when respondents who had received other forms of help had been excluded. The one year follow-up also provided some limited corroboration from personal interviews for the validity of the self-report data used in this study.

Community-Based Interventions

Probably the most successful research demonstration of the potential of brief interventions was conducted in Malmö, Sweden (Kristenson et al., 1982, 1983; Trell, Kristenson, & Fex, 1984). All male residents of Malmö between 45 and 50 years of age were invited to a health screening interview arranged by the local Department of Preventive Medicine. Of these, 585 individuals who were in the top decile of the distribution of GGT readings on two successive occasions were selected for study. Excessive drinking was found to be implicated in the raised GGT of 72% of this sample. Half were then randomly allocated to an intervention group given the procedure described above (p.

105). Control group subjects were simply informed by letter that they showed evidence of impaired liver function and were advised to cut down drinking.

At follow-up two and four years after initial screening, both groups showed significant decreases in GGT levels. However, the control group showed a significantly greater increase in the mean number of sick days per individual, more days of hospitalization in the follow-up period, and a strikingly greater number of days in the hospital for alcohol-related conditions. At a five-year follow-up, the control group showed twice as many deaths, both those probably alcohol-related and not so, as the intervention group. Apart from an unfortunate reluctance to report alcohol consumption figures, Kristenson and his colleagues have undoubtedly produced the most impressive and well-substantiated results to date in the field of brief interventions, with obvious implications for the widespread application of their method in other countries and with other population groups.

Another important set of results was reported by Chick et al. (1985). Seven hundred and thirty-one male inpatients of general hospital wards were screened for problem drinking, excluding those who had received previous treatment for alcoholism or who had little social support. One hundred and fifty-six who agreed to a follow-up interview were randomly allocated to a group which received one session of counseling about their drinking habits from a nurse (see p. 105) or a control group receiving only routine medical care. Results at one-year follow-up showed that both groups showed significant decreases in consumption. However, the intervention group was alone in showing a significant reduction in alcohol-related problems and also contained a significantly higher proportion who were "definitely improved" in terms of GGT and MCV levels.

Miller et al. (1987) have reported a pilot evaluation of the Drinker's Check-up. After a screening session, 42 problem drinkers were randomly assigned to three groups: (a) the Check-up within one week of the screening session; (b) the Check-up plus a comprehensive list of potential sources of help and treatment, given after the feedback session; and (c) a waiting list control who received the Check-up six weeks after the initial session. At a follow-up roughly six weeks after the Check-up, all groups showed modest but significant reductions in alcohol consumption and these were retained at an 18-month follow-up. However, no differences in response are reported between the groups under study. The authors conclude that the Check-up may have a significant impact both in prompting less motivated drinkers to seek help and in modestly suppressing drinking, but that the Check-up itself may be insufficient to alleviate all alcohol-related problems.

One unfortunate gap in the research evidence at present is a lack of data showing the effectiveness of brief interventions compared with controls in a general practice setting. In an evaluation of the Scottish Health Education Group's DRAMS Scheme, Heather et al. (1987) found no clear evidence at six month follow-up of superior outcome in a group given DRAMS compared with one given only simple advice by their doctors and a non-intervention control. However, it might be argued that this study did not represent a fair test of brief interventions in general practice (see Heather et al., 1987). Among other reasons, it is important to note that, since the great majority of patients in the DRAMS evaluation had not visited their doctor to complain specifically of an alcohol problem and were therefore presumably less well motivated to change than, for example, the respondents to newspaper advertisements in Heather et al.'s (1986) self-help manual study, it would take a large sample of subjects to reveal the hypothesized effectiveness of the DRAMS Scheme. There are three other major studies of brief intervention in general practice currently underway in the United Kingdom at present, and their results are awaited with interest.

REFERENCES

Clinical Guidelines

Anderson, P. (1987). A strategy for helping people who are drinking excessively. *The Practitioner, 231,* 297–306. Oriented to general practice intervention.

Chick, J. (1980). Alcohol dependence: methodological issues in its measurement; reliability of the criteria. *British Journal of Addiction, 75,* 175–186. Description of the EADS. Available from Dr. Jonathon Chick, Alcohol Research Group, Royal Edinburgh Hospital, Morningside Terrace, Edinburgh EH10 5HF, UK.

Christensen, A., Miller, W. R., & Muñoz, R. F. (1978). Paraprofessionals, partners, peers, paraphernalia and print: Expanding mental health service delivery. *Professional Psychology,* May 249–270. Still a very useful discussion of its subject.

Heather, N., & Robertson, R. (1983). *Controlled drinking* (revised edition). New York: Methuen. As well as describing the background to the use of controlled drinking treatment, this gives guidance for differential allocation to moderate drinking or abstinence goals (chapter 9).

Mayfield, D., McLeod, G., & Hall, P. (1974). The CAGE questionnaire: Validation of a new alcoholism screening instrument. *American Journal of Psychiatry, 131,* 1121–1123. First description of the CAGE. See also, Ewing, J. A. (1984), Detecting alcoholism—the CAGE questionnaire. *Journal of the American Medical Association, 252,* 1905–1907.

Miller, W. R., & Marlatt, G. A. (1984). *Manual for the Comprehensive Drinker Profile.* Odessa, FL: Psychological Assessment Resources Inc. Source for Ph. Score. Full CDP available from PAR, P.O. Box 98, Odessa, FL 33556.

Miller, W. R., & Marlatt, G. A. (1987). The brief drinker profile. Odessa, FL: Psychological Assessment Resources.

Miller, W. R., & Muñoz, R. F. (1982). *How to control your drinking* (revised edition). Albuquerque, NM: University of New Mexico Press. The original controlled drinking self-help manual. It can be criticized only for being somewhat long for some purposes. Earlier edition (Englewood Cliffs, NJ: Prentice-Hall, 1976) contains useful appendices on controlled drinking therapies and guidelines for therapists.

Miller, W. R., Sovereign, R. G., & Krege, B. V. (1987). Motivational interviewing with problem drinkers: II. The Drinker's check-up as a preventive intervention. Unpublished manuscript, available from Professor W. R. Miller, Department of Psychology, University of New Mexico, Albuquerque, NM 87131. First description of the Drinker's Check-up.

Orford, J., & Edwards, G. (1977). *Alcoholism: A comparison of treatment and advice, with a study of the influence of marriage.* Maudsley Monographs no. 26. Oxford: Oxford University Press. Comprehensive account of the authors' influential research study. Chapter 8 contains a description of the basic treatment method and a wider discussion of the implication of the findings. See also Edwards, G., & Orford, J. (1977), A plain treatment for alcoholism. *Proceedings of the Royal Society of Medicine, 70,* 344–348.

Raistrick, D., Dunbar, G., & Davidson, R. (1983). Development of a questionnaire to measure alcohol dependence. *British Journal of Addiction, 78,* 89–95. Description of the SADD. Available from Lees Addiction Unit, 40 Clarendon Road, Leeds LS2 9PJ, UK.

Robertson, I., & Heather, N. (1985). *So you want to cut down your drinking?* (revised edition). Edinburgh: Scottish Health Education Group. An example of a self-help manual specifically adapted to local culture and conditions. Attractively produced by SHEG. Distributed free in Scotland only, but sample copies obtainable from Scottish Health Education Group, Woodburn House, Canaan Lane, Edinburgh EH10 4SG, UK.

Robertson, I., & Heather, N. (1986). *Let's drink to your health!* Leicester: British Psychological Society Publications. A slightly expanded and up-market version of the manual above.

Ruzek, J. (1987). The Drinkwatchers' experience: A description and progress report on services for controlled drinkers. In T. Stockwell and S. Clement (Eds.), *Helping the problem drinker: New initiatives in community care.* London: Croom Helm. Definitive account of Drinkwatchers in the United Kingdom.

Sanchez-Craig, M. (1982). Teaching controlled drinking and abstinence to early-stage problem drinkers: Self-control strategies for secondary prevention. Unpublished manuscript. Toronto, Canada: Addiction Research Foundation. One of the best therapist manuals in this area. Write to Dr. Martha Sanchez-Craig, ARF, 33 Russell Street, Toronto, Canada M5S 2S1.

Sanchez-Craig, M., Wilkinson, D. A., & Walker, K. (1987). Theory and methods for secondary prevention of alcohol problems: a cognitively-based approach. In W. M. Cox (Ed.), *Treatment and prevention of alcohol problems: A resource manual.* New York: Academic Press. A comprehensive review of this topic.

Saunders, J. B, & Aasland, O. G. (1987). *WHO collaborative project on the identification and treatment of persons with harmful alcohol consumption. Report on phase 1: Development of a screening instrument.* Geneva, Switzerland: World Health Organization. An appendix to the Report gives full details of the two-phase screening procedure. Write to: Mr. Marcus Grant, World Health Organization, Division of Mental Health, Geneva, Switzerland.

Skinner, H. A., & Allen, B. A. (1982). Alcohol dependence syndrome: Measurement and validation. *Journal of Abnormal Psychology, 91,* 199–209. Description of the ADS. Scale and guidelines for use are available from Dr. Harvey Skinner, Addiction Research Foundation, 33 Russell Street, Toronto, Canada M5S 2S1.

Skinner, H. A., & Holt, S. (1983). Early intervention for alcohol problems. *Journal of the Royal College of General Practitioners, 33,* 787–791. Describes a basic strategy for dealing with patients with alcohol problems in general practice.

Skinner, H. A., Holt, S., & Israel, Y. (1981). Early identification of alcohol abuse: 1. Critical issues and psychosocial indicators for a composite index. *The Canadian Medical Association Journal, 124,* 1141–1152. A comprehensive review of its chosen subject. See also, Holt, L., Skinner, H. A., & Israel, Y. (1981). Early identification of alcohol abuse: 2. Clinical and laboratory indicators. *The Canadian Medical Association Journal, 124,* 1279–1295. An essential companion to the paper above.

Skinner, H. A., Holt, S., Sheu, W. J., & Israel, Y. (1986). Clinical versus laboratory detection of alcohol abuse: The alcohol clinical index. *British Medical Journal, 292,* 1703–1708. The index is obtainable from Dr. Harvey A. Skinner, Addiction Research Foundation, 33 Russell Street, Toronto, Ontario, Canada M5S 2S1.

Stockwell, T. R., Hodgson, R. J., Edwards, G., Taylor, C., & Rankin, H. (1979). The development of a questionnaire to measure severity of alcohol dependence. *British Journal of Addiction, 74,* 79–87. Original description of the SADQ.

RESEARCH

Babor, T. F., Treffardier, M., Weill, J., Fegueur, L., & Ferrant, J. P. (1983). The early detection and secondary prevention of alcoholism in France. *Journal of Studies on Alcohol, 44,* 600–616.

Babor, T. F., Ritson, E. B., & Hodgson, R. J. (1986). Alcohol-related problems in the primary health care setting: A review of early intervention strategies. *British Journal of Addiction, 81,* 23–46.

Baldwin, S., & Heather, N. (1987). Alcohol education courses for offenders: A survey of British agencies. *Alcohol and Alcoholism, 22,* 79–82.

Barrison, I. G., Viola, L., Mumford, J., Murray, R. M., Gordon, M., & Murray-Lyon, A. (1982). Detecting excessive drinking among admissions to a general hospital. *Health Trends, 14,* 80–83.

Bernadt, M. W., Mumford, J., Taylor, C., Smith, B., & Murray, R. M. (1982). Comparison of questionnaire and laboratory tests in the detection of excessive drinking and alcoholism. *Lancet, 1,* 325–328.

Buck, K. & Miller, W. R. (1981, November). Why does bibliotherapy work? A controlled study. Paper presented at In W. R. Miller (Chair) Effectiveness of bibliotherapy: Empirical research. Symposium at annual meeting of the Association for Advancement of Behavior Therapy, Toronto.

Chick, J. (1984). Secondary prevention of alcoholism and the Centres D'Hygiene Alimentaire. *British Journal of Addiction, 79,* 221–225.

Chick, J., Lloyd, G., & Crombie, E. (1985). Counselling problem drinkers in medical wards: A controlled study. *British Medical Journal, 290,* 965–967.

Chick, J., Ritson, B., Connaughton, J., Stewart, A., & Chick, J. (1988). Advice versus extended treatment for alcoholism: A controlled study. *British Journal of Addiction, 83*(2), 159–170.

Clement, S. (1986). The identification of alcohol-related problems by general practitioners. *British Journal of Addiction, 81,* 257–264.

Department of Health and Social Security (1978). *The pattern and range of services for problem drinkers.* Report of Advisory Committee on Alcoholism. London: HMSO.

Dow, M. G. T. (1982). Behavioral bibliotherapy: Theoretical and methodological issues in outcome research into self-help programs. In C. J. Main (Ed.), *Clinical psychology and medicine* (pp. 177–204). New York: Plenum.

Edwards, G., Arif, A., & Hodgson, R. (1982). Nomenclature and classification of drug- and alcohol-related problems: A shortened version of a WHO Memorandum. *British Journal of Addiction, 77,* 3–20.

Emrick, C. D. (1975). A review of psychologically oriented treatment of alcoholism: II. The relative effectiveness of different treatment approaches and the effectiveness of treatment versus no treatment. *Quarterly Journal of Studies on Alcohol, 36,* 88–108.

Heather, N. (1986). Minimal treatment interventions for problem drinkers. In G. Edwards (Ed.), *Current issues in clinical psychology* (pp. 171–186). London: Plenum.

Heather, N. (1987). DRAMS for problem drinkers: The potential of a brief intervention by general practitioners and some evidence of its effectiveness. In T. Stockwell & S. Clement (Eds.), *Helping the problem drinker: New initiatives in community care* (pp. 83–104). London: Croom Helm.

Heather, N., Whitton, B., & Robertson, I. (1986). Evaluation of a self-help manual for media-recruited problem drinkers: Six month follow-up results. *British Journal of Clinical Psychology, 25,* 19–34.

Heather, N., Campion, P. D., Neville, R., G., & Maccabe, D. (1987). Evaluation of a controlled drinking minimal intervention for problem drinkers in general practice (the DRAMS Scheme). *Journal of the Royal College of General Practitioners, 37,* 358–363.

Heather, N., Robertson, I., MacPherson, B., Allsop, S., & Fulton, A. (1987). Effectiveness of a controlled drinking self-help manual: One year follow-up results. *British Journal of Clinical Psychology, 26*(4), 279–287.

Hingson, R., Scotch, N., Day, N., & Culbert, A. (1980). Recognizing and seeking help for drinking problems: A study in the Boston metropolitan area. *Journal of Studies on Alcohol, 41,* 1102–1117.

Horn, J. L., Wanberg, K. W., & Foster, F. M. (1987). *The Alcohol Use Inventory.* Minneapolis, MN: National Computer Systems.

Jarman, C. M. B., & Kellett, J. M. (1979). Alcoholism in the general hospital. *British Medical Journal, 285,* 469–472.

Kissin, B. (1977). Comments on "Alcoholism: A controlled trial of treatment and advice." *Journal of Studies on Alcohol, 38,* 1804–1808.

Kristenson, H., Ohlin, H., Hulten-Nosslin, M., Trell, E., & Hood, B. (1983). Identification and intervention of heavy drinking in middle-aged men: Results and follow-up of 24:60 months of long-term study with randomized controls. *Journal of Alcoholism: Clinical and Experimental Research, 20,* 203–209.

Kristenson, H., Trell, E., & Hood, B. (1982). Serum of glutamyl-transferase in screening and continuous control of heavy drinking in middle-aged men. *American Journal of Epidemiology, 114,* 862–872.

Le Gô, P. M. (1976). *Le depistage precoce et systematique du buveur excessif.* Paris: Department d'Alcoologie Therapeutique de Rion Laboratories.

Marlatt, G. A., & Gordon, J. (Eds.). (1985). *Relapse prevention: Maintenance strategies in the treatment of addictive behaviors.* New York: Guilford Press.

Miller, W. R. (1978). Behavioral treatment of problem drinkers: A comparative outcome study of three controlled drinking therapies. *Journal of Consulting and Clinical Psychology, 46,* 74–86.

Miller, W. R. (1983). Motivational interviewing with problem drinkers. *Behavioral Psychotherapy, 11,* 147–172.

Miller, W. R., & Baca, L. M. (1983). Two-year follow-up of bibliotherapy and therapist-directed controlled drinking training for problem drinkers. *Behavior Therapy, 14,* 441–448.

Miller, W. R., Gribskov, C., & Mortell, R. (1981). The effectiveness of a self-control manual for problem drinkers with and without therapist contact. *International Journal of the Addictions, 16,* 829–839.

Miller, W. R., & Saucedo, C. F. (1983). Assessment of neuropsychological impairment and brain damage in problem drinkers. In C. J. Golden, J. A. Moses, Jr., J. A. Coffman, W. R. Miller, & F. D. Strider (Eds.), *Clinical neuropsychology: Interface with neurologic and psychiatric disorders* (pp. 141–195). New York: Grune & Stratton.

Miller, W. R., & Taylor, C. A. (1980). Relative effectiveness of bibliotherapy, individual and group self-control training in the treatment of problem drinkers. *Addictive Behaviors, 5,* 13–24.

Miller, W. R., Taylor, C. A., & West, J. C. (1980). Focused versus broad spectrum behavior therapy for problem drinkers. *Journal of Consulting and Clinical Psychology, 48,* 590–601.

Murray, A., McGarva, A., & Heather, N. (1987). *Staying on the wagon: A guide to living without alcohol.* Keighley: Gunda Press.

Orford, J., Oppenheimer, E., & Edwards, G. (1976). Abstinence or control: The outcome for excessive drinkers two years after consultation. *Behaviour Research and Therapy, 14,* 409–418.

Prochaska, J. O., & DiClemente, C. O. (1986). Toward a comprehensive model of change. In W. R. Miller and N. Heather (Eds.), *Treating addictive behaviors: Processes of change* (pp. 3–27). New York: Plenum.

Quinn, M. A., & Johnston, R. V. (1976). Alcohol problems in acute male medical admissions. *Health Bulletin, 34,* 253–256.

Ritson, B. (1986). Merits of simple intervention. In W. R. Miller and N. Heather (Eds.), *Treating addictive behaviors: Processes of change* (pp. 375–387). New York: Plenum.

Robertson, I., & Heather, N. (1982). An alcohol education course for young offenders. *British Journal on Alcohol and Alcoholism, 17,* 32–38.

Robertson, I., Heather, N., Dzialdowski, A., Crawford, J., & Winton, M. (1986). A comparison of minimal versus intensive controlled drinking treatment interventions for problem drinkers. *British Journal of Clinical Psychology, 22,* 185–194.

Royal College of General Practitioners (1987). *Alcohol: A balanced view.* London: Author.

Royal College of Physicians (1987). *A great and growing evil: The medical consequences of alcohol abuse.* London: Tavistock.

Ryback, R. S., Eckhardt, H. J., & Paulter, C. P. (1980). Biochemical and haematological correlates of alcoholism. *Research Communications in Chemical Pathology and Pharmacology, 27,* 533–550.

Sanchez-Craig, M. (1980). Random assignment to abstinence or controlled drinking in a cognitive–behavioral program: Short-term effects on drinking behavior. *Addictive Behaviors, 5,* 35–39.

Sanchez-Craig, M., Annis, H. M., Bornet, A. R., & MacDonald, K. R. (1984). Random assignment to abstinence and controlled drinking: Evaluation of a cognitive–behavioral program for problem drinkers. *Journal of Consulting and Clinical Psychology, 52,* 390–403.

Sanchez-Craig, M., & Lei, H. (1986). Disadvantages of imposing the goal of abstinence on problem drinkers: An empirical study. *British Journal of Addiction, 81*, 505–512.

Shaw, S., Cartwright, A., Spratley, T., & Harwin, J. (1978). *Responding to drinking problems*. London: Croom Helm.

Skinner, H. A., Holt, S., Schuller, R., Roy, J., & Israel, Y. (1984). Identification of alcohol abuse using laboratory tests and a history of trauma. *Annals of Internal Medicine, 101*, 847–851.

Skinner, H. A., Holt, S., & Israel, Y. (1981). Early identification of alcohol abuse; clinical and laboratory indicators. *Canadian Medical Association Journal, 124*, 1279–1294.

Skutle, A., & Berg, G. (1987). Training in controlled drinking for early-stage problem drinkers. *British Journal of Addiction, 82*, 493–502.

Swenson, P. R., & Clay, T. R. (1980). Effects of short-term rehabilitation on alcohol consumption and drinking-related behaviors: An eight-month follow-up study of drunken drivers. *International Journal of the Addictions, 15*, 821–858.

Taylor, C., Brown, D., Duckitt, A., Edwards, G., Oppenheimer, E., & Sheehan, M. (1985). Patterns of outcome: Drinking histories over ten years among a group of alcoholics. *British Journal of Addiction, 80*, 45–50.

Thom, B. (1986). Sex differences in help-seeking for alcohol problems: 1. The barriers to help-seeking. *British Journal of Addiction, 81*, 777–788.

Trell, E., Kristenson, H., & Fex, G. (1984). Alcohol-related problems in middle-aged men with elevated serum gamma-glutamyltransferase: A preventive medical investigation. *Journal of Studies on Alcohol, 45*, 302–309.

Vogler, R. E., Compton, J. V., & Weissbach, J. A. (1976). The referral problem in the field of alcohol abuse. *Journal of Community Psychology, 4*, 357–361.

Vogler, R. E., Weissbach, T. A., Compton, J. V., & Martin, G. T. (1977). Integrated behavior change techniques for problem drinkers in the community. *Journal of Consulting and Clinical Psychology, 45*, 267–279.

Walker, K., & Shain, M. (1983). Employee assistance programming: in search of effective interventions for the problem-drinking employee. *British Journal of Addiction, 78*, 291–303.

Winters, A. (1978). Review and rationale of the Drinkwatchers International program. *American Journal of Drug and Alcohol Abuse, 5*, 321–326.

CHAPTER 7

Antidipsotropic Medications

Richard K. Fuller

OVERVIEW

Antidipsotropic medications are pharmacological agents whose purpose is to deter the alcoholic from drinking by producing an unpleasant reaction if he or she ingests alcohol. These medications are also called alcohol-sensitizing or deterrent drugs. The reaction they produce is manifested by some or all of the following symptoms: flushing, rapid or irregular heart beat, dizziness, nausea, vomiting, difficulty breathing, and headache. Other pharmacological agents—e.g. lithium—are also used to treat alcoholism, but the antidipsotropic drugs are the only ones currently available that are used solely for the treatment of alcoholism. However, the antidipsotropic medications are not primary treatment by themselves. They are intended to be used as part of a multimodal treatment program to help the patient avoid drinking while he or she is restructuring his or her life.

Disulfiram (Antabuse®) and carbimide (citrated calcium carbimide, Temposil®, Abstem®) are the two antidipsotropic medications used in clinical practice, although the latter is not available in the United States. Disulfiram and carbimide produce the drug–ethanol reaction by

inhibiting the liver enzyme aldehyde-NAD oxireductase (ALDH), which catalyzes the oxidation of acetaldehyde (the major metabolic product of ethanol) to acetate. The resulting accumulation of acetaldehyde is responsible for most of the symptoms of the drug–ethanol reaction. However, there are important pharmacological differences between disulfiram and carbimide. The inhibition of ALDH by disulfiram is irreversible. For this reason the restoration of ALDH activity after disulfiram administration is stopped requires the synthesis of new enzyme, which occurs over several days. The inhibition of ALDH by calcium carbimide is of a mixed reversible–irreversible type and 80% of ALDH activity is restored within 24 hours. This difference in ALDH inhibition has implications for the clinical use of these drugs. Patients cannot drink for four to seven days without having a reaction after stopping disulfiram, whereas they can resume drinking 24 hours after not taking calcium carbimide. The longer duration of action of disulfiram is an advantage because it gives the patient more time to reconsider his or her decision and resume taking the drug.

Disulfiram also inhibits other enzymes, in

cluding dopamine beta-hydroxylase (DBH) and the microsomal mixed function oxidases. Drowsiness is a frequent side effect of disulfiram, and relapse or exacerbation of depression and schizophrenia have been reported with the use of disulfiram. These behavioral toxicities may be the result of altered brain catecholamine levels resulting from the inhibition of DBH by disulfiram. The mixed function oxidases are responsible for the biotransformation of many drugs, and their inhibition by disulfiram can result in toxic levels of those drugs catabolized by these enzymes. Since calcium carbimide does not inhibit these enzyme systems, it has fewer side effects and fewer drug interactions than disulfiram.

Most of the discussion in the following sections will be about disulfiram because the amount of available information about disulfiram is much greater than that about calcium carbimide. Since the disulfiram–ethanol reaction can be fatal and serious adverse reactions have been reported with the use of disulfiram, it is important that patients be evaluated to be sure that disulfiram is appropriate for them before prescribing the drug. This will be discussed more completely in the section on patient selection.

The results of a recent multi-center study of disulfiram suggest that disulfiram is helpful in reducing the frequency of drinking in those who have relapsed, particularly for the slightly older and more socially stable patient. A major problem with disulfiram is that patients often stop taking it; sometimes because of side effects, but usually because of a conscious or subconscious decision to resume drinking. To overcome the problem of poor compliance with the disulfiram regimen, controlled studies have been done in which spouses or treatment staff watch the patient ingest the medication. These studies report better outcomes than if the patient takes disulfiram at his or her discretion. Efforts have been made to develop a long-acting oral antidipsotropic medication, but these have been unsuccessful because of toxicity. Currently, injectable forms of disulfiram are in the developmental stage. The development of such drugs would overcome, to a large degree, the problem of compliance with disulfiram treatment. A guide for using these medications, including the selection of appropriate patients and an analysis of the effectiveness of these drugs, is discussed in the subsequent sections.

SPECIAL CONSIDERATIONS: SELECTION OF PATIENTS

There are two aspects to the appropriate selection of patients. The first is to select those who are more likely to benefit from disulfiram treatment. The second is not to use the medication with those who are at risk for a serious adverse reaction.

Patients Most Likely to Benefit from Disulfiram Treatment

In a recently completed VA multi-center study (Fuller et al., 1986), the addition of disulfiram to multi-modal treatment programs did not result in significantly more patients maintaining continuous abstinence for one year than was achieved without the use of disulfiram. However, a substantial subset of the men who relapsed drank significantly less frequently during the year if they had been given a conventional dose (250 mg) of disulfiram than those who were not given 250 mg of disulfiram. The subset who benefited from disulfiram treatment were older and more socially stable than others who relapsed.

Therefore, I do not recommend disulfiram as part of the initial treatment. I reserve it for those who relapse. The aim of treatment is abstinence, and if an alcoholic can achieve abstinence without disulfiram, there is no need to prescribe a medication which, like most pharmacological agents, has the risk of side effects and adverse reactions. However, alcoholism is a relapsing illness (Peachey & Annis, 1984), and many alcoholics will become candidates for disulfiram therapy.

Similar to the VA multi-center study, Baekeland, Lundwall, Kissin, and Shanahan (1971) found that middle-aged and/or more socially stable men are more likely to benefit from disulfiram than younger, less socially stable men. In addition to age and better social stability (defined as living with someone or being employed), they also found that the following characteristics were associated with a good outcome with disulfiram: (a) a longer history of heavy drinking, (b) a history of delirium tremens, (c) good motivation, manifested by contact with Alcoholics Anonymous and/or abstinence at intake, and (d) not being treated with antidepressant medications. Depressed men, others have reported, do poorly on disulfiram, while a compulsive personality style has been suggested to auger well for disulfiram treatment. Similar data for women currently are not available, and there are currently no empirically based guidelines regarding who is most likely to benefit from calcium carbimide.

In summary, the middle-aged male alcoholic who has relapsed, has some degree of social stability, and is not significantly depressed is the most suitable candidate for disulfiram therapy.

CONTRAINDICATIONS TO DISULFIRAM TREATMENT

Toxicity from disulfiram can occur from the disulfiram–ethanol reaction (DER), an adverse reaction to the drug itself, or interactions with drugs other than alcohol (see Table 7.1). Disulfiram should not be used or used cautiously in any person at increased risk for having a toxic reaction.

Significant drop in blood pressure can occur during the disulfiram–ethanol reaction (DER). Fatal DERs and non-fatal heart attacks and strokes have occurred. Therefore, disulfiram is contraindicated in patients with cardiovascular or cerebrovascular disease. For similar reasons, the presence of severe lung disease and chronic kidney disease is a contraindication to disulfiram administration. Because of the possibility of occult vascular disease I do not prescribe disulfiram for persons over 60 years of age, and others consider diabetes mellitus a contraindication to its use (Sellers, Naranjo, & Peachey, 1981).

Table 7.1. Contraindications to the Use of the Antidipsotropic Medications

---

Disulfiram

Cardiovascular disease
Cerebrovascular disease
Severe chronic pulmonary disease
Chronic renal failure
Neuropsychiatric disease
    Organic brain disease
    Psychosis
    Depression requiring treatment
Idiopathic seizure disorder
Neuropathy
Pregnancy
Chronic liver disease complicated by portal
    hypertension

Calcium Carbimide

Thyroid disease

Disulfiram also is contraindicated in persons with organic brain syndrome because patients who take Antabuse® must fully comprehend the potentially dangerous consequences of the DER. Patients who have a history of, or currently have evidence of, schizophrenia or a major affective illness should not be given disulfiram, because exacerbation or development of serious neuropsychiatric illnesses have been reported with disulfiram. For the same reason the concurrent use of disulfiram and antidepressants is not indicated. Ten patients in the VA multi-center study had neuropsychiatric illnesses requiring hospitalization. However, the illnesses occurred equally among the 250 mg disulfiram patients and the patients in two control groups (Branchey, Davis, Lee, & Fuller, 1987). The fact that the disulfiram-treated patients did not have more serious psychiatric illnesses than the control patients is most likely due to the fact that patients with a history of schizophrenia or major affective disorders were excluded from the study.

Patients who have an idiopathic seizure disorder should not be prescribed disulfiram because it may lower the seizure threshhold (McConchie, Panitz, Sauber, & Shapiro, 1983). If a patient only has alcohol-related seizures, I have prescribed disulfiram after the withdrawal period is finished, since the risk of a seizure from drinking is probably greater than from disulfiram. However, I explain the risk to the patient and follow that person more closely during the first month of treatment. Peripheral neuropathy has been reported with the use of both disulfiram and calcium carbimide. Thus, these drugs should not be prescribed to patients with pre-existing peripheral neuropathy.

Disulfiram should not be used by pregnant women because birth defects have been reported with its use (Nora, Nora, & Blu, 1977).

Disulfiram has to be used carefully in patients taking certain drugs. Disulfiram interferes with the biotransformation of phenytoin (Dilantin®), warfarin (Coumadin®), isoniazid, rifampin, diazepam (Valium®), chlordiazepoxide (Librium®) and the antidepressants: imipramine and desipramine. The concurrent administration of disulfiram may result in toxic levels of these drugs. If it is necessary to prescribe an anti-anxiolytic drug (and the risk of abuse of these drugs usually contraindicates their use in alcoholics), oxazepam (Serax®) can be used because oxazepam is metabolized by glucuronidation and disulfiram does not affect glucuronidation to a significant degree (Mac-Leod et al., 1978). If it is necessary to use disulfiram in patients on the drugs listed above, serum drug levels or the prothrombin time, in the case of those taking Coumadin®, should be monitored. If these tests indicate toxic levels, the dosage of these drugs should be decreased, and if that does not result in resolution of toxic blood levels and/or symptoms disulfiram should be discontinued. If appropriate blood tests are not available, disulfiram should not be used.

Because drugs that impair the regulation of blood pressure (alpha- and beta-adrenergic receptor antagonists and vasodilators) might result in a severe DER, the administration of disulfiram to patients taking these drugs probably is contraindicated. It also has been suggested (Sellers et al., 1981) that drugs that are mediated by norepinephrine or dopamine (e.g. phenothiazines) or inhibit the same enzyme as disulfiram (e.g. monoamine oxidase inhibitors) might result in a serious DER. However, as discussed above, patients with neuropsychiatric illnesses severe enough to require these pharmacological agents should not receive disulfiram.

Liver cirrhosis often is listed as a contraindication to the use of disulfiram. However, evidence for this is scanty. Disulfiram can cause a severe, occasionally fatal hepatotoxic reaction, but this is idiosyncratic and the presence of cirrhosis does not appear to predispose to it. I have prescribed disulfiram to patients with compensated cirrhosis, provided there is no evidence of portal hypertension (ascites, splenomegaly, or esophageal varices by radiology or endoscopy), and have observed no adverse reactions in these patients. I avoid using disulfiram in those with portal hypertension because of the danger of vomiting during the DER and precipitating hemorrhage from esophageal varices.

Since disulfiram causes drowsiness, particularly during the first few weeks of treatment, I do not prescribe it to those whose lives would be endangered if they were drowsy on the job—e.g., house painters working on ladders, window washers. For other potentially dangerous jobs, e.g., driving trucks and working with machinery, I prescribe disulfiram if the patient agrees to begin the medication on a weekend, to take it at bedtime, and to stop it if he or she is still drowsy upon awakening after two or three days on the drug.

Calcium Carbimide

Calcium carbimide has not been released for use in the United States because of an antithyroid effect observed in experimental animals. Otherwise, clinically it appears to be relatively free from side effects. For those who practice in countries in which calcium carbimide is available, it is prudent not to prescribe it for patients with a history of thyroid disease.

DESCRIPTION OF PROTOCOL FOR USE OF THE ANTIDIPSOTROPIC MEDICATIONS

The antidipsotropic medications are not likely to be effective as the only treatment, and should be used as one component of a multimodal treatment program. The steps involved in the use of these medications are: (a) selection of appropriate patients; (b) description of the drug–ethanol reaction; (c) a discussion of the benefits and risks; (d) a decision as to whether the patient will self-medicate or have others administer the medication; and (e) follow-up. Some of these steps overlap. With a patient who is desirous of taking a deterrent drug and comprehends all that is involved, the first four steps may be accomplished in one session. For others it may take several discussions between patient and physician.

Selection of Patients

As described in the preceding section, I reserve disulfiram for the patient who has relapsed. If the patient has relapsed and I am considering using disulfiram, I review the medical record to see whether any of the exclusions listed in the previous section are present. If this review indicates they are not present, I discuss briefly with the patient the benefits and risks of disulfiram. At this point, if the patient is interested in taking disulfiram, I take a medical history, do a physical examination of the heart, abdomen, and nervous system, and order an electrocardiogram and blood tests (serum albumin, serum bilirubin, serum aspartate aminotransferase and serum creatinine). If the history, physical examination, and laboratory tests indicate that the patient is a suitable candidate for disulfiram therapy, I move to the next step.

Description of the Disulfiram-Ethanol Reaction

When disulfiram was first introduced, the practice was to have the patients experience the disulfiram–ethanol reaction. An electrocardiogram and sphygomanometer were attached to the patient, and oxygen and vasopressor agents were available to treat serious hypotensive reactions. This practice has been replaced by vividly describing the disulfiram–ethanol reaction (DER). The patient is informed that if he or she drinks within two weeks of stopping the medication, he or she runs the risk of a DER with all its consequences. In my experience it is unusual for a patient to have a DER if several days have elapsed since the last drink, but the manufacturer advises warning that a DER may occur within two weeks of the last drink. It is important to emphasize that severe hypotension and arrhythmias can occur with the DER, and although rare, there have been fatal DERs. The patient must fully understand the risks of the DER and the severity of the reaction cannot be overemphasized. The patient is also warned not to ingest liquid medications that usually contain alcohol (such as cough syrups and decongestants) or food cooked in wine.

Discussion of Benefits and Risks

Building on the previous discussions, the dialogue between physician and patient proceeds to making a mutual decision to initiate treatment. If a spouse is available, it is useful to have him or her at this session.

It is acknowledged that many people have become abstinent without taking disulfiram. However, since this patient has relapsed, he or she may require something "extra." That something extra may be disulfiram. The simple act of taking a pill daily produces a chemical "fence" for the patient. This can be very helpful if each day is a struggle to avoid taking a drink. Knowing that one will become sick if he or she drinks provides another incentive not to drink. This frees the patients from the struggle of deciding whether to take a drink or not and allows them to devote their emotional energy to restructuring their lives.

If the patient is still ambivalent about taking disulfiram, it is important to explore whether the hesitancy to take disulfiram is a subconscious reluctance to accept the concept of abstinence. Also, the patient may feel he or she is relinquishing control over an aspect of his or her life to an external agent and is relying on a "crutch". Since drinking often results in loss of control over one's life, this reluctance to take disulfiram may not be realistic. I point out that crutches are needed if someone breaks a leg, and, similarly, one may need a crutch in the early months of sobriety. Furthermore, taking disulfiram daily is an act of self-control. On the other hand, a truck driver may be realistic if he expresses concerns about drowsiness being an occupational hazard for him. The possible side effects of disulfiram and the risks of the DER must be acknowledged. However, a discussion of the toxicity of disulfiram has to be balanced against the toxicity of alcohol. To minimize somnolence, the most common side effect, I advise patients to take disulfiram at bedtime.

The pros and cons of taking disulfiram are weighed. I never insist that a patient take disulfiram, but if a person's life is being destroyed by alcoholism and he or she has no contraindication to its use, this could be the step that changes that patient's life.

If after weighing these factors the patient decides to use disulfiram, the next step is to discuss whether the patient will take it himself or have someone at the clinic or a family member administer it to him ("supervised" administration). While controlled studies have indicated that the supervised administration of disulfiram will achieve better results than self-administration, this is not a settled issue (see section on Current Knowledge of the Effectiveness of the Antidipsotropic Medications) and I prefer to use self-administration. Supervised administration has to be done sensitively. It can be demeaning for the patient, because the potential exists for the patient to be reduced to a childlike role. This could be counter-productive to personal growth—i.e., being responsible for one's actions and developing a sense of control of one's life. Furthermore, if there is considerable conflict between the patient and the spouse, the spouse's administration of disulfiram can become another power struggle between the two. Therefore, I initiate disulfiram treatment by prescribing the drug for the patient to self-administer. However, Azrin (1976) has had success with the spouses giving the Antabuse. He emphasizes that treatment is a common goal and works with the patient to view the spouse as a 'helper' or caring friend. If self-administration fails, I discuss supervised disulfiram administration with the patient; I explain that some have found that this method is more effective than giving the pills to the patient to take at his or her discretion, and so deserves serious consideration. I prefer a member of the treatment staff to observe the ingestion because a staff member often is less judgmental than a spouse, and the patient views the staff member as a neutral person whose role is to help him or her to stop drinking. However, if there is a supportive family member who can give positive reinforcement, this person can give the drug.

Dosage

Obviously, disulfiram should not be given until alcohol has been eliminated from the patient's body. To be safe, disulfiram is not given until 24 hours after the last drink. The usual dosage of disulfiram is 250 mg daily.Calcium carbimide is usually given at 50 mg twice daily. The 250 mg disulfiram dose is popular because it is sufficient to cause a DER but side effects appear to be fewer because they are dose-related (Peachey & Annis, 1984). Some side effects have been reported to occur with the 500 mg dose but not with the 250 mg dose (Lake, Major, Ziegler, & Kopin, 1977; Major & Goyer, 1978). In the VA multi-center study, side effects, except for somnolence, were no more common in the 250 mg disulfiram patients than in the members of the two control groups. On the other hand, Brewer (1984) in the United Kingdom has suggested that the 250 mg dose often is not sufficient to result in a DER if an alcoholic drinks. In his study of 63 patients, 17 needed daily doses of disulfiram in the range of 400–500 mg to achieve a disulfiram ethanol reaction, 6 required doses in the range of 600–700 mg, and 7 required 800–1500 mg. This has not been the usual clinical experience, and these results have not been replicated. Srinivasan, Babu, Appaya, and Jubrahmanyam (1986) reported from India that 60 of 61 patients on 500 mg disulfiram daily had a disulfiram ethanol reaction when they drank. All of those who had a reaction experienced flushing, rapid heartbeat, headache, nausea, and a "slight fall in blood pressure." Five patients developed hypotension of sufficient degree to require medical intervention and one patient developed hemorrhage from a tear in the lining of the stomach because of protracted vomiting.

Follow Up

In addition to being involved in a structured treatment program, the patient should return at weekly intervals for the first two weeks, bi-weekly intervals for the next six weeks, monthly for six months, and finally bi-monthly for the remainder of the year. The purpose of these visits is to monitor the response to treatment, assess the occurrence of side effects, and answer questions the patient may have. Wallet-size cards provided by the manufacturer, stating that the patient is taking disulfiram, can be given to the patient to carry on his or her person. If the patient "forgets" to take the medication, this may be a prelude to drinking and should be discussed with the patient. At the end of one year, a discussion about the appropriateness of stopping the disulfiram component of the treatment is held. Most patients, in my experience, elect to stop it, but some feel it is important for their sobriety to continue taking it.

If the patient should drink and have a DER, the treatment is supportive. If the patient is hypotensive, intravenous fluids and a vasopressor are indicated. There is no evidence that either antihistamines or vitamin C are beneficial. Prostaglandin synthetase inhibitors — e.g. aspirin or indomthacin — can ameliorate the flushing.

During the first six months, the patient should also be monitored for the possibility of hepatoxicity secondary to disulfiram. Disulfiram hepatoxicity is rare, but fatal cases have been reported. This is an idiosyncratic reaction, and therefore it is impossible to predict which person will develop it. Most patients who develop hepatoxicity do so within the first three months of treatment; almost all have nausea, malaise, and fatigue preceding the development of jaundice (yellow coloration of eyes, inside of mouth, and skin). Many will also have some arthralgias, rash, or itching. These symptoms and signs should alert the clinician to the possibility that a hepatotoxic reaction is occurring. It is prudent to have baseline liver tests prior to starting treatment and repeating the tests monthly after treatment is initiated for three months. Serum aspartate aminotransferase (AST) is more sensitive than the serum bilirubin or alkaline phosphatase.

An elevated AST which is less than 300 units does not require the automatic termination of disulfiram treatment. Persons who are drinking can have AST levels up to 300 units. Disulfiram hepatoxicity is usually associated with AST values above 300. In the VA cooperative study, in which liver tests were done bimonthly, an increase in the values of the liver tests usually indicated resumption of drinking (Iber, Lee, Lacoursiere, & Fuller, 1987). If the serum AST is below 250 units and the bilirubin less than 3.0 mg/dl, these findings should be discussed with the patient. That discussion often will reveal that the patient is drinking. If the patient insists he is not drinking and there is no other evidence to the contrary, the disulfiram should be discontinued. If the patient has symptoms or signs consistent with a hepatotoxic reaction or the serum AST is above 250 units and serum bilirubin greater than 3 mg/dl, disulfiram should be stopped.

EFFECTIVENESS

Disulfiram was introduced into clinical use in 1948. Many clinical studies initially reported excellent results with the drug. However, most of these studies were uncontrolled. None were double-blinded except for a study evaluating implanted disulfiram, and few monitored compliance with the medication. Reviews of the studies evaluating the efficacy of disulfiram (Lundwall & Baekeland, 1971; Mottin, 1973) have criticized their methodological soundness. Also, pharmacokinetic and formal dose response studies of disulfiram were not done. Thus, this drug was introduced into clinical practice without much of the information that would be considered standard today for introduction of a new drug. In fairness to those who did the initial studies, controlled clinical trials were in their infancy and the methodology for studying the pharmacokinetics of disulfiram was not available at that time.

Two of the earlier studies had shown that disulfiram was not effective in Skid Row-type alcoholics or alcoholics without families. The studies were not blinded, but they were randomized and controlled. Gallant et al. (1968) studied men who were repeated legal offenders. These men had been arrested, on the average, 14 times during the preceding year. They were assigned to disulfiram alone, disulfiram with group counseling, group counseling alone, and routine sentencing. While attrition was high, Gallant and his colleagues achieved a remarkable follow-up rate in a group notori-

ously difficult to locate; they were able to locate more than 90% of the subjects at the end of six months. Unfortunately, almost all of the subjects had resumed drinking. Gerrein, Rosenberg, and Manohar (1973) studied men most of whom lived alone or in a sheltered environment. Again, disulfiram was not effective, except in those men who were observed ingesting the medication by the treatment staff ("monitored" or "supervised" disulfiram treatment). However, the study period was only eight weeks, and, therefore, whether long-term benefit can be achieved with monitored disulfiram in this poor risk group of patients is not known.

The uncertainty about the efficacy of disulfiram treatment stimulated the author and Harold Roth to design a study which we hoped would correct many of the deficiencies identified in previous studies. To that end we designed a double-blind, controlled study. We recruited men who were married because (a) we wanted sources of information about the patients' drinking behavior in addition to self-report and (b) we wanted to study men who had the potential for family support. We employed assessors of treatment outcome who had no involvement in the treatment of the subjects, and built in measures to monitor compliance with the drug regimen (Fuller and Roth, 1979). Furthermore, we used two control groups because of the unique nature of the deterrent drugs—i.e., the basis for their effectiveness being the patient's fear of becoming sick if he or she drinks. This was aptly stated by Enoch Gordis when we wrote ". . . It is probable that it is the patient's belief that he is taking disulfiram (whether or not he actually is) that is therapeutic and not the action itself . . ." (Gordis & Peterson, 1977). Therefore, we had a control group whose members received a 1 mg dose, a dose insufficient to cause a disulfiram--ethanol reaction (DER), and a second control group whose members did not receive disulfiram. Those patients who received either the conventional 250 mg dose or the 1 mg dose were told they were receiving disulfiram but were not told the dose. Thus, the patients receiving the 1 mg dose had the expectation that they would become ill if they drank. Those who were assigned to the no-disulfiram group received riboflavin and were informed that they were not getting Antabuse but were receiving a vitamin. Thus, these patients did not have the expectation of becoming sick if they drank.

However, our study also had a flaw which

was not apparent until it was nearly finished—i.e., insufficient sample size. This occurred because we overestimated the effectiveness of disulfiram when we calculated the sample size prior to initiating the study. We enrolled 128 men and followed them for one year. After one year, 23% of the men given either dose of disulfiram had been continuously abstinent, whereas only 12% of the no-disulfiram men had been totally abstinent. This difference, while twofold, is not statistically significant. Thus, we could not state that disulfiram was effective. On the other hand, if we had claimed that disulfiram was not effective, we would have had a 48% chance of being wrong (a Type II error) because a sample size of 128 men is not large enough to protect against this type of false claim.

This problem has been corrected in a recently reported VA multi-center study (Fuller et al., 1986). In a study whose design was similar to my study with Roth, 605 men were recruited and randomly assigned to a 250 mg disulfiram dose, a 1 mg disulfiram dose, or no disulfiram. All of the patients received the benefit of a multi-modal treatment program. The staff of these programs was multidisciplinary in composition, including physicians, psychologists, nurses, social workers, certified alcoholism counselors, and chaplains. The primary goal of the treatment was abstinence. Most of the patients were treated initially for 2–4 weeks in a hospital setting, where they received education about the deleterious effects of alcohol and were counseled in preventing relapse. After discharge from the hospital, patients were asked to return for clinic visits for counseling, at least weekly for the first six months and bi-weekly for the next six months. Most of the counseling occurred in group sessions led by a psychologist, social worker, nurse, or a certified alcoholism counselor. The discussions in the group sessions were primarily devoted to living a life free of alcohol and coping with personal problems. Individual sessions to address specific psychological and social problems were available if requested by the patients or deemed necessary by the therapist. Attendance at Alcoholics Anonymous (AA) was not mandatory but patients were encouraged to attend AA meetings. The therapists and the interviewers who assessed treatment effect were blinded to the drug treatment the patients were receiving.

The assessment procedures consisted of bi-monthly interviews of the patients and a friend or relative with whom the patient was living. Blood samples analyzed for ethanol were obtained if the patient returned to the clinic for his bi-monthly interview. Whenever a patient returned for a clinic vist, a urine sample was collected and was analyzed for ethanol.

Two hundred and two men were assigned to the 250 mg dose, 204 men to the 1 mg dose, and 199 men to the no-disulfiram group. The three treatment groups were comparable in age, race, marital status, employment status, education, income, and duration of alcohol abuse. After one year of treatment, there were no significant differences among the three groups in continuous abstinence during the year: 18.8% (38/202), 22.5% (46/204), and 16.1% (32/199) were continuously abstinent in the 250 mg disulfiram, 1 mg, and no disulfiram groups, respectively. There were no significant differences in the median time to the first drink, which varied from 41 days in the no-disulfiram group to 65 days in the 1 mg dose group. However, among those patients who drank and supplied all seven scheduled assessment interviews, those in the 250 mg disulfiram group reported significantly fewer drinking days (49 ± 8.4) than the patients in the other two treatment groups (108.7 ± 14.7 and 116.4 ± 16.3 days for the 1 mg disulfiram and no disulfiram groups, respectively). These reports of significantly fewer drinking days in the disulfiram-treated patients were corroborated by the relatives or friends of the patients. The men who relapsed but provided all interviews were slightly but significantly older and had lived longer at their current address than the other patients who had relapsed but did not provide all interviews. On the two parameters of social stability that we measured, continuous employment and remaining with relative or friend during the year, there were no significant differences among the treatment groups.

Compliance with any of the three drug treatments was associated with total abstinence during the year. Overall, 20% of 577 patients who finished the study were judged compliant, and there were no significant differences among the three treatment groups in percent of those who were compliant with the drug regimen. Forty-three percent of the compliers were continuously abstinent whereas only eight percent of the non-compliers were totally abstinent. Assuming that the patients would not have drunk if they continued to take their disulfiram, poor compliance with the disulfiram regimen appears to be a major reason for its failure. However, this problem was not limited to disulfiram alone. Rather, compliance with drug regimen, regardless of medication prescribed, was a marker of success (total abstinence). This suggests that some patients (unfortunately, a minority) entered into the aftercare process with a high degree of zeal and achieved both high compliance and total abstinence.

The results of this large multi-center clinical trial indicate that disulfiram given to patients to take at their discretion is not effective in promoting continuous abstinence. However, there does appear to be a subset of men who will partially benefit from taking disulfiram because they drink less frequently during the year. This suggests that, while disulfiram is not a panacea, it does have a useful role in selected patients. There were no women and relatively few college graduates or professional people in the study, and the results may not be generalizable to these individuals.

Since poor compliance with the drug regimen is the Achilles' heel of conventional disulfiram treatment, several studies have been designed to improve compliance. These studies have used spouses or treatment staff to administer the drug and have reported better abstinence rates in the supervised patients than in the controls. However, these results need to be replicated because follow-up was usually of short duration (less than three months) and selection bias may account for the results since small number of patients (usually less than 40) were studied. Nevertheless, the work of Azrin and his colleagues (1982; see chapter 16) is noteworthy. They randomly assigned 43 patients to "traditional disulfiram" (n = 14), supervised disulfiram (n = 15), and behavior therapy plus supervised disulfiram (n = 14) and followed these men for six months. Those in the supervised disulfiram group consumed their medication at the start of every counseling session and also took their disulfiram in front of a significant other at a set time each day. In addition, the patients role-played with the significant other situations in which the patients felt they would no longer want to take disulfiram. Patients in the behavior therapy plus supervised disulfiram group received all the procedures of the supervised group plus training in preventing relapse, job-finding counseling if unemployed (n = 7), and reci-

procity counseling if drinking had affected their relationships with significant others (n = 8). The patients in the behavior therapy plus supervised disulfiram group were almost continuously abstinent for the six month period. Abstinence declined with time in the other two groups. By six months, those in the supervised only group were abstinent on three-quarters of the days of the sixth month, and those in the unsupervised group were abstinent half of the sixth month. Married patients in the supervised group did as well in terms of abstinence as those in the behavior therapy plus supervised disulfiram group; by four months, none of the 14 men given disulfiram to take at their discretion were taking it, whereas those in the other two groups were taking the drug more than two-thirds of the time. The authors point out that their study was done in a rural area and results may differ with urban clients. They conclude that their works "should be pursued by studies with additional clients and in an urban setting."

Monitored or supervised disulfiram treatment has been used with particular effectiveness in patients over whom the therapist has leverage. This technique has been labelled mandatory disulfiram treatment. Brewer and Smith (1983) reported that nine out of 16 alcoholics who took disulfiram under supervision as a condition of probation were "entirely successful," and the average period of abstinence for all 16 patients was 30 weeks compared with 6 weeks during the previous two years. Brewer (1987) is emphatic that this is the only way to use disulfiram. However, others (Peachey & Annis, 1984; Marco & Marco, 1979; Miller & Hester, 1986) have questioned whether it is legal and ethical to coerce people to take disulfiram. Sereny, Sharma, Holt, and Gordis (1986) studied patients who had failed previous treatment but still wanted to be in the treatment program. These patients were offered supervised disulfiram with the condition that if they did not cooperate, they would be discharged from the program. They observed a 40% (27/68) continuous abstinence rate for one year compared to a 15% rate for their regular outpatient treatment program. Using supervised disulfiram treatment in patients who have failed the regular program but who wish to remain in treatment is less objectionable than coercing patients to undergo this form of treatment, but these results should be replicated in a randomized, controlled study.

In other efforts to correct the problem of poor compliance, disulfiram has been implanted in the subcutaneous fat of the abdominal wall of patients. Because the tablets are dissolved slowly, patients frequently do not experience a DER or have a mild one if they drink. If they experience a DER, the reaction is reported to develop and resolve more slowly than with oral administration. Wilson, Davidson, and Blanchard (1980) randomly assigned 40 patients to a disulfiram implant, 40 to a placebo implant, and 10 to a no implant control group; and also followed 10 patients who refused an implant. Twenty-five percent in both implant groups were lost to follow-up, and corroboration of self-report was possible in only 15 of the original 100 patients. There was no significant difference in continuous abstinence between the two implant groups, although the disulfiram implant patients reported significantly more abstinent days (361 versus 307). None of the non-operated patients remained totally abstinent. A recent double-blind study from Norway (Johnsen et al., 1987) found no significant differences after 20 weeks between disulfiram and placebo implants in number of abstinent weeks, time to first drink, or reduction in average ethanol consumption. None of their disulfiram patients had a DER despite seven intravenous ethanol challenges. Three of the disulfiram implanted patients developed wound infections. None of the placebo patients did. The lack of proven efficacy and the frequent local reactions to implantation justify the policy of prohibiting this form of disulfiram administration in North America. Currently methods are being developed to administer disulfiram either in an intramuscular form or transcutaneously by a patch applied to the skin. When these are available, they should improve the effectiveness of disulfiram therapy. However, reversing a disulfiram–ethanol reaction when the drug is administered parenterally may be a problem that limits this form of treatment.

The preceding discussion has been devoted exclusively to disulfiram because controlled studies of calcium carbimide have not been done. Thus, our knowledge of the effectiveness of calcium carbimide is limited. An advantage to calcium carbimide is that it has relatively few side effects. However, one can drink without having a reaction 24 hours after stopping Temposil®. Since compliance is a problem with disulfiram, this shorter duration of action would appear to limit the effectiveness of calcium carbimide. Temposil® in combination with relapse prevention training is being studied. The patient takes the drug for a short period of time if he or she is entering a situation in which drinking may occur. If this combination proves effective, calcium carbimide would have a place in alcoholism treatment.

In summary, disulfiram remains the model of the antidipsotropic medications. It has been studied the most extensively and there is a very large clinical experience with the drug. One survey (Barchiesi & Varis, 1985) has indicated its use is increasing. Disulfiram should be used always as part of a comprehensive treatment program. In a large, controlled, blinded, multicenter study of disulfiram, the drug did not add additional benefit to counseling in helping patients achieve continuous abstinence. However, the use of disulfiram was accompanied by significant reduction in drinking days in a large subgroup of men who were slightly older and more socially stable. Because of the risk of potential toxicity, patients have to be carefully screened so that the drug is not inappropriately prescribed. The medication usually is given to the patient to take him- or herself, although some studies suggest its effect can be enhanced if the patient ingests it under the supervision of a counselor or significant other. Longer-acting injectable forms are being developed.

REFERENCES

Clinical Guidelines

Peachey, J. E. (1981). A review of the clinical use disulfiram and calcium carbimide in alcoholism treatment. *Journal of Clinical Psychopharmacology, 1,* 368–375. This is an excellent review of the clinical use of the antidipsotropic medications. The author discusses the clinical use, efficacy, factors influencing treatment outcome, treatment strategies, and toxicity. His discussion leads to a recommended treatment plan.

Keiter, R. H. (1983). Principles of disulfiram use. *Psychosomatics, 24,* 483–486. This article provides a guide to the clinical use of disulfiram. The author lists 12 pretreatment steps to disulfiram. These steps are not analogous to the 12 steps of Alcoholic Anonymous, but the symmetry of 12 steps for each is interesting.

Peachey, J. E., and Annis, H. (1984). Pharmacologic treatment of chronic alcoholism. *Psychiatric Clinics of North America, 7,* 745–756. This is the result of a fruitful collaboration between a pharmacologist and a psychologist. They begin their discussion of drug treatments for alcoholism with a section on the antidipotropsic medications. It is a good companion article to Peachey (1981).

Research

Azrin, N. H. (1976). Improvements in the community-reinforcement approach to alcoholism. *Behavioral Research and Therapy, 14,* 339–348.

Azrin, N. H., Sisson, R. W., Meyers, R., & Godley, M. (1982). Alcoholism treatment by disulfiram and community reinforcement therapy. *Journal of Behavioral Therapy and Experimental Psychiatry, 13,* 105–112.

Baekeland, F., Lundwall, L., Kissin, B., & Shananhan, T. (1971). Correlates of outcome in disulfiram treatment of alcoholism. *Journal of Nervous and Mental Diseases, 153,* 1–9.

Barchiesi, A., & Voris, J. C. (1985). Surveying patterns of change in disulfiram use. *VA Practitioner, 2,* 76–78.

Branchey, L., Davis, W., Lee, K. K., Fuller, R. K. (1987). Psychiatric complications following disulfiram treatment. *American Journal of Psychiatry, 144,* 1310–1312.

Brewer, C. (1984). How effective is the standard dose of disulfiram? A review of the alcohol–disulfiram reaction in practice. *British Journal of Psychiatry, 144,* 200–202.

Brewer, C. (1987). Disulfiram treatment of alcoholism. *Journal of the American Medical Association, 257,* 926.

Brewer, C., & Smith, J. (1983). Probation linked supervised disulfiram in the treatment of habitual drunken offenders: results of a pilot study. *British Medical Journal, 287,* 1282–1283.

Fuller, R. K., & Roth, H. P. (1979). Disulfiram for the treatment of alcoholism: an evaluation in 128 men. *Annals of Internal Medicine, 90,* 901–904.

Fuller, R. K., Branchey, L., Brightwell, D. R., Derman, R. M., Emrick, C. D., Iber, F. L., James, K. E., Lacoursiere, R. B., Lee, K. K., Lowenstam, I., Maany, I., Neiderheiser, D., Nocks, J. J., & Shaw, S. (1986). Disulfiram treatment of alcoholism: a Veterans Administration cooperative study. *Journal of Nervous and Mental Diseases, 256,* 1449–1455.

Gallant, D. M., Bishop, M. P., Falkner, M. A., Simpson, L., Cooper, A., Lathrop, D., Brisolara, A. M., & Bossetta, J. B. (1968). A comparative evaluation of compulsory group therapy and/or Antabuse and voluntary treatment of the chronic alcoholic municipal court offender. *Psychosomatics, 9,* 306–310.

Gerrein, J. R., Rosenberg, C. M., & Manohar, V. (1973). Disulfiram maintenance in outpatient treatment of alcoholism. *Archives of General Psychiatry, 28,* 798–802.

Gordis, E., & Peterson, K. (1977). Disulfiram therapy in alcoholism: patient compliance studied with a urine detection procedure. *Alcoholism: Clinical and Experimental Research,* 213–216.

Iber, F., Lee, K., Lacoursiere, R., & Fuller, R. (1987). Liver toxicity encountered in the Veterans Administration trial of disulfiram in alcoholics. *Alcoholism: Clinical and Experimental Research, 11,* 301–304.

Johnsen, J., Stowell, A., Bache-Wig, J. E., Stenstrud, T., Ripel, A., & Morland, J. (1987). A double-blind placebo controlled study of male alcoholics given a subcutaneous disulfiram implantation. *British Journal of Addiction, 82,* 607–613.

Lake, C. R., Major, L. F., Ziegler, M. G., & Kopin, I. J. (1977). Increased sympathetic nervous activity in alcoholic patients treated with disulfiram. *American Journal of Psychiatry, 134,* 1411–1414.

Lundwall, L., & Baekeland, F. (1971). Disulfiram treatment of alcoholism. *Journal of Nervous and Mental Diseases, 153,* 381–394.

MacLoed, S. M., Sellers, E. M., Giles, H. G., Billings, B. J., Martin, P. R., Greenblatt, D. J., & Marshman, J. A. (1978). Interaction of disulfiram with benzodiazepines. *Clinical Pharmacology and Therapeutics, 24,* 583–589.

Major, L. F., & Goyer, P. F. (1978). Effects of disulfiram and pyridoxine on serum cholesterol. *Annals of Internal Medicine, 88,* 53–56.

Marco, C. H., & Marco, J. M. (1979). Antabuse medication in exchange for limited freedom—is it legal? *American Journal of Law and Medicine, 5*(3), 295–330.

McConchie, R. D., Panitz, D. R., Sauber, S. R., & Shapiro, S. (1983). Disulfiram-induced de novo seizures in the absence of ethanol challenge. *Journal of Studies on Alcohol, 44,* 739–743.

Miller, W. R., & Hester, R. K. (1986). The effectiveness of treatment techniques: what the research reveals. In W. R. Miller and N. Heather (Eds.), *Treating addictive behaviors: Process of change* (pp. 121–174). New York: Plenum.

Mottin, J. L. (1973). Drug-induced attenuation of alcohol consumption: a review and evaluation of claimed, potential, or current therapies. *Quarterly Journal of Studies on Alcohol, 34,* 444–472.

Nora, A. H., Nora, J. J., & Blu, J. (1977). Limb-reduction anomalies in infants born to disulfiram-treated alcoholic mothers. *Lancet, 2,* 664.

Peachey, J. E., & Annis, H. (1984). Pharmacologic treatment of chronic alocholism. *Psychiatric Clinics of North America, 7,* 745–756.

Sellers, E. M., Naranjo, C. A., & Peachey, J. E. (1981). Drugs to decrease alcohol consumption. *New England Journal of Medicine, 305,* 1255–1262.

Sereny, G., Sharma, V., Holt, J., & Gordis, E. (1986). Mandatory supervised antabuse therapy in an outpatient alcoholism program: a pilot study. *Alcoholism: Clinical and Experimental Research, 10,* 290–292.

Srinivasan, K., Babu, R. K., Appaya, P., & Subrahmanyam, H. S. (1986). Disulfiram–ethanol reaction. *Journal of Association of Physicians of India, 34,* 505.

Wilson, A., Davidson, W. J., & Blanchard, R. (1980). Disulfiram implantation: a trial using placebo implants and two types of controls. *Journal of Studies on Alcohol, 41,* 429–436.

CHAPTER 8

Aversion Therapies

Carl T. Rimmele
William R. Miller
Michael J. Dougher

OVERVIEW

Aversion therapies are designed to reduce or eliminate an individual's desire for alcohol. A wide variety of methods have been used to decrease urges to drink, based on the pairing of unpleasant stimuli or images with alcohol consumption. The intended result of such treatment is to reduce or eliminate alcohol consumption by producing a negative response to alcohol.

The most common types of aversion therapy are nausea, apnea, electric shock, and imagery; although treatment using an unpleasant odor is also being used currently. Nausea is by far the oldest and most commonly used approach. The induction of nausea is usually done with chemical means, although it is also possible through the use of imagery. The most commonly used drugs are emetine hydrochloride, lithium, and apomorphine. In this approach, the chemical is administered so that violent emesis and nausea occur following and during the tasting, sipping, and swallowing of an alcohol beverage. This form of treatment is used widely in the Soviet Union, and is employed in some U.S. hospitals (e.g., Schick Shadel Hospitals).

Apnea is a form of aversion therapy which produces a terrifying paralysis of breathing for about 60 seconds. During this paralysis, an alcohol beverage is placed on the lips of the patient. This treatment was used experimentally approximately 20 years ago, with mixed results. Because of the severe nature of the treatment, it is no longer used.

Electrical conditioning has been used recently within the context of well-established alcohol treatment centers (e.g., Schick Shadel Hospitals). This approach is based on the same principles of counterconditioning as chemical aversion therapy, but pairs a painful shock with the consumption of alcohol. A shock is usually administered to the hand or arm as the client reaches for or tastes the beverage. Some forms of this treatment include self-administered electrical stimulation.

Each of the procedures mentioned above involves the use of stressful and sometimes painful stimuli. This is especially the case with the chemical and electrical aversion therapies. Because of the stressful nature of these physically aversive treatments, they require adequate medical supervision and often engender high dropout rates. Because of these considerations, it is unlikely that such procedures will be used in most outpatient clinics.

Imagery offers another approach to aversion therapy which is not as painful or invasive as the procedures mentioned above. This approach, called covert sensitization, involves the pairing of imagined unpleasant scenes with the imagery of drinking (Cautela, 1966, 1967, 1970). This treatment typically uses scenes designed to produce nausea, and some treatments have augmented the imagination of nausea with an aversive odor (e.g., Maletzky, 1974). Evaluations have also appeared using scenes depicting plausible "negative consequences" of drinking (Miller & Dougher, in press).

Covert sensitization requires no special equipment, involves minimal risk to patients, and can easily be conducted on an outpatient basis. It is also one of the only known ways to directly impact the *desire* to drink, and has been effectively administered by paraprofessional personnel, given adequate training and supervision (Miller & Dougher, in press). Because of the substantial practical advantages, the bulk of this chapter will be devoted to covert sensitization.

SPECIAL CONSIDERATIONS

Rationale

Initial evaluations of the effectiveness of covert sensitization have yielded mixed results, some finding very favorable outcomes and others less promising effects. Some authors have argued that this is due to the ineffectiveness of the procedures themselves (Little & Curran, 1978). However, others have pointed out that the inconsistent application of the procedures (based on differing theoretical accounts) appears to be at fault (Dougher, Crossen, & Garland, 1986). Indeed, those studies using covert sensitization procedures based on classical conditioning offer the only consistent results (Clarke & Hayes, 1984; Miller & Dougher, in press; Elkins, 1980).

CLIENT SELECTION

The literature has not progressed sufficiently to allow clinicians to determine *before* treatment those clients most likely to benefit from covert sensitization. However, Elkins (Elkins, 1980; Elkins & Murdock, 1977) has derived criteria which allow rapid selection of those clients for whom covert sensitization is *unlikely* to be effective.

Elkins demonstrated that with the use of nausea sensitization, the success of the treatment could be predicted from the degree to which clients experienced conditioned nausea. Conditioned nausea, as with any conditioned response, is considered to have occurred if the client exhibits an aversion response during imagery of drinking. Using the criteria outlined by Elkins, the procedures allow rapid determination within 2–6 sessions of those clients for whom the treatment will not be effective (these criteria will be discussed later). This would allow the therapist to apply a different approach without having to progress through the entire treatment process.

Covert sensitization procedures have been employed in clinical settings for approximately two decades with no reports of major risks, given proper screening. The criteria for exclusion which have been used in clinical *research* settings include (a) history of or current gastrointestinal disorders, (b) history of or current heart disease, (c) current severe depression or suicidal ideation, and (d) current psychosis (Miller & Dougher, in press). However, while these criteria are put forth, there is no literature which indicates that persons with these problems experience complications or have poorer outcomes than other populations.

In addition to these precautions, you (as the therapist) need to be sensitive to any adverse consequences emerging during the course of treatment. The client should be prepared by the therapist to experience nausea or fear during, and possibly for a brief period following the sessions. However, in the unlikely event that the client reports continuing aversive consequences (such as nightmares), the nature of the scenes should be altered or termination of this treatment considered.

Settings and Materials

Covert sensitization can be carried out effectively without any unique materials or settings. A quiet room and a comfortable recliner chair are highly desirable, such as those appropriate for relaxation training, to minimize any discomfort or distraction which may disrupt imagery.

Equipment

Several types of devices can be used to assist you at different points in the treatment process. If you are doing covert sensitization on an outpatient basis, your client could be consuming alcohol prior to treatment. Since intoxication is likely to diminish the effectiveness of this intervention, breath alcohol tests can be used on a routine basis prior to beginning each session. The presence of any measurable alcohol in the breath would be the basis for cancellation of that session, and rescheduling. While you can often detect the presence of high quantities of alcohol, it is useful to use a device for detecting lower blood alcohol levels from breath samples (such as the Intoximeter).

Assisted nausea sensitization (see below) does not necessarily require any additional equipment beyond the chemical used for the noxious odor (valeric acid is commonly used). However, it is necessary to package it in a manner which the therapist can administer. A glass jar with a tight lid may be used to contain a small amount of cotton saturated with valeric acid. This jar can then be opened near the client's nose at the appropriate time during imagery.

As mentioned above, it is sometimes difficult to determine whether the client is actually experiencing a physical reaction to the scenes. This may be an important factor in the successful treatment process (e.g., Elkins, 1980). Several studies have utilized physiological monitoring equipment to aid in this process, reducing the ambiguity of the client's response (Elkins, 1980; Miller & Dougher, in press). A variety of measures have been used, including skin conductance response, skin conductance level, heart rate, and breathing rate. While these measures can be used in unison, it is also possible to use only one or two (e.g., skin conductance response) in conjunction with the client's overt responses to aid in determining conditioning (see below). The equipment for some of these measures may be purchased relatively inexpensively as biofeedback devices.

ADMINISTERING COVERT SENSITIZATION

As mentioned above, covert sensitization primarily involves the pairing in imagery of drinking and unpleasant events. During initial scenes, the client first imagines drinking in a familiar setting, then imagines aversive consequences such as nausea and vomiting or feared natural results of excessive alcohol consumption (Smith & Gregory, 1976). With repeated pairings, the unpleasant images come to be attached to alcohol itself, diminishing the client's desire for, and attraction to, alcohol.

Components of Covert Sensitization

The initial procedure involves a relatively simple pairing of drinking stimuli with the vivid imagination of nausea or uncomfortable consequences of drinking. With the help of the client, construct several typical drinking settings or scenes which you will later describe to the client. You will also solicit the client's description of nausea or fear experiences to assist in describing the second (or sensitization) portion of each scene. For the purpose of this chapter, the presentation of the drinking scenes along with the sensitization portion will be described as the *pairing* phase of covert sensitization.

However, the treatment goal of covert sensitization is to develop an avoidance response in addition to an aversive response. Therefore, in addition to a simple pairing, covert sensitization also involves two other phases: *escape*, and finally *avoidance*.

The *escape* phase begins with imagery of plausible drinking scenes, similar to the *pairing* phase, but when the client begins experiencing discomfort, the scene is altered to include non-drinking alternatives, such as pouring out the drink, leaving the drinking setting, and so forth. Suggestions of relief and positive self-regard are included in these scenes and are called *aversion relief statements*.

Finally, the *avoidance* phase begins with the same imagery of drinking settings. However, in these scenes you will present the non-drinking alternatives *prior* to the client experiencing any significant uncomfortable or aversive reactions. *Aversion relief statements* are also included here.

When to Use Each Component

The sequence of presentation begins with *pairing* scenes, and continues until a *conditioned response* occurs. A conditioned response has occurred when the client experiences nausea or discomfort (determined by client report, behavioral observation, and/or physiological monitoring) when *imagining drinking*. The indications of conditioning and the way in which it may be assessed will be discussed in more detail later.

Once a conditioned response is noted, *escape* scenes begin, allowing your client to exit the drinking setting (in imagination) after beginning to experience some discomfort but before you intensify the aversive response. Alternate *pairing* scenes with *escape* scenes to insure the firm establishment of the conditioned response. Finally, introduce *avoidance* scenes to reinforce avoidance behavior. Covert sensitization treatment is stopped shortly thereafter. Take care to avoid overpracticing the scenes, as this may result in the client becoming used to the aversive elements of the scenes.

This sequence of pairing, escape, and avoidance was used in two studies showing a link between conditioning and successful outcome (Elkins, 1980; Miller & Dougher, in press). Examples of each type of scene will be given later.

We recommend doing covert sensitization on a one-to-one basis. When done on a group basis, it is difficult to incorporate enough detail to ensure realism sufficient to establish or enhance a conditioned response for any given individual client. The effectiveness of this treatment declines significantly when it is done in groups.

Preliminary Assessment

Because the scenes must be individually tailored to each client, it is important to do an in-depth assessment before you begin covert sensitization. During this interview, elicit information regarding your client's most recent drinking pattern, both on a steady and periodic basis. You should also elicit information about the client's beverage preferences, drinking settings, and motivational factors. Additional information about your client's daily habits, hobbies, and interests can be used in building each component of the scenes. A structured interview designed explicitly to provide this information about alcohol consumption is the Comprehensive Drinker Profile (Marlatt & Miller, 1984). Without such detailed information, it is very difficult to structure the scenes in a realistic manner without frequently asking questions during imagery.

When using covert sensitization, it is important to evaluate its effect on both drinking behavior and urges to drink. Self-monitoring is a method which enables you to have access to this information, and it also helps your client to increase his or her awareness of those behaviors that help maintain abstinence. A simple diary card is all that is needed. Include spaces for your client to record the date and time, the type and amount of drink (or the strength of the urge to drink), and aspects of the critical situation, such as setting and companions (Miller & Muñoz, 1982). These cards should be small enough for the client to carry at all times. Instruct your client to record *every* drink and *each* occurrence of an urge to drink at the time it occurs, rather than waiting to reconstruct the event at a later time. Urges are defined as any craving, thought, or desire for a drink, and are best rated using a 1–5 scale for intensity. Anticipate the problems your client may have with self-monitoring ahead of time, and rehearse strategies to deal with those situations.

Constructing Scenes

It is important to prepare a general outline of the scenes to be presented prior to the initial sensitization session. If you have done a detailed evaluation interview, you can prepare initial scripts for the scenes from that information. These scripts are helpful and insure that you are including relevant details which assist the client in vividly imagining the scenes. You will probably make extensive modifications to the scripts in the first few sessions, as you find out which elements are useful and which elements obstruct the client's imagination.

Drinking stimulus scenes

These scenes include details of typical drinking settings for your clients, as well as many details of drinking itself. It is *essential* to include a full range of beverages unique to each client, to insure that the effect of the sensitization will apply to each beverage. This is because it is possible to produce a conditioned aversion to the taste of one alcoholic beverage without affecting the response to others (Quinn & Henbest, 1965; Baker & Cannon, 1979). For the same reason, it is also important to include a variety of drinking settings. This will reduce the monotony of the scene presentations and assist in generalization. In our research, currently underway at the University of New Mexico, we use the full range of each client's beverage preferences within each of three or more drinking settings.

In presenting the scenes, emphasize details which your client would actually *experience* when drinking in each setting. Peter Lang (Lang, Kozak, Miller, Levin, & McLean, 1980) found that doing so enhanced imagery appreciably. While details of the setting (colors, people present, sounds, and so forth) are important in the initial scene elements, major emphasis should be placed on *experiences* your client would have just before and during drinking. Examples of experiences include the feel and the temperature of the container in the client's hand, the sound of ice cubes in the glass, the smell of the beverage as it is brought close to the lips, the taste and feel of sipping and swallowing the drink.

Sensitization Scenes

These scenes should be constructed to produce unpleasant responses themselves, such as anxiety, horror, disgust, or revulsion. There are three general types of sensitization scenes which have been used, each corresponding to a different modality of covert sensitization. *Nausea* sensitization is the form of sensitization most commonly used, and simply involves the presentation of scene elements designed to produce an intense experience of nausea in the client (Elkins, 1980; Miller & Dougher, in press). *Assisted nausea* sensitization is similar, in that the scenes can be identical to those used in nausea sensitization. However, the presentation of a noxious odor (valeric acid) is added during the sensitization portion of the scenes (Maletzky, 1974; Miller & Dougher, in press). The third form of sensitization which has been less frequently used is *emotive* sensitization. This form of covert sensitization uses scenes designed to evoke strong emotions or feelings other than nausea, such as disgust, embarrassment, anxiety, horror, etc. In order to induce such feelings, these scenes use believable negative consequences of heavier drinking (Smith & Gregory, 1976).

Currently it is unclear for whom each type of sensitization scene is most effective, but it appears important to apply only one modality at a time with a client. If one form of sensitization does not appear to be effective, and is not

producing a response, then it may be possible to switch to one of the other modalities. This issue will be addressed below.

When constructing both the drinking scenes and the sensitization scenes, it is necessary to explore with each client exactly what scene elements should be included, and to use the client's own words during the scene. For nausea scenes, ask about your client's responses during the first few sessions. This will help you to tailor the scenes for each client. However, for emotive scenes, it may be helpful to give the Fear Survey Schedule (Wolpe & Lang, 1969) or the Schedule of Aversive Consequences of Drinking (Miller & Olson, 1982) to help you to design initial scene scripts. In any case, unless you ask direct questions about scenes and use the information to refine scene elements, the effectiveness of the sensitization process is compromised.

Common Concerns

Several issues and questions commonly arise about the use of covert sensitization. The first is related to the nausea scenes. Since you are trying to induce intense nausea responses in your clients, you may be concerned that they may actually vomit. This is very rare in both the simple nausea as well as the assisted nausea scenes, but it has been known to happen. As you become more experienced with the nausea reactions of each client, you will be able to detect extraordinarily intense responses in your client, and to terminate the scenes prior to actual vomiting. Since nausea is the desired response to be paired with drinking, vomiting will add little (if anything) to the effectiveness of the procedure. However, it is a good idea to keep a lined wastebasket available in the event your client is especially sensitive, and you do not terminate the sensitization scene early enough.

A second common concern is that you will begin to respond to the scenes yourself. This is also unlikely. As a rule, therapists tend to become desensitized to the scene content as they progress. Within a session, you are constantly monitoring your client's responses and any physiological monitoring equipment used, as well as describing and intensifying the scenes. Also, you have your eyes open and are not reclining in a comfortable chair, both of which inhibit vivid imagination.

Some clients are concerned that the procedures are out of their control, and that the therapist may "hypnotize" them. Reassure your client that the entire procedure is in *his or her* control, and that it is up to him or her to imagine the scenes as vividly as possible.

COVERT SENSITIZATION: STAGES

Initial Session

In the first session, you should elicit the full cooperation of the client. It is important to explain clearly the goal of treatment, emphasizing that covert sensitization is designed specifically to reduce urges or desire to drink by pairing drinking with uncomfortable feelings in imagination. You should also spend some time assisting the client in understanding the effectiveness of imagination in altering feelings, possibly through some examples (imagining biting into a lemon or eating a favorite food results in an increase in saliva).

While explaining the procedure for imagining the scenes, emphasize the client's need to *experience* the scenes for effective treatment, as well as the need for the client to suggest changes in the scenes to enhance vividness. At this time it is important that you emphasize that the treatment is a cooperative effort between you and the client, working together to build scenes which the client finds effective. It is important to minimize the demand characteristics of the procedures as well. You should not tell your client to expect that they will automatically experience an aversion response to the imagery of drinking. Under *no* circumstances should you explain the conditioning process to a client in treatment. Toward these ends, you may find it helpful to describe your client's aversion response simply as "discomfort," and to suggest that they report it *whenever* it occurs. A useful method for signaling is the raising of a number of fingers of the dominant hands; one finger = first indication of any discomfort, two fingers = moderate discomfort, three fingers = severe discomfort, and four fingers = very severe discomfort. Ask the client to hold the appropriate number of fingers elevated until you touch his or her hand. This is to ensure that you saw the signal.

During the first session, you should gather specific information about drinking settings, beverages, and so on. If this session were preceded by a structured interview (e.g., the Comprehensive Drinker Profile), you need only fill in any gaps in the script you have prepared. This session should also be used to gain specifics for the sensitization scenes. Regardless of the type of sensitization to be used, it is important to find out which descriptors your client would actually use, rather than your interpretation of your client's feelings. These points can be fine-tuned in the next several sessions.

Session Two

Starting with the second session, you may present the scenes. However, if physiological monitoring equipment is to be used, you must first extinguish any response your client has to the drinking scenes alone. Do not use any aversive imagery at this time, and explain this to your client in advance. Only the drinking scene components will be presented. Without this step, physiological equipment is useless in determining the initiation of a aversion response, since a client's anticipatory responses may appear identical to aversion responses. During extinction you must present each drinking scene to be used until no response is noted on the monitoring equipment. You may also use this time to intensify the vividness and realism of the drinking scenes through inquiry. When covert sensitization is used on an outpatient basis, there is some concern in letting the client leave after vividly imagining drinking alcohol without any aversive consequence. Thus, this "extinction" session should be extended up to 2 hours, and should be terminated with the presentation of at least three *pairing* scenes.

If no physiological monitoring equipment is to be used, you will begin presenting both drinking and sensitization scene components. It is important in this session to introduce your client to the use of imagery and to assist him or her in overcoming blocks to vivid and realistic imagination. When presenting the scenes, instruct your client to use *active* imagination, as if he or she were really there, seeing the scene through his/her own eyes, experiencing tastes, smells, temperature, sounds and feelings. This means that your client should not "picture" the scene as if he or she were watching it on TV, but should attempt to experience the physical sensations he or she would have if the scene were real.

You should present the scenes at a slow, relaxed, yet deliberate pace while your client reclines in a comfortable chair with his or her eyes closed. It is *vital* to emphasize the sensory aspects of the scenes, especially taste and swallowing when describing the actual consumption of the alcohol. Throughout each of the scenes, it is necessary to use response descriptions, rather than descriptions of the stimulus elements of a scene.

Drinking Scene Components

Below is an example of a drinking scene. Since each client will have different drinking settings and beverage preferences, this is only a sample of how one drinking scene could be constructed.

> It's been a long, hard day at work. You have been driving home thinking about how tired and hot you are, and how good a nice cold drink would taste. You arrive home, unlock the door, and realize you are very hot and sweaty. You wipe your forehead, and feel the moisture on the palm of your hand—you wipe your hand on your pants. Your mouth is dry, and you can feel yourself swallowing. You're thinking now about how much you would like a nice cold beer. You go into the kitchen, to the refrigerator. You grasp the handle, and can feel the coolness of it in your hand. You have to tug a little to break the seal, and then the door opens. Inside, in the light, you can see the six pack of beer. The cans are held together by plastic, and you can see the red and white labels. You can see the beads of moisture on the cans. You reach in, grasp hold of one can, and pry it out of the plastic. You can feel the round coldness of the beer can in your hand, and you can feel the moisture, the condensation against your palm. With the other hand, you lift the pop top, and can hear the hiss as it snaps open. You can see the white bubbles from the beer, and can hear the fizz as you bend the pop top back down. You can almost taste the coolness of the beer already. You bring the can up to your mouth, and feel the cool, round metal on your lips. As you tip the can back, you can feel the bubbles of beer bursting on your lips, and you let it flow into your mouth. It tastes great! You can smell the hops, that heavy good aroma of the beer. You feel the beer in your mouth, all over your tongue, that kind of sharp, cool, bitter, malty taste. You swallow, and feel the coolness spread down your throat and into your stomach. You can still taste and smell the beer in your mouth. This is just what you wanted! You bring the can up to your mouth again, and feel that cool liquid flow over your lips and into your mouth. You take a bigger swallow

this time, and can taste and smell that distinctive aroma of the beer as you swallow.

It is important that you ask your client during a scene, to elaborate on details to assist in intensifying the realism of the scene. However, the questions you ask at this time should only be about the elements of the scene itself, and should not incorporate demand characteristics (i.e.: do not ask "Can you imagine the taste yet?"). For example:

> *Therapist:* You are finally home. You unlock the front door of your house. Would there be anyone else home?
> *Client:* No, just myself.
> *Therapist:* OK, you open the front door, and walk into the house. It's cool and quiet inside. You close the door and walk into the kitchen. You're thinking of that nice, cool drink. You go over to the refrigerator. What color is it?
> *Client:* Green.
> *Therapist:* You can see the green refrigerator. You reach out and grasp the handle. . . .

This interaction will diminish as the scenes progress, but should be encouraged, especially during the first few sessions. The interaction assists both you *and* your client, since it evokes active participation in the imagination process from the client. However, such interaction is more effectively used in the drinking stimulus portion of the scenes than in the sensitization portion.

Drinking scenes should be approximately 2–3 minutes in length. The purpose of these scenes is to allow your client to vividly imagine the drinking setting, and the drink itself. When drinking scenes are longer than this, too many extraneous elements are included, and it quickly becomes unclear what is to be paired with the discomfort. If scenes are much shorter than 2 minutes, it is sometimes difficult for your client to generate the image as vividly or realistically as possible. However, the exact time for each scene will vary as a function of the scene, the individual client's abilities, and the client's experience.

A recording log is useful in tracking client responses, as well as reconstructing previous scenes. Information which you would include on such a log would be the scene number, scene component (pairing, escape, avoidance), client self-report (number of fingers raised, and when), behavioral signs (gag, choke, flushing, squirming), and physiological changes (as shown by monitoring equipment).

Sensitization Scene Elements

Covert sensitization scenes begin with a simple pairing of the drinking and sensitization scene elements. You will present the drinking stimulus portion of each scene exactly as described above, but at the point of the first taste introduce the sensitization scene elements. From that point on, combine elements of the drinking scene, which include the taste and smell of the alcoholic beverage, with the sensitization elements of the scene. It is preferable to continue to mix these elements throughout the entire sensitization scene to insure a pairing of your client's drinking experiences with discomfort.

The sensitization scene elements are designed to evoke vivid and intense responses, and so employ critical elements similar to the drinking stimulus scenes. That is, you should place emphasis on descriptions of what your client would actually experience in each scene: feelings, sights, sounds, tastes, smells, etc.

Below is an example of a sensitization scene using the nausea modality. Such a scene must be individualized within the second session to include elements your client provides. An example is provided below.

> You finish the first sip of beer, and you can feel the coolness spreading down to your stomach. You notice a funny feeling in your stomach, in fact it feels a little queasy. You're not sure what is going on, and you think that maybe you're just a little hungry. Maybe another drink will help. You bring the can up to your lips, and you can feel the coolness against your hand. As you tip it back, you feel the beer pour over your lips, and into your mouth, and you start to swallow. But suddenly, that funny feeling in your stomach is stronger, and you feel like you will have to burp. You can feel the belch coming up, and it meets the beer you just swallowed. You swallow again, trying to force it down, but it doesn't work. You can feel the gas coming up, and you can tell there is some liquid with it, some chunks of food. You swallow more, but suddenly your mouth is filled with a sour liquid that burns the back of your throat, and goes up your nose. You feel you have to cough, and you spew the liquid all over the counter and sink. You can tell that it is vomit mixed with the beer, and you can see the chunks of food and brownish vomit all over the counter and top of the beer can. You can smell the sour odor of the beer and the stench of the vomit. Your throat and nose are really burning now. As you feel the puke running down your chin, you try to wipe it off, but that pressure in your stomach is now a nauseous heaving. You feel your stomach contract, and your throat fills with more burning

vomit. You lean over the sink, and your mouth and nose fill with horrible stinging puke, mixed with the taste of beer. Your stomach heaves uncontrollably, and vomit spews out of your mouth into the sink, splashing back up into your face. You can see the chunks of food and the vomit oozing down the drain, and you notice that there are spots of blood in the vomit as well. You try to spit that sour beer and vomit taste out of your mouth, but your stomach won't quit heaving. Now greenish bile is in your mouth, and running into the sink. Your eyes are watering, and your nose and throat are burning. You can still taste the beer, and you try to spit that taste out as well. The stench from the sink is almost unbearable, the sour odor of vomit, half-digested food and beer. That smell triggers another heave in your stomach, but there is nothing left to come up. Still your stomach continues to churn and heave.

Sensitization scenes using realistic fears of the results of excessive drinking are constructed in a similar manner. The emphasis is on the aspects which your client would *experience*, rather than on the stimulus elements of the scene. As before, you should present the taste and smell of the alcohol beverage throughout the scene.

> You finished that first sip of beer, and now it is a little while later. You have just entered your car, and are preparing to back out of the driveway, on your way to the store. With one hand on the hot steering wheel, you reach forward to insert the key in the ignition. As you feel it slide in, you swallow and notice the taste of beer in your mouth. You can smell it, as if you just swallowed a large sip. You turn the key, and the engine surges to life. As you pull the shift lever into reverse, you glance over your shoulder to make sure it is clear behind the car. You press on the accelerator and begin backing out. Suddenly, there is a blur of motion in the corner of your vision. You jam your foot on the brake as you hear a horrible crunch from behind the car. The car gives a sickening lurch as if you ran over a small bump. The taste of beer is strong in your mouth as you open the door and look toward the back of the car. You are horrified to see a small foot sticking out from behind your rear tire. You jump from the car, and run that small crumpled body pinned under the rear of the car. You're down on your hands and knees, and as you peer under the car, you can clearly see the blood puddling under the small child's body. There is no movement, and you cannot tell if the child is alive. The smell of beer is strong on your breath, and the smell mixes with the warm odor of blood on the ground. You are horrified, you cannot think straight, as you stare at the broken body. You notice that

the child's arms are bent unnaturally, and you see the stark white color of bone protuding through the clothing. The sour taste of beer surges into your mouth, and burning fear and horror fills you, as you see the child's limbs give a series of twitches.

Like the drinking scenes, you should make these scenes 2–3 minutes in length. If they extend beyond this, your client is likely to be unable to sustain a response for the entire period, and is very likely to become used to the scene, rendering it useless. Within this time constraint, clients will differ as to how quickly they will be able to experience a response, and the scene elements should be adapted to this. However, as a general rule, you should initiate the sensitization scene as intensely and rapidly as possible at the first taste of alcohol in the drinking portion of the scene.

You should record each and every scene on a scene log (as mentioned above). This will allow you to monitor the progress of conditioning, and to aid in determining the appropriate time to switch from pairing to escape and to avoidance phases.

CLIENT'S RESPONSE

The initial goal of the pairing phase is to obtain a *response* from your client during the sensitization portion of the scenes. This "unconditioned response" results from the presentation of the sensitization scene alone. Just as an inquiry period following initial drinking scene presentations is required to insure vividness of those scene portions, so too is inquiry needed to modify and tailor the sensitization scenes to incorporate individualized elements. If no unconditioned response is noted within the first 4 scenes, it is possible that you may need to radically alter the sensitization scene elements to produce the realism and vividness necessary to produce an unconditioned response. Should this occur, stop the presentation process, and elicit the assistance of your client in modifying the sensitization scenes.

It is important that you present the *entire* sensitization scene portion when in the pairing phase. Some therapists are tempted to begin terminating the sensitization portion as soon as their client exhibits a significant response. This is likely to be counterproductive, in that the client's response should be intensified to insure that it becomes associated with the imagery of

drinking. However, as mentioned above, with some rare clients, you must walk a fine line between sufficiently intensifying the scene and terminating prior to actual vomiting.

After a scene in which your client has exhibited a response, it is necessary to pause for several minutes to allow the responses to diminish prior to initiating the next scene. This is especially important when physiological monitoring is being used, to allow the readings to stabilize, and/or return to baseline.

What is a Response?

Preliminary research relied primarily on the self-report of the client to determine the presence of discomfort. However, this appears inadequate, and does not control for the demand characteristics of the procedures. In current research, several assessment methods are used, employing client self-report, behavioral observations, and physiological monitoring equipment. We suggest that you use the following guidelines which are currently being used in research at the University of New Mexico, and which allow reliable determination of a client's response:

- *Self-Report:* a finger signal of 2 (moderate discomfort) or more

- *Behavioral Observations:* Noticeable choking coughing, gagging, eyes watering, grimacing, moaning, gasping, panting, swallowing, burping, etc.

- *Physiological Monitoring:*
  Skin Conductance Level: An increase of at least 5 microsiemens relative to baseline.
  Skin Conductance Response: Two discrete phasic changes of at least 0.3 microsiemens within 10 sec.
  Heart Rate: A change of at least 4 beats per min relative to baseline.
  Respiration: A change in breaths per minute or amplitude of breath of at least 30% relative to baseline.

It is not necessary for changes to occur in each of the three areas to consider a significant response as having occurred. A useful criterion includes a change on one physiological measure, and a response on either the self-report or behavioral observations. If your client appears to be responding on physiological measures and/or showing behavioral signs but is not indicating discomfort through the finger signals, spend a few moments between scenes to discuss the self-report signals and ask about his or her subjective experience.

What to do With (or Without) a Conditioned Response

The ultimate goal of the pairing phase is to establish a conditioned response to drinking stimuli. When these responses begin occurring *during the drinking scene, prior to beginning the presentation of the sensitization scene,* a conditioned response is considered to have occurred. This is an important event.

Thus, you should present pairing scenes until one of the following occurs:

1. Until four scenes have been presented with no (unconditioned) response at all. As mentioned above, you should stop the presentation procedure, inquire about vividness and realism, then modify and intensify the scenes. You will then continue within the pairing phase until one of the following occurs.
a. If no *unconditioned response* occurs within 12 scenes, even with intensification of the sensitization scene, terminate treatment within this sensitization modality with an *avoidance* scene. Research indicates that if an *unconditioned response* is to occur, it will occur within this period (Elkins, 1980). Continued presentation of the scenes within the *pairing* phase is extremely unlikely to result in an unconditioned response. However, it is at this time possible to alter the sensitization modality. Thus, if nausea had been tried, it would be possible to introduce assisted nausea or to construct sensitization scenes based on emotive elements. The same criteria for termination of pairing would then apply.
b. If an *unconditioned response* occurs but a *conditioned response* is never established, terminate treatment after 40 scenes (6–8 sessions). This is based on Elkins' (1980) research, confirmed in pilot work at the University of New Mexico, which indicates that if a conditioned response is to occur, it will occur within this period. The final scene should be an *avoidance* scene (see below), to enhance the introduction of non-drinking behavior.

2. If a *conditioned response* occurs, you will begin alternating *escape* scenes and *pairing* scenes. At the point that you note consistent conditioned responding on three consecutive trials, introduce *avoidance* scenes (one *avoidance* scene following each block of three *escape* or *pairing* scenes). Terminate treatment with an *avoidance* scene after the second block of three consecutive conditioned responses.

If, at any point, the conditioned response does not appear, return to the *pairing* phase, intensifying the sensitization scene. When a conditioned response is reestablished, the above criteria are again applicable.

3. In any event, discontinue treatment after 50 scenes (with scene 50 being an *avoidance* scene). These procedures are not any more likely to be successful beyond this limit.

The Escape Phase

Begin escape scenes in the same manner as pairing scenes. The drinking scene elements are initially identical, but at the sign of a significant response from the client, introduce aversion relief and do not begin the sensitization scene. The goal of the escape phase is to allow your client to remove him or herself from the drinking setting (leaving the bar, pouring out the drink) and thus avoid intensification of the aversive response.

The aversion relief elements will not always be identical, and you will need to adjust them to fit into the scene your client is imagining. You should always include statements about feelings of relief and self-confidence. Here is an example of an aversion relief statement:

> You feel the glass in your hand, the moisture of the condensation against your palm. You can smell the tartness of the orange juice and the heavy aroma of the vodka. You can almost taste the drink in your mouth, the coolness, the sweetness. You bring the glass up to your lips, but suddenly you think: What am I doing? I don't want this drink at all, in fact I don't even like the smell! You pour the drink into the sink, and you can see the orange juice, the vodka, and the ice cubes swirling down the drain. You feel a sense of relief, a good feeling as you rinse the glass. You're not quite sure why, but you feel happy, and confident about yourself.

Introduce aversion relief elements (during the Escape phase) at the occurrence of a significant client response. If signs of a response appear but are not significant (e.g., only one finger signal, or a finger signal of 2 but no physiological change), prolong the drinking stimulus portion of the scene to intensify the response. However, if a significant response does not occur, or if you inadvertently begin describing actual alcohol consumption, continue through to the sensitization portion, and present the entire sensitization scene to more firmly establish conditioned responding. In other words, if you do not get a conditioned response and/or begin to describe actual drinking, switch from an escape scene to a pairing scene.

The Avoidance Phase

Your goal in the avoidance phase is to remove your client from the imagined drinking setting *prior* to the conditioned response. This will require you to monitor and record the point at which your client initiates a conditioned response within each scene. Then, just prior to that critical point, introduce the aversion relief element. The aversion relief element can be constructed in exactly the same way as that in which you used in the escape phase.

Occasionally, a client will not consistently exhibit a conditioned response at the same point in a drinking scene, making it difficult for you to predict the appropriate time for an aversion relief element. In such a case, as soon as your client exhibits a response which is *not* significant (a finger signal of only one, or a finger signal of two without a physiological change), immediately introduce the aversion relief element. This allows your client to remove him or herself from the drinking scene without experiencing any significant aversive responses.

LENGTH OF TREATMENT

When applying covert sensitization, it appears optimal to meet with your client fairly often to insure maintenance of the imagery skills as well as the conditioning. We schedule two 60-minute sessions per week as this appears to be the minimum effective frequency. With each scene being a maximum of eight minutes, it is possible to include 6 to 8 scenes per session, including time for inquiry. Thus, it is rare for treatment to extend beyond 8 sessions, or four weeks. If the sessions are scheduled more frequently, treatment will be significantly shorter.

EFFECTIVENESS

The outcome literature for aversion therapies in general is encouraging. Evaluations of chemical aversion therapy have been reported for more than fifty years, with consistently high rates of abstinence (Miller & Hester, 1980). Controlled evaluations have been few, but point to higher rates of abstinence among patients receiving chemical aversion than among those in comparison groups, at least over the 6 months following treatment (Boland, Mellor, & Revusky, 1978; Cannon, Baker, & Wehl, 1981). Cannon's research also supports a relationship between the establishment of a conditioned aversion to alcohol and successful abstinence (Cannon et al., 1981).

Controlled studies to date of the effectiveness of covert sensitization offer mixed results. An early study reported that 40% of the clients receiving covert sensitization were abstinent at 6 months, whereas none of the control group were abstinent (Ashem & Donner, 1968). Similarly, Maletzky (1974) reported that clients undergoing covert sensitization faired better than those randomly assigned to a halfway house program.

Comparative evaluations of covert sensitization have offered somewhat different results. In one study, sensitization resulted in a 74% improvement rate, which was better than that resulting from electrical aversion but poorer than that for family counseling or desensitization (Hedberg & Campbell, 1974). Similarly, Olson, Ganley, Devine, and Dorsey (1981) found that when used as an adjunct to milieu therapy, covert sensitization did not result in different abstinent rates than transactional analysis, which was also provided as an adjunct to milieu therapy.

Two other studies failed to find covert sensitization to be more effective than problem-solving therapy, desensitization, or insight therapy (Fleiger & Zingle, 1973; Piorkorsky & Mann, 1975), although high dropout rates in the latter study make interpretation of the results difficult.

As alluded to earlier in this chapter, these results are confusing. On the one hand, covert sensitization appears to be responsible for 40% abstinence rates and 74% improvement, while on the other hand it is no better than milieu therapy. One reason for these inconsistencies may be the lack of a uniform set of procedures used in "covert sensitization." Studies which have carefully defined sensitization procedures and have documented the occurrence of classical conditioning have shown the most encouraging results. Elkins (Elkins, 1980; Elkins & Murdock, 1977) was the first to demonstrate a relationship between the establishment of a conditioned aversion response and the effectiveness of covert sensitization with alcoholics. Similarly, Miller and Dougher (in press) found that conditioning appeared to play a role in outcome for those clients receiving nausea aversion, whereas conditioning did not appear to play as strong a role for clients receiving covert sensitization using plausible negative consequences of drinking.

Thus, initial research suggests that when the procedures for covert sensitization are well-defined, this treatment can result in a significant reduction in drinking behavior at least for a period of months. However, as suggested by Nathan (1976), unidimensional treatments often do not continue to remain effective without booster sessions. It appears that covert sensitization is an effective way to modify desire for alcohol, but may be most effective when combined with other problem-solving forms of treatment designed to provide alternative coping strategies. The literature also suggests that conditioning is a good predictor of effectiveness, at least with nausea conditioning, and should be corroborated with some form of psychophysiological assessment.

REFERENCES

Clinical Guidelines

Ashem, B., & Donner, L. (1968). Covert sensitization with alcoholics: A controlled replication. *Behaviour Research and Therapy, 6,* 7–12. This is a well-controlled study describing individualized procedures for using covert sensitization with inpatient alcoholics. It also addresses such issues as forward versus backward conditioning.

Elkins, R. L. (1980). Covert sensitization and alcoholism: Contributions of successful conditioning to subsequent abstinence maintenance. *Addictive Behaviors, 5,* 67–89. This article describes in detail Elkins' procedures for conducting covert sensitization with inpatient alcoholics.

Miller, W. R., & Dougher, M. J. (1986). Covert sensitization in alcoholism treatment. Unpublished manual. This manual outlines the procedures used in applying covert sensitization in a research setting at the University of New Mexico. Copies may be obtained by writing William R. Miller, Ph.D., Department of Psychology, University of New Mexico, Albuquerque, NM 87131.

Maletzky, B. M. (1974). Assisted covert sensitization for drug abuse. *International Journal of Addiction, 9,* 411–429. This article briefly describes the manner in which an odor assist is integrated with covert sensitization with outpatients.

Research

Ashem, B., & Donner, L. (1968). Covert sensitization with alcoholics: A controlled replication. *Behaviour Research and Therapy, 6,* 7–12.

Baker, T. B., & Cannon, D. S. (1979). Taste aversion therapy with alcoholics: Techniques and evidence of a conditioned response. *Behaviour Research and Therapy, 17,* 299–242.

Boland, F. J., Mellor, C. S., & Revusky, S. (1978). Chemical aversion treatment of alcoholism: Lithium as the aversive agent. *Behaviour Research and Therapy, 16,* 401–409.

Cannon, D. S., Baker, T. B., & Wehl, C. K. (1981). Emetic and electric shock alcohol aversion therapy: Six- and twelve-month follow-up. *Journal of Consulting and Clinical Psychology, 49,* 360–368.

Cautela, J. R. (1966). Treatment of compulsive behavior by covert sensitization. *Psychological Record, 16,* 33–41.

Cautela, J. R. (1967). Covert sensitization. *Psychological Reports, 20,* 459–468.

Cautela, J. R. (1970). The treatment of alcoholism by covert sensitization. *Psychotherapy: Theory, Research and Practice, 7,* 86–90.

Clarke, J. C., & Hayes, D. (1984). Covert sensitization, stimulus relevance and the equipotentiality premise. *Behaviour Research and Therapy, 22,* 451–454.

Dougher, M. J., Crossen, J. R., & Garland, R. (1986). An experimental test of Cautela's operant explanation of covert conditioning procedures. *Behavioral Psychotherapy, 14,* 226–248.

Elkins, R. L. (1980). Covert sensitization and alcoholism: Contributions of successful conditioning to subsequent abstinence maintenance. *Addictive Behaviors, 5,* 67–89.

Elkins, R. L., & Murdock, R. P. (1977). The contribution of successful conditioning to abstinence maintenance following covert sensitization (verbal aversion) treatment of alcoholism. *IRCS Medical Science: Psychology & Psychiatry: Social & Occupational Medicine, 5,* 167.

Fleiger, D. L., & Zingle, H. W. (1973). Covert sensitization treatment with alcoholics. *Canadian Counsellor, 7,* 269–277.

Hedberg, A. G., & Campbell, L. M. (1974). A comparison of four behavioral treatment approaches to alcoholism. *Journal of Behavior Therapy and Experimental Psychiatry, 5,* 251–256.

Lang, P. J., Kozak, M. J., Miller, G. A., Levin, D. N., & McLean, A. (1980). Emotional imagery: Conceptual structure and pattern of somato-visceral response. *Psychophysiology, 17,* 179–192.

Little, L. M., & Curran, J. P. (1978). Covert sensitization: A clinical procedure in need of some explanations. *Psychological Bulletin, 85,* 513–531.

Maletzky, B. M. (1974). Assisted covert sensitization for drug abuse. *International Journal of Addiction, 9,* 411–429.

Marlatt, G., & Miller, W. R. (1984). *The Comprehensive Drinker Profile*. Odessa, FL: Psychological Assessment Resources.

Miller, W. R., & Dougher, M. J. (1984). Covert sensitization: Alternative treatment procedures for alcoholics. *Alcoholism: Clinical and Experimental Research, 8*, 108.

Miller, W. R., & Muñoz, R. (1982). *How to control your drinking* (Rev. ed.). Albuquerque, NM: University of New Mexico Press.

Miller, W. R., & Olson, J. (1982). *Schedule of aversive consequences of drinking*. Albuquerque, NM: Department of Psychology, University of New Mexico.

Nathan, P. E. (1976). Alcoholism: In H. Leitenberg (Ed.), *Handbook of behavior modification and behavior therapy* (pp. 3–44). Englewood Cliffs, NJ: Prentice-Hall.

Olson, R. P., Ganley, R., Devine, V. T., & Dorsey, G. C., Jr. (1981). Long-term effects of behavioral versus insight-oriented therapy with inpatient alcoholics. *Journal of Consulting and Clinical Psychology, 49*, 866–877.

Piorkorsky, G. K., & Mann, E. T. (1975). Issues in treatment efficacy research with alcoholics. *Perceptual and Motor Skills, 41*, 695–700.

Quinn, J. T., & Henbest, R. (1967). Partial failure of generalization in alcoholics following aversion therapy. *Quarterly Journal of Studies on Alcohol, 28*, 70–75.

Smith, R., & Gregory, P. (1976). Covert sensitization by induced anxiety in the treatment of an alcoholic. *Journal of Behavioral Therapy and Experimental Psychiatry, 7*, 31–33.

Wolpe, J., & Lang, P. L. (1969). *Fear survey schedule*. San Diego, CA: Educational and Industrial Testing Service.

CHAPTER 9

Self-Control Training

Reid K. Hester
William R. Miller

OVERVIEW

Behavioral Self-Control Training (BSCT) is a treatment approach which can be used to pursue either a goal of abstinence or a goal of moderate and nonproblematic drinking. It consists of behavioral techniques which include goal setting, self-monitoring, specific changes in drinking behavior, rewards for goal attainment, functional analysis of drinking situations, and the learning of alternative coping skills. It is educational in that the client is introduced to specific components, one at a time, and is assigned "homework" tasks between sessions. The client maintains primary responsibility for making decisions throughout the training.

Current research suggests that BSCT can be either self-directed (with a self-help manual) or therapist-directed. Controlled outcome research has not found an overall difference in outcome based on whether the treatment is self- or therapist-directed. We conduct therapist-directed treatment in groups of 8–10 which meet weekly for 90 minutes for 8 weeks. Periodic follow-ups are also advisable. In the self-directed format, the client works with minimal therapist consultation, using a self-help manual.

SPECIAL CONSIDERATIONS

Because BSCT has most often been offered with a specific goal of "controlled drinking," it has been a controversial procedure. In fact, the principles of BSCT can be applied as well with a goal of total abstinence (e.g., Graber & Miller, 1987; Sanchez-Craig, Annis, Bornet, & Mac-Donald, 1984). It is appropriate here, however, to consider briefly the treatment issue of moderation goals.

There is little question at this point that following alcoholism treatment at least a few clients do attain and maintain moderate and problem-free drinking outcomes (Heather & Robertson, 1983). Treatment with a goal of moderation, though controversial, has been extensively studied and appears to yield overall success rates comparable to those from abstinence-oriented treatment. Current data suggest that moderation is most likely to be achieved by clients who, at the beginning of treatment, were experiencing less severe alcohol problems and dependence, whereas abstinence is a more stable outcome among more severe alcohol abusers.

There are several reasons to consider offering moderation-oriented treatment as one among a variety of options. Some clients refuse to consider abstinence without at least a reasonable trial at achieving moderation. It has often been suggested, by writers including Marty Mann (1950), that such persons should try to control their drinking as a way of discovering whether or not abstinence is necessary for them. A competent trial with moderation training, then, becomes a diagnostic procedure. If the client succeeds in moderating his or her consumption at a problem-free level, a favorable outcome has been achieved. If not, client and therapist can then together consider a goal of total abstinence. In our long-term follow-up of problem drinkers given BSCT with a goal of moderation, we found that many ultimately chose, achieved, and maintained abstinence (Miller, Leckman, Tinkcom, & Rubenstein, 1986).

Another reason to consider a moderation-goal option is that a broader range of problem drinkers can be attracted and treated. Epidemiological data suggest that within the general population there are far more problem drinkers than severely dependent alcoholics (Cahalan, 1987; Moore & Gerstein, 1981). This problem drinker population has been largely ignored or at least underserved. Less severe problem drinkers (and those who do not consider themselves to be alcoholics or problem drinkers) are more likely to accept services when goals other than lifelong abstinence are possible (see chapter 4). To offer only one alternative, total abstention, is to exclude a large population in need of services.

The data on the characteristics of clients who are most likely to benefit from BSCT are somewhat mixed (Elal-Lawrence, 1986). The most consistent characteristics, however, are a shorter duration of problem drinking and less severe dependence and problems (Miller & Hester, 1986a). Several studies have also found women to be more successful than men in maintaining moderation following BSCT. Research has reflected relatively little success in teaching moderation to severely dependent alcoholics. Some practitioners find it helpful to distinguish, in their own minds, between problem drinkers and true alcoholics, viewing abstinence as the only ultimately feasible goal for the latter. While this distinction is generally consistent with the outcome data, it appears that problem drinking represents a continuum, with severe dependence lying at the upper end.

As treatment begins it is important to emphasize to clients that BSCT is not an effective approach for everyone. Clients need to know that alternatives do exist and that you will continue to work with them if they are not successful with this approach. It has been our experience that if clients do not make substantial progress in reducing their drinking within the first 6–8 weeks of this systematic program, it is unlikely that they will attain stable moderation with more training. If this occurs, it is best to interpret the failure as a lack of an appropriate match between the client and treatment. Explaining a failure in this way will help to maintain motivation for change in the client. Then collaborate with the client in choosing a treatment approach with a goal of abstinence. Referring to the decision tree in Chapter 16 may be helpful at this point.

No special equipment is needed for BSCT. We use only a client self-help manual (Miller & Muñoz, 1982) and self-monitoring cards. It is helpful to give clients a stack of self-monitoring cards rather than asking clients to prepare them; a sample self-monitoring card is presented in the manual. It is also useful for clients to have a summary sheet on which they can keep track of total number of drinks per week, estimated peak Blood Alcohol Concentrations (BACs), and the number of drinks over how many hours to achieve their peak BACs for the week.

When treatment is directed by a therapist, it is usually done in small groups of 8–10 clients. Weekly meetings last 60–90 minutes, and the group runs for 8 weeks. Periodic follow-ups are advisable, in order to reinforce gains made and to determine which clients may need additional interventions.

DESCRIPTION

BSCT involves a number of discrete steps which occur in the following order:

1. Setting limits on the number of drinks per day and on peak BACs
2. Self-monitoring of drinking behaviors
3. Changing the rate of drinking
4. Practicing assertiveness in refusing drinks
5. Setting up a reward system for achievement of goals
6. Learning which antecedents result in overdrinking
7. Learning other coping skills instead of drinking

The remainder of this section will explain these steps in detail.

Setting Limits

To set limits, you first have to agree on what constitutes a "drink." The convention we have adopted defines one drink or SEC (Standard Ethanol Content) as ½ ounce of pure ethanol. That is the amount of alcohol in each of the following: 1 oz of 100 proof distilled spirits, 1.25 oz of 80 proof distilled spirits, 2.5 oz of fortified wine (20% alcohol), 4 oz of table wine (12% alcohol) or 10 oz of beer (5% alcohol). The formula for calculating the number of SECs in a drink is the number of ounces of alcohol times the percent of alcohol times two, divided by 100. For example 12 oz of 5% beer is 1.2 SECs ($12 \times 5 \times 2$ divided by $100 = 1.2$). The easiest way for clients to learn how to calculate SECs is by giving them sample problems and having them work through the formula. We always define a "drink" as 1 SEC.

At this point many clients will realize that they often do not know how much alcohol is in a particular drink. It becomes, then, their responsibility to find out. Assistance in problem solving and role playing is often helpful here to help the clients learn how to get this information, especially when they are drinking at a bar.

To assist clients in deciding what limits they are going to set for themselves, we provide information on the behavioral effects of different BAC levels in persons without significant tolerance to alcohol. They are also given information on the overall rates of consumption in the U.S. adult population. With this information in mind, clients decide on two sets of limits, a regular and an absolute limit. The regular limit is the number of drinks and a peak BAC the client does not want to exceed during the course of an average day. The absolute limits are usually a little higher and are for special occasions, such as weddings, when everyone tends to drink more. Both sets of limits include a maximum number of drinks per day and a maximum peak BAC. Finally, we encourage all clients to set a limit on the total number of drinks per week. As a weekly goal, we recommend that clients set it at or below 21 drinks. While acknowledging that there are no "safe" levels of drinking, when one exceeds 3 drinks per day negative health consequences

increase dramatically (Saunders & Aasland, 1987).

It is important to help clients set realistic goals. If estimated peak BACs for a typical week are 256mg%, it may be unrealistic to set a BAC limit of 40mg% as the first goal. For such clients, setting intermediate goals increases the chances of initial success, which will keep their motivation up. Once clients have met intermediate goals, then they can shoot for lower levels of drinking.

Self-Monitoring

An important step in BSCT is the self-monitoring of drinking. Give your clients enough cards to last for several weeks, and provide additional cards on a regular basis. Emphasize that they need to fill out the information on each drink *before* they begin to drink it. Doing so directs their attention to their drinking and reminds them that they are trying to moderate their consumption. The information includes the date, time, drink type (e.g., beer, scotch), amount of alcohol in the drink, place of drinking, and with whom they are drinking. As they write down the data on each drink, it brings to their attention how long it has been since their last drink and how many drinks they have already had that day. While ongoing self-monitoring is urged, it is always better late than never. If a client realizes when she or he is drinking but not self-monitoring, it is better to try to reconstruct his or her drinking pattern and then go on, rather than to forget the whole matter for the rest of the evening. Similarly if a client realizes that she or he has forgotten to self-monitor, the previous evening, it is better late than never to try to reconstruct the drinking behaviors. In practice, however, this does not occur too often. Once clients have self-monitored for a while, it becomes a habit.

In addition to showing them how to fill out the self-monitoring cards, you will need to address the problems they anticipate experiencing in making this a regular habit. Many clients will anticipate embarrassment or anxiety at the idea of self-monitoring. Role-playing appropriate responses is helpful. Clients will often need a range of responses to the questions of others. Some responses may be humorous (e.g., "I'm working for the CIA and taking notes on some suspects at the end of the bar") while others may be more direct and assertive (e.g., "It's none of your business" or "I'm trying to cut down on my drinking and am keeping track of my drinks"). You can assure them that they will become more comfortable in responding to others after they have done it for a while. Incidently, we often hear from clients that their good friends are supportive of their efforts. On the other hand, some of their "drinking buddies" who are not good friends may continue to hassle them about self-monitoring. Perceptive clients will see that their "drinking buddies" feel threatened by their efforts to reduce their consumption.

Self-monitoring also often results in a number of other realizations about their drinking. While many of these concerns are addressed at different times during the course of the program, it is important to acknowledge these realizations as they occur and help your clients to understand how they fit into the overall pattern of their drinking. As an example, Joe might realize that he always overdrinks at The Watering Hole, but rarely does so at the King's Pub. Armed with this knowledge he might choose not to go to The Watering Hole, try different activities if he goes there, sit in a different place, or visit with someone other than his usual drinking buddies. He might also try to strictly limit the amount of time he spends there by scheduling other activities around his drinking.

Setting goals and self-monitoring are typically covered in the first session. At the beginning of the second and subsequent sessions, have the clients report to the group their total SECs for the previous week and their peak BACs. This allows peer pressure to come into play, and clients who are making progress often receive quite a bit of support for their efforts from other group members at this time.

Rate Control

Once clients have self-monitored their consumption for a week and have set limits for themselves, they are then ready to try some different strategies to control their rate of drinking. We encourage clients to try each different strategy and find out which one(s) works best for them.

The first strategy is to switch from stronger to weaker drinks. Rather than drinking hard li-

quor straight or on ice, switch to highballs (1 ounce of liquor with a glass of mixer). If a client drinks more than 1 ounce of hard liquor in a drink, have him or her reduce it to that amount. (By now he or she should know how much alcohol is in a given drink even if it is served in a bar.) Clients also need to be warned about having drinks which are very tasty and sweet and where the amount of alcohol is masked; these tend to be drunk quickly. Switching to different drinks is to be encouraged. Clients often report that they drink some drinks more slowly than others. While they may have a favorite drink, switching to another, less-favored drink which goes down more slowly will be to their advantage if they want to reduce their consumption.

Another tactic to reduce consumption has to do with sipping. Many clients will tend to gulp their drinks with little time between gulps. To change these behaviors they first need to self-monitor how many sips they take of a drink and how long they wait between sips. They can then try to increase the number of sips per drink to a preferable minimum of 12. This strategy, however, needs to also include a spacing of sips across time lest the clients compensate by sipping faster! A good target to shoot for is 60 seconds between sips. By timing themselves they can get a "feel" for this rate of sipping. It is also helpful to put the glass down when not sipping.

Spacing drinks across time is probably the most frequently used tactic. Have your clients calculate how many drinks they can have over a 4 hour period of time given the regular and absolute BAC limits they have set for themselves. By dividing this number of SECs into 4 hours or 240 minutes, they can determine the average and minimum length of time between drinks to keep their BACs within their limits. Ways to increase the time between drinks include sipping smaller amounts with more time between sips; allowing time to pass between finishing one drink and starting another; having a nonalcoholic drink between drinks; and adding ice or additional mixer to the drink to keep it cool and make it last longer.

Drink Refusal

At some point most clients will have to decline offers of additional drinks, either because they have reached their limit or because they are spacing their drinks out across time. For many of your clients it is not sufficient to tell them to "just say no." Instead, provide them with training in assertiveness skills. Illustrate the verbal and nonverbal components of assertiveness with role playing. Put yourself in the "hot seat" and have a group of clients pressure you to drink while you assertively refuse. Then go back and point out the various components of eye contact, body language, voice tone and volume in addition to the verbal content. Next, go around the group and have each client describe the setting in which they have the greatest difficulty refusing drinks. Then role play that scene with others from the group. After each role play, have group members provide feedback on what the person did well and what aspects need improvement. If a client does poorly during role play, we ask him or her to practice during the week with friends or family. He or she is then given another opportunity to role-play during the next session. The improvement is usually noticeable.

Setting up Reward Systems for Success

As clients progress towards their goals, have them set up a reward system for even minor achievements. Congratulatory self-talk is important after even a minor victory. Assure them that they are not crazy for talking to themselves, and encourage them to give themselves a pat on the back for refusing a drink or keeping their BACs within their limits.

It is also helpful to use tangible rewards. For these rewards to be effective they will need to be "extras," given as soon as possible after the achievement, and tailor-made. By extras, we mean they should be activities, experiences, or objects that the client does not normally do or get. Tailor-made means that the rewards are satisfying and pleasurable to the individual client. (Clearly this means that the rewards need to be developed by the client.) Finally, they need to be readily accessible. A trip to Hawaii next year for success this week is not a timely reward. Here are some examples of material rewards: books, clothes, gadgets, food items such as exotic fruit, fancy meals, and entertainment activities. Rewards involving time (especially for busy clients) might include two hours of doing absolutely nothing or time to read a favorite mystery author.

After clients develop a set of personal rewards, have them draw up a contract with themselves. This contract would specify what reasonable amount of progress is deserving of reward. Then have them write out the contract and have each client tell the group the details of the contract. These latter two actions increase the probability that a client will carry through with the contract.

If and only if a client develops a reward system (which not all will do), then she or he can consider having *penalties* for not achieving his or her goals. A penalty should be something that the client genuinely dislikes but is in some way constructive. Examples might include cleaning out the garage or picking up litter in the neighborhood. Once the penalty is decided upon, have the client write up the agreement just as she or he did with the reward system.

Antecedents to Overdrinking

After clients have self-monitored for several weeks, have them review all their self-monitoring cards and look for patterns in their drinking behaviors. They may have already realized that they tend to drink more at certain bars or with certain people, and that is a good start. Go through each of the different situational factors and have the clients describe how they are associated with overdrinking for them. The factors include day of the week, time of day, places where they drink, people with whom they drink, the presence of hunger and/or thirst, activities associated with drinking (e.g., watching TV), how much money or alcohol they have at their disposal, and the presence of various emotional states.

Once the antecedents to their overdrinking are established, clients can begin to make systematic changes in these situational factors. Strategies include:

1. Avoiding drinking altogether in the presence of a particular antecedent (e.g., after an argument with a spouse).
2. Limiting either the amount of time or money available for drinking.
3. Being aware that overdrinking is especially likely in particular situations and taking extra precautions at these times.
4. Finding alternative ways of coping with particular antecedents, such as anger or frustration.

Alternative Coping Skills

Drinking alcohol results in some positive consequences; otherwise, people would not drink. For some it may result in the achievement of positive mental states, while for others it may help them to avoid negative emotional or physical states. If drinking alcohol is the only way clients can achieve a need, then when they want to fulfill that need, drinking will occur. If, on the other hand, clients have alternative ways to satisfy that need, then the probability of drinking will decrease. Consequently this section deals with identifying the needs that drinking fulfills and developing alternative ways of satisfying those needs.

Many clients will be surprised to hear you say that drinking alcohol has some positive consequences. If you ask them to tell you the positive and desired effects of drinking, they can usually list two or three benefits of drinking. As they list these "desired effects," it is helpful to write them down on a blackboard under this heading. The most frequently cited effects are relaxation, getting a "buzz" on, and some type of disinhibition. After the group has spontaneously given you their list, query them further with the following list of desired effects; courage, avoidance, mood change, increased sociability, consciousness change, sleep, forgetting, and numbing. Next, make a list of the situations when the clients want these desired effects. Some examples include frustration over work, an argument with a spouse, and celebration of a baseball game win. When done, make a third list which notes the feelings the clients are having in these situations. Many of them will be negative feelings but some will be positive. Then start a final list labeled "Alternative Skill." Table 9.1 illustrates how your blackboard might look.

Have the clients brainstorm other ways they could achieve the desired effects without overdrinking. As they produce their own answers, you can also insert the acquisition of various skills, such as relaxation training or self-hypnosis, assertiveness training, systematic desensitization, mood management skills, and social skills training. Emphasize that the more options they have at their disposal to achieve a certain effect, the less likely they are to over-drink in those high risk situations.

In the section of the Miller and Muñoz (1984) self-help manual which deals with alternate skills, at the end of each chapter is a list of additional readings clients can use to develop alternate skills. It is also important to know how to do this training yourself in case a client wishes to do it with you. If you do not know how to conduct this training and do not wish to learn how to do it, then you will need to be knowledgeable about the other competent professionals in your community who do such training.

At this point we provide some training in relaxation skills. The clients are first given instruction in progressive muscle relaxation techniques (Benson, 1975), and are then given exposure to guided visual imagery. They are told that these are but two examples of relaxation techniques chosen from a wide variety.

These seven strategies constitute the course of treatment. Over time, however, we have added a relapse prevention component to the end of the program. The purpose of this is to help clients deal appropriately with relapses, which do occur. The essence of the message is that a relapse is an indication that a client needs to learn to cope more effectively with some antecedent to his or her overdrinking. Follow-ups at regular intervals also focus on relapse prevention. For a thorough discussion of relapse prevention, see chapter 11.

EFFECTIVENESS

The first evaluations of treatments aimed at a goal of moderation appeared in the early 1970s. Lovibond and Caddy (1970) evaluated a complex BSCT program which included actual

Table 9.1. Desired Effects of Alcohol

SITUATIONS	FEELINGS	DESIRED EFFECTS	ALTERNATIVE SKILLS
Fight with spouse	anger, frustration	escape	communication skills, problem solving skills
Frustation with boss	put down, powerless	courage, forgetting	assertiveness training

drinking by clients and electric shock aversion. Of 28 outpatients treated, 21 were reported to have achieved controlled drinking. A replication (Caddy & Lovibond, 1976) yielded somewhat more modest rates of success. Working with a drunk driver population, Lovibond found his moderation training program to be superior to an untreated control condition. Brown (1980) and Coghlan (1979) similarly found that a BSCT program, as compared with an alcohol education program, was significantly more effective in altering the drinking behavior of drunk driving offenders.

A second series of studies was conducted by Vogler and his colleagues. With 12-month follow-ups, Vogler reported rates of controlled drinking ranging from 21% to 68% (Vogler, Compton, & Weissbach, 1975; Vogler, Weissbach, & Compton, 1977; Vogler, Weissbach, Compton, & Martin, 1977). Comparable outcome results were reported by Alden (1978). Other evaluations reported similar outcomes when comparing BSCT procedures with alternative approaches (Hedberg & Campbell, 1974; Miller, 1978; Pomerleau, Pertschuk, Adkins, & d'Aquili, 1978).

The most publicized evaluation of self-control training procedures was conducted by Sobell and Sobell (1973). In a controlled evaluation with inpatient gamma alcoholics, they reported greater improvement in an experimental group receiving controlled drinking training than in three comparison groups in abstinence-focused treatment. The overall success of this treatment was questioned by Pendery, Maltzman, and West (1982), who conducted an independent review of the experimental cases. The controversy surrounding this study is complex (Marlatt, 1985; Sobell & Sobell, 1984). A fair conclusion, in our opinion, is that few of the alcoholics receiving experimental treatment sustained controlled drinking over an extended period, but that they fared no worse than those receiving standard abstinence-oriented treatment. This conclusion is consistent with the findings of a more recent study with a similar inpatient population (Foy, Nunn, & Rychtarik, 1984).

One of the best-designed studies of BSCT procedures was conducted by Sanchez-Craig (1980; Sanchez-Craig et al., 1984). Less severe problem drinkers were assigned at random to controlled drinking or abstinence goals, with both groups receiving outpatient BSCT. Sub-stantial improvement was documented at follow-up to 2 years in both groups, with no significant differences between groups over time. A small-scale replication by Graber and Miller (1987) similarly yielded no differences between groups assigned to abstinence versus moderation goals.

In a series of evaluations, Miller and his colleagues have evaluated alternative modes for offering BSCT to problem drinkers. Controlled comparisons have consistently found no significant differences in effectiveness between a self-administered form of BSCT (Miller & Muñoz, 1982) and a therapist-directed version of the same intervention, with clients in both conditions showing significant improvement at follow-ups to two years (Buck & Miller, 1981; Miller & Baca, 1983; Miller & Taylor, 1980; Miller, Gribskov & Mortell, 1981; Miller, Taylor, & West, 1980). Group and individual therapy formats for BSCT likewise seem to yield comparable results (Miller, Pechacek, & Hamburg, 1981; Miller et al., 1980). Longer-range follow-ups at 3–8 years reflected increasing proportions of clients becoming total abstainers, and a consistent 10–15% of treated outpatients sustaining moderate and problem-free drinking outcomes.

In summary, BSCT procedures have been extensively studied, and have been subjected to more controlled evaluations than any other treatment procedure in the alcoholism field. These studies collectively indicate that some problem drinkers do respond favorably to this approach, sustaining moderate and nonproblematic drinking over extended periods of time. Other clients, following BSCT with a moderation goal, opt for total abstinence, some with and some without additional treatment. When clients are assigned at random to treatment programs with abstinence or moderation goals, long-term results are consistently found to be comparable.

Our overall recommendation is that BSCT procedures should be available as one option among many within a treatment program wishing to serve a broad range of problem drinkers. Moderation-oriented BSCT is most likely to be attractive and effective for less severe problem drinkers. We do not recommend the promotion of a moderation goal with severely dependent alcoholics. BSCT procedures may, however, be useful in pursuing a goal of abstinence.

REFERENCES

Clinical Guidelines

Miller, W. R., & Muñoz, R. F. (1982). *How to control your drinking.* (Rev. ed.). Albuquerque, NM: University of New Mexico Press. This book describes a self-directed program of BSCT for problem drinkers. Its effectiveness has been tested in six studies, which indicate that clients working with minimal therapist supervision and using this manual fare as well, on average, as those receiving a therapist-directed BSCT program. Therapists can also learn the basic outline and procedures of BSCT by reviewing this manual.

Robertson, I., & Heather, N. (1986). *Let's drink to your health:* A self-help guide to sensible drinking. (Published by the British Psychological Society, St. Andrews House, 48 Princess Road East, Leicester, LEI 7DR, U.K.) This cleverly produced self-help manual combines practical information and BSCT techniques with cartoons, drawings, and fill-in boxes. Highly readable and briefer than most other manuals (127 pages + appendices), it is particularly appropriate for British audiences.

Sanchez-Craig, M. (1984). *Therapist's manual for secondary prevention of alcohol problems: Procedures for teaching moderate drinking and abstinence.* Toronto, Canada: Addiction Research Foundation. (May be purchased by writing to the Addiction Research Foundation Bookstore, 33 Russell Street, Toronto, Ontario, M58 2S1, Canada.) This therapist manual provides guidelines for conducting BSCT with either a goal of abstinence or a goal of moderation. Procedures are divided into preparatory, acquisition, and maintenance strategies. The appendices include practical forms, procedures and additional guidelines.

Vogler, R. E., & Bartz, W. R. (1982). *The better way to drink.* New York: Simon & Schuster. (Now available from New Harbinger Publications, 2200 Adeline, Suite 305, Oakland, CA 94607.) Another self-help manual, based on Roger Vogler's research in teaching moderation to problem drinkers.

Research

Alden, L. (1978). Evaluation of a preventive self-management programme for problem drinkers. *Canadian Journal of Behavioural Science, 10,* 258–263.

Benson, H. (1975). *The relaxation response.* New York: William Morrow & Co.

Brown, R. A. (1980). Conventional education and controlled drinking education courses with convicted drunken drivers. *Behavior Therapy, 11,* 632–642.

Buck, K. A., & Miller, W. R. (November, 1981). *Why does bibliotherapy work?* Paper presented at the annual meeting of the Association for Advancement of Behavior Therapy, Toronto.

Caddy, G. R., & Lovibond, S. H. (1974). Self-regulation and discriminated aversive condi-tioning in the modification of alcoholics' drinking behavior. *Behavior Therapy, 7,* 223–230.

Cahalan, D. (1987). *Understanding America's drinking problem: How to combat the hazards of alcohol.* San Francisco, CA: Jossey-Bass.

Coghlan, G. R. (1979). The investigation of behavioral self-control theory and techniques in a short-term treatment of male alcohol abusers. Unpublished doctoral dissertation, State University of New York at Albany, University Microfilms No. 7918818.

Elal-Lawrence, G. (1986). Predictors of outcome type in treated problem drinkers. *Journal of Studies on Alcohol, 47,* 41–47.

Foy, D. W., Nunn, B. L., & Rychtarik, R. G. (1984). Broad-spectrum behavioral treatment for chronic alcoholics: Effects of training controlled drinking skills. *Journal of Consulting and Clinical Psychology, 52,* 213–230.

Graber, R. A., & Miller, W. R. (1987). Abstinence and controlled drinking goals in behavioral self-control training of problem drinkers: A randomized clinical trial. Manuscript submitted for publication.

Heather, N., & Robertson, I. (1983). *Controlled Drinking.* London: Methuen.

Hedberg, A. G., & Campbell, L. M. (1974). A comparison of four behavioral treatment approaches to alcoholism. *Journal of Behavioral Therapy and Experimental Psychiatry, 5,* 251–256.

Lovibond, S. H., & Caddy, G. (1970). Discriminated aversive control in the moderation of alcoholics' drinking behavior. *Behavior Therapy, 1,* 437–444.

Mann, M. (1950). *Primer on alcoholism.* New York: Rinehart.

Marlatt, G. A. (1985). Controlled drinking: The controversy rages on. *American Psychologist, 40,* 374–375.

Miller, W. R. (1978). Behavioral treatment of problem drinkers: A comparative outcome study of three controlled drinking therapies. *Journal of Consulting and Clinical Psychology, 46,* 74–86.

Miller, W. R., & Baca, L. M. (1983). Two-year follow-up of bibliotherapy and therapist-directed controlled drinking training for problem drinkers. *Behavior Therapy, 14,* 441–448.

Miller, W. R., Gribskov, C. J., & Mortell, R. L. (1981). Effectiveness of a self-control manual for problem drinkers with and without therapist contact. *International Journal of the Addictions, 16,* 1247–1254.

Miller, W. R., & Hester, R. K. (1986a). Matching problem drinkers with optimal treatments. In W. R. Miller & N. Heather (Eds.) *Treating addictive behaviors: Processes of change* (pp. 175–204). New York: Plenum.

Miller, W. R., Leckman, A. L., Tinkcom, M., & Rubenstein, J. (1986). Long-term follow-up of controlled drinking therapies. Paper presented at the annual meeting of the American Psychological Association, Washington, DC.

Miller, W. R., & Muñoz, R. F. (1982). *How to control your drinking* (rev. ed.). Albuquerque, NM: University of New Mexico Press.

Miller, W. R., Pechacek, T. F., & Hamburg, S. (1981). Group behavior therapy for problem drinkers. *International Journal of the Addictions, 16,* 827–837.

Miller, W. R., & Taylor, C. A. (1980). Relative effectiveness of bibliotherapy, individual and group self-control training in the treatment of problem drinkers. *Addictive Behaviors, 5,* 13–24.

Miller, W. R., Taylor, C. A., & West, J. C. (1980). Focused versus broad-spectrum behavior therapy for problem drinkers. *Journal of Consulting and Clinical Psychology, 48,* 590–601.

Moore, M. H., & Gerstein, D. R. (Eds.) (1981). *Alcohol and public policy: Beyond the shadow of prohibition.* Washington, DC: National Academy Press.

Pendery, M. L., Maltzman, I. M., & West, L. J. (1982). Controlled drinking by alcoholics? New findings and a reevaluation of a major affirmative study. *Science, 217,* 169–175.

Pomerleau, O., Pertschuk, M., Adkins, D., & d'Aquili, E. (1978). Treatment for middle income problem drinkers. In P. E. Nathan, G. A. Marlatt, & T. Lorberg (Eds.), *Alcoholism: New directions in behavioral research and treatment* (pp. 143–160). New York: Plenum.

Sanchez-Craig, M. (1980). Random assignment to abstinence or controlled drinking in a cognitive-behavioral program: Short-term effects on drinking behavior. *Addictive Behavior, 5,* 35–39.

Sanchez-Craig, M., Annis, H. M., Bornet, A. R., & MacDonald, K. R. (1984). Random assignment to abstinence and controlled drinking: Evaluation of a cognitive–behavioural program for problem drinkers. *Journal of Consulting and Clinical Psychology, 52,* 390–403.

Saunders, J. B., & Aasland, O. G. (Eds.) (1987). *WHO collaborative project on identification and treatment of persons with harmful alcohol consumption: Report on phase I development of a screening instrument.* Geneva, Switzerland: World Health Organization.

Sobell, M. C., & Sobell, L. C. (1984). The aftermath of heresy: A response to Pendery et al.'s (1982) critique of "Individualized behavior therapy for alcoholics". *Behaviour Research and Therapy, 22,* 413–440.

Sobell, M. B., & Sobell, L. C. (1973). Individualized behavior therapy for alcoholics. *Behavior Therapy, 4,* 49–72.

Vogler, R. E., Compton, J. V., & Weissbach, T. A. (1975). Integrated beahvior change techniques for alcoholism. *Journal of Consulting and Clinical Psychology, 43,* 233–243.

Vogler, R. E., Weissbach, T. A., & Compton, J. V. (1977). Learning techniques for alcohol abuse. *Behaviour Research and Therapy, 15,* 31–38.

Vogler, R. E., Weissbach, T. A., Compton, J. V., & Martin, G. T. (1977). Integrated behavior change techniques for problem drinkers in the community. *Journal of Consulting and Clinical Psychology, 45,* 267–279.

PART IV

Additional Interventions

Abuse drinking often does not occur in isolation. Pre-existing deficits or difficulties may precipitate abusive drinking. Conversely, abusive drinking may result in significant life problems. The presence of problems associated with abusive drinking (e.g., unemployment or marital conflict) makes for a poorer prognosis only if they are not effectively addressed.

The interventions in this section provide a way for you to effectively address those problems which are often associated with alcohol abuse.

CHAPTER 10

Self-Help Groups

Barbara S. McCrady
Sadi Irvine

INTRODUCTION

People with pain or distress in their lives seek many routes to alleviate their troubles—they turn inward to their own personal resources, seek the help of family or friends, seek religion, study and acquire knowledge about their problems, seek the help of professionals, or seek the help of others with similar problems. This latter approach, termed self-help or mutual aid (Robinson, 1979), has become an increasingly common source of assistance. Self-help groups have proliferated for persons with a wide array of problems, such as family members of chronic mental patients, widows, and those with serious chronic medical problems.

The earliest of the contemporary self-help groups is Alcoholics Anonymous (AA). Founded in 1935 in Ohio, AA has become a large organization with groups throughout the world. Many persons involved with AA also become involved in other self-help programs for drug abuse, such as Narcotics Anonymous (NA), Cocaine Anonymous (CA), or Potsmokers Anonymous. Special self-help groups for professionals with alcohol and drug problems,

such as International Doctors in AA and the Caduceus groups, have developed.

AA and similar self-help groups have certain characteristics in common. All are voluntary groups, and many of the meetings are open to all who wish to attend. Anyone who expresses the desire to stop drinking (or using drugs) may become a member. There are different kinds of meetings, some emphasizing discussion of a particular topic, some with speakers. AA, NA, CA and similar self-help groups are called Twelve Step programs, because there are twelve defined steps in the program for recovery (described in detail below). AA meetings are held at many different locations, at many different times of the day and evening, and in virtually every city in the United States. There is a wide array of AA literature available, including books, pamphlets, and a monthly magazine, *The Grapevine*.

AA views alcoholism as a physical, mental, and spiritual disease, and sees lifelong abstinence as the only viable alternative. Members give each other strong support for abstinence and many ideas for how to cope with life's problems without alcohol, but there is also a healthy awareness that relapses are common, and no one is excluded from AA for having returned temporarily to drinking. AA views alcoholism as a spiritual illness, and drinking as a symptom of that illness. The central spiritual "defect" of alcoholics is described as an excessive preoccupation with self. Drinking is seen as leading to a physical and psychological illness. Treatment of the preoccupation with self is at the core of AA's approach. The AA program emphasizes abstinence, spirituality, and internal and interpersonal change as important aspects of the program.

The growth of AA has been paralleled by the growth of Alanon, for adult family members and friends of alcoholics, and Alateen and Alatot, for children with alcoholic parents. More recently, Alafam groups for alcoholic families have begun to appear. All of these groups focus on helping family members cope when they have an alcoholic family member. A recent phenomenon has been the development of groups for adults who grew up with an alcoholic parent. These Adult Children of Alcoholics (ACOA) groups are intended to help these adults understand the effects their childhood experience had on their current functioning, and to enable change in maladaptive patterns of behavior believed to be caused by growing up in an alcoholic family.

In addition to these well-known self-help groups, two other self-help approaches to drinking problems should be noted. Drinkwatchers, modeled closely after Weight Watchers, is designed to help people with drinking problems cut down and moderate their alcohol intake. It is more active in European than North American countries. Women for Sobriety is a self-help group for women with drinking problems. The program emphasizes abstinence from alcohol and focuses on problems often experienced by women with drinking problems, such as low self-esteem and difficulties in assertiveness and independence.

In this chapter, we have chosen to focus on AA rather than on the other self-help groups described above. We selected this focus because there is some empirical literature related to the functioning and effectiveness of AA, while there is very little for the other groups. Also, AA has provided the prototype for many of the related self-help groups, and we believe that understanding the functioning of AA and ways that the practitioner can use AA will provide sufficient information to allow a similar understanding of the other self-help groups.

SPECIAL CONSIDERATIONS

In this section, we will discuss the characteristics of patients most likely to be successful in affiliating with AA. The current practice of many clinicians is to refer most or all alcoholic patients to AA. It is not at all clear that this is the optimal procedure, since it has not been established which problem drinkers will benefit from what AA has to offer. The notion that there may be certain individual characteristics associated with successful affiliation with a particular treatment intervention is not new, but clear data to inform treatment matching decisions are lacking. If it were possible to determine what characteristics differentiated potential AA affiliates from non-affiliates, clinicians would be better able to match patients to the most appropriate treatment, thereby increasing their chances of successful recovery.

There are a number of conceptual and methodological problems which surface when attempting to identify characteristics of successful AA affiliates. There is a lack of a consistent definition of what is meant by affiliation. Affiliation may be defined as attending a certain number of AA meetings; joining an AA group; maintaining involvement over a certain length of time; or self-defined AA involvement. Affiliation may not imply successful recovery. Individual characteristics that have been investigated are as varied as the researchers performing the studies. Personality characteristics, as a popular target, differ according to whether the researcher adopts a psychodynamic, social learning, conditioning, or other model of personality development. Ogborne and Glaser (1981) outlined the personality factors that have been considered, including ego strength, identification with mother, dependency needs, locus of control, and the ability to function within groups. Other investigators have considered perceptual and cognitive variables, attitudes, beliefs, values, drinking histories, and degree of impairment in the search for identifiable characteristics of AA affiliates (Fontana, Dowds, & Bethel, 1976; Karp, Witkin, & Goodenough, 1965; Ogborne & Glaser, 1981; Trice, 1957).

In addition to definitional and conceptual problems, there is a lack of valid measures being used to assess the characteristics under investigation. Other problems have resulted from the samples used, which often are not representative of the AA population.

Another set of design problems is related to AA research in general. It is very difficult to randomly assign, perform pre- and post-test measurements on, and follow up members of AA, due to the program's policy of protecting the anonymity of its members. Pre- and post-testing of variables is also arduous if not impossible, since AA membership is not likely to coincide with the beginning and end of formal treatment interventions.

In spite of the many methodological problems, there are some studies which have gathered data relating to well-defined constructs and measured by valid instruments. Using an all male VA sample, O'Leary, Calsyn, Haddock, and Freeman (1980) designed a study to isolate the personality, psychopathology, and drinking behavior correlates associated with successful AA affiliation. They defined affiliation in terms of frequency of AA attendance prior to admission, and developed subcategories of non, low and high affiliation based upon the frequency counts. The Alcohol Use Inventory (AUI) was used to assess drinking chronicity. The Clinical Analysis Questionnaire (CAQ) was employed to assess personality traits and psychopathology. The sample consisted of 76 male veterans from an inpatient alcoholism treatment program. The results indicated that high levels of affiliation were associated with significant differences in the anticipated gains, style, and consequences of alcohol use. High affiliates also reported more anxiety, greater physical, psychological, and social decline, and being more strongly influenced by feelings than by intellect. While there are some biases in the sample, the overall quality of the methodology exceeds many other attempts to identify individual characteristics associated with AA affiliation.

In another descriptive study, Giannetti (1981) collected data from 130 inpatient and outpatient male alcoholics. The purpose of the study was to determine whether there was a relationship between AA affiliation, length of affiliation, and five factors: purpose in life, alienation, locus of control, severity of drinking problem, and socioeconomic status. Five standardized scales were used to measure these factors. Expectations regarding the outcome of treatment were also measured. Global rating scales were used to determine outcome expectations. Although this was not a predictive study, the results showed that AA affiliates displayed a greater purpose in life, held more positive treatment outcome expectations, and showed evidence of a more internal locus of control than non-affiliates. Both internal locus of control and purpose in life increased with longer affiliation with AA. It is not clear if these factors developed as a result of AA involvement or were predictive of successful AA affiliation. Although there were some sampling problems in this study, the measures used were standardized and both affiliation and the constructs being measured were well defined.

In a recent, comprehensive review of the AA literature, Emrick (1987) noted that most demographic variables, characteristics of alcoholism, and mental health variables appeared unrelated to successful AA affiliation across the 10 studies published since 1976 that he summarized. He noted that the data suggest a tendency for older alcoholics to be more likely to become AA members than younger alcoholics, and that certain other characteristics, such as dual addiction to alcohol and other drugs, use of external supports to stop drinking, and warmth of childhood environment were consistently related to successful affiliation in the few studies which examined these particular variables.

In summary, the research to date provides few definitive guidelines for the clinician. Severity of drinking, an affective rather than cognitive focus, and concern about purpose and meaning in life may be client factors that should lead the clinician to be most encouraging of AA involvement. Other variables which as yet have little empirical support include: better social interpersonal skills, limited social support network for abstinence, and high need for affiliation.

Prospective research studies are needed to facilitate prediction of clients most likely to affiliate successfully with AA. With increasing interest in matching patients to treatment, it seems that further research to identify the distinguishing characteristics of AA affiliates is important.

DESCRIPTION OF AA

In these next sections, we will describe AA and then turn to a discussion of how to integrate AA with clinical practice. Although there are many descriptions of AA available to the clinician, there have been fewer attempts to address how AA and clinical practice, especially behaviorally oriented clinical practice, could be integrated.

Table 10.1. The Twelve Traditions of Alcoholics Anonymous

Tradition 1	Our common welfare should come first—personal recovery depends upon AA unity.
Tradition 2	For our group purpose there is but one ultimate authority—a loving God as he may express Himself in our group conscience. Our leaders are but trusted servants; they do not govern.
Tradition 3	The only requirment for AA membership is a desire to stop drinking.
Tradition 4	Each group should be autonomous except in matters affecting other groups or AA as a whole.
Tradition 5	Each group has but one primary purpose—to carry its message to the alcoholic who still suffers.
Tradition 6	An AA group ought never endorse, finance or lend the AA name to any related facility or outside enterprise, lest problems of money, property and prestige divert us from our primary purpose.
Tradition 7	Every AA group ought to be fully self supporting, declining outside contributions.
Tradition 8	Alcoholics Anonymous should remain forever nonprofessional, but our service centers may employ special workers.
Tradition 9	AA, as such, ought never be organized; but we may create service boards or committees directly responsible to those they serve.
Tradition 10	Alcoholics Anonymous has no opinion on outside issues; hence the AA name ought never be drawn into public controversy.
Tradition 11	Our public relations policy is based on attraction rather than promotion: we need always maintain personal anonymity at the level of press, radio and films.
Tradition 12	Anonymity is the spiritual foundation of our traditions, ever reminding us to place principles before personalities.

AA Organization and Principles

If one were to travel around the United States and visit any of the 36,000 Alcoholics Anonymous (AA) meetings, one would encounter some potentially confusing differences. The reason for this is that while there are underlying principles and traditions that hold AA together as a whole, the individual group functions to meet the needs of its members. For this reason, the format and content of each meeting is slightly different, and meetings in different parts of the country may vary significantly. In this section, we will outline some of the similarities and differences among meetings in order to provide a better understanding of the AA group experience. We will then expand our view of AA to include the overall structure of the fellowship as a worldwide service organization.

There are twelve traditions, which are intended to preserve the integrity of the AA program. The fourth AA tradition states that every group is autonomous (see Table 10.1); therefore, a group is free to hold almost any kind of meeting it chooses. However, in general, there are two basic types of AA meetings,

which differ according to who is permitted to attend. *Open* meetings are available to any interested person, regardless of whether or not he or she has a drinking problem. *Closed* meetings are open only to AA members or to people who would like to do something about their drinking. Whenever two or more alcoholics meet together for the purpose of sobriety and are self-supporting and without outside affiliation, they may call themselves an AA group.

When a group is first formed, the members decide whether they would like to have a closed or open meeting and what the format of the meeting should be. Many open meetings choose to have one or more speakers address the group, rather than adopting an interactive format. These AA members may be visitors from another group who are part of a speaker exchange program, referred to as a commitment, or may be a member of the group holding the meeting. These speakers tell the audience what they were like before they stopped drinking, what happened to bring them to AA, and what they are like in recovery. One of the advantages of an open "speaker" meeting is that the newcomer or visitor usually is not asked to speak or even to introduce himself or herself formally as an alcoholic, a sometimes uncomfortable event.

Closed meetings are generally smaller, and each member is more visible to the group as a whole. These meetings are more often "discussion" meetings, which include as many members as possible in active discussion on some chosen topic. The topic may be selected by the chairperson at the beginning of the meeting; or, in the case of step and tradition meetings, the subject of the discussion is one of the twelve steps or twelve traditions. Another type of meeting combines these two formats by having the speaker lead the group in a discussion after the presentation of his or her "story." In recent years there has been an increase in the number of meetings for special populations, including: men, women, alcoholic couples, gays, lesbians, and mentally ill alcoholics. Special beginners meetings are available, which are intended to address the questions and concerns of newcomers.

Taking all of these differences into account, there are certain characteristics of a typical AA meeting which can be found in most meetings. The following is a description of what may transpire during an AA meeting, but the reader should keep in mind that the details may differ according to individual meetings and geographical location. A meeting is usually preceded by a period of social interaction when those who have arrived early greet each other and introduce any new member or visitor. When the meeting time arrives, the chairperson calls it to order and introduces himself or herself to the group by first name and as an alcoholic. After welcoming all members and visitors, some segments may be read from the book *Alcoholics Anonymous* (AA World Services, 1980), which is commonly known as the "Big Book." These might include the AA Preamble, the Twelve Steps, the Twelve Traditions, or the Twelve Promises of AA. At this point, the group's officers are asked to report any AA relevant information, which ranges from announcements about upcoming AA social functions to financial reports. General announcements from the floor are also invited, as well as introductions from anyone who is new or coming back to AA following a relapse. Anniversaries recognizing months or years of continual sobriety in AA are celebrated according to the custom of the group. The celebrant receives a medallion which indicates the length of time that person has abstained from alcohol.

Following a reminder about the importance of anonymity, the meeting begins with the introduction of speakers or discussion leaders. AA meetings often open with the group recitation of a prayer and might close with all present standing, holding hands, and saying the Lord's Prayer.

A very important part of the AA experience is sponsorship. While anyone who wants to stop drinking can join AA, choosing a sponsor as soon as possible is encouraged as a means of maintaining sobriety. The process of sponsorship involves two alcoholics, one of whom has made more progress in recovery and who shares that experience in an ongoing manner with another who is trying to achieve or maintain sobriety. Some groups offer a temporary sponsor program, which matches a newcomer with someone until they are able to meet enough members to make their own choice. The important factor is that a newcomer not be left to flounder without introduction to the program and to each new aspect of recovery as it is experienced for the first time.

Although there are a few basic suggestions which accompany the choice and use of a sponsor, it is up to the individual to establish and maintain the relationship. It is suggested that a sponsor should be of the same gender as the person being sponsored and that he or she be contacted as often as needed. For example, if a person is having an urge to drink or is feeling lonely or sad, he or she is encouraged not to try to "go it alone" but to call the sponsor for help in responding to these feelings. However, it is not just the sponsor who supports the newcomer's sobriety but the entire AA program. In fact, excessive dependence upon a sponsor, or upon any single individual, is seen as a barrier to developing the skills necessary to make decisions and achieve personal independence. Sponsors help with an assortment of problems—ranging from how to stay away from the first drink to what to do if a relapse occurs to how to work the twelve steps of the program and cope with the daily problems of living.

Most groups have officers who fulfill the roles of chairperson, secretary, treasurer, *Grapevine* representative, intergroup representative, and general service representative. Not all groups feel the need to fill all of these positions. Some might decide to elect a special institutions representative, a steering committee, and a hospitality committee. Every officer serves the group for a period of time established by its members, and when his or her term is completed another member takes over the responsibilities. Rotating officers is an important part of the AA program, since it avoids the potential problem of any person or persons gaining too much power and offers more people the opportunity to serve.

The ninth tradition of AA states that "AA as such ought never be organized; but may create service boards or committees directly responsible to those they serve" (Twelve Steps and Twelve Traditions, 1978, p. 172). In 1950, the founders of AA developed a system which was called the conference plan. It was intended to serve not as a legislative body but as the guardian of AA tradition and as a means for carrying out service affairs.

The structure of the conference plan begins at the group level and branches out through the use of elected officials to represent the entire AA "conscience" at an annual General Service Conference. The conscience of AA is an important concept and refers to AA's efforts to base all decisions and actions upon input from its members. Each group that wishes to have its voice heard by AA as a whole elects a general service representative (GSR). The main functions of this officer are to serve as the link between the individual group and AA as a collective entity, and to elect the district committee member (DCM). Approximately once every two years, the GSRs and the DCMs convene for an area assembly in order to elect a delegate who will represent the area at the annual Conference meeting in New York. The officers at each level also have many responsibilities and obligations other than the election of officers.

The purpose of the General Service Conference is to supply the means for the collective group conscience to be heard and to influence the execution of worldwide AA services. Some of the decisions made at this conference include: the approval of AA literature; the establishment of guidelines for the maintenance of anonymity at the level of press, television, and films; and the approval of General Service Board nominees. All delegates have a voice at the Conference and can take the floor on any issue raised.

The General Service Board (GSB) of AA is composed of alcoholic and nonalcoholic trustees who serve as the primary service tool of the Conference. Their duties are basically custodial in nature, and while they may not make decisions which could affect AA as a whole, they are involved in all matters of policy and business matters within the AA service enterprise. The Conference defined the Board as "an agency created and now designated by the Fellowship of Alcoholics Anonymous to maintain services for those who should be seeking, through Alcoholics Anonymous, the means for arresting the disease of alcoholism" (The AA Service Manual, 1982, p. 89).

The Twelve Traditions

The major function of all officers from the General Service Representative to members of the General Service Board is to uphold the Twelve Traditions of AA. We have already referred to three of the twelve traditions in the discussion about the AA structure. These included: tradition three, which states who can be a member; tradition four, which asserts the autonomy of each group; and tradition nine, which deems that AA ought never be organized, in the sense that no one has authority or can govern. The remaining traditions are important to review, since AA's success in remaining in existence is often attributed to its continued adherence to these traditions.

The first tradition emphasizes that AA must put the common welfare of AA as a whole before the welfare of the individual (see Table 10.1 for a listing of the Twelve Traditions). This first tradition views AA unity as the foundation of personal recovery. Tradition two addresses the question of who is in charge of the AA group. The fifth tradition states the primary purpose of each AA group, which is to "carry its message to the alcoholic who still suffers" (AA World Services, 1978, p. 150). In order to insure that AA can carry out this purpose, tradition six addresses "money, power and prestige" (Twelve Steps and Twelve Traditions, 1978, p. 155) as those barriers which may prevent this "spiritual aim" from being realized. This is the reason why the sixth tradition maintains that an AA group should never affiliate itself with any outside organization. The seventh tradition indicates that AA should attempt to avoid any disputes over money, which might also divert AA from its primary purpose of helping the suffering alcoholic. Groups are therefore self-supporting, declining any contributions from sources outside of AA, and it is recommended that groups not accumulate money in their treasuries.

Tradition eight is related to traditions two and nine, which address the issue of how AA can interact with outside organizations without affiliating with them and exploiting the AA name. An important implication of this tradition is that AA members are never to receive payment for doing twelfth step work, which is helping another alcoholic within the AA context. (See below for further descriptions of the AA Twelve Steps.)

The ninth tradition, which stipulates that AA ought never be organized, is directed to the common practice of many other organizations to inflict rules, dues, directives, and punishments on its members. In contrast, no one can decide that someone is not practicing the AA program correctly and should not be allowed to return, nor can any group be told how to function. AA's willingness to allow each member and group to follow or not follow the AA suggestions is founded upon the faith that the AA program works and those who choose not to adhere to its principles are likely to fail. With this knowledge, most AA members and groups approximately conform to the AA traditions and principles.

It is believed that if AA were to become involved in any outside issue, its members might begin to use AA for their own purposes rather than for purposes of AA unity. Therefore, the tenth tradition protects AA unity by sanctioning against its involvement in external affairs.

The eleventh tradition is concerned with public relations policy for AA. AA is willing to publicize its "principles and its work, but not its individual members." From a practical standpoint, if an individual breaks his or her anonymity and is seen as a spokesperson for AA, the entire fellowship may be damaged by the actions of one member. However, AA is quick to point out that anonymity is not only a public relations issue but also a spiritual principle; it discourages personal ambition and self-seeking, which are viewed as deadly to the alcoholic and to AA as a whole.

This brings us to the final tradition, which considers anonymity to be a spiritual concept, which is perpetuated by the willingness of AA members to "give up personal desires for the common good" (*Twelve Steps and Twelve Traditions*, 1978, p. 184). This is a continuing theme throughout the AA principles and steps; it is of critical importance that recovering alcoholics shift their focus from self to others.

The Twelve Steps

The twelve steps of AA are the foundation of the program. Unfortunately, they are often overlooked or referred to in passing, despite the crucial role they play in the acquisition and maintenance of sobriety. Several researchers have offered their interpretation of the steps (Bean, 1975; Brown, 1985) as has AA (Alcoholics Anonymous World Services, 1978), and all differ greatly, depending on the orientation of the author.

Bean supplies a translation of the twelve steps into "psychotherapeutic terms," which emphasizes the breakdown and abandonment of denial, the abdication of personal responsibility and the adoption of a dependency position, "catharsis and confession, penance and undoing" (Bean, 1985, p. 10), the adoption of a new self-image, and the rechanneling of energy through the recruitment of new members.

A different perspective is provided by Brown (1985) in her effort to provide a psychological view of the twelve steps of AA. She emphasizes the twelve steps and the AA program as related to the alcoholic's need to continually reaffirm his or her lack of control over alcohol and need for help from others. This ongoing process begins with the first step through which the alcoholic admits to his or her powerlessness over alcohol. She sees the second step as giving the alcoholic something on which to become dependent, a Higher Power; according to Brown (1985), this dependency is fostered throughout the remaining ten steps. Brown speaks repeatedly of the numerous paradoxes built into the AA program and the twelve steps. The most evident paradox is that becoming dependent upon a "power greater than oneself" enables the alcoholic greater independence from an "ego-centered position in the world." AA as a whole accepts and supports this notion of powerlessness over alcohol, which is seen as a strength rather than weakness.

The Alcoholics Anonymous World Services publishes a book whose purpose is to provide an interpretation of the twelve steps. This book is often used at AA step meetings where a portion or the entire step is read and discussed by the group. Chapters five through seven of the AA "Big Book" (AA World Services, 1980) also provide a practical description of how to implement the steps. The steps are seen as necessary tools to be used by each AA member in the process of recovery. AA offers a developmental model of recovery, which allows for individual differences in when each step is taken. It is suggested that new members start at step one and proceed sequentially and at their own pace through the remaining steps. AA is considered to be a lifetime commitment. At the risk of being too simplistic, the following is a brief outline of the twelve steps as reflected in the AA literature. The twelve steps are outlined in Table 10.2.

Step one is seen as the necessary foundation of the remaining steps, as the AA member admits to complete defeat as far as alcohol was concerned. The notion that alcohol can be overcome by sheer will must be abandoned in order for recovery to begin. The second step is taken when one acknowledges that he or she is not the center of the universe and that there is a power greater than self. This step requires that the AA member acknowledge the fact that life with alcohol is not sane but wrought with mental obsessions, physical maladies, and spiritual deprivation. AA sees the major problem with alcoholics as one of selfishness and obsession with self, a condition which in the organization's view can only be remedied by turning outside of oneself.

The third step requires a decision on the part of the individual. Although the term "God" is often used in AA, there is no prescription as to how one must conceive of his or her Higher Power. AA members are told that if taken "honestly and humbly," the effects of this spiritual step may be felt at once. The notion of complete dependence upon a Higher Power is the major impact of step three. Reliance upon God as each member understands Him in all aspects of daily life is an immense goal, which often begins piecemeal. At this stage of recovery, a new member may be willing to turn his or her drinking over to a Higher Power but not be willing to turn over other aspects of his or her life. These steps have no time limit in which they must be taken, and the amount of time spent varies among individuals. Many AA members make a point of reviewing the steps and attending step meetings throughout their recovery in order to avoid falling back into the cycle of self-absorption and drinking.

Steps four and five involve the implementation of extensive introspective and self-evaluative processes, followed by the disclosure to another person of all that has been uncovered. AA sees alcohol as a symptom of the alcoholic's warped perception of "self," which has a number of cognitive and behavioral manifestations. AA literature (AA World Services, 1980) states that in order for the alcoholic to be free from the compulsion to drink, these underlying "causes and conditions" must be eliminated. For example, resentment is defined as a spiritual malady which, if overcome, will be followed by improvement in the physical and mental realms.

Table 10.2. The Twelve Steps of Alcoholics Anonymous

Step 1	We admitted we were powerless over alcohol—that our lives had become unmanageable.
Step 2	Came to believe that a Power greater than ourselves could restore us to sanity.
Step 3	Made a decision to turn our will and our lives over to the care of God *as we understood Him.*
Step 4	Made a searching and fearless moral inventory of ourselves.
Step 5	Admitted to God, to ourselves and to another human being the exact nature of our wrongs.
Step 6	Were entirely ready to have God remove all these defects of character.
Step 7	Humbly asked Him to remove our shortcomings.
Step 8	Made a list of all persons we had harmed, and became willing to make amends to them all.
Step 9	Made direct amends to such people wherever possible, except when to do so would injure them or others.
Step 10	Continued to take personal inventory and when we were wrong promptly admitted it.
Step 11	Sought through prayer and meditation to improve our conscious contact with God *as we understood Him,* praying only for knowledge of his will for us and the power to carry that out.
Step 12	Having had a spiritual awakening as the result of these steps, we tried to carry this message to alcoholics and to practice these principles in all our affairs.

As a method for taking the fourth step, it is suggested that the alcoholic review his or her life and list the "people, institutions and principles" against which resentments are being held. The purpose of this inventory lies in the discovery that one is responsible for himself or herself, and that the actions of others cannot be used as excuses for resentment, wrongdoing, or drinking. The focus turns to what mistakes the alcoholic made, rather than how he or she was wronged by the rest of the world.

Step five offers the opportunity for the AA member to reinforce the notion that the alcoholic cannot live in a vacuum. AA stresses that the alcoholic who insists on keeping the contents of step four a secret will have grave difficulty maintaining sobriety. The *Twelve Steps and Twelve Traditions* (AA World Services, 1978) refers to the chronic physical and emotional isolation of the active alcoholic and how this can be alleviated by sharing one's worst with another human being. Step five is also seen as a vehicle for allowing the AA member to forgive himself or herself, in addition to the ability to forgive others which was fostered by step four.

Steps six and seven involve the relinquishment, not of responsibility but of control over the "character defects" uncovered in step four. The sixth step refers to the beginning of a lifelong process of spiritual growth. Being ready and open to God's intervention in the removal of the defects that have contributed to past drunkenness requires a spiritual state of willingness. Step seven emphasizes the importance of humility in maintaining sobriety. Humility is defined in spiritual terms, as a reliance upon God as the source of power through which shortcomings can be resolved. The seventh step broadens the perception of powerlessness over alcohol, introduced in step one, to point out the powerlessness of the alcoholic over other problems as well.

The next two steps require that the AA member examine and take action in his or her interpersonal relationships. The eighth step calls for a retrospective examination of one's relationships to determine where one has been at fault. An actual list of persons and situations is constructed, and a willingness to make every effort to correct any wrongdoing is expressed.

The ninth step asks the alcoholic to make every effort to repair the damage which he or she had done to others. This step is not to be interpreted as an attempt to apologize to the wronged parties; it is concerned with making amends and restitution where possible. The AA literature emphasizes that the alcoholic has apologized innumerable times over the years without instituting any actual change. Steps eight and nine demand changes in attitudes and behavior. The AA member is cautioned against unburdening his or her own guilt over some previous action at the expense of another's well-being.

The tenth step encourages the AA member to make daily use of the new way of life established in the first nine steps. Now that measures have been taken to assess character defects, past mistakes and make amends, it is necessary to maintain the associated gains by practicing a daily inventory of attitudes and behaviors. Step ten is seen as a practical means for avoiding a slip back into destructive thinking patterns and drinking.

Step eleven is also concerned with the maintenance of sobriety. Anticipating that the recovering alcoholic might begin to neglect prayer and meditation once his or her life begins to be more satisfying, this step is a reminder of the source of that satisfaction. It also provides guidance about the most effective way to pray, by suggesting that AA members avoid selfish requests and focus instead upon understanding God's will in every situation. This step is related to step three which asks that the alcoholic turn his or her will and life over to the care of God. Both steps serve to counteract the alcoholic's tendency to insist that he or she needs no one, and to foster a dependence upon a Higher Power.

Step twelve states the goal of steps one through eleven. A spiritual awakening is "the result," not an accidental byproduct of following the suggestions of the steps. A spiritual awakening is defined by AA as "a new consciousness and being" (AA World Services, 1978, p. 107). In this new state of awareness, the alcoholic finds meaning and purpose in life where before there was none. This sense of purpose is given an outlet by the portion of the step which encourages the AA member to take the AA message to other alcoholics. This is seen as crucial in maintaining sobriety, and the sentiment is often heard in AA meetings as "you can't keep it unless you give it away." The final suggestion of this step is that the principles acquired by practicing the steps should be practiced in all portions of one's life, and not be limited to contact with AA.

INTEGRATING AA WITH PROFESSIONAL PRACTICE

In the previous section, we described the principles and structure of AA in some detail. In this section, we will consider how the professional practitioner can integrate AA with clinical practice. While some people with drinking problems seek out AA as their primary source of assistance, never using the services of a clinical professional, for this book it is most important to consider how the clinical professional can integrate AA with professional practice. Since the focus of most of the other chapters in this volume is on behavioral approaches to treatment, some serious consideration of the similarities and differences between behavioral approaches and AA is essential.

Theoretical Issues

The differences between AA and behavioral approaches are most apparent at the theoretical level. AA assumes that alcoholism is one disease, with a common set of symptoms, a common genetic basis, and a predictable course. As a progressive disease, cure is not possible, only arrest of the disease. Phenomena such as loss of control and craving are seen as inevitable. As with pregnancy, a person cannot be "a little bit" alcoholic—a person either does or does not have the disease. Thus, the treatment is the same for all—lifelong abstinence and adherence to the AA program. AA focuses on acceptance of the disease, recognizing and dealing with denial, and reliance on others or a Higher Power in order to recover. As an alcoholic remains involved with AA, he or she will learn new ways to respond to situations where alcohol is present, will learn ways to cope with stress and stressful emotions, and will learn to develop healthier relationships with others. The AA program emphasizes acceptance of personal responsibility for one's beliefs, attitudes, and behaviors, while at the same time acknowledging the need for support from others and from a Higher Power.

Behavioral models, while diverse, hold certain assumptions in common that are distinguishable from AA's perspective. Persons may have a diversity of kinds of alcohol problems, with different symptoms and patterns and different underlying etiologies. Some kinds of alcohol problems may have a genetic etiology; others are environmentally based. Thus, de-

pending on the type of problem presented, different treatment goals and methods should be considered. Moderated drinking is seen as a viable goal for certain clients. Loss of control and craving are understood as learned phenomena, although there is disagreement about the underlying learning mechanisms. Treatments vary, and may include stimulus control and consequence control techniques; behavioral skills training to develop skills in refusing drinks, assertiveness, relaxation, or problem solving; and behavioral marital therapy. Some behavioral treatments focus on the classically conditioned aspects of the alcoholic's response to alcohol, and use aversive conditioning or cue exposure and response prevention techniques. Personal control over change and rational decisionmaking are important aspects of treatment.

Common Features of AA and Behavior Therapy

Given the substantial theoretical disagreements between these approaches, how could they possibly be integrated? At the clinical level, there are many more common features than would be expected from a theoretical perspective. However, integration is only possible when treatment is oriented toward abstinence as a goal. AA and behavior therapy are *not* compatible if behavior therapy is directed toward moderated drinking. Even though many members of AA do drink on occasion, the explicit goal is abstinence, and attempts to integrate the approaches with a goal of moderate drinking are probaby futile and confusing for the patient.

Common aspects of the approaches are apparent when considering the role of skills acquisition, affective change, cognitive changes, and use of social supports. At the skills level, both approaches emphasize avoiding drinking environments, developing interests and activities incompatible with drinking, developing skills to use in situations where alcohol is present, and having clearly defined behaviors to draw upon when experiencing a desire to drink. Both approaches emphasize behavior change as preceding cognitive or affective changes (AA uses the expression "fake it until you make it" to convey this concept). Both approaches also consider how to respond to relapses, and neither suggests that relapses indicate a failure of the treatment.

At the affective level, both recognize that negative feelings are a common experience for people who are trying to stop drinking. Both stress that negative affect does not have to become a reason to drink, and that active coping strategies can be used to change or cope with negative feelings.

Cognitive changes are similar in some areas. Both perspectives break down treatment into small steps, and emphasize gradual change (AA advises "don't drink and go to meetings"; a behavioral therapist might advise working on only one problem area at a time). Both also stress the importance of developing a long-term perspective on drinking which incorporates an awareness of the negative consequences, and using this long-term perspective in situations which present a temptation to drink. Both also emphasize the lack of personal responsibility for having developed a drinking problem, although the explanations for etiology are different; both also emphasize personal responsibility for change. AA emphasizes personal powerlessness over alcohol and other people, places, and things, but does not advocate a sense of powerlessness over one's self or one's own actions; similarly, behavioral approaches emphasize personal control but also stress the lack of control that an individual has over others.

Social supports are important to both perspectives. Behavioral approaches emphasize improving marital and family relationships through communication training and relationship enhancement, and also help clients develop effective social skills to be able to access social networks incompatible with drinking. AA does not use formal skills training but provides a social support network of others who are trying not to drink. Relationships with others are an important topic of discussion at AA meetings. However, each family member is encouraged to be involved with their own, separate program of recovery, rather than working on recovery conjointly.

Thus, on the important level of practice, the two approaches have many common goals and some common methods, such as stimulus control, consequence control, and formal or informal covert sensitization. However, many of the methods are different, and the tenor and tone of the treatments are different. AA is a program in which faith, total belief in the program, intense feelings, personal honesty, and closeness to others are central to the experience of the program. This tends to lead to a sense that AA is the only way to recover from alcohol problems. Behavioral approaches tend to explain, teach, and introduce logic to an illogical situation. Behavioral therapists tend to rely on a variety of techniques and approaches to facilitate recovery. Intensity of feeling, passionate belief, and utter commitment to the behavior therapist are rare.

Practice Issues

If the therapist is working toward an abstinence goal with a client, use of AA as a component of the therapy should be considered. AA provides a readily accessible and free support system, and AA members are available to help the alcoholic at any hour, an accessibility that most therapists cannot provide to their clients. In this section, we will discuss some techniques for integrating AA with behavioral treatment. Since there are no empirical studies that guide the methods that a therapist should use in facilitating AA involvement for a client, our proposals here must be viewed as tentative.

Before referring a client to AA, the therapist should develop familiarity with the organization. The therapist should attend some AA meetings and read some of the basic literature, such as *Alcoholics Anonymous* (often called the "Big Book") (AA World Services, 1960) and *Twelve Steps and Twelve Traditions* (AA World Services, 1978). Familiarity with the pamphlets and the *AA Grapevine* is also desirable. The therapist should be aware of the different types of meetings, what the twelve steps are, what a sponsor is, and how a client obtains a sponsor. Familiarity with common terms used in AA is also important, such as "pigeon," "commitment," "easy does it," "higher power," "twelfth step call," and so forth.

When the therapist decides to introduce AA involvement to the client, he or she should provide a clear rationale for involvement. We emphasize that AA is a place where the client can meet others who have had similar problems and experiences, who will be supportive and helpful in sharing their own experiences. We also emphasize that therapy is a time-limited, place-limited proposition, and that AA provides a support system that is available throughout the country and for as long as the client decides to use it. We also emphasize the sense of meaning, the friendships, closeness, and fun that many people experience in AA, and the success that many have had in using the AA program.

Clients often have questions or negative reactions when AA is first suggested. Common reactions include: concern that AA is for deteriorated, skid-row alcoholics, belief that their drinking problem is not "that bad," concern about "religious" aspects of the program, feeling that they can do it on their own, a belief that many people who go to AA are hypocritical because they go to meetings and then drink, or a belief that AA is ineffective because of personal knowledge of someone who relapsed while involved with AA.

These concerns can be addressed in several ways. We emphasize that there is diversity in AA membership, ranging from professionals to economically disadvantaged persons. Meetings vary, and the client is helped to find meetings with members similar in age, sex, and socioeconomic group, as well as meetings with AA members who have been abstinent for a long time. We also emphasize that people have different degrees of severity of alcohol problems, and sometimes review some of the reasons that the client decided to seek treatment and stop drinking. Concerns about religious aspects of the program are common. While AA uses the term "higher power" as well as "God as you understand Him," many experience AA as being closely allied to traditional Christian beliefs. We explain that the emphasis on a "Higher Power" is asking the AA member to rely on something outside of him or herself, recognizing and accepting that change is impossible in a personal vacuum which allows no one else to be involved.

Finally, we address the concerns about success in AA and alternate routes to change. Clearly, many people are successful without AA, many are not successful with AA (see discussion of effectiveness below), and many attend because they have been forced to do so. However, we note that people who remain involved with AA on a long-term basis have a very good chance for continued success, and that the client can affiliate with these successful members. Finally, the most important message we give is that the client try it. In behavioral treatment, there are many new behaviors clients try that feel awkward or unfamiliar, and we are accustomed to encouraging clients to try out and practice new behaviors enough for the behavior to become familiar and comfortable.

AA involvement is treated like other new therapy behaviors in this way.

To facilitate involvement, the therapist can have several tools available. AA meeting books which list the days, times, locations, and types of AA meetings in a particular area are essential, and can be obtained at AA meetings or simply ordered (ordering information on meeting books and other AA publications can be obtained by calling the local AA number in the telephone directory). The therapist and client should examine the book to select a meeting for the client to attend. Some basic introductory AA pamphlets also may help to answer the client's questions. The therapist might have names of several AA members to call upon and arrange for the client and an AA member to meet and go to a meeting together.

A final aspect of helping the client to get to a first AA meeting is to explain what to expect in a meeting. We describe a typical meeting, in which a group of people gather, usually before the scheduled meeting time, and socialize, drink coffee, and greet newcomers. During a typical open meeting, one or more members will tell their story, and others may speak as well. Clients should be told that they do not have to be a member to attend AA meetings, there is no fee, and they do not have to talk during the meeting (they can pass if called upon). We also explain the types of meetings, including open and closed meetings, discussion and speaker meetings, step meetings, and beginners' meetings.

After the client attends a meeting, the therapist should ask about his or her experience and reactions. Concerns and negative reactions should be discussed, and the client should be encouraged to sample a variety of different meetings if the first experience was negative. For some clients, negative reactions to AA meetings allow the therapist to identify interpersonal anxiety or social skills deficits, or to identify significant ambivalence about stopping drinking. These areas then can be worked on fruitfully in the therapy.

As a client continues AA involvement, the therapist should have the client set goals for AA attendance, as he or she would for other behavioral changes, and self-recording forms should include space to record AA attendance. To track the client's progress in becoming involved with AA, the therapist can inquire about whether the client has obtained any AA literature, has begun to speak to people before or after meetings, found a group which is comfortable, joined a group, and obtained a sponsor. All of these are markers of the beginning of more serious involvement with AA. As involvement progresses, attendance at step meetings, speaking at meetings, and going on commitments (where members of one group go to another AA group) are indications of further involvement.

In addition to showing knowledgeable and unambivalent interest in the client's progress in AA, the therapist can facilitate links between therapy and AA. For example, when stimulus control procedures are introduced, AA meetings can be used as an example of an activity incompatible with drinking. Other simple AA suggestions—such as calling an AA member when tempted to drink, reading AA literature, or going to a meeting—are all examples of active behavioral alternatives to drinking.

Rehearsal of the negative consequences of drinking is another behavioral technique closely allied to AA. Writing down a list of aversive consequences of drinking and reviewing it frequently is similar to the fourth step in AA, and also similar to telling one's story in an AA meeting.

Many times, clients begin to identify feelings or areas of concern because of their involvement with AA but do not receive the kind of specific assistance that they need to cope with these problems effectively. The therapist can provide structured behavioral, cognitive, or affective skills training to help clients successfully cope with these concerns.

THE EFFECTIVENESS OF ALCOHOLICS ANONYMOUS

In 1982, Glaser and Ogborne addressed the question, "Does AA really work?" for the "What we would most like to know" section of the *British Journal of Addiction*. They argued that the question needed to be asked because of the preeminence of Alcoholics Anonymous in the North American treatment of drinking problems and because "it has, regrettably, not been answered" (Glaser & Ogborne, 1982, p. 123). In 1988, this question has still not been answered, despite the generally held belief among alcoholism treatment professionals that AA is the most effective treatment. In this section, we will address four major sources of information

about the effectiveness of AA: (a) controlled studies using randomized assignment to experimental groups; (b) quasi-experimental designs comparing AA to other forms of treatment; (c) single group studies which follow subjects after involvement with AA or treatment based on AA principles; and (d) treatment outcome studies which look at the relationships between AA attendance and treatment outcome.

Before addressing the relevant research, it is important to comment upon some of the reasons for the paucity of research on AA. First, as we described above, AA is a program with a variable structure from group to group, making control of the treatment rather difficult to achieve. Second, the traditions of anonymity and not affiliating with other groups make it difficult to keep track of persons involved with AA. However, we believe that these are problems which can be overcome, and the reluctance to research AA has come as much from attitudes about AA as from design problems. In general, AA is a program based on experience and grounded in faith, and the usual kind of objective scrutiny of science is anathema to the values of AA. Because so many clinicians involved in treating alcoholics have themselves successfully recovered through AA, the same faith and acceptance which guided their personal recovery has guided their acceptance of the universal effectiveness of AA. As will become apparent in this section, despite the large membership of AA and the enthusiasm for AA held by so many in the alcoholism field, there is a paucity of scientific studies supporting the superior effectiveness of AA.

Randomized Clinical Trials

Only two studies have randomly assigned subjects to experimental groups which included AA as one of the treatment conditions. An early study (Ditman, Crawford, Forgy, Moskowitz, & MacAndrew, 1967) randomly assigned 301 chronic drunkenness offenders to a no treatment condition, attendance at an alcoholism clinic, or attendance at AA. Subjects had to provide evidence of attendance at a minimum of five AA meetings over a 30 day period. One year after conviction, there were no significant differences in recidivism rates or time to rearrest among the three groups. No data about drinking were reported.

A second randomized clinical trial also used primarily court-referred subjects (Brandsma, Maultsby, & Welsh, 1980). Subjects were assigned to a control group or to one of four experimental groups: AA, insight therapy, rational behavior therapy administered by professionals (RBT-PRO), or rational behavior therapy administered by nonprofessionals (RBT-NON). Of 532 subjects screened for the study, 197 started treatment, and 104 completed at least 10 treatment sessions and were followed for 12 months after treatment. They found that the AA experimental group had the most dropouts from treatment, and that AA and RBT-PRO had the least sessions attended even for those subjects who continued in treatment. All treatment groups did better than controls on drinking measures and legal problems.

These two studies represent the strongest tests of the effectiveness of AA because they attempted to evaluate the outcomes for all subjects who began in AA. Using random assignment also controlled for selection bias in terms of who attended AA. Neither found superior effectiveness of AA, and the Brandsma study found poorer retention in treatment for subjects in the AA condition. The results raise questions about the advisability of mandating AA attendance as a condition of probation.

However, the studies have serious flaws which limit their value as major tests of AA effectiveness. First, both used involuntary treatment populations, who had to involve themselves in treatment as a condition of the courts. AA is a voluntary organization, which is antithetical to mandatory treatment. Also, neither provided a robust test of AA. The Ditman et al. study required only five AA meetings, which is substantially less than the "90 meetings in 90 days" advocated for those new to AA. The Brandsma et al. study had subjects attend only the one AA meeting per week held at their clinic; that meeting only included study subjects, and attendance was taken. These modifications may have significantly changed the subjects' experience of AA, which usually includes involvement with several different and heterogeneous groups. In addition, the Brandsma et al. study had a high dropout rate, which limits the generalizability of the findings to other populations. Thus, while these two studies use the best designs of any AA studies, interpretation of the results must be tempered by the limits of the samples and design.

Quasi-Experimental Studies

Two recent studies (Smith, 1985; 1986) used a quasi-experimental design to compare men (Smith, 1986) and women (Smith, 1985) treated in a halfway house setting to patients treated in a hospital-based detoxification center in the same region in Australia. The author stated that subjects were matched on sex, age, marital status, occupation, education, place of birth, time of treatment, and number of previous treatments, although no matching data were provided. Treatment consisted of daily AA meetings and a work program, as well as contact with recovering alcoholic program staff. Subjects were reinterviewed 14 to 19 months after treatment. Follow-up rates were good (90% of females in the halfway house and 73% of the female controls; 75% of the males in the halfway house and 73% of the male controls). A psychologist conducted the follow-up interviews with the controls, while a program staff member conducted the interviews with the halfway house subjects. Differences in self-reported rates of continuous abstinence were statistically significant and dramatic: 79% of the treated women and 61.8% of the treated men reported abstinence since treatment, compared to 3% of the control women and 5.1% of the control men.

Smith's research represents a serious attempt to identify an appropriate comparison group, even though random assignment to groups was not used, and the comparison group is best seen as a minimal treatment group. The study suggests a high success rate for the particular halfway house studied, but there are problems with the design, in addition to the quasi-experimental nature of the study. Follow-up data were collected by two different interviewers, and one of the interviewers had had a primary clinical relationship with the subjects which could have biased the information obtained. Self-reports were not verified and the lengths of follow-up were somewhat variable. The study is not strictly a test of the effectiveness of AA, because all subjects were in a more comprehensive program which included a group living situation and a work program as well as AA meetings.

Single-group Evaluations of AA

A number of researchers have reported on outcomes of treatment from programs which use many of the principles of AA. In addition,

AA does triennial surveys of the membership, which provide information about abstinence rates reported by members attending meetings. The most recent membership survey (AA World Services, 1984) surveyed a stratified random sample of 7611 AA members in the United States and Canada. Of those surveyed, 38% reported less than one year of continuous abstinence from alcohol and other drugs, 14% reported one to two years abstinence, and 48% reported two or more years of continuous sobriety. An earler AA survey (AA World Services, 1981) reported that 50% of newcomers to AA continue with the program for less than three months. The 1981 survey also reported that AA members with less than one year of sobriety have a 41% chance of remaining abstinent over the next year, but that that chance rose to 86% for those with 1–5 years sobriety and 92% for those with more than 5 years sobriety. Self-reports are not verified in these surveys, and they oversample those persons who become heavily involved with and continue with AA, since they survey only those persons attending AA meetings. Thus, these surveys give us no information about the proportion of persons who become abstinent once they try AA, but rather provide a picture of those who are actively involved, which suggests that those who remain involved are likely to remain sober.

Studies of treatment programs based on AA principles have all derived from inpatient programs. These studies have reported rates of continuous abstinence of 55.4% at one year, (Spicer & Barnett, 1980), 56% at six months (Hoffmann, Harrison, & Belille, 1983) and 51% at two years (Alford, 1980). Of these three studies, only Alford validated self-reports and counted as failures those subjects whom he was unable to locate for follow-up. The other two studies suffer from poor response rates (37% at 12 months for Spicer & Barnett; 71% for Hoffmann et al.) and lack of validation of patient reports. All three studies examined a population which was quite different from that of the randomized clinical trials or the quasi-experimental studies. The subjects in these single-group designs tended to have a significant proportion of female subjects, the majority had at least a high school education, and they tended to be of at least middle class economic status. All were treated at private treatment centers which required either insurance coverage or self-payment for the treatment. Thus, in addition to the problems of unvalidated

self-reports and poor follow-up rates, the lack of an appropriate control group is a serious problem in these studies, as they utilize populations with a higher probability of a positive treatment outcome. In addition, it should be emphasized that none of these studies is an evaluation of AA *per se*, as all report outcomes for comprehensive inpatient treatment programs, which certainly incorporate AA philosophy but also include 30 days in a residential setting, group therapy, lectures and films, and individual counseling in addition to the AA group.

AA Attendance and Treatment Outcome

In this final section, we address the relationship between AA attendance and treatment outcome. A number of studies have reported a significant rate of AA attendance among patients successfully abstaining from alcohol use after treatment. Rates of AA attendance among patients with positive treatment outcomes have varied across studies, ranging from 17.8% (Elal-Lawrence, Slade, & Dewey, 1987) to 84% (Spicer & Barnett, 1980), with a median of about 45% (Bateman & Petersen, 1971; Elal-Lawrence, et al., 1987; Fink et al., 1985; Hoffman et al., 1983; Kolb, Coben, & Heckman, 1981; Polich, Armor, & Braiker, 1980; Rossi, 1970; Spicer & Barnett, 1980; Thorpe & Perret, 1959; Zimberg, 1980).

Finally, in evaluting the effectiveness of AA the work of Vaillant (1983) must be included. In his study of 116 inner city men who evidenced multiple symptoms of problem drinking, Vaillant reported that 49 were able to sustain at least one year of successful abstinence from alcohol, and that 21 had remained abstinent for at least 3 years. Among those ever abstinent for a year, 37% had been actively involved with AA, while 38% of those with long term abstinence were involved with AA.

CONCLUSIONS

The data about the effectiveness of AA are mixed. There are no well-designed, well-executed treatment outcome studies of AA effectiveness which use contemporary standards for treatment outcome research (Emrick & Hansen, 1985). The randomized clinical trials which have been executed find no evidence of AA showing superior effectiveness, these studies had poor outcomes in general and design and clinical problems, as well as using a limited population. Two quasi-experimental studies find support for AA-oriented treatment, but these studies also have substantial design problems. Most studies consistently find an association between AA attendance and positive treatment outcome, suggesting that AA involvement is one factor associated with successful outcome. However, Vaillant's (1983) work has made it clear that multiple methods are used to successfully deal with alcohol problems, including AA, substitute dependencies, "behavior modification," increased religious involvement, and the formation of new love relationships. He has also noted that persons with more severe and extensive drinking problems are more likely to abstain rather than moderate their drinking, which is compatible with AA, but that those with mild problems are more likely to return to social drinking, a goal which is incompatible with AA. Thus, we must conclude that there are some data supportive of AA's role in positive treatment outcomes but that we have insufficient data to determine for whom AA is most effective and under what circumstances. Therefore, although we see AA as an important component of treatment and recovery, the data do not exist to support the widespread belief that AA is the *most* effective treatment for alcoholism.

REFERENCES

Clinical Guidelines

Alcoholics Anonymous World Services (1980). *Alcoholics Anonymous*. New York: Author. This volume is the basic text of Alcoholics Anonymous (AA) and is often referred to as the AA "Big Book". It contains chapters describing AA's perception of alcoholism, the AA program and how it works, and how wives and families might best cope with the alcoholic in recovery. The second portion of the book contains the personal stories of 26 alcoholics who found recovery through the AA program; the authors of these stories represent people of both sexes and from different lifestyles and age groups.

AA World Services (1982). *The AA service manual*. New York: Author. This manual is a comprehensive account of the structure and operation of Alcoholics Anonymous. Following a brief historical account of the development of AA, each of the offices and committees are described in detail. One is able to achieve an understanding of AA from an organizational point of view through this book.

AA World Services (1978). *Twelve steps and twelve traditions*. New York: Author. An interpretation of these basic tenets of the program by one of its cofounders. It describes each step and tradition in a manner which can be useful both to the "newcomer" and the "oldtimer." This book is often used at Step and Tradition meetings as a guide to the discussion.

Brown, S. (1985). *Treating the alcoholic: A developmental model of recovery*. New York: Wiley. The author takes a developmental model of recovery from alcoholism, and discusses the integration of AA with traditional psychotherapy.

Robinson, D. (1979). *Talking out of alcoholism: The self-help process of Alcoholics Anonymous*. London: Croom Helm. The author provides a detailed description of the functioning of AA. This is an excellent book for the reader who is completely unfamiliar with AA.

Research

AA World Services (1978). *Twelve steps and twelve traditions*. New York: Author.

Alcoholics Anonymous World Services (1980). *Alcoholics Anonymous*. New York: Author.

AA World Services (1981). *Analysis of the 1980 survey of the membership of AA*. Unpublished report. New York: Author.

AA World Services (1982). *The AA service manual*. New York: Alcoholics Anonymous World Services, Inc.

AA World Services (1984). *Analysis of the 1983 survey of the membership of AA*. Unpublished report. New York: Author.

Alford, G. S. (1980). Alcoholics Anonymous: An empirical outcome study. *Addictive Behaviors, 5,* 359–370.

Bateman, N. I., & Petersen, D. M. (1971). Variables related to outcome of treatment for hospitalized alcoholics. *International Journal of the Addictions, 6,* 215–224.

Bean, M. (1975). Alcoholics Anonymous, Chapter I: Principles and methods. *Psychiatric Annals, 53(2),* 7–61.

Bean, M. (1975). Alcoholics Anonymous, Chapter II: A critique of AA. *Psychiatric Annals, 5(3),* 7–19.

Brandsma, J. M., Maultsby, M. C., & Welsh, R. J. (1980). *Outpatient treatment of alcoholism. A review and comparative study*. Baltimore, MD: University Park Press.

Ditman, K. S., Crawford, G. C., Forgy, E. W., Moskowitz, H., & MacAndrew, C. (1967). A controlled experiment on the use of court probation for drunk arrests. *American Journal of Psychiatry, 124,* 160–163.

Elal-Lawrence, G., Slade, P. D., & Dewey, M. E. (1987). Treatment and follow-up variables discriminating abstainers, controlled drinkers and relapsers. *Journal of Studies on Alcohol, 48,* 39–46.

Emrick, C. (1987). Alcoholics Anonymous: Affiliation processes and effectivenss as treatment. *Alcoholism: Clinical and Experimental Research, 11,* 416–423.

Emrick, C., & Hansen, J. (1985). Thoughts on treatment evaluation methodology. In: B. S. McCrady, N. E. Noel, & T. D. Nirenberg (Eds.), *Future directions in alcohol abuse treatment research, NIAAA Research Monograph No. 15* (pp. 137–172). Washington, DC: U.S. Government Printing Office.

Fink, E. B., Longabaugh, R., McCrady, B. S., Stout, R. L., Beattie, M., Ruggieri-Authelet, A., & McNeil, D. (1985). Effectiveness of alcoholism treatment in partial versus inpatient settings: Twenty-four month outcomes. *Addictive Behaviors, 10,* 235–248.

Fontana, A. F., Dowds, B. N., & Bethel, M. H. (1976). A.A. and group therapy for alcoholics: An application of the World Hypothesis Scale. *Journal of Studies on Alcohol, 37*(5), 675–682.

Giannetti, V. J. (1981). Alcoholics Anonymous and the recovering alcoholic: An exploratory study. *American Journal of Drug and Alcohol Abuse, 8*(3), 363–370.

Glaser, F. B., & Ogborne, A. C. (1982). Does A.A. really work? *British Journal of Addiction, 77,* 123–129.

Hoffmann, N. G., Harrison, P. A., & Belille, C. A. (1983). Alcoholics Anonymous after treatment: Attendance and abstinence. *International Journal of the Addictions, 18,* 311–318.

Karp, S. A., Witkin, H. A., & Goodenough, D. R. (1965). Alcoholism and psychological differentiation: Effect of alcohol on field dependence. *Journal of Abnormal Psychology, 70*(4), 262–265.

Kolb, D., Coben, P., & Heckman, N. A. (1981). Patterns of drinking and AA attendance following alcohol rehabilitation. *Military Medicine, 146,* 200–204.

Ogborne, A. C., & Glaser, F. B. (1981). Characteristics of affiliates of Alcoholics Anonymous: A review of the literature. *Journal of Studies on Alcohol, 42*(7), 661–675.

O'Leary, M. R., Calsyn, D. A., Haddock, D. L., &

Freeman, C. W. (1980). Differential alcohol use patterns and personality traits among three Alcoholics Anonymous attendance level groups: Further considerations of the affiliation profile. *Drug and Alcohol Dependence, 5,* 135–144.

Polich, J. M., Armor, D. J., & Braiker, H. (1980). *The course of alcoholism: Four years after treatment.* Santa Monica, CA: The Rand Corporation.

Robinson, D. (1979). *Talking out of alcoholism.* London: Croom Helm.

Rossi, J. J. (1970). A holistic program for alcoholism rehabilitation. *Medical Ecology and Clinical Research, 3,* 6–16.

Smith, D. I. (1985). Evaluation of a residential AA program for women. *Alcohol and Alcoholism, 20,* 315–327.

Smith, D. I. (1986). Evaluation of a residential AA program. *International Journal of the Addictions, 21,* 33–49.

Spicer, J., & Barnett, P. (1980). *Hospital-based chemical dependency treatment: A model for outcome evaluation.* Center City, MN: Hazelden Educational Services.

Thorpe, J. J., & Perret, J. T. (1959). Problem drinking. *AMA Archives of Industrial Health, 19,* 24–32.

Trice, H. M. (1957). A study of the process of affiliation with Alcoholics Anonymous. *Quarterly Journal of Studies on Alcohol, 18,* 39–54.

Vaillant, G. E. (1983). *The natural history of alcoholism. Causes, patterns and paths to recovery.* Cambridge, MA: Harvard University Press.

Zimberg, S. (1980). Psychotherapy with alcoholics. In: T. B. Karasu & L. Bellak (Eds.), *Specialized techniques in individual psychotherapy* (pp. 382–399) New York: Brunner/Mazel.

CHAPTER 11

Relapse Prevention

Helen M. Annis
Christine S. Davis

The chronic, relapsing nature of alcohol problems has long been recognized. However, it is only in recent years that research attention has begun to focus on factors affecting the process of relapse (e.g., Litman, Eiser, Rawson, & Oppenheim, 1977; Litman, Stapleton, Oppenheim, Peleg, & Jackson, 1983; Wilson, 1980), and on the development of "relapse prevention" treatment strategies that may be particularly effective in reducing the probability and severity of relapse (Annis, 1986; Marlatt & Gordon, 1985).

Relapse, by definition, involves a failure to maintain behavior change, rather than a failure to initiate change. Social learning theory approaches, and specifically Bandura's theory of self-efficacy, hold that the most powerful procedures for inducing behavior change may not be the most effective techniques for producing generalization and maintenance of treatment effects (Bandura, 1977, 1978, 1986). That is, a treatment strategy may be highly effective in initiating a change in a client's drinking behavior but ineffective at maintaining that change over time and avoiding relapse. This distinction between initiation and maintenance of behavior change was of central importance in our choice of Bandura's theory of self-efficacy

as a framework to guide development of relapse prevention procedures for treatment of alcohol problems. The theoretical derivation of these relapse procedures has been described elsewhere (see Annis, 1986; Annis & Davis, 1988). In this chapter we provide a detailed description of our relapse prevention treatment approach.

OVERVIEW OF THE RELAPSE PREVENTION MODEL

Our model of relapse prevention, based on self-efficacy theory, proposes that when a client enters a high risk situation for drinking, a process of cognitive appraisal of past experiences is set in motion which culminates in a judgment, or efficacy expectation, on the part of the client of his or her ability to cope with the situation. That judgment of personal efficacy determines whether or not drinking takes place (see Figure 11.1). There is now strong empirical evidence of the power of self-efficacy judgments in predicting drinking behavior (e.g., Condra, 1982; Stiemerling, 1983; Rist & Watzl, 1983; Annis & Davis, in press).

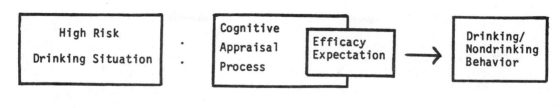

Figure 11.1 Relapse Prevention Model based on self-efficacy theory.

Therapy begins with an analysis of the client's high-risk situations for drinking, as assessed by the Inventory of Drinking Situations (IDS-100; see below), and the establishment of an individual hierarchy of drinking risk situations, from lowest risk to highest risk. The purpose of treatment is to effect an increase in the client's self-efficacy or confidence across all drinking situations in the hierarchy. Because behavioral performance has been shown to have the greatest impact on efficacy judgments, treatment focuses on having clients perform homework assignments involving entry into progressively more risky drinking situations in their natural environment and attempting alternative coping responses. Homework assignments are designed in such a way as to promote maintenance effects which will be reflected in strong gains in the client's confidence or self-efficacy. The Situational Confidence Questionnaire (SCQ-39; see below) is used to monitor progress during treatment in the development of self-efficacy across all drinking risk situations. Because exposure to real life drinking situations is central to these relapse prevention procedures, treatment must take place while the client is at risk in the community. Typically, treatment is completed in eight outpatient treatment sessions, although further sessions may be necessary for some clients.

Each component of the treatment process is described in greater detail below, beginning with a discussion of the type of client for whom this treatment approach is likely to be most effective.

SCREENING FOR CLIENT SUITABILITY

The model of behavior change on which the relapse prevention strategies described in this chapter are based assumes the existence of

adequate motivational incentives; that is, it is assumed that clients perceive some benefit to working with you, as a therapist, toward greater control of their drinking behavior. It is unlikely that the approach would be effective for a homeless alcoholic with few incentives to stop drinking. On the other hand, it should be kept in mind that clients who have a lot to lose in terms of family and work stability, but who are only contemplating change at the time of intake to treatment, may be motivated by the early stages of this treatment approach. In terms of Prochaska and DiClemente's (1984) model of change, some relapse prevention procedures can be seen as ways of narrowing the gap between contemplation and action, of demonstrating to the client that change can be gradual and relatively nonthreatening and thus motivating the client to attempt to control his or her drinking.

It is also important to consider the belief system of the client. Some clients feel strongly that their drinking problem is a reflection of deep-seated psychological conflicts, and may insist on an exclusively psychodynamic approach to therapy. In such cases, it would be unproductive to attempt to apply relapse prevention procedures. More commonly, clients will come to treatment expecting you to take control and solve their drinking problem; such clients must learn that it is necessary for them to take an active role in the design of homework assignments so that they, in effect, become their own therapist or maintenance agent. Clients who believe in the disease model of alcoholism or have a strong adherence to AA philosophy are still likely to be suitable candidates for relapse prevention training; it is only necessary that they accept the value of learning to prevent relapse by dealing more effectively with high risk drinking situations. The client's initial belief in abstinence as a treatment goal should also be assessed to ensure that there is no discrepancy between therapist and client outcome expectancy. The question of a treatment goal should be resolved at the outset of treatment. Relapse prevention training may be directed towards either an abstinence or a moderation goal.

Finally, empirical findings on the relapse model to date suggest that clients who have clearly defined areas of drinking risk, as assessed on the IDS-100, benefit more from brief relapse prevention training than do clients whose drinking is more generalized across situations. Whether clients with generalized (i.e., undifferentiated) profiles on the IDS-100 might show greater gains from more lengthy training is not yet known.

DESCRIPTION OF TREATMENT

Assessment of High Risk Drinking Situations

At intake to treatment, the client should complete the Inventory of Drinking Situations, IDS-100 (Annis, 1982; Annis, Graham, & Davis, 1987). The IDS-100 is a 100-item self-report questionnaire designed to assess situations in which the client drank heavily over the past year. You may administer the questionnaire in either paper and pencil or software versions. Based on a classification developed by Alan Marlatt and his associates (Marlatt & Gordon, 1980, 1985), the client's drinking is assessed in relation to eight categories of drinking situations: unpleasant emotions, physical discomfort, pleasant emotions, testing personal control, urges and temptations, conflict with others, social pressure to drink, and pleasant times with others. You should instruct clients to read each item and indicate the response that most accurately describes their frequency of "heavy drinking" when in that situation during the past year. Clients define "heavy drinking" in terms of their own consumption pattern and perception of what constitutes "heavy" for them. Each of the 100 items is answered on a 4-point scale where 1 = Never, 2 = Rarely, 3 = Frequently, and 4 = Almost Always.

Constructing the Client Profile of Drinking Risk Situations

From the client's responses on the IDS-100, a "problem index" score, varying from 0 to 100, should be calculated for each of the eight cate-gories of drinking situations. By plotting the eight "problem index" scores, you can construct a Client Profile showing the client's areas of greatest risk for heavy drinking. Client Profiles tend to be of two types, Generalized or Differentiated (see Figure 11.2). A generalized profile is relatively flat with no outstanding high or low categories. A differentiated profile, on the other hand, is characterized by peaks and valleys indicating some areas of clearly defined greater drinking risk. The client's profile of risk situations for drinking will serve as the major treatment planning tool.

The Client Profile, with its graphic portrayal of the client's risk situations for drinking, provides an important framework for focusing and structuring treatment in the early phases of therapy. In the initial therapy session, you should present the profile to the client and ask, in effect, "Is this you?". The client should then be encouraged to discuss how his or her drinking varies across different types of situations and to elaborate on areas of particularly high drinking risk. This discussion serves to provide your clients with feedback on their assessment results, introduces clients to the situational approach to viewing their drinking problem, and begins the process of engaging the client as an active collaborator with you in the treatment process.

Working with a Generalized Client Profile

There are no hard and fast rules for determining whether a Client Profile on the IDS-100 is generalized or differentiated. However, if the profile is relatively flat across the eight drinking risk categories, you should consider the profile to be generalized. A generalized profile presents you with a challenge in that it would seem to indicate that no situation is more or less problematic than any other. The profile may be of either high or low elevation. In a generalized profile of high elevation (e.g., "problem index" scores predominantly greater than 60), the client is reporting frequent heavy drinking across all types of situations; whereas in a generalized profile of low elevation, the client is reporting infrequent heavy drinking across all situations.

Initially, you will want to consider, based on other sources of information, whether the profile is an accurate reflection of the client's drinking behavior. In discussing the profile

A) Generalized Profile

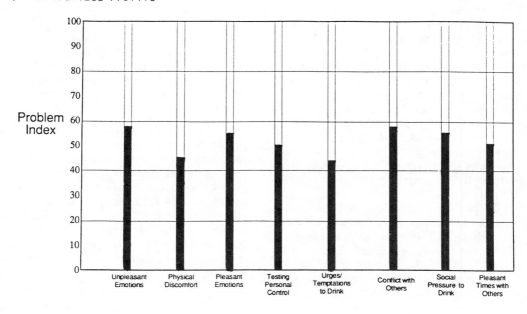

B) Differentiated Profile

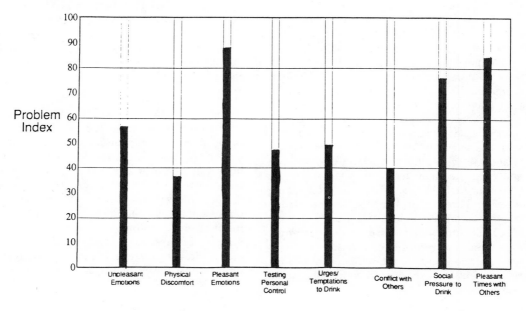

Figure 11.2. Example of a generalized and a differentiated client profile.

with the client, you should attempt to determine whether the client may be trying to present a particularly unfavorable view (high elevation profile) or favorable view (low elevation profile) of his or her drinking behavior. Are there environmental demands or incentives to the client to present in this way? Or, is there reason to believe that drinking has become a highly generalized behavior across all categories of risk situations? In our experience, even clients who have been drinking heavily for years are usually able to identify, under supplementary questioning by the therapist, some examples of situations of particularly high risk for them.

A flat profile should also serve as a signal to you to reconsider whether or not the client is in fact ready to embark on a relapse prevention treatment approach. Are there adequate motivational incentives for change? Is the client at the pre-contemplative or contemplative stage only (see Prochaska & DiClemente, 1984) and unwilling to analyze the situational components of his or her drinking problem? Has a decision to change been made? Should motivational counseling (see chapter 4) be offered before attempting to proceed with relapse prevention training?

With other clients, a flat profile may not reflect a lack of commitment to change but rather a reluctance to view their drinking problem in situational terms, or a lack of awareness of the relevance of situational determinants. In either case, you should explore with the client the situational components present in a few recent examples of drinking episodes he or she has experienced. In many instances, such a discussion will be sufficient to demonstrate to the client the relevance of the approach and help the client learn to differentiate risk situations that play a role in his or her drinking problem. Having the client keep an hourly log in which both emotional states and interpersonal risk situations for drinking are carefully monitored and recorded can also be useful in teaching the client to differentiate the relative risk for drinking experienced within commonly encountered situations.

Working with a Differentiated Client Profile

A differentiated profile, with clearly defined peaks and valleys across drinking categories, makes your treatment planning more straight-

forward because it already suggests areas of high drinking risk for the client. As with generalized profiles, differentiated profiles may be of either relatively high or low elevation. What is important in a differentiated profile is the clear demarcation of peaks indicating areas of increased drinking risk. Differentiated profiles can be of three types: positive, negative or mixed.

Positive Profile. In this type of profile, the client is reporting more frequent heavy drinking in situations that are positive in nature; that is, the peaks occur for one or more of the following: pleasant emotions, testing personal control, social pressure to drink, pleasant times with others; or all of the above. We have found that this type of profile is more common among younger clients and more frequently found in male clients than female clients (Annis, Graham, & Davis, 1987).

Negative Profile. In this type of profile, the client is reporting more frequent heavy drinking in situations which are negative in nature; that is, the peaks occur for unpleasant emotions, physical discomfort, urges and temptations, and/or conflict with others. Our research indicates that heavy drinking in negative situations is more often reported by female clients, by clients who tend to drink alone, and by clients with more years of heavy drinking (Annis, Graham, & Davis, 1987). For these clients, alcohol appears to function as a coping response to negative affect situations.

Mixed Profile. In this type of profile, the client is reporting more frequent heavy drinking in some specific positive and negative situations; that is, the peaks occur for one or more situations that are positive in nature (pleasant emotions, testing personal control, social pressure to drink, pleasant times with others) and one or more situations that are negative in nature (unpleasant emotions, physical discomfort, urges and temptations, conflict with others). In our clinical experience, clearly differentiated profiles of a mixed nature tend to occur relatively rarely.

Developing a Hierarchy of Drinking Risk Situations

Following detailed discussion and elaboration of the client's IDS-100 profile, you should then engage the client in the task of developing a hierarchy of very specific drinking risk situations, from lowest risk to highest risk. The client must understand that this hierarchy will form the basis for the development of homework assignments which will involve entry into progressively more risky drinking situations over the course of treatment. Once success is achieved in coping with situations lower in the hierarchy, homework assignments will involve exposure to more difficult situations in the hierarchy.

Ideally, in collaboration with the client, you will identify two or more specific types of situations within each of the high risk categories on the client's IDS-100 profile. (For example, for a client with a peak on the category *Unpleasant emotions*, one problem situation for drinking may involve coping with feelings of loneliness upon returning to an empty apartment after work, while another may involve drinking in response to feeling depressed about a failure to achieve a particular goal.) Once you have elicited specific recent examples of events within each of the client's high risk categories, a microanalysis of each event should be made. When did the event take place? Where was the client? Who, if anyone other than the client was present? What exactly happened before and after the drinking occurred? How did the client appraise the event—i.e., what were the client's thoughts and feelings before, during, and after the event? What is the client's current level of self-efficacy or confidence that he or she would be able to cope successfully in a similar situation now? Such detailed analyses of recent examples of problem drinking situations often suggest intervention strategies that may be helpful, while at the same time providing information on how the situation should be ranked in terms of difficulty on the client's hierarchy.

As with any treatment plan, the hierarchy is likely to require frequent review and revision over the course of treatment. Nevertheless, the process of establishing a hierarchy is extremely important in that it clarifies for the client how treatment will proceed, provides a series of benchmarks that will indicate progress in treatment as movement proceeds further up the hierarchy, and establishes a common understanding between you and the client of what needs to be accomplished. Because the client is engaged in all aspects of decisionmaking in the formation of the hierarchy, the process is initiated whereby the client will gradually learn to function as his or her own therapist or agent for maintaining change.

Identifying Strengths and Resources

The strengths, supports, and coping responses already available to a client are invaluable in preventing relapse. They form the groundwork for the development of successful homework assignments. The client must become more aware of the wide variety of strengths that he or she possesses and learn to use them effectively. Coping responses that the client may have been using successfully in other areas may be quite effective, with only minor alteration, in addressing problematic drinking situations. Significant others in the client's life, such as a spouse or an employer, may be willing to provide support, encouragement, and even active involvement in helping the client address the drinking problem.

The task, at this point in your treatment planning, is to establish the client's existing repertoire of general coping behaviors, personal strengths, and environmental resources. The process of reviewing the client's repertoire should provide you with a better appreciation of the possibilities open to the client, and should afford the client an opportunity to focus on past successes and enduring capabilities rather than on current failures.

Each of the following resource areas should be explored:

Environmental Supports. Are there friends or family members who have provided support in the past or who would be willing to do so now? Are there people at work who could be called upon when difficulties arise? Are there agencies (AA) or individuals (a local minister) that the client feels comfortable going to?

Behavioral Coping. Has the client ever attempted to solve problems that might have led to drinking, resolved to do something constructive and followed through? Has the client developed any alternative activities or rewards that could take the place of drinking, even if they have not been actively pursued for some time? Has the client ever sought out information or advice from family or friends? Has the client been able to successfully avoid or leave a high risk situation without drinking?

Cognitive Coping. Is the client able to reason things out, see connections between actions and consequences, and plan alternative ways of dealing with a situation? Is the client able to appreciate the positive benefits of not drinking and believe that he or she would personally benefit from abstinence? When confronted by urges or temptations to drink, is the client able to distract him- or herself by thinking of other things or imagining a positive outcome?

Affective Coping. Is the client able to face negative thoughts or emotional turmoil and value feelings of control and self-discipline? Does the client have strong spiritual beliefs that provide comfort? Can the client passively accept things that cannot be changed? Does the client have emotional outlets for releasing tension or anger?

Current strengths of the client in each of the above resource areas should be noted, along with any other ideas that the client would like to try for successful coping. Both you and the client can refer back to this list when discussing the design of homework assignments. The client should be encouraged to use the identified strengths when faced with drinking situations that may not have been anticipated. Because current empirical evidence suggests that reliance on a *wide* range of coping responses, rather than a more restricted repertoire, is related to avoidance of relapse (Litman, Eiser, Rawson, & Oppenheim, 1979; Litman, Stapleton, Oppenheim, Peleg, & Jackson, 1983), the client should be encouraged to draw upon as wide a variety of coping alternatives as possible.

Designing Homework Assignments

Relapse prevention training focuses on having the client enter formerly problematic drinking situations in his or her natural environment and experience success in coping. The client is gradually exposed over the course of treatment to progressively more risky drinking situations in his or her hierarchy until success has been experienced in coping with all identified areas of drinking risk. Particularly in the early stages of treatment, it is critical that homework assignments be designed so that the client experiences "mastery" and begins to build confidence (self-efficacy) in his or her ability to cope in drinking-related situations. Multiple homework assignments (i.e., three or more) should be agreed to at each therapy appointment, so that the client rapidly accumulates evidence of successful coping across a variety of formerly problematic areas. These homework assignments should draw upon as wide a variety of

the client's coping strengths and resources as possible. With the growth of perceived confidence or self-efficacy, movement up the hierarchy to more difficult situations is attempted. At this later stage, a failure experience (i.e., drinking) is unlikely to be the major setback it might have been early in treatment because the client has already initiated a snowball effect in the growth of self-efficacy. Consequently, more "chances" can be taken later in treatment in having the client risk exposure to the most problematic situations in the hierarchy. By the end of treatment, the client should be assuming major responsibility for the design of all homework assignments.

At the outset of treatment, each client should receive a pocket-sized Drinking Log and Weekly Homework Assignment Booklet. All homework assignments for the coming week that have been agreed upon should be entered in the client's booklet. Those assignments, together with detailed entries by the client of any drinking that takes place, will be reviewed at the beginning of the next treatment appointment (see Figure 11.3).

For each problem situation in the client's hierarchy, it is important to have at least a tentative plan of action early in treatment. Discussion thus far has emphasized the highly individual nature of homework assignments that go into relapse prevention training. In our experience, however, there are *five* basic types of homework assignments that are relevant to addressing problems in all categories of drinking risk situations. These basic types are outlined below.

Monitoring specific situations and cognitions. This very basic task is most frequently used early in the treatment process, but it can also serve an important function for some clients throughout the course of treatment. When a client indicates that a particular area is problematic (e.g., the client experiences urges and temptations to drink or feelings of anger or tension leading to drinking) but is unable to describe in detail specific recent examples of this type of event, it can be helpful to have the client monitor on a daily basis all instances in which the situation arises (e.g., all instances in which urges and temptations to drink are experienced, or feelings of anger or tension arise), recording immediate antecedent events, associated thoughts and feelings, and attempted coping responses. The process of monitoring,

WEEKLY DRINKING LOG

NAME: _____

DAY OF WEEK	DATE (month/day)	NUMBER OF DRINKS (Record "0" if you have abstained)
1.		
2.		
3.		
4.		
5.		
6.		
7.		

ASSIGNMENTS: 1. _____

2. _____

3. _____

DAILY DRINKING LOG – A separate page to be completed for each day on which any drinking occurred.

DAY OF WEEK: _____ DATE: _____ NAME: _____
month day

DRINKING OCCASION	TIME			ALCOHOL CONSUMED		SETTING				COMMENT (your thoughts, feelings, etc.)		
	STARTED	STOPPED	TOTAL TIME	TYPE	NO. OF DRINKS	Alone	With others who drank less	With others who drank more	Place: (bar, home, etc.)	BEFORE DRINKING	DURING	AFTER DRINKING
1.												
2.												
3.												
4.												

Figure 11.3. Pocket-sized Client Drinking Log and Weekly Homework Assignment booklet.

with its attendant focusing of the client's attention to the problem area, can be useful in revealing important antecedent triggering events and in initiating the client's planning of alternative ways of handling the situation. Future homework assignments in this problem area will thus be more meaningful to the client because they will be based on a clearer perception of the specific drinking antecedents in his or her current life situation.

Anticipating problem situations. One of the most important skills a client must learn is to anticipate when a difficult drinking situation is likely to arise so that there is time to preplan a coping response before being confronted with the situation. For each major problem area, you should encourage the client to review the likely events of the coming week and note when problematic situations may arise. For example, if social pressure to drink is an identified problem area, the client should try to anticipate for each day when and where he or she may face such pressure. If the client has difficulty anticipating social pressure situations, concurrent monitoring of when these situations arise (see above) is likely to be helpful in revealing patterns predictive of future occurrences. Forewarning frequently makes the critical difference in whether or not a client can successfully implement an appropriate coping response.

Planning and rehearsing alternative responses. Once the client has identified a specific, high-risk drinking situation and when it is likely to occur, the client should be asked to plan and rehearse (at least mentally) a number of possible alternative ways of coping with the situation. For example, if being offered a drink when visiting a particular friend is problematic, the client would be asked to generate a number of possible alternative plans of action. For each plan, exactly what would be done or said. What would be the likely consequences? How would the client feel? Is the client confident that she or he is able to carry out the plan? Of the plans considered, which one would the client like to attempt to implement first? Such assignments allow the client to consider new ways of coping and to become mentally prepared and comfortable with a plan before attempting to put it into action. To the extent possible, rehearsal of proposed plans with you, in the therapeutic session, should be encouraged (e.g., role playing refusing a drink, ordering a non-alcoholic beverage, declining a social invitation, or suggesting an alternative activity for the evening). Being mentally prepared, with well-rehearsed plans of action, increases the client's feelings of control and confidence in being able to confront high-risk situations and experiment with new ways of coping.

The client should also be prepared with plans of action in the event of a drinking slip. If drinking were to occur, what coping strategies has the client considered to help terminate the drinking and avoid a full-blown relapse? Again, you should encourage the client to consider a range of environmental supports and behavioral, cognitive, and affective coping strategies that could be drawn upon (e.g., calling you or a supportive friend, leaving the setting, refusing the next drink, considering the positive benefits of not drinking, taking pride in exercising control). The client must learn to confront the possibility of a drinking slip and to have in place well-developed plans to deal with it con-

structively. It is important for you to convey to the client the belief that he or she is able to exert control and terminate his or her drinking at any point, and that drinking slips present an opportunity for the client to learn about weaknesses and to plan more effective ways of coping.

Practicing new behaviors in increasingly more difficult situations. Having developed and rehearsed coping strategies for dealing with a problematic drinking situation, the client is ready for exposure to such situations so that "mastery" may be experienced in implementing the new coping behaviors. Homework assignments of this type, in which the client enters progressively more risky drinking situations in his or her hierarchy, are the essence of relapse prevention training.

Very difficult assignments should be avoided in the early stages of treatment because it is particularly important that the client experience some early successes. Use of a variety of "external aids" may be helpful to ensure that homework assignments can be successfully performed by the client. These may entail your involvement, that of a spouse, boss, or significant other in accompanying the client on a homework assignment, or the use of an alcohol sensitizing drug (such as Antabuse or Temposil). Having the client avoid certain highly problematic drinking situations is also a useful strategy to initiate a change in drinking behavior early in treatment. However, it is important that you be aware that although these strategies are excellent methods for quickly bringing the client's drinking behavior under control, they are unlikely to have lasting effects on the development of client confidence and the prevention of future relapse. The development of self-efficacy and strong maintenance effects requires that clients attribute improvement in treatment to an increase in their own capability for coping directly with drinking situations. For this reason, you need to ensure that strategies such as the avoidance of common drinking risk situations, the use of an alcohol-sensitizing drug, or excessive reliance on you or the involvement of spouse or significant others in major risk areas have been faded before the client is discharged from treatment.

Particularly in the later stages of treatment, homework assignments should be designed in such a way as to promote strong maintenance effects (reflected in strong gains in self-efficacy, see below) so as to prevent relapse. To have good potential for maintenace or relapse prevention, homework assignments should engender the following self-inferences on the part of the client:

1. The task was challenging (i.e., client perceives that in the past the situation would-likely have resulted in heavy drinking.
2. Only a moderate degree of effort was required to cope effectively (i.e., client assesses the degree of effort expended to control the drinking as not highly aversive).
3. Little external aid was involved in being able to cope successfully (i.e., client appraises the success as a personal victory and not attributable to the therapist, spouse, significant other, a drug, or other external supports.
4. Success on the task was part of an overall pattern of improved performance (i.e., client perceives a pattern of steady improvement in the drinking problem).
5. An increase in personal control was demonstrated (i.e., client attributes the success to a growth in personal capability).
6. The success was highly relevant to the drinking problem (i.e., client perceives the success as reflecting improvement in a critical area of his or her drinking problem).

In instances in which a client is performing homework assignments successfully but does not appear to be gaining in confidence (see monitoring of self-efficacy), your enquiry along these six dimensions of self-inference should reveal where the problem resides and suggest how further homework assignments should be modified.

Noting improved competency. Finally, having the client deliberately note examples of improved competency in handling formerly problematic situations can play an important role in consolidating treatment gains. Throughout therapy, clients should be asked to review how their behavior in different risk situations has changed as a method of reinforcing the progress that they are making. Clients should be encouraged to take a multidimensional view of their drinking problem, and to note examples of improved competency within each of several different risk areas. Failure to progress in one area, or an actual drinking slip, does not negate real gains in competency being made by the client in coping with other types of risk situations. Hence the tendency of some clients

to catastrophize a drinking episode is discouraged. This multidimensional view places both success and failure experiences in context. Any single situation or event, whether it is handled successfully or results in a drinking episode, reflects on only one aspect of the drinking problem. By noting specific examples of improved competency, clients learn that improvement involves incremental gains in coping, with occasional setbacks, across a range of drinking risk situations.

Monitoring Outcome and Changes in Self-Efficacy

At intake, mid-treatment, and towards treatment discharge, the client should complete the Situational Confidence Questionnaire, SCQ-39 (Annis, 1987; Annis & Graham, 1988), which is a 39-item self-report questionnaire designed to assess Bandura's concept of self-efficacy for alcohol-related situations. Clients are asked to imagine themselves in a variety of types of situations, derived from the work of Marlatt and Gordon (1980), and for each situation to indicate on a six-point scale (ranging from 0—not at all confident; 20—20% confident; 40—40% confident; 60—60% confident; 80—80% confident; to 100—very confident) how confident they are that they will be able to resist the urge to drink heavily in that situation. A client's response on the SCQ-39 will allow you to monitor the development of the client's self-efficacy in relation to coping with specific drinking situations over the course of treatment.

The purpose of treatment is to effect a rise in self-efficacy across all areas of perceived drinking risk. If the client fails to show growth of confidence in coping with a particular type of risk situation, further work in this area should be considered before the client is discharged from treatment. You will need to consider possible reasons for the lack of development of confidence in the identified area. Has the client successfully performed homework assignments involving entry into situations of this type? If so, what self-inferences is the client drawing from those experiences? Are the client's self-inferences consistent with the six dimensions (outlined above) that are known to promote gains in self-efficacy? Such an enquiry by you should suggest the reason for the client's lack of confidence in relation to the particular risk area and suggest what further work needs to be done before discharge from treatment.

EFFECTIVENESS

A variety of empirical findings support the principles of self-efficacy theory on which the relapse prevention procedures described in this chapter are based. There is a growing body of evidence in the addictions field that the development of self-efficacy is associated with positive treatment outcome (e.g., Annis & Davis, in press; Coelho, 1984; Colletti, Supnick, & Payne, 1985; Condiotte & Lichtenstein, 1981; DiClemente, 1981; Jeffrey et al., 1984; Marlatt & Gordon, 1985; McIntyre, Lichtenstein, & Mermelstein, 1983; Miller, Ross, Emmerson, & Todt, 1987; Prochaska, Crimi, Lapanski, Martel, & Reid, 1982; and Rist & Watzl, 1983). Morever, there is evidence that a client is most likely to relapse in an area of low perceived self-efficacy (Annis & Davis, in press; Condiotte & Lichtenstein, 1981). Client attribution of the reasons for drinking to external rather than internal causes and heavy consumption of alcohol have both been shown to be associated with low levels of drinking-related self-efficacy (Annis & Graham, 1988; Solomon & Annis, in press). In support of the recommendations of relapse prevention training, patient-generated homework assignments have been found to be somewhat more likely to be completed successfully than therapist-generated tasks (Annis & Davis, in press). There is evidence that client acceptance of the belief of "one drink, a drunk" (i.e., the inevitability of relapse following a single drink and one's inability to exert control) is associated with increased probability of post-treatment relapse (Heather, Rollnick, & Winton, 1983). An inability to deal effectively with high-risk situations involving negative emotional states also has been found to be predictive of relapse (Annis & Davis, in press; Chaney, O'Leary, & Marlatt, 1978).

A recently completed study at the Addiction Research Foundation in Toronto (Annis, Davis, Graham, & Levinson, 1987) was designed to provide a controlled evaluation of the effectiveness of relapse prevention procedures derived from self-efficacy theory. Eighty-three employed alcoholic clients who had completed a three-week inpatient program were randomly assigned to receive relapse prevention training, as described in this chapter, or more traditional counseling on an outpatient basis. On the basis of their scores on the Inventory of Drinking Situations (IDS-100), each client was categorized as having either a "generalized profile" (i.e., similar drinking across all eight types of drinking risk situations), or a "differentiated profile" (i.e., greater drinking risk in some types of situations than in others). All clients received eight treatment sessions over a three month period. Results for the sixty-eight clients (81%) contacted at six month follow-up showed no differences across the two treatment conditions in typical daily quantity of alcohol consumed for clients with *generalized profiles*; however, clients with *differentiated profiles* showed a substantially lower typical daily quantity under relapse prevention treatment than under traditional counseling. This client–treatment matching effect accounted for over 30% of the outcome variance on this measure of consumption.

SUMMARY

The development of relapse prevention procedures, based on self-efficacy theory, has provided a new and promising direction in the treatment of alcohol problems. The treatment strategies described in this chapter are derived from social psychological research investigating the *processes* involved in the initiation versus the maintenance of behavior change. Procedures are outlined for determining a client's suitability for relapse prevention training, for assessing a client's high risk drinking situations, for identifying strengths and resources, for designing individually tailored homework assignments, and for monitoring progress over the course of treatment. Cautionary guidelines are provided on commonly used intervention procedures that are likely to have poor maintenance potential. Client self-inferences related to strong gains in self-efficacy are discussed. Initial findings suggest that the focus on homework assignments, aimed at increasing self-efficacy or confidence in identified areas of drinking risk, is a promising approach to the prevention of future relapse.

REFERENCES

Clinical Guidelines

Annis, H. M. (1982). *Inventory of Drinking Situations (IDS-100)*. Toronto, Canada: Addiction Research Foundation of Ontario. The Inventory of Drinking Situations (IDS) is a situation-specific measure of drinking that can be used to identify a client's high-risk situations for alcoholic relapse. The IDS serves as a treatment planning tool, providing a profile of a client's areas of greatest drinking risk.

Administration may be by paper and pencil questionnaire; computer interactive software also available from Addiction Research Foundation, Dept 897, 33 Russell Street, Toronto, M5S 2S1.

Annis, H. M. (1987). *Situational Confidence Questionnaire (SCQ-39)*. Toronto, Canada: Addiction Research Foundation of Ontario. The Situational Confidence Questionnaire (SCQ-39) is a situation-specific measure of efficacy expectations that is designed to assess Bandura's concept of self-efficacy in relation to a client's perceived ability to cope effectively with alcohol. Administration may be by paper and pencil format or computer interactive software available from Addiction Research Foundation, Dept 897, 33 Russell Street, Toronto, M5S 2S1.

Annis, H. M., & Davis, C. S. (in press). Assessment of expectancies in alcohol dependent clients. In D. M. Donovan & G. A. Marlatt (Eds.), *Assessment of addictive behaviors*. New York: Guilford. This chapter describes the clinical application of relapse prevention procedures directed toward either abstinence or moderation goals. Clinical examples are presented to illustrate the design of homework assignments in relation to each of the eight categories of drinking risk identified on the Inventory of Drinking Situations.

Annis, H. M., & Graham, J. M. (1988). *Situational Confidence Questionnaire (SCQ) user's guide*. Toronto, Canada: Addiction Research Foundation of Ontario. The 45-page User's Guide gives a detailed presentation of the development of the SCQ and presents guidelines for clinical and research applications. Reliability and validity data are summarized and normative data are provided. Available from Addiction Research Foundation, Dept. 897, 33 Russell Street, Toronto, M5S 2S1.

Annis, H. M., Graham, J. M., & Davis, C. S. (1987). *Inventory of Drinking Situations (IDS) user's guide*. Toronto, Canada: Addiction Research Foundation of Ontario. The 50-page User's Guide describes the development of the IDS and its use in clinical and research settings, presents reliability and validity information plus normative data, and provides guidelines for use in paper and pencil or computer interactive format. Available from Addiction Research Foundation, Dept 897, 33 Russell Street, Toronto, M5S 2S1.

Daley, D. C. (1986). *Relapse prevention workbook for recovering alcoholics and drug dependent persons*. Holmes Beach, FL: Learning Publications, Inc. This client workbook presents a number of exercises to help the client identify risk situations for drinking and to plan coping responses for those situations. Other topics covered include use of an emergency sobriety card, lifestyle balancing, and what to do if a relapse occurs.

Marlatt, G. A., & Gordon, J. R. (1985). *Relapse prevention: Maintenance strategies in the treatment of addictive behaviors*. New York: Guilford Press. This book presents a model of relapse prevention based on self-management or self-control procedures. Self-control strategies in three main areas are described: skill-training aimed at the acquisition of adaptive coping skills; cognitive procedures designed to foster new attitudes, attributions, and expectancies; and lifestyle interventions aimed at developing healthy self-care activities).

Research

Annis, H. M. (1986). A relapse prevention model for treatment of alcoholics. In W. R. Miller & N. Heather (Eds.). *Treating addictive behaviors: Processes of change* (pp. 407–433). New York: Plenum.

Annis, H. M., & Davis, C. S. (in press). Self-efficacy and the prevention of alcoholic relapse: Initial findings from a treatment trial. In T. B. Baker & D. Cannon (Eds.), *Addictive disorders: Psychological research on assessment and treatment*. New York: Praeger.

Annis, H. M., Davis, C. S., Graham, M., & Levinson, T. (1987). *A controlled trial of relapse prevention procedures based on self-efficacy theory*. Unpublished manuscript.

Bandura, A. (1977). Self-efficacy: Toward a unifying theory of behavioral change. *Psychological Review, 84*, 191–215.

Bandura, A. (1978). Reflections on self-efficacy. *Advances in Behavioral Research and Therapy, 1*, 237–269.

Bandura, A. (1986). *Social foundations of thought and action: A social cognitive theory*. Englewood Cliffs, NJ: Prentice-Hall.

Chaney, E. F., O'Leary, M. R., & Marlatt, G. A. (1978). Skill training with alcoholics. *Journal of Consulting and Clinical Psychology, 46*, 1092–1104.

Coelho, R. J. (1984). Self-efficacy and cessation of smoking. *Psychological Reports, 54*, 309–310.

Colletti, G., Supnick, J. A., & Payne, T. J. (1985). The Smoking Self-Efficacy Questionnaire: A preliminary validation. *Behavioral Assessment, 7*, 249–254.

Condiotte, M. M., & Lichtenstein, E. (1981). Self-efficacy and relapse in smoking cessation programs. *Journal of Consulting and Clinical Psychology, 49*, 648–658.

Condra, M. St. John (1982). *The effectiveness of relapse-training in the treatment of alcohol problems*. Unpublished doctoral dissertation, Queen's University, Kingston, Canada.

DiClemente, C. C. (1981). Self-efficacy and smoking cessation maintenance: A preliminary report. *Cognitive Research and Therapy, 5*, 175–187.

Heather, N., Rollnick, S., & Winton, M. (1983). A comparison of objective and subjective measures of alcohol dependence as predictors of relapse following treatment. *British Journal of Clinical Psychology, 22*, 11–17.

Jeffrey, R. W., Bjornson-Benson, W. M., Rosenthal, B. S., Lindquist, R. A., Kurth, C. L., & Johnson, S. L. (1984). Correlates of weight loss and its maintenance over two years of follow-up among middle-aged men. *Preventive Medicine, 13*, 155–168.

Litman, G. K., Eiser, J. R., Rawson, N. S. B., & Oppenheim, A. N. (1977). Toward a typology of relapse: A preliminary report. *Drug and Alcohol Dependence, 2*, 157–162.

Litman, G. K., Eiser, J. R., Rawson, N. S. B., & Oppenheim, A. N. (1979). Differences in relapse precipitants and coping behaviours between alcohol relapsers and survivors. *Behaviour Research and Therapy, 17*, 89–94.

Litman, G. K., Stapleton, J., Oppenheim, A. N., Peleg, M., & Jackson, P. (1983). The relationship between coping behaviours, their effectiveness and alcoholism relapse and survival. *British*

Journal of Addiction, 79 (3), 283–291.

Marlatt, G. A., & Gordon, J. R. (1980). Determinants of relapse: Implications for the maintenance of behavior change. In P. Davidson & S. Davidson (Eds.), *Behavioral medicine: Changing health lifestyles* (pp. 410–452). New York: Brunner/Mazel.

McIntyre, D. O., Lichtenstein, E., & Mermelstein, R. J. (1983). Self-efficacy and relapse in smoking cessation: A replication and extension. *Journal of Consulting and Clinical Psychology, 51,* 632–633.

Miller, P. J., Ross, S. M., Emmerson, R. Y., & Todt, E. H. (1987). *Self-efficacy in alcoholics: Clinical validation of the Situational Confidence Questionnaire.* Manuscript submitted for publication.

Prochaska, J. O., Crimi, P., Lapanski, D., Martel, L., & Reid, P. (1982). Self-change processes, self-efficacy and self-concept in relapse and maintenance of cessation of smoking. *Psychological Reports, 51,* 983–990.

Prochaska, J. O., & DiClemente, C. C. (1984). *The transtheoretical approach: Crossing traditional boundaries of therapy.* Homewood, IL: Dow Jones-Irwin.

Rist, F. & Watzl, H. (1983). Self assessment of relapse risk and assertiveness in relation to treatment outcome of female alcoholics. *Addictive Behaviours, 8,* 121–127.

Solomon, K. E., & Annis, H. M. (in press). *Development of a scale to measure outcome expectancies in alcoholics. Cognitive Therapy and Research.*

Stiemerling, N. (1983). *Relapse in alcohol abusers: A short term longitudinal study.* Unpublished doctoral dissertation, Queen's University, Kingston, Canada.

Wilson, G. T. (1980). Cognitive factors in lifestyle changes: A social learning perspective. In P. O. Davidson & S. M. Davidson (Eds.), *Behavioral medicine: Changing health lifestyles* (pp. 3–37). New York: Brunner/Mazel.

CHAPTER 12

Marital and Family Therapy

Timothy J. O'Farrell
Kathleen S. Cowles

OVERVIEW

Marital and family treatment approaches have been called "the most notable current advance in the area of psychotherapy of alcoholism" (Keller, 1974), and enthusiasm derives from several sources. Many alcoholics have extensive marital and family problems (e.g., O'Farrell & Birchler, 1987), and positive marital and family adjustment is associated with better alcoholism treatment outcomes at follow-up (e.g., Finney, Moos, & Mewborn, 1980). Further, there exists growing clinical and research evidence of reciprocal relationships between marital-family interactions and abusive drinking. It is widely known that abusive drinking leads to marital and family discord, among the more serious of which are separation and divorce and child and spouse abuse. At the same time, the role played by marital and family factors in the development and maintenance of alcohol problems is considerable. Individuals reared with an alcoholic parent are themselves at risk for developing alcohol problems, due both to genetic factors and to faulty role modeling. Marital and family problems may stimulate excessive drinking, and family interactions often help to maintain alcohol problems once

they have developed. Excessive drinking may provide more subtle adaptive consequences for the couple or family, such as facilitating the expression of emotion and affection or regulating the amount of distance and closeness between family members. Finally, even when recovery from the alcohol problem has begun, marital and family conflicts may often precipitate renewed drinking by abstinent alcoholics (Maisto, O'Farrell, Connors, McKay, & Pelcovitz, 1988; Marlatt & Gordon, 1985).

This chapter presents marital and family therapy interventions for use with alcohol abusers and alcoholics during three broadly defined stages of recovery (Prochaska & DiClemente, 1983): (a) initial commitment to change—recognizing that a problem exists and deciding to do something about it; (b) the change itself—stopping abusive drinking and stabilizing this change for at least a few months; and (c) the long-term maintenance of change. The focus is primarily on marital or spouse-involved therapy methods drawn from a behavioral orientation because these methods, having been used and studied more extensively than others, have greatest empirical support. This also is the area of our primary

Note: Kathleen Cowles is also a doctoral candidate in clinical psychology at Clark University in Worcester Massachusetts. The Veterans Administration provided partial support for preparation of this chapter. The assistance of Ronald Travaglione is gratefully acknowledged.

expertise. Applications of these methods to family therapy will be noted.[1]

SPECIAL CONSIDERATIONS

Clients Most and Least Likely to Benefit

Unfortunately, studies examining predictors of response to marital and family therapy with alcoholics are not yet available. However, clinical experience and studies of factors that predict alcoholics' acceptance and completion of marital and family therapy (Noel, McCrady, Stout, & Nelson, 1987; O'Farrell, Kleinke, & Cutter, 1986; Zweben, Pearlman, & Li, 1983) provide some informaton on clients most likely to benefit from such treatment, since the clients must accept and stay in therapy to benefit. Clients most likely to accept and complete marital and family therapy have the following characteristics: (a) a high school education or better; (b) employed full-time if able and desirous of working; (c) live together or, if separated, are willing to reconcile for the duration of the therapy; (d) older; (e) have more serious alcohol problems of longer duration; (f) enter therapy after a crisis, especially one that threatens the stability of the marriage; (g) spouse and other family members are not alcoholic; (h) alcoholic, spouse, and other family members without serious psychopathology or drug abuse; and (i) absence of family violence that has caused serious injury or is potentially life-threatening. Further, evidence that the alcoholic is motivated to change and to take an active role in a psychologically oriented treatment approach also suggests potential for benefitting from marital and family therapy. Such evidence includes contact with the treatment program personally initiated by the alcoholic and a history of successful participation in other outpatient counseling or self-help programs (as opposed to those only admitted to detoxification for relief of physical distress due to heavy drinking, without further active ongoing treatment participation). Compliance

---

[1]A list of supplementary readings is available on request from the first author. This list includes (a) material on a family systems approach to alcoholism, which is beyond the scope of the present chapter, and (b) texts on behavioral marital therapy for couples without alcohol problems that contain procedures useful with alcoholics.

with the initial month of outpatient treatment, including abstinence, keeping scheduled appointments, and completing any required assignments are process measures that seem to predict likely benefit on a clinical basis.

These characteristics may sound like those of model clients who are likely to benefit from nearly any treatment method. However, clients do not have to fit these criteria for therapists to use the marital and family therapy methods described in this chapter. Rather, the marital and family methods have to be adapted for some of the more difficult cases—generally by going slower, individualizing the approach to a greater degree, and dealing with more varied and more frequent obstacles and resistances. Strategies for dealing with some of the more difficult cases (e.g., the separated alcoholic, the family with more than one alcohol-abusing member) have been presented elsewhere (O'Farrell, 1986).

Therapist Attributes and Behaviors Needed

Our clinical experience suggests that certain therapist attributes and behaviors are important for successful marital and family therapy with alcoholics. From the outset, the therapist must structure treatment so that control of the alcohol abuse is the first priority, before attempting to help the couple or family with other problems. Many of our clients have had previous unsuccessful experiences with therapists who saw the couple in marital or family therapy without dealing with the alcohol abuse. The hope that reduction in marital or family distress will lead to improvement in the drinking problem is rarely fulfilled. More typically, recurrent alcohol-related incidents and interactions undermine whatever gains have been made in marital and family relationships.

Therapists must be able to tolerate and deal effectively with strong anger in early sessions and at later times of crisis. The therapist can use empathic listening to help each family member feel they have been heard and insist that only one person speaks at a time. Helping the couple or family defuse their intense anger is very important, since failure to do so often leads to a poor outcome (Gurman & Kniskern, 1978).

Therapists need to structure and take control of treatment sessions, especially during the early assessment and therapy phase and at later times of crisis (e.g., episodes of drinking or intense family conflict). Highly structured therapy sessions with a directive, active therapist are more effective for alcoholic families than is a less structured mode of therapy. Many therapists' errors involve difficulty establishing and maintaining control of the sessions and responding to the myriad forms of resistance and noncompliance presented by couples and families. Therapists must steer a middle course between lack of structure and being overly controlling and punitive in response to non-compliance. He or she must clearly establish and enforce the rules of treatment, while offering a "shaping attitude" in which the therapist acknowledges approximation to desired behavior despite significant shortcomings.

Finally, therapists need to take a long-term view of the course of change—both the alcoholism problem and associated marital and family distress may be helped substantially only by repeated efforts, including some failed attempts. Such a long-term view may help the therapist encounter relapse without becoming overly discouraged or engaging in blaming and recriminations with the alcoholic and family. The therapist also should maintain contact with the family long after the problems apparently have stabilized. Leaving such contacts to the family usually means no follow-up contacts occur until they are back in a major crisis again.

DESCRIPTION

Motivating an Initial Commitment to Change in the Alcohol Abuser

For the difficult and all too common case of the alcoholic who is not yet willing to stop drinking, a marital and family therapy approach will try to help the spouse and family members to motivate the uncooperative, denying alcoholic to change his or her drinking. Sisson and Azrin (1986) developed and evaluated a behavior therapy program (see chapter 16) for teaching the following to a nonalcoholic family member (usually the wife of a male alcoholic): (a) how to reduce physical abuse to herself, (b) how to encourage sobriety, (c) how to encourage seeking professional treatment, and (d) how to assist in that treatment. Sisson & Azrin (1986) published the first controlled outcome study of

a method to initiate change in the alcoholic. They concluded that the counseling of concerned family members in the use of appropriate reinforcement procedures can reduce the drinking of unmotivated alcoholics and lead to the initiation of treatment.

Two other approaches have been described in the literature. Vernon Johnson of the Johnson Institute in Minneapolis developed a widely known and used "intervention" procedure. This involves three to four educational and rehearsal sessions with family members prior to the intervention itself, in which the alcoholic is confronted about his or her drinking and strongly encouraged to enter alcoholism treatment (Johnson, 1973; Thorne, 1983). Edwin Thomas and colleagues at the University of Michigan (Thomas & Santa, 1982) have developed their Unilateral Family Therapy approach to the nonalcoholic spouse to strengthen his or her coping capabilities, to enhance family functioning, and to facilitate greater sobriety on the part of the alcohol abuser. The unilateral family therapy approach provides a series of graded steps the spouse can use prior to a confrontation, which may be successful in their own right or will at least pave the way for a positive outcome to a "programmed confrontation" experience similar to the Johnson approach and adapted for use with an individual spouse.

Goals and Preparations for Marital and Family Treatment

Goals

Once the alcoholic has decided to change his or her drinking, marital and family therapy has two basic objectives in order to stabilize short-term change in the alcohol problem and in the alcoholic's marriage and family relationships. The first goal is to reduce or eliminate abusive drinking and support the alcoholic's efforts to change. To this end, a high priority is changing alcohol-related interactional patterns (e.g., nagging about past drinking but ignoring current sober behavior). One can get abstinent alcoholics and their spouses to engage in behaviors more pleasing to each other, but if they continue talking about and focusing on past or "possible" future drinking, frequently such arguments lead to renewed drinking (Maisto et al., 1988; Marlatt & Gordon, 1985). They then feel more discouraged about their relationship and the drinking than before, and are less likely to try pleasing each other again. The second goal involves altering general marital patterns to provide an atmosphere that is more conducive to sobriety. This involves helping the couple repair the often extensive relationship damage incurred during many years of conflict over alcohol, as well as helping them find solutions to relationship difficulties that may not be directly related to the alcoholism. Finally, the couple must learn to confront and resolve relationship conflicts without the alcoholic's resorting to drinking.

After the change in the alcohol problem has been stable for 3 to 6 months, the goals of marital therapy in contributing to long-term maintenance of change are to (a) help the couple prevent relapse to abusive drinking and (b) deal with marital issues frequently encountered during long-term recovery. Methods therapists can use to reach each of these goals will be presented in detail after we consider the initial assessment and crisis intervention sessions that are so important if therapeutic goals are to be accomplished.

Assessment and Crisis Intervention

In the initial interview, the therapist needs to: (a) determine at what stage the alcoholic is in the process of changing his or her alcohol abuse; (b) assess whether there is a need for crisis intervention prior to a careful assessment; and (c) orient the couple to the assessment procedures. If the alcoholic already has initiated changes in the drinking or at least clearly recognizes that a problem exists and may want to change it, then proceeding with the assessment makes sense. If the alcoholic has not yet made a firm decision to change the drinking, then facilitating this decision becomes one of the goals of the assessment. It is very important to give priority to the alcoholic's drinking in the initial sessions. We generally attempt to establish at least a temporary contract of abstinence during the two to four assessment sessions. A minimal requirement is abstinence on the days of assessment sessions, and clients are informed that a portable breath test (Sobell & Sobell, 1975) is a standard feature of all assessment sessions we conduct. An inquiry about the extent of drinking and urges to drink be-

tween sessions is a routine part of each assessment session. We also ask the couple to commit themselves, for the time period needed to complete the assessment, to stay living together, not to threaten separation or divorce, and to refrain from bringing up the past in anger at home.

The therapist evaluates whether any serious negative consequences are likely to occur if two to four assessment sessions are conducted before taking action on the presenting complaints. For example, crisis intervention is necessary for cases in which violence or divorce seem a likely result of delayed action or cases in which an alcoholic is ready to stop drinking but needs immediate hospitalization for detoxification and starting alcoholism treatment. Often the usual assessment can be conducted after the crisis has been resolved. Other issues which also may present obstacles to assessment and require intervention are discussed in more detail below, after considering assessment methods.

Assessment Targets and Procedures

A series of assessment issues or targets are investigated in progressively greater depth as the assessment progresses. In the initial session, the therapist's clinical interview should gather information about (a) the alcoholic's drinking, especially recent quantity and frequency of drinking, whether the extent of physical dependence on alcohol requires detoxification to obtain abstinence during the assessment, what led to seeking help at this time and prior help-seeking efforts, and whether the alcoholic's and spouse's goal is to reduce the drinking or to abstain either temporarily or permanently; (b) the stability of the marriage in terms of current planned or actual separation as well as any past separations; (c) recent violence and any fears of recurrence; and (d) the existence of alcohol-related or other crises that require immediate attention. Allowing 75–90 minutes for the initial session and including 5–10 minutes separately with each spouse alone provides sufficient time to gather the needed information and to learn of important material (e.g., plans for separation, fears of violence) that either spouse may be reluctant to share during the conjoint portion of the interview.

Our own practice makes use of a number of structured assessment instruments and procedures after the initial interview session[2] to explore in greater detail the issues covered in the initial session. The marital relationship is also explored in depth in these subsequent assessment sessions, with special attention being given to the overall level of satisfaction experienced in the relationship, specific changes desired in the relationship, sexual adjustment, and level of communication skills especially when talking about conflicts and problems. The goal of this additional marital assessment is to determine (a) what changes are needed in marital and family life, as well as other day-to-day activities, in order to achieve and maintain the goal for the alcoholic's drinking, and (b) what marital changes are desired to increase marital satisfaction, if one assumes that the drinking goal will be achieved.

After the assessment information has been gathered, the couple and therapist meet for a feedback session in which the therapist shares impressions of the nature and severity of the drinking and marital problems and invites the couple to respond to these impressions. This session allows therapists the opportunity to increase motivation for treatment by reviewing in a nonjudgmental, matter-of-fact manner the negative consequences of the excessive drinking. A second goal of the feedback session is to decide whether or not the couple will begin short-term marital therapy and to prepare them for this if that is the decision. Assuming the decision is to start marital therapy, the therapist usually emphasizes the value of marriage counseling in achieving sobriety and a more satisfying marriage and tries to promote favorable therapeutic expectations. Verbal commitments are obtained from the husband and the wife to live together for at least the initial course of therapy, not to threaten divorce or separation during this period, and to do their best to focus on the future and the present (but not the past) in the therapy sessions and at home. In addition, the couple is asked to agree to do weekly homework assignments as part of the therapy. Finally, the therapist gives an overview of the course of therapy and tells the couple in more detail about the content of the first few sessions.

---

[2]Material describing the assessment process, including the specific questionnaires and structured interviews, used by the authors in our research clinic for alcoholic couples is available on request from the first author.

Obstacles Frequently Encountered During Initial Sessions

Alcohol-related crises. Despite their seeming suitability for marital therapy, many alcoholics and their spouses will present the therapist with substantial obstacles. Common problems encountered during assessment are pressing alcohol-related crises (e.g., actual, impending, or threatened loss of job or home, or major legal or financial problems) that preclude a serious and sustained marital therapy focus. The therapist can help the couple devise plans to deal with the crisis or refer them elsewhere for such help, often after establishing a behavioral contract about drinking and alcohol-related interactions (see below). Other marital assessment and therapy procedures can be started when the crisis has been resolved.

Potential for violence. Many alcoholic couples whose negative interactions escalate quickly have difficulty containing conflict between sessions and pose a potential for violence in some instances. Responses to initial interviews with the couple and with the spouses separately, and further inquiry during subsequent sessions help identify many such violence prone couples during the pretherapy assessment. Once identified, these couples have conflict containment as an explicit goal of their therapy from the outset. For couples with a history of interspousal violence, it is important to determine whether the violence was limited to occasions when the alcoholic had been drinking. If so, then methods to deal with the alcohol abuse may relieve much of the couple's concern about violence. Nonetheless, an additional procedure described by Shapiro (1984) can be very useful in cases where violence still seems likely. This involves a written agreement that spouses are not to hit or threaten to hit each other, and that if they do, one of the spouses (named in the agreement) will leave the home and go to a designated place for 48 to 72 hours. A "time-out" agreement is another useful procedure for containing conflict. In this procedure, if either party gets uncomfortable that a discussion may be escalating, he or she says, "I'm getting uncomfortable,. I want a five-minute time-out." Spouses go to separate rooms and use slow deep breathing to calm themselves. Afterward, the couple may restart the discussion if both desire it. If a second time-out is requested, then the couple definitely must stop the discussion.

The blaming spouse. It usually is not helpful to interpret the nonalcoholic spouse's frequent conversations about past or possible future drinking as an attempt to punish the alcoholic or sabotage the alcoholic's recovery or to overtly disapprove of the spouse's behavior. The therapist can empathize with the spouse by sympathetically reframing the spouse's behavior as trying to protect the couple from further problems due to alcohol. From this perspective, the spouse's talk about drinking is intended to be sure the alcoholic (a) knows fully the negative impact of the past drinking (and this is plausible, since often the drinker does not remember much of what happened); (b) is aware of the full extent of the problem so his or her motivation toward sobriety will be fortified; and (c) is prepared for situations that may lead to a relapse or lapse in motivation. Once the spouse feels understood, he or she becomes more receptive to the therapist's suggestion that the spouse has been "doing the wrong thing for the right reason" and to suggestions about more constructive methods to achieve the same goal.

Typical Structure and Sequence of Therapy Sessions

Once assessment is complete and initial obstacles have been overcome, marital therapy to help stabilize short-term change in the alcoholism and associated marital discord usually consists of 10 to 15 therapy sessions, each of which lasts 60 to 75 minutes. Sessions tend to be highly structured, with the therapist setting the agenda at the outset of each meeting. A typical session begins with an inquiry about any drinking or urges to drink that have occurred since the last session, including compliance with any sobriety contract (see below) that has been negotiated; moves from a review of the homework assignment from the previous session to new material, such as instruction in and rehearsal of skills to be practiced at home during the week; and ends with the assignment of homework and answering questions. Generally, the first few sessions focus on decreasing alcohol-related feelings and interactions and increasing positive exchanges. This decreases tension about alcohol (and the risk of abusive drinking) and builds good will. Both are necessary for dealing with marital problems and desired relationship changes in later sessions, using communication and problem-solving

skills training and behavior change agreements. The following section describes typical interventions used.

Once the alcohol problem has been under control for 3 to 6 months, the structure and content of marital therapy sessions often change as the emphasis of the therapy becomes maintaining gains and preventing relapse. This phase of therapy is described later in the chapter.

PRODUCING SHORT TERM DRINKING AND RELATIONSHIP CHANGES

Alcohol-Focused Interventions

General Goals and Issues

After the alcohol abuser has decided to change his or her drinking, the spouse and other family members can be included in treatment designed to support the alcoholic in adhering to this difficult and stressful decision. The first purpose of such treatment is to establish a clear and specific agreement between the alcohol abuser and family member(s) about the goal for the alcoholic's drinking and the role of each family member in achieving that goal. Behavioral contracting can be very useful for this purpose and is described further below.

Specifying other behavioral changes needed in the alcoholic or the family requires a careful review of individual situations and conditions. Certain issues should be addressed. For instance, possible exposure to alcoholic beverages and alcohol-related situations should be discussed. The spouse and family should decide if they will drink alcoholic beverages in the alcoholic's presence, whether alcoholic beverages will be kept and served at home, if the couple will attend social gatherings involving alcohol, and how to deal with these situations. Particular persons, gatherings, or circumstances that are likely to be stressful should be identified. Couple and family interactions related to alcohol also need to be addressed, because arguments, tensions, and negative feelings can precipitate more abusive drinking. Therapists need to discuss these patterns with the family and suggest specific procedures to be used in difficult situations. The remainder of this section describes specific methods and examples of how to achieve the general goals just described.

Behavioral Contracting

Written behavioral contracts, although different in many specific aspects of the agreements, have a number of common elements that make them useful. The drinking behavior goal is made explicit. Specific behaviors that each spouse can do to help achieve this goal are also detailed. The contract provides alternative behaviors to negative interactions about drinking. Finally, and quite importantly, the agreement decreases the nonalcoholic spouse's anxiety and need to control the alcoholic and his or her drinking.

Structuring the spouse's and the alcoholic's role in the recovery process. Daniel Kivlahan and Elizabeth Shapiro (personal communication, May 18, 1984) have male alcoholics and their spouses engage in what they call a Sobriety Trust Contract. Each day, at a specified time, the alcoholic initiates a brief discussion and reiterates his or her desire not to drink that day. Then the alcoholic asks if the spouse has any questions or fears about possible drinking that day. The alcoholic answers the questions and attempts to reassure the spouse. The spouse is not to mention past drinking or any future possible drinking beyond that day. The couple agrees to refrain from discussing drinking at any other time, to keep the daily trust discussion very brief, and to end it with a positive statement to each other.

Two examples from our practice illustrate other types of contracts we have used with alcoholic couples. In the first case, a male alcoholic, who recognized he had an alcohol problem and had abstained for 3 months in the past year, was trying to engage in "social drinking." Periodically he would drink heavily for a period of 3 to 5 days, and three serious binges had occurred in the past 6 weeks. Each binge ended after an intense fight in which the husband became verbally abusive and the wife threatened to terminate their relationship. At a conjoint session with the wife, the following agreement was negotiated: (a) the husband's goal was at least 6 months' abstinence from alcohol; (b) if he drank before then, he would start daily Antabuse and continue it at least to the end of the 6-month period; (c) if the wife thought he had been drinking, she would remind the husband of their agreement and ask him to start the Antabuse; (d) if the husband refused, the wife would refrain from arguing or threats and leave their home until the husband had stopped drinking and started the Antabuse. Two weeks later, the husband drank and then voluntarily started the Antabuse. Both husband and wife were pleased that their customary intense argument was not necessary to terminate the drinking.

In the second case, a chronic alcoholic with serious liver cirrhosis reported good progress in outpatient sessions but complained that his wife was unfairly accusing him of drinking and they were arguing about financial and other problems. At about the same time, liver function tests showed elevated liver enzymes, most likely indicating recent drinking (O'Farrell & Maisto, 1987). Couple sessions were begun and the following agreement was established: (a) each evening the husband would take an alcohol breath test using a Mobile Breath Alcohol Tester ("Mobat"; Sobell & Sobell, 1975) to verify he had not been drinking; (b) the wife would refrain from accusations about current drinking or complaints about past drinking; (c) the daily Mobat review would continue until normal liver test results, without evidence of drinking, were achieved for two consecutive months; (d) the couple would continue in conjoint sessions about their other relationship problems. Only two isolated instances occurred in which the Mobat indicated the husband had been drinking that day, and the couple conflicts were resolved satisfactorily in later sessions.

Participation in AA and Alanon self-help groups is often part of the behavioral contract we negotiate with couples. As with any other behavior that is part of a "Sobriety Contract," as we call the various forms of behavior contracts we use, attendance at AA and Alanon meetings is reviewed at each therapy session.

Antabuse contracts to promote abstinence. Antabuse (disulfiram), a drug that produces extreme nausea and sickness when the person taking the drug ingests alcohol, is widely used in treatment for persons with a goal of abstinence (see chapter 7). Antabuse therapy often is not always effective because the alcoholic often discontinues the drug prematurely (Lundwall & Baekeland, 1971). The Antabuse Contract, or Disulfiram Assurance Plan, is a procedure that has been used by a number of investigators (e.g., Azrin, 1976; O'Farrell, Cutter, & Floyd, 1985). It is designed to maintain Antabuse ingestion and abstinence from alcohol and to decrease alcohol-related arguments and interactions between the alcoholic and his or her spouse. Before negotiating such a contract, the therapist should be sure that the alcoholic is willing and medically cleared to take Antabuse and that both alcoholic and spouse have been fully informed and educated about the effects of the drug. In the Antabuse Contract, the alcoholic agrees to take Antabuse each day while the spouse observes. The spouse, in turn, agrees to positively reinforce the alcoholic for taking the Antabuse, to record the observation on a calendar provided by the therapist, and not to mention past drinking or any fears about future drinking. It is extremely important that each spouse view the agreement as a cooperative method for rebuilding lost trust and not as a coercive checking-up operation. More details on how to implement the Antabuse Contract and how to deal with common forms of resistance to this procedure are available elsewhere (Azrin, 1976; O'Farrell & Bayog, 1986).

Reducing hazardous drinking. Peter Miller (1972) used contingency contracting with an excessive drinker and his wife to produce reduced consumption and fewer arguments about drinking. The couple signed a contract that required the husband to limit his drinking to between 1 and 3 drinks a day (in the presence of his wife and before the evening meal) and the wife to refrain from negative verbal or nonverbal responses to her husband's drinking. Each partner agreed to pay the other $20 if he or she broke the agreement. Each spouse received a few fines during the first few weeks of the contract, but the infractions rapidly diminished when each partner learned that the contract would, in fact, be enforced.

The alcohol abuser treated by Miller was employed, showed no medical damage from his excessive drinking, and the negative impact of his drinking was confined to the marital relationship. These factors suggested an attempt to reduce rather than eliminate the drinking. Therapists need to choose carefully in each individual case as to whether the goal of treatment should be moderation or total abstinence (see chapters 2, 4, and 9). Although empirical data on which to base this decision are still

being gathered, rational guidelines are available (Heather & Robertson, 1981, pp. 215–240; Miller & Caddy, 1977) and should be used prior to implementing such a behavioral contracting procedure.

Decreasing Family Members' Behaviors that Trigger or Enable Drinking

McCrady (1982) implemented procedures to decrease spouse behaviors that trigger or enable abusive drinking with a male alcoholic and his wife seeking abstinence. The couple identified the wife's behaviors that triggered drinking by the husband (e.g., threatening to leave, pouring alcohol down the sink, or getting rid of it in other ways). The husband reacted by becoming angry or depressed and drinking still more. Moreover, the wife unwittingly reinforced her husband's drinking by protecting him from the consequences of his drinking (e.g., by attempting to make him comfortable when drunk, cleaning up after him when he drank). McCrady helped the couple find mutually comfortable and agreeable methods to reverse the wife's behavior that inadvertently promoted drinking. The wife was also taught to provide positive reinforcers (such as verbal acknowledgement, going to movies and flea markets together, making special dinners and snacks) only when the husband had not been drinking.

Dealing with Drinking During Treatment

Drinking episodes often occur during marital and family therapy with alcoholics. The probability of dealing therapeutically with such drinking is increased if the therapist intervenes before the drinking goes on for too long a period. Having the alcoholic keep a daily record of urges to drink (and any drinking that occurs) and reviewing this record each session can help alert the therapist to the possible risk of a relapse. Between-session phone calls to prompt completion of homework assignments can also alert the therapist to precursors of a drinking episode or to drinking already in progress. Therapists' goals once drinking has occurred should be to get the drinking stopped and the couple to the therapist's office as soon as possible, for a conjoint conference to use the relapse as a learning experience. At the couple session, the therapist must be extremely active in defusing negative hostile or depressive reactions to the drinking. It should be stressed that drinking does not constitute total failure, that inconsistent progress is the rule rather than the exception. The therapist also should try to help the couple identify what couple conflict (or other antecedent) led up to the relapse and generate alternative solutions other than drinking for similar future situations. Finally, the therapist should help the couple decide what they need to do to feel sure that the drinking is over and will not continue in the coming week (e.g., restarting Antabuse, going to AA and Alanon together, reinstituting a Trust Contract, entering a detoxification ward).

Repeated drinking episodes can present a particularly difficult challenge. As indicated above, each drinking episode should be used as a learning experience, and depending on what is discovered, different strategies may be helpful. Sometimes a careful analysis will show that the drinking is being precipitated by factors outside the marital relationship, such as work pressures or job-related drinking situations (see chapter 2). Individual sessions with the alcoholic to devise methods to deal with the nonmarital precipitants often can be useful in such cases. Another nonmarital factor that can lead to repeated drinking episodes is the alcoholic's ambivalence about whether to stop drinking or attempt to drink "socially." Often an individual session with the alcoholic helps the therapist to establish the alcoholic's ambivalence as the basis for the repeated drinking and to matter-of-factly lay out the choices facing the alcoholic about his or her drinking behavior.

At times, repeated drinking episodes are related, at least in part, to marital relationship issues. When the drinking has adaptive consequences for the relationship (e.g., facilitates sexual interaction or emotional communication for one or both spouses), the main strategy is to strengthen controls against drinking while working intensively with the couple to attain the same adaptive relationship consequences without the aid of alcohol. For other couples, repeated drinking episodes are a response to recurring, intense marital conflicts, and the approach is to (a) devise specific methods tailored to their idiosyncratic needs that they can use to contain conflict and that the alcoholic can use to avoid drinking; (b) strengthen nonmarital alcohol coping mechanisms (e.g., AA, Antabuse); and (c) learn alternative communication and problem-solving skills.

Interventions to Improve the Marital and Family Relationship

Once the alcohol abuser has decided to change his or her drinking and has begun successfully to control or abstain from drinking, the therapist can focus on the alcoholic's marital and family relationships. Family members' resentment about past abusive drinking and fear and distrust about the possible return of abusive drinking in the future, coupled with the alcoholic's guilt and desire for recognition of improved drinking behavior, lead to an atmosphere of tension and unhappiness in marital and family relationships. There are problems caused by drinking (e.g., bills, legal charges, embarrassing incidents) that still need to be resolved. There is often a backlog of other unresolved marital and family problems, which the drinking obscured. These longstanding problems may seem to be increasing as drinking declines, when actually the problems are simply being recognized for the first time, now that alcohol cannot be used to excuse them. The family frequently lacks the communication skills and mutual positive feelings needed to resolve these problems. As a result, many marriages and families are dissolved during the first 1 or 2 years of the alcoholic's recovery. In other cases, marital and family conflicts can trigger relapse and a return to abusive drinking by the alcoholic. Even in cases where the alcoholic has a basically sound marriage and family life when he or she is not drinking, the initiation of sobriety can produce temporary tension and role readjustment and provide the opportunity for stabilizing and enriching the marriage and family. For these reasons, many alcoholics can benefit from assistance to improve their marital and family relationships once changes in drinking have begun.

The two major goals of interventions focused on the alcoholic's marital and family relationship are (a) to increase positive feeling, goodwill, and commitment to the relationship and (b) to resolve conflicts, problems, and desires for change. Procedures useful in achieving these two goals will be covered separately, even though they often overlap in the course of actual therapy sessions. More detailed descriptions of the procedures are available elsewhere (O'Farrell, 1986; O'Farrell & Cutter, 1984). The general sequence in teaching couples and families skills to increase positive interchanges and resolve conflicts and problems is (a) therapist instruction and modeling, (b) the couple practicing under therapist supervision, (c) assignment for homework, and (d) review of homework with further practice.

Increasing Positive Interchanges

Increasing pleasing behaviors. A series of procedures can be used to increase a couple's awarness of benefits from the relationship and the frequency with which spouses notice, acknowledge, and initiate pleasing or caring behaviors on a daily basis. *Caring behaviors* are defined to couples as "behaviors showing that you care for the other person," and homework called "Catch Your Spouse Doing Something Nice" is assigned to assist couples in *noticing* the daily caring behaviors in the marriage. This requires each spouse to record one caring behavior performed by the partner each day on sheets provided by the therapist (see Figure 12.1). The couple reads the caring behaviors recorded during the previous week at the subsequent session. Then the therapist models *acknowledging* caring behaviors ("I liked it when you _____ . It made me feel _____ "), noting the importance of eye contact; a smile; a sincere, pleasant tone of voice; and only positive feelings. Each spouse then practices acknowledging caring behaviors from his or her daily list for the previous week. After the couple practices the new behavior in the therapy session, the therapist assigns for homework a 2–5 minute daily communication session at home in which each partner acknowledges one pleasing behavior noticed that day. As couples begin to notice and acknowledge daily caring behaviors, each partner begins *initiating* more caring behaviors. Often the weekly reports of daily caring behaviors show that one or both spouses are fulfilling requests for desired change voiced before the therapy. In addition, many couples report that the 2–5 minute communication sessions serve to initiate conversation about everyday events. A final assignment is that each partner give the other a "caring day" during the coming week by performing special acts to show caring for the spouse. The therapist should encourage each partner to take risks and to act lovingly toward the spouse rather than wait for the other to make the first move. Finally, spouses are reminded that at the start of therapy they agreed to act differently (e.g.,

more lovingly) and then assess changes in feelings, rather than wait to feel more positively toward their partner before instituting changes in their own behavior.

Planning shared recreational and leisure activities. Many alcoholics' families have discontinued or decreased shared leisure activities because in the past the alcoholic has frequently sought enjoyment only in situations involving alcohol and embarrassed the family by drinking too much. Reversing this trend is important because participation by the couple and family in social and recreational activities is associated with positive alcoholism treatment outcome (Moos, Bromet, Tsu, & Moos, 1979). Planning and engaging in Shared Rewarding Activities (SRAs) can be initiated by simply having each spouse make a separate list of possible activities. Each activity must involve both spouses, either by themselves, with their children, or with other adults, and can be at home or away from home. Before giving the couple a homework assignment of planning an SRA, the therapist should model an SRA planning session, illustrating solutions to common pitfalls (e.g., waiting until the last minute so that necessary preparations cannot be made, getting sidetracked on trivial practical arrangements). Finally, the therapist should instruct the couple to refrain from discussing problems or conflicts during their planned SRAs.

Core symbols. Core symbols, or symbols of special meaning, offer another means to enhance positive feelings and interactions in a relationship. A core symbol is any event, place, or object that carries special meaning for the relationship to both marital partners (Liberman, Wheeler, deVisser, Kuehnel, & Kuehnel, 1980). A special song, the honeymoon, the place where the couple met, pictures, eating by candlelight, and wedding rings are examples. Rituals and activities (e.g., going out for breakfast on Sunday morning) which go beyond recreational activities because of their special meaning to the couple can also become a core symbol and represent an intimate shared time set aside for closeness. Core symbols should be introduced with alcoholic couples only after tension over drinking has decreased and the partners are beginning to experience some good will and positive feeling for each other. After each partner gives one example of such a symbol, each spouse lists as many core symbols

"CATCH YOUR SPOUSE DOING SOMETHING NICE"

NAME: Nancy   NAME OF SPOUSE: Mike

DAY	DATE	PLEASING BEHAVIOR
MON.	4/6	He took the kids out for a ride while I finished preparing dinner.
TUES.	4/7	Helped with the chores after dinner.
WED.	4/8	Gave me a kiss when I woke up in the morning.
THUR.	4/9	Took care of the household responsibilities for the evening, allowing me to spend some time alone just pampering myself.
FRI.	4/10	Brought my car to be serviced and paid the bill for me.
SAT.	4/11	Picked up some videos and popcorn and we had a fun time at home.
SUN.	4/12	Brought home flowers, smiled and hugged me tight.

"CATCH YOUR SPOUSE DOING SOMETHING NICE"

NAME: Mike   NAME OF SPOUSE: Nancy

DAY	DATE	PLEASING BEHAVIOR
MON.	4/6	Waited to have dinner with me because I had to stay late at work. Made me feel good.
TUES.	4/7	Told me she loved me.
WED.	4/8	Cooked a delicious Italian dinner and afterwards we had a very romantic evening.
THUR.	4/9	Was patient with me as I came home tired and moody from work.
FRI.	4/10	Enjoyed a walk together around the neighborhood.
SAT.	4/11	Woke me gently and rubbed my back.
SUN.	4/12	Was the perfect hostess for an afternoon party with some friends of ours.

Figure 12.1. Sample record sheets of daily caring behaviors.

as possible for a homework assignment. In subsequent sessions the couple chooses one or more core symbols to reexperience or reestablish in their day-to-day lives together. In relationships where the search for core symbols not poisoned by alcohol proves fruitless, the goal is to help the couple develop and enact new core symbols in their relationship. Identifying and participating in such core symbols can help couples foster positive feelings that have been buried for years under many layers of hostility and disappointment. For some couples, a reestablishment of spiritual and religious practices is an important consideration here.

Applications to family therapy. Core symbols, planning recreational and leisure activities, and increasing positive behaviors can be applied to family therapy in which one or more children are included with their parents. Family therapy sessions are particularly useful and indicated when an adolescent has an alcohol problem or when the alcoholic parent and his or her spouse have made some progress and the therapist wishes then to include the children in the therapy. Using core symbols in family therapy sessions can be very powerful, because special activities and rituals forge strong family ties and traditions. Similarly, planning recreational and leisure activities for the whole family or for selected members (e.g., father and son) can be quite rewarding, and the preceding procedures for couples are directly applicable. The procedures directed to increasing pleasing behavior often can lead to pronounced changes in the emotional tone of the family, especially when the therapist can get the entire family to participate.

Resolving Conflicts and Problems

Training in communication skills. Inadequate communication is a major problem for alcoholic couples (O'Farrell & Birchler, 1987), and the inability to resolve conflicts and problems can cause abusive drinking and severe marital and family tension to recur (Maisto et al., 1988). We generally begin our work on training in communication skills by defining effective communication as "message intended (by speaker) equals message received (by listener)". The chart presented in Figure 12.2 helps explain this definition further, including factors (e.g., "filters") in each person that can impede communication and the need to learn both "listening" and "speaking" skills. Therapists can use in-

structions, modeling, prompting, behavioral rehearsal, and feedback to teach couples and families how to communicate more effectively. Learning communication skills of listening and speaking and how to use planned communication sessions are essential prerequisites for problem solving and negotiating desired behavior changes. The training starts with non-problem areas that are positive or neutral, and moves to problem areas and charged issues only after each skill has been practiced on less problematic topics.

Communication Sessions are planned, structured discussions in which spouses talk privately, face to face, without distractions, and with each spouse taking turns expressing his or her point of view without interruptions. Communication sessions can be introduced for 2–5 minutes daily when couples first practice acknowledging caring behaviors, and in 10- to 15-minute sessions three to four times a week in later sessions when the concern is to practice a particular skill. The therapist discusses with the couple the time and place at which they plan to have their assigned communication practice sessions. The success of this plan is assessed at the next session, and any needed changes are suggested. Just establishing a communication session as a method for discussing feelings, events, and problems can be very helpful for many couples. Couples are encouraged to ask each other for a communication session when they want to discuss an issue or problem and to keep in mind the ground rules of behavior that characterize such a session.

Listening skills help each spouse to feel understood and supported and slow down couple interactions to prevent quick escalation of aversive exchanges. Spouses are instructed to use a listening response ("What I heard you say was . . . Is that right?") to repeat both the words and the feelings of the speaker's message and to check to see if the message they received was the message intended by their partner. When the listener has understood the speaker's message, roles change and the first listener then speaks. Teaching a partner in an alcoholic marriage to communicate support and understanding by summarizing the spouse's message and checking the accuracy of the received message before stating his or her own position is often a major accomplishment that has to be achieved gradually. A partner's failure to separate understanding the spouse's position from agreement with it is often an obstacle that must be overcome.

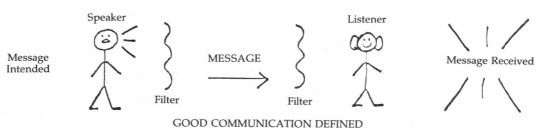

GOOD COMMUNICATION DEFINED

Message Intended equals *Message Received*

Figure 12.2. Illustration of communication used at start of training in communication skills. [Adapted by permission from Gottman, J., Notarius, C., Gonso, J., & Markman, H. (1976). *A couple's guide to communication* (p. 1). Champaign IL: Research Press.]

Speaking skills—expressing both positive and negative feelings directly—can be taught as an alternative to the blaming, hostile, and indirect responsibility-avoiding communication behaviors that characterize many alcoholic marriages (O'Farrell & Birchler, 1987). The therapist instructs that when the speaker expresses feelings directly, there is a greater chance that he or she will be heard because the speaker says these are his or her feelings, his or her point of view, and not some objective fact about the other person. The speaker takes responsibility for his or her own feelings and does not blame the other person for how he or she feels, thus reducing listener defensiveness and making it easier for the listener to receive the intended message. Differences between direct expressions of feelings and those that are indirect, and therefore either ineffective or hurtful, are presented along with examples. The use of statements beginning with "I" rather than "you" is emphasized. After rationale and instructions have been presented, the therapist models correct and incorrect ways of expressing feelings and elicits the couple's reactions to these modeled scenes. Then the couple role-plays a communication session in which spouses take turns being speaker and listener, with the speaker expressing feelings directly and the listener using the listening response. During this role playing, the therapist is poised to prompt, model, stop action, and give feedback to the couple as they practice reflecting the direct expressions of feelings. Similar communication sessions, 10 to 15 minutes each three to four times weekly, are assigned for homework. Subsequent therapy sessions involve more practice with role playing, both during the sessions and for homework, and the topics on which the couple practices increase in difficulty each week.

Problem-solving skills training. After the couple has first learned basic communication skills, they can next learn skills to solve problems stemming from both external stressors (e.g., job, extended family) and relationship conflicts. In solving a problem, the couple should first list a number of possible solutions. Then, while withholding judgment regarding the preferred solution, the couple considers both positive and negative, and short-term and long-term consequences of each solution. Finally, the spouses rank the solutions from most to least preferred and agree to implement one or more of the solutions. Use of problem-solving procedures can help spouses avoid polarizing on one solution or another or the "yes, but . . ." trap, in which one partner points out the negative consequences of the other partner's solution.

Behavior change agreements. Many alcoholics and their spouses need to learn positive methods to change their partner's behavior, to replace the coercive strategies previously used. Many changes that spouses desire from their partners can be achieved through the aforementioned caring behaviors, rewarding activities, and communication and problem-solving skills. However, deeper, emotion-laden conflicts that have caused considerable hostility and coercive interaction for years are more resistant to change. In addition to general communication skills and a spirit of good will, learning to make positive specific requests (PSR) and to negotiate and compromise are prerequisites for making sound behavior-change agreements which may resolve such issues.

Positive specific requests are an alternative to the all-too-frequent practice of couples complaining in vague and unclear terms and trying to coerce, browbeat, and force the other partner to change. The couple is told that "each partner has to learn to state his or her desires in the form of: (a) positive—what you want, not what you don't want; (b) specific—what, where, and when; (c) requests—not demands that use force and threats, but rather requests that show possibility for negotiation and compromise." The therapist gives sample requests that do and do not meet these requirements, and for homework each partner lists at least five PSRs.

Negotiation and compromise comes next. Spouses share their lists of requests, starting with the most specific and positive items, and the therapist gives feedback on the requests presented and helps rewrite items as needed. Then the therapist explains that negotiation and compromise can help couples reach an agreement in which each partner will do one thing requested by the other. After giving instructions and examples, the therapist coaches a couple while they have a communication session, in which requests are made in a positive specific form, heard by each partner, and translated into a mutually satisfactory, realistic agreement for the upcoming week. Finally, the agreement is recorded on a homework sheet that the couple knows will be reviewed during the next session.

Agreements can be a major focus of a number of therapy sessions in which written behavior-change agreements are negotiated for the forthcoming week, often with very good effects on the couple's relationship. Figure 12.3 shows a typical example of a couple agreement. During the sessions, unkept agreements are reviewed briefly, and the therapist provides feedback as to what went wrong and suggests changes needed in the coming week. After completing agreements under therapist supervision, the couple is asked to have a communication session at home to negotiate an agreement on their own and to bring it to the following session for review. A series of such assignments can provide a couple with the opportunity to develop skills in behavior change that they can use after the therapy ends. We encourage good-faith agreements in which each partner agrees to make his or her change independent of whether or not the spouse keeps the agreement and without monetary or other rewards or punishments. This approach, which has been used by others (Turkewitz & O'Leary, 1981), is simpler than other approaches to couple agree-ments and stresses the need for each spouse to freely and unilaterally make the changes needed to improve the marital relationship.

Applications to family therapy. Communication, problem-solving, and behavior change skills are directly applicable to family therapy sessions involving an alcoholic and his or her children and spouse or an adolescent alcohol abuser and his or her parents. We relabel the communicaton sessions as family council meetings or family meetings, and emphasize very strongly some additional ground rules that characterize such a meeting: one person speaks at a time, no interrupting is permitted, and a consensus must be reached to enact a decision. The latter is to guard against parents (or other subgroups) forcing their will on weaker family members. Behavioral family therapy with adolescents and parents, (e.g., Robin, 1981) can be extremely useful for families with alcohol problems because many adult alcoholics have severe problems with their adolescent offspring, and adolescent alcohol abusers (of which there are a growing number) frequently have quite troubled relationships with their parents. Behavior-change agreements are also quite useful with children and their parents, but the behavior changes of the children may be more numerous than those of the parents; generally, reward–punishment contingencies are useful because (unlike a marriage) the parent–child relationship is not one of equal partners.

MAINTAINING DRINKING AND RELATIONSHIP CHANGES

Preventing Relapse

Methods to ensure long-term maintenance of the changes in alcohol problems made through marital and family therapy have received very little attention and need considerable development. We use three general methods during the maintenance phase of treatment, defined somewhat arbitrarily as the phase that begins after at least 6 consecutive months of abstinence or consistent nonproblem drinking have been achieved. First, maintenance must be planned prior to the termination of the active treatment phase. We review the previous marital and family therapy sessions with the clients, to determine which therapeutic interventions or behavior changes (e.g., Antabuse

COUPLE CONTRACT/FULFILLMENT RECORD

Name: ___Mike & Nancy Jones___

Week Beginning ___4/10/87 (Fri.)___

Mike's
RESPONSIBILITIES (Mike checks when performed)

	DAY						
	Fri	Sat	Sun	Mon	Tues	Wed	Thurs
1. Install kitchen appliance on Thursday night.							✓
2. Take Nancy and kids for a ride and visit to her parents on Sunday.			✓				
3.							

Nancy's
RESPONSIBILITIES (Nancy checks when performed)

	Fri	Sat	Sun	Mon	Tues	Wed	Thurs
1. Have a special dinner for the two of us on Wed. night.						✓	
2. Make an effort to have some time alone each day to talk and check in with one another.	✓		✓	✓	✓		
3.							

Figure 12.3. Sample couple agreement.

contract, communication sessions) have been most helpful and plan how the family can continue to engage in the desired new behaviors when needed (e.g., rehearsing how to cope with situations likely to interfere with the new behavior, rereading handouts from the therapy periodically, agreeing to periodic monitoring by the therapist). A second method is to anticipate what high-risk situations for relapse to abusive drinking may be likely to occur after treatment, and to discuss and rehearse possible coping strategies that the alcoholic and other family members can use to prevent relapse when confronted with such situations. A third method is to discuss and rehearse how to cope with a relapse when it occurs. Here, the techniques suggested by Marlatt and Gordon (1985) can be useful: allowing a delay after the first drink; calling the therapist; and engaging in realistic and rational thinking about the slip. A specific couple-family relapse-episode plan, written and rehearsed prior to ending active treatment, can be particularly useful. Early intervention at the beginning of a relapse episode is essential and must be stressed with the couple or family. Often, spouses and family members wait until the drinking has reached dangerous levels again before acting. By then, much additional damage has been done to the marital and family relationship and to other aspects of the drinker's life.

We suggest continued contact with the couple or family via planned in-person and telephone follow-up sessions, at regular and gradually increasing intervals, for 3 to 5 years after a stable pattern of recovery has been achieved. This ongoing contact is useful to monitor progress, to assess compliance with planned maintenance procedures, and to evaluate the need for additional therapy sessions. The therapist must take responsibility for scheduling and reminding the family of follow-up sessions and for placing agreed-upon phone calls if continued contact is to be maintained successfully. The rationale given to couples and families for the continued contact is that alcohol abuse is a chronic health problem that requires active, aggressive, ongoing monitoring by the therapist and family members to prevent or to quickly treat relapses for at least 5 years after an initial stable pattern of recovery has been established. The follow-up contact also provides the opportunity to deal with marital and family issues that appear after a period of recovery.

Marital and Family Issues in Long-Term Recovery

Many alcohol abusers continue to experience significant marital and family difficulties after a period of stable recovery has been established. Although a wide variety of issues can present difficulties during long-term recovery, a number of concerns and life patterns predominate. These problem areas include: (a) role readjustment when the alcoholic tries to regain important family roles lost through drinking; (b) sex and intimacy; and (c) parent–child relationships, especially communication and behavior management with adolescents. Finally, families during the recovery process seem particularly vulnerable to stresses created by critical transitions in the family life cycle (e.g., children leaving home), external life change events (e.g., job loss), or developmental changes in any of the family members (e.g., mid-life crisis). These marital and family issues are by no means unique to alcoholic families, but the therapist has two additional responsibilities when such issues are presented by alcoholic families during long-term recovery. First, the therapist must determine if a relapse is imminent, so that necessary preventive interventions can be instituted immediately. Second, the therapist must (a) determine each family member's view of the relationship between the former alcohol problem and the current marital and family difficulties and (b) carefully assess whether or not he or she shares the family member's view. The latter is important because family members often continue to atrribute difficulties in their relationships to the previous alcohol problem, rather than to their current life situation.

A final problem encountered all too frequently is that even though the alcohol problem is under control, the marriage is no longer viable. We label this "successful sobriety and the bankrupt marriage" to the couples we work with, and consider "breaking up without breaking out" a major accomplishment. Spouses may have grown apart, or one may be unwilling to set aside the past hurts. Whatever the reason, facing the emptiness and inevitable dissolution of the marriage often precipitates a dangerous crisis. If there has been a strong tendency to blame the alcoholic for relationship problems, there is a strong push to want the alcoholic to drink again to provide the reason for the marital breakup. The therapist can try to help the couple confront separation and divorce without requiring the alcoholic to fail again and be the scapegoat for the breakup. If the couple can separate without the alcoholic's drinking, the alcoholic's future relationship with his or her children may be preserved, and both spouses may be able to obtain a realistic assessment of the basis for their divorce. Unfortunately, many couples cannot do this.

EFFECTIVENESS

The present review of outcome research on marital and family therapy with alcoholics covers studies that included a comparison group of some type and at least some follow-up data. Our review is organized according to the stage of change to which the marital and family therapy in each study was directed.

Studies of Marital/Family Therapy to Initiate Change in the Alcoholic

In an early report, Cohen and Krause (1971) evaluated a Family Service Agency program in which a group of social workers were specifically trained in the disease model of alcoholism and techniques for treating the wives of alcohol abusers. Wives who presented the husband's drinking as a major problem at intake were randomly assigned to: (a) caseworkers specially trained in alcoholism (experimental group, N = 146); (b) caseworkers working as usual and aware they were a control group (N = 73); (c) caseworkers unaware of the study (N = 73). Twenty-four additional wives were assessed on the outcome measures before treatment to measure the status of untreated cases. Results showed that fewer experimental than control group cases discontinued treatment after the initial casework contact, experimental group wives attended more treatment sessions than control wives, and more of the alcoholic husbands of women in the experimental group were eventually seen in treatment. Further, the husbands' antisocial behavior improved in more experimental than control cases. There are some indications that wife involvement in treatment can offer therapeutic benefit whether or not the caseworker was specifically trained in alcoholism. Treated wives reported fewer ways their husband's drinking affected the families than did untreated wives. In addition,

treated wives reported improvements in marital problems, the husband's drinking, and their own self-concepts, but the experimental and control groups did not differ.

Thomas and others' work (1987) on Unilateral Family Therapy with the spouses of alcoholics has demonstrated that intervention with the spouse as a change agent around goals of improved spouse coping, reduction of drinking by alcohol abuser, and treatment entry for alcohol abuser can effectively influence the behavior of alcoholics who are uncooperative to treatment. Findings indicated that unilateral family therapy treatment helped move alcohol abusers into treatment, reduced abusers' alcohol intake, and produced decreases in measures of life distress and increases in those of affectional expression and sexual satisfaction. Significant findings in this study indicated that 61% of the alcohol abusers of spouses in the treatment condition improved by decreased drinking and/or movement into treatment, while none of the abusers of spouses in the no-treatment group showed improvement.

Sisson and Azrin (1986) investigated the effect of involvement of family members (usually wives) in a reinforcement program designed to teach interactionally based behavioral contingency skills for coping with the alcoholic. The reinforcement program resulted in significantly more alcoholics entering treatment than did a more traditional program for family members which consisted of alcohol education, individually oriented supportive counseling, and referral to Alanon. In addition, alcoholics with relatives in the reinforcement program showed significantly reduced alcohol use prior to entering treatment, while the control group alcoholics did not.

These studies have demonstrated the sizeable influence of individual family member treatment on the initiation of treatment entry for alcoholics who have not yet sought assistance for recovery.

Studies of Marital/Family Therapy to Stabilize Changes in the Alcoholic

Concurrent Treatment of the Alcoholic and the Spouse

In an early study which analyzed the effects of including the alcoholic's spouse in treatment, Smith (1969) offered wives of hospitalized alcoholics attendance in a weekly therapy group which focused on increasing their understanding of alcoholism and of the role of the marital relationship in the husband's alcoholism. He found that significantly more husbands of wives who attend the therapy group were abstinent or improved at 16 month follow-up than were husbands of wives who did not. Smith's study, however, is difficult to interpret because the contrast group was composed of wives who chose not to attend a therapy group in conjunction with their husband's treatment. The practice of separate and concurrent treatment for the alcoholic and spouse is no longer as popular as it once was (Steinglass, 1976), having been replaced by methods that involve the alcoholic and spouse together in treatment.

Behavioral Contracting to Maintain Antabuse (Disulfiram) Ingestion

Azrin et al. (1982) randomly assigned alcoholic outpatients to one of three treatment groups: (a) traditional, self-initiated disulfiram treatment; (b) disulfiram assurance with a significant other, usually the spouse, observing and reinforcing the ingestion of the medication; and (c) disulfiram assurance plus a multifaceted behavior therapy program. At six-month follow-up, the behavior therapy plus disulfiram assurance group was almost fully abstinent, drinking on the average 0.4 days a month. The traditional group, in contrast, had stopped disulfiram and was drinking on the average 16.4 days a month. Although follow-up measures for the disulfiram assurance group as a whole were intermediate between the other two groups, for married alcoholics disulfiram assurance alone was sufficient to produce almost total abstinence.

Keane, Foy, Nunn, and Rychtarik (1984) randomly assigned male alcoholics being discharged from a four-week behaviorally oriented inpatient alcoholism treatment program to one of three treatment conditions: (a) disulfiram prescription and contract with significant other, usually the wife, plus instructions for the wife to use positive reinforcement for contract compliance; (b) disulfiram prescription and contract with significant other; and (c) disulfiram prescription without contract. At three month follow-up, 84% of all subjects were still abstinent and taking disulfiram daily by collateral report, with no siginificant differences among treatment groups. A greater proportion of sub-

jects in the contract groups had filled all three monthly prescriptions of disulfiram, but this difference did not significantly distinguish the groups.

The Azrin et al. (1982) and Keane et al. (1984) studies of spouse behavioral contracting to maintain disulfiram ingestion reach opposite conclusions about the usefulness of such procedures. A number of differences in the studies may explain the differing results. The Azrin et al. study was with applicants for outpatient treatment who received 5 weekly outpatient sessions, the spouse was not involved in the prescription only condition, and data were gathered for 6 months follow-up. In the Keane et al. study, subjects started disulfiram after at least 4 weeks of inpatient treatment; the spouse and patient together received a videotape on the use of disulfiram and its effects in all conditions, including the prescription only group and only 3 months follow-up data were gathered. Given these differing results, the evidence from other studies showing that patients who stay on disulfiram have better alcoholism treatment outcomes (Fuller et al., 1986), and the good outcomes produced by programs that have included a disulfiram contract as part of the program (e.g., Azrin, 1976; O'Farrell, Cutter, & Floyd, 1985; O'Farrell & Cutter, 1982), further research is needed.

Multiple Couples Group Therapy

Burton and Kaplan (1968) contacted 179 couples to obtain their evaluations of their treatment experience. Forty-eight of the couples had been treated with multiple couples group therapy; the rest of the sample had received individual treatment for the alcoholic and spouse. Overall, 76% of couples treated in multiple couple groups reported that counseling had been a positive experience, while only 57% of couples in which the alcoholic and/or spouse had been treated in individual counseling felt similarly. These results should be viewed cautiously, since cases were not randomly assigned to treatments, the length of follow-up varied considerably (from 2–12 years), and data were limited to client satisfaction reports. Nonetheless, this early enthusiasm for couples group treatment is supported by later, more controlled studies.

Corder, Corder, and Laidlaw (1972) studied the effects of spouse inclusion on treatment outcome in an investigation that added a four-day intensive residential marital couples group workshop to a standard three-week inpatient alcohol rehabilitation program. In contrast to a control group which was treated only with the standard individual inpatient rehab program, the experimental groups showed significant improvement at six-month follow-up: 11 of 19 in the experimental group and only 3 in the control group had maintained sobriety. In addition, the couples of the experimental group were participating in significantly more recreational activities together at six-month follow-up than were couples of the control group.

Cadogan (1973) treated a group of 20 alcoholics and their spouses with marital group interactive therapy and compared them with a group of 20 couples "waiting for treatment." The marital group therapy focused on marital communication and problem-solving, with goals of improvement in marital problem-solving and continued abstinence from alcohol. At six months post-treatment, the experimental and control groups differed significantly: 9 subjects of the couples' treatment group remained abstinent, 4 subjects reported some drinking, and 7 subjects had relapsed, while in the control condition only 2 subjects remained abstinent, 5 subjects reported some drinking, and 13 subjects had relapsed. Although the effect of marital group treatment on drinking behavior appears to be fairly powerful in this study, due to the lack of pre- and post-treatment assessment of marital relationship variables, the effects of the intervention on the marital relationship remain unclear.

In the Counseling for Alcoholics' Marriages (CALM) Project, O'Farrell and his colleagues (O'Farrell & Cutter, 1982; O'Farrell, Cutter, & Floyd, 1985) investigated the effect of adding marital group treatment to individually oriented outpatient treatment of married male alcoholics. Thirty-six couples, in which the husband had recently begun individual alcoholism counseling that included an Antabuse prescription, were randomly assigned to a no-marital-treatment control group or to 10 weekly sessions of either a behavioral (Antabuse Contract plus behavioral rehearsal of communication skills and marital agreements) or an interactional (largely verbal interaction and sharing of feelings and Antabuse without spouse involvement) couples group. Assessment of marital and drinking adjustment provided comparison data pre- and post-treatment and at two and six months follow-up. Results for marital adjust-

ment showed the behavioral marital therapy (BMT) couples: (a) improved from pre- to post-treatment on a variety of measures and remained significantly improved at follow-ups; (b) did better than control couples who did not improve on any measures; and (c) did better than interactional couples (whose improvement on two measures was not sustained at follow-up) although the superiority of the BMT group was reduced to nonsignificant trends at follow-up. On drinking adjustment, alcoholics in all three treatments showed significant improvements sustained at follow-up and BMT subjects did better than interactional subjects at post-treatment and at two months follow-up. O'Farrell and his colleagues concluded that adding a BMT couples group to outpatient alcoholism counseling showed clear advantages for the alcoholics' marital relationships but no additional gains in drinking adjustment. The less positive results for the interactional couples group suggested that just talking about relationship problems without making specific changes may lead to conflict and drinking, and that the Antabuse Contract protected the BMT couples while they learned new skills to confront their problems without alcohol.

Other Studies

Hedberg and Campbell (1974) compared behavioral family counseling with various individually oriented behavioral treatments. Subjects were randomly assigned to (a) systematic desensitization, (b) covert sensitization, (c) electric shock avoidance conditioning, or (d) behavioral family counseling in communication skills and learning principles, with use of behavioral contracts with each family member. At six-month follow-up, Behavioral Family Counseling (BFC) was the most effective treatment for all patients, regardless of whether the patients' goal was abstinence or controlled drinking; and BFC was particularly effective for patients with abstinence goals.

In a study examining the effects of joint hospitalization and couples treatment for alcoholism, McCrady, Paolino, Longabough, and Rossi (1979) evaluated the relative effectiveness of couples and individual treatment for alcoholics. Subjects were randomly assigned to (a) individual involvement, in which only the alcoholic attended group therapy; (b) couples involvement in which the alcoholic and spouse participated in an outpatient interactional couples therapy group, in addition to concurrent individual treatment groups for each spouse; or (c) joint admission, in which both partners were initially hospitalized and then participated in both the couples group therapy and individual therapy groups following discharge. At six-month follow-up, findings indicated significant decreases in alcohol intake for both the couples involvement and joint admission treatment groups but not for the individual treatment group. All groups showed signficant decreases in marital problems.

The Program for Alcoholic Couples Treatment (PACT) study compared three types of spouse involvement. McCrady and her colleagues (1986) randomly assigned alcoholics and spouses to one of three outpatient behavioral treatments: (a) minimal spouse involvement (MSI), in which the spouse simply observed the alcoholic's individual therapy; (b) alcohol-focused spouse involvement (AFSI), which included teaching the spouse specific skills to deal with alcohol-related situations plus the MSI interventions; (c) alcohol behavioral marital therapy (ABMT), in which all skills taught in the MSI and AFSI conditions were included, as well as BMT. Results at six-month follow-up indicated that all subjects had decreased drinking and reported increased life satisfaction, and suggested that ABMT led to better treatment outcomes than the other spouse-involved therapies. Specifically, ABMT couples better maintained their marital satisfaction after treatment and tended to have more stable marriages than the other two groups; were more compliant with homework assignments; decreased the alcoholics' number of drinking days during treatement; and increased post-treatment drinking more slowly than AFSI couples.

Studies of Marital and Family Therapy and Long-Term Maintenance

Research is just starting to focus on the effects of marital and family therapy during long-term recovery. The available data come from long-term follow-up outcomes of recent studies, the intermediate-term outcomes of which have just been reviewed. Four-year follow-up data from the McCrady et al. (1979) joint hospitalization and couples therapy outcome study (McCrady, Moreau, Paolino, & Longabaugh, 1982) showed there were no longer any significant differences among the different treatment groups in the study on either marital or drinking adjustment. The results of this study also show a commonly observed pattern of decay in outcomes over time, with more than 75% of the subjects showing improvement at 6 month follow-up but less than one-third functioning consistently well over the four years.

Two-year follow-up data from the PACT study (McCrady et al., 1986) show a somewhat surprising result. Time trend statistics showed that patients who received marital therapy (i.e,. ABMT group) gradually decreased their drinking over time after treatment, whereas those who received alcohol-focused therapy only (MSI group) showed the more usual pattern of a gradual increase in drinking. According to Stout, McCrady, Longabaugh, Noel, & Beattie (1987), this pattern suggests that the primary impact of marital therapy is on the long-term maintenance of improvements resulting from treatment, rather than on the initial level of short-term improvement. Stout et al. (1987) analyzed follow-up data over two years from married alcoholics, in the ongoing Butler Hospital Environmental Treatment for Alcoholism (BETA) project, and found similar results. BETA patients receiving marital therapy initially have slightly higher levels of drinking than those in alcohol-focused therapy, but this difference reverses over time. Treatment group differences on measures of marital functioning have not yet been published for these two studies.

Eighteen-month follow-up data from the Project CALM study (O'Farrell & Cutter, 1982) showed BMT superior to no marital treatment controls on marital adjustment and stability up to 18-month follow-up, but the superiority of BMT over the interactional group faded as a function of time after treatment. On drinking, BMT remained superior to interactional treatment for part of the first year after treatment, but by 18 months follow-up there were no differences between groups, all of which remained significantly improved from pretreatment levels. O'Farrell and Cutter (1982) also examined trend lines over the 18 months after treatment in a manner similar to that used by Stout et al. (1987), but did not find similar results for drinking outcomes. The two marital plus individual therapy conditions (i.e., BMT and interactional) deteriorated gradually, as did the individual therapy only patients. However, the two marital therapy conditions showed a less precipitous deterioration on amount of time separated than did the individual therapy only control patients. In addition, at 18-month follow-up, the behavioral group was superior to and the interactional group nearly better than the controls on time separated, suggesting that the common effect of both types of marital therapy in this study may have been to promote relationship stability during the long and arduous period of recovery from alcoholism.

Summary and Conclusions on Marital and Family Therapy Outcome Research

Two studies show that marital and family therapy can be used effectively to motivate an initial commitment to change in the alcoholic (Thomas et al., 1987; Sisson & Azrin, 1986). Replication of these results and evaluation of the widely used Johnson Institute intervention are needed.

Evidence is accumulating that marital and family therapy helps stabilize marital and family relationships and supports improvements in alcoholics' drinking during the 6 month period following treatment entry for alcoholism. Marital and family therapy produces better results during this time period than methods that do not involve the spouse or other family members. Recent studies suggest that the most promising marital therapy approach combines a focus on the drinking and drinking-related communications with work on more general marital relationship issues. Tentative support is found for superior results with more structured, directive, behaviorally oriented marital therapy methods as compared to other marital therapy methods.

Studies of long-term recovery are just beginning to appear. Although they suggest that behaviorally oriented marital therapy with both an alcohol and relationship focus may reduce marital or drinking deterioration or both during long-term recovery, considerably more research is needed to substantiate this conclusion.

REFERENCES

Clinical Guidelines

Azrin, N. H. (1976). Improvements in the community-reinforcement approach to alcoholism. *Behaviour Research and Therapy, 14*, 339–348.

Comprehensive behavioral treatment program that included Antabuse contract and marital therapy is described and evaluated.

Johnson, V. A. (1973). *I'll quit tomorrow.* New York: Harper & Row. Detailed account of alcoholism treatment approach at the Johnson Institute in Minneapolis, where the "intervention" method is used with significant others to motivate the alcoholic to seek treatment.

McCrady, B. S. (1982). Conjoint behavioral treatment of an alcoholic and his spouse. In W. M. Hay & P. E. Nathan (Eds.), *Clinical case studies in the behavioral treatment of alcoholism* (pp. 127–156). New York: Plenum. Presents a case study in which a multifaceted behavioral approach to decreasing spouse behaviors that cue or enable drinking is used.

Miller, P. M. (1972). The use of behavioral contracting in the treatment of alcoholism: A case report. *Behavior Therapy, 3*, 593–596. Presents case in which a behavioral contract between an alcohol abuser and his wife is used to reduce problem drinking to an acceptable level.

O'Farrell, T. J. (1986). Marital therapy in the treatment of alcoholism. In N. S. Jacobson & A. S. Gurman (Eds.), *Clinical handbook of marital therapy* (pp. 513–535). New York: Guilford Press. Provides a detailed consideration of marital therapy for alcoholics using a behavioral approach. Case illustrations and considerable procedural detail are included.

O'Farrell, T. J., & Bayog, R. D. (1986). Antabuse contracts for married alcoholics and their spouses: A method to insure Antabuse taking and decrease conflict about alcohol. *Journal of Substance Abuse Treatment, 3*, 1–8. Presents step by step instructions on how to implement an Antabuse contract with alcoholic couples and how to deal with common resistances to this procedure.

O'Farrell, T. J., & Cutter, H. S. G. (1984). Behavioral marital therapy couples groups for male alcoholics and their wives. *Journal of Substance Abuse Treatment, 1*, 191–204. Provides detailed description, including session by session outline, of a 10-week couples group specifically for alcoholics.

Robin, A. (1981). A controlled evaluation of problem-solving communication training with parent–adolescent conflict. *Behavior Therapy, 12*, 593–609. Describes and evaluates communication training with parents and adolescents, not specific to but useful with alcoholic families.

Shaprio, R. J. (1984). Therapy with violent families. In S. Saunders, A. Anderson, C. Hart, & G. Rubenstein (Eds.), *Violent individuals and families: A handbook for practitioners* (pp. 112–136). Springfield, IL: Charles C. Thomas. Describes methods for use with marital and family violence, many of which are applicable to alcoholics.

Sisson, R. W., & Azrin, N. H. (1986). Family-member involvement to initiate and promote treatment of problem drinkers. *Journal of Behavior Therapy and Experimental Psychiatry, 17*, 15–21. Presents treatment procedures and outcome data on a behavior therapy program for teaching the alcoholic's spouse how to reduce physical abuse and encourage sobriety and treatment entry by the alcoholics.

Sobell, M. B., & Sobell, L. C. (1975). A brief technical

report on the MOBAT: An inexpensive portable test for determining blood alcohol concentration. *Journal of Applied Behavioral Analysis, 8,* 117–120. Describes a Mobile Breath Alcohol Test useful in assessment and treatment with alcoholic couples.

Thomas, E. J., & Santa, C. A. (1982). Unilateral family therapy for alcohol abuse: A working conception. *American Journal of Family Therapy, 10,* 49–60. Presents the goals and methods for working with the alcoholic's spouse to aid the spouse's coping and motivate the resistant alcoholic to change the drinking.

Thorne, D. R. (1983). Techniques for use in intervention. *Journal of Alcohol and Drug Education, 28,* 46–50. Provides session-by-session description of the Johnson Institute "intervention" method for motivating the alcoholic to stop drinking.

Research

Azrin, N. H., Sisson, R. W., Meyers, R., & Godley, M. (1982). Alcoholism treatment by disulfiram and community reinforcement therapy. *Journal of Behavior Therapy and Experimental Psychiatry, 13,* 105–112.

Burton, G., & Kaplan, H. M. (1968). Group counseling in conflicted marriages where alcoholism is present: Client's evaluation of effectiveness. *Journal of Marriage and the Family, 30,* 74–79.

Cadogan, D. A. (1973). Marital group therapy in the treatment of alcoholism. *Quarterly Journal of Studies on Alcohol, 34,* 1187–1194.

Cohen, D. C., & Krause, M. S. (1971). *Casework with the wives of alcoholics.* New York: Family Service Assoc. of America.

Corder, B. F., Corder, R. F., & Laidlaw, N. D. (1972). An intensive treatment program for alcoholics and their wives. *Quarterly Journal of Studies on Alcohol, 33,* 1144–1146.

Finney, J. W., Moos, R. H., & Mewborn, C. R. (1980). Posttreatment experiences and treatment outcome of alcoholic patients six months and two years after hospitalization. *Journal of Consulting and Clinical Psychology, 48,* 17–29.

Fuller, R. K., Branchey, L., Brightwell, D. R., Derman, R. M., Emrick, C. D., Iber, F. L., James, K. E., Lacoursiere, R. B., Lee, K. L., Lowenstam, I., Maany, I., Neiderhister, D., Nocks, J. J., & Shaw, S. (1986). Disulfiram treatment of alcoholism. *Journal of the American Medical Association, 256,* 1449–1455.

Gurman, A. S., & Kniskern, D. P. (1978). Deterioration in marital and family therapy: Empirical, clinical, and conceptual issues. *Family Process, 17,* 3–20.

Heather, N., & Robertson, I. (1983) (rev. ed.). *Controlled drinking.* London: Methuen.

Hedberg, A. G., & Campbell, L. (1974). A comparison of four behavioral treatments of alcoholism. *Journal of Behavior Therapy and Experimental Psychiatry, 5,* 251–256.

Keane, T. M., Foy, D. W., Nunn, B., & Rychtarik, R. G. (1984). Spouse contracting to increase Antabuse compliance in alcoholic veterans. *Journal of Clinical Psychology, 40,* 340–344.

Keller, M. (Ed.). (1974). Trends in treatment of alcoholism. In *Second special report to the U.S. Congress on alcohol and health.* (pp. 145–167). Washington, DC: Department of Health, Education, and Welfare.

Liberman, R. P., Wheeler, E. G., de Visser, L. A. Kuehnel, J., & Kuehnel, T. (1980). *Handbook of marital therapy: A positive approach to helping troubled relationships.* New York: Plenum.

Lundwall, L., & Baekeland, F. (1971). Disulfiram treatment of alcoholism. *Journal of Nervous and Mental Disease, 153,* 381–394.

Maisto, S. A., O'Farrell, T. J., Connors, G. J., McKay, J., & Pelcovitz, M. A. (1988). Alcoholics' attributions of factors affecting their relapse to drinking and reasons for terminating relapse events. *Addictive Behaviors, 13,* 79–82.

Marlatt, G. A., & Gordon, J. (1985). *Relapse prevention: Maintenance strategies in the treatment of addictive behaviors.* New York: Guilford Press.

McCrady, B. S., Moreau, J., Paolino, T. J., Jr., & Longabaugh, R. (1982). Joint hospitalization and couples therapy for alcoholism: A four-year follow-up. *Journal of Studies on Alcohol, 43,* 1244–1250.

McCrady, B. S., Noel, N. E., Abrams, D. B., Stout, R. L., Nelson, H. F., & Hay, W. M. (1986). Comparative effectiveness of three types of spouse involvement in outpatient behavioral alcoholism treatment. *Journal of Studies on Alcohol, 47,* 459–467.

McCrady, B. S., Paolino, T. J., Jr., Longabough, R., & Rossi, J. (1979). Effects of joint hospital admission and couples treatment for hospitalized alcoholics: A pilot study. *Addictive Behaviors, 4,* 155–165.

Miller, W. R., & Caddy, G. R. (1977). Abstinence and controlled drinking in the treatment of problem drinkers. *Journal of Studies on Alcohol, 38,* 986–1003.

Moos, R. H., Bromet, E., Tsu, V., & Moos, B. (1979). Family characteristics and the outcome of treatment for alcoholism. *Journal of Studies on Alcohol, 40,* 78–88.

Noel, N. E., McCrady, B. S., Stout, R. L., & Nelson, H. F. (1987). Predictors of attrition from an outpatient alcoholism treatment program for alcoholic couples. *Journal of Studies on Alcohol, 48,* 229–235.

O'Farrell, T. J., & Birchler, G. R. (1987). Marital relationships of alcoholic, conflicted, and nonconflicted couples. *Journal of Marital and Family Therapy, 13,* 259–274.

O'Farrell, T. J., & Cutter, H. S. G. (1982, November). Effect of adding a behavioral or an interactional couples group to individual outpatient alcoholism counseling. In T. J. O'Farrell (Chair), *Spouse-involved treatment for alcohol abuse.* Symposium conducted at the Sixteenth Annual Convention of the Association for the Advancement of Behavior Therapy, Los Angeles.

O'Farrell, T. J., Cutter, H. S. G., & Floyd, F. J. (1985). Evaluating behavioral marital therapy for male alcoholics: Effects on marital adjustment and communication from before to after therapy. *Behavior Therapy, 16,* 147–167.

O'Farrell, T. J., Kleinke, C., & Cutter, H. S. G. (1986). Differences between alcoholic couples accepting and rejecting an offer of outpatient marital therapy. *The American Journal of Drug and Alcohol Abuse, 12,* 301–310.

O'Farrell, T. J. & Maisto, S. A. (1987). The utility of

self-report and biological measures of alcohol consumption in alcoholism treatment outcome studies. *Advances in Behaviour Research and Therapy, 9,* 91–125.

Prochaska, J. O., & DiClemente, C. C. (1983). Stages and processes of self-change of smoking: Toward an integrative model of change. *Journal of Consulting and Clinical Psychology, 51,* 390–395.

Smith, C. G. (1969). Alcoholics: Their treatment and their wives. *British Journal of Psychiatry, 115,* 1039–1042.

Steinglass, P. (1976). Experimenting with family treatment approaches to alcoholism, 1950–1975: A review. *Family Process, 15,* 97–123.

Stout, R. L., McCrady, B. S., Longabaugh, R., Noel, N. E., & Beattie, M. C. (1987). Marital therapy enhances the long-term effectiveness of alcohol treatment. *Alcoholism: Clinical and Experimental Research, 11,* 213 (Abstract).

Thomas, E. J., Santa, C. A., Bronson, D., Oyserman, D. (1987). Unilateral family therapy with spouses of alcoholics. *Journal of Social Service Research, 10,* 145–163.

Zweben, A., Pearlman, S., & Li, S. (1983). Reducing attrition from conjoint therapy with alcoholic couples. *Drug and Alcohol Dependence, 11,* 321–331.

CHAPTER 13

Social Skills Training

Edmund F. Chaney

OVERVIEW

Skills training has received attention over the last decade as an effective behavior-therapeutic technique for a wide range of populations with social skills deficits. These groups include psychiatric patients (Hogarty et al., 1986), and children (Gresham, 1986), as well as substance abusers. In alcoholism treatment, there has been an increased awareness of the importance of considering relapse in all phases of intervention. Improving coping skills is now thought to be an important part of initial addiction treatment to reduce the risk of relapse (Brownell, Marlatt, Lichtenstein, & Wilson, 1986). This chapter will present one empirically validated model of skills training for alcoholics and will consider the current state of the art and some future directions in this area. In spite of recent work, there are, of course, many questions yet to be answered in maximizing the cost-effectiveness of skills training in combination with other forms of treatment.

Coping skill, as used in this chapter, refers to the ability to use thought, emotion, and action effectively to solve intrapersonal and interpersonal problems and to achieve personal goals. A cognitive social learning model can be used to analyze relapse determinants and formulate appropriate skills training techniques. Within this model, skillful behavior is an interaction of the individual's cognitions, affect, and behavior with the environment and particularly with other individuals. Everyone possesses coping skills to some degree. In addition to possible genetic differences in abilities and susceptibilities to stress, everyone has had both common and unique learning experiences. Social skills are, to some extent, specific to particular types of situations, such as public speaking or dating. However, people also vary in the extent to which they can act skillfully in relatively novel situations. In part, this is due to the effectiveness with which new problems can be analyzed. Also important is the extent to which emotions such as anxiety or depression interfere with coping.

For problem drinkers, alcohol consumption often becomes a preferred way of coping with unpleasant situations and feelings. This can be true for several reasons. Alcohol consumption alters mood, structures time, anesthetizes the central nervous system (reduces pain), serves as the cue for a variety of cultural and personal expectations (relaxation, friendliness), organizes interpersonal relationships (drinking friends), and provides a universally applicable rationale for failure. On the other hand, alcohol consumption is problematic as a coping mechanism. Its use may change or allow negative emotions, which are cues that there are problems to be solved, to be ignored. Alcohol as a drug has a biphasic stimulant–depressant effect, in which a letdown follows the initial positive sensation. The positive sensation lessens and the letdown worsens with repeated use. Since the letdown can be postponed by keeping the blood alcohol level up, chronic drinking comes more and more to be self-motivated, regardless of the initial circumstances. Finally, alcohol is a chronic central nervous system depressant that increases impulsivity and reduces thinking and problem-solving abilities.

The problems raised by excessive use of alcohol are sufficiently similar for different individuals to make possible situational analyses relevant to groups of problem drinkers. It is important to remember that problem drinkers are not necessarily deficient in general social skills (Twentyman, et al., 1982). The generality and severity of social skills deficits are likely to be related to parental drinking through genetic and *in utero* influences (in extreme), environmental deprivation, and modeling. Age of onset and length of drinking also affects individuals' opportunities to learn social skills (O'Leary, O'Leary, & Donovan, 1976). Different treatment populations of alcoholics will differ on these and other factors and will require different amounts and types of skills training.

The skills training methods for problem drinkers are in principle the same as those applied to other patient groups. Coping skills training methods, particularly for alcoholics, have grown out of assertiveness training and have benefited from assertiveness research and treatment outcome studies. However, the theoretical framework is more comprehensive. The desired outcome of skills training is to improve coping strategies. For problem drinkers, this means a shift from a maladaptive strategy, in which drinking can be characterized as avoidant coping, to active behavioral or cognitive coping methods.

SPECIAL CONSIDERATIONS

Skills training is compatible with, and has been used in, both in- and outpatient settings, including partial hospitalization. It is applicable to both goals of abstinence and of moderate drinking, although the content obviously has to be modified in accordance with the treatment goals. Characteristics of both the target population and the setting in which skills training is to be administered will be considered.

Some have argued that problem drinkers will become overconfident if a skills training approach is used, particularly if training is within the context of a goal of moderate drinking. There is, at least, the logical danger that a behaviorally ineffective program applied to the wrong clients could lead to clients placing themselves in high-risk situations which they otherwise might have avoided and then failing to behave skillfully in the situation, but there is little evidence to support this contention (Nathan & Skinstad, 1987; Rychtarik, Foy, Scott, Lokey, & Prue, 1987).

Client Characteristics

Relevant client characteristics for skills training are those which are related to general social skill level, to specific anti-relapse skill level, and to the ability to learn, remember, and use new skills. Riley, Sobell, Leo, Sobell, and Klajner (1987) have suggested that cognitive techniques used in skills training may not be appropriate for cognitively impaired populations. Given that between 50% and 85% of alcoholics score in the impaired range on neuropsychological tests (Parsons, 1986), at least when recently detoxified, this issue needs to be addressed.

Skills training involves the learning of coping strategies of various levels of complexity; therefore, the presence of neuropsychological impairment should be a relevant factor in the appropriateness and effectiveness of this type of treatment (Wilkinson & Sanchez-Craig, 1981). Commonly found types of deficits relevant here are abstraction-ability/concept-formation and memory/learning (Grant, 1987). The few studies now available do not show conclusively that alcoholics perform more poorly than nonalcoholics on interpersonal problem-solving tasks of the type used to measure adaptive skill level (Parsons, 1986). However, it is clear that the more impaired the alcoholic's performance on neuropsychological tests, the less he or she is likely to benefit from treatment in general and the poorer the prognosis (Kupke & O'Brien, 1985; O'Leary, Donovan, Chaney, & Walker, 1979; Walker, Donovan, Kivlahan, & O'Leary, 1983).

Neuropsychological deficits cannot be predicted reliably from drinking history variables (Grant, 1987). However, they do improve with abstinence, most dramatically over the first month (Goldman, 1983) but continuing over perhaps months to years (Grant & Reed, 1985). Results of skills training are therefore likely to vary depending on whether it is administered to still-drinking individuals, those who are early in treatment, or those who have been abstinent for at least 2–3 weeks (Becker & Jaffe, 1984).

Since the few published skills training studies that are methodologically adequate and employ both cognitive and behavioral techniques have generated positive results (see Effectiveness section), it would appear the method is useable at least in the context of inpatient alcohol treatment. Individuals demonstrating marked cognitive deficits which would interfere with independent functioning constitute a special population. Neuropsychological rehabilitation (Meier, Benton, & Diller, 1987) or a protective environment to encourage extended abstinence may be necessary before the type of skills training discussed here is indicated. At the other extreme, high-functioning clients who are employed and have intact relationships may require fewer training sessions or a different mix of cognitive and behavioral components (Jones, Kanfer, & Lanyon, 1982). It has not been established that it is cost-effective to screen patients on some coping skill assessment instrument, although with advances in measurement technology this may become possible in the future.

Setting Variables

Where possible, a group is suggested as the preferred setting for skills training (Kelly, 1985). There are three specific reasons for this recommendation. First, many of the skills to be improved are interpersonal, and the context of a group provides a realistic and yet, if properly managed, "safe" setting for practice. Second, the methods found to be effective in skills training—modeling, rehearsal, and feedback—probably occur more powerfully in a group setting. A client model whose skill level is only somewhat greater than that of the observer is likely to have more impact than the skilled therapist. Rehearsal with and feedback from peers is likely to be more realistic than individual treatment, and may facilitate generalization. Third, cost-effectiveness is higher, since therapists can treat more clients in the same amount of time in group as compared to individual treatment. A group focus may also capitalize on non-specific factors in motivation ("I can't let my group down") and the development of a support network. Finally, group settings provide more opportunity for therapist training than do individual sessions.

In many settings, you may not have complete control over procedural variables such as selection of group members, open or closed group format, size of group, number of therapists, and group duration. Indeed, definitive guidelines for group-administered skills training do not exist (Kelly, 1985), but the following are offered as suggestions until more empirical information is available. Group members may have heterogeneous skill levels, but should not be so disparate so that your attention becomes focused on a group minority. If at all possible, skills training should not be started until 2 to 3 weeks after cessation of heavy drinking.

Both open (enter any time) and closed (cohorts of patients) groups have been used (Chaney, O'Leary, & Marlatt, 1978; McCrady, Dean, Dubreuil, & Swanson, 1985). Closed groups have the advantages of building on earlier sessions, of maximizing group cohesion to encourage the operation of nonspecific factors (Yalom, 1975), and probably of being easier on your morale.

Two cotherapists are preferable. The therapists can thus role-play dyadic situations, and one can be active while the other monitors group process and assesses the comprehension of the clients. One cotherapist should be experienced both in cognitive behavioral therapy and in group treatment. The other may be a trainee or, when possible, a program graduate whose successful use of the skills being taught will motivate and lend credence to the treatment. There may be merit in having the therapists be male and female rather than a same-sex pair to facilitate realism in interpersonal problem solving. This, however, has not been systematically investigated. Coping skills training can be done with couples groups (see chapter 12), although this changes the nature of the group significantly. There will be ongoing relationship issues which will need to be dealt with in group and a more flexible and longer format is likely to be necessary. For this type of group, at least one of the therapists should be experienced in family treatment.

A group size of four to six is suggested for skills training, to provide enough time for role playing. If a group this size is not feasible, a larger group may be broken into subgroups, with actors and observers for behavioral rehearsal. Outpatient groups in most settings usually suffer some initial attrition, so if a closed-end group is used, its initial size should be greater than the target size. Groups of 1.5 hours duration with a short break allow enough time for the cognitive–behavioral process described here without being too fatiguing. Most skills training groups run 8 to 12 sessions, weekly for outpatients and biweekly to daily for inpatients. Ideally, groups would continue until clients are able to demonstrate skillful behavior in the variety of high-risk situations they are likely to encounter. In practice, an alternative is to integrate skill training techniques into continued aftercare or support group meetings through the first few high-risk months of the post-treatment period.

To promote generalization, the training setting should be as lifelike as possible (Scott, Himadi, & Keane, 1983). For problem drinking-related coping skills training, this might be accomplished for some of the high-risk situations by simulating a restaurant or bar and by using real alcoholic beverages as props. This type of simulation may be quite problematic, particularly in inpatient settings. There is insufficient research at this time to support the utility of these methods to enhance realism in the context of skill training.

Patient crises will arise inevitably in outpatient settings and occasionally in inpatient treatment. You should consider whether the format of the skills training group can be used to problem solve the crisis. If so, such a crisis can provide a valuable opportunity to increase group relevance and client involvement. If it is too early in the course of training or if the client is not willing to discuss the problem in the group, other arrangements must be made. In an inpatient program, the group usually should be informed that there is a problem and how it is being dealt with. In an outpatient setting, one of the group therapists can coordinate with, or refer to, another therapist or arrange to see the client individually, on a time-limited basis, outside of the group.

What should alcoholics be trained to do? As yet there is little systematic information about what behaviors are most effective in preventing relapse in particular types of situations. Much empirical work on typologies of high risk situations also remains to be done. The most widely used model for assessing social competence (Goldfried & D'Zurilla, 1969) has been used productively to generate standard training materials for group comparison treatment studies. To make sure content of training is relevant in treating a particular individual, however, you should determine in which types of high risk situations a person's coping skills are likely to be deficient, even if the training package samples across all situation types.

DESCRIPTION

Assessment

Before presenting treatment techniques, a sample instrument for assessing clients' initial levels of high risk situation-related coping skills will be presented. Something like the Situational Competency Test (SCT) (Chaney et al., 1978), presented below, should be given prior to and after training and the results discussed with the patient. For clinical purposes, both the client and you should rate the adequacy of the responses using a simple 5-point scale (no response or not adequate to very skillful) and compare your ratings, before and after treatment. Before treatment, this rating can be useful to orient and motivate the client for treatment and to point out weaknesses of coping in certain types of situations. After treatment this scale can be used to document progress, and to identify situation types to which the client may still be vulnerable.

The SCT can be administered using one of three techniques. The preferred method, although also the most complex, is to present the situations orally, either live or from a tape, and tape-record the responses. The simplest method is as a paper-and-pencil questionnaire with written responses. A reasonable compromise is a mixed format, with the situations presented on a written form and the client giving oral answers that are written down verbatim by the interviewer, possibly with comments about the client's body language.

Whichever method is chosen, the following paragraph gives a suggested assessment orientation for the client.

Situational Competency Test Orientation

As part of matching the treatment program to your needs, we want to find out how you react to some real-life everyday situations that you might find outside the hospital. I will play a tape recording of a situation. As you listen carefully to each situation, I want you to imagine that it is actually happening to you. Each situation will end with the question, "What would you say or do?" and a bell will ring. After the bell rings, I want you to say the words you would normally say if you were actually in that situation. If the situation requires doing something rather than saying something, then just describe what you would actually do, but remember that we want you to imagine that the situation is actually happening to you while it is being described and that when you hear the bell you are to speak as if the situation were happening to you right now here in this room. Some situations may not seem to fit you too well, but do your best to reply to all of the situations. Do not take more time to respond that you would in real life. There are sixteen situations in all. Signal me when you have finished responding to each situation. Do you have any questions?

If the patient has failed to respond to any of the situations or if some replies were ambiguous in meaning, ask the patient why responses were not given and what ambiguous responses meant.

Situational Competency Test Situations

Practice Situation.

Tomorrow morning you have to get to work early. You had some trouble falling asleep last night, but finally dozed off about midnight. The sound of your telephone ringing wakes you up. As you get up to answer it, you notice that it is 2:00 a.m. The person on the other end of the line is someone you know slightly, but he sounds like he is high on something, and he doesn't make much sense. What do you say to him?

Test Situations.

1. It is Friday night and you are home alone. You've finished eating dinner and you start to look through a magazine, but you hear the sound of a party going on a couple of houses away. You begin to feel very lonely and really feel the need to be around people. What do you do?

2. You have several bills to pay, but a check you have been expecting has not come on time. What do you do?

3. You are taking a walk after work. You walk by a bar and think how much you want a drink. You find yourself heading for the entrance. What do you do?

4. Everything has been going so well for you lately that you feel like having a drink or two to celebrate. What do you do?

5. You are sitting at home alone in a bad mood thinking about the failures in your life. You are getting pretty depressed. What do you do?

6. You are driving down the highway within the speed limit when the police stop you, say you were speeding, and prepare to give you a ticket. What do you say?

7. You have taken your car to be repaired and the mechanic gave you an estimate. When you return to pick up your car, you find that the bill is for twice as much as what the mechanic told you before and is much more than you think it should be. What do you do?

8. You are at a big family party. You are being careful not to drink even though almost everyone else is drinking. A relative who knows you have a drinking problem comes over. He says, "Why not have a couple of drinks with the rest of us and then quit? Just one or two won't hurt." What do you say to him?

9. You are sitting at home alone one evening and there is nothing on TV which you want to watch. As you are sitting there doing nothing, you think about the bottle of booze which you hid before you went to the hospital. You remember that you never got rid of it. The idea of getting the bottle and having a drink is very tempting. What do you do?

10. It is a Monday morning and you are out of work. You are sitting around thinking about getting out and looking for a job. You know you are running out of money, but the idea of looking for work turns you off. What do you do?

11. Before you entered the alcoholism treatment program, your employer, who knew about your drinking problem, said that you could have your job back when you got out

of the hospital. When you leave the program you find that the company has hired someone to take your place. What do you do?

12. Your boss invites you and some of the other people at work out to lunch. People are ordering drinks. Not knowing about your drinking problem, the boss asks you what you will have. What do you say?

13. You get up Saturday morning and realize that you don't have anything planned to do during the day. You sit around for a while, but you begin to feel bored and restless. What do you do?

14. You are eating at a good restaurant on a special occasion with some friends. The waitress comes over and says, "Drinks before dinner?" Everyone else orders one. All eyes seem to be on you. What do you do?

15. You've been feeling lonely lately, but the only friends you can think of getting in touch with are your old drinking buddies. You give one of them a call. He starts to invite you out for a drink. What do you say to him?

16. You have been out of the hospital a couple of months now and haven't taken a single drink. However, you've been wondering how well the treatment really worked and you feel like taking a drink to test it out. What do you do?

Therapy Procedures

The description of skills training given here is based largely on the therapist manual used for the Chaney, et al. (1978) study with an inpatient Veterans Administration alcoholic population. Changes have been made which reflect increased knowledge about high-risk relapse situations (Marlatt & Gordon, 1985) and increased flexibility of administration. The description is designed to provide instruction and motivation for the therapist, an orientation for the clients, and step-by-step guide to group content. Finally, sample high-risk situations are given using Marlatt's typology (Marlatt & Gordon, 1985) with suggested coping strategies.

Therapist Orientation and Instructions

There is a high probability that an alcoholic, once released from an inpatient treatment program, will relapse into drinking within the first six months after treatment. The situations in which people take their first drink following a period of abstinence after treatment have been examined. It has been found that there are common patterns in the relapse situations and that these situations can be classified into a small number of categories. Relapse may often occur in response to certain types of situations rather than at random. The training procedures used here will focus on the types of situations found to have a high risk of relapse.

The assumption underlying skills training treatment is that alcoholics tend to use alcohol, rather than other coping skills, in response to certain types of interpersonal and intrapersonal situations. Because they cannot deal with certain situations satisfactorily, they turn to alcohol to allay anxiety or to produce a feeling of power or control. They may lack the skills, or if they do possess the necessary cognitive and behavioral skills to deal with situations that present high risk of relapse, feelings such as anger, anxiety, dependency, or depression may interfere with the effective use of the skills that they have. If the skills are in fact present, examination of the problem situations and the feelings that are present at those times may be sufficient to give the patient a new way to think about (appraise) the situation, which will reduce negative affect and promote more effective coping behavior in the future.

The focus of the skills training group is to initiate and strengthen adequate coping behavior in problem situations through *demonstration* and *practice*. The skills training package nominally consists of eight 90-minute sessions for a group size of four to six patients. The first group begins with introductions and an orientation for the group members. Each succeeding group begins with the presentation of a situation. Each member of the group is asked for suggestions on how he or she might cope with that situation if it were to happen. The leader then models an effective response to the situation, incorporating whichever group suggestions are judged most appropriate. If the situation is an interpersonal one, the cotherapist or a group member can be used as a foil. The leader explains what the response was intended to accomplish and how its form was generated. This phase should take about fifteen minutes.

Each member of the group is then asked to role-play the situation, following the behaviors suggested by the group. If it is an interpersonal situation, one of the leaders or other group members takes the other role. After each member's role performance, the leader asks the group to evaluate the member's performance in terms of how well suggestions made earlier were carried out and whether paralinguistic aspects—i.e., volume and tone of voice, gestures, and emotions—were appropriate and effective. The leaders should be explicit in their own feedback, indicating when responses are convincing and adequate (and why) and requiring repetition of the role performance to incorporate suggestions for improvement. About ten minutes should be allowed for each subject. Each member should be encouraged to adapt the role to their own situation, so as to maximize the relevance of the problem situation. The basic outline of the problem situation should be retained, however. After all members have rehearsed a situation, the leaders should have a group member summarize the method for generating and evaluating an adequate response for that situation. Copies of the corresponding part of Table 13.1 can be given to the clients for this phase, so that they can have a written reminder of response guidelines and can individualize the situation by adding any additional points the group generated. Over sessions, each group member should be asked to summarize an equal number of times. The therapist should also vary the order of rehearsal from session to session.

Over the course of the group, all patients are requested to make up their own problem situations and present them to the group. Responsibility for presenting a situation should be assigned to a patient during the preceding session as homework. Once the patient has presented the situation, the session continues as previously outlined, with the leader serving as moderator as all of the patients rehearse the presented situation after generating ways of coping with it. Once clients have demonstrated some facility with the problem-solving approach, they can be assigned, as homework, coping with actual situations outside the group. This is particularly relevant in outpatient groups, since each client probably will experience several high-risk situations while attending the group. If it is at all possible, less difficult real situations should be assigned first to make a success experience more likely. The assignment should follow group practice of the situation, and the client's experiences should be debriefed in the following session.

Although the group format is a structured one, shaping clients' involvement in the process should not be neglected. The therapists should present the group as a cooperative effort in which they and the members work together to improve coping skills. The clients should have an investment in participating in the group. One way to facilitate this is to use an assessment and treatment planning process which culminates in individualized treatment goals and activities, of which the group is one. By emphasizing problem drinking as maladaptive coping behavior, the clients are encouraged to think of their drinking as a decisionmaking process for which they have responsibility and which can be modified. If the group members do not already know each other (as in an outpatient program), an introductory exercise should be used so that background information can be shared. If clients become familiar with each others' situations, this should make role playing easier and increase the impact of peer feedback.

Patient Orientation

One of the therapists gives the following introduction to the group members at the beginning of the first group.

> This is the special training group that you have agreed to participate in. It will meet twice a week, for an hour and a half for four weeks. Each person is expected to attend all eight meetings. Each of you has been chosen especially for this group and I think it will be productive for you. In here we will concentrate on certain types of situations that present problems for recovering alcoholics. In other words, these types of situations often lead to a person taking the first drink after a period of abstinence. By practicing ways to handle these situations while you are in the program, we think you will be better able to cope with these or similar situations should they arise after you leave the hospital. As we discuss and practice these situations, you may find that some of the situations seem more real to you than others. You will receive the maximum benefit from the group if you attempt to relate the situations as closely as possible to your own life. I am not here to lecture you about what to do in these types of situations. Rather, I feel that the group working together can come to understand each situation.

> Each group will go something like this: I will present a type of situation and will ask all of you to think for a couple of minutes about various ways to handle it, decide on one way, and be ready to explain why you would deal

Table 13.1. Skill Training Situations for Alcoholics

CATEGORY	EXAMPLE	RESPONSE GUIDELINES
	Intrapersonal-Environmental Situations	
Frustration, anger	It is Monday morning. You have been out of work for a while and your money is running low. The rent is due and you haven't paid child support in a while. You are going to have to get a job soon and you aren't looking forward to job hunting.	How are you feeling—frustrated? That is a signal that you need to act now! What are the various ways of finding a job? Pick one, and practice preparing for it and doing it in detail.
Other negative emotional states	It is Friday evening and you realize that you are feeling kind of depressed and lonely.	Figure out what kind of activity will make you feel better. Should you seek out old friends or make some new acquaintances? Practice in detail doing whatever you decide upon: Where to go, what to say, and so on. What are the sources of satisfaction for you? Generate ways you could obtain more satisfaction (hobbies, better job, more activities) and role-play setting up at least one.
Physical states associated with prior substance use	It has been quite a while since you had anything to drink but you feel like you have a hangover.	Stop! You don't have a hangover—it just feels that way. Is there anything that has happened recently that might be affecting you? Anything that reminds you of your drinking days? If so, get rid of it or leave the situation. Or, are you mixing up another feeling for a hangover? Do you have the flu? If so, take the proper medicine.
Other negative physical-physiological states	You are in physical pain or discomfort (from a toothache, sore throat, strain, or old injury acting up).	After identifying the problem, evaluate the need for intervention and treat it appropriately—with relaxation, medication, making a doctor's appointment or whatever is necessary.
Enhancement of positive emotional state	Something good happens—you get some extra money, for example, and you feel like celebrating.	Think of ways to celebrate that don't involve drinking. Practice making a detailed plan of how you are going to celebrate and role play setting it up.
Testing personal control	You've been out of the hospital a couple of months now and haven't taken a single drink. However, you've been wondering how well the treatment really worked and you get to feeling like taking a drink to test it out.	Stop! Is this straight thinking? Call up someone who will understand (an AA buddy or your counselor) right now and talk to them. Make a specific plan to do something that will make you feel in control.
Temptations or urges in the presence of substance cues	You get a bottle of your favorite booze for a present.	Get rid of it right now. Throw it away or give it to somebody else. Thank the giver but inform him of your abstinence.
Urges in the absence of substance cues	You are sitting home alone one evening and there is nothing on TV that you want to watch. As you are sitting there doing nothing, you think about the bottle which you hid before you went to the hospital. You remember that you never got rid of it. The idea of getting it and having a drink is very tempting.	Call up a friend who will understand how you are feeling. Review the past few days aloud to see if you have unfinished business or unrecognized stresses building up. Make a plan for getting rid of the bottle with the friend and build in something fun to do afterwards.

Continued

213

Table 13.1. Skill Training Situations for Alcoholics (*Continued*)

CATEGORY	EXAMPLE	RESPONSE GUIDELINES
	Interpersonal Determinants	
Frustration, anger	During the last few months your drinking problem has kept you from holding onto a job. You are now interviewing for a job and the interviewer says, "It doesn't look like you have been able to stay with a job very long lately."	You want something the other person has control over. To get it, you need to impress the interviewer that you are in control of your actions. Therefore, handle the implied criticism directly by explaining that you have had a drinking problem and that is the main reason for your unemployment. Don't get trapped in lies. Mention that you are going through an alcohol treatment program and indicate what your employment goals are.
Other interpersonal conflict	You go to a party with a date. He or she appears to ignore you during the course of the evening. You are on your way home and feel hurt because of his or her behavior.	You want to change the way you feel. Check your perception of the situation with the other person. Express the way you feel ("I feel . . ."). Ask the other to clarify what he or she is saying so that you are sure you understand his or her point of view. State where you agree and disagree about what he or she has said and how it has made you feel. Try to reach agreement on the reasons for the situation. Share the responsibility. Stay on the topic. Compromise. Step back from the situation if necessary. Try to see the other person's point of view, but don't lose sight of your own needs. State what you will and will not do in response to his/her request and how you would like to see his/her behavior toward you change in the future. Agree on a specific course of action that you feel OK about, which will remedy the situation or prevent its recurrence.
Direct social pressure	One of the people at the halfway house where you are staying suggests you and he go have a drink.	Politely refuse. Point out the consequences of breaking the house rules and getting caught. Suggest an alternative activity which you would enjoy doing. Change the subject decisively.
Indirect social pressure	You are at a party (or on a hunting or fishing trip) where several people are drinking. You're beginning to feel like having one yourself.	Recognize relevant cues for drinking. Formulate and rehearse past consequences of drinking, reasons for ("no one will know") and against, and the payoffs of not drinking. Act out a way of reducing temptation (leaving the situation, for example). Enlist the help of others.
Enhancement of positive emotional state	You are with a group of people who are having a good time. You start to feel like having a drink.	Stop! How are you feeling? If you are feeling good, talk through the urge with someone there who will understand. If you aren't having a good time, then leave and visit or call someone with whom you can have a drink-free party.

with the situation in that particular way. In order to give everyone a chance to participate, I'll ask various members of the group for their ideas. Using the ideas that the group has proposed, I will act out the situation here in the group, and then each person will have the opportunity to practice responding to the situation. Not everyone can recreate a situation equally convincingly. Some people may think that they can do better than they really do the first time. Each person will have the opportunity to practice responding in each situation, until the group feels that the performance is convincing and shows that the person could respond in the same manner if the situation happened outside the hospital. I realize that you may be doing some similar things in some of the groups that you will be attending here at the hospital. I think, however, that you will find that our group will be different, since we focus on coming up with practical solutions to problems *before* they happen and we give each group member a chance to practice these solutions. In addition to the situations that I will present, each of you will be given the opportunity to and be expected to come up with problem situations of your own, ones with which you have had difficulty in the past or anticipate having difficulty in the future and wish to have the group help you practice.

In conclusion, we have several ground rules. Everyone is expected to participate. All criticisms offered should be constructive — that is, the person who criticizes should be able to say in what way the criticism is helpful. Everything said in the group is confidential; it should not be discussed outside the group by patients, and it will not be used by the staff to evaluate you in any way.

Guidelines for Evaluating Group-Generated Situation Responses

All categories of training situations can be conceptualized in a problem-solving context. The group's task is to solve the problem presented by generating cognitive or behavioral alternatives. Then each member's task is to successfully role play the chosen alternative. (Read the referenced article by D'Zurilla and Goldfried [1971] for a conceptualization of the 5 steps in problem solving behavior: orientation, definition, generation of alternatives, decision-making, and verification.) In using this procedure in the skills-training group, one of the therapists provides the orientation or set. The group and cotherapists together define and formulate the problem and generate alternatives. Each member makes a decision on the basis of their own values. Verification is carried

out through role playing by each individual, with the group and trainers providing feedback.

Comments would be more effective if they came from other members of the group, and suggestions made should be left open for group confirmation or disagreement. Suggestions and comments should be offered by the group in a helpful manner, not as the final word. An approximately equal amount of time should be spent with each member, realizing that multiple situations will be covered and that there is more than one situation to be practiced in each high-risk situation category.

The problem situations (Table 13.1) are divided into two groups, depending on whether they are intrapersonal and likely to require active-cognitive coping or interpersonal, requiring active-behavioral coping. Subcategories in common to the two groups are: (a) situations that produce feelings of frustration and anger for most people if not handled satisfactorily; (b) situations in which the person is in a negative emotional state, i.e., depression, loneliness, boredom, or feelings of uselessness; (c) situations where alcohol is usually used to enhance a positive emotional state. Categories unique to intrapersonal determinants are: (a) situations where the individual is in a negative physical state, either related to withdrawal cues or for reasons unrelated to substance use; (b) testing personal control; (c) situations that represent a temptation to resume drinking, either in the presence of cues — i.e., television commercials, thirst, or the ready availability of alcohol — or in the absence of preexisting cues. The final category, unique to interpersonal determinants, involves social pressure to resume drinking, either directly or through the influence of modeling.

For frustration or anger situations, if intrapersonal, focus the group's attention on determinants of feelings — i.e., unrealistic or resented demands from self or environment, guilt, inaccurate expectations, and blocked activities. If interpersonal, identify the important aspects of the situation, such as put-downs, tangles with authority figures, and unresolved arguments. The general goal of responses will be to reduce or eliminate the environmental or interpersonal block to achieving the person's own goal, whether it be to get or retain a job, avoid a ticket, or get back together with a spouse. In most cases, the strategy decided upon will involve an assertive response on the part of the patient.

For situations that represent a negative emotional state, help people try to pinpoint what it is about the situation that made them feel depressed, lonely, and so forth, with a view to helping them recognize the initial stages of the onset of these feelings. Negative emotional state situations require generating an activity that is likely to change the individual's affective state. Depending on the emotions being experienced, this might involve practicing self-reinforcement in low self-esteem situations or initiating conversations for loneliness situations.

For positive emotional state enhancement situations, after analyzing the situation, identify the short and long-term consequences of use in that situation, examining the rationale for giving up a short term "high" for the longer term good. Identify alternatives, including acknowledgement and discussion of the feelings.

For negative physical–physiological state situations, identify the pain. If it is not withdrawal-related, decide on and apply appropriate remedies if any. If there are no specific actions to be taken or if the state is one of physical craving or withdrawal cues, the client needs to relax or engage in an alternate competing activity. This has the advantage of helping to extinguish the craving cues.

In testing-personal-control situations, attempt to make the thought process explicit. The group will usually fairly readily label this testing as "stinking thinking." Clients should be encouraged to generate other methods of asserting personal control, such as physical activity of a competitive or noncompetitive nature.

For situations that involve intrapersonal temptation to resume drinking, help people classify these kinds of situations in terms of the feelings aroused and recognize those emotions as they shape up. Often feelings of hopelessness, "what's the use," false confidence, "I can stop after one," or impulsive recklessness may be present. Help clients analyze these feelings as products of day-to-day events and as cues that there are unrecognized problems to be solved. Other group members' reactions can be particularly helpful here. Solutions might involve seeking help from a variety of sources or generating behavior that makes drinking less desirable or available, or that involves the individual in an alternate, satisfying activity.

It is especially important in intrapersonal situations to carefully explore and define whatever initially unrecognized interpersonal or environmental cues there may be for the feelings, so that the agreed-upon strategy can include an attempt to eliminate these cues or make their influences less likely.

For the social pressure situations, the goal is usually to get or retain friendship (or other relationships) with other people without drinking. Where appropriate, practice confrontation of the person who is doing the pressuring, refusing to drink in what used to be a drinking situation, and building up a repertoire of alternative activities.

Group Termination and Generalization

The last group session should allow for measuring clients' progress and giving feedback to the therapists. The SCT can be readministered prior to the last session, and results discussed in the group. Ideally, written results should also be given to each client. After this phase, therapists should solicit client perceptions of the group—what was particularly helpful to them, comments on therapist style, suggested modifications in format or content, and other observations. This material is often useful in increasing the relevance and effectiveness of future groups and provides a final verification that the clients and therapists have been working together and are mutually accountable for the progress achieved.

Generalization of training is built into the group through peer role playing, systematically practicing the range of high-risk situation exemplars, and encouraging clients to adapt the situations to their circumstances. It is highly recommended that if the training is administered as part of an inpatient program, the therapeutic contract involve participation in a weekly aftercare group for at least three to six months. Many clients will use this group as an informal extension of the coping skills training. Involvement of significant others in this type of aftercare group is another way to promote generalization, with therapeutic support available.

EFFECTIVENESS

Before reviewing investigations of the efficacy of skills training for problem drinkers, some methodological comments are in order. Although there have been controlled investigations of skills training in alcoholics, it is difficult to arrange appropriate treatment controls. As for other interventions, adding skills training to a "standard" treatment package and comparing it with the package alone does not control for nonspecific effects. Merely assessing drinking-related outcome also does not show that clients learned anything and that the extent of skill improvement was related to outcome. Different problem-drinking populations are likely to need skills training interventions differing in content, depending on their level of general social skills and environmental supports. Clinically it is a very different enterprise to engage an individual in skills training who is unemployed, has poor job skills, is divorced or never married, has few or no sober friends or family, and has no place to live than to treat someone whose addiction-related problems in these areas are basically one of fine tuning activities and relationships rather than creating or rebuilding skills and social supports.

When studies have assessed the direct outcome of skills training in alcohol treatment, analogue role-playing tasks have most commonly been assessed. The acceptable level of sophistication of such tasks has increased (Bellack, 1983) in the quest for improved external validity. There have been two contrasting approaches to the measurement of skill level. Behavior can be appraised at either the molecular or molar level. Molecular elements, such as gaze, response duration, latency, and voice volume are presumed to be the building blocks of skilled behavior, whereas molar ratings attempt to qualitatively consider the totality of the behavior. The effectiveness of skills training will be advanced by studies that attempt to specify the cognitive, affective, and behavioral components of skilled performance (Bellack, 1983).

Some research studies have attended to the relevance of training situations to the target populations, often through the procedure originally codified by Goldfried and D'Zurilla (1969). In clinical settings, limitations in resources make it an attractive option to borrow a treatment package "whole cloth" from an extant study. If this is done, the similarities and differences of the treatment setting, therapist background and skills, and the target population's socioeconomic level, cultural background, age, race, sex, and level of functioning should be considered very carefully.

With these cautions in mind, there continues to be a slow stream of reports supporting the effectiveness of skills training. Early social skills training studies (several under the rubric of assertiveness training) for alcoholics have been reviewed previously (Van Hasselt, Hersen, & Milliones, 1978; Miller & Hester, 1980). Only controlled outcome studies will be mentioned here.

Freedberg and Johnston (1981) reported on the results of a three-week residential program for employed alcoholics, comparing the program plus assertion training (n = 56) to the program alone (n = 45). As the program structure was "closed," four separate patient cohorts receiving each treatment were compared (nonrandom assignment). No behavioral measure of assertiveness was used, but the subjects who received assertion training in addition to the rest of the program had better drinking and employment status over the year follow-up period.

Ferrell and Galassi (1981) randomly assigned 22 alcoholics scoring low on an assertion scale to assertion training or human relations training groups in the context of an inpatient alcohol rehabilitation center. After treatment, the assertion training subjects behaved more assertively than the controls on a role-play test and had higher sobriety rates at six-month and one- and two-year follow-ups.

Oei and Jackson (1982) compared social skills training, cognitive restructuring, and traditional supportive therapy with inpatient alcoholics selected for low social skills. The results indicated that skills training and cognitive interventions were superior to supportive therapy at discharge and follow-up as assessed by interview, staff rating, and self-report measures including alcohol intake. In addition, at the three-month follow-up the cognitive restructuring group appeared to be doing better than the skills-training group. The skills-training intervention consisted of direct training on a variety of social and assertive skills, with no direct manipulation of cognitions. The cognitive restructuring group involved direct manipulation of cognitive beliefs but no direct skills training. The authors concluded that although both approaches were individually useful, maladaptive cognitions may inhibit the individual's use of new responses, suggesting that a combination of the two approaches would be advisable at least for some alcoholics.

Intagliata (1978) reported on 64 male veterans in inpatient alcoholism treatment assigned to a control group or to 10 sessions of behavioral group therapy specifically designed to improve interpersonal problem-solving thinking skills. Evaluation at program discharge found that problem-solving training subjects showed significantly greater improvement on the Means–Ends Problem Solving measure (Platt, Prout, & Metzger, 1986) than controls. Follow-up at one month indicated that 64% of the treatment subjects contacted described using the problem-solving methods to deal with real life problems.

Chaney and his colleagues (Chaney et al., 1978) evaluated an eight-session skills-training group intervention with hospitalized male alcoholics. Groups were designed to teach the problem-solving steps of (a) orientation, (b) definition, (c) generation of alternatives, (d) decisionmaking, and (e) verification. The teaching used instruction, modeling, behavioral rehearsal, and coaching, both of actual response behavior and of the cognitive process for generating the response. Goldfried and D'Zurilla's (1969) model for identifying ecologically relevant problematic situations was used to generate relevant training and testing tasks. These tasks were assembled into both a manual and the Situational Competency Test (SCT), a role-playing instrument designed to assess the skillfulness of verbal behavior. Forty subjects were assigned randomly to one of three groups: skills training, discussion control, or no additional treatment control. The three most important findings were that the skills-training subjects showed significant improvement as compared with the other groups in handling difficult tasks as measured by the SCT. Second, during the one-year follow-up period the skills-training group, on the average, drank one-fourth as much as the pooled control groups, spent one-sixth as many days drunk, and had an average drinking period length less than one eighth as long. Finally, measures from the predischarge SCT (particularly response latency) were comparable or superior to demographic and drinking history measures in predicting drinking behaviors during the one-year follow-up period, accounting for from 16% to 53% of the variance of specific indices. In other words, predischarge social skill level was an important determinant of treatment outcome.

Jones et al. (1982) partially replicated the Chaney et al. (1978) study by randomly assigning 20 female and 48 male alcoholic inpatients to skills-training, discussion control, or no additional treatment groups using the training procedures developed by Chaney. Subjects' problem-solving skills were assessed using the Adaptive Skills Battery, an instrument similar to the SCT but scored somewhat differently. All three groups showed a significant increase in level of coping skills during treatment. The one-year follow-up found that both the skills-training and discussion groups drank less and had fewer days drunk than the control group. Unfortunately, the follow-up comprised only 46% of the sample. Jones and colleagues suggest that their sample may have been sufficiently well functioning prior to treatment to benefit equally from either identifying problematic situations or actually practicing solutions.

Sanchez-Craig and Walker (1982) evaluated the teaching of coping skills to unselected chronic alcoholics over a three week period in the context of a coeducational halfway house. In the experimental phase, 90 subjects (56 men and 34 women) were assigned to one of three treatment groups—coping skills, covert sensitization, or discussion control. A planned no-additional-treatment condition could not be implemented. The results of a one-month interview assessment procedure showed poor retention of the content of the coping skills intervention. There were no differences among the three groups on outcome variables during an 18-month period. As the authors point out, their subjects tended to be more chronic than those in other studies, the intervention began immediately upon admission, and the program context was shorter and less intensive than those of most of the other studies reviewed here. The coping skills groups were also primarily cognitively oriented, rather than incorporating modeling and structured rehearsal.

Eriksen, Björnstad, and Götestam (1986) compared 24 alcoholic clients, randomly assigned to an eight-session social skill training package or a discussion control group, in the context of a long-stay rehabilitation program. Treatment was abstinence oriented; clients had to have been in treatment for eight weeks and had to be actively seeking employment. They were followed for one year with 96% retention, and confirming information was gathered from significant others for 88% of the sample. The skills-training group had two-thirds the alcohol consumption of the control group (which put them very close to the Norwegian nonabstainer national average) and twice as many sober days and working days. Skills-training clients did drink an average of twice as much as controls (4 drinks versus 2 drinks) on drinking days, but their drinking was judged by significant others as socially appropriate and qualitatively improved from baseline levels in almost all cases.

A recent study of drug abusers (Hawkins, Catalano, & Wells, 1986) bears mentioning because of its scope and the population overlap between alcohol and drug abuse. This study was designed to test the effectiveness of adding skill training and social network development components to the pre-entry phase of treatment in residential therapeutic communities. Clients (n = 130) were assigned, using a randomized block design, to either receive the additional component (n = 70) or not. Experimental subjects (n = 47) and 42 controls completed "full treatment," which consisted of biweekly two-hour skills training sessions for ten weeks, seven sessions of which were used to plan community activities with an assigned volunteer partner. Treatment resulted in improved coping skills in several areas, as measured by a specially developed instrument, the Problem Situations Inventory. Follow-up data soon will be available to indicate to what extent treatment affected substance use.

Monti, Rohsenow, Abrams, and Binkoff (in press) report preliminary results of a study comparing individual social skill training, family skills training, and cognitive–behavioral mood management in the context of a VA inpatient alcohol treatment program. All three patient groups improved coping skills as measured on an Alcohol-Specific Role Play Test (ASRPT). The family skills group (which included a significant other in treatment) drank less during a six-month follow-up period than the mood management group, with the individual social skill group's performance being intermediate. Greater skill as measured by the ASRPT was also predictive of less drinking during follow-up.

In summary, the strongest evidence for the efficacy of social skill training comes from studies conducted in the context of inpatient alcohol programs in which there are additional treatment components and some degree of screening of patients. The literature also suggests that for most client populations the cognitive and behavioral components of treatment should both be employed. More outcome re-

search needs to be done, particularly in outpatient settings. Future studies should incorporate process measures such as the SCT, ASB, or ASRPT, and should work toward improving the assessment of social skill level and increasing the cost-effectiveness of training by matching content of training to clients' skill deficits. Overall, skills training has received sufficient empirical validation to be ensured a permanent role in alcoholism treatment.

REFERENCES

Clinical Guidelines

D'Zurilla, T. J., & Goldfried, M. R. (1971). Problem solving and behavior modification. *Journal of Abnormal Psychology, 78,* 107–126. The first statement of the operations involved in effective problem solving in a manner allowing incorporation into the cognitive component of skills training.

Goldfried, M. R., & Davison, G. C. (1976). *Clinical behavior therapy.* New York: Holt, Rinehart & Winston. Chapter 9 on problem solving elaborates on D'Zurilla and Goldfried (1971) and gives additional practical material.

Kelly, J. A. (1985). Group social skills training. *The Behavior Therapist, 8,* 93–95. Practical suggestions with regard to group social sills training procedures.

Marlatt, G. A., & Gordon, J. R. (1985). *Relapse prevention: Maintenance strategies in the treatment of addictive behaviors.* New York: Guilford. A watershed book in the cognitive-behavioral approach to problem drinking, smoking, and obesity, with a wealth of clinical and theoretical ideas and reviews.

McCrady, B. S., Dean, L., Dubreuil, E., & Swanson, S. (1985). The problem drinkers' project: A programmatic application of social-learning-based treatment. In G. A. Marlatt & J. R. Gordon (Eds.), *Relapse prevention: Maintenance strategies in the treatment of addictive behaviors* (pp. 417–471). New York: Guilford. Details the clinical application of skills training and other cognitive behavioral techniques in an abstinence-oriented partial hospitalization setting.

Moos, R. H., & Billings, A. G. (1982). Conceptualizing and measuring coping resources and processes. In L. Goldberger & S. Breznitz (Eds.), *Handbook of stress: Theoretical and clinical aspects* (pp. 212–230). New York: Free Press. Presents a typology of coping strategies, including both focus and method of coping. Coping can be oriented to changing appraisal (cognitive), problem-solving (behavioral), or regulating affect.

Platt, J. J., Prout, M. F., & Metzger, D. S. (1986). Interpersonal cognitive problem-solving therapy (ICPS). In W. Dryden & W. Golden (Eds.), *Cognitive behavioral approaches to psychology* (pp. 261–289). London: Harper & Row. Reviews 15 years of investigation of the role of problem solving in socially competent behavior for substance abusers and other groups, and presents a treatment method based on this research.

Roskies, E., & Lazarus, R. S. (1980). Coping theory and the teaching of coping skills. In P. O. Davidson & S. M. Davidson (Eds.), *Behavioral medicine: Changing health lifestyles* (pp. 38–79). New York: Brunner/Mazel. Integrative article bridging coping theory literature and cognitive behavior therapy approaches to improving coping and pointing out commonalities.

Wilkinson, J., & Canter, S. (1982). *Social skills training manual.* New York: Wiley. Practical exposition of behavioral techniques concentrating on psychiatric populations.

Yalom, I. D. (1975). *The theory and practice of group psychotherapy.* New York: Basic Books. Perhaps the best single reference on the practice of group psychotherapy with applicability to substance abusing clients.

Research

Becker, J. T., & Jaffe, J. H. (1984). Impaired memory for treatment-relevant information in inpatient men alcoholics. *Journal of Studies on Alcohol, 45,* 339–343.

Bellack, A. S. (1983). Recurrent problems in the behavioral assessment of social skill. *Behaviour Research and Therapy, 21,* 29–41.

Brownell, K. D., Marlatt, G. A., Lichtenstein, E., & Wilson, G. T. (1986). Understanding and preventing relapse. *American Psychologist, 41,* 765–782.

Chaney, E. F., O'Leary, M. R., & Marlatt, G. A. (1978). Skill training with alcoholics. *Journal of Consulting and Clinical Psychology, 46,* 1092–1104.

Curran, J. P., & Monti, P. M. (1982). *Social skills training.* New York: Guilford.

Eriksen, L., Björnstad, S., & Götestam, K. G. (1986). Social skills training in groups for alcoholics: One-year treatment outcome for groups and individuals. *Addictive Behaviors, 11,* 309–329.

Ferrell, W. L., & Galassi, J. P. (1981). Assertion training and human relations training in the treatment of chronic alcoholics. *The International Journal of the Addictions, 16,* 959–968.

Freedberg, E. J., & Johnston, W. E. (1981). Effects of assertion training within context of a multi-modal alcoholism treatment program for employed alcoholics. *Psychological Reports, 48,* 379–386.

Goldfried, M. R., & D'Zurilla, T. J. (1969). A behavior analytic model for assessing competence. In C. D. Spielberger (Ed.), *Current topics in clinical and community psychology (Vol. 1)* (pp. 151–196). New York: Academic.

Goldman, M. S,. (1983). Cognitive impairment in chronic alcoholics: Some cause for optimism. *American Psychologist, 38,* 1045–1054.

Grant, I. (1987). Alcohol and the brain: Neuropsychological correlates. *Journal of Consulting and Clinical Psychology, 55,* 310–324.

Grant, I., & Reed, R. (1985). Neuropsychology of alcohol and drug abuse. In A. I. Alterman (Ed.), *Substance abuse and psychopathology* (pp. 289–341). New York: Plenum.

Gresham, F. (1986). Conceptual and definitional is-sues in the assessment of children's social skills: Implications for classification and training. *Journal of Clinical Child Psychology, 15,* 3–15.

Hawkins, J. D., Catalano, R. F., & Wells, E. A. (1986). Measuring effects of a skills training intervention for drug abusers. *Journal of Consulting and Clinical Psychology, 54,* 661–664.

Hogarty, G. E., Anderson, C. M., Reiss, D. J., Kornblith, S. J., Greenwald, D. P., Javna, C. D., Madonia, M. J. (1986). Family psychoeducation, social skills training, and maintenance chemotherapy in the aftercare treatment of schizophrenia. *Archives of General Psychiatry, 43,* 633–642.

Intagliata, J. C. (1978). Increasing the interpersonal problem-solving skills of an alcoholic population. *Journal of Consulting and Clinical Psychology, 46,* 489–498.

Jones, S. L., Kanfer, R., & Lanyon, R. I. (1982). Skill training with alcoholics: A clinical extension. *Addictive Behaviors, 7,* 285–290.

Kupke, T., & O'Brien, W. (1985). Neuropsychological impairment and behavioral limitations exhibited within an alcohol treatment program. *Journal of Clinical and Experimental Neuropsychology, 7,* 292–304.

Ladd, G. W., & Mize, J. (1983). A cognitive–social learning model of social-skill training. *Psychological Review, 90,* 127–157.

McFall, R. M. (1982). A review and reformulation of the concept of social skills. *Journal of Behavioral Assessment, 4,* 1–33.

Meier, M., Benton, A., & Diller, L. (1987). *Neuropsychological rehabilitation.* New York: Guilford.

Miller, W. R., & Hester, R. K. (1980). Treating the problem drinker: Modern approaches. In W. R. Miller (Ed.), *The addictive behaviors* (pp. 11–142). New York: Pergamon.

Monti, P. M., Rohsenow, D. J., Abrams, D. B.,. & Binkoff, J. A. (1988). Social learning approaches to alcohol relapse: Selected illustrations and implications. In B. Ray (Ed.), *Learning factors in substance abuse.* NIDA Research Monograph Series. Washington, DC: U. S. Government Printing Office.

Nathan, P. E., & Skinstad, A. H. (1987). Outcomes of treatment for alcohol problems: Current methods, problems and results. *Journal of Consulting and Clinical Psychology, 55,* 332–340.

Oei, T. P. S., & Jackson, P. R. (1982). Social skills and cognitive behavioral approaches to the treatment of problem drinking. *Journal of Studies on Alcohol, 43,* 532–547.

O'Leary, M. R., Donovan, D. M., Chaney, E. F., & Walker, R. D. (1979). Cognitive impairment and treatment outcome with alcoholics: Preliminary findings. *Journal of Clinical Psychiatry, 42,* 230–243.

O'Leary, D. E., O'Leary, M. R., & Donovan, D. M. (1976). Social skill acquisition and psychosocial development of alcoholics: A review. *Addictive Behaviors, 1,* 111–120.

Parsons, O. A. (1986). Alcoholics' neuropsychological impairment: Current findings and conclusions. *Annals of Behavioral Medicine, 8,* 13–19.

Riley, D. M., Sobell, L. C., Leo, G. I., Sobell, M. B., & Klajner, F. (1987). Behavioral treatment of alcohol problems: A review and comparison of behavioral and nonbehavioral studies. In W. M. Cox (Ed.), *Treatment and prevention of alcohol prob-*

lems: *A resource manual* (pp. 73–115). Orlando, FL: Academic.

Rychtarik, R. G., Foy, D. W., Scott, T., Lokey, L., & Prue, D. M. (1987). Five six year follow-up of broad-spectrum behavioral treatment for alcoholism: Effects of training controlled drinking skills. *Journal of Consulting and Clinical Psychology, 55,* 106–108.

Sanchez-Craig, M., & Walker, K. (1982). Teaching coping skills to chronic alcoholics in a coeducational halfway house: I. Assessment of programme effects. *British Journal of Addiction, 77,* 35–50.

Scott, R. R., Himadi, W., & Keane, T. M. (1983). A review of generalization in social skills training: Suggestions for future research. In M. Hersen, R. Eisler, & P. Miller (Eds.), *Progress in behavior modification* (Vol. 15) (pp. 114–172). New York: Academic.

Twentyman, C. T., Greenwald, D. P., Greenwald, M. A., Kloss, J. D., Kovalski, M. E., & Zibung-Hoffman, P. (1982). An assessment of social skills deficits in alcoholics. *Behavioral Assessment, 4,* 317–326.

Van Hasselt, V. B., Hersen, M., & Milliones, J. (1978). Social skills training for alcoholics and drug addicts: A review. *Addictive Behaviors, 3,* 221–233.

Walker, R. D., Donovan, D. M., Kivlahan, D. R., & O'Leary, M. R. (1983). Length of stay, neuropsychological performance, and aftercare: Influence on alcohol treatment outcome. *Journal of Consulting and Clinical Psychology, 51,* 900–911.

Wilkinson, D. A., & Sanchez-Craig, M. (1981). Relevance of brain dysfunction to treatment objectives: Should alcohol-related cognitive deficits influence the way we think about treatment? *Addictive Behaviors, 6,* 253–260.

CHAPTER 14

Anxiety and Stress Management

Tim Stockwell
Carole Town

OVERVIEW

Drinking in order to reduce anxiety and cope with stressful situations is one of the most common reasons given by heavy social drinkers and problem drinkers for their behavior. Agoraphobia, social phobias, panic disorders, and generalized anxiety are all more commonly reported by heavy drinkers than in the general population. Research in this area has shown that for many people, alcohol can be a powerful anxiolytic, although paradoxically, if taken in large quantities for a prolonged period, it may actually *elevate* anxiety levels. This simple concept of opposing short-term and long-term consequences of alcohol consumption is central to the following account of assessment and treatment of the anxious problem drinker.

The terms "anxiety" and "stress" are frequently used very loosely in everyday language. For present purposes, we will employ the term "stress" when referring to an entire process of interaction between external "stressors" (e.g., work commitments, criticism, unrealistic demands) and an individual's reactons to these, or "stress responses." Anxiety, fear, anger, or depression are all examples of stress responses. Anxiety and stress management approaches attempt to enable individuals to gain control of their reactions to stress in the following ways:(a) by altering their perception of the degree of threat posed by the stressor: (b) by altering their lifestyle to reduce both the frequency and severity of external stressors: and (c) by enabling them to utilize active coping strategies which inhibit or replace disabling stress responses such as extreme anxiety or fear.

Other chapters in this book deal with methods for helping a person to modify a tendency towards depressed mood states and for reducing social anxiety by training assertiveness and other social skills (see chapter 13). While this chapter will focus more specifically on lifestyle modification and anxiety management techniques, it should be borne in mind that a flexible, individualized treatment will always draw upon ideas and methods from many other sources.

The fascinating two-way relationship between the experience of anxiety and the consumption of alcohol is well illustrated when a heavy drinker ceases to drink. The extent to which this "withdrawal" period will be characterized by raised anxiety levels, or even panic attacks, will be determined by many factors: the extent of uninterrupted prior drinking, pre-existing anxiety levels, current stresses, and degree of learned dependence upon alcohol. While only a small minority of drinkers experience severe withdrawal or "rebound anxiety" when stopping drinking for a period, many such individuals who seek help at clinics will do so. Thus, anxiety and stress management procedures may be needed both to enable a reduction in drinking to occur and also to maintain this reduction subsequently.

SPECIAL CONSIDERATIONS

There are many instances when treating anxiety in a problem drinker will be ineffective or even counterproductive. It is likely that millions of hours of therapy have been wasted with this client group by not observing certain basic ground rules. It should also be said that in many instances this will be due to the therapist being *unaware* of their client's drinking habits. There is persuasive evidence that only a small minority of problem drinkers are identified as such, but continue to be heavy users of physical and mental health care resources which are directed at correcting the *consequences* of excessive drinking. Thus the first ground rule must be that any treatment—whether pharmacological, psychotherapeutic or behavioral—aimed at anxiety or stress reduction should not be delivered without a prior assessment of the recipient's drinking *and* drug use. Numerous simple and non-threatening assessment methods have been designed for this purpose, including the Health Questionnaire (Wallace and Haynes, 1985) which enquires about a variety of health-related behaviors including alcohol consumption. To continue to heroically treat anxiety levels that are being continuously fueled by heavy alcohol consumption is almost invariably futile, and, in the case of drug treatments, downright dangerous.

The following ground rules assume that the client or patient has both been asked and is open about her or his alcohol and drug intake.

Client's Motivational Status

As with all addictive or dependency problems, an assessment of the client's perception of the relative balance of the benefits and drawbacks of their alcohol or drug use is an early treatment priority (see chapter 4). If the client is unwilling to reduce or stop excessive drinking as a condition of treatment, it is either necessary to dedicate time towards persuading them further or to firmly refuse treatment. If need be, they can be invited to attempt to reduce their intake as an "experiment" to discover the subsequent effect upon their anxiety.

Client's Drinking and Drug Use Status

Many clients who drink heavily or abuse other anxiolytic drugs will experience substantial or complete recovery from extreme anxiety following successful detoxification. It is prudent to focus initially upon achieving an alcohol and drug-free state of at least two weeks' duration before assessing the need for offering intensive anxiety management treatment. Heavy alcohol use over a prolonged period of time stimulates the autonomic nervous system, often causing symptoms of severe anxiety. Such overstimulation gradually subsides and may disappear altogether after a two week "rest" from drinking (often termed "alcohol withdrawal").

Further research is needed to discover the exact levels and patterns of consumption which worsen rather than alleviate anxiety. We recommend the following guidelines based on our clinical experience:

1. Clients are advised to avoid entirely alcohol and drug use that is intended to help cope with anxiety or another stress response.
2. Otherwise, clients are advised to reduce their consumption to below 5 standard drinks per day for men and 4 standard drinks for women—for *less* than 5 days per week in each case. (One "standard drink" in the UK contains 10cc of alcohol.)
3. Use of other anxiolytic medication is to be avoided unless for a specific and time-limited therapeutic purpose—e.g., detoxification or *occasional* facilitation of sleep.

Cognitive Impairment

Many heavy and problem drinkers suffer from a degree of cognitive impairment ranging in severity from forgetfulness ("the morning after the night before") to the permanent loss of ability to remember new information, as displayed in full blown Korsakoff's Psychosis. Rapid recovery of learning and problem-solving abilities are the norm following reduced intake or abstinence. However, the level at which any individual client is performing should be assessed and taken into account when designing a treatment program. A particular emphasis on simple instructions, readily understood written materials, and audiotapes can generally be recommended.

Screening out Specific Clinical Conditions

Anxiety-related symptoms are perhaps the most common across the whole range of mental health problems. As a consequence, when an individual complains of high levels of anxiety, these may be related to an underlying psychiatric condition. Panic attacks may be a feature of an "agitated" depression; neurological impairment and psychotic illness can also be the underlying cause of clinically severe anxiety. A thorough psychiatric and psychological assessment will be needed if these causes are to be excluded.

In summary, there are several special considerations to be borne in mind before including a problem drinker in an anxiety and stress management program:

1. Certain types of cause for the anxiety need to be excluded.
2. It is essential that the client is sufficiently motivated to tackle his or her drinking problem.
3. Drug and alcohol use should be under control before anxiety-focused work need begin.

DESCRIPTION

It is not possible to describe a precise set of procedures or a "recipe" for the treatment of every case where an anxiety-related problem is responsible for an individual's excessive drinking. Rather, a set of principles can be outlined and a range of alternative procedures described which may or may not be applicable for a particular client.

As indicated above, anxiety and stress management procedures are indicated for problem drinkers (a) to aid short-term drinking reduction or 'withdrawal' and (b) to minimize the possibility of future relapse. Accordingly, this

section will be subdivided under these headings, and assessment and management issues examined separately in each case.

Anxiety Management during Alcohol Withdrawal

It is normal, though by no means universal, practice to provide anxiety-reducing medication on a reducing schedule to ensure a smooth withdrawal from alcohol. In Britain, the drugs chlordiazepoxide or chlormethiazole tend to be preferred, and are reduced over a period of up to seven days according to severity of withdrawal symptoms. Alternative, drug-free methods are increasingly being employed, such as electro-acupuncture and intensive social and emotional support. The risks of a drug-free withdrawal include grand mal seizures and the bizarre behavior associated with delerium tremens.

A useful assessment tool for predicting severity of withdrawal symptomatology is the Severity of Alcohol Dependence Questionnaire, or SADQ (Stockwell, Murphy, & Hodgson, 1983). This 20-item questionnaire assesses degree of alcohol dependence on a 0 to 60 scale for the client's most recent month of heavy drinking. Higher scores have been shown to predict severe withdrawal. It should be borne in mind that alcohol withdrawal symptoms consist mainly of the psychophysiological signs of extreme anxiety—viz. trembling, sweating, racing pulse, subjective experience of anxiety, and even panic. During the withdrawal phase, an excellent instrument for monitoring symptoms is the Selected Symptom Checklist (Murphy, Shaw, & Clarke, 1983); both objective and subjective signs, plus overall severity, can be assessed continuously as an easily administered scale.

Since the drinker who is undergoing withdrawal will be having to cope with uncomfortable levels of anxiety—even on the best medication regime—it is important to give psychological assistance as well. A number of psychological principles can be applied to ensure that anxiety is minimized and chances of success are maximized.

Removal of Alcohol and Alcohol-related Cues

Procedures which help the recovering drinker to actively cope with available alcohol are not appropriate at this stage. Normally it is necessary for alcohol to be removed from the drinker's house and for steps to be taken to reduce the likelihood of family members or friends bringing in new supplies or inviting them out for a drink. When the home carries too many associations with drinking or too easy access to alcohol, then admission to hospital at a detoxification unit may be needed. In most cases this will be unnecessary and withdrawal can be supervised in the client's home.

Reduction of Social and Environmental Stress

Careful attention needs to be given to the setting for alcohol withdrawal. A busy general or psychiatric hospital ward is often too noisy, frightening, impersonal, and unsupportive. Continuing to work may either provide vital distraction or create intolerable stress. Staying at home may be counterproductive if there are severe tensions in the marriage or family. In general, a quiet environment without social stress or demands, low lighting, warmth, and company available if needed constitute ideal conditions for minimizing stress.

Reducing Conflict about Whether or Not to Drink Alcohol

The experience of conflict between two competing and quite incompatible courses of action is notoriously stressful. The problem drinker is well used to such stress in relation to his or her drinking. Again, the importance of establishing the individual's commitment or motivation cannot be overemphasized; the stronger the commitment then the less the decisional conflict that will be experienced. Having the individual client elect for alcohol and alcohol-related cues to be absent will also minimize the experience of such conflict. Some may even find talking or thinking about alcohol produces such conflicts. One advantage of an institutional setting can be the existence of a firm "no drinking" rule (i.e., instant discharge if it is broken), which can also minimize such conflict.

Provision of Accurate Information to Prevent Faulty Attributions

The individual needs to be able to discuss the symptoms he or she is experiencing—to have these explained if need be, but to ideally have been well prepared for these from the outset.

Very often the tendency is to wrongly attribute anxiety symptoms either to an external cause or to an enduring feature of the experience of abstinence. The importance of simplicity, clarity, and repetition of such information must again be stressed, as cognitive impairment will be maximal at this point.

Avoiding Stimulants as Far as Possible

Many people cope with alcohol withdrawal by consuming large quantities of non-alcoholic drinks. Unfortunately, this often leads to taking great amounts of caffeine, which may both intensify the experience of anxiety and render sleeping very difficult. It should be remember that many soft drinks contain caffeine—not just tea and coffee. The great majority of heavy drinkers also smoke cigarettes, and will also greatly increase their smoking during alcohol withdrawal. While it is not generally advisable to press for these to be given up at the same time as alcohol, it may be advisable to limit smoking, as nicotine is also a powerful stimulant. It is an intriguing possibility that much anxiety associated with alcohol withdrawal is caused by clients substituting these stimulant drugs for alcohol.

Use of Simple Relaxation Methods

Cognitive coping strategies, other than the very simplest, may be impractical at this stage. However, practicing simple relaxation techniques and deep breathing exercises may be invaluable. These will be discussed shortly.

Anxiety Management and Relapse Prevention

One of the most common causes of relapse into heavy drinking is known to be the experience of negative emotions—often those caused by "interpersonal stress." Many people ca.. successfully "dry out" or temporarily reduce their consumption to safe levels, but it can be far harder to sustain reduced consumption in the face of life's inevitable stresses and anxieties.

For many drinkers, the experience of extreme anxiety is only a feature of a heavy drinking period or of withdrawal. Subsequently, they may need only to practice coping with normal levels of anxiety in the absence of alcohol a few times for their discomfort and urge to drink to disappear or "extinguish."

It is usually possible to predict the extent of recovery from anxiety following reduced alcohol intake and, hence, to judge the subsequent need for the input of anxiety management training. The best approach is to take a detailed history which explores relative changes in drinking, alcohol dependence, and anxiety—giving the most weight to recent experiences. The retrospective use of the SADQ and the Fear Questionnaire (Marks and Mathews, 1979) are valuable assessment tools for this. The latter instrument is particularly useful, as it picks up not only a wide range of fears and anxieties but also the extent of avoidance provoked by each and an overall rating of different mood states. The extent to which heavy drinking developed as an attempt to obtain relief from anxiety symptoms and to which the anxiety symptoms were created or "fueled" by heavy drinking will usually become readily apparent. In general, clients with severe degrees of alcohol dependence will experience the greatest reduction in fear and anxiety by simply stopping drinking.

It is vital to make the above assessment in order to make an important clinical decision— how soon to recommend active coping strategies, as opposed to avoidance strategies, for dealing with anxiety-provoking situations. In this context, *active* coping strategies involve confronting and experiencing those situations which most tempt the client to take a drink— e.g., social drinking situations. The rule of thumb is to plan avoidance strategies during the initial recovery phase but then to gradually introduce active coping strategies at a pace with which the individual drinkers is comfortable (see chapter 11).

At a more practical level, it is important to assess whether there are pressing external worries concerning court cases, family problems, work, or financial problems. Often, simple, short-term actions will reduce worry and uncertainty, and hence the stressfulness of such difficulties.

A formal assessment of the very anxious problem drinker will itself frequently raise anxiety levels. A long list of worries and anxieties may be generated. It is vital to be aware of this and to help the client to order and place priorities on what might otherwise feel a totally overwhelming set of problems. As discussed in

chapter 4, if the client is helped to feel valued and optimistic, then raising such anxieties can *increase* his or her motivation to find alternative coping methods to drinking alcohol.

Some basic anxiety management procedures will now be outlined. More detailed discussions of these can be found in the reference section.

Exercises to Induce a State of Relaxation

There are many relaxation, breathing, yoga, and meditation techniques which are widely practiced and written about. Different methods will appeal to different individuals, and the provision of a wide range of choices is ideal. Methods which can be practiced in real-life anxiety-provoking situations are the most effective—possibly because they provide an active coping response and lower anxiety by inducing a sense of control.

A classic example is learning to control one's breathing to cope with panic attacks. A frequently experienced aspect of panic is for breathing to become fast, shallow, and erratic— such breathing (or hyperventilation) may even *cause* a panic attack by lowering levels of carbon dioxide. A simple remedy is to breathe into a paper bag to restore carbon dioxide levels. Learning to recognize incorrect breathing patterns and instituting a series of controlled, deep breaths is also of value. One method is to place your hands on your abdomen and breathe in to a slow count of ten. If correctly done you will feel your abdomen expand. Hold the breath for a further count of ten and release it slowly, also to a count of ten. You will feel your abdomen contracting as you do this.

Most relaxation exercises are more difficult to utilize in actual anxiety-provoking situations. For example, a classic exercise involves tensing and then relaxing various muscles in the body one by one, thus gradually inducing a state of relaxation. On occasion, it is possible to find a quiet place to practice a speeded up version of what normally takes 15 minutes. Using the same breathing pattern outlined above, you can simultaneously tense *all* your muscles while breathing in, then hold the tension and gradually release it while breathing out. Repeating this process several times can often counteract quite high levels of anxiety.

Another effective technique, which can be applied instantly when experiencing a stress response, has been called Autogenic Training.

It is more akin to self-hypnosis or autosuggestion, and involves concentrating on different parts of the body (arms, legs, abdomen, chest, neck, head) in turn and making suggestions to oneself of sensations being experienced there: mainly sensations of warmth and heaviness. Involving no active effort or movement, repeated practice can create a powerful relaxation response in association with such simple suggestions as "my whole body feels calm and relaxed" or "my arms feel warm and heavy". Another advantage of this method is that clients find it less effortful and are more likely to practice it regularly. The use of an audiotape in order to learn the instructions is also a popular choice among clients.

As in any area of psychological treatment, people vary widely in their response to different relaxation techniques. An alternative method known as progressive muscle relaxation, or PMR, may be preferred. It is a very flexible technique in that the basic principle is to tense and then relax individual muscle groups. Many clients discover they have particular areas of muscle tension that cause them difficulties (e.g., the hands and arms for those with writer's cramp, or the neck and head for those with tension headaches). They may find it sufficient to only work on these muscle groups or to give them extra attention while undergoing a full PMR procedure.

The usual routine for training yourself in PMR is as follows:

1. Lie down or sit in a comfortable chair in a quiet room, free from distractions. Do not cross your arms or legs.
2. To the count of ten, gradually tense the following muscle groups, hold that tension for a further ten seconds, and then relax gradually, also for a count of ten seconds. Do this for your hands (clench them into fists), your arms (raise your hands to your shoulders), your shoulders (hunch them), your neck (press your head backwards against the bed or chair), your face (screw up all facial muscles and close your eyes), your chest (take in a deep breath), your abdomen (pull it in tightly), your buttocks (clench them tightly), your thighs (clench), your calves (point feet upwards, bending from ankle) and your feet (clench toes together)
3. It is important to make positive suggestions

about "letting go of tension" as you relax each muscle group. Try to concentrate on the exercise and shut out other thoughts and worries.
4. Two repetitions of these exercises should be sufficient to attain a deep state of relaxation. Some anxious clients may take several attempts to benefit from this exercise, as they find it very hard to let go of their exaggerated self-control. Such clients often report upsetting thoughts and images entering their mind as soon as they begin to relax successfully. It is important to help clients verbalize these thoughts and to deal with them.

Behavioral Strategies

Where a high level of avoidance of fear or anxiety arousing situations has been evident, a behavioral program may be needed to help the drinker cope with such situations. In this context, avoidance should not merely be construed as physical avoidance; using alcohol or anxiety-reducing drugs to feel courageous are other methods of avoiding the *experience* of fear and anxiety. Indeed, one of the more common anxiety related disorders associated with problem drinking, agoraphobia, is now known to constitute a "fear of fear" and the associated avoidance behaviors to be designed to avoid experiencing fearfulness.

A very powerful therapeutic principle here is to facilitate the client remaining in fear-arousing situations long enough for the fearfulness to subside. Short exposures may actually *worsen* a phobia, whereas exposures in excess of 30 minutes—and often of several hours— represent an ideal target. A closely related therapeutic principle involves the extinction of craving for alcohol in such situations; it has been found that long exposures to craving does enable it to be extinguished. In such cases, a behavioral approach must involve graded and prolonged exposures to cues for drinking while preventing *any* avoidance response, be it physical avoidance or use of anxiety-reducing substances.

The exact procedures utilized closely mirror those described elsewhere for the treatment of phobic anxiety states and obsessional disorders. However, a few novel considerations apply when alcohol or drug use needs to be prevented for treatment to be successful. First, as described above, there is usually no point in encouraging such exposure and response prevention approaches until the full benefits of reducing alcohol intake have been appreciated—i.e. rebound anxiety has returned to "normal" levels. By contrast, avoidance strategies should be actively recommended during this initial phase to give such recovery processes the best chance of occurring.

Second, when embarking on an active exposure program it is important to consider the extent of *craving* a particular task will generate as well as the level of fear or anxiety. For example, walking into a bar may arouse only moderate anxiety but very high levels of craving for alcohol. Tasks need to be graded, therefore, in terms of both these considerations, then approached and mastered starting with the least challenging. A number of strategies may be used to reduce the likelihood of drinking occurring: involving family, friends, or volunteer helpers in accompanying the client and the use of an alcohol-sensitizing agent (e.g., disulfiram) are two very good ones. In Exeter we make use of an alcohol-free pub, "The Milestone," to enable anxious clients to adjust to socializing without being tempted to drink alcohol.

Again, the rehearsal of assertiveness and social skills will often be very valuable before entering situations alcohol and drug free. Very often it is not skills which are lacking with problem drinkers but confidence in being able to *use* their existing skills without alcohol. Thus, guided practice, with plenty of support and positive feedback, is strongly indicated. Having clients attend group therapy—ideally based upon problem-solving and behavioral principles—is another method of enabling them to learn to communicate in a sober state.

Cognitive Strategies

Recently, many investigators have realized that many negative mood states result from a tendency to misconstrue events and communications in a negative way. Cognitive therapies have been developed which focus upon identifying distorted and negative patterns of perception and then teaching methods of correcting these patterns.

Thought patterns which lead to excess anxiety are characterized by an exaggerated perception of the likelihood of negative consequences or eventualities—e.g., having a panic attack, being criticized, or failing in the eyes of important other people.

There are excellent manuals that explain these new and sophisticated cognitive therapies in detail (e.g., Beck & Emery, 1979). Such therapy proceeds by explaining the rationale very carefully, using general examples and, ideally, those drawn from the client's experience. Next, the client is helped to be aware of negative automatic thoughts or images associated with acute anxiety. Access to these may often be difficult, and the use of diaries, guided fantasies, and role play may be needed. (One of our clients discovered she always had a fleeting image of her stepmother scolding her when she felt anxious—even though she hadn't lived with her for 20 years. She developed a strategy of mentally shouting at her to "leave me alone!") The next step is to train clients to step back from their negative thoughts, to devise alternative constructions, and to challenge their negative thinking. A simple example is to learn that social anxiety normally declines after an initial high—even if you do not drink alcohol. Very often anxiety reduction is incorrectly attributed to alcohol when alcohol may merely, by an act of faith or placebo effect, enable a person to remain long enough in a situation for anxiety to naturally subside.

Bibliotherapy

Many readable self-help guides have been written and are widely available. Some of these (e.g., *Living with Fear* by Isaac Marks) are based on cognitive and behavioral principles similar to those outlined above.

Lifestyle Management

Many aspects of one's lifestyle may contribute to the experience of stress. Most common are those involving the acceptance of unrealistic workloads and responsibility—whether at work or at home. These are, of course, avoidable, and enabling a person to be aware of this and encouraging them to assertively resist pressure may be sufficient.

There are many "naturally" occurring, positively therapeutic processes which serve to prevent or reduce anxiety: satisfying social and sexual relationships, regular physical exercise, and regular sleep. A great many activities and interests are intrinsically relaxing, but very often anxious individuals fail to plan in sufficient time for these. A full assessment of all these factors—as well as of the use of psychotropic substances—will invariably point to several effective methods for rapidly reducing anxiety and stress.

EFFECTIVENESS

Given the variety of therapeutic principles and procedures outlined above, it is not surprising that no single controlled study can be cited to support the overall approach. The two studies which come the closest to this ideal were performed by Rohsenow, Smith, & Johnson (1985) and McLellan, Woody, & Luborsky (1983). Rohsenow and her colleagues tested a comprehensive cognitive–affective stress management package for heavy social drinking male college students. The training combined deep muscle relaxation, meditation, cognitive restructuring, and the rehearsal of coping skills while experiencing anxiety. Significant short-term changes in subjects' drinking behavior occurred, despite their not being explicitly motivated towards this end. Only modest longer term changes occurred, which may, once more, underline the need for first working on clients' motivation to reduce drinking if durable treatment effects are to be obtained.

McLellan and his colleagues (1983) evaluated a sophisticated cognitive-behavioral package designed for drug and alcohol abusers which was contrasted with supportive psychotherapy and counseling from volunteers. Although this treatment focused on anxiety and stress management as but *one* major problem area, the rigor of the research design—including screening for high motivation and random assignment to groups—provided an exacting test of the overall approach. It was found that both cognitive-behavioral therapy and supportive psychotherapy were significantly superior to counseling.

Oei and Jackson (1982) have also produced encouraging evidence of the efficacy of a cognitive–behavioral approach for treating social anxieties in problem drinkers.

An abundance of research evidence exists to support some of the therapeutic principles described in the previous section. The evidence that prolonged alcohol consumption raises anxiety levels while abstinence reliably reduces them has been reviewed elsewhere (Stockwell & Bolderston, 1987). Ashton (1987) recently reviewed an extensive literature on the health consequences of caffeine intake, including studies linking caffeine to sleep disorders. Litman, Stapleton, Oppenheim, Peleg, and Jackson (1984) found that "survivors" (as opposed to "relapsers") of alcoholism treatment were characterized by an early phase of reliance on avoidance strategies, and then, between 6 weeks and 4 months, by an increase in the use of active coping strategies (e.g., refusing drinks at parties instead of avoiding parties). Stern and Marks (1973) and Rankin, Hodgson, and Stockwell (1983) have demonstrated the value of long exposures to cues triggering fear and craving, respectively. There is also much basic research linking certain cognitive coping styles with the experience of fear and anxiety (e.g., Clark, 1986).

There is clearly a need for further, well-designed treatment studies. These would need to control for the various drinking, drug use, and motivational variables described earlier, and ensure that all subjects still experienced a significant level of anxiety prior to treatment. While there are always further research questions to pursue, it is possible to confidently assert that assessing and treating anxiety should be an integral part of any comprehensive alcohol treatment program.

REFERENCES

Clinical Guidelines

Self-help and Treatment Manuals

Annis, H. (1983). *A Relapse prevention model for the treatment of alcoholics*. Addiction Research Foundation, 33 Russell St., Toronto, Ontario, Canada. A clear account of a cognitive–behavioral approach to help problem-drinkers cope in a variety of high-risk situations.

Beck, A. T., and Emery, G. (1979). *Cognitive therapy of anxiety and phobic disorders*. Philadelphia, PA: Center for Cognitive Therapy. Everything one needs to know about cognitive therapy in relation to anxiety!

Rosa, K. (1976). *You and A.T. Autogenic Training* New York: Dutton. A straightforward account of this very useful relaxation technique.

Marks, I. (1978). *Living with fear*. New York: McGraw-Hill. A clearly written self-help guide written by an expert in the field.

Miller, W. R., and Muñoz, R. F. (1982). *How to control your drinking* (Rev. ed.). Albuquerque, NM: University of New Mexico Press. See section on Relaxation Training.

Assessment Questionnaires.

Marks, I., and Mathews, A. (1979). Brief standard self-rating for phobic patients. *Behavior Research and Therapy, 17,* 263–267. The "Fear Questionnaire" described in this chapter.

Stockwell, T., Murphy, D., & Hodgson, R. (1983). The Severity of Alcohol Dependence Questionnaire. Its use, reliability and validity, *British Journal of Addiction, 78,* 2, 145–155. Useful for predictive severity of alcohol withdrawal (especially anxiety components) and longer-term recovery from alcohol induced fear and anxiety.

Murphy, D., Shaw, C., & Clarke, I. (1983). Tiapride and chlormethiazole in alcohol withdrawal: A double-blind trial. *Alcohol & Alcoholism, 18,* 227–237. An easy to use and well-researched assessment of alcohol withdrawal severity.

Wallace, P, and Haines, A. (1985). Use of a questionnaire in general practice to increase the recognition of problem drinkers. *British Medical Journal, 290,* 1949–1953.

Research

Ashton, C. H. (1987). Caffeine and health. *British Medical Journal, 295,* 1293–1294.

Clark, D. M. (1986). A cognitive approach to panic. *Behaviour Research and Therapy, 24,(4)* 461–470.

Litman, G. L., Stapleton, J., Oppenheim, A., Peleg, M., & Jackson, P. (1984). The relationship between coping behaviors, their effectiveness and alcoholism relapse and survival, *British Journal of Addiction, 79, 3,* 283–292.

Oei, T. P. S., & Jackson, P. R. (1982). Social skills and cognitive behavioral approaches to the treatment of problem drinking. *Journal of Studies on Alcohol, 43,* 532–547.

Rankin, H., Hodgson, R., & Stockwell, T. (1983). Cue exposure and response prevention with alcoholics: A controlled trial. *Behaviour Research and Therapy, 21,* 435–446.

Rohsenow, D. J., Smith, R. E., and Johnson, S. (1985). Stress management training as a prevention program for heavy social drinkers: Cognitive affect, drinking and individual differences, *Addictive Behaviors, 10,* 45–54.

Stern, R., and Marks, I. (1973). Brief and prolonged flooding. *Archives of General Psychiatry, 28,* 270–276.

Stockwell, T., and Bolderston, H. (1987). Alcohol and phobias. *British Journal of Addiction, 82, 9,* 971–981.

CHAPTER 15

Psychotropic Medications

Sheldon I. Miller
Richard J. Frances
Donna J. Holmes

OVERVIEW

Interest in the use of psychotropic (psychologically active) drugs has a long history in the treatment of alcoholism (for reviews, see Charnoff, Kissin, & Reed, 1963; Ditman, 1967; Kissin, 1975; Kissin & Gross, 1968; W. R. Miller & Hester, 1986; Peachey & Naranjo, 1984) for three main reasons. First, there is the need for medications to ameliorate symptoms of withdrawal during alcohol detoxification. Second is the close association between alcoholism and other psychiatric problems, such as depression and anxiety, for which psychotropics are clearly a useful form of treatment. Third, there is continuing interest in drugs, including psychotropics, which may have the potential to reduce alcohol consumption or to attenuate its effects, even in the absence of other psychopathology.

The efficacy of psychotropics, particularly the benzodiazepines, is well established in the treatment of alcohol withdrawal syndromes (for reviews, see Favazza, 1982; Schuckit, 1984; Thompson, 1978; Zimberg, 1982). However, no psychotropic has been proven useful as a primary therapeutic tool in alcoholism treatment and rehabilitation. Though several promising lines of evidence have emerged recently, experimental data to support the efficacy of any of these drugs in the reduction of drinking are still lacking or at best equivocal. Psychoactive medications in general will probably always play an important role in alcoholism treatment, but only as adjuncts to behavioral and psychosocial therapies.

In this chapter, we will outline procedures for using psychotropics during detoxification, as well as reviewing some of the most important recent experimental research indicating the potential utility of these medications in alcohol rehabilitation. The antidipsotropic drugs, including disulfiram (Antabuse), will not be discussed here, since they are covered in detail in chapter 7.

SPECIAL CONSIDERATIONS

Along with the normal risks and side effects associated with drug therapy of any kind, the use of psychotropic medications carries with it some special considerations when treating alcoholics. This is particularly true for sedatives and hypnotics, which are cross-reactive with alcohol. When used in detoxification or in treating patients with psychiatric diagnoses in addition to alcoholism, drugs should be prescribed conservatively, and patients closely monitored to prevent abuse or the development of cross-dependency. This is particularly important for alcoholics who also abuse other substances, and such patients represent an increasingly large proportion of the clinical population of alcoholics (Schuckit, 1984; Zimberg, 1982). As Peachey and Naranjo (1984) have pointed out, the primary criterion for any successful therapy in alcoholism treatment is the facilitation of continued abstinence, not the creation of new dependencies.

Although psychotropics have no place in the rehabilitative treatment of the uncomplicated alcoholic after detoxification, alcoholism is often not a unitary disorder. Wherever possible, the clinician should attempt to distinguish between primary and secondary alcoholism. Primary alcoholism, though not incorporated into DSM-III-R due to its implication of etiological diagnosis, is generally defined as that which is unaccompanied by a prior history of other psychiatric illness (Allen & Frances, 1985; Goodwin & Guze, 1977; Schuckit, 1973, 1983, 1984, 1986; Schuckit & Winokur, 1972; Solomon, 1982; Zimberg, 1982). In studies conducted to date, the majority (approximately 70 percent) of alcoholics fall into this category (Cadoret & Winokur, 1974; Schuckit & Winokur, 1972; Sedlacek & S. I. Miller, 1982). Although primary alcoholics may present with other psychopathology, successful cessation of drinking will often bring about improvement in other problem areas, including life problems in general (W. R. Miller, Hedrick, & Taylor, 1983).

Secondary alcoholism, on the other hand, is that which accompanies a preexisting psychiatric disorder. Most secondary alcoholics are diagnosed as having an underlying primary affective illness, but schizophrenia, anxiety, attention deficit disorder, and other personality disorders may also present with alcoholism (for a review, see Allen & Frances, 1985). The term "secondary alcoholism" in no case implies a less severe or less important form of alcohol abuse.

It may be difficult, in many cases, to get a clear picture retrospectively of which came first—the primary disorder or the alcoholism. The continuation of psychopathology during alcohol-free intervals coupled with family history of psychiatric disorder can help to make a firm diagnosis of secondary alcoholism.

Even if alcoholism is secondary to another illness, treatment of the underlying psychopathology may not in itself be successful in controlling drinking. Although alcohol may have been used initially to self-medicate underlying psychiatric problems, in many cases abuse becomes an "autonomous," self-perpetuating disorder (Sedlacek & S. I. Miller, 1982; Woodruff, Guze, Clayton, & Carr, 1973).

Depression, either primary or secondary, is commonly associated with alcoholism (Allen & Frances, 1985; Keeler, Taylor, & W. R. Miller, 1979; Weissman & Myers, 1980). Hence, the dangers of overdose and abuse are important factors to consider when prescribing psychotropics. In alcoholics also suffering from affective disorders, suicidal ideation and delusions or hallucinations are not uncommon. Actual incidence of suicide in alcoholics is as high as 15 percent (Frances, Franklin, & Flavin, 1987), and the majority of successful suicides overall are either alcoholic, depressed, or both (Barraclough, Bunch, Nelson, & Sainsbury, 1974; Dorpat & Ripley, 1960; Robins, Murphy, Wilkinson, Gassner, & Kayes, 1959). Careful monitoring of patients' medical and psychiatric status during treatment is essential, including (a) compliance with therapy in general; (b) use of alcohol and other drugs (as reported by family members or significant others, as well as the patient); (c) status of social and family relations; (d) financial and employment status; (e) medical and psychiatric status in general; and (f) any adverse effects of medication.

DESCRIPTION

Psychotropics in Detoxification

The first phase of treatment of acutely intoxicated patients should include a test for blood alcohol level, a drug screen, and a physical examination. (Readers interested only in the use of medications for post-detoxification treatment may wish to skip to the next section.) Psychotropics, particularly the benzodiazepine tranquilizers, are frequently indicated during detoxification to treat symptoms of withdrawal, including confusion, agitation, anxiety, irritability, sleeplessness, tremors, and, in more severe cases, cognitive impairment, hallucinations, or seizures (Favazza, 1982; Schuckit, 1984; Sellers & Kalant, 1978). Such symptoms usually become most pronounced within 12 to 60 hours of withdrawal.

Nonpharmacological inpatient "social setting" detoxification is effective for uncomplicated cases of mild withdrawal, as described by Femino and Lewis (1982). This approach involves keeping patients who are undergoing withdrawal in a quiet, secure hospital setting for two to seven days, during which they are helped to achieve nonpharmacological control.

If other supportive therapy fails within the first few hours of treatment, benzodiazepines should be administered. The use of benzodiazopine derivatives for treatment of withdrawal is particularly desirable because they are pharmacologically similar to alcohol, are long-lasting, have low liver toxicity, and carry a low risk of respiratory depression or overdose. They are effective (a) in reducing anxiety, including that associated with depression and other primary affective disorders; (b) as hypnotics; (c) in reducing tremor and autonomic hyperactivity; and (d) in preventing convulsions. Meprobamate (Miltown®, Equanil®) is to be strictly avoided because of its high addiction potential and low therapeutic value. Although barbiturates (e.g., phenobarbital) have a history of use in treatment of withdrawal (and many practitioners still prescribe them), they have a low margin of safety, carrying a serious risk of overdose and respiratory failure, as well as high addiction and cross-addiction potential.

Vegetative symptoms of withdrawal indicating a need for medication include tachycardia, fever, systolic hypertension, gastrointestinal distress, tremor, and perspiration (Favazza, 1982; Greenblatt, Divoll, Abernethy, Ochs, & Shader, 1984; Peachey & Naranjo, 1984). The overall mental status of the patient, including any impairment in orientation, should also be evaluated, and the decision to continue drug treatment based on the patient's response and any adverse clinical effects that ensue. Although these medications are relatively safe, overdose of depressants or cross-reaction between benzodiazepines and abused substances can result in respiratory depression and ataxia. Moreover, they have a considerable potential for addiction, particularly in substance abusers, and should be prescribed for as short a period as possible to avoid the development of new drug dependencies.

After making as complete a medical and psychiatric assessment of the patient as possible, mild withdrawal symptoms may be treated on an outpatient basis with oral benzodiazepines (e.g., 100–200 mg daily of chlordiazepoxide). Outpatient detoxification requires daily follow-up and a good support system. In cases where alcohol use is likely to be continued, medications abused, or alcoholism is accompanied with other serious medical problems, including psychiatric illnesses, inpatient or social setting detoxification is indicated. Patients with withdrawal syndromes severe enough to require hospitalization may be given oral or intravenous diazepam (2.5 mg/min) or intravenous (12.5 mg/min) or oral (25–100 mg every 4–8 hrs) chlordiazepoxide. Most patients tolerate oral medication, but the intravenous route of administration can be used when there is severe vomiting, the patient is at risk of developing delirium tremens, or there is concern about oral medications not reaching therapeutic levels quickly enough. In any case, the dosage should be reduced gradually (20 percent daily) over a period of days. More gradual dose reduction (e.g., 10 percent per day) is needed for patients cross-addicted to other substances. Although as a group the benzodiazepines are similar in their anxiolytic, sedative/hypnotic, and anticonvulsant properties, their pharmacokinetic profiles differ substantially (Greenblatt et al., 1984; Peachey & Naranjo, 1984). Diazepam, for example, is longer acting and has particular value as a muscle relaxant and anticonvulsant. Because alcoholics like its euphoric effects better than chlordiazepoxide, however, it carries a greater risk of abuse and dependence. Oxazepam (Serax®), with its short half-life, is particularly useful for insomnia as well as for patients with liver or respiratory problems, since it is excreted via the kidney. It is often helpful in elderly patients. Flurazepam (Dalmane®) is longer acting and accumulates in the bloodstream. In general, benzodiazepines should not be administered intramuscularly, since absorption via this route can be unpredictable.

Elevation of body temperature and heart rate indicate the need for a higher dose of medication, but patients should be monitored carefully for respiratory depression, ataxia, confusion, or other signs of overdose.

If a patient in severe withdrawal has epilepsy, a history of withdrawal seizures, or appears to be at risk for developing grand mal seizures, an anticonvulsant medication should be administered. Diazepam (IV) is recommended over intravenous phenytoin (Dilantin®) initially, as diazepam is safer and provides multiple therapeutic effects. This can be followed with oral benzodiazepines and oral phenytoin (100 mg three times daily) for one to two weeks. Magnesium sulfate is also effective for seizure prevention, and can be administered intramuscularly for the first two to three days of detoxification.

If primarily associated with alcohol withdrawal, the risk of seizures should subside as detoxification continues. Seizures that persist after this time, however, suggest the need for a thorough neurologic evaluation.

It has been suggested that benzodiazepines may also be useful in the treatment of so-called "protracted withdrawal syndrome" (Gorski, 1977; Kielholz, 1970; Peachey & Naranjo, 1984). In general, however, the long-term prescription of depressants in the treatment of alcoholism is to be avoided.

Although the benzodiazepines are the primary psychotropic tool in treating withdrawal, producing the fewest complications, a variety of other drugs, including other antipsychotics, are also frequently used. We should stress, however, that the use of neuroleptics in the treatment of uncomplicated withdrawal should in general be avoided. Some antipsychotics (e.g., phenothiazine), in addition to carrying the risk of causing tardive dyskinesia, can decrease the threshold for seizures. If these drugs are prescribed at all for alcoholics in withdrawal, it should be for as brief a period as possible.

The administration of vitamins has become routine in most detoxification centers, and has significantly reduced the risk of patients developing severe neurological problems (e.g., Wernicke-Korsakoff syndrome) (Frances & Franklin, 1987). Thiamine can be administered at 100 mg IM for the first two days of detoxification, accompanied by an oral preparation of B-vitamins and Vitamin C.

Distinguishing between primary psychosis and the hallucinosis and delusions that can accompany severe alcohol withdrawal can be problematic (Peachey & Naranjo, 1984; Schuckit, 1982; Zimberg, 1982). Although alcoholic hallucinosis and paranoia may in some cases be symptomatic of organic psychosis, fewer than 10 percent (no greater than the

general population) of alcoholics are schizophrenic (Goodwin & Guze, 1977; Peachey & Naranjo, 1984; Schuckit, 1984). Symptoms of alcoholic psychosis generally subside as detoxification procedes.

Psychotropics in Rehabilitation

Although intoxication makes accurate psychiatric diagnosis more difficult, rehabilitation can be started during detoxification, provided the patient has a relatively clear mental status. After intoxication clears, the patient should undergo a complete psychiatric assessment, including life history of drinking and any other psychiatric problems or other substance abuse.

Despite tentative evidence that some psychotropics reduce alcohol consumption or intoxication, none has yet been established as a primary agent for treatment in the rehabilitative phase of uncomplicated primary alcoholism. The once prevalent idea that alcoholism is a symptom of an additional psychiatric disorder, and that treatment of underlying psychopathology would alleviate the drinking problem, is outmoded (Sellers, Naranjo, & Peachey, 1981). In cases of primary alcoholism, successful reduction of drinking will often bring about improvement in other problem areas. In studies conducted to date, approximately 70 to 80 percent of alcoholics fall into this category (Allen & Frances, 1985; Cadoret & Winokur, 1974; W. R. Miller, Hedrick, & Taylor, 1983; Schuckit, 1973, 1983, 1984; Sedlacek & S. I. Miller, 1982; Woodruff et al., 1973). Of the remaining 20 to 30 percent, the secondary alcoholics, the majority are likely to present with an underlying primary affective disorder and the remainder with other psychiatric illnesses, including personality disorders. Depression, anxiety, or other affective symptoms which have occurred for a sustained period when the patient was not drinking or before the onset of major life problems associated with alcoholism, or a family history of such problems, suggests the possibility of primary affective disorder accompanied by secondary alcoholism.

If indicated for treatment of concomitant psychiatric illness, psychotropics should be continued in conjunction with behavioral and psychosocial alcohol rehabilitation therapies. For example, a well-diagnosed bipolar patient with a good history of response to lithium should be maintained on it, and lithium may be needed to treat acute mania in alcoholics. Similarly, a patient with diagnosed schizophrenia will need to be maintained on neuroleptics. Treatment for other patients may involve use of tricyclic antidepressants or monoamine oxidase inhibitors (with care) for panic disorder, anticonvulsants for seizure disorder, pemoline for adult attention disorder, and methadone for opiate addiction. In general, an alcoholic patient who meets clinical criteria for major affective disorder with alcoholism should be treated accordingly, with medication trials started after a drug-free interval unless there is a clear diagnosis of primary depression. If psychotropic medications are prescribed, particular care should be taken to guard against the possibility of cross-tolerance, abuse, or dangerous side effects that can result from administration of such medications to drinking alcoholics or multidrug users. Because the complex effects of alcohol on the liver may lead to either increased or decreased drug metabolism, close monitoring of the patient's condition and blood levels of drugs is important. Moreover, patients should be counseled carefully to resist efforts of well-meaning peers to make them discontinue all medications, including those essential for treating concomitant psychiatric problems.

EFFECTIVENESS

Detoxification

In general, the effectiveness of psychotropics, particularly the benzodiazepines, for relieving symptoms of withdrawal is well established (see, for example, Favazza, 1982; Schuckit, 1984; Thompson, 1978; Zimberg, 1982). A variety of other psychoactive agents is also used by many practitioners. In some cases their efficacy has not been firmly established; in others, the associated risks and side effects outweigh their potential benefits.

Clonidine (Catapres®), an alpha-agonist antihypertensive medication, can be an aid in treating symptoms of narcotic withdrawal (Charney et al., 1982; Charney, Sternberg, Kleber, Heninger, & Redmond, 1981; Franz, Hare, & McCloskey, 1982; Gold, Pottash, & Kleber, 1981). Recent evidence that it may also be helpful in treating alcohol withdrawal, while promising, is still preliminary (Peachey & Naranjo, 1984). Propranolol, a beta-blocker, can be used in small doses (0.1 or 0.5 mg IV) in

detoxification to control tremor and tachycardia, and there is some evidence that it is effective in alleviating other withdrawal symptoms as well (Carlsson, 1971; Carlsson & Johansson, 1971; Gallant, 1982; Zilm, Sellers, McLeod, & Degani, 1975). The efficacy of propranolol is controversial, however (e.g., Favazza, 1982; Peachey & Naranjo, 1984; Thompson, 1978), and its use in detoxification is not routinely advocated.

Paraldehyde has historically been used as a hypnotic during detoxification (Gallant, 1982; Schuckit, 1984), but, like barbiturates, it is far more addictive and dangerous in terms of risk of overdose than the benzodiazepines. The use of antihistamines as hypnotics is sometimes recommended as an alternative to other psychoactive medications (e.g., Gallant, 1982). The anticholinergic effects of these drugs can be a problem, however (Favazza, 1982).

There is some evidence that lithium can suppress symptoms of withdrawal (Ho & Tsai, 1976; McMillan, 1981; Sellers, Cooper, Sen, & Zilm, 1974; Sellers, Cooper, Zilm, & Shankes, 1976). Lithium is not a simple drug to administer, however, since blood levels must be monitored to prevent toxic reactions. The toxicity of lithium is a particular problem in severe cases of withdrawal, which may be complicated by fluid and electrolyte imbalances. Lithium is not recommended currently for treatment of withdrawal, and more research is needed into the possible usefulness of this drug in detoxification.

Research is also in progress to explore the possibility that opiate antagonists (e.g., Naloxone and Naltrexone) may be useful in counteracting alcohol intoxication. A growing number of studies have shown that the adverse effects of acute alcohol intoxication, including coma, can be reduced or reversed by Naloxone (Cholewa, Pach, & Macheta, 1983; Ducobu, 1984; Guerin & Friedberg, 1982; Jeffreys, Flanagan, & Volans, 1980; Lyon & Anthony, 1982; Mackenzie, 1979; Moss, 1973; Schenk, Engelmeir, Maltz, & Pach, 1978; Sorenson & Mattison, 1978), although this finding has been refuted by others (Mackenzie, 1983; Nuotto, Palva, & Lahdenranta, 1983). To date, these agents have only been used experimentally, and have not been proven suitable for routine application in alcohol or narcotic detoxification.

Chlormethiazole is being used successfully for treatment of alcohol withdrawal in other countries, but it has not been approved in the

U.S. due to concern about reports of deaths, addiction, and problems associated the use of this drug in patients with liver disease (Peachey & Naranjo, 1984).

Rehabilitation

There are a number of problems associated with evaluating experimental data pertaining to the efficacy of psychotropic medications in alcohol rehabilitation. These include: (a) differences in subject populations (e.g. depressed vs. nondepressed); (b) inadequate or no controls; (c) high dropout and noncompliance rates; (d) inconsistencies in outcome measures; (e) inadequate follow-up period; and (f) possible interactions between pharmacological and psychosocial therapies when they are combined in the same study. It is also difficult to control for variability in socioeconomic environments among subjects undergoing experimental treatment. It is important to be aware of these problems when evaluating the validity of recent research findings concerning the usefulness of psychotropics in alcohol rehabilitation.

Lithium

There is evidence that lithium can prevent the deficits in cognitive and motor performance produced by alcohol (Judd, Hubbard, Huey, Attewell, Janowsky, & Takahashi, 1977; Judd & Huey, 1984; Linnoila, Saario, & Maki, 1974), and that it can alter the subjective experience of intoxication, including perceived self-control over drinking. Since lithium is well established as an effective medication for bipolar affective disorder as well as unipolar illness (Baastrup, Poulsen, Schou, Thomsen, & Amdisen, 1970; Coppen et al., 1971, 1973; Coppen, Montgomery, Gupta, & Bailey, 1976), it is not surprising that it has also been shown experimentally to be useful in treating a portion of the alcoholic population (for reviews, see McMillan, 1981; W. R. Miller & Hester, 1986; Pond et al., 1981; Schou, 1978). In general, controlled studies indicate that lithium is more helpful than placebo in reducing drinking in depressed alcoholics (e.g., Fawcett et al., 1984; Kline, Wren, Cooper, Varga, & Canal, 1974; Merry, Reynolds, Bailey, & Coppen, 1976; Wren, Kline, & Cooper, 1974; but see Pond et al., 1981). Differences among studies with respect to psychiatric characteristics of subjects, outcome measures,

and high noncompliance and dropout rates make comparison of experimental results difficult, however, and the efficacy of lithium in rehabilitation of nondepressed alcoholics relative to other psychotropics has not been clearly established. Although some workers remain optimistic, others (e.g., Schou, 1978; Young and Keeler, 1977) have suggested that only a segment of the alcoholic population will clearly benefit from lithium therapy, and that this segment is most likely the manic–depressive subgroup.

Lithium has been shown to reduce alcohol consumption in laboratory animals (Ho & Tsai, 1976; Truitt & Vaughen, 1976). Some workers have suggested it may prove useful as an antidipsotropic for humans (Revusky, 1973; Revusky, Parker, Coombes, & Coombes, 1976; Revusky & Taukulis, 1975). At this point, however, it would clearly be inappropriate to routinely prescribe lithium to alcoholics with no diagnosis of a primary affective disorder. Data supporting the efficacy of lithium as an aversive agent are equivocal, since toxic levels of lithium may produce nausea unrelated to any specific aversive effect (McMillan, 1981; Schou, 1978). Moreover, lithium is a potentially dangerous medication. The therapeutic dose for manic–depressive disorder closely approaches toxicity, and blood levels of the drug must be closely monitored in patients receiving lithium therapy. Until such time as the usefulness of lithium is firmly established experimentally, the potential risks of using it in alcohol rehabilitation outweigh any clear benefit.

Antidepressants

Depression is the most common psychiatric problem among alcoholics, and can be an impediment to effective treatment. Though there is no indication that antidepressants should be routinely prescribed for uncomplicated alcoholism, concurrent major depressive disorder may be treated accordingly after a two- to four-week detoxification period, provided there are no medical or psychosocial contraindications.

Depression generally remits in two to four weeks and is usually secondary to alcoholism. In cases of a clear diagnosis of an additional illness based on past history, patients who have been treated successfully in the past with lithium, antidepressants, or anticonvulsants (in instances of a diagnosed seizure disorder rather than withdrawal seizures) can be given these same medications during detoxification.

There is some experimental evidence that antidepressants, as well as lithium, can be helpful in the rehabilitation of some alcoholics (for reviews, see Baekeland, 1977; W. R. Miller & Hester, 1986). In general, however, though they may alter *mood*, neither tricyclic antidepressants nor monoamine oxidase inhibitors have been shown to consistently alter drinking *behavior* per se. Comparison of results of the relatively few controlled experimental studies carried out on antidepressants thus far is rendered more difficult by (a) a lack of consistency in study design (e.g. antidepressants used as an experimental treatment alone or in combination with another psychotropic), (b) subject population (e.g. depressed vs. nondepressed, inpatients vs. outpatients, male vs. female, or psychotic vs. nonpsychotic), (c) outcome measurements (e.g. reduction of drinking rate vs. amelioration of anxiety or depression), and (d) adequacy and length of follow-up period. Moreover, the problem of effective dosage, as well as that of possible drug interactions in a number of studies which combined antidepressants with other psychotropics (usually benzodiazepines or phenothiazines), has not always been adequately addressed (Baekeland, 1977).

Nialamide, a monoamine oxidase inhibitor, was no more effective in preventing recurrence of drinking than placebo in an early study by Shaffer, Freinek, Wolf, Foxwell, and Kurland (1964). The tricyclic antidepressant imipramine (Tofranil®), however, has been shown to be more effective than placebo in a number of studies, either when administered separately (Baekeland & Lundwall, 1975; Butterworth, 1971; Shaw, Donley, Morgan, & Robinson, 1975; Wilson, Alltop, & Riley, 1970) or in combination with chlordiazepoxide (Librium®) (Kissin & Gross, 1968; Kissin, Platz, & Su, 1970). Outcome measures in these studies varied, however, from reduction of drinking or amelioration of anxiety or depression to some unspecified "improvement" measure (Butterworth, 1971).

Butterworth and Watts (1971) found doxepin (Sinequan®), another tricyclic, was more effective than chlordiazepoxide in reducing anxiety and depression in male alcoholics. This finding was consistent with that of Overall, Brown, Williams, and Neil (1973), who found that chlordiazepoxide was less effective than either mesoridazine (a phenothiazine antipsychotic)

or amitryptiline (Elavil®). There are no data, however, which indicate that antidepressants are more effective in controlling alcohol consumption than psychosocial therapies; in fact, Kissin et al. (1970) found that a combination of imipramine and chlordiazepoxide was less effective than psychotherapy.

Until more unequivocal experimental data are available, antidepressants should continue to be used only in treating persistent major depression in alcoholics after sobriety has been achieved, rather than as a primary medication in rehabilitation. Since alcoholics may be less compliant than other patients with dietary restrictions, they are at particular risk for the "wine and cheese" reaction (tyramine-induced hypertensive crisis) that can occur in patients on monoamine oxidase inhibitors.

Tranquilizers

As a rule, the use of sedatives, hypnotics, and antianxiety agents (including meprobamate, paraldehyde, and barbiturates, as well as the benzodiazepine derivatives) is to be avoided in the treatment of alcoholics in the rehabilitative phase, because of their potential for producing dependence, synergism with alcohol, and the danger of overdose (Zimberg, 1982). Although the benzodiazepines are extremely useful in detoxification, controlled studies have provided only weak or equivocal evidence of their efficacy in rehabilitation. Hoff (1961) initially found a higher proportion (72%) of patients with reduced drinking after being given chlordiazepoxide relative to matched controls (52% reduction in drinking scores). Subsequent studies, however, have failed to show significant differences between chlordiazepoxide-treated subjects and controls on measures either of drinking or psychosocial functioning (Bartholomew & Guile, 1961; Charnoff et al., 1963; Mooney, Ditman, & Cohen, 1961; Rosenberg, 1974; Shaffer et al., 1964). Although there are some data suggesting that chlordiazepoxide given to alcoholics in combination with imipramine was more effective than placebo or imipramine alone (Kissin & Gross, 1968), there is by and large no compelling evidence to support the efficacy of benzodiazepines in alcoholism treatment after detoxification. In fact, as stated earlier, these depressants are strongly contraindicated for alcoholics, because of their potential for abuse, addiction, and cross-reactivity (W. R. Miller & Hester, 1986; Schuckit, 1984; Zimberg, 1982).

Antipsychotics

Neuroleptics, including the antipsychotics chlorpromazine (Thorazine®), thioridazine (Mellaril®) and haloperidol (Haldol®), are also generally contraindicated in the rehabilitation of primary, uncomplicated alcoholism. Besides the fact that their effectiveness has not been established experimentally, they have a relatively high risk of side effects, including tardive dyskinesia. Small doses (25 to 50 mg) of Mellaril® are sometimes used as a hypnotic for newly detoxified patients or those with prolonged withdrawal symptoms (Zimberg, 1982). Antipsychotic medications or increased doses of benzodiazepines may be indicated for psychotic patients during both detoxification and rehabilitation. In general, however, the administration of these medications to recovering alcoholics should be avoided.

Even though early reports were hopeful (e.g., Fox & Smith, 1959), there is no conclusive evidence that any antipsychotic, including thiothixene (Navane®) or trifluoperazine (Stelazine®), clearly has utility in treating nonpsychotic alcoholics.

Opiate Antagonists and Other Psychotropics

Drugs affecting neurotransmitter action, uptake, and metabolism represent one of the most exciting experimental frontiers in the treatment of alcoholism. Recent evidence, though not as extensive as that for other psychoactive agents, indicates that opiate antagonists show some promise in the rehabilitation of alcoholics, as well as in the treatment of intoxication. Naloxone has been shown to decrease alcohol consumption in animals (Altshuler, Phillips, & Feinhandler, 1980; Ross, Hartmann, & Geller, 1976), and also to block psychomotor impairment in human subjects (Jeffcoate, Cullen, Herbert, Hastings, & Walder, 1979). These results are controversial, however (see, for example, Bird, Chester, Perl, & Starmer, 1982; Catley, Jordan, Frith, Lehane, Rhodes, & Jones, 1981; Mattila, Nuotto, & Seppala, 1981; Whalley, Freedman, & Hunter, 1981).

Borg (1983) found that zimelidine, an inhibitor of serotonin reuptake, can reduce drinking in alcoholics. Bromocriptine, an ergot derivative that acts as a dopamine agonist, has been found to reduce alcohol consumption by heavy social drinkers (Naranjo et al., 1983), although it may simply produce an aversion to alcohol unrelated to specific neuropharmacological effects. GABA agonists (e.g., calcium bis acetyl homotaurine) are also suspected to have some potential for preventing relapse drinking in recovering alcoholics (Lhuintire et al., 1985). Even more recently, Klotz, Ziegler, Rosenkranz, and Mikus (1986) have investigated the possibility that a benzodiazepine antagonist, RO 15-1788, antagonizes the action of alcohol at the receptor level. It would be premature at this point, however, to suggest that these drugs be administered to recovering alcoholics. Even if they are eventually proven effective as anti-intoxication agents, such medications carry with them the substantial risk of encouraging an increase in alcohol consumption and resultant organ damage, since they can give alcoholics a false sense of security about the physiological impact of continued drinking.

Investigators are clearly still seeking new pharmacological therapies for alcoholism. To date, however, the utility of any psychoactive drug in the treatment of uncomplicated alcoholism has yet to be unequivocally established. Until such time as their safety and efficacy has been proven, our position remains that psychotropics are contraindicated for uncomplicated recovering alcoholics.

REFERENCES

Clinical Guidelines

Favazza, A. R. (1982). The alcohol withdrawal syndrome and medical detoxification. In E. M. Pattison & E. Kaufman (Eds.), *Encyclopedic handbook of alcoholism* (pp. 1068–1075). New York: Gardner Press. Provides guidelines for identifying patients in need of detoxification and for medical management of alcohol withdrawal, particularly the administration of benzodiazepine tranquilizers.

Forest, J. L., Frances, R. J., & Mooney, III, A. J. (1987). Alcoholism Rx: How you can help. *Patient Care*, Jan, 92–97. Provides detailed sample inpatient detoxification protocol, including dosages for magnesium sulfate and vitamins.

Frances, R. J., & Franklin, J. E. (1987). Alcohol-induced organic mental disorders. In R. E. Hales & S. C. Yudofsky (Eds.), *Textbook of neuropsychiatry* (pp. 410–431). Washington, DC: APP Press. Gives criteria for distinguishing between patients in need of inpatient vs. outpatient treatment for withdrawal and detailed descriptions of withdrawal syndromes. Also provides background necessary for diagnosing specific alcohol-related organic mental illnesses, as well as detailed regimes—both inpatient and outpatient—for the management of withdrawal.

Zimberg, S. (1982). *The clinical management of alcohol-*

ism. New York: Brunner/Mazel Inc. A thorough guide to the diagnosis and treatment of alcoholism in general, including detoxification, management of psychiatric–neurological complications, and various alternative approaches to rehabilitation.

Research

Allen, M. H., & Frances, R. J. (1985). Varieties of psychopathology found in patients with addictive disorders: A review. In R. Meyer (Ed.), *Psychopathology of addiction* (pp. 17–38). New York: Guilford.

Altshuler, H. L., Phillips, P. E., & Feinhandler, D. A. (1980). Alteration of ethanol self-administration by Naltrexone. *Life Sciences, 26,* 679–688.

Baastrup, P. C., Poulson, J. C., Schou, M., Thomsen, K., & Amdisen, A. (1970). Prophylactic lithium: Double blind discontinuation in manic–depressive and recurrent-depressive disorders. *Lancet, 2,* 326.

Baekeland, F. (1977). Evaluation of treatment methods in chronic alcoholism. In B. Kissin & H. Begleiter (Eds.), *The Biology of Alcoholism. Vol. 5. Treatment and rehabilitation of the chronic alcoholic* (pp. 385–440). New York: Plenum.

Baekeland, F., & Lundwall, L. K. (1975). Effects of discontinuity of medication on the results of a double-blind drug study in outpatient alcoholics. *Journal of Studies on Alcohol, 36,* 1268–1272.

Barraclough, J., Bunch, J., Nelson, D., & Sainsbury, P. (1974). 100 cases of suicide: Clinical aspects. *British Journal of Psychiatry, 125,* 355–373.

Bartholomew, A. A., & Guile, L. A. (1961). A controlled evaluation of "Librium in the treatment of alcoholics." *Medical Journal of Australia, 2,* 578–581.

Bird, K. D., Chester, G. B., Perl, J., & Starmer, G. A. (1982). Naloxone has no effect on ethanol-induced impairment of psychomotor performance in man. *Psychopharmacology, 76,* 193–197.

Borg, A. (1983). Bromocriptine in the prevention of alcohol abuse. *Acta Psychiatrica, 68,* 100–110.

Butterworth, A. T. (1971). Depression associated with alcohol withdrawal: Imipramine therapy combined with placebo. *Quarterly Journal of Studies on Alcohol, 32,* 343–348.

Butterworth, A. T., & Watts, R. D. (1971). Treatment of hospitalized alcoholics with doxepin and diazepam: a controlled study. *Quarterly Journal of Studies on Alcohol, 32,* 78–81.

Cadoret, R., & Winokur, G. (1974). Depression in alcoholism. *Annals of the New York Academy of Science, 233,* 34–39.

Carlsson, C. (1971). Haemodynamic effects of adrenergic beta-receptor blockade in the withdrawal phase of alcoholism. *International Journal of Clinical Pharmacology,* Supplement No. 3, 61–63.

Carlsson, C., & Johansson, T. (1971). The psychological effects of propranolol in the abstinence phase of chronic alcoholics. *British Journal of Psychiatry, 119,* 605–606.

Catley, D. H., Jordan, C., Frith, C. D., Lehane, J. R., Rhodes, A. M., & Jones, J. G. (1981). Alcohol induced discoordination is not reversed by naloxone. *Psychopharmacology, 75,* 65–68.

Charney, D. S., Riordan, C. E., Kleber, H. D., Murburg, M., Braverman, P., Sternberg, D. E.,

Heninger, G. R., & Redmond, D. E. (1982). A safe, effective, and rapid treatment of abrupt withdrawal from methadone therapy. *Archives of General Psychiatry, 39,* 1327–1332.

Charney, D. S., Sternberg, D. E., Kleber, H. D., Heninger, G. R., & Redmond, D. E. (1981). The clinical use of clonidine in abrupt withdrawal from methadone. *Archives of General Psychiatry, 38,* 1273–1277.

Charnoff, S. M., Kissin, B., & Reed, J. I. (1963). An evaluation of various psychotherapeutic agents in the long-term treatment of chronic alcoholism. *American Journal of Medical Sciences, 246,* 172–179.

Cholewa, L., Pach, J., & Macheta, A. (1983). Effects of naloxone on ethanol-induced coma. *Human Toxicology, 2,* 217–219.

Coppen, A. Montgomery, S. A., Gupta, R. K., & Bailey, J. E. (1976). A double-blind comparison of lithium carbonate and maprotiline in the prophylaxis of affective disorders. *British Journal of Psychiatry, 128,* 479.

Coppen, A., Noguera, R., Bailey, J., Burns, B., Swani, M., Hare, E., & Gardner, R. (1971). Prophylactic lithium in affective disorders. *Lancet, 2,* 275.

Coppen, A., Peet, M., Bailey, J., Nogura, R., Burns, B., Swani, M. S., Maggs, R., & Gardner, R. (1973). Double-blind and open prospective studies of lithium prophylaxis in affective disorders. *Psychiatria, Neurologia, Neurochirugia, 76,* 501.

Ditman, K. S. (1967). Review and evaluation of current drug therapies in alcoholism. *International Journal of Psychiatry, 3,* 248–258.

Dorpat, T. L., & Ripley, H. S. (1960). A study of suicide in the Seattle area. *Comprehensive Psychiatry, 1,* 349–359.

Ducobu, J. (1984). Naloxone and alcohol intoxication. *Annals of Internal Medicine, 100,* 617–618.

Favazza, A. (1982). The alcohol withdrawal syndrome and medical detoxification. In E. M. Pattison & E. Kaufman (Eds.), *Encyclopedic Handbook of Alcoholism* (pp. 1068–1075). New York: Gardner Press.

Fawcett, J., Clark, D. C., Gibbons, R. D., Aagesen, C. A., Pisani, V. D., Tilkin, J. M., Sellers, D., & Stutzman, D. (1984). Evaluation of lithium therapy for alcoholism. *Journal of Clinical Psychiatry, 45,* 494–499.

Femino, J., & Lewis, D. C. (1982). Clinical pharmacology and therapeutics of the alcohol withdrawal syndrome (Report No. 0372). Rockville, MD: National Institute on Alcohol Abuse and Alcoholism.

Fox, V., & Smith, M. A. (1959). Evaluation of a chemopsychotherapeutic program for the rehabilitation of alcoholics: Observations over a two-year period. *Quarterly Journal of Studies on Alcohol, 20,* 767–780.

Frances, R. J., & Franklin, J. E. (1987). Alcohol-induced organic mental disorders. In R. E. Hales and S. C. Yudofsky (Eds.), *Textbook of neuropsychiatry* (pp. 410–431). Washington, DC: APP Press.

Frances, R. J., Franklin, J., & Flavin, D. K. Suicide and alcoholism. *American Journal of Alcohol and Drug Abuse, 13,* 327–341.

Franz, D. N., Hare, B. D., & McCloskey, K. L. (1982). Spinal sympathetic neurons: Possible sites of opiate-withdrawal suppression by clonidine. *Sci-*

ence, 215, 1643–1645.

Gallant, D. M. (1982). Psychiatric aspects of alcohol intoxication, withdrawal, and organic brain syndromes. In J. Solomon (Ed.), *Alcoholism and clinical psychiatry* (pp. 141–162). New York: Plenum.

Gold, M. S., Pottash, A. C., & Kleber, H. D. (1981). Outpatient clonidine detoxification. *Lancet 1,* 621.

Goodwin, D. W., & Guze, S. B. (1977). *Psychiatric diagnosis* (2nd ed.). New York: Oxford University Press.

Gorski, T. T. (1977). *Neurologically-Based Alcoholism Diagnostic Systems (NADS).* Harvey, IL: Ingalls Memorial Hospital.

Greenblatt, D. J., Divoll, M., Abernethy, D. R., Ochs, H. R., & Shader, R. I. (1984). Benzodiazepine pharmokinetics: An overview. In G. D. Burrows, T. R. Norman, & B. Davies (Eds.), *Antianxiety agents* (pp. 79–92). Amsterdam: Elsevier.

Guerin, J. M., & Friedberg, G. (1982). Naloxone and ethanol intoxication. *Annals of Internal Medicine, 97,* 932.

Ho, A. K. S., & Tsai, C. S. (1976). Effects of lithium on alcohol preference and withdrawal. *Annals of the New York Academy of Science, 273,* 371–377.

Hoff, E. C. (1961). The use of pharmacological adjuncts in the psychotherapy of alcoholics. *Quarterly Journal of Studies on Alcohol,* Suppl. No. 1, 138–150.

Jeffcoate, W. J., Cullen, M. A., Herbert, M., Hastings, A. G., & Walder, C. P. (1979). Prevention of effects of alcohol intoxication by Naloxone. *Lancet, 1,* 1157–1159.

Jeffreys, D. B., Flanagan, R. F., & Volans, G. W. (1980). Reversal of ethanol induced coma with naloxone. *Lancet, 1,* 308–309.

Jeffreys, D. B., & Volans, G. W. (1983). An investigation of the role of the specific opioid antagonist naloxone in clinical toxicology. *Human Toxicology, 2,* 227–231.

Judd, L. L., Hubbard, R. B., Huey, L. Y., Attewell, P. A., Janowsky, D. S., & Takahashi, K. I. (1977). Lithium carbonate and ethanol induced "highs" in normal subjects. *Archives of General Psychiatry, 34,* 463–467.

Judd, L. L, & Huey, L. Y. (1984). Lithium antagonizes ethanol intoxication in alcoholics. *American Journal of Psychiatry, 141,* 1517–1521.

Keeler, M. H.,Taylor, C. I., & Miller, W. R. (1979). Are all recently detoxified alcoholics depressed? *American Journal of Psychiatry, 1136,* 586–588.

Kielholz, P. (1970). Alcohol and depression. *British Journal of Addiction, 65,* 187–193.

Kissin, G. (1975). The use of psychoactive drugs in the long-term treatment of chronic alcoholics. *Annals of the New York Academy of Science, 252,* 385–395.

Kissin, B., & Gross, M. M. (1968). Drug therapy in alcoholism. *American Journal of Psychiatry, 125,* 31–41.

Kissin, B., Platz, & Su, W. H. (1970). Social and psychological factors in the treatment of chronic alcoholism. *Journal of Psychiatric Research, 8,* 13–27.

Kline, N. S., Wren, J. C., Cooper, T. B., Varga, E., & Canal, O. (1974). Evaluation of lithium therapy in chronic alcoholism. *American Journal of the Medical Sciences, 268,* 15–22.

Klotz, U., Ziegler, G., Rosenkranz, B., & Mikus, G. (1986). Does the benzodiazepine antagonist RO

15-1788 antagonize the action of ethanol? *British Journal of Pharmacology, 22,* 513–520.

Lhuintire, J. P., Moore, N. D., Saligaut, C., Boismare, F., Dauoust, M., Chretien, P., Tran, G., & Hillemand, B. (1985). Ability of calcium bis acetyl homotaurine, a GABA agonist, to prevent relapse in weaned alcoholics. *Lancet, 1,* 1014–1016.

Linnoila, M., Saario, I., & Maki, M. (1974). Effect of treatment with diazepam and alcohol on psychomotor skills related to driving. *European Journal of Clinical Pharmacology, 7,* 337–342.

Lyon, L. J., & Anthony, J. (1982). Reversal of alcoholic coma by naloxone. *Annals of Internal Medicine, 96,* 464–465.

Mackenzie, A. I. (1979). Naloxone in alcohol intoxication. *Lancet, 1,* 733–734.

Mackenzie, A. I. (1983). Naloxone for ethanol intoxication? *Lancet, 2,* 145–146.

Mattila, M. J., Nuotto, E., & Seppala, T. (1981). Naloxone is not an effective antagonist of ethanol. *Lancet, 1,* 775–776.

McMillan, T. M. (1981). Lithium and the treatment of alcoholism: A critical review. *British Journal of Addiction, 76,* 245–258.

Merry, J., Reynolds, C. M., Bailey, J., & Coppen, A. (1976). Prophylactic treatment of alcoholism by lithium carbonate: a controlled study. *Lancet, 2, 481–482.*

Miller, W. R., Hedrick, K. E., & Taylor, C. A. (1983). Addictive behaviors and life problems before and after treatment of problem drinkers. *Addictive Behaviors, 8,* 403–412.

Miller, W. R., & Hester, R. K. (1986). The effectiveness of alcoholism treatment: What research reveals. In W. R. Miller & N. Heather (Eds.), *Treating Addictive Behaviors: Processes of Change* (pp. 121–174). New York: Plenum.

Mooney, H. B., Ditman, K. S., & Cohen, S. (1961). Chlordiazepoxide in the treatment of alcoholics. *Diseases of the Nervous System, 22* (Supplement), 44–51.

Moss, L. M. (1973). Naloxone reversal of non-narcotic induced apnea. *Journal of the American College of Emergency Physicians, 2,* 46–48.

Naranjo, C. A., Lawrin, M., Addison, D., Roach, C. A., Harrison, M., Sanchez-Craig, M., & Sellers, E. M. (1983). Zimelidine decreases alcohol consumption in non-depressed heavy drinkers. *Clinical Pharmacology and Therapeutics, 33,* 241.

Nuotto, E., Palva, E. S., & Lahdenranta, U. (1983). Naloxone fails to counteract heavy alcohol intoxication. *Lancet, 2,* 167.

Overall, J. E., Brown, D., Williams, J. D., & Neill, L. T. (1973). Drug treatment of anxiety and depression in detoxified alcoholic patients. *Archives of General Psychiatry, 29,* 218–221.

Peachey, J. E., & Naranjo, C. A. (1984). The role of drugs in the treatment of alcoholism. *Drugs, 27(2)* 171–182.

Pond, S. M., Becker, C. E., Vandervoort, R., Phillips, M., Bowler, R., & Peck, C. C. (1981). An evaluation of the effects of lithium in the treatment of chronic alcoholism. I. Clinical results. *Alcoholism: Clinical and Experimental Research, 5,* 247–251.

Revusky, S. (1973). Some laboratory paradigms for chemical aversion treatment of alcoholism. *Journal of Behavioural Therapy and Experimental Psychiatry, 14,* 15.

Revusky, S., Parker, L. A., Coombes, J., & Coombes, S. (1976). Rat data which suggest alcoholic beverages should be swallowed during chemical aversion therapy, not just tasted. *Behavioural Research and Therapy, 14,* 189.

Revusky, S., & Taukalis, H. (1975). Effects of alcohol and lithium habituation on the development of alcohol aversions through contingent lithium injection. *Behaviour Research and Therapy, 13,* 163.

Robins, E., Murphy, G. E., Wilkinson, R. H., Jr., Gassner, S., & Kayes, J. (1959). Some clinical consideration in the prevention of suicide based on a study of 134 successful suicides. *American Journal of Public Health, 49,* 888–889.

Rosenberg, C. M. (1974). Drug maintenance in the outpatient treatment of chronic alcoholism. *Archives of General Psychiatry, 30,* 373–377.

Ross, D., Hartmann, R. J., & Geller, I. (1976). I. Ethanol preference in the hamster: effects of morphine sulfate and Naltrexone, a long-acting morphine antagonist. *Proceedings of the Western Pharmacological Society, 19,* 326–330.

Schenk, G. K., Engelmeier, M. P., Maltz, D., & Pach, J. (July, 1978). High dosage Naloxone treatment in acute alcohol intoxication. *Proceedings of the CINP (Collegium Internationale Neuropsychopharamcologicum) Congress,* Vienna, p. 386 (Abstract).

Schou, M. (1978). The range of clinical uses of lithium. In F. N. Johnson & S. Johnson (Eds.), *Lithium in medical practice* (pp. 21–40). Baltimore: University Park Press.

Schuckit, M. A. (1973). Alcoholism and sociopathy: Diagnostic confusion. *Quarterly Journal of Studies on Alcohol, 34,* 157–164.

Schuckit, M. A. (1983). A study of alcoholics with secondary depression. *American Journal of Psychiatry, 140,* 711–714.

Schuckit, M. A. (1984). *Drug and Alcohol Abuse: A Clinical Guide to Diagnosis and Treatment.* New York: Plenum.

Schuckit, M. A. (1986). Genetic and clinical implications of alcoholism and affective disorder. *American Journal of Psychiatry, 143*(1), 140–147.

Schuckit, M. A., & Winokur, G. (1972). A short-term follow-up of women alcoholics. *Diseases of the Nervous System, 33,* 672–678.

Sedlacek, D., & Miller, S. I. (1982). A framework for relating alcoholism and depression. *Journal of Family Practice, 14*(1), 41–44.

Sellers, E. M., Cooper, S. D., Sen, A. K., & Zilm, D. H. (1974). Lithium treatment of alcohol withdrawal. *Clinical Pharmacology and Therapeutics, 15,* 218 (Abstract).

Sellers, E. M., Cooper, S. D., Zilm, D. H., & Shanks, C. (1976). Lithium treatment during alcohol withdrawal. *Clinical Pharmacology and Therapeutics, 20,* 199.

Sellers, E. M., & Kalant, H. (1978). Pharmacology of acute and chronic alcoholism and alcohol withdrawal syndrome. In A. J. Clark and J. del Guidice (Eds.), *Principles of Pharmacology* (2nd ed.) (pp. 721–740). New York: Academic Press.

Sellers, E. M., Naranjo, C. A., & Peachey, J. E. (1981). Drugs to decrease alcohol consumption. *New England Journal of Medicine, 305,* 1255–1262.

Shaffer, J. W., Freinek, W. R., Wolf, S., Foxwell, N. H., & Kurland, A. A. (1964). Replication of a study of nialamide in the treatment of convalescing alcoholics with emphasis on prediction of response. *Current Therapeutic Research, 6,* 521–531.

Shaw, J. A., Donley, P., Morgan, D. W., & Robinson, J. A. (1975). Treatment of depression in alcoholics. *American Journal of Psychiatry, 132,* 641–644.

Shaw, J. M., Kolesar, G. S., Sellers, E. M., Kaplan, H. I., & Sandor, P. (1981). Development of optimal treatment tactics for alcohol withdrawal. I. Assessment and effectiveness of supportive care. *Journal of Clinical Pharmacology, 1,* 382–389.

Solomon, J. (1982). Alcoholism and affective disorders: Methodological considerations. In J. Solomon (Ed.), *Alcoholism and clinical psychiatry* (pp. 81–95). New York: Plenum.

Sorenson, S. C., & Mattison, K. W. (1978). Naloxone as an antagonist of severe alcohol intoxication. *Lancet, 2,* 688–689.

Thompson, W. L. (1978). Management of alcohol withdrawal syndromes. *Archives of Internal Medicine, 138,* 278–283.

Truitt, E. B., & Vaughen, C. M. (1976). Effects of lithium on chronic ethanol consumption and behavior. *Federal Proceedings, 35,* 814 (Abstract).

Weissman, M. M., & Myers, J. K. (1980). Clinical depression in alcoholism. *American Journal of Psychiatry, 137,* 372–373.

Whalley, L. J., Freedman, C. P.,& Hunter, J. (1981). Role of endogenous opioids in alcoholic intoxication. *Lancet, 2,* 89.

Wilson, I. C., Alltop, L. B., & Riley, L. (1970). Tofranil in the treatment of post alcoholic depressions. *Psychosomatics, 11,* 488–494.

Woodruff, R. A., Jr., Guze, S. B., Clayton, P. J., & Carr, D. (1973). Alcoholism and depression. *Archives of General Psychiatry, 28,* 97–100.

Wren, J. C., Kline, N. S., Cooper, T. B., Varga, E., & Canal, O. (1974). Evaluation of lithium therapy in chronic alcoholism. *Clinical Medicine, 81,* 33–36.

Young, L. D., & Keeler, M. M. (1977). Sobering data on lithium in alcoholics. *Lancet, 1,* 144.

Zilm, D. H., Sellers, F. M., MacLeod, S. M., & Degani, N. C. (1975). Propranolol effect on tremor in alcoholic withdrawal. *Annals of Internal Medicine, 83,* 234–236.

Zimberg, S. (1982). *The clinical management of alcoholism.* New York: Brunner/Mazel.

CHAPTER 16

The Community Reinforcement Approach

Robert W. Sisson
Nathan H. Azrin

OVERVIEW

The Community Reinforcement Approach (CRA) to the treatment of alcoholism is a set of behaviorally based treatment procedures designed to enable the alcoholic to have a more rewarding and meaningful life without alcohol. The treatment concept was developed in 1973 by George Hunt and Nathan Azrin, working with inpatient alcoholics. With ongoing improvements and refinements, the use of this approach made it possible to treat people on an outpatient basis who might otherwise have normally gone into a residential setting. In addition, procedures have been developed for family members of active alcoholics to teach them how to encourage their loved one to seek treatment (Sisson & Azrin, 1986).

The complete CRA, as currently offered, includes the following components:

1. A prescription for disulfiram (Antabuse)
2. A positive program to encourage the client to continue to take disulfiram
3. Reciprocity marriage counseling

4. A job club for unemployed clients
5. Social skills training
6. Advice on social and recreational activities
7. Help with controlling urges to drink

An important aspect of the CRA is its intensity. Intervention is rapid, affects a broad range of areas of the person's life, and is typically accomplished in a relatively brief period (4–6 weeks, with periodic follow-ups). Treatment outcome research has documented its effectiveness in comparison with traditional treatment approaches (see section on effectiveness).

SPECIAL CONSIDERATIONS

Although not a component of the original program, Antabuse, and behavioral procedures to assure the client will take this medication daily, have become a critical part of the CRA. Although the alcohol-Antabuse reaction can make an individual extremely ill, it is a safe medication when the client is well informed about its use (see chapter 7). However, clients who are medically unable to use this medication, or who refuse to use it, can still benefit from the CRA.

Simply prescribing Antabuse is usually insufficient to achieve effective compliance and abstinence (Azrin, Sisson, Meyers, & Godley, 1982); therefore, an assurance program accompanies the medication within the CRA. In order to facilitate the implementation of the Antabuse assurance procedure, it is helpful to have made prior arrangements with a local physician who understands alcoholism and the role of Antabuse in its treatment. In this way, once clients have agreed to take Antabuse, they can begin it without unnecessary delay. Clients can feel that they have made a decision about stopping drinking and that they have made a concrete step in the right direction to accomplish this goal. If the Antabuse procedures can be accomplished in the first session, it not only gives the client a sense of accomplishment but provides an opportunity for family and friends to comment on the commitment the client has made, providing immediate social support for the client.

Socially Isolated Clients

A special consideration is the client who lacks social support. Some individuals, because of the number of years of their excessive drinking, repeated moves, and job changes, have lost contact with their families and have few, if any, friends who are not excessive drinkers. The CRA attempts to rearrange the individual's social environment so that it is supportive of sobriety. For clients without a social support network, that social environment must be developed almost from scratch.

The Antabuse monitor, described below, is the first aspect to consider. One possible solution is to have a former successful client serve as a "buddy" to the new client. One of the "buddy's" roles is to monitor the client's Antabuse. If the client is living in a halfway house, it could be monitored daily by a house staff member. If there is no alternative, the therapist can monitor the Antabuse daily.

Generally, the next pressing need is to help the client find a job. The type of job is very important. It should be one in which the client has a sense of a future, encouraging social stability.

The United Club, if available (see below), is a great place for the client to make new friends. Another role for the "buddy" is to make sure the client has transportation to the club. The client can also be trained in the same positive request procedures as for married couples (see below) to facilitate interactions.

If the client lives alone, consider having the client get a dog or another pet. In addition to companionship, the client has a reason to stay sober—Who else will take care of the dog? Using the same principle, the client may obtain plants for home, or anything requiring regular care and responsibility.

If funds are available, pay for the client to try out new activities while she or he is trying to obtain employment. Pay for their first month in an apartment, first month for the phone, magazine subscriptions, and so forth. If the client is able to get a driver's license, help him or her through the process.

Working with socially isolated clients is a time-consuming but extremely rewarding experience. Most have had several treatment failures. They have been "kicked to the curb" by friends, family, and usually many treatment professionals. They are used to failing. In order for them to remain in an area and stay sober, they must "buy into" something—that is, they must find something reinforcing to them. It might be a job, the club, a pet, a friend, a place to live, a counselor, or a combination of these.

PROGRAM REQUIREMENTS

The CRA treatment regimen is one that is designed to be implemented rapidly and intensively to provide the client with immediate success and social reinforcement for his or her decision to stop drinking. In order to effectively implement this program, a few systems should be established before the counselor begins to see clients using this approach.

1. Every effort should be made to see the client the same day or at latest the next day when he or she calls for an outpatient appointment. Inpatients should be seen as early as possible during the residential phase of treatment.
2. Clients should be strongly encouraged to bring a person significant to them to the sessions. This approach is more effectively implemented when the client has an already existing relationship with another person who is invested in him or her remaining sober.
3. Once the client agrees to take Antabuse, he

or she should be seen immediately by a physician. The prescription is then filled immediately, so the client can take the Antabuse. Under optimal conditions, this can all be accomplished during or right after the first visit.

4. Although not necessary, it is convenient if the alcohol treatment center has a Job Finding Club into which unemployed clients can be referred (see below). Otherwise, the primary counselor may provide individual or group training in the Job Club procedures.

Once these programmatic steps are in place, counselors can begin to use the specific procedures described in the next section.

DESCRIPTION

The actual procedures of the CRA consist of a number of relatively discrete components. They include the intake procedure, the Antabuse program with its assurance subcomponent, reciprocity marriage counseling, drink refusal training, the Job Club for unemployed clients, social and recreational counseling, and strategies for controlling urges to drink. This section describes in detail how to implement these components. They are discussed in the chronological order in which they usually occur. Once the intake and Antabuse procedures have been completed, however, continue treatment by implementing first those procedures which will be the most reinforcing and helpful for the client.

Intake

Probably the most important and critical session is the first. It is here that the groundwork is laid to motivate the client by providing him or her with immediate success. Optimally, clients are seen the day they call or as soon as possible after admission. They have brought in with them someone they know cares about them and who is invested in their stopping drinking. Often they have just decided to seek help. They may be motivated to stop drinking at this time because they have just had an excessive drinking bout, done something that they dislike while intoxicated (e.g. strike their spouse), or are genuinely concerned about their health. Whatever the motivation, it is impor-

tant for you to understand it so you can use it to help the client remain sober. Introduce yourself to the client and explain the intake package (see Appendix to this chapter). The intake package includes a life history questionnaire, an inconvenience review checklist, and a drinking inventory which asks quantity and frequency questions concerning the prior month, along with the question "Why did you decide to do something about drinking now?" Ask the client to fill these out alone, and while he or she is doing that tell him or her that you are going to chat alone with the significant other.

Interviewing the significant other

The goal of speaking with the significant other is to develop an alliance. Generally, this ally is the spouse. To enhance motivation, ask about the difficulties the spouse's drinking has caused. Discuss what attempts she or he has made in the past to help stop the drinking to determine what attempts have been successful in the past.

Then describe in some detail the CRA in the treatment of alcoholism. Discuss the role of Antabuse and how it would help their particular situation. The importance of his or her role in monitoring the Antabuse is emphasized, as well as what to do if the client doesn't want to take it. Once all of his or her questions are answered and the client has finished filling out the intake forms, see them together. (Note: be careful not to assume that it is only the identified spouse who has the alcohol problem, that the spouse does not have an alcohol or drug problem too. One unassertive husband agreed to take the Antabuse, got the prescription filled, and actually took Antabuse in the first session before he finally exploded at his wife, "What about you? You're the one drinking a quart of vodka a day!") Next, review the intake forms in detail with the client and his or her significant other. The inconvenience review checklist is gone over by discussing each item to discover more about the extent of the alcohol problem and to motivate the client by reminding him or her of all the problems alcohol consumption has caused.

Bring the significant other into the conversation as much as possible and attempt to have him or her talk directly to the client, particularly if the client is minimizing the extent of the problem. Alcohol and drug consumption questions are then asked, emphasizing the extent of the problem in the recent past. Generally, what is motivating the client to come in can be determined in the first session by asking "What made you decide to come in now? Why didn't you call last week or wait another month?" The answer to this question is quite important. In order to provide the necessary reinforcement to the client, you need to know what the client sees as his or her immediate needs. The client who is going to appear in front of a judge for driving under the influence would view a letter to the court stating they are participating in the program as a powerful reinforcer. The client whose wife has just left him needs assistance in rebuilding their marriage. Work with the client on these immediate needs and develop reinforcement contingencies that promote continuing sobriety. You may be able to work with the district attorney to postpone the court case so the client may have time to demonstrate his or her sobriety for the court. A wife may be willing to return as long as she is assured the client will remain sober by taking Antabuse daily and attending counseling sessions.

Presenting Antabuse

Explain that you are going to speak for a few minutes and that you would like the client and his or her significant other to listen carefully. Begin by restating many of the problems the client has experienced. A typical example might proceed like this:

> You have told me that you have blackouts, your personality changes when you drink, your wife is afraid of you. You've lost several jobs as a result of your drinking, and you spend lots of money at bars. You say that before you only needed a six pack to get high and now you can drink a case with no problems, which means you have a much higher tolerance to alcohol. You have trouble waking up in the middle of the night and you get jittery when you don't drink. These are signs of withdrawal and signs of addiction. In addition, you have (stating motivation for coming in) just gotten your second DUI and your license is revoked, and your attorney has recommended you see a counselor immediately so you can demonstrate to the judge that you are trying to change. What I would recommend that you do is consider seeing a physician to determine if you could take Antabuse. (At this time the client may try to make some comment about not having a problem or that he or she heard of Antabuse and objects to taking it. It is important for the counselor to continue making the presentation by simply

stating, "Let me finish, then I'll be happy to answer any questions you might have.") Antabuse is a little white pill that works by making you very ill if you take even small amounts of alcohol. It does this by working in the liver to make it impossible for your body to digest alcohol. If you were taking Antabuse every day and you drank alcohol, in about five minutes or less you would start to feel extremely hot and sweaty, your heart would pound. The symptoms get much worse as you continue to drink. You start vomiting and you feel faint. So it's a very good medication for those people who are serious about wanting to stay sober.

> One of the important characteristics of Antabuse which can really help you is that once you're taking Antabuse regularly, even if you decide to stop taking it and go back to drinking, you can't go back to drinking for approximately five days. In those days a lot can happen for you to change your mind. The way we set it up is as an early warning system when your spouse (or significant other) will help you take it every day. This way, when you really feel like drinking again, you have to let someone else know who cares about you, and talk about what's going on. For you, taking Antabuse would have a couple of benefits. First it's going to make your spouse less afraid of you because she (or he) doesn't have to worry about you; she (or he) is going to know you're not drinking, so it will help you get your family back together. Also, right now you have to demonstrate to the court that you're serious about staying sober. Taking Antabuse is a concrete step which demonstrates you're serious about staying sober.

Generally you can determine by watching the client whether she or he is willing to take Antabuse. If you feel the client is going to say yes, simply ask if he or she would like to see a physician. If you feel the client is going to say "no," ask the significant other how she or he would feel if the client were to take it. Then have the significant other state directly to the client why she or he would like the client to take Antabuse. (This is often a very emotional time particularly with married couples.) In our experience, about 90% of the time the client agrees to take Antabuse. If the client agrees, immediately have him or her seen by the necessary medical staff, obtain the prescription, and have it filled so that the client can take the medication before leaving the clinic. (See Antabuse assurance procedure). Some clients at first say they don't want to take Antabuse. Some legitimate concerns are medical and can be allayed by the physician. Often having the client agree to try it for a specified period of time, as short as a week or even one day, is enough to have the client begin. If a client is still adamant in refusing and stresses that he or she can do it "by willpower", get the client to agree that if he or she returns to drinking, he or she automatically will take Antabuse. Here you must work closely with the spouse or other significant person so that all parties understand the agreement. Then carry on with the other reinforcement procedures (see below). If the client returns to drinking, remind the significant other and client of the agreement. If the client then agrees to take Antabuse, do the Antabuse assurance procedures. If he or she refuses, consider informing him or her that it is obvious he or she will not be successful without Antabuse and you feel that it would be a waste of time to continue counseling until they make that commitment. It is important in any event that you continue to see the significant other (see Sisson & Azrin, 1986).

Antabuse Assurance

It is important to complete this procedure within the first day if at all possible, to provide the client with an immediate start on sobriety. Once the client has seen the physician and has had the prescription filled, start the Antabuse assurance program. Take out the Antabuse tablets and show the client and significant other what they look like. Point out that it's smooth, like an aspirin, and that each pill should be checked when administered. Place the Antabuse in a ceramic coffee cup with about one ounce of warm water. Wait about one minute for it to begin to dissolve, then gently tap the pill with a spoon until it completely dissolves. Next add about two ounces of a preferred juice, stir and have the client drink in one gulp. Most hesitate when confronted with actually taking it for the first time. While the client is staring at the mug realizing his or her drinking is actually over for a while, praise him or her, and have the spouse provide the encouragement or praise. Let him or her know that you understand that this is tough, that it is difficult and courageous to take such a serious step. Once he or she takes it, make sure he or she is sincerely praised by the significant other. Invite them to hug, make it a celebration that they have made a concrete step for a new life. Encourage him or her to feel proud of taking this step. (Note: Individuals cannot take Antabuse until they have a blood alcohol level of zero.)

The next task is getting the client and significant other to agree on a set time and place to take Antabuse daily. Generally time of day isn't as important as a time that a regularly occurring event happens. Good times to take Antabuse are right before going to bed, at supper, at breakfast or morning coffee. Instruct them also to bring the Antabuse to every counseling session, and to start each session by taking Antabuse. Depending upon the length of time that has transpired since the start of the session and how emotionally daring it has been, this is a good place to end the first session after briefly describing the other components of the CRA — i.e., relaxation training, job club, marriage counseling, social skills, and so forth. If you stop here, have them return the very next day.

The next component of the Antabuse assurance program is role-playing what to do if either party decides not to be involved in the Antabuse procedure. Surprisingly, just as often as the client refuses to take Antabuse, the significant other refuses to administer it.

After the client has taken Antabuse in the session with the significant other administering it, discuss with them the circumstances under which the client might feel like drinking. Let them know that this is normal and is to be expected. Ask him or her to remember times in the past when he or she has decided to stop drinking and then returned. Let them know that wanting to return to drinking can happen around good times, as well as around stressful time. (Consider using a relapse prevention checklist to identify high risk situations — see chapter 11). Ask the client how he or she might try to avoid taking Antabuse and what the circumstances would be. Then ask how he or she would like the significant other to respond. Remind them that the critical characteristic of Antabuse is that it will stay in the system for at least five days, and that the client cannot drink for that time period.

Next, have them role play a conversation in which the client refuses to take Antabuse. After this first, uninstructed practice, instruct them in positive communication techniques in which any request is prefaced with an understanding statement, accepting partial responsibility, and offering to help. Ask the significant other if she or he has ever gone on a diet or had to give up something he or she really liked. Then demonstrate a positive request. Here is an example: "I understand that work has been hard lately and you're feeling frustrated, but things have been going much better between us since you've stopped drinking. Maybe I haven't been as much help as I could be in supporting you. Why don't I get a baby sitter and we'll go out and have dinner and relax. Why not take your Antabuse today so we can relax." Ask the client to compare this request to the one previously role played before your instructions. Have them practice once more with the spouse using the positive communication technique.

Next, using the same techniques, discuss under what circumstances the significant other might not want to be involved with administering Antabuse. Ask them if the partner has ever gotten mad at the drinker or not wanted to be around him or her. Then do the role play, modeling and instruction, and directed practice again. The added step here is that in this practice the drinker should role play taking Antabuse anyway in front of the partner. Instruct them that if either the spouse or drinker doesn't want to follow through with this assurance plan at any time in the future, they should immediately call and make an appointment to see you.

Cultural Considerations

Although it is important for the client to have someone monitor the Antabuse, it is just as important that the client "buy into" the program by feeling that the partner is someone who legitimately is concerned about him or her. A client, because of the culture in which he or she was raised, may not feel that certain people can legitimately be concerned about their alcohol consumption. In helping the client choose a monitor, cultural considerations must be taken into account.

Cape Verdeans, for example, are a minority in Southeastern Massachusetts. Some Cape Verdean men do not feel comfortable speaking to a professional woman about any problem — medical, financial, or alcohol-related. A male counselor has much more success, and selecting a male Antabuse partner is in keeping with the cultural heritage. Such issues may arise when working with other cultural groups. Fair generalizations cannot be made. The important point is to help the client decide who would be the best monitor. If the client has brought someone along to the first session, it can usually be that person, because his or her presence means the client feels he or she is someone who can legitimately be concerned about the client's alcohol consumption.

Other Reinforcement Procedures

The Antabuse assurance procedures are the first of the reinforcement procedures. The following is a description of the other procedures which comprise the CRA. Each client will not need each procedure. Obviously, if a client is single and employed, the reciprocity marriage counseling and Job Club would not be part of the treatment plan, but the others might. Use those procedures which are applicable to your client. Again as a rule of thumb, first work with the client on areas which will be the most reinforcing for the client. Remember that it is important for CRA procedures to be begun in a rapid, intensive fashion. It is not unusual to see clients daily or every other day for the first week.

Reciprocity Marriage Counseling

Reciprocity Marriage Counseling is a set of procedures designed to teach people how to communicate better. It can be used with married couples, roommates, people who are dating but live separately or together, and with gay or lesbian couples. It has often been used with married couples who were about to separate because of one partner's excessive use of alcohol. The procedures follow naturally from the Antabuse assurance procedures and are usually begun the next day after the Antabuse assurance procedures have been taught.

At the start of this session, and the start of each session, have both clients fill out the Marriage Happiness Scales (see Appendix) in which their scores on a ten point scale show how happy they are with various categories of their lives. Collect the completed scales from the clients during the session. It only takes a few minutes to fill out this questionnaire.

In each and every session, have the clients do the Antabuse assurance procedure at the beginning. Watch to make sure the partner dissolves the Antabuse in liquid and praises the client when he or she drinks the solution.

Next, ask the couple to recount what it was like when they first started seeing each other. Ask what they liked about each other and have them talk directly to each other. Ask them what they like about one another now. Explain to them that because of the impact alcohol has had on their lives, they may not have been communicating with each other the way that they have done in the past.

Give the clients a copy of the "Daily Reminder Sheet." The sheet contains a description of several positive behaviors that couples can practice (see Appendix). It includes giving compliments, showing appreciation, giving pleasant surprises, and offering to help. Ask each person how he or she would feel if his or her partner performed these behaviors every day. Have the clients speak directly to one another to tell each other specifically what behaviors they would like the other to do. For example one partner may want the other to sit next to them touching, while watching TV, but not to engage in sex. The other partner may like the other to show appreciation more by saying "Thank you" and giving more compliments. The mood in this session should be light and fun. Instruct the clients to record each day on the sheet whether they performed each of the positive behaviors.

This should be a fun session. Remember the "drinker" is now on Antabuse and feels he or she is making a step in the right direction. The partner is often ecstatic because finally he or she feels relaxed and not worried that the client is going to drink. After this session, give the couple four or five days before the next session so that they have time to be with one another and some naturally occurring reinforcers can take place. It may have been years since the couple went out to dinner without the drinker becoming inebriated. Because the drinker has more free time now, more time can be spent doing interesting recreational activities with the partner or family. Making love may be more enjoyable for the nondrinker because his or her partner is not intoxicated.

When the couple comes in for their next session have them fill out the Happiness Scale, then begin the session with the Antabuse Assurance Procedure. Next, review their Daily Reminder Sheets. Have each partner tell specifically what behaviors he or she performed and have the other partner respond by saying how that made him or her feel. In this way, the session begins on a positive note. Tell the clients to continue to do the Daily Reminder Sheets.

Hand the clients the Perfect Marriage form which lists several areas of marital life: household responsibilities, money management, child rearing, sex, social activities, communica-

tion, and others. Instruct them to fill out the line under "household responsibilities." Tell them they are going to write down what behaviors they would like their partner to perform in that category. Tell them it should be specific, and worded in the positive (to do more of something, not less of something). Give them an example: "Say for instance you wanted your husband to stop tracking in mud on his work shoes. You would write: take your shoes off and leave them inside the door when you come home from work at night." Make sure both partners understand being "specific and positive," and give more examples if needed.

Then ask one of the partners if he or she has specific household behavior he or she would like the other to perform. Work with him or her to word it so that it is specific and positive. Have that partner write it down. Repeat with the other partner.

After they both have written down the behaviors, tell them you are going to teach them how to make a "positive request." Tell them this is important because often couples stop communicating positively and keep things inside when people are drinking heavily.

Tell them there are ways to make a request that are more pleasant than others and that make it more likely that the request will be acted upon. "Before even making the request, you should think about a few things. First try to take the other person's point of view and try to understand how they feel. Maybe he or she is busy, maybe he or she does not realize what you want. Perhaps you can take partial responsibility and offer to help him or her so it is easy for him or her to comply with the request."

Next give an example of what you want. "Suppose you really did want your partner to stop tracking mud through the house. First, he must be tired at the end of the day because he works hard to make money to run the house and relax, and that's a lot better than going to a bar. Second, there really isn't a place to take his shoes off at the door because there is no place to sit. These are the things you should think about, then plan how to word your request."

Next look at the other partner and speak to him directly. "Which one of these two requests are you more likely to respond to? First: 'John, I know you're tired when you get home and you're anxious to just sit down and relax. If I put a chair in the entry way, would you take your shoes off before you come inside so it doesn't track mud in the house?' Or, second: 'John stop tracking mud through the house!' " John will probably say he prefers the wording of the first request better.

Tell the couple that when one of them makes a request the other should try not to refuse it outright, but instead come up with an alternative solution if the request is not acceptable as it is. In making an alternative solution, he or she should follow the same steps as above: Take the other's point of view, take partial responsibility, or offer to help. Then plan what to say. For example John might respond, "You're right, I am tired at night, thanks for understanding that. But I shouldn't make more work for you by tracking mud. How about if I leave my boots in the car, I'll take them off at work and change into my sneakers."

Tell the couple that this is one part of effective communication. Now have them make a household responsibility request from their lists. Help them first by going over what they should think about. Then help them first by reviewing what they should think about. Then help them word the request in a specific and positive manner. Have the clients talk to one another and have each make a request. Record the request, and tell them you'll be interested in hearing next session how it went. Tell the clients to fill out the rest of the Perfect Marriage form and bring it next time. Schedule the next session in about a week.

This is the basic reciprocity marriage procedure. Have the couple continue making agreements in the various areas. On about the fourth session, talk to each partner individually to make sure both have had an opportunity to discuss sensitive issues with you alone. Then have your regular session with both. Use the Happiness Scale to determine which areas might need more work.

The first month of this counseling is generally very upbeat. It's sort of a "honeymoon" period in which the couple is in some ways getting reacquainted. Be careful not to conclude prematurely that counseling is no longer necessary. Continue to work with the couple until both feel more satisfied with their relationship and then "wean" away from the number of sessions. See them biweekly, then monthly, then once every three months, then six months. Make sure both partners realize you are still working with them and that they can call at any time.

The Job Club

Clients who are unemployed should be referred to the Job Club. The purpose of the Job Club is to help the client identify a job which would help promote the client's sobriety and then to help the client obtain that job.

The Job Club is the only set of procedures which need not be performed by the primary therapist. Because the Job Club itself can be a separate full time job for a counselor, it would be helpful if your treatment program or another community program had a counselor assigned full time to do this training.

The Job Club procedures can be implemented with your client as soon as is feasible for the client and your treatment plan. Generally, it has been found to be effective to start a new group of clients each Monday.

The Job Club for non-alcoholics has been detailed by Azrin and Besalel (1980). For alcoholics, the first session of the Job Club is devoted to analyzing with the client the relationship between their work history and their alcohol consumption. For many people, the characteristics of their career choice promote their excessive use of alcohol, despite the fact that the job may be well-paying. For example, master electricians who work construction sites around the country are generally very well paid. The job requires travel away from home, long work hours, and sometimes no days off. Electricians may work 7–12s — that is 7 days a week, twelve hours a day. They may work this for weeks at a time until the job is completed and then be without work for a month until the union calls them back again. The work is deservedly well paid. However, for a person trying to stop drinking, it can be very difficult. On lonely nights away from home, it can be tempting to spend time at a bar where it is easier to meet people. The boredom during the hiatus from work waiting for another job may likewise lead to drinking, spending some of the money made from the last job.

This is no way to imply all members of certain professions have drinking problems. It is important, however, for you to educate the client on how a job affects his or her drinking. Actively recommend to the client, if necessary, that he or she consider a career change if the characteristics of their job are obviously interfering with his or her goal to stop drinking.

Generally a job that promotes sobriety is one

that the client enjoys, finds rewarding, is regular, non-seasonal, and full time. Risky characteristics include self-employment and lack of observation or accountability while the client is working. Traditionally, bad jobs for people trying to stop drinking include any construction job that requires traveling, lawn and tree care (because it is seasonal), self-employed mechanical work (because the client need not respond to a routine), and night guard work because of boredom and lack of supervision.

Once the client has determined the type of job he or she wants to obtain, the procedures are the same as in Azrin and Besalel (1980). Briefly, the procedures are to teach the client how to find a job lead and how to speak on the telephone to get a job interview. Looking for a job becomes a full-time job itself and the client works at it 8 hours every day, making phone contacts in the morning and going out on interviews in the afternoon.

Finding a job lead. Tell the client most jobs aren't advertised. The best place to find the job lead no one else knows about is in the phone book. Have the client use the phone book to find the telephone numbers of companies that have jobs like the one they are looking for. Other potential sources for job leads are friends, relatives, and former employers. Of course, the newspaper want ads is another resource.

Making the call. Once the client has several numbers to call, instruct him or her what to say on the phone. First, he or she must get past the person answering the phone and talk directly to the person in charge—not the personnel office. This is done by asking for the name of the person in charge and then asking to speak to him or her directly. Second, once the client is speaking to the person in charge, the client states his or her name and briefly describes the skills he or she possess that could benefit that company. He or she then asks to make an appointment to meet directly with the person to discuss her or his job abilities in more detail. At this point, the person on the other end of the phone can say: (a) yes, come in at such and such a time or (b) no, we're not hiring. If the person said the former, the client thanks him or her and now has a job interview to go to. If the person says the latter, the client asks if he or she can come in anyway to speak to the person

in case a job does open up at a later date. If the person responds yes, the client has an interview. If the person still says no, the client asks if the person knows of anyone else who may be hiring. Nine times out of ten, the person will give the name of another person in the same field. The client then asks if it is OK to use the person's name when the client calls. Now for the next call, the client can begin by asking for the person in charge directly and tell him or her who he or she was referred by, which is much more personable. The client repeats this process every day in order to get more interviews.

Once you've instructed the client in this process, model a phone call. Using two phones, you play the client, and the client plays the person answering the phone and the person in charge. You say "Hello, who is in charge of the parts department?" (Mr. Mendoza) "Could I speak to Mr. Mendoza please." (Just a moment) "Hello, Mr. Mendoza, my name is John Jones. I have worked in parts departments for several years. I know how to handle invoices, shipping and receiving, and customer relations. I would like to set up an appointment with you to speak further about my job qualification." (No, we're not hiring) "Could I come in anyway in case something opens up?" (No) "Well do you know anyone who may be hiring someone with my experience?" (Try Sears, the manager there is Jim Riley) "Thank you. Do you mind if I tell him you suggested I call?" (No go ahead, goodbye.)

Once you've modeled the procedure, help the client write down what he or she is going to say. Then role play again, this time with you as the person answering the phone and the boss. Make a game out of it to make the client feel comfortable. Then have the client actually make calls to real companies. If possible, listen in on an extension phone and provide feedback.

The client should be able to get at least one interview the first day. The client should make a minimum of ten calls a day.

Job interviewing. Going on the interview is the obvious next step for which the client should be trained. Instruct the client to dress the way they would if they were going to work at that job. Again role play with the client some of the typical questions asked on job interviews. Instruct the client to answer every question with a positive remark. For example, if asked if they are married they can respond either "Yes I am—

I am a family oriented person, and have two children," or "No I am not, so I am able to work any hours, and working overtime is not a problem." Or if asked how long they have lived in the area: "I've lived here all my life" or else "I've just moved here and really enjoy the area, and I'm looking forward to putting down some roots here."

Often, individuals who have had a serious alcohol problem over an extended number of years have a sporadic work history and no real job skills. They may be living at a halfway house and may be well known in the area as someone who has a serious alcohol problem. Ask the client, if he or she feels comfortable, to speak to this issue directly. The client may state assertively in the interview that he or she has had a serious problem with alcohol, is taking Antabuse to assure abstinence, and is participating in an alcohol treatment program to start a new life. This approach is often quite effective because the person to whom he or she is speaking may have a friend or family member with the same problem and may be sympathetic to helping the client. The potential employer may even be recovering from the same problem himself or herself.

The Job Club consists of these procedures. The client should devote 8 hours a day 5 days a week until he or she finds employment. Virtually all clients find a job within 2–3 weeks. This program is very effectively done in groups of up to 10 clients. When the client gets a job, make a celebration out of it.

Drink Refusal Training

At times, people trying to maintain their abstinence feel pressure from others to return to drinking. This can be very subtle and unspoken, such as not being asked to a social function by friends because alcohol will be present, or it can be blatant, such as a friend saying "What are you, too good to drink with me now?"

The CRA approach to this problem is the following. First, review with the client times when he or she really didn't feel like drinking, but did so because he or she was with friends and it was expected. Talk to the client about how he or she felt. Next, tell the client that a good way to handle this issue is to take control of the situation. Tell him or her, "Contact your friends and relatives to inform them of your desire to stop drinking. You can then enlist

your friends' support by requesting that your friends do not offer you drinks. Tell them that you are still friends, but you can't drink. If you don't feel comfortable telling them why, just say it's for health reasons. In this way, by taking the initiative, you won't hurt your friends' feelings by not drinking with them and if they are really your friends, they'll help. You'll be surprised how many will congratulate you and try to help." Such conversations can be practiced in sessions.

This procedure can be done any time after the first session. Have the client tell you how it went in the next session, and praise him or her for handling such a challenging social situation.

Social and Recreational Counseling

Discuss with your client the relationship between his or her alcohol consumption and his or her recreational or social life, as in the Job Club procedures. Have the client identify friends and activities which are always associated with heavy drinking. Tell your client, "These activities and people are not supportive of your goal of sobriety and you probably should consider avoiding them." Examples of recreational activities to avoid include going to bars or playing pool with former drinking buddies.

Then have your client identify friends and activities that are not related to heavy alcohol consumption even though alcohol may be present. Tell the client "It's important to understand that drinking played an important role in your recreational life, and provided a way to spend a lot of your time. Drinking was a way to have fun. It's important now that you develop new ways to spend time without sacrificing any fun. You can be having more fun now because you'll be straight and you've got time now to try new things."

Stress that having a good social and recreational life is extremely important and a critical area on which to focus new efforts. After identifying friends and activities not associated with drinking, have your client specify a particular activity he or she wants to attend and with whom he or she would like to do it. Record this. Have the client contact that person, attend the activity, and tell you how it went next session. If the client feels uncomfortable calling the other person, role-play the call until he or she feels comfortable.

Help your client make a list of activities that he or she has wanted to do but never had the time. Then have him or her pick one and try it. Examples could be anything: square dancing, playing chess, carving duck decoys, lifting weights, joining a health club, cross-country skiing, becoming involved in PTA, learning karate, or parachuting. It is essential that the client do things that are fun and exciting for him or her. Sobering up and being bored is not conducive to continued sobriety.

Because some clients have been so involved in alcohol they had no other friends except heavy drinkers, the CRA has usually had a social club associated with it. If it is feasible in your area, such a "United Club" can be an important asset in maintaining sobriety. The United Club is a dry bar where alcoholics can come with their families on a Saturday night to have fun. A meal is always provided, and people bring a dish to share. There was frequently a live band, a juke box, pool table, and a card game going on in the back. The United Club is operated solely by alcoholics and is officially incorporated as a not-for-profit organization. The only rules at the club are that you must be straight to attend, and no alcohol or drugs are allowed on the premises. Special events at the club can be such fun at times that people who are just bar-hopping try to come in because they thought it was an actual bar.

The United Club provides a place where people can get social support, have fun, and develop non-drinking friendships. To develop such a club requires some organization. To get started, you need only have a small group of people willing to participate and meet on Saturday night to do things together. As the group gets bigger, you'll need a building to meet in. Try to get a building associated with recreational activities, such as an old bar or VFW hall—preferably not a building associated with religion or treatment.

Next, seek a band to play for free and have a dance. (Musicians are generally very supportive of such organizations.) The group may want to legally incorporate, so host a meeting to discuss it. Once incorporated, organize fund raisers such as bake sales or raffles. You can have special events, such as Halloween and Christmas parties, and go on field trips to ball games and concerts. Such a club offers a variety of activities, which helps people structure their time and recreation in a meaningful way.

Controling Urges to Drink

Even if clients are abstinent, employed, are enjoying improved marital relations, and are effectively refusing pressures to drink, they may continue to experience urges to drink. If your clients have these urges, try these simple strategies. (If these are not completely successful you might consider covert sensitization—see chapter 8.)

Tell the client, "From time to time you may get serious urges to drink. You may be feeling bad about something, or you may be feeling great and want to celebrate something. There may be no reason at all. It's not unusual for people stopping drinking to feel these urges.

"When you have these feelings you can reassure yourself by remembering that you are on Antabuse and so your early warning system is working for you. Review in your mind the progress you have made since you decided to stop drinking. You can relax yourself by becoming conscious of your breathing. Concentrate on taking slower deep breaths which you let out slowly. Think about the muscles in your shoulders and let them droop and relax. Let the muscles that control your jaw relax. Repeat the words 'relax' as you let out a long slow breath. Now think of something pleasant." Have clients practice this as you instruct them through it, then have them do it themselves. (See also chapter 14 for more detailed relaxation instructions.)

EFFECTIVENESS

Several studies have evaluated the effectiveness of the CRA, from its inception through its stages of evolution. Compared to traditional treatment approaches, the CRA has been shown to be a more successful way to help inpatient or outpatient alcoholics remain sober, employed, and out of institutions. Few other treatment approaches for alcoholism have been so carefully evaluated.

In 1973, Hunt and Azrin, in their original study, compared the CRA with a standard hospital program, with dramatic results. After six months, the CRA treated patients were drinking on 14% of days compared with 79% drinking days in the hospital-treated control group. Unemployed days were 12 times higher in the traditional treatment group, and institutionalized days were 15 times higher relative to those in CRA.

In 1976, Azrin evaluated improvements in CRA including the use of Antabuse. Working with hospitalized clients he compared the CRA with the standard hospital program. At six months follow-up, the CRA clients showed fewer than 1% drinking days per month, compared to 55% in the control group; 20% unemployment, compared to 56%; and 7% of days away from home, vs. 67% in the traditional group.

After working with inpatient alcoholics, it became apparent that these procedures could be used with alcoholics on an outpatient basis as well. Mallams, Godley, Hall and Meyers (1982) tested the effects of encouraging outpatients to attend the United Club. At follow-up, they found that clients who were encouraged to attend the club (random assignment) showed less behavioral impairment, drank less, and spent less time in heavy drinking contexts than clients who were not encouraged to attend the club.

In 1982, Azrin and his colleagues (Azrin, Sisson, Meyers, & Godley, 1982) evaluated the relative contributions of different components of the CRA. Treatment groups received either (a) traditional treatment plus traditional Antabuse (clients took it themselves), (b) traditional treatment plus the Antabuse assurance procedures, or (c) Antabuse assurance procedures plus other reinforcement procedures (the Job Club, marriage counseling, relaxation training, drink refusal training, and recreational counseling). At six-month follow-up, the traditionally treated group reported over 50% drinking days and about one third of their days unemployed and intoxicated. The Antabuse assurance procedures resulted an almost total sobriety for married or cohabitating clients but had little effect for single people. The full CRA produced near total sobriety for all clients, married or single. A conclusion of this study, then, is that for clients who have someone in their lives whom they see everyday and for whom they care about, the Antabuse Assurance Program may be all that is required. This finding is one that warrants replication in different settings, but it makes sense from a behavioral point of view. Social and job-finding skills have already been acquired by most adults, and taking Antabuse requires clients to use these skills. Then the natural positive consequences (spouse, ju-

dicial, self-approval, monetary) take effect. Single, isolated clients who have never acquired these skills need to be helped systematically to acquire them, or they are likely to relapse back to what is familiar and comfortable—drinking.

To be sure, the CRA needs further evaluation. The four controlled studies completed to date, however, have all found the CRA to be significantly more effective than traditional treatment methods. It is designed to bring about changes in the client's lifestyle that are important in maintaining sobriety. Overall, the CRA need not take much more time than would be spent in traditional counseling. Given the apparently substantial improvement in outcome, the effort required of both therapist and client in the CRA seems well justified.

REFERENCES

Clinical Guidelines

Azrin, N. H., & Besalel, V. A. (1980). *Job Club Counselor's Manual*. Baltimore, MD: University Park Press. Detailed procedures for setting up and conducting the Job Club component of the CRA.

Azrin, N. H., Naster, B. J., & Jones, R. (1973). Reciprocity counseling: A rapid learning based procedure for marital counseling. *Behaviour Research and Therapy, 11*, 364–382. A description of the couples counseling procedures used in the CRA.

Sisson, R. W., & Azrin, N. H. (1986). Family-member involvement to initiate and promote treatment of problem drinkers. *Journal of Behavior Therapy and Experimental Psychiatry, 17*(1), 15–21. A procedure for working with the partner of an alcoholic to create motivation for change and treatment, even when the alcoholic is initially uncooperative.

Research References

Azrin, N. H. (1976). Improvements in the community-reinforcement approach to alcoholism. *Behaviour Research and Therapy, 14*, 339–348.

Azrin, N. H., Sisson, R. W., Meyers, R., & Godley, M. (1982). Alcoholism treatment by disulfiram and community reinforcement therapy. *Journal of Behavior Therapy and Experimental Psychiatry, 13*, 105–112.

Hunt, G. M., & Azrin, N. H. (1973). A community-reinforcement approach to alcoholism. *Behaviour Research and Therapy, 11*, 91–104.

Mallams, J. H., Godley, M. D., Hall, G. M., & Meyers, R. A. (1982). A social-systems approach to resocializing alcoholics in the community. *Journal of Studies on Alcohol, 43*, 1115–1123.

APPENDIX

Marriage Agreements

State how you would like your partner to behave in the following areas:

1. **Household Responsibilities**

_____
_____
_____
_____
_____
_____
_____
_____
_____
_____

2. **Money Management**

_____
_____
_____
_____
_____
_____

3. **Social/Recreational Activities**

_____
_____
_____
_____
_____
_____
_____
_____

4. **Job**

_____
_____
_____
_____
_____
_____
_____
_____

5. **Child Rearing**

_____
_____
_____
_____
_____
_____

6. **Affection**

_____
_____
_____
_____
_____
_____
_____

7. **Communication**

_____
_____
_____
_____
_____
_____

8. **Sex/Affection**

_____
_____
_____
_____
_____

9. **Independence**

_____
_____
_____
_____

10. **Other**

_____
_____
_____
_____
_____

		Week of _____

Marriage Self Reminder

Description	Mon.	Tues.	Wed.	Thurs.	Fri.	Sat.	Sun.
Compliments							
Appreciation							
Pleasant Surprise							
Affection							
Pleasant Conversation							
Offer to Help							
Understanding							
Other							

Inconvenience Review Checklist

Do you have an alcohol problem?

This program is not only for the full-fledged alcoholic, but also for the person experiencing problems with alcohol. Below is a listing of situations commonly agreed upon by others as alcohol problems and reasons for counseling. Please indicate which of the following situations apply to you and *you feel* are a problem, by placing an "X" in the space in front of the number which applies.

Remember, the questionnaire concerns only those situations you feel are problems with alcohol and reasons why *you* would like counseling.

_____ 1. Being hospitalized for alcohol-related problems.
_____ 2. Being physiologically addicted to alcohol and unable to stop drinking without a physician's help or the help of a hospital or detox center.
_____ 3. Being in jail for alcohol-related arrests.
_____ 4. Suffering severe withdrawal symptoms (i.e., tremors, hallucinations, stomach cramps, nausea, vomiting, etc.)
_____ 5. Having an automobile accident while under the influence of alcohol.
_____ 6. Being sent home or fired because of hangovers or drinking.
_____ 7. Being arrested for driving while under the influence of alcohol.
_____ 8. Missing work or school because of hangovers or drinking.
_____ 9. Acting foolish and/or aggressive at parties or in bars.
_____ 10. Having financial difficulties as a result of drinking.
_____ 11. Not being able to remember what you did while drunk.
_____ 12. Having difficulty in sleeping due to drinking.
_____ 13. Having family problems due to drinking.
_____ 14. Not getting promoted at work due to drinking.
_____ 15. Losing driving privileges due to alcohol-related arrests.
_____ 16. Suffering severe hangovers after drinking.
_____ 17. Having lapses of memory due to drinking (blackouts).
_____ 18. Being committed to a detox center, hospital, or alcoholism treatment program because of drinking.
_____ 19. Having decreased ambition since drinking.
_____ 20. Having decreased sexual drive or impotency due to drinking.
_____ 21. Feeling guilty about drinking.
_____ 22. Having poor health or alcohol-related problems.
_____ 23. Being disowned by friends or family over drinking.
_____ 24. Losing trust and respect of family, friends, fellow employees, or relatives due to drinking.
_____ 25. Being divorced or separated due to drinking.
_____ 26. Having severe shakes or tremors (DT's) due to alcoholism.
_____ 27. Feeling sad, depressed, or unhappy over drinking.
_____ 28. Having suicidal thoughts because of alcohol problems.
_____ 29. Being arrested or doing things while drinking (i.e., assault, disorderly conduct, battery, etc.)
_____ 30. Having to pay for high risk insurance because of alcohol-related traffic arrests.
_____ 31. Dropping out or not doing well in school because of drinking.
_____ 32. Having a poor reputation as a heavy drinker.
_____ 33. Needing a drink in the morning to overcome hangover or shakes.
_____ 34. Getting violent or into fights while drinking.
_____ 35. Having friends, family, or your children afraid of you when drinking.
_____ 36. Not being able to get a good job due to a reputation as a heavy drinker.
_____ 37. Spending money foolishly while drinking.
_____ 38. Fear of becoming an alcoholic (unable to control your drinking or worrying about drinking too much.)
_____ 39. Suffering personal injury or hurting others while drinking.
_____ 40. Having emotional problems due to drinking (i.e., anxieties).
_____ 41. Others (Specify) _____

HAPPINESS SCALE

This scale is intended to estimate your *current* happiness with your life on each of the ten dimensions listed. You are to circle one of the numbers (1–10) beside each area. Numbers toward the left end of the ten unit scale indicate some degree of unhappiness and checks toward the right end of the scale reflect varying degrees of happiness. Ask yourself this question as you rate each life area: "If things continue in the future as they are today, how happy will I be *with this area of my life?*" In other words, state according to the numerical scale (1–10) exactly how you feel today. Try to exclude all feelings of yesterday and concentrate only on the feelings of today in each of the life areas. Also try *not* to allow one category to influence the results of the other categories.

		Completely Unhappy									Completely Happy
1.	Drinking/sobriety	1	2	3	4	5	6	7	8	9	10
2.	Job or educational progress	1	2	3	4	5	6	7	8	9	10
3.	Money Management	1	2	3	4	5	6	7	8	9	10
4.	Social Life and new friends	1	2	3	4	5	6	7	8	9	10
5.	Personal Habits	1	2	3	4	5	6	7	8	9	10
6.	Marriage/Family relationships	1	2	3	4	5	6	7	8	9	10
7.	Sex	1	2	3	4	5	6	7	8	9	10
8.	Emotional Life	1	2	3	4	5	6	7	8	9	10
9.	Communication	1	2	3	4	5	6	7	8	9	10
10.	General Happiness	1	2	3	4	5	6	7	8	9	10

Name _____

Date _____

PART V

Client Treatment Matching

CHAPTER 17

Matching Individuals with Interventions

William R. Miller

THE CASE FOR MATCHING

Problems

Procrustes, as the Greek legend goes, was not known for accepting people as they are. He is remembered for the iron bed to which he tied all of his hapless victims. Those who were too short to fit the bed were stretched until they matched it in length. Those too tall, he accommodated to the bed by amputation. He met his own end at the hands of the hero Theseus, who dispatched Procrustes by reshaping him to his own berth.

Few people would argue with the common-sense idea that treatment should be individualized to the needs and characteristics of clients. If one surveys alcoholism treatment programs with the question, "Do you tailor your treatment to the individual?", nearly all will answer "Yes." Yet many programs still consist of a relatively invariant set of treatment experiences offered to almost all clients.

Furthermore, the treatment recommended to a client after evaluation is often determined by the door through which the person walked for assessment. Each program tends to find most clients it evaluates in need of the very kind of treatment it happens to offer (Hansen & Emrick, 1983). Inpatient programs tend to judge people to be in need of inpatient treatment; outpatient programs recommend outpatient treatment. Disease model programs recommend Alcoholics Anonymous (AA); behavioral programs advise behavioral treatment. Procrustes would be proud.

The fact is that matching is not easy, and there are many obstacles. First, one must recognize and have at one's disposal a variety of different treatment options. The preceding chapters of this book attest to the range of potentially effective alternatives, but such options are still unknown or unavailable in many areas. Second, one needs some reasonable system for matching individuals to interventions. That is the purpose of this chapter. The guidelines presented here must be considered tentative, the best advice based on currently available research. Certainly a chapter of this kind written ten years from now should be able to offer substantially more accurate and helpful advice.

Still other obstacles pertain to the economics

261

of health care delivery. Will programs really turn away paying clients because they are judged more appropriate for another program? Will capitation-based systems receiving a fixed amount for every subscriber, tend to avoid more expensive forms of treatment when they are truly needed? Can for-profit treatment programs be expected to give due emphasis to brief, self-directed treatment options such as those described in chapter 6? Considerations such as these raise the question of *who* should do the matching. Where feasible, matching might be accomplished most objectively by an independent evaluation system with no allegiances to or biases toward particular treatment programs or approaches. In practice, this kind of objectivity is difficult to obtain.

Benefits

Given that matching is so challenging and difficult to accomplish, why bother? Why not just offer everyone the best and most comprehensive treatment package we can put together?

First, there is evidence that many individuals do not *need* extensive treatment. In fact, some seem to fare worse in intensive treatment than if they had been given brief intervention (Miller & Hester, 1986b). Matching offers the hope of avoiding unnecessarily expensive treatment. Those who can do well with less intervention are given no more than they need, while others genuinely in need of more intensive care receive it. The economic principle here is that of the *least sufficient* effort. Treatment outcomes are not compromised; in fact, they are likely to improve on an absolute basis. The major difference is in cost savings and increased efficiency of treatment.

Second, it appears that different kinds of people do in fact need different types of treatment. Some who do well in one particular type of treatment fare poorly in another. Different approaches seem to succeed best with different kinds of clients (Miller & Hester, 1986c). Offering a person the wrong kind of treatment can have adverse effects. It is a waste of time and expense; further, it is a discouragement for both clients and staff. To the individual, a treatment failure may be incorrectly interpreted as meaning that his or her case is hopeless, and that there is no point in trying. (A more benign

attribution would be that it was not the right treatment approach, and that it is time to try something else.) To the staff, therapeutic failures may reinforce the mistaken notion that alcoholism treatment is ineffective, or that alcoholics are perniciously resistant to recovery.

Client–treatment matching, then, offers the hope of increased cost-effectiveness and also of avoiding unnecessary therapeutic failures, by identifying the right treatment the first time. Beyond this, a matching system is likely to promote a more healthy and more accurate perception of treatment. In a competitive health care economy, there is great temptation to oversell one's own approach and to demean alternative treatments. Yet the fact remains that no alcoholism treatment method has been shown to be superior to all others (Miller & Hester, 1986a). There simply is no single outstandingly effective approach to be recommended as best for all candidates. A sound basis for hope lies in the variety of treatment methods currently available, a number of which already have promising empirical evidence to support their effectiveness. Acknowledgment of the validity of matching opens the door for an alternative to cutthroat competition for the same population of potential clients. Each program, rather than competing for *all* individuals with alcohol problems, might identify the types of individuals with whom its approach is particularly effective. This perspective could serve to increase cooperation among programs, while avoiding the unnecessary and ineffective treatment inherent in free-for-all competition.

SELF-MATCHING

One approach for individualizing treatment is *self-matching*. Here the client is presented with an array of options, is given a fair and accurate description of each, and is encouraged to choose among them the approach that seems most appropriate.

There are several reasons for giving serious consideration to a self-matching approach. First, it happens whether or not we acknowledge it. Though some might argue that one cannot "allow" alcoholics to choose their own treatment, the truth is that one is hard pressed to prevent it. Unless aggressively coerced, people will not comply with treatment ap-

proaches they find inappropriate or unacceptable. Substantial population differences are
evident across alcoholism treatment programs
and AA groups (e.g., Bromet, Moos, Wuthe-
mann, & Bliss, 1977; Finney & Moos, 1979),
suggesting that informal self-matching is already occurring. Self-matching, then, is an inevitable condition of the freedom to choose.
Treatment professionals can choose to deny
and ignore this, or can work with the self-
matching process to optimize it.

Second, there is reason to believe that self-
matching may be a very effective approach for
selecting optimal treatment. Research on
human motivation clearly indicates that people
are more likely to carry through when they
perceive that they have chosen a course of
action from among options (Deci, 1975). Compliance is known to be a powerful predictor of
positive treatment outcome (e.g., Fuller et al.,
1986; Fawcett et al., 1987). A self-chosen approach, then, may be more effective precisely
because it *is* self-selected and thereby more
likely to be followed. In addition, it is reasonable to believe that individuals have some
wisdom about which approaches are most
likely to work for them. This may explain why
alcoholics given a choice among alternative
treatments seem to fare better than those assigned without choice to a particular approach
(Kissin, Platz, & Su, 1971).

An argument sometimes made against self-
matching is that alcoholics are characterologi-
cally incapable of making otpimal choices for
themselves because of their inherent denial,
which leads them to take all possible escapes to
avoid change. Though this description may
aptly fit particular individuals, evidence does
not support a unique characterological structure for all alcoholics (Miller, 1976). The defense
mechanism of denial has not been found to be
more prevalent among alcoholics than among
others (Chess, Neuringer, & Goldstein, 1971;
Donovan, Rohsenow, Schau, & O'Leary, 1977;
Skinner & Allen, 1983). Indeed, there is reason
to believe that strong resistance to treatment is
driven not by client personality but rather by
characteristics of therapists and treatments
themselves (Miller, 1983, 1985; Patterson &
Forgatch, 1984; Sovereign & Miller, 1987). A
third important reason to consider self-
matching, then, is the possibility that it will
reduce resistance and thereby improve the
chances for recovery.

Negotiation

Acknowledging the importance or inevitability
of self-matching is not the same as abandoning
the client to his or her own resources. An
informed choice among options requires that the
client be given a fair and accurate description of
the alternatives available. This would include
information about the known overall effectiveness of each approach, as well as current
knowledge about the likelihood of success of
each approach given the client's individual
characteristics. These are standard components
of informed consent procedures for participation in any treatment research program. Unfortunately, the same standards are rarely followed when treatment is given outside the
context of research. Informed consent is a requirement only when the effectiveness of treatment is being studied.

Self-matching is current practice in many
areas of medicine. A patient with cancer is
informed of alternative treatments available
and of the likelihood that each might be successful given the nature of the person's condition. The patient has the right to choose among
options, and to accept or refuse any particular
treatment that is offered. It would be irrespon-
sible to provide the patient with only a list of all
possible treatments and no information about
their relative curative potential. Self-matching
is aided by the best available research information, and the physician's personal opinion may
carry quite a bit of weight in the patient's final
decision.

A similar approach would be sensible within
the alcoholism field. The person could be given
a fair and honest description of alternative
avenues to change (including minimal and self-
directed options, such as those described in
chapter 6). This would include an accurate
accounting of current evidence about the
overall efficacy of each approach. Where available, information could also be provided about
the likelihood of success of each approach
given the characteristics of the individual and
his or her alcohol problems. What follows this
informational stage is a process of negotiation,
in which alternatives are discussed and evaluated. The goal of this process is the mutual
selection of an appropriate change strategy for
the individual. The client agrees and consents
to this approach. The negotiation process leads
to *informed consent*. An approach so chosen,

through a free process of informing and negotiation, may be more likely to evoke motivation, compliance, and positive outcomes (Miller, 1985).

I wonder, in fact, whether any system of matching could be superior to such a process of self-matching. It would be conceivable, for example, to develop a computer-driven expert decision system, which matches individuals to optimal treatments based upon the most current research information. Yet if the client were then offered only this computer-chosen option, it would lack the motivational properties of a self-chosen path. Further, it is quite possible that the individual would have access to relevant matching information not available to the computer. In other areas, computer-based decision systems have been found superior to human clinical judgments (Goldberg, 1968), but these have not required the motivation to carry out a decision. It is an interesting question for future research: Could an actuarial computer-matching system surpass self-matching on ultimate treatment outcomes?

In any event, the conditions of freedom in our society make self-matching inevitable. Clients are free to heed or reject the advice given to them, whether by a psychologist, their physician, a counselor, or a computer. The process of negotiation occurs, whether or not it is overtly acknowledged by treatment professionals.

TENTATIVE GUIDELINES FOR MATCHING INDIVIDUALS WITH INTERVENTIONS

Many articles and chapters end with the statement that "more research is needed." That is true enough in the area of matching. Yet an encouraging amount of information is already available, enough to form at least some tentative guidelines for matching individuals to types of intervention.

The range of possible alternatives is wide. As a help in organization, I will present four levels of matching which involve different types of decisions. The first is negotiation of the *goals* of treatment. Second is a decision about the *level* or optimal intensity of intervention. Third, and perhaps most difficult at this point, is a choice of the *type* or content of treatment. Finally, there are *maintenance* arrangements: What kinds of continued contact, if any, are needed

to help sustain change? Needless to say, decisions such as these will require a competent and comprehensive assessment of the client and her or his problems (see chapters 2 and 3). For reasons discussed in chapter 5, systematic follow-up is also desirable for maintaining treatment gains. Figure 17.1 illustrates the sequence and types of decisions involved in assessment, treatment, and followup.

Treatment Goals

The first level of negotiation involves selection of the *goals* of treatment. Individuals enter the evaluation process with initial goals of their own. Some come already having decided that they want to change their drinking. Some are concerned about other drugs. Some hope for changes in other areas of their lives, and give little priority to changing their drinking or drug use habits.

The client's initial goals need not be accepted at face value. The therapist may well perceive a need for change that is not shared by the client. If the need for change is supported by a competent assessment (chapters 2 and 3), the ther-

Figure 17.1. The process of matching.

apist's challenge becomes one of creating motivation for change in the client (chapter 4). If successful, this alters the client's goal structure, giving higher priority to a type of change not previously valued. Suppose, for example, that a client is seeking help for depression. Evaluation reveals a pattern of steady and heavy alcohol consumption, though the client does not perceive this to be a problem. The therapist knows that heavy drinking is a significant contributing factor in depression. The therapist's task is not to change the client's goal of decreasing depression, but rather to persuade the client that changing alcohol use is an important part of achieving that goal.

Motivational interventions may or may not succeed. After a process of negotiation, the therapist and client may still differ on perceived goals. At this point the therapist has at least three options: (a) decline to help the person toward his or her goals; (b) accept the client's goals as at least provisional objectives; or (c) attempt to coerce the client into accepting the therapist's goals. This choice is essentially an ethical one. The first of these options would be chosen if the therapist felt ethically constrained from pursuing or otherwise supporting the client's chosen goals. The third would be chosen if the therapist felt an ethical obligation (and ability) to rescue the client despite the client's own wishes.

Between these two extremes is the option of "rolling with" the client's insistence, as a strategy for reducing resistance (Haley, 1963). Consider the client who cannot be dissuaded from a goal of moderate drinking. An alternative to abandonment or coercion is to offer the client a fair trial at his or her chosen goal. This was early recommended by Marty Mann (1950) as an acid test of the necessity for abstinence. If the client succeeds in sustaining moderate and problem-free drinking, the goal has been achieved and, as the "big book" of Alcoholics Anonymous (1955) states, "Our hats are off to him" (or her). If the client fails to achieve control over his or her drinking, it can be a persuasive diagnostic experience, and the door is open to discuss abstinence anew (Miller & Caddy, 1977).

Alcohol Use

There are at least three relevant areas to consider in clarifying the goals for change. First, is there a need to eliminate hazardous

alcohol consumption? Is change in drinking a goal? If so, the type of change requires clarification. Is the goal total abstention from alcohol? If not, what changes in the person's drinking pattern would eliminate hazards and problems? Some examples of such goals would be: (a) never to consume alcohol before driving or other risk situations; (b) to increase the number of alcohol-free days; (c) to eliminate heavy drinking binges; (d) to set an upper limit for consumption on any drinking day; (e) to keep blood alcohol concentration within a low level on any drinking day (e.g., Miller & Muñoz, 1982). Close monitoring of progress is important to determine progress (or lack thereof) toward the goal. The common objective underlying all of these goals is the elimination of hazardous and problematic alcohol use.

Current evidence from treatment studies provides one clear guideline for helping clients choose between abstinence and moderation goals. With remarkable consistency, these studies have found a relationship between pretreatment severity of alcohol problems and abstinence versus moderation outcomes. Those who succeed in maintaining moderate and problem-free drinking over long spans of time tend to be those who had less severe alcohol problems and dependence before treatment. Individuals with more severe alcohol problems and dependence are unlikely to achieve stable moderation, and fare best with total abstinence (Armor, Polich, & Stambul, 1978; Edwards, Duckitt, Oppenheimer, Sheehan, & Taylor, 1983; Finney & Moos, 1981; Miller & Joyce, 1979; Miller & Baca, 1983; Miller, Leckman, Tinkcom, & Rubenstein, 1987; Orford, Oppenheimer, & Edwards, 1976; Polich, Armor, & Braiker, 1981; Smart, 1978; Vogler, Compton, & Weissbach, 1975; Vogler, Weissbach, Compton, & Martin, 1977). There is also evidence that moderation outcomes are more likely among women and those with less family history of alcoholism (Miller et al., 1986).

Other Drug Use

A second goal area regards change in the use of other drugs. A person may perceive a need for change in one area (drinking) but not another (marijuana use). What changes are needed in the person's use of drugs other than alcohol? Consideration here should include not only illicit drugs, but also prescription medications and socially sanctioned drugs such as nicotine and caffeine. Are certain medications needed for legitimate medical reasons, and unlikely to cause problems of abuse (cf. Chapter 15)? Would stopping smoking increase or decrease the chances of staying sober? Is heavy caffeine use increasing arousal and agitation, and thus contributing to the likelihood of relapse? Goals again may be total cessation of the drug, modification of use, or no change.

Other Life Problems

A third and likewise important consideration is the need for change in other life problem areas. Clients may be brought to treatment by concern about problems other than drinking or drug use: marital difficulties, mood problems, medical concerns, conflicts with the law, social problems, or anxiety. Direct treatment of these concerns is appropriate, particularly if they persist after alcohol and drug abuse have been addressed (see chapters 10–16). Indeed, research indicates that alcoholics are more likely to stay sober when such concerns are effectively addressed (Miller & Hester, 1986a). Figure 17.2 illustrates how goals in the areas of alcohol consumption, other drug use, and other life problems can be negotiated on three dimensions.

Level of Intervention

How much outside help does the person need to achieve her or his goals? Here one chooses along a continuum of intensity of intervention: no formal treatment, brief intervention, self-help groups, outpatient consultation, intensive nonresidential night- or day-treatment, and residential care in a hospital or specialized treatment setting.

Three general guidelines can be commended at this point for choosing level of intervention, beyond the self-selection factors discussed earlier. First, it is prudent to try the *least intensive* intervention likely to be sufficient to the client's needs and goals. If a person might be helped either by outpatient consultation or inpatient treatment, it is sensible to try the outpatient alternative first, because it is generally much less expensive and intrusive. Indeed, controlled studies comparing more with less intensive treatment approaches have consistently found no significant overall differences in effectiveness (Miller & Hester, 1986b). Given this, it

is reasonable to begin with a less intensive approach and, if this fails, step up to the next level of intensity until the desired results are obtained. A progression of this type is illustrated in Figure 17.3.

Second, a leap to more supervised care may be warranted by special conditions. A client who is acutely suicidal or violent, for example, may require inpatient treatment. Severe alcohol dependence warrants closely supervised detoxification, although safe alternatives to hospitalization are available (Sparadeo et al., 1982; Whitfield et al.,1978). Medical or psychological conditions which would otherwise justify hospitalization should be similarly treated when concomitant to alcohol problems.

Third, there is evidence that more intensive treatment approaches are differentially effective for persons who have severe levels of alcohol problems and dependence, or who are socially unstable (homeless, unemployed, indigent). Conversely, more socially intact individuals with less severe dependence tend to fare better in *less* intensive treatment settings (McLellan, Luborsky, Woody, O'Brien, & Druley, 1983; Orford et al., 1976). Combining this with the "least intensive" principle outlined above, it suggests that it is particularly wise to try simpler interventions first when treating socially stable people who are not severely addicted to alcohol.

It is worth noting here that formal outpatient treatment is about halfway up the continuum of intervention intensity. Many people succeed in changing addictive behaviors with only brief intervention, self-help groups, or no formal intervention at all (Heather, 1986; Peele, 1985; Prochaska & DiClemente, 1986; cf. chapters 6 and 10). Outpatient treatment thus should not be thought of as the lowest level of entry onto the continuum of intervention.

Finally, it must be acknowledged that other pragmatic factors are important determinants of the level of intervention finally chosen. These include the client's preferences, legal mandates, economic feasibility, and the availability of alternatives.

Type of Intervention

Much less is known currently about how to match individuals with specific types of treatment. The authors of Chapters 6–16 in this volume were asked to describe the types of

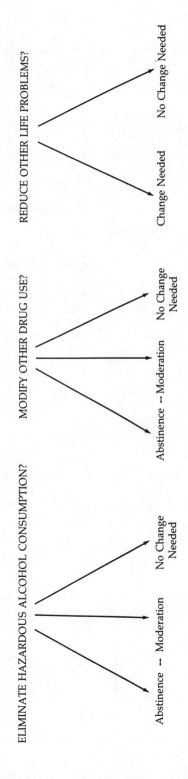

Figure 17.2. Negotiation of treatment goal.

267

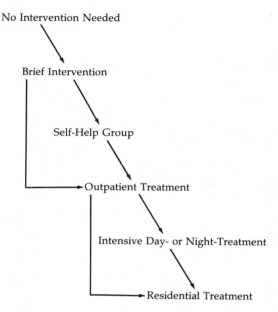

Figure 17.3. Selection of level of intervention.

individuals for whom each treatment approach might be optimal. Among the factors considered are personality variables, cognitive functioning, social stability, severity of alcohol dependence, family cooperation, and concurrent psychopathology. Within a given *level* of intervention (e.g., outpatient treatment), client preference, socioeconomic, and arbitrary factors may play substantial roles in determining the type of treatment chosen.

One important matching consideration that emerges from current research is the presence of concomitant problems beyond alcohol abuse. Emotional and interpersonal problems have been implicated as major precipitants of relapse to drinking (Marlatt & Gordon, 1985). Treatment approaches that address life problems as well as alcohol abuse itself have been found to increase the rate of successful outcomes (e.g., Azrin, Sisson, Meyers, & Godley, 1982). The available data indicate that these additional interventions (represented in Part IV of this volume) are effective primarily for individuals who show higher levels of the concomitant problem that each treatment addresses. For example, studies showing positive benefits of social skills training (chapter 13) have been conducted with populations of alcoholics who are generally deficient in social skills (Chaney, O'Leary, & Marlatt, 1978; Ferrell & Galassi, 1981; Freedberg & Johnston, 1978). Stress management (chapter 14) appears to aid sobriety most in those individuals who show high levels of anxiety (Rosenberg, 1979). Antidepressant medications are beneficial primarily to alcoholics who have concomitant depression (chapter 15). The Community Reinforcement Approach (chapter 16) differentially benefited unmarried alcoholics (Azrin et al., 1982). The practical implication of this is straightforward: If a person has another significant life problem beyond alcohol abuse, particularly one which persists into sobriety, treat it! A listing of alternative types of interventions, with corresponding chapters, is shown in Figure 17.4.

Another guideline can be considered once a specific treatment strategy has been initiated. *Compliance* with treatment has been found, across a variety of strategies, to be a strong predictor of successful outcome (e.g., Fawcett et al., 1987; Fuller et al., 1986). Client noncom-

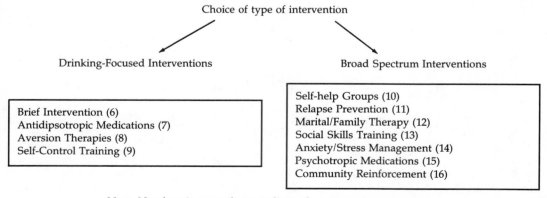

Note: Numbers in parentheses indicate chapters in this volume

Figure 17.4.

pliance with a particular approach, then, indicates a need to reevaluate and perhaps renegotiate the change strategy. There are also, for certain treatments, significant milestones that can be used to judge whether the strategy will "take" or not. In aversion therapies (chapter 8), for example, the emergence of conditioning appears to be a key determinant of treatment success (Elkins, 1980; Miller & Dougher, 1984). In self-control training with a moderation goal (chapter 9), failure to modulate drinking within 6–8 weeks is a strong predictor of long-term inability to control one's drinking (Miller et al.. 1986). Thus noncompliance, client dissatisfaction, or early poor response to a particular treatment may signal the need to switch modalities.

Research data are currently insufficient to recommend particular approaches based on client traits. The "goodness of fit" of an intervention may be determined more by therapist characteristics than by the specific content of treatment (Miller, 1985). McLachlan (1972, 1974) reported a strong post-hoc interaction of client personality with therapist style in determining treatment outcome. Clients assigned to therapists whose style matched their personality showed much higher rates of success. This suggests that it is important to consider matching not only to type of treatment, but also to therapist style. Until more data become available, the best markers of goodness of fit are likely to be those discussed above: client compliance, satisfaction, and early treatment response.

Maintenance Arrangements

What arrangements are optimal for continued contact and care following the formal termination of treatment? Just as it is unreasonable to expect that one treatment will be most effective for all types of individuals, it is unlikely that uniform maintenance arrangements are acceptable in heterogeneous populations. McLachlan (1972, 1974) reported an interaction between type of aftercare (regular groups versus periodic telephone contact) and client cognitive style. Some apparently responded better to a more structured aftercare approach, whereas others fared best with the less intensive approach.

Very little is known at present about how to optimize maintenance arrangements for individual clients. A range of options exist, varying in intensity (no contact, mail contact, telephone calls, reading material, individual follow-up visits, self-help groups, regular therapist-led groups) and content (supportive, relapse prevention, didactic, twelve-step, interpersonal, cognitive, emotive). Attendance at scheduled aftercare events may be heavily determined by very practical considerations, such as how far away the client lives (Prue, Keane, Cornell, & Foy, 1979).

There is some consensus within the field that continued follow-up contacts are beneficial in maintaining positive outcomes (chapter 5). At the very least, brief regular contacts offer the opportunity to detect impending relapses. Voluntary participation in aftercare and "booster" sessions has been found to be predictive of sustained sobriety, again underlining the value of compliance as a predictor of outcome.

In the absence of reliable empiricial guidelines for matching to maintenance arrangements, individual negotiation and self-matching remain the state of the art. Procedures similar to those described above can be employed. A range of options can be presented, and individual arrangements negotiated based on client preferences, experience, and other available information. A minimal "early warning system" may be advisable, in which the individual monitors his or her own condition for signs of relapse and initiates renewed contact if such signs appear. Periodic check-up visits are also feasible. (The parallels to medical care are again apparent.) Client dissatisfaction, noncompliance, or poor response to a designated maintenance arrangement may signal the need for reconsideration.

SUMMARY

The individualization of intervention is a complex process that operates from initial assessment through follow-up. The goal of matching is to provide each individual with the most cost-effective intervention that will lead to successful change. Matching involves a process of negotiation that includes the goals of treatment, level of intervention, the type of intervention, and maintenance arrangements. The implementation of an optimal system for matching would involve a radical departure from the status quo of self-contained and competing programs offering relatively consistent treatment to most or all clients.

REFERENCES

Alcoholics Anonymous (1955). *Alcoholics Anonymous: The story of how many thousands of men and women have recovered from alcoholism.* (rev. ed.) New York: Author.

Armor, D. J., Polich, J. M., & Stambul H. B. (1978). *Alcoholism and treatment.* New York: Wiley.

Azrin, N. H., Sisson, R. W., Meyers, R., & Godley, M. (1982). Alcoholism treatment by disulfiram and community reinforcement therapy. *Journal of Behavior Therapy and Experimental Psychiatry, 13,* 105–112.

Bromet, E., Moos, R., Wuthmann, C., & Bliss, F. (1977). Treatment experiences of alcoholic patients: An analysis of five residential alcoholism programs. *International Journal of the Addictions, 12,* 953–958.

Cannon, D. S., Baker, T. B., & Wehl, C. K. (1981). Emetic and electric shock aversion therapy: Six- and twelve-month follow-up. *Journal of Consulting and Clinical Psychology, 49,* 360–368.

Chaney, E. G., O'Leary, M. R., & Marlatt, G. A. (1978). Skill training with alcoholics. *Journal of Consulting and Clinical Psychology, 46,* 1092–1104.

Chess, S. B., Neuringer, C., & Goldstein, G. (1971). Arousal and field dependence in alcoholics and nonalcoholics. *Journal of Studies on Alcohol, 37,* 990–994.

Deci, E. L. (1975). *Intrinsic motivation.* New York: Plenum.

Donovan, D. M., Rohsenow, D. J., Schau, E. J., & O'Leary, M. R. (1977). Defensive style in alcoholics and nonalcoholics. *Journal of Studies on Alcohol, 38,* 465–470.

Edwards, G., Duckitt, A., Oppenheimer, E., Sheehan, M., & Taylor, C. (1983). What happens to alcoholics? *Lancet, 2,* 269–271.

Elkins, R. L. (1980). Covert sensitization treatment of alcoholism: Contributions of successful conditioning to subsequent abstinence maintenance. *Addictive Behaviors, 5,* 67–89.

Fawcett, J., Clark, D. C., Aagesen, C. A., Pisani, V. D., Tilkin, J. M., Sellers, D., McGuire, M., & Gibbons, R. D. (1987). A double-blind, placebo-controlled trial of lithium carbonate therapy for alcoholism. *Archives of General Psychiatry, 44,* 248–256.

Ferrell, W. L., & Galassi, J. P. (1981). Assertion training and human relations training in the treatment of chronic alcoholics. *International Journal of the Addictions, 16,* 959–968.

Finney, J. W., & Moos, R. H. (1979). Treatment and outcome for empirical subtypes of alcoholic patients. *Journal of Consulting and Clinical Psychology, 47,* 25–38.

Finney, J. W., & Moos, R. H. (1981). Characteristics and prognoses of alcoholics who become moderate drinkers and abstainers after treatment. *Journal of Studies on Alcohol, 42,* 94–105.

Freedberg, E. J., & Johnston, W. E. (1978). The effects of assertion training within the context of a multimodal alcoholism treatment program for employed alcoholics. Toronto, Canada: Alcoholism and Drug Addiction Research Foundation, Substudy No. 796.

Fuller, R. K., Branchey, L., Brightwell, D. R., Derman, R. M., Emrick, C. D., Iber, F. L., James, K. E., Lacoursiere, R. B., Lee, K. K., Lowenstam, I., Maany, I., Neiderhiser, D., Nocks, J. J., & Shaw, S. (1986). Disulfiram treatment of alcoholism: A Veterans Administration cooperative study. *Journal of the American Medical Association, 156,* 1449–1455.

Goldberg, L. R. (1968). Simple models or simple processes? Some research on clinical judgments. *American Psychologist, 23,* 483–496.

Haley, J. (1963). *Strategies of psychotherapy.* New York: Grune & Stratton.

Hansen, J., & Emrick, C. D. (1983). Whom are we calling "alcoholic"? *Bulletin of the Society of Psychologists in Addictive Behaviors, 2,* 164–178.

Heather, N. (1986). Change without therapists: The use of self-help manuals by problem drinkers. In W. R. Miller & N. Heather (Eds.), *Treating addictive behaviors: Processes of change* (pp. 331–359). New York: Plenum.

Kissin, B., Platz, A., & Su, W. H. (1971). Selective factors in treatment choice and outcome in alcoholics. In N. K. Mello & J. H. Mendelson (Eds.), *Recent advances in studies of alcoholism* (pp. 781–802). Washington, DC: U.S. Government Printing Office.

Mann, M. (1950). *Primer on alcoholism.* New York: Rinehart.

Marlatt, G. A., & Gordon, J. R. (Eds.) (1985). *Relapse prevention.* New York: Guilford Press.

McLachlan, J. F. C. (1972). Benefit from group therapy as a function of patient–therapist match on conceptual level. *Psychotherapy: Theory, Research and Practice, 9,* 317–323.

McLachlan, J. F. C. (1974). Therapy strategies, personality orientation and recovery from alcoholism. *Canadian Psychiatric Association Journal, 19,* 25–30.

McLellan, A. T., Luborsky, L., Woody, G. E., O'Brien, C. P., & Druley, K. A. (1983). Predicting response to alcohol and drug abuse treatments: Role of psychiatric severity. *Archives of General Psychiatry, 40,* 620–625.

McLellan, A. T., Woody, G. E., Luborsky, L., O'Brien, C. P., & Druley, K. A. (1983). Increased effectiveness of substance abuse treatment: A prospective study of patient–treatment "matching." *Journal of Nervous and Mental Disease, 171,* 597–605.

Miller, W. R. (1976). Alcoholism scales and objective assessment methods: A review. *Psychological Bulletin, 83,* 649–674.

Miller, W. R. (1983). Motivational interviewing with problem drinkers. *Behavioural Psychotherapy, 11,* 147–172.

Miller, W. R. (1985). Motivation for treatment: A review with special emphasis on alcoholism. *Psychological Bulletin, 98,* 84–107.

Miller, W. R., & Baca, L. M. (1983). Two-year follow-up of bibliotherapy and therapist-directed controlled drinking training for problem drinkers. *Behavior Therapy, 14,* 441–448.

Miller, W. R., & Caddy, G. R. (1977). Abstinence and controlled drinking in the treatment of problem drinkers. *Journal of Studies on Alcohoi, 38,* 986–1003.

Miller, W. R., & Dougher, M. J. (in press). Covert sensitization: Alternative treatment procedures for alcoholism. *Behavioural Psychotherapy.*

Miller, W. R., & Hester, R. K. (1986a). The effectiveness of alcoholism treatment: What research reveals. In W. R. Miller & N. Heather (Eds.), *Treating addictive behaviors: Processes of change* (pp. 121–174). New York: Plenum.

Miller, W. R., & Hester, R. K. (1986b). Inpatient alcoholism treatment: Who benefits? *American Psychologist, 41,* 794–805.

Miller, W. R., & Hester, R. K. (1986c). Matching problem drinkers with optimal treatments. In W. R. Miller & N. Heather (Eds.), *Treating addictive behaviors: Processes of change* (pp. 175–203). New York: Plenum.

Miller, W. R., Leckman, A. L., Tinkcom, M., & Rubenstein, J. (1986). Long-term follow-up of controlled drinking therapies. Paper presented at the annual meeting of the American Psychological Association, Washington, DC.

Miller, W. R., & Muñoz, R. F. (1982). *How to control your drinking* (rev. ed.). Albuquerque, NM: University of New Mexico Press.

Miller, W. R., & Joyce, M. A. (1979). Prediction of abstinence, controlled drinking, and heavy drinking outcomes following behavioral self-control training. *Journal of Consulting and Clinical Psychology, 47,* 773–775.

Orford, J., Oppenheimer, E., & Edwards, G. (1976). Abstinence or control: The outcome for excessive drinkers two years after consultation. *Behaviour Research and Therapy, 14,* 409–418.

Patterson, G. R., & Forgatch, M. S. (1984). Therapist behavior as a determinant for client noncompliance: A paradox for the behavior modifier. *Journal of Consulting and Clincal Psychology, 53,* 846–851.

Peele, S. (1985). *The meaning of addiction: Compulsive experience and its interpretation.* Kensington, MA: D. C. Heath.

Polich, J. M., Armor, D. J., & Braiker, H. B. (1981). *The course of alcoholism: Four years after treatment.*

New York: Wiley.

Popham, R. E., & Schmidt, W. (1976). Some factors affecting the likelihood of moderate drinking by treated alcoholics. *Journal of Studies on Alcohol, 37,* 868–882.

Prochaska, J. O., & DiClemente, C. C. (1986). Toward a comprehensive model of change. In W. R. Miller & N. Heather (Eds.), *Treating addictive behaviors: Processes of change* (pp. 3–27). New York: Plenum.

Prue, D. M., Keane, T. M., Cornell, J. E., & Foy, D. W. (1979). An analysis of distance variables that affect aftercare attendance. *Community Mental Health Journal, 15,* 149–154.

Rosenberg, S. D. (1979). Relaxation training and a differential assessment of alcoholism. Unpublished doctoral dissertation, California School of Professional Psychology, San Diego. (University Microfilms No. 8004362)

Skinner, H. A., & Allen, B. A. (1983). Differential assessment of alcoholism. *Journal of Studies on Alcohol, 44,* 852–862.

Smart, R. G. (1978). Characteristics of alcoholics who drink socially after treatment. *Alcoholism: Clinical and Experimental Research, 2,* 49–52.

Sovereign, R. G., & Miller, W. R. (1987). Effects of therapist style on resistance and outcome among problem drinkers. Paper presented at the Fourth International Conference on Treatment of Addictive Behaviors, Os/Bergen, Norway.

Sparadeo, F. R., Zweck, W. R., Ruggiero, S. D., Meek, D. A., Carloni, J. A., & Simone, S. S. (1982). Evaluation of a social-setting detoxication program. *Journal of Studies on Alcohol, 43,* 1124–1136.

Vogler, R. E., Compton, J. V., & Weissbach, T. A. (1975). Integrated behavior change techniques for alcoholism. *Journal of Consulting and Clinical Psychology, 43,* 233–243.

Vogler, R. E., Weissbach, T. A., Compton, J. V., & Martin, G. T. (1977). Integrated behavior change techniques for problem drinkers in the community. *Journal of Consulting and Clincal Psychology, 45,* 267–279.

Whitfield, C. L., Thompson, G., Lamb, A., Spencer, V., Pfeifer, M., & Browning-Ferrando, M. (1978). Detoxification of 1,024 alcoholic patients without psychoactive drugs. *Journal of the American Medical Association, 239,* 1409–1410.

Author Index

Subject Index

About the Editors

Reid K. Hester received his Ph.D. in clinical psychology from Washington State University in 1979. He has been involved in research in alcohol abuse since 1974 and has published a number of literature reviews of alcoholism treatment. He is currently Director of the Alcohol Self-Control Program at Behavior Therapy Associates in Albuquerque, NM, and a Clinical Associate in the departments of Psychology and Psychiatry at the University of New Mexico. He has been a consultant to the National Institute of Alcohol Abuse and Alcoholism and the National Institute of Drug Abuse. He is also actively involved in professional training at the national level.

William R. Miller is Professor of Psychology and Psychiatry and Director of Clinical Training at the University of New Mexico. He has published over 100 professional articles and chapters and has held a number of federal grants for research on the effectiveness of treatment and prevention programs. His books include *The Addictive Behaviors* (1980), *How to Control Your Drinking* (1982 with Ricardo Muñoz) and *Treating Addictive Behaviors* (1986, with Nick Heather). He has been a consultant to the National Academy of Sciences, the U.S. Senate Committee on Governmental Affairs, The National Institute on Alcohol Abuse and Alcoholism, and the National Institute on Drug Abuse. He received his Ph.D. in clinical psychology from the University of Oregon in 1976.

Contributors

Helen M. Annis, Addiction Research Foundation and University of Toronto, Toronto, Ontario, Canada.

Nathan H. Azrin, Department of Psychology, Nova University, Fort Lauderdale, Florida.

Edmund F. Chaney, Department of Psychiatry and Behavioral Sciences, University of Washington and Veterans Administration Medical Center, Seattle, Washington.

Kathleen S. Cowles, Department of Psychiatry, Harvard Medical School, Boston, Massachusetts and the Veterans Administration Medical Center, Brockton and West Roxbury, Massachusetts.

Christine S. Davis, Addiction Research Foundation, Toronto, Ontario, Canada.

Michael J. Dougher, Department of Psychology, University of New Mexico, Albuquerque, New Mexico.

Richard Francis, Department of Psychiatry and Mental Health Science, University of Medicine and Dentistry of New Jersey, New Jersey Medical School, Newark, New Jersey.

Richard K. Fuller, Veterans Administration Medical Center, Cleveland, Ohio.

Nick Heather, National Drug and Alcohol Research Centre, University of New South Wales, Kensington, New South Wales, Australia.

Reid K. Hester, Behavior Therapy Associates, Albuquerque, New Mexico.

Donna J. Holmes, Department of Psychiatry and Mental Health Science, University of Medicine and Dentistry of New Jersey, New Jersey Medical School, Newark, New Jersey.

Sadi Irvine, Department of Psychology and Center of Alcohol Studies, Rutgers University, Piscataway, New Jersey.

George R. Jacobson, Division of Alcoholism and Chemical Dependency, Department of Psychiatry and Mental Health Sciences, Medical College of Wisconsin.

Daniel J. Lettieri, National Institute on Alcohol Abuse and Alcoholism, Rockville, Maryland.

Barbara S. McCrady, Center of Alcohol Studies and Graduate School of Applied and Professional Psychology, Rutgers University, Piscataway, New Jersey.

Sheldon Miller, Department of Psychiatry, University of Medicine and Dentistry of New Jersey, New Jersey Medical School, Newark, New Jersey.

William R. Miller, Department of Psychology, University of New Mexico, Albuquerque, New Mexico.

Timothy J. O'Farrell, Department of Psychiatry, Harvard Medical School, Boston, Massachusetts and the Veterans Administration Medical Center, Brockton and West Roxbury, Massachusetts.

Carl T. Rimmele, Veterans Administration Medical Center, Palo Alto, California.

Robert W. Sisson, Eastern Massachusetts Correctional Alcohol Center, Bristol County

Sheriff's Department, New Bedford, Massachusetts.

Tim Stockwell, Exeter Health Authority, Exeter, United Kingdom.

Carole Town, Exeter Health Authority, Exeter, United Kingdom.

Pergamon General Psychology Series

Editors: **Arnold P. Goldstein,** Syracuse University
Leonard Krasner, Stanford University &
SUNY at Stony Brook

*Out of print in original format. Available in custom reprint edition.